The Weather-Conditioned House

The Weather-Conditioned House

Groff Conklin

Revised and updated by
S. Blackwell Duncan

VNR Van Nostrand Reinhold Company
New York Cincinnati Toronto London Melbourne

Printed in the United States of America

Published by Van Nostrand Reinhold Company
135 West 50th Street, New York, NY 10020

Van Nostrand Reinhold Limited
1410 Birchmount Road
Scarborough, Ontario M1P 2E7, Canada

Van Nostrand Reinhold Australia Pty. Ltd.
17 Queen Street
Mitcham, Victoria 3132, Australia

Van Nostrand Reinhold Company Limited
Molly Millars Lane
Wokingham, Berkshire, England

16 15 14 13 12 11 10 9 8 7 6 5 4 3 2 1

Library of Congress Cataloging in Publication Data

Conklin, Groff, 1904–1968.
    The weather - conditioned house.

    Bibliography: p.
    Includes index.
    1. Dwellings—Environmental engineering.
2. House construction. I. Duncan, S. Blackwell.
II. Title.
TH6057.A6C66   1981   690'.837   81–3012
ISBN 0-442-22655-1   AACR2

Contents

Preface

A little over three decades ago, Groff Conklin set about the tremendous task of assembling, in logical and readable sequence, a substantial body of facts and general information about the design and construction of what he called the weather-conditioned house. His intent was to outline processes by which a residence could be well constructed, comfortable, environmentally oriented, and maintained/operated at reasonable cost. After some six years of research and two more of writing, he succeeded, and the result was the original edition of this book, first published in 1956.

At that time, the subject was not a particularly popular one. The environment was little more than a word in the dictionary, and environmental consciousness as we know it today existed only in a very limited way. Fuels were abundant and cheap, construction and housing costs were relatively low, conservation and preservation were not causes for popular consideration, and residential housing, with all its attendant ramifications, was simply not the concern that it is nowadays. Research and development programs in such matters as alternative fuels, super-efficient heating/cooling systems, high-performance insulations, thermally efficient windows and doors, methods of solar control, and dozens of other similar matters in the area of residential design and construction, were limited, desultory, and such results as were obtained were slow in making their appearance and gaining acceptance.

Since that time, the building industry has come a long, long way. At present, pushed hard by the necessities of the times, we are in the midst of an explosion of ideas, general information, specific data, new materials and methods, and practical applications of old ones, that is unprecedented and also sufficient, as the old saying goes, to truly boggle the mind. Never before has the residential housing industry been in such a state of development and change, almost entirely for the better (except, of course, for the dismayingly high costs involved). And yet, the basics of this book, in its original edition as written thirty years ago, are as pertinent now as they were then.

As Mr. Conklin wrote in the original Preface:

[There are] two distinct aspects of the ever-present problem of achieving comfort in the immoderate climate in which we human beings have evolved from the changeless deeps of the primordial seas. The first is that ingenuity plus labor has always found a way, even as today, to improve on Nature; and the second is that being cool during hot weather is just as important as being warm during cold winters. This has always been true, of course, but it was not until after World War II that invention and capital combined to give us year-round domestic living comfort at a reasonable cost, through the creation of an artificial indoor climate, controlled as to temperature, humidity, air cleanliness, and sound.

However, this book is not entirely devoted to the artifices of climate control. As the first chapter points out in some detail, living companionably with the natural environment, making full use of the desirable qualities of any climate while diminishing the less pleasant ones, can be achieved to a very great degree by care in planning and by knowledge of the goals to be sought and the methods of gaining them. It is one purpose of this book (among many others) to outline those goals and to explain how they are to be achieved. It also, of course, deals at length with the creation of artificial indoor weather, since no matter how carefully we study our climate and try to adapt to it, we still find that it cares not about our ways, and goes on being thoroughly intractable when it chooses. Therefore it covers central heating and cooling, humidifiers and dehumidifiers, double glazing and insulating materials, and the whole arsenal of materials and equipment that go into the making of *the weather-conditioned house*.

This book, then, is about both aspects of this complex problem. I have made an effort to present the material in an informal and readable manner, even in the chapters that are most formidably technical. It is hoping for the impossible to expect to find any sex appeal in a table of coefficients of heat transmission. . . .

Indeed. But the table remains, in updated form, along with many others of similar nature. The entire text, and all of the illustrations, have been checked for veracity, timeliness, and current usefulness, and, as might be expected, numerous changes have been made. What is surprising is not that changes were necessary, but that so few, comparatively speaking, had to be made. With a few exceptions, most were in the area of specific details and numbers, not in basic premises or points. Those portions of original text that are still valid—and there are many—have been left intact. Those illustrations that still put across their points—and there are many—have remained in place. Thus the revised and updated edition reflects well the thinking of the author, a man whose thoughts extended well into the future, while at the same time incorporating the views of the reviser and the necessary up-to-date factual information.

There is one point that must be made with regard to the Bibliography. In the original work, this list was quite lengthy and included a great many technical papers, articles from periodicals, bulletins, studies, and the like. Nearly all of these items have been deleted from the revised Bibliography, primarily because, from a practical standpoint, they are no longer readily available for reference. In point of fact, much of that old information still exists in various libraries and archives about the country, some of it on microfiche or similar storage media, and it can be obtained at the expense of considerable time and a certain amount of cash. For anyone who might be interested in doing so, a caution is in order: much of the information contained in those materials is no longer valid, much of it is, and some is in limbo. Care, judgment, and, usually, further research as well is needed in order to determine which is which. The current Bibliography, on the other hand, is comprised of works that are in current circulation, for the most part, and are readily obtainable for further research. All of the works listed were used during the course of revising the original edition of this book.

In the course of writing *The Weather-Conditioned House,* Groff Conklin was aided by hundreds of people who answered inquiries, furnished research data, supplied illustrative material, and helped out in a good many different ways, to whom he expressed his heartfelt thanks in the original Preface. I too have been helped by dozens of willing and cooperative folks at various organizations, institutions, companies, and government agencies all over the country—in particular, Carl MacPhee and his staff at the American Society of Heating, Refrigerating and Air-Conditioning Engineers (ASHRAE). Without their unfailing aid, the task of revising this book would have been extremely difficult. Or more likely—impossible.

And finally, I think it fitting that Mr. Conklin close this revised Preface:

I hope that this book proves useful to the reader. And I hope that the readers eventually include not only professional men and women—architects, builders, engineers, planners, and the pre-professionals in the colleges and technical schools of the country, but also the intelligent laymen and women upon whose tastes and decisions, in the long run, the future of good house design and building will rest. It is they who will foot the bill: and I believe that they will make their decisions more intelligently if they, too, have some grasp of what constitutes a house that lives with and takes advantage of its environment.

I concur.

S. Blackwell Duncan
Snowmass, Colorado

Chapter 1

The Elements of
Environmental Control
for Houses

No one need be told that we are in the midst of a revolution in residential design and building. In the past two decades or so, new materials (fiberglass shingles), new techniques (truss-framing), new types of equipment (solar collectors), and new design concepts (earth-sheltered houses) have changed the whole scheme of house building as well as the appearance and the functioning of the house itself. And the changes show few signs of slowing down.

Actually, this is not one revolution, but at least two. On the one hand, we have seen an unprecedented development of mass-produced houses with new methods of rationalized building bringing the dwelling to the status of an assembly line product—as, indeed, it has already become in the latest methods of factory prefabrication. The primary effect of this particular revolution has been relative cost reduction, especially for the manufacturer/builder in "tract-type" houses; only secondarily, if at all, does it involve any measureable increase in overall amenity.

On the other hand, new materials, new uses of conventional materials (such as glass), and new labor-saving devices and types of equipment to increase comfort have made possible, for those who can afford them, levels of indoor (and indoor/outdoor) living ease and luxury undreamed of a generation ago. From prefabricated triple glazing to microwave ovens, from gadgets such as house-and-perimeter security systems to seminecessities such as automated mechanical cooling, the march of technology continues to enrich, and complicate, our houses.

But despite all the glitter of these new methods and new things, we still have to face the fact that the house *in relation to its environment* has made little progress—indeed, has in some ways retrogressed—from the older days when land was more living place than a speculative football. Once upon a time houses, even for

common folk, were built with an innate understanding of the need for space aroung the house: plenty of backyard for gardening and for children to play in, plenty of trees to sit under and to shade the house, plenty of lawn in which to set up a croquet game or across which one could exercise one's eyes with the curiosity of one intimate with, and fond of, the outdoors, or with the viewless gaze of contemplation.

Today, "lower-cost," "compact," and "tract" houses are denied land, trees, or vista because these have become luxuries (Figure 1-1), while houses in the upper brackets all too often depend upon costly mechanical refinements for their comfort and ignore, or misuse, the natural environment.

The enviroment *is* considered, of course, particularly in individually designed houses and in many of the newer, "environment conscious" subdivisions. (It often is almost completely destroyed in tract housing developments.) Since mechanical cooling to increase summer comfort has come into widespread use, and particularly since the advent of solar heating and solar-assist heating concepts have gained popularity, attention to the thermal aspects of the environment—sun, wind, rain, and the relation of the house to these elements—has greatly increased. Economical air conditioning is impossible without this stepped-up attention to siting, building orientation, and structural efficiencies. Likewise, effective solar heating, even in a minimal degree, cannot be accomplished without proper orientation. But there are other environmental aspects that, while perhaps not always having a direct economical effect on cooling and heating costs, are important in improving livability. Not every house in every American climate really needs mechanical cooling. Nor can every house, whether existing or about to be built, effectively utilize solar heat. But *all* houses, without exception, should be designed and built to take every ad-

1-1. A typical modern subdivision. (Duncan Photos)

1-2. Air view of Hollin Hills, Virginia, an environmentally integrated subdivision. (Robert C. Lautman)

vantage of nature's innate "cooling and heating capacities," just as they are built, as a matter of course, to protect against the inclemencies of the temperate zone's often intemperate climate.

Unfortunately, other aspects of environmental control are often neglected and a preponderance of the emphasis is placed upon those aspects of the problem that involve structure: management of the external conditions of heat, cold, wind, and moisture. No one needs to be told that these are important; indeed, this book is for the most part devoted to them. But the human animal has other senses besides those relating to temperature and humidity. In thinking of the house primarily as shelter against the elements, we are em-

phasizing the negative aspects of the environment, aspects that can physically damage us unless we are protected against them. Shelter against the weather is the primary purpose of the house, but there are other, positive environmental elements, those affecting privacy, visual and aural (and even olfactory) impacts, health, safety, and overall quality of home living, which can also be controlled by good planning and good construction. These "secondary" environmental factors are analyzed in this chapter just as thoroughly as are those bearing primarily on thermal control, and they should be just as carefully considered in the planning and building of the house (Figure 1-2).

IMPORTANCE OF THERMAL CONTROL

Control of the thermal aspects of shelter has become increasingly important over the past three decades, as mechanical summer cooling has evolved into a "necessity." Before that, almost the whole emphasis (in central and northern zones of the country) was on developing types of construction that would provide reasonable winter comfort and only incidentally reduce plant and operating costs for heating. Today, even more concentrated attention must be devoted to that process in *every* part of the country for both heating *and* cooling, and far more consideration must be given to the technical problems of orientation, design and engineering, and environmental integration than ever has been done before. This is essential not just to make heating and cooling (whether natural, mechanical, or a combination) as economical and affordable as possible, but also to further the ever-increasing necessity to carefully husband fuel and energy supplies. To that end, much thought must also be given to the development and use of multiple-fuel, solar, and other so-called alternative heating/cooling systems.

To take a simple example, it used to be said that the value of thermal insulation was limited almost entirely to somewhat improved economy of winter heating. It might also provide a slightly cooler house in the summer, but not enough to be important in itself. One used just enough insulation to reduce heat loss in winter to manageable proportions. But one of the startlingly new aspects of thermal conditioning, one that we Americans are thoroughly unaccustomed to, is the now shockingly high and steadily increasing cost of operation. At present, energy costs for conventional heating systems are three times or more greater than they were just a few years ago. To make matters worse, now that we have accepted mechanical cooling systems as necessities rather than luxuries, the cost of removing heat from many houses during hot weather is considerably more than adding heat during cold weather. For many homeowners, heating/cooling expenses are virtually a year-round burden, one that is becoming increasingly difficult to bear. Thus, greater thermal efficiency and high quality, weathertight construction have become economic imperatives of modern-day living.

Important as high thermal efficiency and excellence of construction are, they should not be the only areas of concern. All possible methods that will, or even might, protect the house against variations in the thermal environment must be considered if maximum heating/cooling benefits are to be realized. It now appears that many houses built in the immediate future will be of unconventional design, and most of them will include technologically advanced equipment and/or systems for cold-weather heating, hot-weather cooling, or year-round air conditioning. That being so, such factors as design, engineering, orientation, and environmental integration to make the cost of installing and operating such equipment and systems as low as possible, and also to make them fully functional with minimum difficulties, take on tremendous importance.

Though low operating cost for heating cooling systems is of primary importance (along with providing a healthful and comfortable indoor environment for the occupants of the house, of course), there is another, allied economic factor that must be considered. Even as little as a decade ago, house planning and construction for effective thermal control and high thermal efficiency had little bearing upon the market value, or the general desirability, of a house. Today, that is no longer true. Houses so planned and built almost invariably have not only a higher resale value, but also enhanced marketability—they will sell faster and more readily than neighboring houses that have demonstrably lower thermal efficiency and higher heating/cooling costs. An owner who can guarantee that a dwelling has been designed for the most economical use of heating/cooling energy will usually be able to obtain a measurably higher price for it than otherwise.

Effective thermal control is also important from the standpoint of self-protection against such circumstances as rapidly increasing unit costs of energy to an unaffordable level, potential spot shortages or cutbacks that can occur at any time for particular fuels, or interruptions of fuel or energy supply services. These and similar possibilities, all too real nowadays, dictate that a house must be as efficiently and effectively protected from variations in the thermal environment as is practically possible. In addition, both the techniques of heating/cooling and the equipment employed in the systems must be of the highest caliber and include at least some versatility of energy sources and operating modes in order to be wholly dependable and economically suitable.

ELEMENTS OF ENVIRONMENTAL CONTROL

As emphasized previously, this analysis is concerned not only with external thermal factors, but also with the broader spectrum of *total* environment: sound as well as heat, deterioration of materials as well as humidity, and so on. In the discussion that follows, equal attention is given to all of these, not just to those that influence heating and cooling.

There are ten factors of environment that can be brought more or less under control through the use of sound planning principles and construction techniques: temperature, humidity, moisture, insolation, air motion, pests and contaminants, sound, vision, wind and snow load, and fire. And there are, in each case, up to six methods of achieving the best measure of control, in relation to the house: site selection, orientation, planning, construction, landscaping, and mechanical equipment.

In analyzing these environmental factors and the methods of controlling them, it is important to remember that nature is always presenting us with extraordinarily complex and often contradictory situations. Almost no factor of the environment can be brought under measurable control without affecting other factors. If you orient the house to take advantage of prevailing summer breezes, you may later find that the structure is cruelly vulnerable to wintry blasts and snowstorms. On the other hand, it may not be: the microclimate of the immediate locality may indicate prevailing winds from one direction in warm weather and from an entirely different direction when it is cold. Similar inconsistencies will be found in many other aspects of the environment. More generally, a dwelling in the Texas Panhandle will require an entirely different program from one in a Vermont valley. Regional as well as local variations must be carefully analyzed before a house can be effectively fitted into its environment. This is a truism, but one that is forgotten with astonishing frequency.

The following is a brief examination of the ten factors of environmental control and, for each, the methods of achieving that control. The following descriptive examples of the purposes and techniques of controlling each environmental factor must be read with the knowledge that the variations and permutations of those factors are practically infinite and that many adjustments may have to be made before the general pattern can be applied to a specific dwelling on a specific site. Also, other particular possibilities not mentioned here might well exist in certain individual circumstances.

Control of Interior Temperature on a Year-Round Basis. In order to provide comfort within the house regardless of outside temperatures (see chapters 3 and 5), the following methods should be used:

Site selection: Near a lake or running stream, if possible, since bodies of water tend to even off extremes in temperature (but a low area close to the water may entrap a layer of air that is relatively colder than surrounding higher elevations during winter weather). Under the lee of a hill, if there is one (but *not* in a low, breathless pocket of land). In a region known to possess good prevailing summer breezes. In an area with plenty of natural foliage—healthy trees and shrubs—if it can be found. Preferably not flat, both for visual variety and for the protection from boreal blasts that a sheltered hillside site affords.

Orientation: Major glass areas located to receive maximum sun in winter and minimum in summer. Correct southerly orientation where solar heating is a design consideration; openings to be protected against winter winds and to admit summer breezes.

Planning: Arrangement of rooms so that living areas face sheltered exposures and bedrooms, garage, kitchen, etc., face less sheltered areas (at least in climates with severe winters and strong winds). Fenestration to avoid excess exposure of large glass areas to winter winds and summer sun, if local climate makes this possible. In hot climates, a relatively open plan, to make best use of natural ventilation; but in cold climates, the plan should ideally approach the square, perhaps with an interior, protected court (a dome is also feasible). In dry, hot climates, the square plan with an interior court is also often desirable. In either cold or dry, hot climates, the underground house is a viable alternative style.

Landscaping: Deciduous trees for sunlight in winter, shade in summer; evergreen trees for windbreak in winter, shade in summer. Minimum of heat-reflecting drives and terraces or patios, and a maximum of grassy lawns and flower gardens immediately around the house, for low heat gain in summer. Climbing vines (on trellises or arbors) close to the house as summer sunshades.

Mechanical equipment: Heating system in winter; mechanical cooling in summer if necessary; mechanical ventilation as required for both seasons.

Control of Relative Humidity Within the House. This has several purposes: to maintain the relative humidity at a more or less constant level the year round; to reduce or eliminate the danger of damage to house construction from winter condensation, high cooling bills from excess air moisture and latent heat in the summer, and high heating costs in the winter resulting from relatively higher thermostat settings to compensate for the feeling of chilliness imparted by too-dry interior air; to provide enough humidity for people and plants, which need a goodly amount in wintertime (chapters 4 and 5); to ensure a healthful environment; and to reduce or eliminate potential damage to furnishings caused by excessive drying in winter or damage to furnishings, possessions or house construction in summer because of excessive moisture and mildew. The following are methods by which this can be achieved:

Site selection: Not in a low, damp pocket of land. Good prevailing summer breezes desirable. Above or away from excessive groundwater conditions. Apart from watershed or water runoff areas.

Planning: Maximum utilization of natural ventilation in winter and summer through planned fenestration and ventilating methods (exception: in regions of severe storms and winds, a compromise will have to be arrived at between optimum ventilation and storm protection).

Construction: Effective vapor barriers at top, sides, and bottom of the house. Attic and other ventilation to reduce vapor pressure in winter and sunheat load in summer. Reduction in moisture released into the house by venting stoves, laundry equipment, etc., and by providing powered exhaust ventilation in baths, kitchens, and laundries. Weatherstrips and double or triple glazing to help maintain higher winter humidity and lower heat loss.

Landscaping: Shrubbery and trees kept sufficiently distant from the house to permit adequate air circulation and evaporation of water vapor in summer; in some climates this will mean avoiding trees that overhang the roof, since they can make the house uncomfortably damp during the summer.

Mechanical equipment: Forced exhaust ventilation for attic or roof, kitchen, bath, laundry, etc., primarily in summer. Humidifiers (winter) and dehumidifiers (summer) (but only if the conditions within the house are so severe that they cannot be remedied in other ways).

Control of Free Moisture. As means of control of free moisture to prevent external damage of the structure by precipitation and water penetration through cracks and joints, and to minimize the danger of groundwater, runoff and floods (chapters 2, 4 and 9), the following methods should be considered:

Site selection: Location sheltered from driving rains and winds. Well above any conceivable high water mark along streams that have history of flooding. Avoid damp or swampy areas and sites that have poor natural drainage. Avoid watershed and runoff areas, or snowdrift pockets.

Orientation: Location on the lot to take full advantage of natural shelter against storms (lee of hills, existing vegetated windbreaks) and to minimize the danger of rain or groundwater collecting around or under the house. If the site is near a running stream, runoff course, or dry wash, locate the house at the highest point to minimize flood danger.

Planning: Ventilation and fenestration protected by roof overhang, gutters, and other means. Roof profile planned to avoid snowdrifts and pockets, and standing pools of rainwater. Complete drainage systems utilized to divert or carry away free-running surface and subsurface water.

Construction: Tight and weatherproof (waterproof wherever possible) materials and techniques. Quality flashing at all roof and wall openings and at foundations where necessary. Guttering system, with polypropylene or other mesh screen over gutters to prevent leaves from clogging and causing water and snow backup. Subsurface rainwater and groundwater drains, both direct and diversion, to carry water away from the house. Moisture-resistant or moisture-proof exterior treatments such as paints, stains or sealers, masonry damp-proofing or waterproofing materials, and, where needed, waterproof caulking, grouting, or putty.

Landscaping: Moderately dense planting along, but not too close to, the sides of the house on which worst storms usually beat (but sufficiently distant to permit efficient drainage around house). Grading down and away from the house on all sides to prevent collection of rainwater around the foundation. Thick sod around the house perimeter to reduce the danger of water seepage into the foundation.

Mechanical equipment: Sump pumps if the area under the house (basement or crawl space) cannot be kept dry otherwise.

Note that if a private sewage disposal system must be used, locate it a safe distance from the house and design it so that the effluent will drain away from the house and from the domestic water supply.

Control of Insolation. The sun's direct rays should supplement the heating system during the winter and should be kept out of the house in the summer as much as possible (chapters 2, 3, 5, and 6). The methods of control are essentially the same as with temperature, except that (air temperatures being equal) sun control devices and heat-blocking glass or glass-applied films can be very important in certain regions (hot, arid, and treeless) and less so in others (temperate, humid, with adequate natural shade). Those houses that are so designed as to depend partially or entirely upon insolation for interior comfort heating require special attention in the way of equipment and techniques, as well as construction, to achieve precise control. It should also be pointed out that house locations too close to *unshaded* bodies of water, wide sand beaches, expanses of pavement, etc., will suffer considerable addition to summer cooling load by radiant heat reflection, although a waterfront location may be good for the non-air-conditioned house because of water-cooled breezes. In very hot regions that have an ample water supply, a roof pool or sprinkler system will help reduce the cooling load and increase comfort.

It should be noted that there is no mention here of glare control or "daylighting." This is intentional. Scientific distribution of sunlight within rooms is often important in nonresidential buildings, but in houses it does not, in most instances, require separate consideration. The kinds of landscape and structural treatments required to reduce insolation as a heat factor also automatically take care of glare. As for distribution of daylight in rooms, most people would not like an even daytime illumination. Daylight variety within a room is psychologically important; light and shadow are desirable, in homes if not elsewhere.

Control of Air Motion. This is necessary to reduce vapor pressure in the house in winter and cooling load in summer; to add to summer comfort in non-air-conditioned houses (chapters 2, 3, 4 and 5); and to reduce or eliminate cold air infiltration and subsequent drafts within the house during stormy or windy winter weather. The methods of control are:

Site selection: Region or locale of good natural breeze in summer, but minimal boreal winds in winter.

Orientation: House located so prevailing summer winds will blow through rather than bypass, but strongest winter winds will be kept out, if possible.

Planning: Location of sleeping rooms to obtain maximum benefit from prevailing summer breeze in non-air-conditioned house. Fenestration in such a house planned to provide through or cross ventilation wherever possible. Elimination of "dead" spots, areas without air motion, by provision of extra louvers or windows if necessary. Note that in houses with mechanical cooling, summer breezes are important only to the degree that they help reduce the cooling load, which they do mainly by ventilating the attic space, or, in mild weather, by allowing the occupants to turn off the mechanical cooling equipment and open the windows instead.

Construction: Even in houses with year-round air conditioning, operable windows or adjustable louvers or vents below or above fixed windows for comfort during periods of moderate weather. Inclusion of specially placed air intake and exhaust vents to take advantage of natural cooling drafts from cool side to warm side of the house; adequate screened openings in flat or pitched roofs, eaves, clerestories, and basements and crawl spaces, for air circulation to reduce condensation danger in winter and make full use of prevailing breezes in summer. Weatherstripping, insulating window shutters, etc., to keep out winter drafts and reduce cold air drop.

Landscaping: When it does not interfere with winter functions as wind- and storm-break, elimination of thick plantings close to the house that might hinder penetration of summer breezes. Evergreen plantings of suitable height and at the proper distance from the house to act as winter windbreaks.

Mechanical equipment: Powered exhaust fans in attic or in the roof space where there is no attic (the latter with powered rotary ventilators exposed on the roof as required); small exhaust fans in bath, kitchens, laundries. Adequate intake vents to supply proper air circulation. Correctly designed air supplies in standard heating and cooling equipment. Where possible, large-bladed, low-speed circulating ceiling fans to evenly distribute warm air in winter and to provide additional cooling in summer.

Control of Pests and Contaminants. The following methods may be used to reduce airborne dirt and odors, eliminate flying insects, to keep earth-bound pests such as termites, ants, and rats from damaging the structure, and to reduce the danger of decay (chapter 9):

Site selection: Safe distance from industrial and other air and water polluting sources, including garbage dumps, feed lots, etc. (always remember that prevailing winds are a factor in these situations). Out of and away from areas noted for accumulation of smog, or high levels of acid-rain precipitation. A site naturally protected against termites, carpenter ants, and other pests, i.e., not too damp or too thickly wooded, and known to be uninfested.

Orientation: Location as high as possible on a well-drained plot, safely distant from surrounding woods, marshes, or swamps, if any.

Planning: Location of incinerator or other odor-and-dirt-producing equipment and activities (compost pile, corral, auto shop) a safe distance from the house and in the direction toward which the prevailing winds blow. Placement of doors, windows, and other openings so that pests cannot enter (that is, moderately above ground level). In mild climates, *completely* screened outdoor living areas with free passage to and from enclosed rooms.

Construction: Weathertight, rodent-proof construction. Adequate termite-proof building techniques. Wood near the ground dipped or pressure-treated with preservatives when conditions require. Use of impervious building materials wherever possible. Screens at all windows, exterior doors, and ventilating louvers or windows in attics, basements, and crawl spaces, and on all chimneys and stacks. A minimum of six inches of clearance between the earth and any wood construction, with no wood in direct contact with the earth in termite country. Thorough clearing away of dead organic material from the periphery of the house and from backfill.

Landscaping: Plantings a safe distance from walls and foundations to reduce danger from termites, ants, and other pests.

Mechanical equipment: Electrostatic or other air cleaning equipment when needed, particularly in houses without air conditioning units that filter incoming air. Regularly maintained filters on furnace blowers and similar equipment. If the basement is damp or parts of the living quarters are overly humid, dehumidifiers to keep wood dry and reduce danger of decay, mildew growth, and termites. Outdoor insect traps, electrical or chemical, when conditions require.

Control of Sound, External and Internal. Use the following methods to provide a quiet and restful environment in the house and in each room of the house where quiet is desired (chapter 8):

Site selection: Greatest possible distance from airports and heavily traveled airlanes, noise-producing industrial and transportation activities (factories, railroads, major highways), shopping centers and other commercial areas, and schools. A lot large enough to permit ample space between houses. If possible, a site that has good natural acoustical protection, such as hills, thick shrubs, and trees, etc.

Where feasible, a site where unobtrusive and continuous background sound ("white noise") such as ocean surf, wind sighing through pine boughs, or a running stream, will mask other unavoidable and obtrusive noises.

Orientation: Windowless wall or garage, or both, facing unavoidable sources of noise. House set as far back from the street as practical. House set as far away from other noise sources as practical. Location to take fullest possible advantage of natural barriers to sound.

Planning: For outdoor noise sources, organizing rooms so that those needing the most quiet are as far as possible from the street and from nearby houses or other potential noise sources; provision for tall, heavy perimeter fences or walls facing unavoidable noise sources. For indoor noise sources, segregation of quiet rooms from potentially noisy one, such as music room, kitchen, playroom, etc. Within rooms, dimensioning and designing music rooms, recreation rooms, workshops, etc., to minimize reverberation and sound transference.

Construction: For outdoor noise sources, structural cross sections designed to reduce sound transmission such as masonry, heavy frame construction with lath and plaster, double or triple glazing, heavy exterior doors, heavy sound and thermal insulation. For indoor noise sources, sound-transmission-reducing partitions or sound-walls when a noisy room has a common wall with a quiet one (bathroom, bedroom, study), and, in two-story houses, floors designed to reduce sound transmission by impact. For noise within a room, acoustical insulation in ceilings of noisy rooms; slightly off-angle and/or off-plumb construction (possibly coupled with curvilinear components) to interrupt sound waves and reduce reverberation, and selection and arrangement of furniture and major room components or elements for the same reason; sound-deadening wall and window treatment (particularly for music rooms); carpeting or large rugs on the floors; and sound-absorbing draperies or wall hangings. For equipment noise, acoustical mounting of laundry equipment, air conditioning equipment, etc.; isolation of equipment when possible; selection of quiet type of equipment if available; use of acoustical insulation and noise baffles in air ducts for heating and cooling equipment. Proper placement and mounting, and the use of plastic pipes wherever possible, in plumbing systems.

Landscaping: Wood or, preferably, masonry wall between the house and areas of objectionable noise (streets, house next door, playgrounds). Separation of play and other noise-producing areas from the house by distance, if possible. Dense plantings of evergreens (not deciduous trees, which lose their slight acoustical value in the winter), both for privacy and for minor sound reduction as well, around the lot boundaries that are exposed to noise sources.

Mechanical equipment: None. There is no machine (except in science fiction!) that produces silence. On the other hand, a good many people who live in areas where noise is inescapable, particularly sudden or piercing noises such as street traffic or children at play, have found that the relatively low and even hum of a fan or air conditioning unit has a desirable effect. For these people, this background noise level so reduces the contrast between outdoor and indoor sounds that they cease to be a hazard, particularly at night. A steady, low-pitched sound is never as disturbing as an infrequent, sudden, loud sound, abruptly breaking the silence. Thus, situations of irreducibly high exterior noise level can be easily and effectively combatted by a radio, television or stereo played constantly at low volume. Under such circumstances, piping of soft music into all of the principal rooms of the house can be advantageous.

Control of the Visual Environment. In order to provide the best possible relation of the house to the landscape and to assure the neccessary privacy, thus eliminating wherever possible the less attractive aspects of the surroundings, the following methods should be considered:

Site selection: Zoning controls or land-use regulations governing present or future use of adjacent land areas that might adversely affect the character of the architecture and the landscaping, or the continued potential enjoyability, livability, and reasonable property value of the home. A lot size sufficiently large and correctly shaped to make good views possible and at the same time preclude too much inspection of activities in and around the house by neighbors or the general public. A site that is initially pleasing to the eyes or can obviously and readily be made so. A site so located that obtrusive or unsavory uses of adjacent land areas do not or cannot detract from the site itself.

Orientation: Segregation of all outdoor work areas and service yards from view areas; placing the house so that the most used windows get the best views and windowless walls (such as garages) face areas subject to public inspection—not always possible, however, in view of other requirements listed previously.

Planning: The design of the house should be no less attractive than the views from its windows, since it is a part of the visual environment. Good planning will also relate windows and glass areas, decks and patios, etc., to the most enjoyable and private views and grounds areas.

Construction: Placement of ample glass areas at strategic locations. Use of nondistorting window glass and nonglare glass if necessary. Installation of high-visibility, nonglare screening.

Landscaping: For good views, planting (or thinning) to the owner's taste. For privacy, decorative but dense shrubbery or, if necessary, wood or masonry walls between the house and the street or the neighbors. For beauty, plantings of flowers, flowering shrubs, and flowering vines. For interest, plantings that will attract wild birds and small animals.

Mechanical equipment: Sequester all exterior equipment and machinery out of sight of the best views. Conceal by plantings or trellises or other means those which must be exposed. Otherwise, no application.

Control of Wind and Snow Loads. To assure a dwelling that is secure against all foreseeable hazards of the elements, insofar as is possible. Note: the control of these climatic aspects is the same as for temperature or for free moisture, except in:

Construction: Careful adherence to accepted general (and, when conditions are extraordinary, local) engineering and building code requirements for dimensioning structural members and for general building design. Meticulous attention to adequate nailing practices throughout the structure, as outlined in the nailing schedule in L. O. Anderson's *Wood-Frame House Construction* (Agriculture Handbook No. 73, slightly revised April 1975, available from the Forest Products Laboratory), or in other standard house-building reference books. Local records for extremes of wind and snow loads should be checked before making final specifications. The profile and plan relative to the collecting of snow in pockets and internal angles should be considered. In areas where earthquakes, hurricanes, exceptionally severe storms, or tornados are prevalent or potentially expectable, local building designs, techniques, and practices should be closely followed.

Control of Fire Hazards. The following methods should be used to protect dwellings—and, more importantly, occupants—from external hazards such as brush and forest fires, fires in other houses, lightning, etc., and from internal hazards arising from poor wiring, poor ventilation, poor construction practices, etc. (chapter 9):

Site selection: Avoidance of sites too hedged in by forests or brush in areas subject to seasonal dry spells and consequent wild fires.

Orientation: A wide belt of mowed field, open lawn and flower beds, or vegetable gardens between the house and any fire hazardous brush, meadows, or woods.

Planning: Provision of means of egress from basements, whether used as living quarters or not, and every habitable room in the house, particularly bedrooms and all second-floor rooms. The establishment of preplanned methods and means of rapid

evacuation of occupants under both daytime and night conditions; this is especially important where youngsters or elderly or infirm persons are involved.

Construction: Specification and use of fire-resistant, fire-retardant, and, when economically feasible, fireproof, exterior materials and methods such as slate, metal, or tile roofing. Exterior masonry or other fire-resistant wall surfaces. Lightning rods and protection systems in all areas where lightning is known to be a particular hazard and, especially, in rural communities where proper municipal or volunteer fire fighting equipment is not within quick and easy reach. Fire-safe interior construction techniques, including ample firestopping, top-grade wiring and approved electrical equipment, fire-resistant wall and ceiling materials, and specially fireproofed areas around heating and cooking equipment, fireplaces (whether masonry, built-in, or freestanding), and wood stoves or ranges.

Landscaping: Location of fire hazardous materials such as oil tanks, gas bottles or tanks, woodpiles, rubbish piles, paint supplies, etc., in protected areas safely away from the house. Wide lawns (which should be kept well mowed!) in areas subject to brush fires. If economically feasible, a swimming pool or farm pond as a source of water for fire fighting, provided local water sources are inadequate, as they usually are in country communities.

Mechanical equipment: Fire warning systems. Portable fire extinguishers indoors and out, of types that will control various types of fires (oil and other "wet" materials, electrical materials, dry stuffs, and a special type for chimney fires). In rural areas, pumps and hoses to lift water from the pond or pool to the structure with sufficient pressure and volume to quench the fire.

Summary

The immense subject discussed above concerning the natural environment and its relation to houses is, of course, covered in this book in only a small way; reams of detailed and technical information are available covering most of this subject material in mind-boggling depth. Nevertheless, almost all of the factors described will be discussed, if only briefly in some cases, in the various chapters to which reference is made. Our hope is to present a rounded picture of the basic elements that comprise a weather-conditioned house, and to present a platform made up of fundamental house-design-and-construction planks that will at once afford the reader a solid knowledge base and the first step toward further, more detailed investigation of those aspects that may be of particular concern. The only exceptions are the allied subjects of wind and snow load, and special constructions employed in known areas of such violent phenomena as tornados, earthquakes, and hurricanes. It has been considered unnecessary to go into the subject of structural strength required under these conditions because this is a basic part of every architect's and builder's training, because the requirements are practically always stipulated in building codes and government regulations, and because the various aspects of strength of buildings have been exhaustively treated elsewhere. For those who are interested in reviewing the latest data on the subject, direct contact is suggested with any or several of the various agencies and associations active in building-trade affairs. In addition, in-depth and up-to-date information on *all* of the subject material covered in this book can be obtained from the sources and publications referenced in the text, Bibliography, and Further Reference List.

It is a fact that research and development in the areas of building techniques and designs, strengths and uses of materials, and new building products continues apace, and keeping up with this explosion of knowledge and information is difficult. Witness, for instance, the recent increase in availability of and popular interest in the geodesic dome style of house, new development of comfortable and attractive earth-sheltered houses, experimentation by the Forest Products Laboratory with truss-framing for houses, the increased availability of high-performance roofing, exterior siding, and various building materials, and other such matters. As the years slide by and we grope our hesitant way toward the twenty-first century, rest assured that we will see an incredible number of changes, improvements, and startling new developments in the field of environmentally related residence construction.

Chapter 2

Orientation and Climate

Architect-builder Ken Kern writes in *The Owner Built Home* (Charles Scribner's Sons, New York, 1975), "Architecture these days ignores environment: witness the growth of the world's cities, which violate natural principles of summer cooling, for instance. Contrast the cool, shady woodland found in nature with the exposed acres of urban pavement, concrete buildings, and reflecting rooftops. Compatibility of the building with its environment is currently neglected as modern designers devote a disproportionate amount of attention to appearance and fashion—which, of course, boost the sale value of the package." Nothing, in the short time that has elapsed since that writing, has happened to change that situation.

More revealing comments were made more than *thirty years ago* by Professor James M. Fitch of Columbia University's School of Architecture:

Architectural inattention to a meteorological fact [that climates are never symmetrical] is possible today only because of the materials made available to the building field by science and technology. It was never possible before. If we look at all the periods prior to the last one hundred years, we find close attention being paid to climate in all buildings. In fact, this seems to be the distinctive quality of all national and regional architectural styles. Whether men built a palm-thatched cottage or a house of stone or wood is of secondary importance. What really deserves our admiration is the way in which they use the materials at hand to ameliorate a given complex of climatic conditions [Figures 2-1, 2-2].

Today this is no longer necessary. We can erect identically the same building in Portland, Maine, and in Brownsville, Texas. Indeed, we do it all the time. We can even maintain exactly the same internal conditions inside the same two buildings, thanks to the level of our engineering sciences. But does the fact that this is technically possible mean that it is economically or even philosophically correct? . . . It causes many buildings to be over-engineered—that is, mechanical means are used to correct conditions which reasonable attention to site, orientation, path of sun and wind, even proper use of vegetation might well prevent. In other words, this mechanistic concept tends to produce buildings which are always fighting their environment instead of trying to work with it. . . . Internal balance can only be maintained by the use of a wide range of auxiliary equipment and the consumption of immense amounts of energy.

Since these comments were published in the Building Research Advisory Board Conference Report No. 1, *Weather and the Building Industry* (National Research Council, Washington, D.C., 1950), Professor Fitch's comments have only been reinforced by three decades of residential construction that for the most part has little concern for meaningful symbiotic relationships with the environment. It is only recently that an extensive awareness of such matters has begun to develop, and there is little doubt now that it will continue to burgeon in the future.

2-1. Eskimo igloo. (American Museum of Natural History)

2-2. Native village in Aitape, New Guinea. (U.S. Army)

It is not to be assumed from Professor Fitch's comments that the full practice of the principles of orientation will make summer cooling (or winter heating, for that matter) unnecessary in most American climates. What it does mean is that such practice can markedly reduce the costs of installing and operating such "auxiliary equipment," and can, furthermore, in some areas of the country, make summer living comfortable without mechanical cooling of any sort, except possibly some artificial ventilation.

Careful and scientific orientation, in the fullest meaning of the term, will influence almost every structural or mechanical specification for a house, from size and location of windows to tonnage of refrigeration for summer cooling. It will not perform miracles, but it can and will increase living comfort and often decrease construction and equipment costs to a degree not always easy to imagine. Furthermore, maintenance and operating costs can be lowered as well, much greater overall energy efficiency can be realized, and the conservation of fuels, energy, and raw materials (which concern will be a highly visible part of our everyday lives from now on) will be accomplished. For these reasons, proper orientation deserves the close attention of everyone interested in and concerned with the livable and affordable private residence.

CLIMATIC DATA

Though many studies have been done, perhaps one of the best general summaries of the effect of climate on houses appeared in a series on climate control in *House Beautiful* and in the American Institute of Architects' *Bulletin* from 1948 to 1950. The regional climatic charts prepared for the project by Dr. Paul Siple and others, and published in the AIA *Bulletin*, were of particular value to everyone interested in the design and construction of houses that benefit from, and do not fight, the natural environment. The study is still valid, and *Regional Climate Analyses and Design Data* are still available for the following: *Denver, Colorado; Mid-Ohio Region; Mid-Mississippi Basin; Gulf Coast; Chicago Area; Washington, D.C. Area; Boston Area; Pittsburgh Area; Portland, Oregon Area; Charleston, S.C. Area; Albany Area.* Availability is limited, and inquiries can be addressed to *House Beautiful*, 717 Fifth Avenue, New York, NY 10022.

It should be borne in mind that these are essentially *regional* climatic studies. As with all such studies, they do not attempt to detail the subject down to the finest possible point. Within the large area treated, natural features such as hills and valleys, ponds and running streams, trees and meadows, and local wind and rain variations arising from the action of these topographical factors as well as artificial elements such as paved streets, terraces and driveways, adjacent buildings, and the like, will all make measurable changes in the general climatic picture. In other words, while the Siple charts, or studies of similar nature, are of great value as guides to relatively large regions, they should be carefully evaluated and modified in terms of special conditions that may exist in a given area.

An excellent example of this is shown in Figure 2-3. In the same Building Research Advisory Board Conference Report cited earlier in this chapter, Dr. Helmut Landsberg describes the influence of a large body of water—Lake Ontario in this case—on the temperature of the region. The figure, he states, "shows the temperatures recorded on a clear winter night at right angles to the lake shore. It shows the warmest temperatures near the lake, which acts as a large reservoir of heat. Then we notice a gradual decrease of temperature with distance from the lake. Finally, we can observe the effects of a pool of cold air which has drained into the narrow valley of the Don River. Only seven miles from the lake, the temperature is 34° lower. Both the lakeshore and the Don River valley show considerable differences against the official weather stations of the city. . . ."

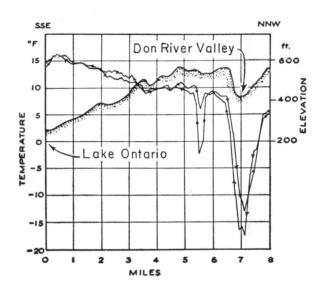

2-3. Temperature profile at right angles to the shore of Lake Ontario near Toronto, Canada. (Building Research Advisory Board, "Weather and the Building Industry")

On a truly microclimatic scale, the effect of grass and trees between a street and a house in hot weather is shown in Figure 2-4. The moral: set the house back on its lot!

These two examples, just as valid now as they were when the research was originally done, effectively define the outer and inner limits of the microclimatic problem. On the one hand, there are the often large temperature and humidity effects arising from the relation of the house to bodies of water, stands of trees, elevations of hills, and the like; and on the other hand, there are controllable—but often forgotten or ignored—effects that arise on the site and are alleviated by landscaping, by careful planning of exterior paved surfaces, by relation to other buildings, and by such architectural minutiae as sun control overhangs and exterior wall and roof colors.

2-4. A microclimatic weather effect. (BRAB Conference Report, op. cit.)

The whole business of relating building design to environment is a most difficult and involved procedure, riddled with complexities that until recently have not come to light nor received much consideration. Now, however, a relatively new building science, variously called climate control or building climatology, has come into being. In the past few years, particularly, extensive research and development programs have been initiated in this field, but, as yet, comprehensive and meaningful design data remain scattered and a bit confusing. We do know, however, that there are a great many low-technology, commonsense, and inexpensive devices and expedients that can be fully utilized in more consequential design and construction features by which residential climates can be practically, effectively, and economically controlled.

SITE AMENITIES

Though every effort should be made in that direction, it is not always possible to justify the time and expense that must be devoted to microclimatic studies solely on the basis of actual savings in the design and building of the structure or in the specification of equipment. However, there are other acceptable justifications besides those that are solely economic. A strategically located tree may be worth saving not because it will reduce solar radiation through a window or against a wall, but because it provides a visual delight—and a place to be comfortable under on a hot day—for the occupants of the building. Subdividers who ruthlessly strip wooded land of every tree and level small hills with thundering bulldozers simply to save a few dollars in hewing out foundations are forgetting the fact that the natural environment is a desirable one, "good for the soul." Furthermore, due attention to the preservation of a large part of the environment, where it has desirable features, will pay dividends by giving each house an immediate naturalness and beauty that, under other circumstances, could not be achieved within a generation.

Much of this will sound to the reader like a platitude. The tragedy is that only too often immediate economic considerations blind one to the long-range benefits of preserving the natural environment of the building site and surrounding area as much as possible.

There is another reason for emphasizing the point. Ignoring existing contours often results in houses that do not sit well on their sites. A common example is the "split-level" on a flat site. We are all familiar with the semisunken garage that is part of such a house, with the driveway lined on both sides by masonry walls or hazardously steep sodded banks—serious dangers to playing children, to elderly persons, and to anyone trying to find the front door on a dark night.

SITE SELECTION

Many other aspects besides comfort may enter into the selection of a building site, of course. Type of neighborhood, nearness to work, availability and price of land, existence and nearness of schools and stores, personal tastes and requirements, all may lead to the choice of a site that is far from perfect from the viewpoint of effective orientation. It would thus be futile to outline the optimum qualities of a good site because they will differ from person to person and because it is increasingly difficult, and in many areas almost impossible, to find building sites that meet all climatic, social, and economic requirements, particularly within the suburban precincts of our large cities.

Once a site has been selected, its purely physical attributes should be carefully analyzed. In addition to the metes and bounds described in the deed and outlined on the surveyor's plat, the following types of information should be obtained:

A contour survey if the land is at all irregular;

An inventory, best done in sketch-map fashion, of principal natural features, including trees and large shrubs, streams, springs, and "wild garden" areas;

The relation of the site to adjacent properties and structures as they might affect the house location;

Front, back, and side lot setbacks, as required in local codes or zoning ordinances, accurately marked on the plat;

An assessment of potential view planes;

An evaluation of existing and/or potential public access and a preferred driveway location;

Locations of all existing utilities (electric lines, telephone lines, water and sewer mains), together with predetermined tap-on points, if any, and a judgment as to the most appropriate courses the utilities might take to reach the building site; and

For rural and exurban sites, an investigation of potential water sources, and a complete analysis of the soils as regards landscaping and gardening capabilities, foundation design, and, more important, percolation rates for a sewage disposal system.

With these basic benefits and limitations in mind, it now becomes possible to study placing the house from the point of view of the weather.

CLIMATIC FACTORS

A thorough study of weather patterns affecting a given site is essential as a planning preliminary. Without it, errors in house orientation, room location, landscaping, and construction detailing may be made that make the resultant house uncomfortable to live in and uneconomical to heat and cool. There may also be a failure to maximize existing beneficial site aspects, or to minimize poor ones, that can make for a less workable and comfortable house than might otherwise have been the case.

The most important climate aspects affecting houses are as follows:

Temperature extremes, averages, and duration. Highest and lowest temperatures, how frequently they occur, mean highs and lows for summer and winter seasons, and duration of these extremes and means. These data are essential for economic scaling of heating and cooling plants, for computing heating/cooling loads, and for determining the relative thermal efficiencies and cost-effectiveness of various building section constructions and design details to be used in house design. The figures are of a general nature, applying to whole regions, and should be refined by obtaining specific information on conditions in the immediate vicinity of the site, since local variations often considerably modify the more general averages in the area.

Hours of sunshine, number of clear, cloudy, and partly cloudy days, and clearness of air. These figures are not important in heating and cooling load calculations and in the selection of conventional heating/cooling equipment, since these elements are based primarily on temperature extremes rather than on variations in insolation. The solar data are absolutely essential, however, in planning solar heating/cooling systems and then the selection of that equipment, and as design data for the planning of so-called solar houses whether they be of active, passive, or hybrid type. This data is also needed in planning fenestration and sun-control devices, whether or not the proposed house is to include solar or solar-assist heating/cooling means and mechanisms. In climates with much cloudiness, it may be well to permit sunlight in the rooms at almost all times except around the summer solstice, when natural shade or artificial overhangs should keep the sun out of exposed windows for around a month. In hot, dry climates it may be preferable to keep the sun out the year round. Air clarity can have an influence on both solar-control and solar-utilization design details, too, through its effect upon insolation in any given locale.

Solar angles in the various seasons. These factors of climate control are invariable, and from them stem the planning of solar collection devices, windows, and the location and extent of natural or artificial shade over and around the windows. They may also have a bearing upon house orientation, roof design, window placement, porch or deck locations, and other factors. Further information is contained in chapter 5, and a wealth of specific details and design considerations can be found in *The Solar Home Book* by Bruce Anderson (Brick House Publishing Co., Inc., 1976), the *ASHRAE HANDBOOK & Product Directory* (American Society of Heating, Refrigerating and Air-Conditioning Engineers, Inc.) and numerous other sources, including government agency and equipment manufacturers' association publications.

Direction and velocity of prevailing winds at different seasons and different hours of the day. These are modified by a study of local changes in wind patterns due to hills, bodies of water, other buildings, etc., and by transient variations that may occur during violent storms and breeze patterns, especially in summer. They are of great importance in providing comfortable living in nonmechanically cooled houses. Construction materials and techniques sufficiently strong to withstand winds of gale force are taken for granted here (a whole gale on the Beaufort scale is 55 to 63 mph wind).

One interesting aspect of the "prevailing winds" concept is the extent to which these winds vary over a twenty-four hour period, as well as from season to season. Though many people may indeed be familiar with the prevailing winds in their locality, oftentimes they think only of the daytime hours and pay no attention to prevailing nighttime breezes, and even less to prevailing cool air flow patterns, which often are quite different. For example, in many locales a breeze will typically blow up a valley during the day but reverse itself in the evening. In mountainous country, a chilling "cold air fall" may roll downslope at 1 to 2 mph all night, during otherwise calm conditions and irrespective of normal prevailing breezes.

There are some important points that should be noted about the use of wind data. Intelligent use can be made of wind behavior patterns when the specific house site is chosen and the building itself is oriented. House design can also be coordinated with these factors, so that prevailing winds, as well as storm tracks, will have a minimum physical impact upon the structure, and so that fenestration and exterior doors can be so arranged as to minimize wind effect. For example, with such knowledge a roof design/orientation can be so arranged as to prevent, or at least minimize, the deep drifting of snow onto a leeward roof section, with possible consequent damage.

In addition, when new sites are cleared, existing vegetation, particularly trees and tall shrubbery, can be left toward the direction of the coldest winds to serve as a natural windbreak. The same information can be taken into consideration for planning new planting. Trees, shrubbery, and lawns or pastures, besides providing protection from wind, are effective in filtering pollution products from the air, retaining cool air and some degree of moisture during the warm months, and reducing and dispersing cool air drainage during the colder months; conversely, vegetation can be so arranged as to allow adequate air motion in low areas that might otherwise entrap cool, stagnant, or humid air. In short, by coordinating the typical wind behavior and air current patterns in a given microclimate with either the existing vegetation or plans for planting new vegetation, or both, maximum benefits of the site can be derived that will enhance the livability and comfort, both indoors and out, of the residence.

Amount of rainfall, snowfall, number of thunderstorms, and periods of fog. Local rainfalls may vary considerably from the figures for the larger region. For example, in many hilly areas, there is often a good deal more rain on one side of a hill than on the other. Mountain weather is extremely variable, even from one valley or ridgeline to another, even though the separation may only be a half mile or less. These variations should be taken into account primarily when locating the house on the site and when locating the openings in the house, but not as an aspect of weatherproofing of materials or of construction techniques. In *any* region that experiences heavy precipitation (whether rain or snow and even if only once or twice a year, as in some semiarid parts of the country), the house must be able to withstand it. The pervasive soaking effects of fog must likewise be guarded against. Where applicable, of course, additional factors concerning the possibility of seismic, tornadic, or hurricane activity should be included in house design.

Good orientation will also, of course, assure that the house is located so that effective drainage away from the foundation will take place under the heaviest conceivable deluge of rain or the melting of large accumulations of snow. Dry washes, watercourses, small drainage watersheds, and the like must be avoided, and siting should never be done on unstable soil (complete soil analyses are often advisable in the immediate area of the building site).

Seasonal variation in humidity. Much hot weather discomfort is due not only to high temperatures, but also to an excessive amount of water vapor in the air. In orienting a house on its site, particularly in humid regions, the largest possible amount of natural ventilation should be encouraged by placing the openings so that the prevailing winds will pass through unimpeded. Even in houses with mechanical summer cooling, free passages of breezes through the attic may reduce the heat load on the air conditioning unit and cut operating costs. Powered ventilation is, at best, a supplement to the winds of nature and an expensive one at that.

Outdoor humidity in wintertime, on the other hand, is not usually a problem. Indeed, indoor humidification often becomes necessary to provide a healthful and comfortable atmosphere during cold weather, as is more fully explained in chapter 4.

Moderately complete data on these and a few other aspects of climate are compiled in the Regional Climatic Analyses and Design Data (AIA *Bulletin*) previously referred to. Other sources of information can be tapped: The National Climatic Center, the U.S. Department of Agriculture, the U.S. Department of Energy, the National Solar Information Center, various state and local agencies, public utility companies, manufacturers of heating and cooling equipment and their trade associations, and the like. With the rapidly increasing interest in such matters, a substantial amount of specific and detailed information is now available to the general public in a great many books dealing with heating and cooling, especially of the solar and alternative-energy variety; a representative selection of such volumes can be found at most public libraries.

Contradictions often arise when one tries to put into effect the oftentimes conflicting climatic requirements of summer and winter comfort, and of economy in operating heating and cooling systems. In general, it is best to lean toward planning for maximum summer comfort from the point of view of design and orientation, since structural methods and materials can much more economically cope with cold than with heat. Moreover, it still is true that many regions in the temperate zone can provide a comfortable indoor summer climate without mechanical cooling—*if* the natural environment is fully exploited. This is not true of winter conditions.

Therefore, if there is a choice, locate the house where it will receive the most natural shade and breezes on hot days. This rule is worth observing not only in those regions where heat is the principal problem, as in the southern tier of states, but also elsewhere, even where winter conditions are severest. Like most generalities, this one has exceptions, but usually it is worth observing.

NONCLIMATIC FACTORS IN HOUSE ORIENTATION

Although control of the thermal environment is the most important problem in orienting a house, there are other aspects to be considered, and they have been outlined in chapter 1. They include protection against noise and smells, and provision of visual pleasure in and from the house, including, where needed, landscaping or structural elements that afford the occupants privacy from neighbors and passersby. It is not necessary to expatiate further on these elements, except to emphasize that they *should not* be forgotten in the overall planning of the house and its environs.

One of the best ways to account for all relevant orientation factors and site features is to commit them to a pair of sketch maps. These need not be fancy, so long as they are complete. The first (which is not always necessary, as in the case of a small urban site) should consist of a composite overview of the site and the surrounding area, as shown in Figure 2-5. The second is similar but more microcosmic, taking into account only the immediate area, as in Figure 2-6. Between the two sketches, all basic climatic factors should be indicated, as well as all pertinent data from the site analysis discussed earlier in this chapter. If warranted, the sketch maps can be transformed into formal large-scale drawings by a draftsman and detailed to any reasonable degree.

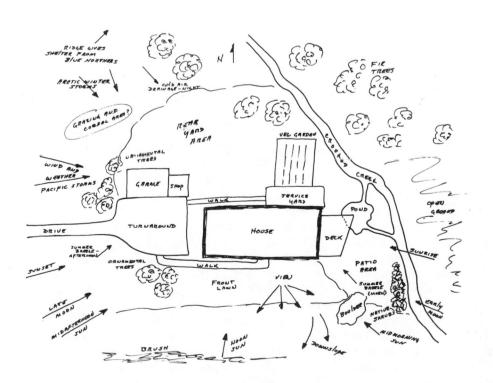

2-5. Typical informal sketch map showing overview of building site, land tract, and surrounding area.

2-6. Typical informal sketch map showing building site and immediate area, with orientation and climatic information.

Chapter 3

Principles of Thermal Control: Winter

Optimum orientation, according to best scientific principles and data (study in the area goes on continually, and findings are updated regularly), of a house on a well-selected site can eliminate almost entirely the environmental problems of sight, sound, smell, and privacy. By the same means, the summer cooling load can be substantially reduced by keeping at least a portion of the solar energy out of the structure. Although the impact of low winter temperatures on a house can only be alleviated to a relatively small degree, orientation does play a definite part in this aspect of weather conditioning, too. In this chapter and the next, the overall problems of thermal control will be analyzed, with specific emphasis upon winter conditions. Since the basic task to be performed in summer (cooling), is in many ways diametrically the opposite of that in winter (heating), construction for summer comfort and for economy in cooling equipment is described separately in chapter 4.

THE MODERN CONCEPT OF SHELTER

A house is nothing but a hollow shell. The word "shelter" does not derive from the same Anglo-Saxon root as "shell" (*scyll*), but it well could have. After all, a shell is all that a house, or any other structure in which humans live or work, really is. And most natural shells are extraordinarily inefficient barriers to cold or heat, as are most primitive types of man-made shelter.

Certain animals hibernate in the winter. Their metabolism has been modified through evolution so that they can sleep through many weeks or months without additional nourishment. But they cannot live during cold weather behind a thin-shell structure such as an unheated house. Nature has given hibernators the instinct to bury themselves deep away from winter—in caves, or in the ground, with several feet of earth be-

tween them and the outer cold (Figure 3-1), or in the hollow trunks of trees, with thick layers of insulating wood protecting them from the raw blasts of January.

Other animals, particularly some birds and fish, migrate. They cannot hibernate, so they take wing or fin or foot to find warmer climates. And still other creatures, as for example many of those in the arctic regions, provide their own insulation with thick layers of fat and fur.

But man is basically defenseless against low temperatures. His ingenuity as an intelligent animal has, over the centuries, provided him with fire, clothing, and elaborate structures within which he can use the fire and clothing to keep himself warm. Why the human animal ever left the year-round salubriousness of the warmer regions in which civilization first arose is a question for the anthropologists (and also frequently wailed about every February by the denizens of the Dakotas, Vermont, Minnesota, et al.); we only know that western civilization is primarily a temperate zone phenomenon. In fact, the challenge of cold has been one of the important drives that has made man into the aggressive, energetic, exploring being that he is.

In the past, cold was conquered by relatively primitive methods that served well enough for the rugged and inevitably cruel early human societies that hardened preindustrial man (Figure 3-2). But today, the advance of modern technology has successfully beaten back and warded off Old Man Winter, and the further continuation of that process remains a goal of paramount importance in the development of building construction, particularly houses.

In the latter half of the nineteenth century and the first quarter of the twentieth, advances in thermal control involved first and foremost the invention of central heating equipment and methods of heat distribution. It was enough, at that time, to produce great quantities of

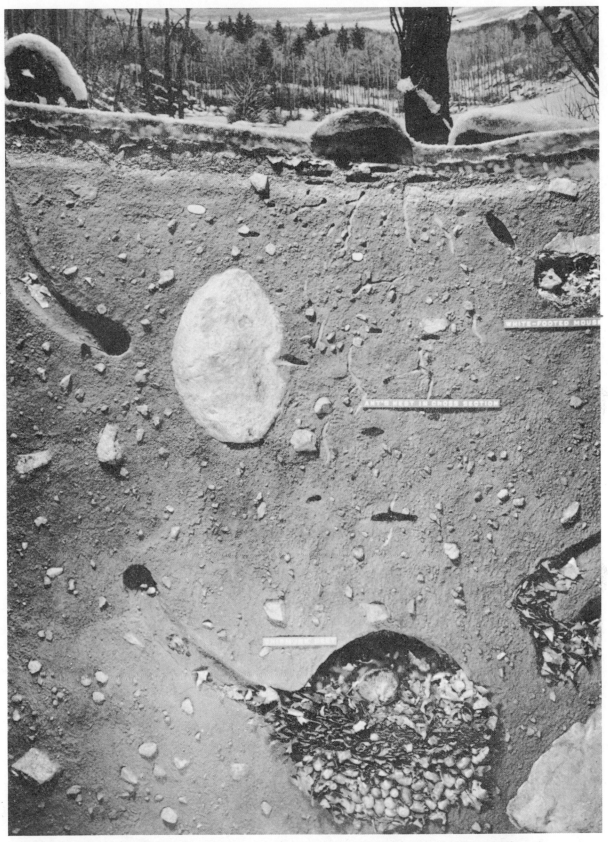

3–1. Model showing how and where a chipmunk hibernates. (American Museum of Natural History)

lovely, hot heat that, by one means or another, could be spread throughout the house. Those were the days when all architects and builders had to do was to enclose space fairly aesthetically, or fairly cheaply. Sometimes they did both, and were called geniuses. Specifications simply called for oversized furnaces or boilers, ducts or pipes—and the average citizen spent lots of money for cordwood or coal in the winter. In the summer, he just sweltered, for free.

But along with a general rise in price levels during the period after World War I came a rapid increase in the costs of fuels. Furthermore, the explosive expansion of postwar technology, especially after World War II, brought with it a whole series of new methods for combating cold, methods that had two basic purposes. The first was to increase the efficiency and ease of operation of the heating plant, and the second was to improve the thermal efficiency of the structure in which it was housed, thus reducing the amount of fuel needed and also increasing comfort. Then came the energy crisis of 1973, followed by even more serious and widespread acknowledgement of a continuing and deepening shortage and dislocation of traditional energy supplies and sources during the late 1970's, accompanied by heretofore undreamed-of upward spiraling of energy costs of all kinds. This resulted in a rapid intensification of research and development in the thermal control field. Conventional and familiar materials, methods,

and techniques were (and are being) reviewed, retested, and updated, while unconventional and alternative ones, including entirely new designs and systems, were (and are being) brought forth. This, in turn and in all its horrendous complexity, has amounted to no less than a revolution in the building industry, again particularly affecting houses.

Today, architects and builders have to be more than aesthetic, economical, and aware of a few important engineering principles. The days are past when a man who carried a rafter table in his hip pocket was counted as a leader in the business. The fellow who leads these days is the type who can rattle off "U" factors for complicated wall sections, chart a sun track for July 19 at latitude 33° 17′ 21″, discuss "therms" and "perms" and "STC's" and "insolation," and carries a slide rule in his hip pocket.

This chapter is concerned with *structural* methods of increasing heat efficiency. They are not the whole story, of course; the heating plant and associated equipment is the heart of the system, and a brief review of modern heating methods is found in chapter 7. Likewise, orientation of a house to take advantage of the winter sun *can* cut heating costs appreciably, but *not* necessarily the initial cost of heating equipment or design/materials related to high thermal efficiency. Conventional heating plants must be sized for worst, rather than average, weather conditions, though in certain

3–2. Indian village in winter. (The Bettman Archive)

specific cases allowances may be made for beneficial climate effects. And unconventional heating systems, as well as the construction of unconventional or specialized structural designs such as the solar-heated or earth-sheltered houses, are still in the main more costly at the outset than their comparable conventional counterparts. Total costs, calculated over the projected life of an unconventional building are, however, another matter. But in any case, the thermal efficiency of structures in this book—houses—is primarily a matter of the intelligent use of both old and new building materials and construction techniques.

HEAT LOSS

The basic principle behind construction for efficient heat conservation in a house is simple: prevent as much as possible of the heat created, or entrapped within the structure, by whatever means, from escaping outdoors, and reduce to a minimum the infiltration of cold outer air into the structure.

Before final design specifications for a house and its heating/cooling equipment can be laid down, a reasonably accurate estimation of the rate of heat loss/gain through the components of the structure must be obtained. This in turn requires a knowledge of house design, construction techniques, and the characteristics (thermally speaking) of the building materials being contemplated for use, as well as the different effects that can be gained by combinations thereof. Comparisons must also often be made, in order to determine the points of diminishing returns, where further thermal "tightening up" by one means or another will prove to be more expensive than the fuel consumed over a given (usually long) period of time, and so perhaps not worth the additional effort/cost.

The calculations that must be made to determine heat loss for a given structure in a given location and operating under given conditions are most important if optimum operation at high efficiency and low cost is to be realized, and they should be done as carefully and with as much specific information in hand as possible. But, it is equally important to realize that the final results will remain only an estimation, nothing more. The degree of accuracy obtained when the proper procedures are followed can be, especially when verified over a long period of time, surprisingly high; still, the figures are only approximate and the calculations cannot be made with great precision, at least from a practical standpoint. Carefully controlled laboratory experiments and tests using all of the latest scientific techniques can indeed lead to pinpoint data, but few of us live in laboratories. There are so many variables involved in heat loss calculations for real buildings in the real world that complete accuracy is physically impossible, and a reasonably definitive set of numbers upon which acceptable design specifications and construction details can be based is about the best one can hope for.

Among those variables that can never be fully ascertained are:

Climatic and microclimatic conditions that vary constantly: wind direction and speed, duration of sunshine, intensity of sunshine, outside ambient temperatures, numbers and duration of storms, etc.;

Natural or production variations in building materials that make for slightly different thermal characteristics from sample to sample;

Variations in quality levels of building materials and commercially made component sections or parts;

Quality of workmanship in construction of the building;

Effects of aging and weathering on the building; and

Living habits of the occupants as regards cooking, ventilation, frequency of exterior door operation, etc.

It is also important to understand that heat loss calculations can be made in a number of ways (though they follow the same basic pattern) and in numerous varying degrees of complexity. Highly sophisticated procedures have been developed that involve complete, hour-by-hour calculations, extending over several months of heating time and including dozens of factors and subcalculations, that must be analyzed by computer. The results are extremely detailed and, comparatively speaking, quite accurate. On the other hand, heat loss calculations for houses can be worked out on a far simpler basis and including far fewer specifics and more averages and generalizations, with results that are perfectly acceptable and, from a practical standpoint, can be relied upon quite satisfactorily for house design and construction purposes. The basic methods of making those calculations follow.

HEAT TRANSMISSION COEFFICIENTS

Heat flows through different materials at different rates. For instance, an inch thickness of common brick may transmit more than six times as much heat per hour as an inch thickness of plywood. For materials that are of a more or less uniform internal structure, such as wood, brick, or particle board, the rate of heat flow, or thermal transmission, is known as the thermal conductivity, or k. This k is expressed as the amount of heat that passes in 1 hour through 1 square foot of a homogeneous material 1 inch thick. Our customary measure is the quantity of heat in British thermal units (Btu—see Glossary) that is transmitted per degree Fahrenheit of temperature difference from the warm side to the cool side of the material. One shorthand way of writing this definition is Btu/hr/sq ft/° F diff/in.

Thus the k of a piece of plywood 1 inch thick and 1 foot square, with a density per cubic foot of 34 pounds, is known to average 0.80, which means that eight-tenths of a Btu will pass through that piece every hour, for each degree of temperature difference between its two sides. The 0.80 figure will vary with a number of factors, including the kind of wood and the moisture content of the plywood, but since such factors also change the specified weight of a cubic foot of the material, the value remains correct *for the specific sample.*

For example, if the temperature on one side of the piece of plywood is 70° F and 20° F on the other, the heat loss per hour is a total of 40 Btu (50 times 0.80)—enough heat to raise the temperature of a pound (approximately 1 pint) of water by 40° F. This is a considerable heat loss for one small square foot of material, considering today's fuel prices.

The *k* for an inch thickness of molded-bead expanded polystyrene insulating board with a density of 1 pound per cubic foot is only 0.28; for interior-finish insulating board (plank, tile) with a density of 15 pounds per cubic foot it is 0.35 (and of course less for lesser densities). For exfoliated vermiculite loose-fill insulation at 7.0 to 8.2 pounds per cubic foot density, the *k is* 0.47. The smaller the number, the lower the heat transmission through the material; note the considerable, and sometimes extreme, differences between the common structural building materials and the thermal insulating materials. Note, too, that these figures are based upon a calculation mean temperature of 75° F, and changes in that temperature, the specific density, and other test parameters will result in changes in *k*.

Many materials are not homogeneous or, if they are, are not normally available an inch thick. In this case the heat transfer is measured for the stated thickness and material structure and is called the thermal conductance, or *C*. For asbestos-cement shingles with a density of 120 pounds per cubic foot, the *C* is 4.76, expressed as heat transfer in Btu/hr/sq ft/° F diff/*standard thickness.* For three-oval-core concrete blocks made from sand and gravel aggregate in an 8-inch thickness, the *C* is 0.90; for 1 × 8-inch wood drop siding it is 1.27.

Obviously, all building materials transfer heat to a greater or lesser extent. The same is true of air in contact with (surface conductance) or inside of (air space conductance) a complex of building materials. When the surface of a building section is indoors, the air is treated as still; the conductance of still air varies, depending upon the orientation of the section and the emittance (ε) of the surface.

Emittance is the ratio of heat radiated by a surface to that radiated by a theoretical black body that would absorb *all* radiation falling upon it. *Effective emittance (E)* is the combined effect of the surface emittances of the parallel boundary surfaces of an air space of large dimensions compared to the distance between the surfaces. Emittance and effective emittance values for a few materials are given in Table 3-1.

A different situation prevails when the surface is outdoors. Film or surface conductance, symbolized as *h*, now comes into play. This is the heat transfer, over a certain time period, to or from a surface that is in contact with the air, for the difference between the temperature of the surface and the air temperature, written Btu/hr/sq ft/° F. The conductance of moving air varies with speed (Figure 3-3) and, to a lesser degree, with temperature and surface roughness. This complex relationship remains under study, and further information can be obtained through the American Society of Heating, Refrigerating and Air Conditioning Engineers, Inc. (ASHRAE), in the *1977 Fundamentals*

Reflectivity and Emittance Values of Various Surfaces and Effective Emittances of Air Spaces

Surface	Reflectivity in Percent	Average *Emittance ε*	Effective *Emittance E* of Air Space — One surface emittance ε; the other 0.90	Effective *Emittance E* of Air Space — Both surfaces emittances ε
Aluminum foil, bright	92 to 97	0.05	0.05	0.03
Aluminum sheet	80 to 95	0.12	0.12	0.06
Aluminum coated paper, polished.	75 to 84	0.20	0.20	0.11
Steel, galvanized, bright. . .	70 to 80	0.25	0.24	0.15
Aluminum paint	30 to 70	0.50	0.47	0.35
Building materials: wood, paper, masonry, nonmetallic paints	5 to 15	0.90	0.82	0.82
Regular glass	5 to 15	0.84	0.77	0.72

Table 3-1. (Reprinted with permission from the *1977 Fundamentals Volume, ASHRAE HANDBOOK & Product Directory)*

3-3. Surface conductance for different 12-inch square surfaces as affected by air movement. (Reprinted with permission from the *1977 Fundamentals Volume, ASHRAE HANDBOOK & Product Directory)*

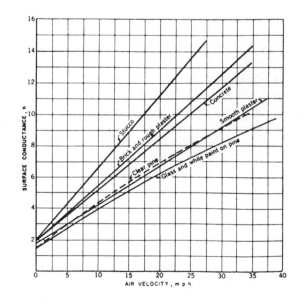

Volume, ASHRAE HANDBOOK & Product Directory. From a practical standpoint affecting heat loss calculations for houses, air is considered to be moving over outside surfaces, during the winter heating season, at an average 15 miles per hour. In this case, the surface conductance h_o is given as 6.0, regardless of building section orientation or surface type. This figure is used in the same manner as k or C in making calculations. There are some localities, however, where a wind speed basis of 15 mph could be incorrect. Refer to Table 3-2 for the proper conversion factors needed for other wind velocities. The table should be used only if it is certain that the *average* wind velocities on a winter-long basis are noticeably higher or lower than 15 mph. Table 3-3 contains values of surface conductances and resistances.

Air space conductance reduces heat loss through a volume of still air. Air enclosed between two surfaces—wall, floor, or ceiling—is classed as still, even though there may be some slight motion in it. The reduction depends upon the width and orientation of the air space, temperature differences between the surfaces, the mean temperature within the enclosed space, and the effective emittance (E) of the space. The thermal resistances of various air spaces can be determined by first finding the value of E in Table 3-1, and then relating it to the values given in Table 3-4.

Once the values just discussed have been determined, the next step, that of finding the *resistances* of the materials, or R, can take place. In our calculations for heat loss, we are interested in the ability of a material to hold back heat rather than to transmit it, and the R, or R-factor, is a universal, additive measure for heat resistance—the more R's are added together, the more heat will be held back and the more effective the material or section will be as a thermal insulator. In order

to obtain R, we need only to take the reciprocal of k, C, or h. And to find a reciprocal of a given number, one merely divides that number into 1.000, a simple matter with a pocket calculator. Thus, the reciprocal of 5.0, the k of common brick or stucco, is 1.000 divided by 5.0, or 0.20. The reciprocal of the k for molded-bead expanded polystyrene insulating board, 0.28, is 3.57. The greater the R number, the greater the insulating value of the material; note the substantial difference between brick and bead-board. C's, k's and R's of various building materials are given in Table 3-5.

Knowing the R of a given material is all well and good, but houses are not built of sheets of single

Surface Conductances and Resistances

Position of Surface	Direction of Heat Flow	Non-reflective $\varepsilon = 0.90$		Reflective $\varepsilon = 0.20$		Reflective $\varepsilon = 0.05$	
		h_i	R	h_i	R	h_i	R
STILL AIR							
Horizontal ..... Upward		1.63	0.61	0.91	1.10	0.76	1.32
Sloping—45 deg Upward		1.60	0.62	0.88	1.14	0.73	1.37
Vertical .... Horizontal		1.46	0.68	0.74	1.35	0.59	1.70
Sloping—45 deg Downward		1.32	0.76	0.60	1.67	0.45	2.22
Horizontal ..... Downward		1.08	0.92	0.37	2.70	0.22	4.55
		h_0	R	h_0	R	h_0	R
MOVING AIR (Any Position)							
15-mph Wind (for winter)	Any	6.00	0.17				
7.5-mph Wind (for summer)	Any	4.00	0.25				

Table 3–3. (Reprinted with permission from the *1977 Fundamentals Volume, ASHRAE HANDBOOK & Product Directory*)

Conversion Table for Wall Coefficient U for Various Wind Velocities

U for 15 mph	U for 0 to 30 mph Wind Velocities						U for 15 mph	U for 0 to 30 mph Wind Velocities					
	0	5	10	20	25	30		0	5	10	20	25	30
0.050	0.049	0.050	0.050	0.050	0.050	0.050	0.290	0.257	0.278	0.286	0.293	0.295	0.296
0.060	0.059	0.059	0.060	0.060	0.060	0.060	0.310	0.273	0.296	0.305	0.313	0.315	0.317
0.070	0.068	0.069	0.070	0.070	0.070	0.070	0.330	0.288	0.314	0.324	0.333	0.336	0.338
0.080	0.078	0.079	0.080	0.080	0.080	0.080	0.350	0.303	0.332	0.344	0.354	0.357	0.359
0.090	0.087	0.089	0.090	0.090	0.091	0.091	0.370	0.318	0.350	0.363	0.375	0.378	0.380
0.100	0.096	0.099	0.100	0.100	0.101	0.101	0.390	0.333	0.368	0.382	0.395	0.399	0.401
0.110	0.105	0.108	0.109	0.110	0.111	0.111	0.410	0.347	0.385	0.402	0.416	0.420	0.422
0.130	0.123	0.127	0.129	0.131	0.131	0.131	0.430	0.362	0.403	0.421	0.436	0.441	0.444
0.150	0.141	0.147	0.149	0.151	0.151	0.152	0.450	0.376	0.420	0.439	0.457	0.462	0.465
0.170	0.158	0.166	0.169	0.171	0.172	0.172	0.500	0.410	0.464	0.487	0.509	0.514	0.518
0.190	0.175	0.184	0.188	0.191	0.192	0.193	0.600	0.474	0.548	0.581	0.612	0.620	0.626
0.210	0.192	0.203	0.208	0.212	0.213	0.213	0.700	0.535	0.631	0.675	0.716	0.728	0.736
0.230	0.209	0.222	0.227	0.232	0.233	0.234	0.800	0.592	0.711	0.766	0.821	0.836	0.847
0.250	0.226	0.241	0.247	0.252	0.253	0.254	0.900	0.645	0.789	0.858	0.927	0.946	0.960
0.270	0.241	0.259	0.266	0.273	0.274	0.275	1.000	0.695	0.865	0.949	1.034	1.058	1.075

Table 3–2. (Reprinted with permission from the *1977 Fundamentals Volume, ASHRAE HANDBOOK & Product Directory*)

materials. They are comprised of sections made up of several materials arranged in different ways and in varying complexity. In order to develop usable figures, the next step is to convert the R's to a value called U, which is the symbol for *thermal transmittance*. This is the overall coefficient of heat transfer, the amount of heat flow through given building sections made up of combinations of materials, and also some single materials such as glass. It includes the surface conductance on both sides of the section and is expressed as Btu per hour per square foot per degree F temperature difference between the air on the inside and the air on the outside (Btr/hr/sq ft/° F diff).

The U, or U-value as it is sometimes called, of a particular building section is not difficult to determine and can be worked out for virtually any combination of materials. In fact, during the house design process, it may be investigated for several possible combinations in order to discover which might be the most efficient, effective, and cost-effective. To find U, add all of the individual R values of the components of the section to find R_t, or total thermal resistance. U is then the reciprocal of R_t, or $U = 1/R_t$.

For example, the wall of a typical frame house might consist, between studs, of a layer of 1 × 8-inch wood drop siding, another of ½-inch fiberboard sheathing, 3½ inches of mineral fiber blanket insulation, a layer of ½-inch plasterboard, and a finish of ¼-inch plywood paneling, plus an air film both inside and outside. Table 3-6 shows how the U-value is determined. But note that the U for those points where studs occur in the wall section is different, because the 3½-inch thickness of the wood stud is substituted there for the 3½ inches of insulation. Another formula can be employed to correct for this; more about that a bit later. Predetermined U values for a great many different typical section constructions can be found in *Insulation Manual; Homes, Apartments*, prepared by The National Association of Home Builders Research Foundation, Inc., and available from them or from the Mineral Insulation Manufacturers Association, Inc.

Thermal Resistances of Plane Air Spaces[d,e*]

All resistance values expressed in (hour)(square foot)(degree Fahrenheit temperature difference) per Btu
Values apply only to air spaces of uniform thickness bounded by plane, smooth, parallel surfaces with no leakage of air to or from the space.
Thermal resistance values for multiple air spaces must be based on careful estimates of mean temperature differences for each air space.
See the Caution section, under Overall Coefficients and Their Practical Use.

Position of Air Space	Direction of Heat Flow	Air Space Mean Temp,[b] (F)	Air Space Temp Diff,[b] (deg F)	0.5-in. Air Space[d] Value of E[b,c]					0.75-in. Air Space[d] Value of E[b,c]				
				0.03	0.05	0.2	0.5	0.82	0.03	0.05	0.2	0.5	0.82
Horiz.	Up	90	10	2.13	2.03	1.51	0.99	0.73	2.34	2.22	1.61	1.04	0.75
		50	30	1.62	1.57	1.29	0.96	0.75	1.71	1.66	1.35	0.99	0.77
		50	10	2.13	2.05	1.60	1.11	0.84	2.30	2.21	1.70	1.16	0.87
		0	20	1.73	1.70	1.45	1.12	0.91	1.83	1.79	1.52	1.16	0.93
		0	10	2.10	2.04	1.70	1.27	1.00	2.23	2.16	1.78	1.31	1.02
		−50	20	1.69	1.66	1.49	1.23	1.04	1.77	1.74	1.55	1.27	1.07
		−50	10	2.04	2.00	1.75	1.40	1.16	2.16	2.11	1.84	1.46	1.20
45° Slope	Up	90	10	2.44	2.31	1.65	1.06	0.76	2.96	2.78	1.88	1.15	0.81
		50	30	2.06	1.98	1.56	1.10	0.83	1.99	1.92	1.52	1.08	0.82
		50	10	2.55	2.44	1.83	1.22	0.90	2.90	2.75	2.00	1.29	0.94
		0	20	2.20	2.14	1.76	1.30	1.02	2.13	2.07	1.72	1.28	1.00
		0	10	2.63	2.54	2.03	1.44	1.10	2.72	2.62	2.08	1.47	1.12
		−50	20	2.08	2.04	1.78	1.42	1.17	2.05	2.01	1.76	1.41	1.16
		−50	10	2.62	2.56	2.17	1.66	1.33	2.53	2.47	2.10	1.62	1.30
Vertical	Horiz.	90	10	2.47	2.34	1.67	1.06	0.77	3.50	3.24	2.08	1.22	0.84
		50	30	2.57	2.46	1.84	1.23	0.90	2.91	2.77	2.01	1.30	0.94
		50	10	2.66	2.54	1.88	1.24	0.91	3.70	3.46	2.35	1.43	1.01
		0	20	2.82	2.72	2.14	1.50	1.13	3.14	3.02	2.32	1.58	1.18
		0	10	2.93	2.82	2.20	1.53	1.15	3.77	3.59	2.64	1.73	1.26
		−50	20	2.90	2.82	2.35	1.76	1.39	2.90	2.83	2.36	1.77	1.39
		−50	10	3.20	3.10	2.54	1.87	1.46	3.72	3.60	2.87	2.04	1.56
45° Slope	Down	90	10	2.48	2.34	1.67	1.06	0.77	3.53	3.27	2.10	1.22	0.84
		50	30	2.64	2.52	1.87	1.24	0.91	3.43	3.23	2.24	1.39	0.99
		50	10	2.67	2.55	1.89	1.25	0.92	3.81	3.57	2.40	1.45	1.02
		0	20	2.91	2.80	2.19	1.52	1.15	3.75	3.57	2.63	1.72	1.26
		0	10	2.94	2.83	2.21	1.53	1.15	4.12	3.91	2.81	1.80	1.30
		−50	20	3.16	3.07	2.52	1.86	1.45	3.78	3.65	2.90	2.05	1.57
		−50	10	3.26	3.16	2.58	1.89	1.47	4.35	4.18	3.22	2.21	1.66
Horiz.	Down	90	10	2.48	2.34	1.67	1.06	0.77	3.55	3.29	2.10	1.22	0.85
		50	30	2.66	2.54	1.88	1.24	0.91	3.77	3.52	2.38	1.44	1.02
		50	10	2.67	2.55	1.89	1.25	0.92	3.84	3.59	2.41	1.45	1.02
		0	20	2.94	2.83	2.20	1.53	1.15	4.18	3.96	2.83	1.81	1.30
		0	10	2.96	2.85	2.22	1.53	1.16	4.25	4.02	2.87	1.82	1.31
		−50	20	3.25	3.15	2.58	1.89	1.47	4.60	4.41	3.36	2.28	1.69
		−50	10	3.28	3.18	2.60	1.90	1.47	4.71	4.51	3.42	2.30	1.71

Table 3–4. (Reprinted with permission from the *1977 Fundamentals Volume, ASHRAE HANDBOOK & Product Directory*)

Table 3-4 continued

Position of Air Space	Direction of Heat Flow	Air Space Mean Temp,[b] (F)	Air Space Temp Diff,[b] (deg F)	1.5-in. Air Space[d] Value of E[b,c] 0.03	0.05	0.2	0.5	0.82	3.5-in. Air Space[d] Value of E[b,c] 0.03	0.05	0.2	0.5	0.82
Horiz	Up	90	10	2.55	2.41	1.71	1.08	0.77	2.84	2.66	1.83	1.13	0.80
		50	30	1.87	1.81	1.45	1.04	0.80	2.09	2.01	1.58	1.10	0.84
		50	10	2.50	2.40	1.81	1.21	0.89	2.80	2.66	1.95	1.28	0.93
		0	20	2.01	1.95	1.63	1.23	0.97	2.25	2.18	1.79	1.32	1.03
		0	10	2.43	2.35	1.90	1.38	1.06	2.71	2.62	2.07	1.47	1.12
		−50	20	1.94	1.91	1.68	1.36	1.13	2.19	2.14	1.86	1.47	1.20
		−50	10	2.37	2.31	1.99	1.55	1.26	2.65	2.58	2.18	1.67	1.33
45° Slope	Up	90	10	2.92	2.73	1.86	1.14	0.80	3.18	2.96	1.97	1.18	0.82
		50	30	2.14	2.06	1.61	1.12	0.84	2.26	2.17	1.67	1.15	0.86
		50	10	2.88	2.74	1.99	1.29	0.94	3.12	2.95	2.10	1.34	0.96
		0	20	2.30	2.23	1.82	1.34	1.04	2.42	2.35	1.90	1.38	1.06
		0	10	2.79	2.69	2.12	1.49	1.13	2.98	2.87	2.23	1.54	1.16
		−50	20	2.22	2.17	1.88	1.49	1.21	2.34	2.29	1.97	1.54	1.25
		−50	10	2.71	2.64	2.23	1.69	1.35	2.87	2.79	2.33	1.75	1.39
Vertical	Horiz.	90	10	3.99	3.66	2.25	1.27	0.87	3.69	3.40	2.15	1.24	0.85
		50	30	2.58	2.46	1.84	1.23	0.90	2.67	2.55	1.89	1.25	0.91
		50	10	3.79	3.55	2.39	1.45	1.02	3.63	3.40	2.32	1.42	1.01
		0	20	2.76	2.66	2.10	1.48	1.12	2.88	2.78	2.17	1.51	1.14
		0	10	3.51	3.35	2.51	1.67	1.23	3.49	3.33	2.50	1.67	1.23
		−50	20	2.64	2.58	2.18	1.66	1.33	2.82	2.75	2.30	1.73	1.37
		−50	10	3.31	3.21	2.62	1.91	1.48	3.40	3.30	2.67	1.94	1.50
45° Slope	Down	90	10	5.07	4.55	2.56	1.36	0.91	4.81	4.33	2.49	1.34	0.90
		50	30	3.58	3.36	2.31	1.42	1.00	3.51	3.30	2.28	1.40	1.00
		50	10	5.10	4.66	2.85	1.60	1.09	4.74	4.36	2.73	1.57	1.08
		0	20	3.85	3.66	2.68	1.74	1.27	3.81	3.63	2.66	1.74	1.27
		0	10	4.92	4.62	3.16	1.94	1.37	4.59	4.32	3.02	1.88	1.34
		−50	20	3.62	3.50	2.80	2.01	1.54	3.77	3.64	2.90	2.05	1.57
		−50	10	4.67	4.47	3.40	2.29	1.70	4.50	4.32	3.31	2.25	1.68
Horiz.	Down	90	10	6.09	5.35	2.79	1.43	0.94	10.07	8.19	3.41	1.57	1.00
		50	30	6.27	5.63	3.18	1.70	1.14	9.60	8.17	3.86	1.88	1.22
		50	10	6.61	5.90	3.27	1.73	1.15	11.15	9.27	4.09	1.93	1.24
		0	20	7.03	6.43	3.91	2.19	1.49	10.90	9.52	4.87	2.47	1.62
		0	10	7.31	6.66	4.00	2.22	1.51	11.97	10.32	5.08	2.52	1.64
		−50	20	7.73	7.20	4.77	2.85	1.99	11.64	10.49	6.02	3.25	2.18
		−50	10	8.09	7.52	4.91	2.89	2.01	12.98	11.56	6.36	3.34	2.22

[b] Interpolation is permissible for other values of mean temperature, temperature differences, and effective emittance E. Interpolation and moderate extrapolation for air spaces greater than 3.5 in. are also permissible.

[c] Effective emittance of the space E is given by $1/E = 1/e_1 + 1/e_2 - 1$, where e_1 and e_2 are the emittances of the surfaces of the air space.

[d] Credit for an air space resistance value cannot be taken more than once and only for the boundary conditions established.

[e] Resistances of horizontal spaces with heat flow downward are substantially independent of temperature difference.

[f] Thermal resistance values were determined from the relation $R = 1/C$, where $C = h_c + Eh_r$, h_c is the conduction-convection coefficient, Eh_r is the radiation coefficient $\cong 0.00686\, E\,[(460 + t_m)/100]^3$, and t_m is the mean temperature of the air space.

[*] Based on National Bureau of Standards data presented in Housing Research Paper No. 32, Housing and Home Finance Agency 1954, U. S. Government Printing Office, Washington 20402.

Thermal Properties of Typical Building and Insulating Materials—(Design Values)[a]

(For Industrial Insulation Design Values, see Table 3B). These constants are expressed in Btu per (hour) (square foot) (degree Fahrenheit temperature difference). Conductivities (k) are per inch thickness, and conductances (C) are for thickness or construction stated, not per inch thickness. All values are for a mean temperature of 75 F, except as noted by an asterisk (*) which have been reported at 45 F. The SI units for Resistance (last two columns) were calculated by taking the values from the two Resistance columns under Customary Unit, and multiplying by the factor 1/k (r/in.) and 1/C (R) for the appropriate conversion factor.

Description	Density (lb/ft³)	Conductivity (k)	Conductance (C)	Resistance[b] (R) Per inch thickness (1/k)	Resistance[b] (R) For thickness listed (1/C)	Specific Heat, Btu/(lb) (deg F)	SI Unit Resistance[b] (R) (m·K) / W	SI Unit Resistance[b] (R) (m²·K) / W
BUILDING BOARD								
Boards, Panels, Subflooring, Sheathing Woodboard Panel Products								
Asbestos-cement board	120	4.0	—	0.25	—	0.24	1.73	
Asbestos-cement board ... 0.125 in.	120	—	33.00	—	0.03			0.005
Asbestos-cement board ... 0.25 in.	120	—	16.50	—	0.06			0.01
Gypsum or plaster board ... 0.375 in.	50	—	3.10	—	0.32	0.26		0.06
Gypsum or plaster board ... 0.5 in.	50	—	2.22	—	0.45			0.08
Gypsum or plaster board ... 0.625 in.	50	—	1.78	—	0.56			0.10
Plywood (Douglas Fir)	34	0.80	—	1.25	—	0.29	8.66	
Plywood (Douglas Fir) ... 0.25 in.	34	—	3.20	—	0.31			0.05
Plywood (Douglas Fir) ... 0.375 in.	34	—	2.13	—	0.47			0.08
Plywood (Douglas Fir) ... 0.5 in.	34	—	1.60	—	0.62			0.11
Plywood (Douglas Fir) ... 0.625 in.	34	—	1.29	—	0.77			0.19

Table 3-5. (Reprinted with permission from the *1977 Fundamentals Volume, ASHRAE HANDBOOK & Product Directory*)

Continued on next page

Table 3–5 continued

Description	Density (lb/ft³)	Conductivity (k)	Conductance (C)	Resistance[b] (R) Per inch thickness (1/k)	Resistance[b] (R) For thickness listed (1/C)	Specific Heat, Btu/(lb)(deg F)	SI Unit Resistance[b] (R) (m·K)/W	SI Unit Resistance[b] (R) (m²·K)/W
Plywood or wood panels..............0.75 in.	34	—	1.07	—	0.93	0.29		0.16
Vegetable Fiber Board								
Sheathing, regular density............0.5 in.	18	—	0.76	—	1.32	0.31		0.23
............0.78125 in.	18	—	0.49	—	2.06			0.36
Sheathing intermediate density........0.5 in.	22	—	0.82	—	1.22	0.31		0.21
Nail-base sheathing...................0.5 in.	25	—	0.88	—	1.14	0.31		0.20
Shingle backer.....................0.375 in.	18	—	1.06	—	0.94	0.31		0.17
Shingle backer....................0.3125 in.	18	—	1.28	—	0.78			0.14
Sound deadening board ....0.5 in.	15	—	0.74	—	1.35	0.30		0.24
Tile and lay-in panels, plain or acoustic	18	0.40	—	2.50	—	0.14	17.33	
....................0.5 in.	18	—	0.80	—	1.25			0.22
....................0.75 in.	18	—	0.53	—	1.89			0.33
Laminated paperboard.....................	30	0.50	—	2.00	—	0.33	13.86	
Homogeneous board from repulped paper	30	0.50	—	2.00	—	0.28	13.86	
Hardboard								
Medium density	50	0.73	—	1.37	—	0.31	9.49	
High density, service temp. service underlay	55	0.82	—	1.22	—	0.32	8.46	
High density, std. tempered	63	1.00	—	1.00	—	0.32	6.93	
Particleboard								
Low density	37	0.54	—	1.85	—	0.31	12.82	
Medium density	50	0.94	—	1.06	—	0.31	7.35	
High density	62.5	1.18	—	0.85	—	0.31	5.89	
Underlayment....................0.625 in.	40	—	1.22	—	0.82	0.29		0.14
Wood subfloor....................0.75 in.		—	1.06	—	0.94	0.33		0.17
BUILDING MEMBRANE								
Vapor—permeable felt......................	—	—	16.70	—	0.06			0.01
Vapor—seal, 2 layers of mopped 15-lb felt	—	—	8.35	—	0.12			0.02
Vapor—seal, plastic film	—	—	—	—	Negl.			
FINISH FLOORING MATERIALS								
Carpet and fibrous pad	—	—	0.48	—	2.08	0.34		0.37
Carpet and rubber pad	—	—	0.81	—	1.23	0.33		0.22
Cork tile.........................0.125 in.	—	—	3.60	—	0.28	0.48		0.05
Terrazzo...............................1 in.	—	—	12.50	—	0.08	0.19		0.01
Tile—asphalt, linoleum, vinyl, rubber	—	—	20.00	—	0.05	0.30		0.01
vinyl asbestos						0.24		
ceramic...............................						0.19		
Wood, hardwood finish ....0.75 in.			1.47		0.68			0.12
INSULATING MATERIALS								
Blanket and Batt								
Mineral Fiber, fibrous form processed from rock, slag, or glass								
approx.[e] 2–2.75 in......................	0.3–2.0	—	0.143	—	7[d]	0.17–0.23		1.23
approx.[e] 3–3.5 in......................	0.3–2.0	—	0.091	—	11[d]			1.94
approx.[e] 5.50–6.5	0.3–2.0	—	0.053	—	19[d]			3.35
approx.[d] 6–7 in.	0.3–2.0		0.045		22[d]			3.87
approx.[d] 8.5 in.	0.3–2.0		0.033		30[d]			5.28
Board and Slabs								
Cellular glass	8.5	0.38	—	2.63	—	0.24	18.23	
Glass fiber, organic bonded	4–9	0.25	—	4.00	—	0.23	27.72	
Expanded rubber (rigid)...................	4.5	0.22	—	4.55	—	0.40	31.53	
Expanded polystyrene extruded Cut cell surface	1.8	0.25	—	4.00	—	0.29	27.72	
Expanded polystyrene extruded Smooth skin surface....................	2.2	0.20	—	5.00	—	0.29	34.65	
Expanded polystyrene extruded Smooth skin surface....................	3.5	0.19	—	5.26	—		36.45	
Expanded polystyrene, molded beads..........	1.0	0.28	—	3.57	—	0.29	24.74	
Expanded polyurethane[f] (R-11 exp.)	1.5	0.16	—	6.25	—	0.38	43.82	
(Thickness 1 in. or greater)	2.5							

Description	Density (lb/ft³)	Conductivity (k)	Conductance (C)	Resistance[b] (R) Per inch thickness (1/k)	Resistance[b] (R) For thickness listed (1/C)	Specific Heat, Btu/(lb) (deg F)	SI Unit Resistance[b] (R) (m·K) W	SI Unit Resistance[b] (R) (m²·K) W
Mineral fiber with resin binder	15	0.29	—	3.45	—	0.17	23.91	
Mineral fiberboard, wet felted								
Core or roof insulation.	16–17	0.34	—	2.94	—		20.38	
Acoustical tile.	18	0.35	—	2.86	—	0.19	19.82	
Acoustical tile.	21	0.37	—	2.70	—		18.71	
Mineral fiberboard, wet molded								
Acoustical tile[g]	23	0.42	—	2.38	—	0.14	16.49	
Wood or cane fiberboard								
Acoustical tile[g] . . . . 0.5 in.	—	—	0.80	—	1.25	0.31		0.22
Acoustical tile[g] . . . . 0.75 in.	—	—	0.53	—	1.89			0.33
Interior finish (plank, tile)	15	0.35	—	2.86	—	0.32	19.82	
Wood shredded (cemented in preformed slabs).	22	0.60	—	1.67	—	0.31	11.57	
LOOSE FILL								
Cellulosic insulation (milled paper or wood pulp)	2.3–3.2	0.27–0.32	—	3.13–3.70	—	0.33	21.69–25.64	
Sawdust or shavings.	8.0–15.0	0.45	—	2.22	—	0.33	15.39	
Wood fiber, softwoods	2.0–3.5	0.30	—	3.33	—	0.33	23.08	
Perlite, expanded.	5.0–8.0	0.37	—	2.70	—	0.26	18.71	
Mineral fiber (rock, slag or glass)								
approx.[e] 3.75–5 in.	0.6–2.0	—	—		11	0.17		1.94
approx.[e] 6.5–8.75 in.	0.6–2.0	—	—		19			3.35
approx.[e] 7.5–10 in.	0.6–2.0	—	—		22			3.87
approx.[e] 10.25–13.75 in.	0.6–2.0	—	—		30			5.28
Vermiculite, exfoliated.	7.0–8.2	0.47	—	2.13	—	3.20	14.76	
	4.0–6.0	0.44	—	2.27	—		15.73	
ROOF INSULATION[h]								
Preformed, for use above deck								
Different roof insulations are available in different			0.72		1.39		—	0.24
thicknesses to provide the design C values listed.[h]			to		to		—	to
Consult individual manufacturers for actual			0.12		8.33			1.47
thickness of their material.								
MASONRY MATERIALS								
CONCRETES								
Cement mortar.	116	5.0	—	0.20	—		1.39	
Gypsum-fiber concrete 87.5% gypsum,								
12.5% wood chips	51	1.66	—	0.60	—	0.21	4.16	
Lightweight aggregates including ex-	120	5.2	—	0.19	—		1.32	
panded shale, clay or slate; expanded	100	3.6	—	0.28	—		1.94	
slags; cinders; pumice; vermiculite;	80	2.5	—	0.40	—		2.77	
also cellular concretes	60	1.7	—	0.59	—		4.09	
	40	1.15	—	0.86	—		5.96	
	30	0.90	—	1.11	—		7.69	
	20	0.70		1.43			9.91	
Perlite, expanded.	40	0.93		1.08			7.48	
	30	0.71		1.41			9.77	
	20	0.50		2.00		0.32	13.86	
Sand and gravel or stone aggregate (oven dried)	140	9.0	—	0.11		0.22	0.76	
Sand and gravel or stone aggregate (not dried)	140	12.0	—	0.08			0.55	
Stucco	116	5.0	—	0.20			1.39	
MASONRY UNITS								
Brick, common[i]	120	5.0	—	0.20	—	0.19	1.39	
Brick, face[i]	130	9.0	—	0.11	—		0.76	
Clay tile, hollow:								
1 cell deep . . . . 3 in.	—	—	1.25	—	0.80	0.21		0.14
1 cell deep . . . . 4 in.	—	—	0.90	—	1.11			0.20
2 cells deep. . . . . 6 in.	—	—	0.66	—	1.52			0.27
2 cells deep. . . . . 8 in.	—	—	0.54	—	1.85			0.33
2 cells deep. . . . . 10 in.	—	—	0.45	—	2.22			0.39
3 cells deep. . . . . 12 in.	—	—	0.40	—	2.50			0.44

Continued on next page

Table 3–5 continued

Description	Density (lb/ft³)	Conductivity (k)	Conductance (C)	Resistance[b] (R) Per inch thickness (1/k)	Resistance[b] (R) For thickness listed (1/C)	Specific Heat, Btu/(lb) (deg F)	Resistance[b] (R) (m·K)/W	Resistance[b] (R) (m²·K)/W
Concrete blocks, three oval core:								
Sand and gravel aggregate .... 4 in.	—	—	1.40	—	0.71	0.22		0.13
.... 8 in.	—	—	0.90	—	1.11			0.20
.... 12 in.	—	—	0.78	—	1.28			0.23
Cinder aggregate .... 3 in.	—	—	1.16	—	0.86	0.21		0.15
.... 4 in.	—	—	0.90	—	1.11			0.20
.... 8 in.	—	—	0.58	—	1.72			0.30
.... 12 in.	—	—	0.53	—	1.89			0.33
Lightweight aggregate .... 3 in.	—	—	0.79	—	1.27	0.21		0.22
(expanded shale, clay, slate .... 4 in.	—	—	0.67	—	1.50			0.26
or slag; pumice) .... 8 in.	—	—	0.50	—	2.00			0.35
.... 12 in.	—	—	0.44	—	2.27			0.40
Concrete blocks, rectangular core.*j								
Sand and gravel aggregate								
2 core, 8 in. 36 lb.k* .:	—	—	0.96	—	1.04	0.22		0.18
Same with filled coresj*	—	—	0.52	—	1.93	0.22		0.34
Lightweight aggregate (expanded shale,								
clay, slate or slag, pumice):								
3 core, 6 in. 19 lb.k*	—	—	0.61	—	1.65	0.21		0.29
Same with filled coresl*	—	—	0.33	—	2.99			0.53
2 core, 8 in. 24 lb.k*	—	—	0.46	—	2.18			0.38
Same with filled coresl*	—	—	0.20	—	5.03			0.89
3 core, 12 in. 38 lb.k*	—	—	0.40	—	2.48			0.44
Same with filled coresl*	—	—	0.17	—	5.82			1.02
Stone, lime or sand.	—	12.50	—	0.08	—	0.19	0.55	
Gypsum partition tile:								
3 × 12 × 30 in. solid	—	—	0.79	—	1.26	0.19		0.22
3 × 12 × 30 in. 4-cell	—	—	0.74	—	1.35			0.24
4 × 12 × 30 in. 3-cell	—	—	0.60	—	1.67			0.29

METALS
(See Chapter 37, Table 3)

PLASTERING MATERIALS

Description	Density (lb/ft³)	Conductivity (k)	Conductance (C)	Resistance[b] (R) Per inch thickness (1/k)	Resistance[b] (R) For thickness listed (1/C)	Specific Heat, Btu/(lb) (deg F)	Resistance[b] (R) (m·K)/W	Resistance[b] (R) (m²·K)/W
Cement plaster, sand aggregate	116	5.0	—	0.20	—	0.20	1.39	
Sand aggregate .... 0.375 in.	—	—	13.3	—	0.08	0.20		0.01
Sand aggregate .... 0.75 in.	—	—	6.66	—	0.15	0.20		0.03
Gypsum plaster:								
Lightweight aggregate. .... 0.5 in.	45	—	3.12	—	0.32			0.06
Lightweight aggregate .... 0.625 in.	45	—	2.67	—	0.39			0.07
Lightweight agg. on metal lath .... 0.75 in.	—	—	2.13	—	0.47			0.08
Perlite aggregate.	45	1.5	—	0.67	—	0.32	4.64	
Sand aggregate.	105	5.6	—	0.18	—	0.20	1.25	
Sand aggregate .... 0.5 in.	105	—	11.10	—	0.09			0.02
Sand aggregate .... 0.625 in.	105	—	9.10	—	0.11			0.02
Sand aggregate on metal lath. .... 0.75 in.	—	—	7.70	—	0.13			0.02
Vermiculite aggregate.	45	1.7	—	0.59	—		4.09	

ROOFING

Description	Density (lb/ft³)	Conductivity (k)	Conductance (C)	Resistance[b] (R) Per inch thickness (1/k)	Resistance[b] (R) For thickness listed (1/C)	Specific Heat, Btu/(lb) (deg F)	Resistance[b] (R) (m·K)/W	Resistance[b] (R) (m²·K)/W
Asbestos-cement shingles.	120	—	4.76	—	0.21	0.24		0.04
Asphalt roll roofing.	70	—	6.50	—	0.15	0.36		0.03
Asphalt shingles.	70	—	2.27	—	0.44	0.30		0.08
Built-up roofing .... 0.375 in.	70	—	3.00	—	0.33	0.35		0.06
Slate. .... 0.5 in.	—	—	20.00	—	0.05	0.30		0.01
Wood shingles, plain and plastic film faced	—	—	1.06	—	0.94	0.31		0.17

SIDING MATERIALS (On Flat Surface)
Shingles

Description	Density (lb/ft³)	Conductivity (k)	Conductance (C)	Resistance[b] (R) Per inch thickness (1/k)	Resistance[b] (R) For thickness listed (1/C)	Specific Heat, Btu/(lb) (deg F)	Resistance[b] (R) (m·K)/W	Resistance[b] (R) (m²·K)/W
Asbestos-cement.	120	—	4.75	—	0.21	0.24		0.04
Wood, 16 in., 7.5 exposure.	—	—	1.15	—	0.87	0.31		0.15
Wood, double, 16-in., 12-in. exposure	—	—	0.84	—	1.19	0.28		0.21
Wood, plus insul. backer board, 0.3125 in.	—	—	0.71	—	1.40	0.31		0.25
Siding								
Asbestos-cement, 0.25 in., lapped.	—	—	4.76	—	0.21	0.24		0.04
Asphalt roll siding	—	—	6.50	—	0.15	0.35		0.03
Asphalt insulating siding (0.5 in. bed.)	—	—	0.69	—	1.46	0.35		0.26
Hardboard siding, 0.4375 in.	40	1.49	—	0.67	—	0.28	4.65	
Wood, drop, 1 × 8 in.	—	—	1.27	—	0.79	0.28		0.14
Wood, bevel, 0.5 × 8 in., lapped	—	—	1.23	—	0.81	0.28		0.14
Wood, bevel, 0.75 × 10 in., lapped	—	—	0.95	—	1.05	0.28		0.18
Wood, plywood, 0.375 in., lapped	—	—	1.59	—	0.59	0.29		0.10

Description	Customary Unit						SI Unit	
	Density (lb/ft³)	Conductivity (k)	Conductance (C)	Resistance[b] (R)		Specific Heat, Btu/(lb) (deg F)	Resistance[b] (R)	
				Per inch thickness (1/k)	For thickness listed (1/C)		(m·K) / W	(m²·K) / W
Aluminum or Steel[m], over sheathing								
Hollow-backed..........................	—	—	1.61	—	0.61	0.29		0.11
Insulating-board backed nominal								
0.375 in............................	—	—	0.55	—	1.82	0.32		0.32
Insulating-board backed nominal								
0.375 in., foil backed....................			0.34		2.96			0.52
Architectural glass..........................	—	—	10.00	—	0.10	0.20		0.02
WOODS								
Maple, oak, and similar hardwoods..............	45	1.10	—	0.91	—	0.30	6.31	
Fir, pine, and similar softwoods.................	32	0.80	—	1.25	—	0.33	8.66	
Fir, pine, and similar softwoods...........0.75 in.	32	—	1.06	—	0.94	0.33		0.17
.........................1.5 in.		—	0.53	—	1.89			0.33
.........................2.5 in.		—	0.32	—	3.12			0.60
.........................3.5 in.		—	0.23	—	4.35			0.75

Notes for Table

[a] Representative values for dry materials were selected by ASHRAE TC4.4, Insulation and Moisture Barriers. They are intended as design (not specification) values for materials in normal use. For properties of a particular product, use the value supplied by the manufacturer or by unbiased tests

[b] Resistance values are the reciprocals of C before rounding off C to two decimal places.

[c] Also see Insulating Materials, Board.

[d] Does not include paper backing and facing, if any. Where insulation forms a boundary (reflective or otherwise) of an air space, see Tables 3-1, 3-3, and 3-4 for the insulating value of air space for the appropriate effective emittance and temperature conditions of the space.

[e] Conductivity varies with fiber diameter. Insulation is produced by different densities; therefore, there is a wide variation in thickness for the same R-value among manufacturers. No effort should be made to relate any specific R-value to any specific thickness. Commercial thicknesses generally available range from 2 to 8.5.

[f] Values are for aged board stock.

[g] Insulating values of acoustical tile vary, depending on density of the board and on type, size, and depth of perforations.

[h] The U. S. Department of Commerce, *Simplified Practice Recommendation for Thermal Conductance Factors for Preformed Above-Deck Roof Insulation,* No. R 257-55, recognizes the specification of roof insulation on the basis of the C-values shown. Roof insulation is made in thicknesses to meet these values.

[i] Face brick and common brick do not always have these specific densities. When density is different from that shown, there will be a change in thermal conductivity.

[j] Data on rectangular core concrete blocks differ from the above data on oval core blocks, due to core configuration, different mean temperatures, and possibly differences in unit weights. Weight data on the oval core blocks tested are not available.

[k] Weights of units approximately 7.625 in. high and 15.75 in. long. These weights are given as a means of describing the blocks tested, but conductance values are all for 1 ft² of area.

[l] Vermiculite, perlite, or mineral wool insulation. Where insulation is used, vapor barriers or other precautions must be considered to keep insulation dry.

[m] Values for metal siding applied over flat surfaces vary widely, depending on amount of ventilation of air space beneath the siding; whether air space is reflective or nonreflective; and on thickness, type, and application of insulating backing-board used. Values given are averages for use as design guides, and were obtained from several guarded hotbox tests (ASTM C236) or calibrated hotbox (BSS 77) on hollow-backed types and types made using backing-boards of wood fiber, foamed plastic, and glass fiber. Departures of ±50% or more from the values given may occur.

Derivation of U Factor for a Standard Wall Section

Construction Elements	k or C	R
Outside surface (15 mph wind)	6.00.	0.17
Wood siding ½″ × 8″ lapped	1.23	0.81
Sheathing, 0.5″ asphalt impregnated	0.76	1.32
Insulation 3.5″ blanket	0.91	11.00
Wallboard 0.5″ gypsum	2.22	0.45
Inside surface (still air)	1.47	0.68
Total of resistances		14.43

Reciprocal, $14.43 \sqrt{1.00000}$, or U factor = 0.069

Table 3-6.

THERMAL INSULATING MATERIALS

Of all the various materials employed in residential construction, those that are classed as thermal insulating materials are of the greatest importance insofar as the thermal efficiency of the structure is concerned. Through judicious use of these materials, practically any desired final heat loss characteristics can be built into the structure. A brief look at the common types in use today is in order.

Batt and blanket. Perhaps the most widely used of all thermal insulations, batts and blankets are composed of fine, inorganic fibers made of rock, glass, or slag. The fibers are woven loosely into strips of various widths and thicknesses, and packaged in standard quantities. The blanket type is continuous, while the batts are clipped into short lengths, usually four feet. While some are unfaced, many are faced on one side with kraft vapor barrier paper, with stapling flanges, and a few include a breathable paper backing as well. Other types are faced with aluminum-foil vapor barrier material. The passage of heat from warm to cold side is inhibited primarily by entrapping it in millions of tiny dead air pockets that are an inherent characteristic of these materials. The insulating value is almost entirely convective, unless a reflective outer surface is present, along with an air space. But insulating efficiency is almost equal whether there is an air space or not, and regardless of the position or orientation of the material.

Both blankets and batts have relatively good thermal resistance, and they are rated specifically for the manufactured thicknesses by R-value.

Board and slab. Many different kinds, sizes, and types of board and slab insulating materials are available for various purposes. They may be either rigid or semirigid, and are made of such materials as mineral fiber or wool, expanded or extruded polystyrene, polyurethane, polyisocyanurate, expanded rubber, and wood or cane fiberboard. Applications for these insulations include exterior wall sheathing, facing for interior walls of crawl spaces, foundation insulation, perimeter insulation for slab-on-grade construction, roof insulation, acoustical ceiling tiles, and interior-finish wall planking. Thermal resistance varies widely. The lowest value is about equivalent to an R-7 blanket insulation, per inch of installed thickness. Expanded polyurethane, at the other end of the scale, has an R-value of about 6.25 per inch of thickness, one of the best available except for the expensive polyisocyanurate at 7.2.

Loose-fill. Loose-fill insulations are relatively free-flowing materials that can be emplaced by hand. They are generally used in such applications as unfloored attics and to fill the open cores of concrete blocks. Exfoliated vermiculite, running from R-2.13 to R-2.27 per inch of installed thickness, is widely used for this purpose, and, surprisingly enough, sawdust or wood shavings packed to a density of 8 to 15 pounds per cubic foot have almost the same thermal resistance per inch of thickness. Chopped paper, generally known as cellulose insulation, and mineral wool can also be used as loose-fill insulation, but both types are more effective if blown in place.

Blown. Blown insulations are emplaced pneumatically with special equipment, principally in floor, wall, and ceiling cavities. While widely used to insulate existing houses that previously were uninsulated, blown insulations are also commonly installed in new construction. Mineral wool and cellulose are widely used. Density of blown mineral wool plays an important part in its thermal resistance, as does fiber diameter. Generally speaking, 7.5 to 10.0 inches of wool is required to reach an equivalent R-value (R-22) of about 6 to 7 inches of blanket or batt insulation. However, assigning any specific R-value to any specific thickness is most difficult. Cellulose, on the other hand, ranges in R-value from 2.9 to 3.7 per inch of thickness, depending upon density and the specific product.

Foamed-in-place. This class of thermal insulations is relatively new to the scene and has yet to be fully proven. Though there are numerous advantages, some drawbacks to their use have also been discovered. Foamed-in-place insulations must be installed by qualified personnel with special equipment and are designed to be injected or sprayed into building cavities (stud, joist, and rafter spaces, for instance) as a liquid or semiliquid. The foam expands, fills, and seals the cavities, cures to a rigid layer that adheres to the building surfaces, and soon provides a good *R*-value. Urea-formaldehyde foams, or urea-based foams, are one type now in use; they have an *R* of 4.17 per inch of thickness, as tested by the National Bureau of Standards. However, the foam has a tendency to shrink after installation, which has led the Department of Housing and Urban Development (HUD) to recommend derating the thermal performance of UF foams to 72 percent, or *R*-3. The Canadian Goverment Specifications Board recommends reduction to 60 percent, or *R*-2.5. There are other problems as well, such as possible toxicity of the outgassing formaldehyde after application, low service temperature and deterioration under high temperature and high humidity, reaction of the foam to other building materials, water vapor transmission, and so on. The NBS recommends that UF foams not be installed in attics and ceilings, nor in any exposed locations, primarily because of these and other difficulties. However, foams do have a number of advantages, especially in retrofitting and in special applications. Research and development in this area continues apace, and more information is brought forth continually; in due course, foamed-in-place insulations may become as widely used and accepted as the batt and blanket types.

Deck. Deck, or roof, insulations are available in a number of specific thicknesses and panel sizes, all depending upon the individual manufacturer. These insulations are especially made to cover roof decks, acting as a combined structural material and thermal insulation. A number of different methods and materials are used in their construction, and *R*-values range from as little as 1.25 or so to 8.0 or better. Application of deck insulations depends as much upon the required characteristics of the material from a construction standpoint as from thermal performance, so they must be chosen on the basis of availability, overall usefulness, design requirements, and the manufacturer's specifications.

Reflective. Once in relatively widespread use, reflective insulations are now installed only on a limited basis. Unlike other types, they have very little mass and make use of the fact that bright metallic foil surfaces reflect a large proportion of any heat directed against them, provided they face an air space at least ½ inch wide, preferably more. The air space is critical, since without one the foil has no insulating value at all. Because of cost, difficulties in installation, longevity problems, and the ready availability of equal or better thermal barriers (as determined on an overall, practical basis), reflective insulations will probably slip from the scene.

Insulation Applications

No single thermal insulation can adequately handle every kind of insulating job, and choosing the best one for each given application can make a substantial difference in the overall effectiveness and performance of the thermal barrier in a house. It is entirely conceivable, in fact, that one or more specific types from each of the classes of thermal insulations just discussed could be used in a single residence. Since each has different characteristics, and different advantages and disadvantages, using each type to its best advantage and in an application where it will do the most good (and more good than another type) makes sense. For example, in modern house construction one might employ one kind of rigid board insulation around the foundation, another at a slab perimeter edge, a third as exterior wall sheathing, blanket or batts in the wall cavities, deck insulation (perhaps in combination with rigid foam slabs) on the roof, loose-fill in masonry cavities, blown cellulose in inaccessible cavity areas, small quantities of canned foam to seal awkward openings, and so on. Logical choices that make full use of all the particular characteristics of each given kind of insulation can do much to maximize the thermal performance of a house.

Nonthermal Characteristics

Obviously, the thermal characteristics of an insulating material are of paramount importance. So are physical characteristics, insofar as specific applications are concerned: blue bead-board tacked to the interior living room walls would not be very attractive but interior finish insulating plank would, and insulating between the floor joists over a crawl space with chopped cellulose would be a bit of a struggle but installing friction-fit batts would not. But there are other factors that should be considered as well when choosing insulations.

Fire safety is one factor. UF foams, for instance, as well as rigid plastic boards or panels, are combustible and can give off toxic gasses. Mineral wool will not burn, nor will vermiculite. But the paper backing or facing on mineral wool batts and blankets certainly will. Cellulose is supposed to be chemically treated to be fire resistant (it is *not* fireproof), but the process often does not come up to standards.

Moisture absorption and retention should also be considered; some insulations are prone to this and others are not. Moisture in insulation diminishes, and can even negate, the thermal performance of the material. Odor is also a factor; UF foams, for instance, can give off a malodorous gas. Reactions of the insulation with surrounding building materials can occur, too; some of the chemicals used in cellulose insulation fire retardants are corrosive. And then there is the pest problem; mice love to nest in mineral wool, and certain insects will breed there. The presence of starch or other organic compounds, as in cellulose, sawdust, or woodshavings insulation, can serve as a food attractant for insects. In short, the various nonthermal properties of insulations must be investigated to ascertain that misapplication, which might result in unforseen problems of an expensive nature, does not take place.

Insulation Installation

Much of the theoretical efficiency of any insulating material can be dissipated if it is put into a structure incorrectly. There are three factors involved: proper placement in the structure, correct installation procedures undertaken with top-quality workmanship, and the proper use and installation of vapor barriers. Insulation installation goes, in large measure, hand in hand with proper placement of vapor barriers, which are described in the next chapter. Correct methods of placing both insulation and vapor barriers are discussed there.

DESIGN CONDITIONS

Before work can continue in making heating load calculations, or heat loss calculations, two sets of detailed information must be established. The first concerns the building design, which includes not only the general plan of the house, but also sets of building material/thermal insulation material combinations for various building sections; these must be calculated to determine the most practical overall thermal efficiency for the structure, if and as necessary or desirable. We will assume this information to be a part of the house plan package developed by the architects/designers/engineers.

The second set of data concerns design weather conditions, from which further heat loss calculations can be made. It is possible to estimate with reasonable accuracy the probable heat loss from a house by working with a given number of degrees temperature difference between indoors and outdoors and by adding other weather factors as necessary.

But how can one know what the "given number of degrees" is? It changes almost every hour. However, the calculations must assume adverse rather than average climatic conditions, since heat is needed most when weather is worst. Therefore, the problem is reduced to: What figure can be used for "worst weather"?

Outdoor Design Temperature

The concept of design temperature is based on known winter extremes for a given climate or geographical location. It is a pragmatic simplification of those figures, which has been found to work well in almost all house heating situations. The winter outdoor design temperatures recommended by ASHRAE for making heat loss calculations are presented in Table 3-7. There are two levels given for each station, 99 percent and 97.5 percent, to represent the temperatures that equalled or exceeded those portions of the total hours (2160) in the months of December, January, and February. The 99 percent figure makes a reasonable

choice, unless the building happens to have a particularly high thermal mass, a situation untrue of most houses. Choosing Douglas, Arizona, for example, the 99 percent column shows an average temperature of 27° F, and the temperature can reasonably be expected to fall below that figure for only 1 percent of the 2160 hours, or about 22 hours. The 97.5 percent column shows the average temperature as 31° F, which means that the temperature would fall below that point for perhaps 55 hours, on the average. The practical result would be, if a heating plant were designed for 27° F, that the inside temperature of the house might fall a bit during those 22 colder hours, and for 31° F, for about 55 hours. But, depending upon just when those colder hours might fall and for what duration, the homeowner might never notice any appreciable difference, or might easily correct the situation with some inexpensive auxiliary heating.

For a house located at or quite near one of the stations listed in Table 3-7, the recommended design temperature should serve quite well, especially since the entire heat loss calculation is an estimation anyway. Even so, it should be realized that a given microclimate only a mile away from the reporting station might be different, and adjustments should be made for conditions that are obviously dissimilar, especially in the "worse" direction. Even more caution should be exercised in using the listed figures for locations other than the immediate area of the reporting station. Some adjustments for the figures can be made for altitude by adding or subtracting 1°F for every 200-foot change in elevation. However, cold air drainage or radiational cooling resulting from open expanses surrounding the site, especially in mountainous areas, negate the adjustments and, in fact, the listed temperature figures as well.

Choosing an outdoor design temperature for a site removed from the listed stations in Table 3-7 can start with some interpolation from the Table, but should be based largely on local conditions. These must be determined in the best way possible by consulting every available source of weather data, including local weather stations, heating fuel dealers, private sources of weather data, local newspaper files, etc. Scaling the heating equipment to record-low temperatures, which occur only infrequently, is generally a waste of money because the system will most likely be greatly oversized for average needs. However, sizing to the average low temperature for the three-month period including December, January, and February is a reasonable solution in lieu of other, more definitive data. It is even quite possible for the site-owner to personally record daily low temperatures right at the building site during one winter season for that period. Since in most locales the average monthly low for those months seldom swings up or down more than 4 to 5 degrees, the average low for the period, minus 3 or 4 degrees as a safety factor, would doubtless prove satisfactory as an outside design temperature. And irrespective of where the final figure is derived from, or how, judgement can be used to temper the final selection. For instance, the temperature might be lowered a few degrees, and the heating plant consequently oversized a bit, just to be on the safe side. Or, the outside design temperature could be raised a few degrees, with the thought of saving a bit on initial heating plant costs and employing some auxiliary heating means, such as a woodstove, if and as necessary.

CLIMATIC CONDITIONS FOR THE UNITED STATES[a]

						Winter[d]		Summer[e]						
Col. 1	Col. 2		Col. 3		Col. 4	Col. 5		Col. 6			Col. 7	Col. 8		
State and Station	Lati-tude[b]		Longi-tude[b]		Eleva-tion[c]	Design Dry-Bulb		Design Dry-Bulb and Mean Coincident Wet-Bulb			Mean Daily Range	Design Wet-Bulb		
	°	′	°	′	Ft	99%	97.5%	1%	2.5%	5%		1%	2.5%	5%
ALABAMA														
Alexander City	33	0	86	0	660	18	22	96/77	93/76	91/76	21	79	78	78
Anniston AP	33	4	85	5	599	18	22	97/77	94/76	92/76	21	79	78	78
Auburn	32	4	85	3	730	18	22	96/77	93/76	91/76	21	79	78	78
Birmingham AP	33	3	86	5	610	17	21	96/74	94/75	92/74	21	78	77	76
Decatur	34	4	87	0	580	11	16	95/75	93/74	91/74	22	78	77	76
Dothan AP	31	2	85	2	321	23	27	94/76	92/76	91/76	20	80	79	78
Florence AP	34	5	87	4	528	17	21	97/74	94/74	92/74	22	78	77	76
Gadsden	34	0	86	0	570	16	20	96/75	94/75	92/74	22	78	77	76
Huntsville AP	34	4	86	4	619	11	16	95/75	93/74	91/74	23	78	77	76
Mobile AP	30	4	88	2	211	25	29	95/77	93/77	91/76	18	80	79	78
Mobile CO	30	4	88	1	119	25	29	95/77	93/77	91/76	16	80	79	78
Montgomery AP	32	2	86	2	195	22	25	96/76	95/76	93/76	21	79	79	78
Selma-Craig AFB	32	2	87	0	207	22	26	97/78	95/77	93/77	21	81	80	79
Talladega	33	3	86	1	565	18	22	97/77	94/76	92/76	21	79	78	78
Tuscaloosa AP	33	1	87	4	170r	20	23	98/75	96/76	94/76	22	79	78	77
ALASKA														
Anchorage AP	61	1	150	0	90	−23	−18	71/59	68/58	66/56	15	60	59	57
Barrow (S)	71	2	156	5	22	−45	−41	57/53	53/50	49/47	12	54	50	47
Fairbanks AP (S)	64	5	147	5	436	−51	−47	82/62	78/60	75/59	24	64	62	60
Juneau AP	58	2	134	4	17	−4	−1	74/60	70/58	67/57	15	61	59	58
Kodiak	57	3	152	3	21	10	13	69/58	65/56	62/55	10	60	58	56
Nome AP	64	3	165	3	13	−31	−27	66/57	62/55	59/54	10	58	56	55
ARIZONA														
Douglas AP	31	3	109	3	4098	27	31	98/63	95/63	93/63	31	70	69	68
Flagstaff AP	35	1	111	4	6973	−2	4	84/55	82/55	80/54	31	61	60	59
Fort Huachuca AP (S)	31	3	110	2	4664	24	28	95/62	92/62	90/62	27	69	68	67
Kingman AP	35	2	114	0	3446	18	25	103/65	100/64	97/64	30	70	69	69
Nogales	31	2	111	0	3800	28	32	99/64	96/64	94/64	31	71	70	69
Phoenix AP(S)	33	3	112	0	1117	31	34	109/71	107/71	105/71	27	76	75	75
Prescott AP	34	4	112	3	5014	4	9	96/61	94/60	92/60	30	66	65	64
Tuscon AP (S)	32	1	111	0	2584	28	32	104/66	102/66	100/66	26	72	71	71
Winslow AP	35	0	110	4	4880	5	10	97/61	95/60	93/60	32	66	65	64
Yuma AP	32	4	114	4	199	36	39	111/72	109/72	107/71	27	79	78	77
ARKANSAS														
Blytheville AFB	36	0	90	0	264	10	15	96/78	94/77	91/76	21	81	80	78
Camden	33	4	92	5	116	18	23	98/76	96/76	94/76	21	80	79	78
El Dorado AP	33	1	92	5	252	18	23	98/76	96/76	94/76	21	80	79	78
Fayetteville AP	36	0	94	1	1253	7	12	97/72	94/73	92/73	23	77	76	75
Fort Smith AP	35	2	94	2	449	12	17	101/75	98/76	95/76	24	80	79	78
Hot Springs	34	3	93	1	535	17	23	101/77	97/77	94/77	22	80	79	78
Jonesboro	35	5	90	4	345	10	15	96/78	94/77	91/76	21	81	80	78
Little Rock AP (S)	34	4	92	1	257	15	20	99/76	96/77	94/77	22	80	79	78
Pine Bluff AP	34	1	92	0	204	16	22	100/78	97/77	95/78	22	81	80	80
Texarkana AP	33	3	94	0	361	18	23	98/76	96/77	93/76	21	80	79	78
CALIFORNIA														
Bakersfield AP	35	2	119	0	495	30	32	104/70	101/69	98/68	32	73	71	70
Barstow AP	34	5	116	5	2142	26	29	106/68	104/68	102/67	37	73	71	70
Blythe AP	33	4	114	3	390	30	33	112/71	110/71	108/70	28	75	75	74
Burbank AP	34	1	118	2	699	37	39	95/68	91/68	88/67	25	71	70	69
Chico	39	5	121	5	205	28	30	103/69	101/68	98/67	36	71	70	68

[a] Table 1 was prepared by ASHRAE Technical Committee 4.2, Weather Data, from data compiled from official weather stations where hourly weather observations are made by trained observers.

[b] Latitude, for use in calculating solar loads, and longitude are given to the nearest 10 minutes. For example, the latitude and longitude for Anniston, Alabama are given as 33 34 and 85 55 respectively, or 33° 40, and 85° 50.

[c] Elevations are ground elevations for each station. Temperature readings are generally made at an elevation of 5 ft above ground, except for locations marked r, indicating roof exposure of thermometer.

[d] Percentage of winter design data shows the percent of the 3-month period, December through February.

[e] Percentage of summer design data shows the percent of 4-month period, June through September.

Table 3–7. (Reprinted with permission from the *1977 Fundamentals Volume, ASHRAE HANDBOOK & Product Directory*)

Continued on next page

Table 3-7 continued

State and Station	Latitude °	'	Longitude °	'	Elevation Ft	Winter Design Dry-Bulb 99%	97.5%	Summer Design Dry-Bulb and Mean Coincident Wet-Bulb 1%	2.5%	5%	Mean Daily Range	Design Wet-Bulb 1%	2.5%	5%
Concord	38	0	122	0	195	24	27	100/69	97/68	94/67	32	71	70	68
Covina	34	0	117	5	575	32	35	98/69	95/68	92/67	31	73	71	70
Crescent City AP	41	5	124	0	50	31	33	68/60	65/59	63/58	18	62	60	59
Downey	34	0	118	1	116	37	40	93/70	89/70	86/69	22	72	71	70
El Cajon	32	4	117	0	525	42	44	83/69	80/69	78/69	30	71	70	68
El Centro AP (S)	32	5	115	4	−30	35	38	112/74	110/74	108/74	34	81	80	78
Escondido	33	0	117	1	660	39	41	89/68	85/68	82/68	30	71	70	69
Eureaka/ Arcata AP	41	0	124	1	217	31	33	68/60	65/59	63/58	11	62	60	59
Fairfield- Travis AFB	38	2	122	0	72	29	32	99/68	95/67	91/66	34	70	68	67
Fresno AP (S)	36	5	119	4	326	28	30	102/70	100/69	97/68	34	72	71	70
Hamilton AFB	38	0	122	3	3	30	32	89/68	84/66	80/65	28	72	69	67
Laguna Beach	33	3	117	5	35	41	43	83/68	80/68	77/67	18	70	69	68
Livermore	37	4	122	0	545	24	27	100/69	97/68	93/67	24	71	70	68
Lompoc, Vandenburg AFB	34	4	120	3	552	35	38	75/61	70/61	67/60	20	63	61	60
Long Beach AP	33	5	118	1	34	41	43	83/68	80/68	77/67	22	70	69	68
Los Angeles AP (S)	34	0	118	2	99	41	43	83/68	80/68	77/67	15	70	69	68
Los Angeles CO (S)	34	0	118	1	312	37	40	93/70	89/70	86/69	20	72	71	70
Merced-Castle AFB	37	2	120	3	178	29	31	102/70	99/69	96/68	36	72	71	70
Modesto	37	4	121	0	91	28	30	101/69	98/68	95/67	36	71	70	69
Monterey	36	4	121	5	38	35	38	75/63	71/61	68/61	20	64	62	61
Napa	38	2	122	2	16	30	32	100/69	96/68	92/67	30	71	69	68
Needles AP	34	5	114	4	913	30	33	112/71	110/71	108/70	27	75	75	74
Oakland AP	37	4	122	1	3	34	36	85/64	80/63	75/62	19	66	64	63
Oceanside	33	1	117	2	30	41	43	83/68	80/68	77/67	13	70	69	68
Ontario	34	0	117	36	995	31	33	102/70	99/69	96/67	36	74	72	71
Oxnard	34	1	119	1	43	34	36	83/66	80/64	77/63	19	70	68	67
Palmdale AP	34	4	118	1	2517	18	22	103/65	101/65	98/64	35	69	67	66
Palm Springs	33	5	116	4	411	33	35	112/71	110/70	108/70	35	76	74	73
Pasadena	34	1	118	1	864	32	35	98/69	95/68	92/67	29	73	71	70
Petaluma	38	1	122	4	27	26	29.	94/68	90/66	87/65	31	72	70	68
Pomona CO	34	0	117	5	871	28	30	102/70	99/69	95/68	36	74	72	71
Redding AP	40	3	122	1	495	29	31	105/68	102/67	100/66	32	71	69	68
Redlands	34	0	117	1	1318	31	33	102/70	99/69	96/68	33	74	72	71
Richmond	38	0	122	2	55	34	36	85/64	80/63	75/62	17	66	64	63
Riverside- March AFB (S)	33	5	117	2	1511	29	32	100/68	98/68	95/67	37	72	71	70
Sacramento AP	38	3	121	3	17	30	32	101/70	98/70	94/69	36	72	71	70
Salinas AP	36	4	121	4	74	30	32	74/61	70/60	67/59	24	62	61	59
San Bernardino, Norton AFB	34	1	117	1	1125	31	33	102/70	99/69	96/68	38	74	72	71
San Diego AP	32	4	117	1	19	42	44	83/69	80/69	78/68	12	71	70	68
San Fernando	34	1	118	3	977	37	39	95/68	91/68	88/67	38	71	70	69
San Francisco AP	37	4	122	2	8	35	38	82/64	77/63	73/62	20	65	64	62
San Francisco CO	37	5	122	3	52	38	40	74/63	71/62	69/61	14	64	62	61
San Jose AP	37	2	122	0	70r	34	36	85/66	81/65	77/64	26	68	67	65
San Luis Obispo	35	2	120	4	315	33	35	92/69	88/70	84/69	26	73	71	70
Santa Ana AP	33	4	117	5	115r	37	39	89/69	85/68	82/68	28	71	70	69
Santa Barbara MAP	34	3	119	5	10	34	36	81/67	77/66	75/65	24	68	67	66
Santa Cruz	37	0	122	0	125	35	38	75/63	71/61	68/61	28	64	62	61
Santa Maria AP (S)	34	5	120	3	238	31	33	81/64	76/63	73/62	23	65	64	63
Santa Monica CO	34	0	118	3	57	41	43	83/68	80/68	77/67	16	70	69	68
Santa Paula	34	2	119	0	263	33	35	90/68	86/67	84/66	36	71	69	68
Santa Rosa	38	3	122	5	167	27	29	99/68	95/67	91/66	34	70	68	67
Stockton AP	37	5	121	2	28	28	30	100/69	97/68	94/67	37	71	70	68
Ukiah	39	1	122	4	620	27	29	99/69	95/68	91/67	40	70	68	67
Visalia	36	2	119	1	354	28	30	102/70	100/69	97/68	38	72	71	70
Yreka	41	4	122	4	2625	13	17	95/65	92/64	89/63	38	67	65	64
Yuba City	39	1	121	4	70	29	31	104/68	101/67	99/66	36	71	69	68
COLORADO														
Alamosa AP	37	3	105	5	7536	−11	−6	84/57	82/57	80/57	35	62	61	60
Boulder	40	0	105	2	5385	−6	0	93/59	91/59	89/59	27	64	63	62
Colorado Springs AP	38	5	104	4	6173	−3	2	91/58	88/57	86/57	30	63	62	61
Denver AP	39	5	104	5	5283	−5	1	93/59	91/59	89/59	28	64	63	62
Durango	37	1	107	5	6550	−6	−1	89/59	87/59	85/59	30	64	63	62

	Col. 2		Col. 3		Col. 4	Winter[d] Col. 5		Summer[e] Col. 6			Col. 7	Col. 8		
Col. 1	Lati-tude[b]		Longi-tude[b]		Eleva-tion[c]	Design Dry-Bulb		Design Dry-Bulb and Mean Coincident Wet-Bulb			Mean Daily	Design Wet-Bulb		
State and Station	°	'	°	'	Ft	99%	97.5%	1%	2.5%	5%	Range	1%	2.5%	5%
Fort Collins	40	4	105	0	5001	−5	1	93/59	91/59	89/59	28	64	63	62
Grand Junction AP (S)	39	1	108	3	4849	2	7	96/59	94/59	92/59	29	64	63	62
Greeley	40	3	104	4	4648	−2	4	96/60	94/60	92/60	29	65	64	63
La Junta AP	38	0	103	3	4188	−3	3	100/68	98/68	95/67	31	72	70	69
Leadville	39	2	106	2	10177	−18	−14	84/52	81/51	78/50	30	56	55	54
Pueblo AP	38	2	104	2	4639	−7	0	97/61	95/61	92/61	31	67	66	65
Sterling	40	4	103	1	3939	−7	−2	95/62	93/62	90/62	30	67	66	65
Trinidad AP	37	2	104	2	5746	−2	3	93/61	91/61	89/61	32	66	65	64
CONNECTICUT														
Bridgeport AP	41	1	73	1	7	6	9	86/73	84/71	81/70	18	75	74	73
Hartford, Brainard Field	41	5	72	4	15	3	7	91/74	88/73	85/72	22	77	75	74
New Haven AP	41	2	73	0	6	3	7	88/75	84/73	82/72	17	76	75	74
New London	41	2	72	1	60	5	9	88/73	85/72	83/71	16	76	75	74
Norwalk	41	1	73	3	37	6	9	86/73	84/71	81/70	19	75	74	73
Norwich	41	3	72	0	20	3	7	89/75	86/73	83/72	18	76	75	74
Waterbury	41	3	73	0	605	−4	2	88/73	85/71	82/70	21	75	74	72
Windsor Locks, Bradley Field (S)	42	0	72	4	169	0	4	91/74	88/72	85/71	22	76	75	73
DELAWARE														
Dover AFB	39	0	75	3	38	11	15	92/75	90/75	87/74	18	79	77	76
Wilmington AP	39	4	75	3	78	10	14	92/74	89/74	87/73	20	77	76	75
DISTRICT OF COLUMBIA														
Andrews AFB	38	5	76	5	279	10	14	92/75	90/74	87/73	18	78	76	75
Washington National AP	38	5	77	0	14	14	17	93/75	91/74	89/74	18	78	77	76
FLORIDA														
Belle Glade	26	4	80	4	16	41	44	92/76	91/76	89/76	16	79	78	78
Cape Kennedy AP	28	3	80	3	16	35	38	90/78	88/78	87/78	15	80	79	79
Daytona Beach AP	29	1	81	0	31	32	35	92/78	90/77	88/77	15	80	79	78
Fort Lauderdale	26	0	80	1	13	42	46	92/78	91/78	90/78	15	80	79	79
Fort Myers AP	26	4	81	5	13	41	44	93/78	92/78	91/77	18	80	79	79
Fort Pierce	27	3	80	2	10	38	42	91/78	90/78	89/78	15	80	79	79
Gainesville AP (S)	29	4	82	2	155	28	31	95/77	93/77	92/77	18	80	79	78
Jacksonville AP	30	3	81	4	24	29	32	96/77	94/77	92/76	19	79	79	78
Key West AP	24	3	81	5	6	55	57	90/78	90/78	89/78	9	80	79	79
Lakeland CO (S)	28	0	82	0	214	39	41	93/76	91/76	89/76	17	79	78	78
Miami AP (S)	25	5	80	2	7	44	47	91/77	90/77	89/77	15	79	79	78
Miami Beach CO	25	5	80	1	9	45	48	90/77	89/77	88/77	10	79	79	78
Ocala	29	1	82	1	86	31	34	95/77	93/77	92/76	18	80	79	78
Orlando AP	28	3	81	2	106r	35	38	94/76	93/76	91/76	17	79	78	78
Panama City, Tyndall AFB	30	0	85	4	22	29	33	92/78	90/77	89/77	14	81	80	79
Pensacola CO	30	3	87	1	13	25	29	94/77	93/77	91/77	14	80	79	79
St. Augustine	29	5	81	2	15	31	35	92/78	89/78	87/78	16	80	79	79
St. Petersburg	28	0	82	4	35	36	40	92/77	91/77	90/76	16	79	79	78
Sanford	28	5	81	2	14	35	38	94/76	93/76	91/76	17	79	78	78
Sarasota	27	2	82	3	30	39	42	93/77	92/77	90/76	17	79	79	78
Tallahassee AP (S)	30	2	84	2	58	27	30	94/77	92/76	90/76	19	79	78	78
Tampa AP (S)	28	0	82	3	19	36	40	92/77	91/77	90/76	17	79	79	78
West Palm Beach AP	26	4	80	1	15	41	45	92/78	91/78	90/78	16	80	79	79
GEORGIA														
Albany, Turner AFB	31	3	84	1	224	25	29	97/77	95/76	93/76	20	80	79	78
Americus	32	0	84	2	476	21	25	97/77	94/76	92/75	20	79	78	77
Athens	34	0	83	2	700	18	22	94/74	92/74	90/74	21	78	77	76
Atlanta AP (S)	33	4	84	3	1005	17	22	94/74	92/74	90/73	19	77	76	75
Augusta AP	33	2	82	0	143	20	23	97/77	95/76	93/76	19	80	79	78
Brunswick	31	1	81	3	14	29	32	92/78	89/78	87/78	18	80	79	79
Columbus, Lawson AFB	32	3	85	0	242	21	24	95/76	93/76	91/75	21	79	78	77
Dalton	34	5	85	0	720	17	22	94/76	93/76	91/76	22	79	78	77
Dublin	32	3	83	0	215	21	25	96/77	93/76	91/75	20	79	78	77
Gainesville	34	2	83	5	1254	16	21	93/74	91/74	89/73	21	77	76	75
Griffin (S)	33	1	84	2	980	18	22	93/76	90/75	88/74	21	78	77	76

Continued on next page

Table 3-7 continued

State and Station	Lati-tude°	Lati-tude'	Longi-tude°	Longi-tude'	Eleva-tion Ft	Design Dry-Bulb 99%	Design Dry-Bulb 97.5%	Design Dry-Bulb and Mean Coincident Wet-Bulb 1%	2.5%	5%	Mean Daily Range	Design Wet-Bulb 1%	2.5%	5%
	Col. 2		**Col. 3**		**Col. 4**	**Col. 5**		**Col. 6**			**Col. 7**	**Col. 8**		
La Grange	33	0	85	0	715	19	23	94/76	91/75	89/74	21	78	77	76
Macon AP	32	4	83	4	356	21	25	96/77	93/76	91/75	22	79	78	77
Marietta, Dobbins AFB	34	0	84	3	1016	17	21	94/74	92/74	90/74	21	78	77	76
Moultrie	31	1	83	4	340	27	30	97/77	95/77	92/76	20	80	79	78
Rome AP	34	2	85	1	637	17	22	94/76	93/76	91/76	23	79	78	77
Savannah-Travis AP	32	1	81	1	52	24	27	96/77	93/77	91/77	20	80	79	78
Valdosta-Moody AFB	31	0	83	1	239	28	31	96/77	94/77	92/76	20	80	79	78
Waycross	31	2	82	2	140	26	29	96/77	94/77	91/76	20	80	79	78
HAWAII														
Hilo AP (S)	19	4	155	1	31	61	62	84/73	83/72	82/72	15	75	74	74
Honolulu AP	21	2	158	0	7	62	63	87/73	86/73	85/72	12	76	75	74
Kaneohe Bay MCAS	21	2	157	5	18	65	66	85/75	84/74	83/74	12	76	76	75
Wahiawa	21	3	158	0	900	58	59	86/73	85/72	84/72	14	75	74	73
IDAHO														
Boise AP(S)	43	3	116	1	2842	3	10	96/65	94/64	91/64	31	68	66	65
Burley	42	3	113	5	4180	−3	2	99/62	95/61	92/66	35	64	63	61
Coeur d'Alene AP	47	5	116	5	2973	−8	−1	89/62	86/61	83/60	31	64	63	61
Idaho Falls AP	43	3	112	0	4730r	−11	−6	89/61	87/61	84/59	38	65	63	61
Lewiston AP	46	2	117	0	1413	−1	6	96/65	93/64	90/63	32	67	66	64
Moscow	46	4	117	0	2660	−7	0	90/63	87/62	84/61	32	65	64	62
Mountain Home AFB	43	0	115	5	2992	6	12	99/64	97/63	94/62	36	66	65	63
Pocatello AP	43	0	112	4	4444	−8	−1	94/61	91/60	89/59	35	64	63	61
Twin Falls (AP (S)	42	3	114	3	4148	−3	2	99/62	95/61	92/60	34	64	63	61
ILLINOIS														
Aurora	41	5	88	2	744	−6	−1	93/76	91/76	88/75	20	79	78	76
Belleville, Scott AFB	38	3	89	5	447	1	6	94/76	92/76	89/75	21	79	78	76
Bloomington	40	3	89	0	775	−6	−2	92/75	90/74	88/73	21	78	76	75
Carbondale	37	5	89	1	380	2	7	95/77	93/77	90/76	21	80	79	77
Champaign/Urbana	40	0	88	2	743	−3	2	95/75	92/74	90/73	21	78	77	75
Chicago, Midway AP	41	5	87	5	610	−5	0	94/74	91/73	88/72	20	77	75	74
Chicago, O'Hare AP	42	0	87	5	658	−8	−4	91/74	89/74	86/72	20	77	76	74
Chicago CO	41	5	87	4	594	−3	2	94/75	91/74	88/73	15	79	77	75
Danville	40	1	87	4	558	−4	1	93/75	90/74	88/73	21	78	77	75
Decatur	39	5	88	5	670	−3	2	94/75	91/74	88/73	21	78	77	75
Dixon	41	5	89	3	696	−7	−2	93/75	90/74	88/73	23	78	77	75
Elgin	42	0	88	2	820	−7	−2	91/75	88/74	86/73	21	78	77	75
Freeport	42	2	89	4	780	−9	−4	91/74	89/73	87/72	24	77	76	74
Galesburg	41	0	90	3	771	−7	−2	93/75	91/75	88/74	22	78	77	75
Greenville	39	0	89	2	563	−1	4	94/76	92/75	89/74	21	79	78	76
Joliet	41	3	88	1	588	−5	0	93/75	90/74	88/73	20	78	77	75
Kankakee	41	1	87	5	625	−4	1	93/75	90/74	88/73	21	78	77	75
La Salle/Peru	41	2	89	1	520	−7	−2	93/75	91/75	88/74	22	78	77	75
Macomb	40	3	90	4	702	−5	0	95/76	92/76	89/75	22	79	78	76
Moline AP	41	3	90	3	582	−9	−4	93/75	91/75	88/74	23	78	77	75
Mt Vernon	38	2	88	5	500	0	5	95/76	92/75	89/74	21	79	78	76
Peoria AP	40	4	89	4	652	−8	−4	91/75	89/74	87/73	22	78	76	75
Quincy AP	40	0	91	1	762	−2	3	96/76	93/76	90/76	22	80	78	77
Rantoul, Chanute AFB	40	2	88	1	740	−4	1	94/75	91/74	89/73	21	78	77	75
Rockford	42	1	89	0	724	−9	−4	91/74	89/73	87/72	24	77	76	74
Springfield AP	39	5	89	4	587	−3	2	94/75	92/74	89/74	21	79	77	76
Waukegan	42	2	87	5	680	−6	−3	92/76	89/74	87/73	21	78	76	75
INDIANA														
Anderson	40	0	85	4	847	0	6	95/76	92/75	89/74	22	79	78	76
Bedford	38	5	86	3	670	0	5	95/76	92/75	89/74	22	79	78	76
Bloomington	39	1	86	4	820	0	5	95/76	92/75	89/74	22	79	78	76
Columbus, Bakalar AFB	39	2	85	5	661	3	7	95/76	92/75	90/74	22	79	78	76
Crawfordsville	40	0	86	5	752	−2	3	94/75	91/74	88/73	22	79	77	76
Evansville AP	38	0	87	3	381	4	9	95/76	93/75	91/75	22	79	78	77
Fort Wayne AP	41	0	85	1	791	−4	1	92/73	89/72	87/72	24	77	75	74
Goshen AP	41	3	85	5	823	−3	1	91/73	89/73	86/72	23	77	75	74
Hobart	41	3	87	2	600	−4	2	91/73	88/73	85/72	21	77	75	74
Huntington	40	4	85	3	802	−4	1	92/73	89/72	87/72	23	77	75	74
Indianapolis AP (S)	39	4	86	2	793	−2	2	92/74	90/74	87/73	22	78	76	75
Jeffersonville	38	2	85	5	455	5	10	95/74	93/74	90/74	23	79	77	76
Kokomo	40	3	86	1	790	−4	0	91/73	90/73	88/73	22	77	75	74
Lafayette	40	2	86	5	600	−3	3	94/74	91/73	88/73	22	78	76	75

	Col. 2		Col. 3		Col. 4	Winter[d] Col. 5		Summer[e] Col. 6			Col. 7	Col. 8		
Col. 1	Lati-tude[b]		Longi-tude[c]		Eleva-tion[c]	Design Dry-Bulb		Design Dry-Bulb and Mean Coincident Wet-Bulb			Mean Daily Range	Design Wet-Bulb		
State and Station	°	'	°	'	Ft	99%	97.5%	1%	2.5%	5%		1%	2.5%	5%
La Porte	41	3	86	4	810	−3	3	93/74	90/74	87/73	22	78	76	75
Marion	40	3	85	4	791	−4	0	91/74	90/73	88/73	23	77	75	74
Muncie	40	1	85	2	955	−3	2	92/74	90/73	87/73	22	76	76	75
Peru, Bunker Hill AFB	40	4	86	1	804	−6	−1	90/74	88/73	86/73	22	77	75	74
Richmond AP	39	5	84	5	1138	−2	2	92/74	90/74	87/73	22	78	76	75
Shelbyville	39	3	85	5	765	−1	3	93/74	91/74	88/73	22	78	76	75
South Bend AP	41	4	86	2	773	−3	1	91/73	89/73	86/72	22	77	75	74
Terre Haute AP	39	3	87	2	601	−2	4	95/75	92/74	89/73	22	79	77	76
Valparaise	41	2	87	0	801	−3	3	93/74	90/74	87/73	22	78	76	75
Vincennes	38	4	87	3	420	1	6	95/75	92/74	90/73	22	79	77	76
IOWA														
Ames (S)	42	0	93	4	1004	−11	−6	93/75	90/74	87/73	23	78	76	75
Burlington AP	40	5	91	1	694	−7	−3	94/74	91/75	88/73	22	78	77	75
Cedar Rapids AP	41	5	91	4	863	−10	−5	91/76	88/75	86/74	23	78	77	75
Clinton	41	5	90	1	595	−8	−3	92/75	90/75	87/74	23	78	77	75
Council Bluffs	41	2	95	5	1210	−8	−3	94/76	91/75	88/74	22	78	77	75
Des Moines AP	41	3	93	4	948r	−10	−5	94/75	91/74	88/73	23	78	77	75
Dubuque	42	2	90	4	1065	−12	−7	90/74	88/73	86/72	22	77	75	74
Fort Dodge	42	3	94	1	1111	−12	−7	91/74	88/74	86/72	23	77	75	74
Iowa City	41	4	91	3	645	−11	−6	92/76	89/76	87/74	22	80	78	76
Keokuk	40	2	91	2	526	−5	0	95/75	92/75	89/74	22	79	77	76
Marshalltown	42	0	92	5	898	−12	−7	92/76	90/75	88/74	23	78	77	75
Mason City AP	43	1	93	2	1194	−15	−11	90/74	88/74	85/72	24	77	75	74
Newton	41	4	93	0	946	−10	−5	94/75	91/74	88/73	23	78	77	75
Ottumwa AP	41	1	92	2	842	−8	−4	94/75	91/74	88/73	22	78	77	75
Sioux City AP	42	2	96	2	1095	−11	−7	95/74	92/74	89/73	24	78	77	75
Waterloo	42	3	92	2	868	−15	−10	91/76	89/75	86/74	23	78	77	75
KANSAS														
Atchison	39	3	95	1	945	−2	2	96/77	93/76	91/76	23	81	79	77
Chanute AP	34	4	95	3	977	3	7	100/74	97/74	94/74	23	78	77	76
Dodge City AP (S)	37	5	100	0	2594	0	5	100/69	97/69	95/69	25	74	73	71
El Dorado	37	5	96	5	1282	3	7	101/72	98/73	96/73	24	77	76	75
Emporia	38	2	96	1	1209	1	5	100/74	97/74	94/73	25	78	77	76
Garden City AP	38	0	101	0	2882	−1	4	99/69	96/69	94/69	28	74	73	71
Goodland AP	39	2	101	4	3645	−5	0	99/66	96/65	93/66	31	71	70	68
Great Bend	38	2	98	5	1940	0	4	101/73	98/73	95/73	28	78	76	75
Hutchinson AP	38	0	97	5	1524	4	8	102/72	99/72	97/72	28	77	75	74
Liberal	37	0	101	0	2838	2	7	99/68	96/68	94/68	28	73	72	71
Manhattan, Fort Riley (S)	39	0	96	5	1076	−1	3	99/75	95/75	92/74	24	78	77	76
Parsons	37	2	95	3	908	5	9	100/74	97/74	94/74	23	79	77	76
Russell AP	38	5	98	5	1864	0	4	101/73	98/73	95/73	29	78	76	75
Salina	38	5	97	4	1271	0	5	103/74	100/74	97/73	26	78	77	75
Topeka AP	39	0	95	4	877	0	4	99/75	96/75	93/74	24	79	78	76
Wichita AP	37	4	97	3	1321	3	7	101/72	98/73	96/73	23	77	76	75
KENTUCKY														
Ashland	38	3	82	4	551	5	10	94/76	91/74	89/73	22	78	77	75
Bowling Green AP	37	0	86	3	535	4	10	94/77	92/75	89/74	21	79	77	76
Corbin AP	37	0	84	1	1175	4	9	94/73	92/73	89/72	23	77	76	75
Covington AP	39	0	84	4	869	1	6	92/73	90/72	88/72	22	77	75	74
Hopkinsville, Campbell AFB	36	4	87	3	540	4	10	94/77	92/75	89/74	21	79	77	76
Lexington AP (S)	38	0	84	4	979	3	8	93/73	91/73	88/72	22	77	76	75
Louisville AP	38	1	85	4	474	5	10	95/74	93/74	90/74	23	79	77	76
Madisonville	37	2	87	3	439	5	10	96/76	93/75	90/75	22	79	78	77
Owensboro	37	5	87	1	420	5	10	97/76	94/75	91/75	23	79	78	77
Paducah AP	37	0	88	4	398	7	12	98/76	95/75	92/75	20	79	78	77
LOUISIANA														
Alexandria AP	31	2	92	2	92	23	27	95/77	94/77	92/77	20	80	79	78
Baton Rouge AP	30	3	91	1	64	25	29	95/77	93/77	92/77	19	80	80	79
Bogalusa	30	5	89	5	103	24	28	95/77	93/77	92/77	19	80	80	79
Houma	29	3	90	4	13	31	35	95/78	93/78	92/77	15	81	80	79
Lafayette AP	30	1	92	0	38	26	30	95/78	94/78	92/78	18	81	80	79
Lake Charles AP (S)	30	1	93	1	14	27	31	95/77	93/77	92/77	17	80	79	79
Minden	32	4	93	2	250	20	25	99/77	96/76	94/76	20	79	79	78
Monroe AP	32	3	92	0	78	20	25	99/77	96/76	94/76	20	79	79	78
Natchitoches	31	5	93	0	120	22	26	97/77	95/77	93/77	20	80	79	78

Continued on next page

Table 3-7 continued

Col. 1	Col. 2		Col. 3		Col. 4	Col. 5 Winter[d]		Col. 6 Summer[e]			Col. 7	Col. 8		
	Lati-tude[b]		Longi-tude[c]		Eleva-tion[c]	Design Dry-Bulb		Design Dry-Bulb and Mean Coincident Wet-Bulb			Mean Daily	Design Wet-Bulb		
State and Station	°	'	°	'	Ft	99%	97.5%	1%	2.5%	5%	Range	1%	2.5%	5%
New Orleans AP	30	0	90	2	3	29	33	93/78	92/78	90/77	16	81	80	79
Shreveport AP(S)	32	3	93	5	252	20	25	99/77	96/76	94/76	20	79	79	78
MAINE														
Augusta AP	44	2	69	5	350	−7	−3	88/73	85/70	82/68	22	74	72	70
Bangor, Dow AFB	44	5	68	5	162	−11	−6	86/70	83/68	80/67	22	73	71	69
Caribou AP (S)	46	5	68	0	624	−18	−13	84/69	81/67	78/66	21	71	69	67
Lewiston	44	0	70	1	182	−7	−2	88/73	85/70	82/68	22	74	72	70
Millinocket AP	45	4	68	4	405	−13	−9	87/69	83/68	80/66	22	72	70	68
Portland (S)	43	4	70	2	61	−6	−1	87/72	84/71	81/69	22	74	72	70
Waterville	44	3	69	4	89	−8	−4	87/72	84/69	81/68	22	74	72	70
MARYLAND														
Baltimore AP	39	1	76	4	146	10	13	94/75	91/75	89/74	21	78	77	76
Baltimore CO	39	2	76	3	14	14	17	92/77	89/76	87/75	17	80	78	76
Cumberland	39	4	78	5	945	6	10	92/75	89/74	87/74	22	77	76	75
Frederick AP	39	3	77	3	294	8	12	94/76	91/75	88/74	22	78	77	76
Hagerstown	39	4	77	4	660	8	12	94/75	91/74	89/74	22	77	76	75
Salisbury (S)	38	2	75	3	52	12	16	93/75	91/75	88/74	18	79	77	76
MASSACHUSETTS														
Boston AP (S)	42	2	71	0	15	6	9	91/73	88/71	85/70	16	75	74	72
Clinton	42	2	71	4	398	−2	2	90/72	87/71	84/69	17	75	73	72
Fall River	41	4	71	1	190	5	9	87/72	84/71	81/69	18	74	73	72
Framingham	42	2	71	3	170	3	6	89/72	86/71	83/69	17	74	73	71
Gloucester	42	3	70	4	10	2	5	89/73	86/71	83/70	15	75	74	72
Greenfield	42	3	72	4	205	−7	−2	88/72	85/71	82/69	23	74	73	71
Lawrence	42	4	71	1	57	−6	0	90/73	87/72	84/70	22	76	74	73
Lowell	42	3	71	2	90	−4	1	91/73	88/72	85/70	21	76	74	73
New Bedford	41	4	71	0	70	5	9	85/72	82/71	80/69	19	74	73	72
Pittsfield AP	42	3	73	2	1170	−8	−3	87/71	84/70	81/68	23	73	72	70
Springfield, Westover AFB	42	1	72	3	247	−5	0	90/72	87/71	84/69	19	75	73	72
Taunton	41	5	71	1	20	5	9	89/73	86/72	83/70	18	75	74	73
Worcester AP	42	2	71	5	986	0	4	87/71	84/70	81/68	18	73	72	70
MICHIGAN														
Adrian	41	5	84	0	754	−1	3	91/73	88/72	85/71	23	76	75	73
Alpena AP	45	0	83	3	689	−11	−6	89/70	85/70	83/69	27	73	72	70
Battle Creek AP	42	2	85	2	939	1	5	92/74	88/72	85/70	23	76	74	73
Benton Harbor AP	42	1	86	3	649	1	5	91/72	88/72	85/70	20	75	74	72
Detroit	42	2	83	0	633	3	6	91/73	88/72	86/71	20	76	74	73
Escanaba	45	4	87	0	594	−11	−7	87/70	83/69	80/68	17	73	71	69
Flint AP	42	0	83	4	766	−4	1	90/73	87/72	85/71	25	76	74	72
Grand Rapids AP	42	5	85	3	681	1	5	91/72	88/72	85/70	24	75	74	72
Holland	42	5	86	1	612	2	6	88/72	86/71	83/70	22	75	73	72
Jackson AP	42	2	84	2	1003	1	5	92/74	88/72	85/70	23	76	74	73
Kalamazoo	42	1	85	3	930	1	5	92/74	88/72	85/70	23	76	74	73
Lansing AP	42	5	84	4	852	−3	1	90/73	87/72	84/70	24	75	74	72
Marquette CO	46	3	87	3	677	−12	−8	84/70	81/69	77/66	18	72	70	68
Mt Pleasant	43	4	84	5	796	0	4	91/73	87/72	84/71	24	76	74	72
Muskegon AP	43	1	86	1	627	2	6	86/72	84/70	82/70	21	75	73	72
Pontiac	42	4	83	2	974	0	4	90/73	87/72	85/71	21	76	74	73
Port Huron	43	0	82	3	586	0	4	90/73	87/72	83/71	21	76	74	73
Saginaw AP	43	3	84	1	662	0	4	91/73	87/72	84/71	23	76	74	72
Sault Ste. Marie AP (S)	46	3	84	2	721	−12	−8	84/70	81/69	77/66	23	72	70	68
Traverse City AP	44	4	85	4	618	−3	1	89/72	86/71	83/69	22	75	73	71
Yipsilanti	42	1	83	3	777	1	5	92/74	89/71	86/70	22	75	74	72
MINNESOTA														
Albert Lea	43	4	93	2	1235	−17	−12	90/74	87/72	84/71	24	77	75	73
Alexandria AP	45	5	95	2	1421	−22	−16	91/72	88/72	85/70	24	76	74	72
Bemidji AP	47	3	95	0	1392	−31	−26	88/69	85/69	81/67	24	73	71	69
Brainerd	46	2	94	2	1214	−20	−16	90/73	87/71	84/69	24	75	73	71
Duluth AP	46	5	92	1	1426	−21	−16	85/70	82/68	79/66	22	72	70	68
Fairbault	44	2	93	2	1190	−17	−12	91/74	88/72	85/71	24	77	75	73
Fergus Falls	46	1	96	0	1210	−21	−17	91/72	88/72	85/70	24	76	74	72
International Falls AP	48	3	93	2	1179	−29	−25	85/68	83/68	80/66	26	71	70	68

	Col. 1	Col. 2		Col. 3		Col. 4	Winter[d] Col. 5		Summer[e] Col. 6			Col. 7	Col. 8		
		Lati-tude[b]		Longi-tude[c]		Eleva-tion[c]	Design Dry-Bulb		Design Dry-Bulb and Mean Coincident Wet-Bulb			Mean Daily	Design Wet-Bulb		
	State and Station	°	′	°	′	Ft	99%	97.5%	1%	2.5%	5%	Range	1%	2.5%	5%
	Mankato	44	1	94	0	785	−17	−12	91/72	88/72	85/70	24	77	75	73
	Minneapolis/ St Paul AP	44	5	93	1	822	−16	−12	92/75	89/73	86/71	22	77	75	73
	Rochester AP	44	0	92	3	1297	−17	−12	90/74	87/72	84/71	24	77	75	73
	St Cloud AP (S)	45	4	94	1	1034	−15	−11	91/74	88/72	85/70	24	76	74	72
	Virginia	47	3	92	3	1435	−25	−21	85/69	83/68	80/66	23	71	70	68
	Willmar	45	1	95	0	1133	−15	−11	91/74	88/72	85/71	24	76	74	72
	Winona	44	1	91	4	652	−14	−10	91/75	88/73	85/72	24	77	75	74
MISSISSIPPI															
	Biloxi, Keesler AFB	30	2	89	0	25	28	31	94/79	92/79	90/78	16	82	81	80
	Clarksdale	34	1	90	3	178	14	19	96/77	94/77	92/76	21	80	79	78
	Columbus AFB	33	4	88	3	224	15	20	95/77	93/77	91/76	22	80	79	78
	Greenville AFB	33	3	91	1	139	15	20	95/77	93/77	91/76	21	80	79	78
	Greenwood	33	3	90	1	128	15	20	95/77	93/77	91/76	21	80	79	78
	Hattiesburg	31	2	89	2	200	24	27	96/78	94/77	92/77	21	81	80	79
	Jackson AP	32	2	90	1	330	21	25	97/76	95/76	93/76	21	79	78	78
	Laurel	31	4	89	1	264	24	27	96/78	94/77	92/77	21	81	80	79
	McComb AP	31	2	90	3	458r	21	26	96/77	94/76	92/76	18	80	79	78
	Meridian AP	32	2	88	5	294	19	23	97/77	95/76	93/76	22	80	79	78
	Natchez	31	4	91	3	168	23	27	96/78	94/78	92/77	21	81	80	79
	Tupelo	34	2	88	4	289	14	19	96/77	94/77	92/76	22	80	79	78
	Vicksburg CO	32	2	91	0	234	22	26	97/78	95/78	93/77	21	81	80	79
MISSOURI															
	Cape Girardeau	37	1	89	3	330	8	13	98/76	95/75	92/75	21	79	78	77
	Columbia AP (S)	39	0	92	2	778	−1	4	97/74	94/74	91/73	22	78	77	76
	Farmington AP	37	5	90	3	928	3	8	96/76	93/75	90/74	22	78	77	75
	Hannibal	39	4	91	2	489	−2	3	96/76	93/76	90/76	22	80	78	77
	Jefferson City	38	4	92	1	640	2	7	98/75	95/74	92/74	23	78	77	76
	Joplin AP	37	1	94	3	982	6	10	100/73	97/73	94/73	24	78	77	76
	Kansas City AP	39	1	94	4	742	2	6	99/75	96/74	93/74	20	78	77	76
	Kirksville AP	40	1	92	4	966	−5	0	96/74	93/74	90/73	24	78	77	76
	Mexico	39	1	92	0	775	−1	4	97/74	94/74	91/73	22	78	77	76
	Moberly	39	3	92	3	850	−2	3	97/74	94/74	91/73	23	78	77	76
	Poplar Bluff	36	5	90	3	322	11	16	98/78	95/76	92/76	22	81	79	78
	Rolla	38	0	91	5	1202	3	9	94/77	91/75	89/74	22	78	77	76
	St Joseph AP	39	5	95	0	809	−3	2	96/77	93/76	91/76	23	81	79	77
	St Louis AP	38	5	90	2	535	2	6	97/75	94/75	91/74	21	78	77	76
	St Louis CO	38	4	90	2	465	3	8	98/75	94/75	91/74	18	78	77	76
	Sedalia, Whiteman AFB	38	4	93	3	838	−1	4	95/76	92/76	90/75	22	79	78	76
	Sikeston	36	5	89	3	318	9	15	98/77	95/76	92/75	21	80	78	77
	Springfield AP	37	1	93	2	1265	3	9	96/73	93/74	91/74	23	78	77	75
MONTANA															
	Billings AP	45	5	108	3	3567	−15	−10	94/64	91/64	88/63	31	67	66	64
	Bozeman	45	5	111	0	4856	−20	−14	90/61	87/60	84/59	32	63	62	60
	Butte AP	46	0	112	3	5526r	−24	−17	86/58	83/56	80/56	35	60	58	57
	Cut Bank AP	48	4	112	2	3838r	−25	−20	88/61	85/61	82/60	35	64	62	61
	Glasgow AP (S)	48	1	106	4	2277	−22	−18	92/64	89/63	85/62	29	68	66	64
	Glendive	47	1	104	4	2076	−18	−13	95/66	92/64	89/62	29	69	67	65
	Great Falls AP (S)	47	3	111	2	3664r	−21	−15	91/60	88/60	85/59	28	64	62	60
	Havre	48	3	109	4	2488	−18	−11	94/65	90/64	87/63	33	68	66	65
	Helena AP	46	4	112	0	3893	−21	−16	91/60	88/60	85/59	32	64	62	61
	Kalispell AP	48	2	114	2	2965	−14	−7	91/62	87/61	84/60	34	65	63	62
	Lewiston AP	47	0	109	3	4132	−22	−16	90/62	87/61	83/60	30	65	63	62
	Livingston AP	45	4	110	3	4653	−20	−14	90/61	87/60	84/59	32	63	62	60
	Miles City AP	46	3	105	5	2629	−20	−15	98/66	95/66	92/65	30	70	68	67
	Missoula AP	46	5	114	1	3200	−13	−6	92/62	88/61	85/60	36	65	63	62
NEBRASKA															
	Beatrice	40	2	96	5	1235	−5	−2	99/75	95/74	92/74	24	78	77	76
	Chadron AP	42	5	103	0	3300	−8	−3	97/66	94/65	91/65	30	71	69	68
	Columbus	41	3	97	2	1442	−6	−2	98/74	95/73	92/73	25	77	76	75
	Fremont	41	3	96	3	1203	−6	−2	98/75	95/74	92/74	22	78	77	76

Continued on next page

Table 3-7 continued

State and Station	Lati-tude[b] °	'	Longi-tude[c] °	'	Eleva-tion[c] Ft	Winter[d] Design Dry-Bulb 99%	97.5%	Summer[e] Design Dry-Bulb and Mean Coincident Wet-Bulb 1%	2.5%	5%	Mean Daily Range	Design Wet-Bulb 1%	2.5%	5%
Grand Island AP	41	0	98	2	1841	−8	−3	97/72	94/71	91/71	28	75	74	73
Hastings	40	4	98	3	1932	−7	−3	97/72	94/71	91/71	27	75	74	73
Kearney	40	4	99	1	2146	−9	−4	96/71	93/70	90/70	28	74	73	72
Lincoln CO (S)	40	5	96	5	1150	−5	−2	99/75	95/74	92/74	24	78	77	76
McCook	40	1	100	4	2565	−6	−2	98/69	95/69	91/69	28	74	72	71
Norfolk	42	0	97	3	1532	−8	−4	97/74	93/74	90/73	30	78	77	75
North Platte AP (S)	41	1	100	4	2779	−8	−4	97/69	94/69	90/69	28	74	72	71
Omaha AP	41	2	95	5	978	−8	−3	94/76	91/75	88/74	22	78	77	75
Scottsbluff AP	41	5	103	4	3950	−8	−3	95/65	92/65	90/64	31	70	68	67
Sidney AP	41	1	103	0	4292	−8	−3	95/65	92/65	90/64	31	70	68	67
NEVADA														
Carson City	39	1	119	5	4675	4	9	94/60	91/59	89/58	42	63	61	60
Elko AP	40	5	115	5	5075	−8	−2	94/59	92/59	90/58	42	63	62	60
Ely AP (S)	39	1	114	5	6257	−10	−4	89/57	87/56	85/55	39	60	59	58
Las Vegas AP (S)	36	1	115	1	2162	25	28	108/66	106/65	104/65	30	71	70	69
Lovelock AP	40	0	118	3	3900	8	12	98/63	96/63	93/62	42	66	65	64
Reno AP (S)	39	3	119	5	4404	5	10	95/61	92/60	90/59	45	64	62	61
Reno CO	39	3	119	5	4490	6	11	96/61	93/60	91/59	45	64	62	61
Tonopah AP	38	0	117	1	5426	5	10	94/60	92/59	90/58	40	64	62	61
Winnemucca AP	40	5	117	5	4299	−1	3	96/60	94/60	92/60	42	64	62	61
NEW HAMPSHIRE														
Berlin	44	3	71	1	1110	−14	−9	87/71	84/69	81/68	22	73	71	70
Claremont	43	2	72	2	420	−9	−4	89/72	86/70	83/69	24	74	73	71
Concord AP	43	1	71	3	339	−8	−3	90/72	87/70	84/69	26	74	73	71
Keene	43	0	72	2	490	−12	−7	90/72	87/70	83/69	24	74	73	71
Laconia	43	3	71	3	505	−10	−5	89/72	86/70	83/69	25	74	73	71
Manchester, Grenier AFB	43	0	71	3	253	−8	−3	91/72	88/71	85/70	24	75	74	72
Portsmouth, Pease AFB	43	1	70	5	127	−2	2	89/73	85/71	83/70	22	75	74	72
NEW JERSEY														
Atlantic City CO	39	3	74	3	11	10	13	92/74	89/74	86/72	18	78	77	75
Long Branch	40	2	74	0	20	10	13	93/74	90/73	87/72	18	78	77	75
Newark AP	40	4	74	1	11	10	14	94/74	91/73	88/72	20	77	76	75
New Brunswick	40	3	74	3	86	6	10	92/74	89/73	86/72	19	77	76	75
Paterson	40	5	74	1	100	6	10	94/74	91/73	88/72	21	77	76	75
Phillipsburg	40	4	75	1	180	1	6	92/73	89/72	86/71	21	76	75	74
Trenton CO	40	1	74	5	144	11	14	91/75	88/74	85/73	19	78	76	75
Vineland	39	3	75	0	95	8	11	91/75	89/74	86/73	19	78	76	75
NEW MEXICO														
Alamagordo, Holloman AFB	32	5	106	1	4070	14	19	98/64	96/64	94/64	30	69	68	67
Albuquerque AP (S)	35	0	106	4	5310	12	16	96/61	94/61	92/61	27	66	65	64
Artesia	32	5	104	2	3375	13	19	103/67	100/67	97/67	30	72	71	70
Carlsbad AP	32	2	104	2	3234	13	19	103/67	100/67	97/67	28	72	71	70
Clovis AP	34	3	103	1	4279	8	13	95/65	93/65	91/65	28	69	68	67
Farmington AP	36	5	108	1	5495	1	6	95/63	93/62	91/61	30	67	65	64
Gallup	35	3	108	5	6465	0	5	90/59	89/58	86/58	32	64	62	61
Grants	35	1	107	5	6520	−1	4	89/59	88/58	85/57	32	64	62	61
Hobbs AP	32	4	103	1	3664	13	18	101/66	99/66	97/66	29	71	70	69
Las Cruces	32	2	107	0	3900	15	20	99/64	96/64	94/64	30	69	68	67
Los Alamos	35	5	106	2	7410	5	9	89/60	87/60	85/60	32	62	61	60
Raton AP	36	5	104	3	6379	−4	1	91/60	89/60	87/60	34	65	64	63
Roswell, Walker AFB	33	2	104	3	3643	13	18	100/66	98/66	96/66	33	71	70	69
Santa Fe CO	35	4	106	0	7045	6	10	90/61	88/61	86/61	28	63	62	61
Silver City AP	32	4	108	2	5373	5	10	95/61	94/60	91/60	30	66	64	63
Socorro AP	34	0	106	5	4617	13	17	97/62	95/62	93/62	30	67	66	65
Tucumcari AP	35	1	103	4	4053	8	13	99/66	97/66	95/65	28	70	69	68
NEW YORK														
Albany AP (S)	42	5	73	5	277	−6	−1	91/73	88/72	85/70	23	75	74	72
Albany CO	42	5	73	5	19	−4	1	91/73	88/72	85/70	20	75	74	72
Auburn	43	0	76	3	715	−3	2	90/73	87/71	84/70	22	75	73	72
Batavia	43	0	78	1	900	1	5	90/72	87/71	84/70	22	75	73	72
Binghamton AP	42	1	76	0	1590	−2	1	86/71	83/69	81/68	20	73	72	70
Buffalo AP	43	0	78	4	705r	2	6	88/71	85/70	83/69	21	74	73	72
Cortland	42	4	76	1	1129	−5	0	88/71	85/71	82/70	23	74	73	71
Dunkirk	42	3	79	2	590	4	9	88/73	85/72	83/71	18	75	74	72
Elmira AP	42	1	76	5	860	−4	1	89/71	86/71	83/70	24	74	73	71
Geneva (S)	42	5	77	0	590	−3	2	90/73	87/71	84/70	22	75	73	72

Col. 1	Col. 2		Col. 3		Col. 4	Winter[d] Col. 5		Summer[e] Col. 6			Col. 7	Col. 8		
	Latitude[b]		Longitude[c]		Elevation[c]	Design Dry-Bulb		Design Dry-Bulb and Mean Coincident Wet-Bulb			Mean Daily	Design Wet-Bulb		
State and Station	°	′	°	′	Ft	99%	97.5%	1%	2.5%	5%	Range	1%	2.5%	5%
Glen Falls	42	2	73	4	321	−11	−5	88/72	85/71	82/69	23	74	73	71
Gloversville	43	1	74	2	790	−8	−2	89/72	86/71	83/69	23	75	74	72
Hornell	42	2	77	4	1325	−4	0	88/71	85/70	82/69	24	74	73	72
Ithaca (S)	42	3	76	3	950	−5	0	88/71	85/71	82/70	24	74	73	71
Jamestown	42	1	79	2	1390	−1	3	88/70	86/70	83/69	20	74	72	71
Kingston	42	0	74	0	279	−3	2	91/73	88/72	85/70	22	76	74	73
Lockport	43	1	78	4	520	4	7	89/74	86/72	84/71	21	76	74	73
Massena AP	45	0	75	0	202r	−13	−8	86/70	83/69	80/68	20	73	72	70
Newburg-Stewart AFB	41	3	74	1	460	−1	4	90/73	88/72	85/70	21	76	74	73
NYC-Central Park (S)	40	5	74	0	132	11	15	92/74	89/73	87/72	17	76	75	74
NYC-Kennedy AP	40	4	73	5	16	12	15	90/73	87/72	84/71	16	76	75	74
NYC-La Guardia AP	40	5	73	5	19	11	15	92/74	89/73	87/72	16	76	75	74
Niagra Falls AP	43	1	79	0	596	4	7	89/74	86/72	84/71	20	76	74	73
Olean	42	1	78	3	1420	−2	2	87/71	84/71	81/70	23	74	73	71
Oneonta	42	3	75	0	1150	−7	−4	86/71	83/69	80/68	24	73	72	70
Oswego CO	43	3	76	3	300	1	7	86/73	83/71	80/70	20	75	73	72
Plattsburg AFB	44	4	73	3	165	−13	−8	86/70	83/69	80/68	22	73	72	70
Poughkeepsie	41	4	73	5	103	0	6	92/74	89/74	86/72	21	77	75	74
Rochester AP	43	1	77	4	543	1	5	91/73	88/71	85/70	22	75	73	72
Rome-Griffiss AFB	43	1	75	3	515	−11	−5	88/71	85/70	83/69	22	75	73	71
Schenectady (S)	42	5	74	0	217	−4	1	90/73	87/72	84/70	22	75	74	72
Suffolk County AFB	40	5			57	7	10	86/72	83/71	80/70	16	76	74	73
Syracuse AP	43	1	76	1	424	−3	2	90/73	87/71	84/70	20	75	73	72
Utica	43	1	75	2	714	−12	−6	88/73	85/71	82/70	22	75	73	71
Watertown	44	0	76	0	497	−11	−6	86/73	83/71	81/70	20	75	73	72
NORTH CAROLINA														
Ashville AP	35	3	82	3	217r	10	14	89/73	87/72	85/71	21	75	74	72
Charlotte AP	35	0	81	0	735	18	22	95/74	93/74	91/74	20	77	76	76
Durham	36	0	78	5	406	16	20	94/75	92/75	90/75	20	78	77	76
Elizabeth City AP	36	2	76	1	10	12	19	93/78	91/77	89/76	18	80	78	78
Fayetteville, Pope AFB	35	1	79	0	95	17	20	95/76	92/76	90/75	20	79	78	77
Goldsboro, Seymour-Johnson AFB	35	2	78	0	88	18	21	94/77	91/76	89/75	18	79	78	77
Greensboro AP (S)	36	1	80	0	887	14	18	93/74	91/73	89/73	21	77	76	75
Greenville	35	4	77	2	25	18	21	93/77	91/76	89/75	19	79	78	77
Henderson	36	2	78	2	510	12	15	95/77	92/76	90/76	20	79	78	77
Hickory	35	4	81	2	1165	14	18	92/73	90/72	88/72	21	75	74	73
Jacksonville	34	5	77	3	24	20	24	92/78	90/78	88/77	18	80	79	78
Lumberton	34	4	79	0	132	18	21	95/76	92/76	90/75	20	79	78	77
New Bern AP	35	1	77	0	17	20	24	92/78	90/78	88/77	18	80	79	78
Raleigh/Durham AP (S)	35	5	78	5	433	16	20	94/75	92/75	90/75	20	78	77	76
Rocky Mount	36	0	77	5	81	18	21	94/77	91/76	89/75	19	79	78	77
Wilmington AP	34	2	78	0	30	23	26	93/79	91/78	89/77	18	81	80	79
Winston-Salem AP	36	1	80	1	967	16	20	94/74	91/73	89/73	20	76	75	74
NORTH DAKOTA														
Bismark AP (S)	46	5	100	5	1647	−23	−19	95/68	91/68	88/67	27	73	71	70
Devil's Lake	48	1	98	5	1471	−25	−21	91/69	88/68	85/66	25	73	71	69
Dickinson AP	46	5	102	5	2595	−21	−17	94/68	90/66	87/65	25	71	69	68
Fargo AP	46	5	96	5	900	−22	−18	92/73	89/71	85/69	25	76	74	72
Grands Forks AP	48	0	97	2	832	−26	−22	91/70	87/70	84/68	25	74	72	70
Jamestown AP	47	0	98	4	1492	−22	−18	94/70	90/69	87/68	26	74	74	71
Minot AP	48	2	101	2	1713	−24	−20	92/68	89/67	86/65	25	72	70	68
Williston	48	1	103	4	1877	−25	−21	91/68	88/67	85/65	25	72	70	68
OHIO														
Akron-Canton AP	41	0	81	3	1210	1	6	89/72	86/71	84/70	21	75	73	72
Ashtabula	42	0	80	5	690	4	9	88/73	85/72	83/71	18	75	74	72
Athens	39	2	82	1	700	0	6	95/75	92/74	90/73	22	78	76	74
Bowling Green	41	3	83	4	675	−2	2	92/73	89/73	86/71	23	76	75	73
Cambridge	40	0	81	4	800	1	7	93/75	90/74	87/73	23	78	76	75

Continued on next page

Table 3-7 continued

State and Station	Lati-tude[b] °	'	Longi-tude[c] °	'	Eleva-tion[c] Ft	Design Dry-Bulb 99%	97.5%	Design Dry-Bulb and Mean Coincident Wet-Bulb 1%	2.5%	5%	Mean Daily Range	Design Wet-Bulb 1%	2.5%	5%
Chillicothe	39	2	83	0	638	0	6	95/75	92/74	90/73	22	78	76	74
Cincinnati CO	39	1	84	4	761	1	6	92/73	90/72	88/72	21	77	75	74
Cleveland AP (S)	41	2	81	5	777r	1	5	91/73	88/72	86/71	22	76	74	73
Columbus AP (S)	40	0	82	5	812	0	5	92/73	90/73	87/72	24	77	75	74
Dayton AP	39	5	84	1	997	−1	4	91/73	89/72	86/71	20	76	75	73
Defiance	41	2	84	2	700	−1	4	94/74	91/73	88/72	24	77	76	74
Findlay AP	41	0	83	4	797	2	3	92/74	90/73	87/72	24	77	76	74
Fremont	41	2	83	1	600	−3	1	90/73	88/73	85/71	24	76	75	73
Hamilton	39	2	84	3	650	0	5	92/73	90/72	87/71	22	76	75	73
Lancaster	39	4	82	4	920	0	5	93/74	91/73	88/72	23	77	75	74
Lima	40	4	84	0	860	−1	4	94/74	91/73	88/72	24	77	76	74
Mansfield AP	40	5	82	3	1297	0	5	90/73	87/72	85/72	22	76	74	73
Marion	40	4	83	1	920	0	5	93/74	91/73	88/72	23	77	76	74
Middletown	39	3	84	2	635	0	5	92/73	90/72	87/71	22	76	75	73
Newark	40	1	82	3	825	−1	5	94/73	92/73	89/72	23	77	75	74
Norwalk	41	1	82	4	720	−3	1	90/73	88/73	85/71	22	76	75	73
Portsmouth	38	5	83	0	530	5	10	95/76	92/74	89/73	22	78	77	75
Sandusky CO	41	3	82	4	606	1	6	93/73	91/72	88/71	21	76	74	73
Springfield	40	0	83	5	1020	−1	3	91/74	89/73	87/72	21	77	76	74
Steubenville	40	2	80	4	992	1	5	89/72	86/71	84/70	22	74	73	72
Toledo AP	41	4	83	5	676r	−3	1	90/73	88/73	85/71	25	76	75	73
Warren	41	2	80	5	900	0	5	89/71	87/71	85/70	23	74	73	71
Wooster	40	5	82	0	1030	1	6	89/72	86/71	84/70	22	75	73	72
Youngstown AP	41	2	80	4	1178	−1	4	88/71	86/71	84/70	23	74	73	71
Zanesville AP	40	0	81	5	881	1	7	93/75	90/74	87/73	23	78	76	75
OKLAHOMA														
Ada	34	5	96	4	1015	10	14	100/74	97/74	95/74	23	77	76	75
Altus AFB	34	4	99	2	1390	11	16	102/73	100/73	98/73	25	77	76	75
Ardmore	34	2	97	1	880	13	17	100/74	98/74	95/74	23	77	77	76
Bartlesville	36	5	96	0	715	6	10	101/73	98/74	95/74	23	77	77	76
Chickasha	35	0	98	0	1085	10	14	101/74	98/74	95/74	24	78	77	76
Enid-Vance AFB	36	2	98	0	1287	9	13	103/74	100/74	97/74	24	79	77	76
Lawton AP	34	3	98	2	1108	12	16	101/74	99/74	96/74	24	78	77	76
Mc Alester	34	5	95	5	760	14	19	99/74	96/74	93/74	23	77	76	75
Muskogee AP	35	4	95	2	610	10	15	101/74	98/75	95/75	23	79	78	77
Norman	35	1	97	3	1109	9	13	99/74	96/74	94/74	24	77	76	75
Oklahoma City AP (S)	35	2	97	4	1280	9	13	100/74	97/74	95/73	23	78	77	76
Ponca City	36	4	97	0	996	5	9	100/74	97/74	94/74	24	77	76	76
Seminole	35	2	96	4	865	11	15	99/74	96/74	94/73	23	77	76	75
Stillwater (S)	36	1	97	1	884	8	13	100/74	96/74	93/74	24	77	76	75
Tulsa AP	36	1	95	5	650	8	13	101/74	98/75	95/75	22	79	78	77
Woodward	36	3	99	3	1900	6	10	100/73	97/73	94/73	26	78	76	75
OREGON														
Albany	44	4	123	1	224	18	22	92/67	89/66	86/65	31	69	67	66
Astoria AP (S)	46	1	123	5	8	25	29	75/65	71/62	68/61	16	65	63	62
Baker AP	44	5	117	5	3368	−1	6	92/63	89/61	86/60	30	65	63	61
Bend	44	0	121	2	3599	−3	4	90/62	87/60	84/59	33	64	62	60
Corvallis (S)	44	3	123	2	221	18	22	92/67	89/66	86/65	31	69	67	66
Eugene AP	44	1	123	1	364	17	22	92/67	89/66	86/65	31	69	67	66
Grants Pass	42	3	123	2	925	20	24	99/69	96/68	93/67	33	71	69	68
Klamath Falls AP	42	1	121	4	4091	4	9	90/61	87/60	84/59	36	63	61	60
Medford AP (S)	42	2	122	5	1298	19	23	98/68	94/67	91/66	35	70	68	67
Pendleton AP	45	4	118	5	1492	−2	5	97/65	93/64	90/62	29	66	65	63
Portland AP	45	4	122	4	21	17	23	89/68	85/67	81/65	23	69	67	66
Portland CO	45	3	122	4	57	18	24	90/68	86/67	82/65	21	69	67	66
Roseburg AP	43	1	123	2	505	18	23	93/67	90/66	87/65	30	69	67	66
Salem AP	45	0	123	0	195	18	23	92/68	88/66	84/65	31	69	68	66
The Dalles	45	4	121	1	102	13	19	93/69	89/68	85/66	28	70	68	67
PENNSYLVANIA														
Allentown AP	40	4	75	3	376	4	9	92/73	88/72	86/72	22	76	75	73
Altoona CO	40	2	78	2	1468	0	5	90/72	87/71	84/70	23	74	73	72
Butler	40	4	80	0	1100	1	6	90/73	87/72	85/71	22	75	74	73
Chambersburg	40	0	77	4	640	4	8	93/75	90/74	87/73	23	77	76	75
Erie AP	42	1	80	1	732	4	9	88/73	85/72	83/71	18	75	74	72
Harrisburg AP	40	1	76	5	335	7	11	94/75	91/74	88/73	21	77	76	75
Johnstown	40	2	78	5	1214	−3	2	86/70	83/70	80/68	23	72	71	70
Lancaster	40	1	76	2	255	4	8	93/75	90/74	87/73	22	77	76	75
Meadville	41	4	80	1	1065	0	4	88/71	85/70	83/69	21	73	72	71
New Castle	41	0	80	2	825	2	7	91/73	88/72	86/71	23	75	74	73

Col. 1	Col. 2		Col. 3		Col. 4	Col. 5 (Winter[d])		Col. 6 (Summer[e])			Col. 7	Col. 8		
State and Station	Latitude[b]		Longitude[c]		Elevation[c]	Design Dry-Bulb		Design Dry-Bulb and Mean Coincident Wet-Bulb			Mean Daily Range	Design Wet-Bulb		
	°	'	°	'	Ft	99%	97.5%	1%	2.5%	5%		1%	2.5%	5%
Philadelphia AP	39	5	75	2	7	10	14	93/75	90/74	87/72	21	77	76	75
Pittsburgh AP	40	3	80	1	1137	1	5	89/72	86/71	84/70	22	74	73	72
Pittsburgh CO	40	3	80	0	749r	3	7	91/72	88/71	86/70	19	74	73	72
Reading CO	40	2	76	0	226	9	13	92/73	89/72	86/72	19	76	75	73
Scranton/ Wilkes-Barre	41	2	75	4	940	1	5	90/72	87/71	84/70	19	74	73	72
State College (S)	40	5	77	5	1175	3	7	90/72	87/71	84/70	23	74	73	72
Sunbury	40	5	76	5	480	2	7	92/73	89/72	86/70	22	75	74	73
Uniontown	39	5	79	4	1040	5	9	91/74	88/73	85/72	22	76	75	74
Warren	41	5	79	1	1280	-2	4	89/71	86/71	83/70	24	74	73	72
West Chester	40	0	75	4	440	9	13	92/75	89/74	86/72	20	77	76	75
Williamsport AP	41	1	77	0	527	2	7	92/73	89/72	86/70	23	75	74	73
York	40	0	76	4	390	8	12	94/75	91/74	88/73	22	77	76	75
RHODE ISLAND														
Newport (S)	41	3	71	2	20	5	9	88/73	85/72	82/70	16	76	75	73
Providence AP	41	4	71	3	55	5	9	89/73	86/72	83/70	19	75	74	73
SOUTH CAROLINA														
Anderson	34	3	82	4	764	19	23	94/74	92/74	90/74	21	77	76	75
Charleston AFB (S)	32	5	80	0	41	24	27	93/78	91/78	89/77	18	81	80	79
Charleston CO	32	5	80	0	9	25	28	94/78	92/78	90/77	13	81	80	79
Columbia AP	34	0	81	1	217	20	24	97/76	95/75	93/75	22	79	78	77
Florence AP	34	1	79	4	146	22	25	94/77	92/77	90/76	21	80	79	78
Georgetown	33	2	79	2	14	23	26	92/79	90/78	88/77	18	81	80	79
Greenville AP	34	5	82	1	957	18	22	93/74	91/74	89/74	21	77	76	75
Greenwood	34	1	82	1	671	18	22	95/75	93/74	91/74	21	78	77	76
Orangeburg	33	3	80	5	244	20	24	97/76	95/75	93/75	20	79	78	77
Rock Hill	35	0	81	0	470	19	23	96/75	94/74	92/74	20	78	77	76
Spartanburg AP	35	0	82	0	816	18	22	93/74	91/74	89/74	20	77	76	75
Sumter-Shaw AFB	34	0	80	3	291	22	25	95/77	92/76	90/75	21	79	78	77
SOUTH DAKOTA														
Aberdeen AP	45	3	98	3	1296	-19	-15	94/73	91/72	88/70	27	77	75	73
Brookings	44	2	96	5	1642	-17	-13	95/73	92/72	89/71	25	77	75	73
Huron AP	44	3	98	1	1282	-18	-14	96/73	93/72	90/71	28	77	75	73
Mitchel	43	5	98	0	1346	-15	-10	96/72	93/71	90/70	28	76	75	73
Pierre AP	44	2	100	2	1718r	-15	-10	99/71	95/71	92/69	29	75	74	72
Rapid City AP (S)	44	0	103	0	3165	-11	-7	95/66	92/65	89/65	28	71	69	67
Sioux Falls AP	43	4	96	4	1420	-15	-11	94/73	91/72	88/71	24	76	75	73
Watertown AP	45	0	97	0	1746	-19	-15	94/73	91/72	88/71	26	76	75	73
Yankton	43	0	97	2	1280	-13	-7	94/73	91/72	88/71	25	77	76	74
TENNESSEE														
Athens	33	3	84	4	940	13	18	95/74	92/73	90/73	22	77	76	75
Bristol- Tri City AP	36	3	82	2	1519	9	14	91/72	89/72	87/71	22	75	75	73
Chattanooga AP	35	0	85	1	670	13	18	96/75	93/74	91/74	22	78	77	76
Clarksville	36	4	87	2	470	6	12	95/76	93/74	90/74	21	78	77	76
Columbia	35	4	87	0	690	10	15	97/75	94/74	91/74	21	78	77	76
Dyersburg	36	0	89	3	334	10	15	96/78	94/77	91/76	21	81	80	78
Greenville	35	5	82	5	1320	11	16	92/73	90/72	88/72	22	76	75	74
Jackson AP	35	4	88	5	413	11	16	98/76	95/75	92/75	21	79	78	77
Knoxville AP	35	5	84	0	980	13	19	94/74	92/73	90/73	21	77	76	75
Memphis AP	35	0	90	0	263	13	18	98/77	95/76	93/76	21	80	79	78
Murfreesboro	35	5	86	2	608	9	14	97/75	94/74	91/74	22	78	77	76
Nashville AP (S)	36	1	86	4	577	9	14	97/75	94/74	91/74	21	78	77	76
Tullahoma	35	2	86	1	1075	8	13	96/74	93/73	91/73	22	77	76	75
TEXAS														
Abilene AP	32	3	99	4	1759	15	20	101/71	99/71	97/71	22	75	74	74
Alice AP	27	4	98	0	180	31	34	100/78	98/77	95/77	20	82	81	79
Amarillo AP	35	1	101	4	3607	6	11	98/67	95/67	93/67	26	71	70	70
Austin AP	30	2	97	4	597	24	28	100/74	98/74	97/74	22	78	77	77
Bay City	29	0	96	0	52	29	33	96/77	94/77	92/77	16	80	79	79
Beaumont	30	0	94	0	18	27	31	95/79	93/78	91/78	19	81	80	80
Beeville	28	2	97	4	225	30	33	99/78	97/77	95/77	18	82	81	79
Big Springs AP (S)	32	2	101	3	2537	16	20	100/69	97/69	95/69	26	74	73	72
Brownsville AP (S)	25	5	97	3	16	35	39	94/77	93/77	92/77	18	80	79	79
Brownwood	31	5	99	0	1435	18	22	101/73	99/73	96/73	22	77	76	75
Bryan AP	30	4	96	2	275	24	29	98/76	96/76	94/76	20	79	78	78

Continued on next page

Table 3-7 continued

State and Station	Lati-tude[b] °	'	Longi-tude[c] °	'	Eleva-tion[c] Ft	Winter[d] Col. 5 Design Dry-Bulb 99%	97.5%	Summer[e] Col. 6 Design Dry-Bulb and Mean Coincident Wet-Bulb 1%	2.5%	5%	Col. 7 Mean Daily Range	Col. 8 Design Wet-Bulb 1%	2.5%	5%
Corpus Christi AP	27	5	97	3	43	31	35	95/78	94/78	92/78	19	80	80	79
Corsicana	32	0	96	3	425	20	25	100/75	98/75	96/75	21	79	78	77
Dallas AP	32	5	96	5	481	18	22	102/75	100/75	97/75	20	78	78	77
Del Rio, Laughlin AFB	29	2	101	0	1072	26	31	100/73	98/73	97/73	24	79	77	76
Denton	33	1	97	1	655	17	22	101/74	99/74	97/74	22	78	77	76
Eagle Pass	28	5	100	3	743	27	32	101/73	99/73	98/73	24	78	78	77
El Paso AP (S)	31	5	106	2	3918	20	24	100/64	98/64	96/64	27	69	68	68
Fort Worth AP (S)	32	5	97	0	544r	17	22	101/74	99/74	97/74	22	78	77	76
Galveston AP	29	2	94	5	5	31	36	90/79	89/79	88/78	10	81	80	80
Greenville	33	0	96	1	575	17	22	101/74	99/74	97/74	21	78	77	76
Harlingen	26	1	97	4	37	35	39	96/77	94/77	93/77	19	80	79	79
Houston AP	29	4	95	2	50	27	32	96/77	94/77	92/77	18	80	79	79
Houston CO	29	5	95	·2	158r	28	33	97/77	95/77	93/77	18	80	79	79
Huntsville	30	4	95	3	494	22	27	100/75	98/75	96/75	20	78	78	77
Killeen-Gray AFB	31	0	97	4	1021	20	25	99/73	97/73	95/73	22	77	76	75
Lamesa	32	5	102	0	2965	13	17	99/69	96/69	94/69	26	73	72	71
Laredo AFB	27	3	99	3	503	32	36	102/73	101/73	99/74	23	78	78	77
Longview	32	2	94	4	345	19	24	99/76	97/76	95/76	20	80	79	78
Lubbock AP	33	4	101	5	3243	10	15	98/69	96/69	94/69	26	73	72	71
Lufkin AP	31	1	94	5	286	25	29	99/76	97/76	94/76	20	80	79	78
Mc Allen	26	1	98	1	122	35	39	97/77	95/77	94/77	21	80	79	79
Midland AP (S)	32	0	102	1	2815r	16	21	100/69	98/69	96/69	26	73	72	71
Mineral Wells AP	32	5	98	0	934	17	22	101/74	99/74	97/74	22	78	77	76
Palestine CO	31	5	95	4	580	23	27	100/76	98/76	96/76	20	79	79	78
Pampa	35	3	101	0	3230	7	12	99/67	96/67	94/67	26	71	70	70
Pecos	31	2	103	3	2580	16	21	100/69	98/69	96/69	27	73	72	71
Plainview	34	1	101	4	3400	8	13	98/68	96/68	94/68	26	72	71	70
Port Arthur AP	30	0	94	0	16	27	31	95/79	93/78	91/78	19	81	80	80
San Angelo, Goodfellow AFB	31	2	100	2	1878	18	22	101/71	99/71	97/70	24	75	74	73
San Antonio AP (S)	29	3	98	3	792	25	30	99/72	97/73	96/73	19	77	76	76
Sherman Perrin AFB	33	4	96	4	763	15	20	100/75	98/75	95/74	22	78	77	76
Snyder	32	4	101	0	2325	13	18	100/70	98/70	96/70	26	74	73	72
Temple	31	1	97	2	675	22	27	100/74	99/74	97/74	22	78	77	77
Tyler AP	32	2	95	2	527	19	24	99/76	97/76	95/76	21	80	79	78
Vernon	34	1	99	2	1225	13	17	102/73	100/73	97/73	24	77	76	75
Victoria AP	28	5	97	0	104	29	32	98/78	96/77	94/77	18	82	81	79
Waco AP	31	4	97	0	500	21	26	101/75	99/75	97/75	22	78	78	77
Wichita Falls AP	34	0	98	3	994	14	18	103/73	101/73	98/73	24	77	76	75
UTAH														
Cedar City AP	37	4	113	1	5613	−2	5	93/60	91/60	89/59	32	65	63	62
Logan	41	4	111	5	4775	−3	2	93/62	91/61	88/60	33	65	64	63
Moab	38	5	109	3	3965	6	11	100/60	98/60	96/60	30	65	64	63
Ogden AP	41	1	112	0	4455	1	5	93/63	91/61	88/61	33	66	65	64
Price	39	4	110	5	5580	−2	5	93/60	91/60	89/59	33	65	63	62
Provo	40	1	111	4	4470	1	6	98/62	96/62	94/61	32	66	65	64
Richfield	38	5	112	0	5300	−2	5	93/60	91/60	89/59	34	65	63	62
St George CO	37	1	113	4	2899	14	21	103/65	101/65	99/64	33	70	68	67
Salt Lake City AP (S)	40	5	112	0	4220	3	8	97/62	95/62	92/61	32	66	65	64
Vernal AP	40	3	109	3	5280	−5	0	91/61	89/60	86/59	32	64	63	62
VERMONT														
Barre	44	1	72	3	1120	−16	−11	84/71	81/69	78/68	23	73	71	70
Burlington AP (S)	44	3	73	1	331	−12	−7	88/72	85/70	82/69	23	74	72	71
Rutland	43	3	73	0	620	−13	−8	87/72	84/70	81/69	23	74	72	71
VIRGINIA														
Charlottsville	38	1	78	3	870	14	18	94/74	91/74	88/73	23	77	76	75
Danville AP	36	3	79	2	590	14	16	94/74	92/73	90/73	21	77	76	75
Fredericksburg	38	2	77	3	50	10	14	96/76	93/75	90/74	21	78	77	76
Harrisonburg	38	3	78	5	1340	12	16	93/72	91/72	88/71	23	75	74	73
Lynchburg AP	37	2	79	1	947	12	16	93/74	90/74	88/73	21	77	76	75
Norfolk AP	36	5	76	1	26	20	22	93/77	91/76	89/76	18	79	78	77
Petersburg	37	1	77	3	194	14	17	95/76	92/76	90/75	20	79	78	77

	Col. 2		Col. 3		Col. 4	Winter[d] Col. 5 Design Dry-Bulb		Summer[e] Col. 6 Design Dry-Bulb and Mean Coincident Wet-Bulb			Col. 7 Mean Daily	Col. 8 Design Wet-Bulb		
State and Station	Latitude[b] °	'	Longitude[c] °	'	Elevation[c] Ft	99%	97.5%	1%	2.5%	5%	Range	1%	2.5%	5%
Richmond AP	37	3	77	2	162	14	17	95/76	92/76	90/75	21	79	78	77
Roanoke AP	37	2	80	0	1174r	12	16	93/72	91/72	88/71	23	75	74	73
Staunton	38	2	78	5	1480	12	16	93/72	91/72	88/71	23	75	74	73
Winchester	39	1	78	1	750	6	10	93/75	90/74	88/74	21	77	76	75
WASHINGTON														
Aberdeen	47	0	123	5	12	25	28	80/65	77/62	73/61	16	65	63	62
Bellingham AP	48	5	122	3	150	10	15	81/67	77/65	74/63	19	68	65	63
Bremerton	47	3	122	4	162	21	25	82/65	78/64	75/62	20	66	64	63
Ellensburg AP	47	0	120	3	1729	2	6	94/65	91/64	87/62	34	66	65	63
Everett- Paine AFB	47	5	122	2	598	21	25	80/65	76/64	73/62	20	67	64	63
Kennewick	46	0	119	1	392	5	11	99/68	96/67	92/66	30	70	68	67
Longview	46	1	123	0	12	19	24	88/68	85/67	81/65	30	69	67	66
Moses Lake, Larson AFB	47	1	119	2	1183	1	7	97/66	94/65	90/63	32	67	66	64
Olympia AP	47	0	122	5	190	16	22	87/66	83/65	79/64	32	67	66	64
Port Angeles	48	1	123	3	99	24	27	72/62	69/61	67/60	18	64	62	61
Seattle- Boeing Fld	47	3	122	2	14	21	26	84/68	81/66	77/65	24	69	67	65
Seattle CO (S)	47	4	122	2	14	22	27	85/68	82/66	78/65	19	69	67	65
Seattle- Tacoma AP (S)	47	3	122	2	386	21	26	84/65	80/64	76/62	22	66	64	63
Spokane AP (S)	47	4	117	3	2357	−6	2	93/64	90/63	87/62	28	65	64	62
Tacoma- Mc Chord AFB	47	1	122	3	350	19	24	86/66	82/65	79/63	22	68	66	64
Walla Walla AP	46	1	118	2	1185	0	7	97/67	94/66	90/65	27	69	67	66
Wenatchee	47	2	120	2	634	7	11	99/67	96/66	92/64	32	68	67	65
Yakima AP	46	3	120	3	1061	−2	5	96/65	93/65	89/63	36	68	66	65
WEST VIRGINIA														
Beckley	37	5	81	1	2330	−2	4	83/71	81/69	79/69	22	73	71	70
Bluefield AP	37	2	81	2	2850	−2	4	83/71	81/69	79/69	22	73	71	70
Charleston AP	38	2	81	4	939	7	11	92/74	90/74	87/72	20	76	75	74
Clarksburg	39	2	80	2	977	6	10	92/74	90/73	87/72	21	76	75	74
Elkins AP	38	5	79	5	1970	1	6	86/72	84/70	82/70	22	74	72	71
Huntington CO	38	2	82	3	565r	5	10	94/76	91/74	89/73	22	78	77	75
Martinsburg AP	39	2	78	0	537	6	10	93/75	90/74	88/74	21	77	76	75
Morgantown AP	39	4	80	0	1245	4	8	90/74	87/73	85/73	22	76	75	74
Parkersburg CO	39	2	81	3	615r	7	11	93/75	90/74	88/73	21	77	76	75
Wheeling	40	1	80	4	659	1	5	89/72	86/71	84/70	21	74	73	72
WISCONSIN														
Appleton	44	2	88	2	742	−14	−9	89/74	86/72	83/71	23	76	74	72
Ashland	46	3	90	5	650	−21	−16	85/70	82/68	79/66	23	72	70	68
Beloit	42	3	89	0	780	−7	−3	92/75	90/75	88/74	24	78	77	75
Eau Claire AP	44	5	91	3	888	−15	−11	92/75	89/73	86/71	23	77	75	73
Fond du Lac	43	5	88	3	760	−12	−8	89/74	86/72	84/71	23	76	74	72
Green Bay AP	44	3	88	1	683	−13	−9	88/74	85/72	83/71	23	76	74	72
La Crosse AP	43	5	91	2	652	−13	−9	91/75	88/73	85/72	22	77	75	74
Madison AP (S)	43	1	89	2	858	−11	−7	91/74	88/73	85/71	22	77	75	73
Manitowoc	44	1	87	4	660	−11	−7	89/74	86/72	83/71	21	76	74	72
Marinette	45	0			605	−15	−11	87/73	84/71	82/70	20	75	73	71
Milwaukee AP	43	0	87	5	672	−8	−4	90/74	87/73	84/71	21	76	74	73
Racine	42	4	87	4	640	−6	−2	91/75	88/73	85/72	21	77	75	74
Sheboygan	43	4	87	4	648	−10	−6	89/75	86/73	83/72	20	77	75	74
Stevens Point	43	0	89	3	1079	−15	−11	92/75	89/73	86/71	23	77	75	73
Waukesha	43	0	88	1	860	−9	−5	90/74	87/73	84/71	22	76	74	73
Wausau AP	44	6	89	4	1196	−16	−12	91/74	88/72	85/70	23	76	74	72
WYOMING														
Casper AP	42	5	106	3	5319	−11	−5	92/58	90/57	87/57	31	63	61	60
Cheyene AP	41	1	104	5	6126	−9	−1	89/58	86/58	84/57	30	63	62	60
Cody AP	44	3	109	2	5090	−19	−13	89/60	86/60	83/59	32	64	63	61
Evanston	41	2	111	0	6860	−9	−3	86/55	84/55	82/54	32	59	58	57
Lander AP (S)	42	5	108	4	5563	−16	−11	91/61	88/61	85/60	32	64	63	61
Laramie AP (S)	41	2	105	3	7266	−14	−6	84/56	81/56	79/55	28	61	60	59
Newcastle	43	5	104	1	4480	−17	−12	91/64	87/63	84/63	30	69	68	66
Rawlins	41	5	107	1	6736	−12	−4	86/57	83/57	81/56	40	62	61	60
Rock Springs AP	41	4	109	0	6741	−9	−3	86/55	84/55	82/54	32	59	58	57
Sheridan AP	44	5	107	0	3942	−14	−8	94/62	91/62	88/61	32	66	65	63
Torrington	4	0	104	1	4098	−14	−8	94/62	91/62	88/61	30	66	65	63

Indoor Design Temperature

Selecting an indoor design temperature is much simpler than selecting an outside one. This temperature must be decided upon in the light of personal convictions, susceptibility to heat/cold discomfort, and living habits, and also with the knowledge that it too will affect the size and capability of the heating system. This temperature is used to find the design temperature difference, or ΔT, used in many of the heat load calculations. Normally 70° F is chosen but this figure could just as easily be 68° F or 65° F in the interest of energy conservation, or set at 75° F or even higher in circumstances where invalids or elderly persons are among the occupants of the house. Whatever temperature is chosen should be the one at which the homeowner anticipates maintaining the indoor temperature the greater part of the time during occupancy.

Wind Speed and Direction

Under most circumstances, wind direction is not much considered in the construction of houses, though it is (or should be) during siting and orientation and in the house design (fenestration, for instance). Wind speed, as mentioned earlier, is usually taken as 15 mph, and calculations are made on that basis. However, if average wind speed at the site is appreciably higher or lower than 15 mph, the correction factors in Table 3-2 can be used. If wind velocity and impact upon a particular part of a structure seems sufficient to alter normal thermal efficiency for that section, adjustments might be entered into the calculations in compensation. However, such changes should be approached with caution, especially when aimed in the direction of lowering thermal efficiency.

Unheated Space Temperatures

Frequently, unheated spaces are adjacent to heated spaces in a house, and temperatures for them must also be calculated. Obviously, the outside design temperature is more often than not incorrect by a wide margin, so individual temperatures must be assigned to each adjacent unheated space; these should be used in conjunction with the indoor design temperature in arriving at an intermediate ΔT for the calculations needed to determine heat loss for the boundary building sections. Since heat loss is always to the colder area, heat will travel from the heated area to the adjacent unheated area, and from there to the outside. The result is that the temperature of the adjacent spaces will lie somewhere between the inside and the outside temperatures. The question is, where? This depends upon a number of factors, including thermal effectiveness of the boundary walls, relative positions of the heated and unheated spaces, the amount of infiltration involved, and so on.

The *1977 Fundamentals Volume, ASHRAE HANDBOOK & Product Directory* offers a formula, not as complicated as it looks, by which these intermediate design temperatures can be estimated. First, if "the respective surface areas adjacent to the heated room and exposed to the outdoors are the same, and if the heat transfer coefficients are equal, the temperature in the unheated space may be assumed to be almost equal to the mean of the indoor and outdoor design temperatures." However, this situation obtains rather infrequently: generally the surface areas are unequal and the heat transfer coefficients different. In that case, use the formula:

$$t_u = \frac{t_i (A_1 U_1 + A_2 U_2 + A_3 U_3 + \text{etc.}) + t_o (2.16 V_o + A_a U_a + A_b U_b + A_c U_c + \text{etc.})}{A_1 U_1 + A_2 U_2 + A_3 U_3 + \text{etc.} + 2.16 V_o + A_a U_a + A_b U_b + A_c U_c + \text{etc.}}$$

where

t_u	=	temperature in unheated space, ° F
t_i	=	indoor design temperature of heated room, ° F
t_o	=	outdoor design temperature, ° F
A_1, etc.	=	areas of surface of unheated space adjacent to heated space, square feet
A_a, etc.	=	areas of surface of unheated space exposed to outdoors, square feet
U_1, etc.	=	heat transfer coefficients of surfaces of A_1, etc.
U_a, etc.	=	heat transfer coefficients of surfaces of A_a, etc.
V_o	=	rate of introduction of outside air into the unheated space by infiltration and/or ventilation, cubic feet per minute

Unheated ground surface space, such as the floor of an unheated garage adjacent to a heated room, can usually be disregarded. In many instances, the factor V_o can also be left out of the calculations.

Though this calculation can be used with great effectiveness, sometimes the results are not worth the time and effort. There are some conventional practices, rules of thumb, and judgemental decisions that can be used in certain instances to arrive at reasonable, and workable, intermediate design temperatures for particular adjacent unheated spaces. These will be noted as the occasions arise in the next section.

HEAT LOSS CALCULATIONS

Heat loss calculations, which in turn lead to a determination of the total heating load for sizing heating equipment and also for costing of seasonal heating fuel or energy requirements, are made piecemeal for each space or room of the structure to be heated. The estimated maximum probable heat loss for each space or room is calculated in conjunction with the established design temperatures to determine heat load. Those heat losses are brought about in two principal ways: transmission losses and infiltration losses. The former consist of heat transferred through the building sections: walls, floors, windows, doors, roofs, etc. The latter consist of heat transported out by air flow via ventilating fans, opening doors, open chimney dampers, structural cracks, and the like, and by the heat needed to warm cold air introduced from the outside via cracks, doors, windows, and such.

Transmission Losses

Heat transmission losses must be figured for all of the various different building sections of each heated room or space that are exposed on a regular basis during the heating season to any temperature lower than approximately 10° F below the established indoor design temperature. Since these building sections are handled somewhat differently, we will examine them separately.

Heat loss through walls. Some typical examples of calculations of coefficients of transmission for above-grade wall constructions are shown in Tables 3-8 through 3-13. All of these examples are calculated in two ways: first in a basic configuration (1), and then with added insulation (2). Note the substantial elevation in total *R*-value when insulation is added, resulting in a substantially lower *U*, or overall thermal transmittance.

The wall construction shown in Table 3-8 is a popular one in house construction. In (1), the calculations are made on the basis of a nonreflective air space within the wall, first for the section between the wall studs, then for the section including a wall stud. Note the *R* for a section including a wall stud is considerably higher than that between studs. In (2), the only difference in the example is the replacement of the air space with 3.5-inch *R*-11 blanket insulation. Note that while the stud section *R* remains the same, the between-framing area *R* is 3¼ times greater than for the air space construction.

The notes below the example show how the *U* is determined. First the reciprocals of the *R*'s in (1) are found, then each *U* is corrected to make allowance for the framing. The two are added together to determine the average *U* for an entire wall made in this manner. The *U* given is for one square foot, and the factor is applicable to an identical wall construction of any size. The same process is employed to find the *U* for (2), the insulated wall. In this example, the *U* of the uninsulated wall is shown as 0.206, which means that 0.206 Btu of heat will pass through each square foot of this wall construction every hour. The insulated wall, however, has an average *U* of 0.081, and so each square foot will pass only 0.081 Btu every hour. In both cases, the amount of heat passed is for each degree F of temperature difference between the inside surface and the outside surface. If there were 1000 square feet of wall area, and the average temperature difference were 50°, the uninsulated wall in 10 hours time would transmit 1000 × 0.206 × 50 × 10, or 103,000 Btu. For the insulated wall it would be 1000 × 0.081 × 50 × 10, or 40,500

Btu. The difference of 62,500 Btu represents about 18.3 kwh of electric heat energy, or about a dollar's worth depending upon specific utility rates. Consider that continually wasted dollar—a dime an hour—for one small section of wall, multiply by the substantial remaining area of a house, and relate that to the one-time cost of 3.5-inch blanket insulation of about 25 cents per square foot; the logical choice is obvious.

The business of correcting for the effect of framing members in building sections affords a more accurate *U* than would otherwise be obtained (though it is often disregarded). A simple formula given in the *1977 Fundamentals Volume,* ASHRAE *HANDBOOK & Product Directory* can be used for this purpose:

$$U_{av} = \frac{S}{100}(U_s) + 1 - \frac{S}{100}(U_i)$$

where

U_{av} = average *U* value for building section
U_i = *U* value for area between framing members
U_s = *U* value for area backed by framing members
S = percentage of area backed by framing members

In calculating the area backed by framing members, the actual width of the members is used, not the nominal thickness or trade size. Thus, the thickness of a two-by-four is not really 2 inches, but approximately 1.5 inches. In practice, framing is usually considered to be 20 percent of the total wall area for typical 16-inch-on-center framing, which includes multiple studs, plates, sills, headers, etc. The percentage for 24-inch o.c. construction is usually estimated at 15.

Tables 3-8 through 3-13 can serve as guidelines in making calculations for wall sections of slightly different construction simply by substituting materials as necessary. They can also be used to draw comparisons between sections built with different materials, and with more or less insulation. Table 3-14 affords a method of determining *U* values resulting from the addition of insulation to a given building section. First find the *U* of the building section in question—say, 0.20. Enter the left-hand column under *U* at 0.20 and move right along that line. The addition of *R*-4 insulation will improve the *U* to 0.11, *R*-6 to 0.09, and so forth. Or, if an existing building section has a *U* of 0.50 and it is desired to raise the performance to 0.10, enter the left-hand column at 0.50 and read right to 0.10; the required amount of added insulation is *R*-8. This table can also be used when the building section *R* is known.

For walls exposed to unheated areas, calculations for intermediate design temperature can be made as noted earlier. However, an assumption can also be made with little consequential loss in accuracy. The temperature of the unheated space may be assumed to be, according to the *Manual For Electric Comfort Heating* of the National Electrical Manufacturers Association (NEMA), "one-third as much above the outside

53

Coefficients of Transmission (U) of Frame Walls

These coefficients are expressed in Btu per (hour) (square foot) (degree Fahrenheit) difference in temperature between the air on the two sides), and are based on an outside wind velocity of 15 mph

Construction	1 Resistance (R)		2	
Replace Air Space with 3.5-in. R-11 Blanket Insulation (New Item 4)	Between Framing	At Framing	Between Framing	At Framing
1. Outside surface (15 mph wind)	0.17	0.17	0.17	0.17
2. Siding, wood, 0.5 in.× 8 in. lapped (average)	0.81	0.81	0.81	0.81
3. Sheathing, 0.5-in. asphalt impregnated	1.32	1.32	1.32	1.32
4. Nonreflective air space, 3.5 in. (50 Fmean; 10 deg F temperature difference)	1.01	—	11.00	—
5. Nominal 2-in. × 4-in. wood stud	—	4.38	—	4.38
6. Gypsum wallboard, 0.5 in.	0.45	0.45	0.45	0.45
7. Inside surface (still air)	0.68	0.68	0.68	0.68
Total Thermal Resistance (R)	R_i=4.44	R_s=7.81	R_i=14.43	R_s=7.81

Construction No. 1: U_i = 1/4.44=0.225; U_s=1/7.81 =0.128. With 20% framing (typical of 2-in. × 4-in. studs @ 16-in. o.c.), U_{av} = 0.8 (0.225) + 0.2 (0.128) = 0.206

Construction No. 2: U_i = 1/14.43 = 0.069; U_s = 0.128. With framing unchanged, U_{av} = 0.8(0.069) + 0.2(0.128) = 0.081

Table 3–8. (Reprinted with permission from the *1977 Fundamentals Volume, ASHRAE HANDBOOK & Product Directory*)

Coefficients of Transmission (U) of Solid Masonry Walls

Coefficients are expressed in Btu per (hour) (square foot) (degree Fahrenheit difference in temperature between the air on the two sides), and are based on an outside wind velocity of 15 mph

Construction	1 Resistance (R)		2
Replace Furring Strips and Air Space with 1-in. Extruded Polystyrene (New Item 4)	Between Furring	At Furring	
1. Outside surface (15 mph wind)	0.17	0.17	0.17
2. Common brick, 8 in.	1.60	1.60	1.60
3. Nominal 1-in. ×3-in. vertical furring	—	0.94	—
4. Nonreflective air space, 0.75 in. (50 F mean; 10 deg F temperature difference)	1.01	—	5.00
5. Gypsum wallboard, 0.5 in.	0.45	0.45	0.45
6. Inside surface (still air)	0.68	0.68	0.68
Total Thermal Resistance (R)	R_i = 3.91	R_s = 3.84	R_i = 7.90 = R_s

Construction No. 1: U_i = 1/3.91=0.256; U_s=1/3.84=0.260. With 20% framing (typical of 1-in. × 3-in. vertical furring on masonry @ 16-in. o.c.) U_{av} = 0.8 (0.256) + 0.2 (0.260) = 0.257
Construction No. 2: U_i = U_s = U_{av} = 1/7.90 = 0.127

Table 3–9. (Reprinted with permission from the *1977 Fundamentals Volume, ASHRAE HANDBOOK & Product Directory*)

Coefficients of Transmission (U) of Frame Partitions or Interior Walls

Coefficients are expressed in Btu per (hour) (square foot) (degree Fahrenheit difference in temperature between the air on the two sides), and are based on still air (no wind) conditions on both sides

Replace Air Space with 3.5-in. R-11 Blanket Insulation (New Item 3)

	1 Resistance (R)		2	
Construction	Between Framing	At Framing	Between Framing	At Framing
1. Inside surface (still air)	0.68	0.68	0.68	0.68
2. Gypsum wallboard, 0.5 in.	0.45	0.45	0.45	0.45
3. Nonreflective air space, 3.5 in. (50 F mean; 10 deg F temperature difference)	1.01	—	11.00	—
4. Nominal 2-in. × 4-in. wood stud	—	4.38	—	4.38
5. Gypsum wallboard 0.5 in.	0.45	0.45	0.45	0.45
6. Inside surface (still air)	0.68	0.68	0.68	0.68
Total Thermal Resistance (R)	R_i= 3.27	R_s= 6.64	R_i=13.26	R_s= 6.64

Construction No. 1: U_i= 1/3.27 = 0.306; U_s= 1/6.64 = 0.151. With 10% framing (typical of 2-in. × 4-in. studs @ 24-in. o.c.), U_{av}= 0.9 (0.306) + 0.1 (0.151) = 0.290

Construction No. 2: U_i = 1/13.26 = 0.075, U_s = 1/6.64 = 0.151. With framing unchanged, U_{av} = 0.9(0.075) + 0.1(0.151) = 0.083

Table 3–10. (Reprinted with permission from the *1977 Fundamentals Volume, ASHRAE HANDBOOK & Product Directory*)

Coefficients of Transmission (U) of Masonry Walls

Coefficients are expressed in Btu per (hour) (square foot) (degree Fahrenheit difference in temperature between the air on the two sides), and are based on an outside wind velocity of 15 mph

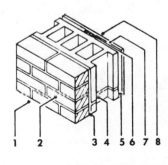

Replace Cinder Aggregate Block with 6-in. Light-weight Aggregate Block with Cores Filled (New Item 4)

	1 Resistance (R)		2	
Construction	Between Furring	At Furring	Between Furring	At Furring
1. Outside surface (15 mph wind)	0.17	0.17	0.17	0.17
2. Face brick, 4 in.	0.44	0.44	0.44	0.44
3. Cement mortar, 0.5 in.	0.10	0.10	0.10	0.10
4. Concrete block, cinder aggregate, 8 in.	1.72	1.72	2.99	2.99
5. Reflective air space, 0.75 in. (50 F mean; 30 deg F temperature difference)	2.77	—	2.77	—
6. Nominal 1-in. × 3-in. vertical furring	—	0.94	—	0.94
7. Gypsum wallboard, 0.5 in., foil backed	0.45	0.45	0.45	0.45
8. Inside surface (still air)	0.68	0.68	0.68	0.68
Total Thermal Resistance (R)	R_i= 6.33	R_s= 4.50	R_i= 7.60	R_s= 5.77

Construction No. 1: U_i= 1/6.33 = 0.158; U_s = 1/4.50 = 0.222. With 20% framing (typical of 1-in. × 3-in. vertical furring on masonry @ 16-in. o.c.), U_{av} = 0.8 (0.158) + 0.2 (0.222) = 0.171

Construction No. 2: U_i = 1/7.60 = 0.132, U_s = 1/5.77 = 0.173. With framing unchanged, U_{av} = 0.8(0.132) + 0.2(0.173) = 1.40

Table 3–11. (Reprinted with permission from the *1977 Fundamentals Volume, ASHRAE HANDBOOK & Product Directory*)

Coefficients of Transmission *(U)* of Masonry Cavity Walls

Coefficients are expressed in Btu per (hour) (square foot) (degree Fahrenheit difference in temperature between the air on the two sides), and are based on an outside wind velocity of 15 mph

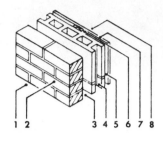

| | Resistance (R) | | |
| Replace Furring Strips and Gypsum Wallboard with 0.625-in. Plaster (Sand Aggregate) Applied Directly to Concrete Block-Fill 2.5-in. Air Space with Vermiculite Insulation (New Items 3 and 7.) | **1** | | **2** |
Construction	Between Furring	At Furring	
1. Outside surface (15 mph wind)	0.17	0.17	0.17
2. Common brick, 8 in.	0.80	0.80	0.80
3. Nonreflective air space, 2.5 in. (30 F mean; 10 deg F temperature difference)	1.10*	1.10*	5.32**
4. Concrete block, stone aggregate, 4 in.	0.71	0.71	0.71
5. Nonreflective air space 0.75 in. (50 F mean; 10 deg F temperature difference)	1.01	—	—
6. Nominal 1-in. × 3-in. vertical furring	—	0.94	—
7. Gypsum wallboard, 0.5 in.	0.45	0.45	0.11
8. Inside surface (still air)	0.68	0.68	0.68
Total Thermal Resistance (R)	$R_i = 4.92$	$R_s = 4.85$	$R_i = R_s = 7.79$

Construction No. 1: $U_i = 1/4.92 = 0.203$; $U_s = 1/4.85 = 0.206$. With 20% framing (typical of 1-in. × 3-in. vertical furring on masonry @16-in. o.c.), $U_{av} = 0.8(0.203) + 0.2(0.206) = 0.204$
Construction No. 2: $U_i = U_s = U_{av} = 1.79 = 0.128$

* Interpolated value from Table 3–2

** Calculated value from Table 3–5

Table 3–12. (Reprinted with permission from the *1977 Fundamentals Volume, ASHRAE HANDBOOK & Product Directory*)

Coefficients of Transmission *(U)* of Masonry Partitions

Coefficients are expressed in Btu per (hour) (square foot) (degree Fahrenheit difference in temperature between the air on the two sides), and are based on still air (no wind) conditions on both sides

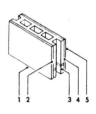

Replace Concrete Block with 4-in. Gypsum Tile (New Item 3) Construction	1	2
1. Inside surface (still air)	0.68	0.68
2. Plaster, lightweight aggregate, 0.625 in.	0.39	0.39
3. Concrete block, cinder aggregate, 4 in.	1.11	1.67
4. Plaster, lightweight aggregate, 0.625 in.	0.39	0.39
5. Inside surface (still air)	0.68	0.68
Total Thermal Resistance(R)	3.25	3.81

Construction No. 1: $U = 1/3.25 = 0.308$
Construction No. 2: $U = 1/3.81 = 0.262$

Table 3–13. (Reprinted with permission from the *1977 Fundamentals Volume, ASHRAE HANDBOOK & Product Directory*)

Determination Of *U*-Value Resulting From Addition Of Insulation to the Total Area of Any Given Building

Given Building Section Property[a,b]		Added *R*[c,d,e]						
		R = 4	R = 6	R = 8	R = 12	R = 16	R = 20	R = 24
U	R	U	U	U	U	U	U	U
1.00	1.00	0.20	0.14	0.11	0.08	0.06	0.05	0.04
0.90	1.11	0.20	0.14	0.11	0.08	0.06	0.05	0.04
0.80	1.25	0.19	0.14	0.11	0.08	0.06	0.05	0.04
0.70	1.43	0.18	0.13	0.11	0.07	0.06	0.05	0.04
0.60	1.67	0.18	0.13	0.10	0.07	0.06	0.05	0.04
0.50	2.00	0.17	0.13	0.10	0.07	0.06	0.05	0.04
0.40	2.50	0.15	0.12	0.10	0.07	0.05	0.04	0.04
0.30	3.33	0.14	0.11	0.09	0.07	0.05	0.04	0.04
0.20	5.00	0.11	0.09	0.08	0.06	0.05	0.04	0.03
0.10	10.00	0.07	0.06	0.06	0.05	0.04	0.03	0.03
0.08	12.50	0.06	0.05	0.05	0.04	0.04	0.03	0.03

[a] For *U*- or *R*-values not shown in the table, interpolate as necessary.

[b] Enter column 1 with *U* or *R* of the design building section.

[c] Under appropriate column heading for added *R*, find *U*-value of resulting design section.

[d] If the insulation occupies previously considered air space, an adjustment must be made in the given building section *R*-value.

[e] If insulation is applied between framing members, correction for effect of framing members must be made.

Table 3-14. (Reprinted with permission from the *1977 Fundamentals Volume, ASHRAE HANDBOOK & Product Directory)*

temperature as the heated space is above the outside temperature.'' Thus, if the inside design temperature is 70° F and the outside design temperature is 10° F, the intermediate design temperature for the unheated space can be taken as ⅓ of the inside/outside temperature difference of 60° F, or 20° F, plus the outside design temperature, for a total of 30° F.

Heat loss through floors. Exactly the same kind of figuring is needed to establish heat losses through floors. Table 3-15 shows a typical calculation for a floor/ceiling construction, while Table 3-16 lists *U*'s in a somewhat different fashion for numerous typical floor constructions. Note that this information concerns frame construction; concrete floors will be considered later.

Heat loss through floors over ventilated, unheated crawl spaces should be figured as though the temperature in the crawl space is the same as the outside design temperature, *if* the space is very well ventilated or fully open (pier construction). If the ventilation is partial, the calculations *may* be made the same way, with only a small overall error, or may be calculated with other formulae for greater accuracy. The heat loss should be calculated the same as it is in walls and ceilings, except that the surface resistance should be 0.92 instead of 0.61, conductance 1.08 instead of 1.63, because of the different behaviour of heat flowing downward, as indicated in Table 3-3.

Coefficients of Transmission (*U*) of Frame Construction Ceilings and Floors

Coefficients are expressed in Btu per (hour) (square foot) (degree Fahrenheit difference between the air on the two sides), and are based on still air (no wind) on both sides

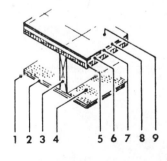

	Assume Unheated Attic Space above Heated Room with Heat Flow Up—Remove Tile, Felt, Plywood, Subfloor and Air Space—Replace with R-19 Blanket Insulation (New Item 4)			
Heated Room Below Unheated Space	1		2	
	Resistance (R)			
Construction (Heat Flow Up)	Between Floor Joists	At Floor Joist	Between Floor Joists	At Floor Joists
1. Bottom surface (still air)	0.61	0.61	0.61	0.61
2. Metal lath and lightweight aggregate, plaster, 0.75 in.	0.47	0.47	0.47	0.47
3. Nominal 2-in. × 8-in. floor joist	—	9.06	—	9.06
4. Nonreflective airspace, 7.25-in.	0.93*	—	19.00	—
5. Wood subfloor, 0.75 in.	0.94	0.94	—	—
6. Plywood, 0.625 in.	0.78	0.78	—	—
7. Felt building membrane	0.06	0.06	—	—
8. Resilient tile	0.05	0.05	—	—
9. Top surface (still air)	0.61	0.61	0.61	0.61
Total Thermal Resistance (R)	R_i= 4.45	R_s= 12.58	R_i= 20.69	R_s=10.75

Construction No. 1 U_i = 1/4.45= 0.225; U_s= 1/12.58= 0.079. With 10% framing (typical of 2-in. joists @ 16-in. o.c.), U_{av} = 0.9 (0.225) + 0.1 (0.079)= 0.210

Construction No. 2 U_i = 1/20.69 = 0.048; U_s = 1/10.75 = 0.093. With framing unchanged, U_{av} = 0.9 (0.048) + 0.1 (0.093) = 0.053

* Use largest air space (3.5 in.) value shown in Table 3-4.

Table 3-15. (Reprinted with permission from the *1977 Fundamentals Volume, ASHRAE HANDBOOK & Product Directory*)

TYPE OF FLOOR COVERING[b]	INSULATION R-VALUE	TYPE OF SUBFLOOR					
		Single Layer			Double Layer		
		1/2" PLYWOOD	5/8" PLYWOOD	3/4" PLYWOOD	PARTICLEBOARD OVER PLYWOOD	PLYWOOD OVER PLYWOOD	HARDBOARD OVER PLYWOOD
Carpet with fibrous pad	R-11	0.067	0.067	0.066	0.064	0.065	0.066
	R-19	0.046	0.045	0.045	0.044	0.045	0.045
Carpet with foam pad	R-11	0.072	0.071	0.070	0.068	0.069	0.070
	R-19	0.048	0.047	0.047	0.046	0.047	0.047
Hardwood strip	R-11	0.075	0.074	0.073	0.070	0.072	0.073
	R-19	0.049	0.049	0.048	0.047	0.048	0.048
Resilient tile or sheet	R-11	0.078	0.077	0.077	0.074	0.076	0.077
	R-19	0.051	0.050	0.050	0.049	0.049	0.050

[a]Based on 2″ × 10″ (1½″ × 9¼″ actual) floor joists, 16″ o.c. For other joist depths no adjustment is necessary. For insulated floors over basements and unvented crawl spaces use *less* than a full temperature difference, as these spaces are at an intermediate temperature and not at the outside design temperature.

[b]While residences may have several floor coverings (carpet in living room, hall, and bedroom areas; and resilient tile in kitchen and bathroom areas), it is common practice in calculating heat losses to use the single U-value representing the most prevalent covering.

Table 3–16. (NAHB *Insulation Manual,* 1979)

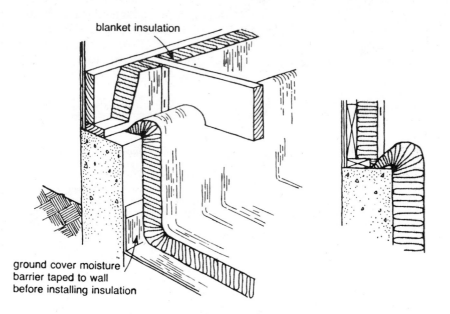

3-4. Method of insulating unvented crawl space. (NAHB *Insulation Manual,* 1979)

Floors over heated basements are generally assumed to have no heat loss through the floor into the basement, and this is true to a satisfactory degree if the basement temperature remains no more than 10° to 20° below the first-floor space. But, if temperature levels fall much lower than that, there is downward heat loss. The same is true of floors over insulated crawl spaces (Figure 3-4) fitted with vapor barriers over the ground and with no vents, and, as mentioned earlier, of floors over unheated, ventilated crawl spaces. Computations for these situations can be made with formulae for calculating intermediate temperatures of unheated adja-

cent spaces, which must be adjusted to reflect the presence of any heat that might be escaping from warm pipes, ducts, etc., that might be housed in those spaces.

Along with the calculations, a certain amount of judgement must be used to evaluate the given conditions. Ground temperatures must be substituted for the normal outdoor design temperatures in portions of the building section computations, and the whole affair becomes quite complex and a bit tenuous. In practice, crawl space temperatures are generally arrived at by estimation. Floors over unheated basements that are substantially below-grade are often considered as having an intermediate design temperature on the cool side, half as much above the outside design temperature as the inside design temperature is above the outside. Thus, if the inside temperature above the floor is 70° F and the chosen outside design temperature is 10° F, the difference is 60° F. Half of that is 30° F; this, added to the outdoor temperature, equals 40° F for the intermediate design temperature.

Heat loss through roofs. Though the same basic sorts of calculations are involved in determining heat losses through roofs, here the cross sections are often more complicated than walls, and the calculations consequently become somewhat more difficult. Tables 3-17 through 3-20 show the calculations for some typical roof constructions.

For unventilated flat, shed and vaulted roofs, assuming that there is no crawl or access space between the ceiling and the roof of any substantial depth, the *U* is derived as for walls. In winter, the effect of the sun beating on the roof is ignored except in a few special instances, since overall heat loss is based upon adverse conditions—no sun.

The common approach to making calculations for pitched-roof heat losses in houses having unheated, well-ventilated attics, and insulation between the ceiling joists, is to proceed as though the roof does not exist. There is one minor exception: the conductance of the attic floor surfaces, or of the top of the insulation, if there is no attic floor, should be treated as inside surfaces, not outside. This situation is not entirely correct;

for the best estimation, the attic intermediate temperature, which actually is not equal to the chosen outside design temperature, should be calculated with a special formula. If there is little or no insulation in the attic floor this formula should be used, and can be found on page 24.2 in chapter 24 of the *1977 Fundamentals Volume, ASHRAE HANDBOOK & Products Directory*. In other cases, however, disregarding these complex calculations will introduce only a very minor error into the heat loss calculations. In fact, the National Association of Home Builders (NAHB) states that if calculations are made with the figures shown in Table 3-21, the calculated heat losses will be within 3 percent of those made by the more complex methods. Bearing in mind that the final results are still approximations either way, this error factor is unlikely to bear any serious results.

Heat loss through basements. Calculating the heat losses for basements that are to be heated to a specific temperature is done in much the same way as for other building sections, but there are some differences and the computations have to be broken down into several parts. First, the portions of the basement walls that stand above grade are assessed for *U*, just as would be any exterior wall. Next, the portions of the basement walls that lie below grade are calculated for *U*, in conjunction with ground temperature for the surfaces in contact with the soil. Last, the same procedure is followed for the basement floor.

The heat flow pattern from a basement is shown in

Coefficients of Transmission *(U)* **of Flat Masonry Roofs with Built-up Roofing, with and without Suspended Ceilings** **(Winter Conditions, Upward Flow)**

These Coefficients are expressed in Btu per (hour) (square foot) (degree Fahrenheit difference in temperature between the air on the two sides), and are based upon an outside wind velocity of 15 mph

Add Rigid Roof Deck Insulation, $C = 0.24$ ($R = 1/C$) (New Item 7) Construction (Heat Flow Up)	1	2
1. Inside surface (still air)	0.61	0.61
1. Metal lath and lightweight aggregate plaster, 0.75 in.	0.47	0.47
3. Nonreflective air space, greater than 3.5 in. (50 F mean; 10 deg F temperature difference)	0.93*	0.93*
4. Metal ceiling suspension system with metal hanger rods	0**	0**
5. Corrugated metal deck	0	0
6. Concrete slab, lightweight aggregate, 2 in.	2.22	2.22
7. Rigid roof deck insulation (none)	—	4.17
8. Built-up roofing, 0.375 in.	0.33	0.33
9. Outside surface (15 mph wind)	0.17	0.17
Total Thermal Resistance (R)	4.73	8.90

Construction No. 1: $U_{av} = 1/4.73 = 0.211$
Construction No. 2: $U_{av} = 1/8.90 = 0.112$

* Use largest air space (3.5 in.) value shown in Table 3-4.

** Area of hanger rods is negligible in relation to ceiling area.

Table 3-17. (Reprinted with permission from the *1977 Fundamentals Volume, ASHRAE HANDBOOK & Product Directory*)

Coefficients of Transmission (U) of Wood Construction Flat Roofs and Ceilings
(Winter Conditions, Upward Flow)

Coefficients are expressed in Btu per (hour) (square foot) (degree Fahrenheit difference in temperature between the air on the two sides), and are based upon an outside wind velocity of 15 mph

Replace Roof Deck Insulation and 7.25-in. Air Space with 6-in. R-19 Blanket Insulation and 1.25-in. Air Space (New Items 5 and 7)

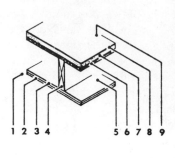

Construction (Heat Flow Up)	1 Resistance (R) Between Joists	At Joists	2 Between Joists	At Joists
1. Inside surface (still air)	0.61	0.61	0.61	0.61
2. Acoustical tile, fiberboard, glued, 0.5 in.	1.25	1.25	1.25	1.25
3. Gypsum wallboard, 0.5 in.	0.45	0.45	0.45	0.45
4. Nominal 2-in. × 8-in. ceiling joists	—	9.06	—	9.06
5. Nonreflective air space, 7.25 in. (50 F mean; 10 deg F temperature difference)	0.93*	—	1.05**	—
6. Plywood deck, 0.625 in.	0.78	0.78	0.78	0.78
7. Rigid roof deck insulation, c = 0.72, ($R = 1/C$)	1.39	1.39	19.00	—
8. Built-up roof	0.33	0.33	0.33	0.33
9. Outside surface (15 mph wind)	0.17	0.17	0.17	0.17
Total Thermal Resistance (R)	R_i=5.91	R_s=14.04	R_i=23.64	R_s=12.65

Construction No. 1 U_i = 1/5.91 = 0.169; U_s = 1/14.04 = 0.071. With 10% framing (typical of 2-in. joists @ 16-in. o.c.), U_{av} = 0.9 (0.169) + 0.1 (0.071) = 0.159

Construction No. 2 U_i = 1/23.64 = 0.042; U_s = 1/12.65 = 0.079. With framing unchanged, U_{av} = 0.9 (0.042) + 0.1 (0.079) = 0.046

*Use largest air space (3.5 in.) value shown in Table 3–4.
**Interpolated value (0 F mean; 10 deg F temperature difference).

Table 3–18. (Reprinted with permission from the *1977 Fundamentals Volume, ASHRAE HANDBOOK & Product Directory*)

Coefficients of Transmission *(U)* of Metal Construction Flat Roofs and Ceilings
(Winter Conditions, Upward Flow)

Coefficients are expressed in Btu per (hour) (square foot) (degree Fahrenheit difference in temperature between the air on the two sides), and are based on upon outside wind velocity of 15 mph

Replace Rigid Roof Deck Insulation (C = 0.24) and Sand Aggregate Plaster with Rigid Roof Deck Insulation, C = 0.36 and Lightweight Aggregate Plaster (New Items 2 and 6)

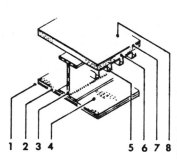

Construction (Heat Flow Up)	1	2
1. Inside surface (still air)	0.61	0.61
2. Metal lath and sand aggregate plaster, 0.75 in.	0.13	0.47
3. Structural beam	0.00	0.00
4. Nonreflective air space (50 F mean; 10 deg F temperature difference	0.93**	0.93**
5. Metal deck	0.00	0.00
6. Rigid roof deck insulation, C = 0.24($R = 1/c$)	4.17	2.78
7. Built-up roofing, 0.375 in.	0.33	0.33
8. Outside surface (15 mph wind)	0.17	0.17
Total Thermal Resistance (R)	6.34	5.29

Construction No. 1: U = 1/6.34 = 0.158
Construction No. 2: U = 1/5.29 = 0.189

** Use largest air space (3.5 in.) value shown in Table 3–4.

Table 3–19. (Reprinted with permission from the *1977 Fundamentals Volume, ASHRAE HANDBOOK & Product Directory*)

Coefficients of Transmission (U) of Pitched Roofs [b]

Coefficients are expressed in Btu per (hour) (square foot) (degree Fahrenheit difference in temperature between the air on the two sides), and are based on an outside wind velocity of 15 mph for heat flow upward and 7.5 mph forheat flow downward

Find U_{av} for same Construction 2 with Heat Flow Down (Summer Conditions)

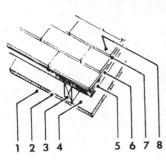

Construction 1 (Heat Flow Up) (Reflective Air Space)	1 Between Rafters	1 At Rafters	2 Between Rafters	2 At Rafters
1. Inside surface (still air)	0.62	0.62	0.76	0.76
2. Gypsum wallboard 0.5 in., foil backed	0.45	0.45	0.45	0.45
3. Nominal 2-in. × 4-in. ceiling rafter	—	4.38	—	4.38
4. 45 deg slope reflective air space, 3.5 in. (50 F mean, 30 deg F temperature difference)	2.17	—	4.33	—
5. Plywood sheathing, 0.625 in.	0.78	0.78	0.78	0.78
6. Felt building membrane	0.06	0.06	0.06	0.06
7. Asphalt shingle roofing	0.44	0.44	0.44	0.44
8. Outside surface (15 mph wind)	0.17	0.17	0.25**	0.25**
Total Thermal Resistance (R)	R_i=4.69	R_s=6.90	R_i=7.07	R_s=7.12

Construction No. 1: U_i=1/4.69= 0.213; U_s = 1/6.90 = 0.145. With 10% framing (typical of 2-in. rafters @16-in. o.c.), U_{av}= 0.9 (0.213) + 0.1 (0.145) = 0.206

Construction No. 2: U_i=1/7.07= 0.141; U_s = 1/7.12 = 0.140. With framing unchanged, U_{av} = 0.9 (0.141) + 0.1 (0.140) = 0.141

Find U_{av} for same Construction 2 with Heat Flow Down (Summer Conditions)

Construction 1 (Heat Flow Up) (Non-Reflective Air Space)	3 Between Rafters	3 At Rafters	4 Between Rafters	4 At Rafters
1. Inside surface (still air)	0.62	0.62	0.76	0.76
2. Gypsum wallboard, 0.5 in.	0.45	0.45	0.45	0.45
3. Nominal 2-in. × 4-in. ceiling rafter	—	4.38	—	4.38
4. 45 deg slope, nonreflective air space, 3.5 in. (50 F mean; 10 deg F temperature difference)	0.96	—	0.90*	—
5. Plywood sheathing, 0.625 in.	0.78	0.78	0.78	0.78
6. Felt building membrane	0.06	0.06	0.06	0.06
7. Asphalt shingle roofing	0.44	0.44	0.44	0.44
8. Outside surface (15-mph wind)	0.17	0.17	0.25**	0.25**
Total Thermal Resistance (R)	R_i=3.48	R_s=6.90	R_i=3.64	R_s=7.12

Construction No. 3: U_i= 1/3.48 = 0.287; U_s = 1/6.90 = 0.145. With 10% framing typical of 2-in. rafters @ 16-in. o.c.), U_{av}= 0.9 (0.287)+ 0.1 (0.145) = 0.273

Construction No. 4: U_i= 1/3.64 = 0.275; U_s = 1/7.12 = 0.140. With framing unchanged, U_{av}= 0.9 (0.275) + 0.1 (0.140) = 0.262

[b] Pitch of roof—45 deg.

* Air space value at 90 F meann, 10 F dif. temperature difference.

** 7.5-mph wind.

Table 3–20. (Reprinted with permission from the *1977 Fundamentals Volume, ASHRAE HANDBOOK & Product Directory*)

U-Values of Ceiling Sections

TYPE OF INSULATION	TYPE OF ROOF CONSTRUCTION[b]	INSULATION R-VALUE R-19	R-22	R-26	R-30	R-38
Blanket	Trusses	0.056	0.050	0.044	0.040	0.034
	Joists and rafters	0.052	0.047	0.041	0.037	0.031
Blown[c]	Trusses	0.049	0.043	0.036	0.032	0.026
	Joists and rafters	0.053	0.045	0.038	0.033	0.026

[b] 2" × 4" bottom chords, 24" o.c.; 2" × 8" ceiling joists, 16" o.c.

[c] Application ± 0.001 to loose fill insulations with thermal resistances up to R-2.8 per inch.

Table 3–21. (NAHB Insulation Manual 1979)

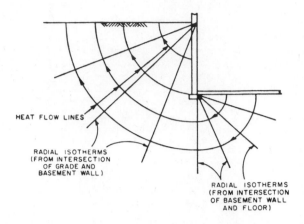

3-5. Heat flow from basement. (Reprinted with permission from the *1977 Fundamentals Volume, ASHRAE HANDBOOK & Product Directory*)

Soil Temperature Distribution

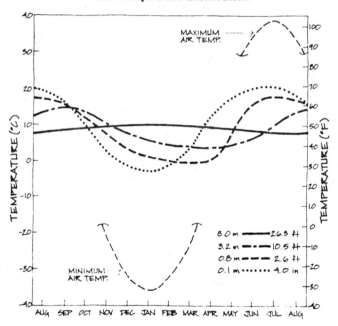

Table 3-22. (*Earth Sheltered Housing Design,* Van Nostrand Reinhold, 1979)

Figure 3-5; the rate of heat flow depends upon the conductivity of the soil, the material from which the walls or floor is made, the temperature difference between the air in the basement and that of the ground, and the presence or absence of insulating materials. The rate of heat loss also diminishes as the depth below grade increases, a very important factor for establishing insulation design specifications for the below-grade walls of earth-sheltered houses. This is because of the changing relationship of soil temperatures to surface temperatures as depth increases (Table 3-22). Study in this important area continues, and more information can be found through the ASHRAE and the Underground Space Center of the University of Minnesota, among others.

At present, about the easiest way to calculate the heat loss of below-grade basement (or other) walls is to consult Table 3-23. The heat loss for each level of the wall section can be found there, based upon an average soil conductivity of 9.6 Btu/hr/in/sq ft/° F. Insulation for the purposes of the table was assumed to have a thermal conductivity of 0.24 Btu/hr/in/sq ft/° F; other values can be substituted for k or C vis-a-vis thickness. Once the proper value is found for each wall level, they are added together to find the total Btu/hr loss per linear foot of wall, and then multiplied by the perimeter of the house, or foundation, to find the total wall heat loss in Btu/hr/(° F).

Concrete basement floors, uninsulated and poured on the ground well below grade, are often assigned an

Heat Loss through Basement Floors
[Btu/(h)(ft²)(F)]

Depth of Foundation Wall below Grade (ft)	Width of House			
	20 (ft)	24 (ft)	28 (ft)	32 (ft)
5	0.032	0.029	0.026	0.023
6	0.030	0.027	0.025	0.022
7	0.029	0.026	0.023	0.021

Table 3-24. (Reprinted with permission from the *1977 Fundamentals Volume, ASHRAE HANDBOOK & Product Directory*)

Heat Loss below Grade in Basement Walls[a] [Btuh/(ft²)(F)]

Depth (ft)	Path Length through Soil (ft)	Heat Loss			
			Insulation		
		Uninsulated	1-in.	2-in.	3-in.
0–1 (1st)	0.68	0.410	0.152	0.093	0.067
1–2 (2nd)	2.27	0.222	0.116	0.079	0.059
2–3 (3rd)	3.88	0.155	0.094	0.068	0.053
3–4 (4th)	5.52	0.119	0.079	0.060	0.048
4–5 (5th)	7.05	0.096	0.069	0.053	0.044
5–6 (6th)	8.65	0.079	0.060	0.048	0.040
6–7 (7th)	10.28	0.069	0.054	0.044	0.037

[a] k_{soil} = 9.6(Btuh)(in.)/(ft²)(F); $k_{insulation}$ = 0.24(Btuh)(in.)/(ft²)(F).

Table 3-23. (Reprinted with permission from the *1977 Fundamentals Volume, ASHRAE HANDBOOK & Product Directory*)

arbitrary *U* of 0.10, and this is a safe enough figure to use. Table 3-24 shows other values that can be used to calculate heat losses through concrete floors in basements. By choosing one of the per-square-foot values and multiplying by the floor area, the heat loss in Btu/hr/(° F) can be found. This figure and the total below-grade wall heat loss can then be added together. When multiplied by the chosen design temperature difference, the result is the below-grade heat loss for the basement.

The outside design temperature that must be used in these calculations is that of the contacting soil surface, and from a practical standpoint, only a rough estimate can be used. According to the *1977 Fundamentals Volume, ASHRAE HANDBOOK & Products Directory,* page 24.4, a suitable figure can be determined by first choosing an amplitude *A*, at which the ground surface temperature fluctuates about a mean temperature value that varies with surface cover and geographical location. Then the mean annual air temperature, $\overline{t}_a$, must be obtained for the site from weather records. Amplitude *A* can be selected from Figure 3-6. *A* is then subtracted from $\overline{t}_a$ to find the external design temperature.

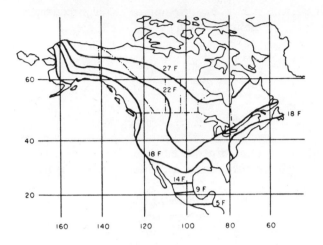

3-6. (Reprinted with permission from the *1977 Fundamentals Volume, ASHRAE HANDBOOK & Product Directory*)

U-Values at Band Joists and Sills at the Top of Foundation Walls

TYPE OF EXTERIOR FINISH	INSULATION R-VALUE	TYPE OF EXTERIOR SHEATHING				
		None	1/2″ Fiberboard	1/2″ Plywood	1/2″ Gypsumboard	3/4″ Polyurethane or 1″ Polystyrene
Wood siding or shingles	R-11	0.077	0.070	0.074	0.075	0.055
	R-13	0.071	0.065	0.067	0.068	0.051
	R-19	0.056	0.052	0.054	0.054	0.042
Metal or vinyl insulated siding	R-11	0.071	0.066	0.068	0.069	0.052
	R-13	0.066	0.060	0.063	0.063	0.049
	R-19	0.052	0.049	0.050	0.051	0.040
3/8″ Plywood	R-11	0.079	0.072	0.076	0.077	0.056
	R-13	0.072	0.066	0.069	0.070	0.052
	R-19	0.057	0.053	0.055	0.055	0.043
7/16″ Hardboard	R-11	0.078	0.071	0.074	0.075	0.056
	R-13	0.071	0.065	0.068	0.069	0.052
	R-19	0.056	0.052	0.054	0.055	0.043
Asbestos cement siding or shingles	R-11	0.083	0.075	0.078	0.079	0.058
	R-13	0.075	0.068	0.071	0.072	0.054
	R-19	0.059	0.054	0.056	0.057	0.044
Metal or vinyl uninsulated siding	R-11	0.079	0.071	0.075	0.076	0.056
	R-13	0.072	0.065	0.068	0.069	0.052
	R-19	0.056	0.052	0.054	0.055	0.043
3/4″ Stucco	R-11	0.081	0.074	0.077	0.078	0.057
	R-13	0.074	0.067	0.070	0.071	0.053
	R-19	0.058	0.054	0.056	0.056	0.043
Face brick veneer on wood frame	R-11	0.080	0.072	0.076	0.077	0.056
	R-13	0.073	0.066	0.069	0.070	0.052
	R-19	0.057	0.053	0.055	0.056	0.043
Common brick veneer on wood frame	R-11	0.078	0.071	0.074	0.075	0.055
	R-13	0.071	0.065	0.068	0.068	0.052
	R-19	0.056	0.052	0.054	0.054	0.042

ªFloor joists occupying 6% of perimeter included with R-11 and R-13 insulation, joists 16″ o.c., 2″ × 6″ sill. Floor joists occupying 4% of perimeter included with R-19 insulation; joists 24″ o.c., 2″ × 6″ sill.

Table 3-25. (NAHB Insulation Manual, 1979)

Once the intermediate design temperature of the ground has been found, it is subtracted from the interior design temperature in the usual way to find the temperature difference ° F; the inside temperature for a basement might well be the same as the rest of the heated space in the house (approximately 70° F), but can be any other desired temperature as well. Then the total heat loss in Btu's per square foot of the floor can be added to the loss in Btu per linear foot for the below-grade portions of the walls, and the total multiplied by the ΔT (design temperature difference) to find the total maximum rate of heat loss. This figure added to the maximum rate of heat loss (calculated in the usual manner) for the above-grade portions of the walls results in the total heat loss for the basement.

Further refinements can be made in these calculations. There are instances where the basement is heated to a higher temperature than a space above part of the basement ceiling. In that case, there would also be an upward heat loss through that portion of the basement ceiling which must be included in the calculations. In all but small basements, it is also well to consider the heat loss that occurs through the area of the sills and the end and header joists, just atop the foundation walls; the larger the basement, the more consequential these losses become. Just where and how this loss occurs, and its magnitude, depends upon the specifics of the house construction. Table 3-25 shows various possibilities.

Heat loss through slabs. Many houses (as well as heated garages, workshops, barns, etc.) are built upon concrete slabs in direct contact with the earth. Some have heating pipes or ducts in them; some do not. The words of the *1977 Fundamentals Volume, ASHRAE HANDBOOK & Products Directory,* Chapter 24, on these types of floors are worth quoting directly.

For unheated slab floors, "Floor heat loss generally comprises only about 10 percent of total heat loss of the house. For comfort, however, it may be the most important, since houses with cold floors are difficult to heat. Note that a well-insulated floor does not in itself assure comfort if downdrafts from windows or exposed walls create pools of chilly air over considerable areas of the floor. Therefore [an unheated slab] floor should not be used in a severe climate, except with a heating system that delivers enough heat near the floor to counteract the downdrafts of exterior walls and heat transmission through the floor." In other words, perimeter heat (see chapter 7), in addition to edge insulation, should be installed.

Heat loss in a slab takes place predominantly around its outer edges. For this reason, ample perimeter insulation should always be used in such constructions (Figure 3-7). The value of such insulation can readily be seen in Table 3-26, which the *1977 Fundamentals Volume, ASHRAE HANDBOOK & Products Directory* recommends as being sufficiently accurate for design calculations. Heat loss is given directly in Btu/hr

loss per linear foot; simply multiply the chosen figure by the number of linear feet of exposed concrete slab edge. The figures in the table are predicated upon the insulation extending under the floor for 2 feet, but the insulation will have approximately equal effectiveness if applied to the foundation vertical wall, provided that it extends 2 feet below floor level. Other specific heat loss figures can be found by using the formula:

$$q = F_2 P(t_i - t_o)$$

where

q = heat loss of floor, Btu per hour

F_2 = heat loss coefficient, Btu per hour per linear foot of exposed edge per ° F temperature difference between the indoor air and the outdoor air

P = perimeter or exposed edge of floor, linear feet

t_i = indoor air temperature, ° F.

t_o = outdoor air temperature, ° F

The situation is somewhat different with slabs that are heated. The heat loss is increased because of the presence of a heat source within the slab, and good insulation is imperative. A 1-inch minimum thickness should be used, and 2-inch is recommended; the slab should be laid several inches above grade, on a 4-inch gravel cushion for moisture protection, with a waterproof membrane over the gravel . The figures in Table 3-27 can be used for design calculations for heated slabs. For example, if the outdoor design temperature is 10° F and the slab has 2-inch L-type insulation along the perimeter, the heat loss is 55 Btu's per linear foot of slab for every degree of temperature difference between the inside and the outside temperatures, per hour. These figures assume a standard average slab heat loss to the ground within the perimeter, and therefore an average ground temperature. If there is no reason to believe that the ground temperature is markedly below the temperate zone average, so that heat loss through the parts of the slab inward from the perimeter may be more than is usually found in the north-central U.S.A. (as, for example, in areas in Alaska where permafrost is a problem), calculations made with the information given above will result in a reasonably accurate comfort figure for heat loss and for warm floors over concrete slabs.

Heat loss through windows and doors. A vertical sheet of glass is the least efficient heat barrier of any building section normally found in a house. Its overall heat transmission is given as 1.10 in winter conditions (R-0.91), whereas even the uninsulated between-framing portion of the wall in Table 3-8 has a U of 0.225 (R-4.44).

A window cannot be insulated with standard materials, of course, since its transparency would be lost. But by doubling or tripling the layers of glass, the heat loss can be considerably reduced, though by no

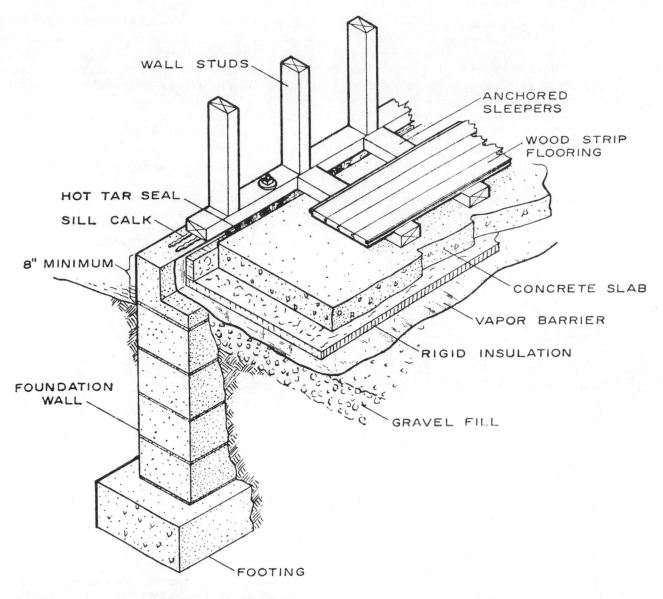

WALL STUDS

ANCHORED SLEEPERS

WOOD STRIP FLOORING

HOT TAR SEAL

SILL CALK

8" MINIMUM

CONCRETE SLAB

VAPOR BARRIER

RIGID INSULATION

FOUNDATION WALL

GRAVEL FILL

FOOTING

3-7. Perimeter insulation under concrete slab. (USDA)

Heat Loss of Concrete Floors at or Near Grade Level per Foot of Exposed Edge		
	Heat Loss per Foot of Exposed Edge, Btuh	
Outdoor Design Temperature, F	Recommended 2-in. Edge Insulation	1-in. Edge Insulation
−20 to −30	50	55
−10 to −20	45	50
0 to −10	40	45
Outdoor Design Temperature, F	1-in. Edge Insulation	No Edge Insulation[a]
−20 to −30	60	75
−10 to −20	55	65
0 to −10	50	60

[a]This construction not recommended; shown for comparison only.

Table 3-26. (Reprinted with permission from the *1977 Fundamentals Volume, ASHRAE HANDBOOK & Product Directory*)

Floor Heat Loss to be Used When Warm Air Perimeter Heating Ducts Are Embedded in Slabs[a]			
Btuh per (linear foot of heated edge)			
	Edge Insulation		
Outdoor Design Temperature, F	1-in. Vertical Extending Down 18 in. Below Floor Surface	1-in. L-Type Extending at Least 12 in. Deep and 12 in. Under	2-in. L-Type Extending at Least 12 in. Down and 12 in. Under
−20	105	100	85
−10	95	90	75
0	85	80	65
10	75	70	55
20	62	57	45

[a] Factors include loss downward through inner area of slab.

Table 3-27. (Reprinted with permission from the *1977 Fundamentals Volume, ASHRAE HANDBOOK & Product Directory*)

means as efficiently as with opaque materials. The *U* values for various types of glazing appear in Table 3-28; surface conductances are included in the figures given and need not be separately calculated. The adjustment factors listed in *Part C* of the table should be used as required in order to take into consideration the different thermal characteristics of the sash that holds the glazing. The NAHB *Insulation Manual* offers an extensive table, arranged somewhat differently, of heat loss values for numerous glazings that is quite useful.

It should be noted that, while these figures are suitable for making calculations, the values are approximate. Situations can occur, however, where glazing can have a much higher or lower *U*, such as when a particular window is exposed to a nearby heat-radiating source, or where there is air movement (as from a grille) across the inside surface. In such cases where an unusual situation occurs, judgement must be used in making assessments of the true *U*.

It is bad practice to assume any heat gain from

Coefficients of Transmission *(U)* of Windows, Skylights, and Light-transmitting Partitions

PART A—VERTICAL PANELS (EXTERIOR WINDOWS, SLIDING PATIO DOORS, AND PARTITIONS)— FLAT GLASS, GLASS BLOCK, AND PLASTIC SHEET

Description	Exterior[a] Winter	Summer	Interior
Flat Glass[b]			
single glass	1.10	1.04	0.73
insulating glass—double[c]			
0.1875-in. air space[d]	0.62	0.65	0.51
0.25-in. air space[d]	0.58	0.61	0.49
0.5-in. air space[e]	0.49	0.56	0.46
0.5-in. air space, low emittance coating[f]			
$e = 0.20$	0.32	0.38	0.32
$e = 0.40$	0.38	0.45	0.38
$e = 0.60$	0.43	0.51	0.42
insulating glass—triple[c]			
0.25-in. air spaces[d]	0.39	0.44	0.38
0.5-in. air spaces[g]	0.31	0.39	0.30
storm windows			
1-in. to 4-in. air space[d]	0.50	0.50	0.44
Plastic Sheet			
single glazed			
0.125-in. thick	1.06	0.98	—
0.25-in. thick	0.96	0.89	—
0.5-in. thick	0.81	0.76	—
insulating unit—double[c]			
0.25-in. air space[d]	0.55	0.56	—
0.5-in. air space[e]	0.43	0.45	—
Glass Block[h]			
6 × 6 × 4 in. thick	0.60	0.57	0.46
8 × 8 × 4 in. thick	0.56	0.54	0.44
—with cavity divider	0.48	0.46	0.38
12 × 12 × 4 in. thick	0.52	0.50	0.41
—with cavity divider	0.44	0.42	0.36
12 × 12 × 2 in. thick	0.60	0.57	0.46

PART B—HORIZONTAL PANELS (SKYLIGHTS)— FLAT GLASS, GLASS BLOCK, AND PLASTIC DOMES

Description	Exterior[a] Winter[i]	Summer[j]	Interior
Flat Glass[e]			
single glass	1.23	0.83	0.96
insulating glass—double[c]			
0.1875-in. air space[d]	0.70	0.57	0.62
0.25-in. air space[d]	0.65	0.54	0.59
0.5-in. air space[c]	0.59	0.49	0.56
0.5-in. air space, low emittance coating[f]			
$e = 0.20$	0.48	0.36	0.39
$e = 0.40$	0.52	0.42	0.45
$e = 0.60$	0.56	0.46	0.50
Glass Block[h]			
11 × 11 × 3 in. thick with cavity divider	0.53	0.35	0.44
12 × 12 × 4 in. thick with cavity divider	0.51	0.34	0.42
Plastic Domes[k]			
single-walled	1.15	0.80	—
double-walled	0.70	0.46	—

PART C—ADJUSTMENT FACTORS FOR VARIOUS WINDOW AND SLIDING PATIO DOOR TYPES (MULTIPLY *U* VALUES IN PARTS A AND B BY THESE FACTORS)

Description	Single Glass	Double or Triple Glass	Storm Windows
Windows			
All Glass[l]	1.00	1.00	1.00
Wood Sash—80% Glass	0.90	0.95	0.90
Wood Sash—60% Glass	0.80	0.85	0.80
Metal Sash—80% Glass	1.00	1.20[m]	1.20[m]
Sliding Patio Doors			
Wood Frame	0.95	1.00	—
Metal Frame	1.00	1.10[m]	—

[a] See Part C for adjustment for various window and sliding patio door types.
[b] Emittance of uncooled glass surface = 0.84.
[c] Double and triple refer to the number of lights of glass.
[d] 0.125-in. glass.
[e] 0.25-in. glass.
[f] Coating on either glass surface facing air space; all other glass surfaces uncoated.
[g] Window design: 0.25-in. glass—0.125-in. glass—0.25-in. glass.
[h] Dimensions are nominal.
[i] For heat flow up.
[j] For heat flow down.
[k] Based on area of opening, not total surface area.
[l] Refers to windows with negligible opaque area.
[m] Values will be less than these when metal sash and frame incorporate thermal breaks. In some thermal break designs, *U*-values will be equal to or less than those for the glass. Window manufacturers should be consulted for specific data.

Table 3–28. (Reprinted with permission from the *1977 Fundamentals Volume, ASHRAE HANDBOOK & Product Directory*)

sunlight through glass during cold weather when calculating total heat load for a house. The most adverse (average, not record-breaking) climatic conditions must be assumed. The heating plant, whether conventional, solar, or combined-method, may then be *theoretically* larger than necessary, but people do not live theoretically in houses. They want to be warm when conditions are at their worst as well as when they are average. The bright winter sun can indeed save quite a bit of fuel, depending upon the design of the house, and can provide quite a bit of useful and usable heat, but the full heating capacity must be there to take care of the cold night, the blizzardy day.

By the same token, various kinds of shading devices or closures can be used to make substantial reductions in U values of windows. Well-made, tight-fitting devices such as draperies, venetian blinds, or roller shades *can* reduce the U value of vertical exterior single glazing by as much as 25 percent. Special insulating draperies, thermally insulated heavy shutters, and similar devices can effect a much greater reduction. *But only when they are in place,* which, a great part of the time, they are not. So again, such adjustments should not be considered in determining the heating load and choosing the heating equipment, but rather as heat-conservation measures. (They can, however, be used in figuring cooling loads.)

U's for slab doors appear in Table 3-29. If the doors are glass, use the U for glass; if they are part wood and part glass, use a combination of wood and glass factors in proportion to the areas of each material. In practice, exterior doors containing any glass are frequently calculated as though they were all glass.

Double glazing. In studying the problem of double glazing, a number of factors should be borne in mind. The insulating value of either storm sash (Figure 3-8) or integral double or triple glazing (Figures 3-9, 3-10) is not only high in winter, but also in the mechanically cooled house in the summer. Indeed, it can be shown that double glazing will pay for itself in a very short time in fuel savings and possibly in smaller heating and cooling plant initial cost. Triple glazing is somewhat less cost-effective, but well worth installing in areas of severe winter weather. Integrally manufactured double and triple glazing is generally preferable to storm sash because of greater effectiveness and less maintenance. However, there are also situations where storm sash should be considered as an alternative, especially in retrofitting an existing house.

| Thickness[a] | Winter | | | Summer |
| | Solid Wood, No Storm Door | Storm Door[b] | | No Storm Door |
		Wood	Metal	
1-in.	0.64	0.30	0.39	0.61
1.25-in.	0.55	0.28	0.34	0.53
1.5-in.	0.49	0.27	0.33	0.47
2-in.	0.43	0.24	0.29	0.42
Steel Door[14]				
1.75 in.				
A[c]	0.59	—	—	0.58
B[d]	0.19	—	—	0.18
C[e]	0.47	—	—	0.46

[a] Nominal thickness.
[b] Values for wood storm doors are for approximately 50% glass; for metal storm door values apply for any percent of glass.
[c] A = Mineral fiber core (2 lb/ft^3).
[d] B = Solid urethane foam core with thermal break.
[e] C = Solid polystyrene core with thermal break.

Table 3-29. (Reprinted with permission from the *1977 Fundamentals Volume, ASHRAE HANDBOOK & Product Directory)*

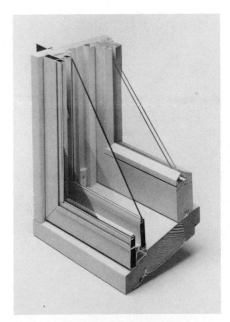

3-8. Double-glazed sash equipped with 2-track combination storm sash and screen. (Courtesy, Andersen Corporation, Bayport, MN 55003)

3-9. Typical double-glazing sash arrangement. (Courtesy, Andersen Corporation, Bayport, MN 55003)

3-10. Triple-glazing arrangement, with removable outer glazing panel. (Courtesy, Andersen Corporation, Bayport, MN 55003)

Glass blocks, the properties of which appear in Table 3-28, *Part B*, insulate with about the same efficiency as double ¼-inch insulating glass. They permit light to enter while barring vision, which makes them useful in certain special situations such as foyers, bathrooms, and the like (Figure 3-11).

A recent development in double glazing deserves mention here. The Beadwall was designed by Zomeworks primarily for solar-design houses, but is actually applicable to any kind of house. This arrangement consists of two large glazing panels of glass or plastic, with a wide air space between them. Whenever prevention of undesirable heat loss is wanted, a quantity of small polystyrene beads is blown into the air space, completely filling the void. When not needed, the beads are sucked out of the space under vacuum by a small motor and returned to a storage container. The system can be operated manually or automated by light-sensitive controls with a manual override. When manually controlled, the system should be considered in the same light as any other shutter device, but, if automated, it might reasonably be intergrated into the heating load calculations in the same manner as double or triple glazing, with the appropriate values being used. The total *R* of the Beadwall depends upon its thickness and other design characteristics, but a 3-inch wall has a value of about *R*-10 or so.

Solar houses. We have remarked that it is a bad practice to assume a heat gain from the sun during cold weather. It is true that in many instances double-glazed windows facing anywhere in the range from south-southeast to south-southwest will gain more heat during a sunny day than they will lose during the night. But not every day is sunny during the winter, and the result is a net heat loss, especially through glazing that faces in other directions. Draperies and similar devices will cut night heat loss, true. But experience has shown that, unless automation is part of the scheme, no net improvement in heat loss will occur; indeed, there will still be a substantial net loss because the occupants of the house never exercise sufficient discipline and regularity in closing and opening drapes or in similar heat-saving activities. In fact, occupants often are not present when such activities should be taking place, and, in any event, a computer would be necessary to monitor all of the subtle heat loss/gain changes that occur during every 24-hour period, even in a small and simple building. (And the day may come when the heating/ cooling systems in our houses are controlled in just that way.) Thus, even though a glass wall or substantial areas of glazing are part of the design—for certainly this increases livability—it never should be reason to reduce the winter heat load.

3-11. Glass block wall construction. (Courtesy, Pittsburgh Corning Corporation)

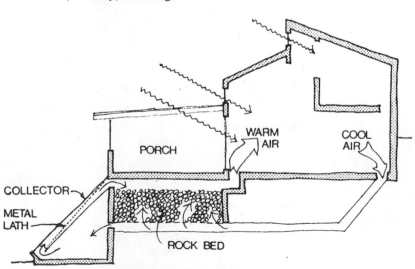

3-12. Solar house designed for collecting and storing heat. (USDOE)

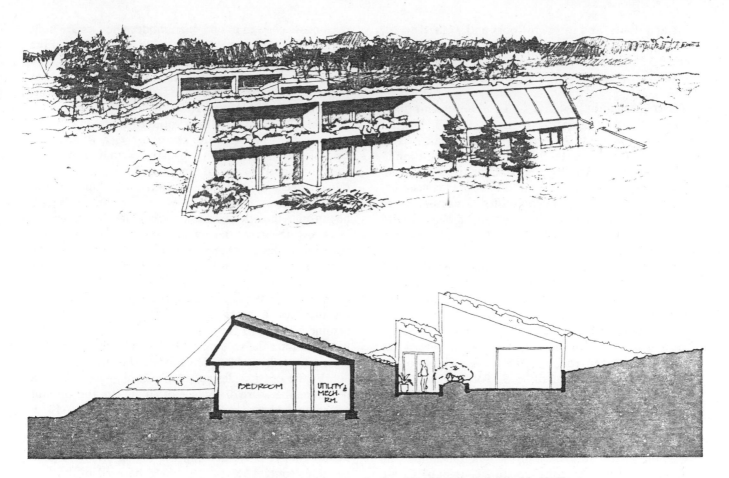

3-13. Earth sheltered house design. (*Earth Sheltered Housing Design,* Van Nostrand Reinhold, 1979)

But houses specifically designed to *collect and store* solar energy (Figure 3-12) are quite another matter. The time has come when this technique can eliminate a large part of the heating bill. Though in many areas of the country, especially in the northern climates, supplementary heating methods are needed, even so, heating fuel costs can be drastically cut. It is possible to design solar installations to provide 100 percent of heating needs, including domestic hot water, and indeed there are numerous solar houses about the country, even in the cold climes, that are today operating sucessfully on that basis. In general practice, though, solar heating systems are usually sized at about 75 percent of total heating requirements, or thereabouts. And since solar heating techniques and equipment are so flexible and varied, they can be integrated with house design to provide for virtually any needs in literally thousands of permutations. Further information on basic solar heating is contained in chapter 7.

Earth-sheltered houses. The thermal characteristics of earth-sheltered houses (Figure 3-13) can range anywhere from mildly to vastly different than conventional, above-ground houses. In cases where the earth-sheltering consists only of a relatively small area of berming or when just a few portions of the structure are below grade, heating load calculations can be made in about the same manner as a conventional house with a fully below-grade basement, for example. But houses that are more or less fully earth-sheltered must be handled differently.

Building sections that are exposed to the outdoors are calculated in the usual fashion for heat loss. However, other sections that are in contact with the earth must be specially calculated, with an eye toward the depth of the section in the earth, variations in depth, conductivity of the surrounding soil, the thermal mass of both the structure and the surrounding soil, moisture content of the soil, configurations of the building sections, and so on. Roof designs warrant special consideration; waterproofing and insulation placement below grade is very important; internal heat gains must be acknowledged; and window and door placement is important. In short, the subject is a complex one and is currently undergoing extensive study. Further specifics can be obtained from *Earth Sheltered Housing Design, Guidelines, Examples, and References,* The Underground Space Center of the University of Minnesota (Van Nostrand Reinhold, 1979).

Infiltration Losses

Infiltration is the second important factor to be taken into account in the calculation of a house's overall heat loss. Infiltration refers to the inflow of cold air through cracks and interstices in the construction, around windows and doors, and through floors and walls. This includes *natural ventilation*, or intentional air displacement as through a window, door, or ventilator, and *mechanical ventilation* by fans of whatever sort or purpose.

The coefficient of heat loss, or U, of infiltrating air is given as 0.018. This is the result of multiplying the specific heat of air (0.24) by the density of air (which averages 0.075). The total heat loss from infiltration is then 0.018 multiplied by the volume of outside air entering the house, then by the difference between indoor and outdoor design temperatures. This calculation determines the *sensible* heat loss, or the amount of heat needed to bring the cold infiltrating air up to the indoor air temperature.

In cases where moisture must be added to the indoor air by mechanical humidification for winter comfort, calculations must also be made for *latent* heat loss, the energy needed to evaporate an amount of water equal to that lost by infiltration. Here the latent heat of vapor is assumed to be 1060 Btu/lb, and the air density, as before, is assumed to be 0.075 lb/ft³. The two are multiplied to get a factor of 79.5. To find latent heat loss for any particular space, simply multiply 79.5 by the volume in cubic feet per hour of outdoor air entering the space, and multiply the result by the humidity ratio difference between inside and outside air, pound per pound of dry air. The result will be the amount of heat required to increase the moisture content of the air entering the house from its usually dry state at outdoor cold temperatures to the desired moisture content of the warmer indoor air. Note that it is not common practice to include the energy needed to occasionally operate small portable humidifiers or vaporizers, nor is it necessary to make additional calculations for latent heat losses where the humidifying equipment already has that factor included in its rating, as is usually the case.

Making infiltration calculations can be extremely complex when all of the detailed factors are taken into consideration, and the *1977 Fundamentals Volume, ASHRAE HANDBOOK & Product Directory* presents an exhaustive analysis of infiltration minutiae, along with methods of making computations. But such analyses are generally of greatest value with respect to large and/or commercial buildings, and the methods for calculating infiltration in houses is nearly always simplified, with no consequential error factor introduced into the final results. As with transmission heat losses, those results are at best an educated estimation anyway.

There are two ways of simply figuring infiltration losses for houses. The first is by the *air change* method. One possibility is to assume one complete air change per hour throughout the structure. This means that once every hour there is an intake of air at outdoor temperature equal to the total volume of warm air enclosed in the house. Though that assumption was

reasonable enough at one time, modern houses are built tighter than they were only a decade or so ago, and the air change is now less. For that reason, NEMA recommends using ½ to ¾ air changes per hour for houses that are constructed in average fashion with average insulation. ASHRAE suggest following the figures listed in Table 3-30 and making a room-to-room assessment that can then be related to the house as a whole. It is possible, for a house of up-to-date design built with extreme care and the best of materials, to achieve an ACH (air change per hour) of somewhat less than ½, and research shows that an ACH as low as ¼ is still healthful, though perhaps somewhat odoriferous. Whatever the case, once a determination is made, the fraction of the air change per hour is entered into the formulae noted above to find the sensible heat loss, or latent heat loss, or both, of infiltration. In the latter case, the latent and sensible heat losses are added together for a total infiltration loss. For example, assume a room 10 feet wide and 20 feet long, with an 8-foot ceiling; the volume of the room is 1600 cubic feet (10 × 20 × 8 = 1600). The inside design temperature is 70° F, the outside design temperature −10° F, for a design temperature difference of 80° F. So, the amount of energy needed to raise the incoming cold air at −10° F to 70° F in Btu/hr (q_s) equals 0.018 (coefficient of heat loss) times 1600 cu. ft. (V) times 80° F (ΔT), or 2304, if the air change is 1.0 per hour. If the air change is 0.75 per hour, only 1200 cu. ft. would be used in the formula (0.75 × 1600 = 1200).

Note that separate calculations for latent heat loss are, in practice, seldom made for residential heating loads.

The second way of figuring infiltration losses is by the *crack* method. Properly done, this method can be more accurate, but is more complex. Basically, the calculations consist of analyzing the various cracks in the exterior walls through which air can flow, such as around windows and doors; determining the pressures under which the air will flow through them; referring to specific air leakage data (or developing new data by

Air Changes Occurring Under Average Conditions in Residences, Exclusive of Air Provided for Ventilation[a]	
Kind of room	Number of Air Changes per hour
Rooms with no windows or exterior doors	0.5
Rooms with windows or exterior doors on one side	1
Rooms with windows or exterior doors on two sides	1.5
Rooms with windows or exterior doors on three sides	2
Entrance halls	2

[a] For rooms with weatherstripped windows or with storm sash, use two-thirds these values.

Table 3–30. (Reprinted with permission from the *1977 Fundamentals Volume, ASHRAE HANDBOOK & Product Directory*)

testing); and finally making an estimate of the total crackage infiltration. The heat loss is usually expressed in terms of Btu/hr/crack length; tables for infiltration contain values in cubic feet of air passage per hour per unit (foot of crack, square foot of section, etc.).

Sometimes the use of additional factors is recommended when computing infiltration losses, especially with the air change method, in order to increase the calculated heat loss in compensation for prevailing winds, certain construction features, and the like. While not generally necessary in making house heat-load calculations, especially for small or average-size structures of conventional design, these added factors can do no harm and may be regarded as a safety factor. NEMA, for instance, choose to include *construction feature losses* in their calculations for heat loss in houses using electric comfort heating. Thus, they include a direct heat loss of 50 Btu/hr per degree of temperature difference for a fireplace with an average-fitting damper, for example, and 40 Btu/hr for each exhaust fan without automatic damper, and so on. These losses are added directly to the air infiltration factor of 0.0088 Btu/hr per ° F difference, per cubic foot for a ½ air change per hour, or 0.0132 Btu/hr for a ¾ ACH.

Weatherstrips. Notice that the footnote to Table 3-30 states that infiltration values can be cut to two-thirds "for rooms with weatherstripped windows or storm sash." This would seem to indicate that one does not need weatherstrips if storm windows are used. This is not the intent of the footnote, however. Because of variations in workmanship and material quality, the full value of storm sash and weatherstrips may not actually be realized. In estimating the size of heating plant this factor has to be taken into account. A really good job of weatherstripping, and of caulking all accessible air leaks, will enhance thermal performance of a house considerably. But the savings will be realized in lower fuel consumption, not in a smaller heating plant—mainly because it is impossible to tell in advance what the living habits of the occupants of the house are going to be. There should always be a margin for carelessness, for the blithe inattention of children (and many adults), for the inevitable air leakage through a fireplace chimney or cracks that develop in a structure with age, and for similar factors.

Thus, weatherstripping is an extremely valuable adjunct to any house in the northern climates, especially in conjunction with liberal air-leak caulking. It has been estimated that infiltration can be responsible for as much as 50% of total heating costs, and can be substantial even in a so-called "tight" house. In the average house, the total amount of crackage continually leaking cold air in can be the equivalent of leaving a small window open all the time.

The best weatherstrips are made from spring metal, and, though high in cost, they are easy to install, provide an excellent seal, and have a life expectancy of about twenty years. Other types in common use are felt, tubular vinyl gasket, foam-filled tubular gasket, and pressure-sensitive foam. Though less expensive yet capable of providing a good seal, these have to be replaced often and have life spans of only two to six years or so.

Emphasis should hardly have to be placed on the fact that all windows and doors must be weatherstripped whenever there is year-round air conditioning or mechanical summer cooling, and not only in severe climates where the only problem is cold air.

AVERAGE THERMAL TRANSMITTANCE

In times past, building codes paid little attention to thermal performance of houses. But times have changed, and so have thermal performance standards. Nowadays various national code bodies recommend certain levels of thermal performance, and many local building codes specify them in detail. In some cases these regulations take the form of minimum U or R values for particular sections: $R - 12.5$ or $U - 0.08$ for a stud wall, for instance. However, such individual stipulations sometimes interfere with the design of a house and are being recognized as unnecessary restrictions; a log-construction wall, for instance, with an R of 9 would not meet that code requirement, and the addition of thermal insulation to bring it into compliance would destroy the appearance of one side or the other of the wall.

The concept of combined or average thermal transmittance gets around this problem neatly and is now becoming more widely recognized as an effective method of establishing minimum thermal performance standards for structures without interfering unduly with design. The concept merely establishes an overall average U, known as U_o, that can be applied to any building section, part of a building, or an entire building, without regard to the makeup of specific component parts thereof.

Thus, the equation for a wall would be:

$$U_o = \frac{U_{wall}A_{wall} + U_{window}A_{window} + U_{door}A_{door}}{A_o}$$

where

U_o = the average thermal transmittance of the gross wall area, Btu/h/ft²/° F

A_o = the gross area of exterior wall, sq. ft.

U_{wall} = the thermal transmittance of all elements of the opaque wall area, Btu/h/ft²/° F

U_{window} = the thermal transmittance of the window area, Btu/h/ft²/° F

A_{wall} = opaque wall area, sq. ft.

A_{window} = window area (including sash), sq. ft.

A_{door} = door area, sq. ft.

If there is more than one type of wall, window, or door in the particular section under consideration, then the $U \times A$ term is expanded to include the different elements:

$$U_{\text{wall}_1} A_{\text{wall}_1} + U_{\text{wall}_2} A_{\text{wall}_2} + \text{etc.}$$

By extending the formula sufficiently, or running a series of calculations for the various parts of the house under consideration and averaging them, an ultimate U_o, or average thermal performance, can be determined, even for an entire house.

THERMAL MASS

There is nothing new about the concept of thermal mass; the Romans and other ancient cultures probably used it to their benefit, and certainly many early American homes incorporated the principle into their design and construction. The concept is based upon the fact that all materials have the ability, to a greater or lesser degree, to retain or store a certain quantity of heat. The heat is absorbed from the material's surroundings or from direct heat sources, such as the sun or a stove, and remains in the material until the heat source is removed and/or the surroundings become cooler than the material. Then the heat begins to radiate back to the cooler surroundings. Many early Cape Cod houses, to take one example, were constructed with massive center chimneys that often contained several fireplaces. The heat of the fires during the day warmed the masonry mass, which was contained almost entirely within the structure of the house. At night, when the fires were dying or banked, the stored heat would radiate back into the house, keeping inside temperature levels reasonable enough (for those days) until the fires were started up again next morning.

But, for the most part, the thermal mass concept has not been a part of our house design programs until recently. Today, it is this principle that makes successful solar heating a viable possibility and, indeed, a practical reality. And, in a somewhat different fashion, it is also an important consideration in the design and construction of earth-sheltered houses. The fact that thermal mass comes in for little or no consideration in conventional residential design and construction is most unfortunate because it is an excellent design tool of great worth. One of the principal difficulties at the present is that the concept is not well understood; the effects upon overall heat consumption and other factors have not been studied in depth; and there is no great body of information available on the subject. Complete analyses, especially for large buildings, can be so complex for in-depth studies that the help of sophisticated computers is needed. In due course, thermal mass is quite likely to become part and parcel of ordinary building construction. Meanwhile, there is no gainsaying the fact that, from a practical standpoint, thermal mass is being used to great advantage, based upon relatively simple designs and calculations plus a bit of common sense and experimentation.

Every material can store some heat, and this ability is expressed as the *specific heat* of the material, or the number of Btu's required to raise the temperature of the material 1° F. For instance, water has a specific heat of 1.0 at a temperature of 40 ° F, so 1 Btu is needed to raise the temperature 1° F. Every material also has a density, which is expressed in terms of pounds of weight per cubic foot of material. The density of water is 62.5, for example. Table 3-5, which lists the thermal properties of various building materials, also shows the specific heat and the density values for those materials. Every material also has a certain capacity for holding heat, and some do so much better than others. This *heat capacity* is expressed in terms of the number of Btu's retained per cubic foot, per ° F, and can be found for any material simply by multiplying the specific heat by the density. Thus, for water, the result would be $1.0 \times 62.5 = 62.5$ Btu per cubic foot per ° F. Steel has a far higher density (489) but a much lower specific heat (0.12), so it has a heat capacity less than water (58.7).

When large masses of material with high, or relatively high, heat capacities are integral with the building design and construction and are *included within the insulated building envelope*, they will become charged with a sizable quantity of stored heat absorbed from the heat sources within the building, or from sunlight shining into the building. This heat can then be radiated back into the living spaces, in either regulated or unregulated fashion, as other heat sources diminish or turn off. In a house heated in the passive solar mode, the thermal mass might consist of thick concrete floors, massive concrete or rock walls, drums or cylinders of water, etc. In a house heated in the active solar mode, the thermal mass is a storage center usually consisting of a large quantity of rock in a heavily insulated bin, a huge tank of water, or, in some cases, containers of eutectic salts in a special storage vault. Heat is transferred from storage to living quarters by mechanical means as the need for heat arises. In earth-sheltered houses, the situation is somewhat different, since not only the heavy concrete structure itself, but also the surrounding earth, becomes a thermal mass.

In all cases, the thermal mass must lie *within* the heated space and the thermal insulation must be on the *outside* of the structure for the effect to be worthwhile. This, of course, is contrary to conventional construction practices, where the insulation is almost invariably fitted within or to the inside of the building sections. And, most conventionally built small buildings, especially houses, are so lightly constructed and make such little use of heavy, massive building materials that their total thermal mass is ineffective from a practical standpoint. Yet, thermal mass is a critical and essential part of the design and construction of solar and earth-sheltered houses. Though it should be considered in heating-load calculations, especially in regard to its impact upon the overall livability of the house, it still is inherently a heat-conserving principle and should not markedly alter the sizing of the heating equipment; that still must be capable of handling average adverse weather conditions.

There is another aspect of thermal mass that deserves consideration, too, and that is *thermal lag*. This simply means that the greater the thermal mass, the slower the temperature change in that mass will be with relation to changes in the surrounding ambient temperature. When the heat goes off in a frame-construction house of low thermal mass on a cold day, the inside temperature begins to drop rather rapidly, slowing its rate of decline somewhat as the inside and outside temperatures approach one another. The time lag for a house with a large thermal mass, however, is much greater; the rate of inside temperature drop is also much slower. In an earth-sheltered house set deep in the ground, the lag is even greater and the fluctuations in temperatures can be practically nonexistent. Thus, experience has shown beyond any doubt that, if thermal lag and thermal mass factors are taken into account and the house is properly designed and integrated with its environment and with its heating/cooling/ventilation systems, and of course properly constructed, a remarkably small heating system can keep a sizable house more than adequately comfortable for an astonishingly small operating cost.

This completes the survey of winter heat losses in a house. Vapor already in the indoor air adds to cooling load in the summer but does not affect winter heating load. For example, vapor in the exhalations from the lungs of people and animals, transpiration from plants, steam from pots on the stove, vapor from the shower in the bathroom, etc., are at room temperature or higher, and do not have to be heated. All that this moisture in a heated house can do is eventually damage the structure and its inner and outer surfaces, unless they are protected against this by vapor barriers and/or other means, as outlined in the next chapter.

Not all of the aspects of heat loss have been examined here, by any means; this is an extremely complex field in which new findings are continually being added to the current knowledge. On the other hand, heat loss calculations made by means of the foregoing information will result in perfectly adequate and acceptable results for houses and similar small buildings. And there are some aspects of heat loss that cannot be evaluated. These include the length of time the outer door is kept open, or the extent to which youngsters lean out of their windows to yell at the neighbor's children. These minor losses create irregular loads which the heating plant can handle well enough. The same goes for fireplaces: simply assume that the damper should be closed at all times when there is no fire on the hearth; the loss through this opening can be very large, but it is up to the occupants of the house to keep it down by tending to the damper. And so it is for storm doors, and undampered dryer vents, and letting the dog in and out and in and out. . . .

TOTAL HEAT LOAD

The fact must be emphasized that calculating the general heat loss for a whole structure is not enough. For the efficient layout of a heating plant and its distribution system, as well as the most effective thermal design, the heat loss of *each room or heated space*

Data for Uninsulated Sample House

Outside design temperature	-10°F
Outdoor wind speed	11 mph
Indoor design temperature	75°F
Ground temperature under basement and garage floors	50°F
Ground temperature, adjoining basement walls	32°F
Attic—unheated	
Infiltration losses—ACH method	
No insulation, but storm sash on all first and second floor windows, except garage.	

Building Construction	U Factors
Walls: Brick veneer, building paper, wood sheathing, studding, metal lath, and plaster.	0.29 .
Dormer walls over garage: Same, except wood siding instead of brick.	0.26
Attic walls: Brick veneer, building paper, wood sheathing on studding.	0.42
Basement walls: 10″ concrete.	0.10
Roof: Asphalt shingles on wood sheathing on rafters.	0.44
Second-floor ceiling: Metal lath and plaster.	0.74
Floor (bedroom D): Maple floor on yellow pine subfloor, metal lath and plaster ceiling below.	0.26
Floor (basement and garage): 4″ stone concrete on 3″ cinder concrete.	0.10
Windows: Double-hung wood, 70% glass, with storm sash.	0.45[1]
Windows, basement and garage: steel casement.	1.13[2]
French doors, dining room: 50% glass, no storm sash.	0.85[3]

1. 0.53 times application factor which, by interpolation, is found to be 0.85.
2. 1.13, single glass, times application factor of 1.00.
3. 1.13, all glass, times application factor which, by interpolation, is found to be 0.75.

Table 3–31. (Reprinted with permission from the *1977 Fundamentals Volume, ASHRAE HANDBOOK & Product Directory*)

must be determined. *Then*, if the situation warrants, an overall heat loss value for the entire structure can be determined, with thermal design adjustments made to individual building sections as necessary. The room-by-room system of determining total heat load is illustrated in the following example.

(For purposes of example, heat loss data for a typical residence of specific design and construction (Table 3-31), located in the Syracuse, New York area, as published in the *1977 Fundamentals Volume, ASHRAE HANDBOOK & Product Directory* have been modified for use in this book.)

The Uninsulated House

The data on the uninsulated house for which the heat loss is estimated appear in Table 3-32, and heat losses are summarized in Table 3-33. The totals in Column F of the latter table are the result of multiplying Column C by Column D by Column E and rounding totals to the nearest 10 Btu/hr.

Note that the house is fitted with storm windows. The heat losses through the glass and doors are only 19.8 percent, much smaller than would have been the case without the storm closures. Infiltration losses (14 percent) are also low, since the storm closures equal weatherstripping as a means of reducing infiltration.

In the summarized data in Table 3-33, note that in the final calculation *only one half of the total infiltration loss* is included on the *Operating Totals* line. The reason is simple: Air cannot leak into a house on all sides at the same time, for otherwise there would be a net increase in air pressure, like blowing up a balloon.

The assumption is, therefore, that the amount of air escaping from the sides of the house away from the wind balances the amount infiltrating the sides facing the wind. Thus, *effective* infiltration equals half the total amount.

		Ceiling and		Glass and	Infil-	
Room or Space	Walls	Roof	Floor	Door	tration	Totals
Bedroom A	5870	8350	—	1530	3080	18,830
Bedroom B	3840	5630	—	1530	2080	13,080
Bedroom C	2810	4280	—	1030	1580	9,700
Bedroom D	2910	3640	1140	770	1350	9,810
Bathroom 1	740	1820	—	540	670	3,770
Bathroom 2	1750	1190	360	340	430	4,070
Living Room	8050	—	—	1910	5730	15,690
Dining Room	4090	—	—	3300	3270	10,660
Kitchen	3170	—		1040	2440	6,650
Lavette	3350	—	—	1160	590	5,100
Entrance Hall	960	2990	—	680	1700	6,330
Garage	−1180[a]	−1500[b]	1180	4120	2120	4,740
Recreation	950	—	720	770	3080	5,520
Design Totals	37,310	26,400	3,400	18,720	28,120	113,950
Operating Totals[c]	37,310	26,400	3,400	18,720	14,060	99,890
Percentages[d]	37	27	3	19	14	100

Summary of Heat Losses of Uninsulated Residence (Btuh)

[a] Wall heat loss of 2420 Btuh minus wall heat gains of 1470, 800, and 1330 Btuh.
[b] Heat gains of 1140 and 360 Btuh.
[c] Based on 0.5 computed infiltration.
[d] Based on operating totals.

Table 3–33. (Reprinted with permission from the *1977 Fundamentals Volume, ASHRAE HANDBOOK & Product Directory*)

Heat Loss Calculation Sheet for Uninsulated Residence

A Room or Space	B Part of Structure or Infiltration Air Changes	C Net Exterior Area and Air Volume	D U-value Coefficient, (Btuh)/(ft²)(F)	E Temp. Diff.,[a] F	F Heat Loss, (Btuh)	G Totals, (Btuh)
Bedroom A and Closet	Walls	238 ft²	0.29	85	5870	
	Glass	40 ft²	0.45	85	1530	
	Ceiling	252 ft²	0.74	44.8[d]	8350	
	Infiltration (1)[g]	2016 cfh[b]	0.018[c]	85	3080	18,830
Bedroom B and Closet	Walls	156 ft²	0.29	85	3840	
	Glass	40 ft²	0.45	85	1530	
	Ceiling	170 ft²	0.74	44.8[d]	5630	
	Infiltration (1)[g]	1360 cfh[b]	0.018[c]	85	2080	13,080
Bedroom C and Closet	Walls	114 ft²	0.29	85	2810	
	Glass	27 ft²	0.45	85	1030	
	Ceiling	129 ft²	0.74	44.8[d]	4280	
	Infiltration (1)[g]	1032 cfh[b]	0.018[c]	85	1580	9,700
Bedroom D and Closet	Walls	118 ft²	0.29	85	2910	
	Glass	20 ft²	0.45	85	770	
	Ceiling	110 ft²	0.74	44.8[d]	3640	
	Floor over garage	110 ft²	0.26	40[e]	1140[p]	
	Infiltration (1)[g]	880 cfh[b]	0.018[c]	85	1350	9,810
Bathroom 1	Walls	30 ft²	0.29	85	740	
	Glass	14 ft²	0.45	85	540	
	Ceiling	55 ft²	0.74	44.8[d]	1820	
	Infiltration (1)[g]	440 cfh[b]	0.018[c]	85	670	3,770

Table 3–32. (Reprinted with permission from the *1977 Fundamentals Volume, ASHRAE HANDBOOK & Product Directory*)

Table 3–32 continued

A	B	C	D	E	F	G
Room or Space	**Part of Structure or Infiltration Air Changes**	**Net Exterior Area and Air Volume**	**U-value Coefficient, (Btuh)/(ft²)(F)**	**Temp. Diff.,[a] F**	**Heat Loss, (Btuh)**	**Totals, (Btuh)**
Bathroom 2	Walls	79 ft²	0.26	85	1750	
	Glass	9 ft²	0.45	85	340	
	Ceiling	35 ft²	0.74	44.8[d]	1190	
	Floor over garage	35 ft²	0.26	40[e]	360	
	Infiltration (1)[g]	280 cfh[b]	0.018[c]	85	430	4,070
Living Room	Walls	267 ft²	0.29	85	6580	
	Walls (adjoining garage)	94 ft²	0.39[f]	40[e]	1470	
	Glass	50 ft²	0.45	85	1910	
	Floor	294 ft²				
	Infiltration (1.5)[h]	3745 cfh[b]	0.018[c]	85	5730	15,690
Dining Room	Walls	166 ft²	0.29	85	4090	
	Glass (doors)	35 ft²	0.85	85	2530	
	Glass (windows)	20 ft²	0.45	85	770	
	Floor	168 ft²				
	Infiltration (1.5)[i]	2140 cfh[b]	0.018[c]	85	3270	10,660
Kitchen and Entrance to Garage	Walls	96 ft²	0.29	85	2370	
	Walls (adjoining garage)	51 ft²	0.39[f]	40[e]	800[p]	
	Glass	18 ft²	0.45	85	690	
	Door	17 ft²	0.51	40	350	
	Floor	125 ft²				
	Infiltration (1.5)[j]	1595 cfh[b]	0.018[c]	85	2440	6,650
Lavette and Vestibule	Walls	82 ft²	0.29	85	2020	
	Walls (adjoining garage)	85 ft²	0.39[f]	40[e]	1330[p]	
	Glass	9 ft²	0.45	85	340	
	Door	19 ft²	0.51	85	820	
	Floor	30 ft²				
	Infiltration (1.5)[k]	383 cfh[b]	0.018[c]	85	590	5,100
Entrance Hall	Walls	39 ft²	0.29	85	960	
	Door	21 ft²	0.38	85	680	
	Ceiling[r]	87 ft²	0.74	44.8[d]	2990	
	Infiltration (2)[l]	1110 cfh[b]	0.018[c]	85	1700	6,330
Garage	Walls	167 ft²	0.29	50[e]	2420	
	Glass	53 ft²	1.13	50	3000	
	Doors	44 ft²	0.51	50	1120	
	Infiltration (1.5)[m]	2360 cfh[b]	0.018[c]	50	2120	
	Floor	29 ft[s]	0.81	50	1180	
	Gain adjoining rooms				−5100[p]	4,740
Recreation Room[q]	Walls	220 ft²	0.10	43	950	
	Glass	8 ft²	1.13	85	770	
	Floor	287 ft²	0.10	25	720	
	Infiltration (1)[n]	2010 cfh[b]	0.018[c]	85	3080	5,520
					TOTAL	**113,950**

[a] The indoor-outdoor temperature difference is [75—(− 10)] or 85 F, except where otherwise noted.

[b] Volume of infiltration, cfh = (number of air changes) × (floor or ceiling area) × (ceiling height).

[c] From $q_s = 0.018V(t_i − t_o)$

[d] The ceiling heat losses are calculated by estimating the attic temperature and then calculating the loss through the ceiling using the proper temperature difference. This unheated attic is not ventilated during winter months. The attic temperature is estimated to be 30.2 F when the outdoor temperature is − 10 F and room temperature is 75 F. The temperature difference is then (75− 30.2) or 44.8 deg F. For the insulated residence, the attic temperature becomes 4.6 F, and the temperature difference, 75 − 4.6 = 70.4 deg F.

[e] Temperature in garage selected to be 35 F.

[f] Coefficient for wall adjoining garage calculated on basis of metal lath and plaster on both sides of studs [U = 0.39 Btuh/(ft²) (F)].

[g] Two-thirds of value Table 3–30, for storm windows or weather-stripping.

[h] Exposed on two sides; weatherstripped windows offset by fireplace. Use 1.5.

[i] Window on one side weatherstripped but double-doors are hard to close tightly. Hence, conservative value of 1.5.

[j] Assuming kitchen vent door to vestibule usually open, allow full table value of 1.5.

[k] Value in Table 3–30 increased to 1.5 by nearby outside door in the vestibule.

[l] Value in Table 3–30.

[m] Two sides exposed; large doors but large volume. Use value 1.5, as given in Table 3–30.

[n] Two small unweatherstripped windows in protected location, but fireplace, indicate one change.

[p] Heat losses from these rooms into garage are heat gains for garage.

[q] Neglect heat loss to basement, as losses from boiler, piping, etc., will probably keep basement near, if not above, 75 F.

[r] Upstairs hall ceiling figures with downstairs. Heat should be provided downstairs for both.

[s] Linear feet of exposed edge.

The Fully Insulated House

Now, suppose the house is insulated to average standards. In this context, that means the equivalent of 4 to 6 inches of mineral blanket in the ceiling or roof, 3½ inches in the walls, and 2 to 3 inches in the floors over unheated spaces. This arrangement is typical of houses built in cold country over the past three or four decades, and is also common to retrofittings of older, uninsulated houses. Just within the past few years have insulating standards been upgraded to allow substantially better thermal performance, primarily in recognition of the fact that extra-heavy insulation pays for itself in reducing cooling unit sizes and also, of course, cutting operating costs for both heating and cooling and conserving substantial amounts of energy on a nationwide basis. Past custom of installing light or barely adequate insulation is an unwise building economy today and indeed is not permitted by building codes in some areas, since it means not only higher heating and cooling bills for the life of the house, but also an extravagant and unnecessary waste of fuels. Additional data supporting the modern definition of proper insulation appear in chapter 5.

The insulated house is of the same design and construction as the uninsulated one, but improvements have been made, primarily by adding thermal insulation, to upgrade the overall heat transfer coefficients of various building sections as follows (design data used in calculations for Table 3-34): Walls: 0.13; walls of dormer over garage: 0.12; attic walls: 0.28; walls adjoining garage: 0.18; basement walls (recreation room): 0.10; roof: 0.53; ceiling (second floor): 0.15; windows: same; floor (Bedroom D): 0.18. The procedure for calculating the heat losses is the same as for the uninsulated house, and the results are summarized in Table 3-34. Note that the losses are considerably less than two-thirds of those in the same house with no insulation. Extra-heavy insulation would, of course, widen the gap much further and result in substantial savings in cost and energy.

Surface Temperatures

Insulation, particularly in walls and floors, not only saves on fuel bills, but also increases human comfort by raising the inside wall and floor surface temperatures. This higher inside surface temperature often results in further fuel savings, since many people find that they do not have to maintain a 70° F air temperature if the walls and floors are warmer.

In uninsulated houses, an air temperature as high as 85° F may not be enough to keep people from getting chilled, since their bodies lose heat by radiation to the cold walls and floors and they cannot absorb enough by convection from the warm air to counterbalance the loss. The walls in the uninsulated house just analyzed have a surface temperature of 58.2° F, too cold for comfort. This temperature is found as follows:

Inside surface temperature equals inside design temperature (75° F) minus inside surface resistance (0.68) times the U of the wall (0.29) times the difference between indoor and outdoor design temperature (85° F). In equation form this reads $T_s = t_i - (R_i \times U)(t_i - t_o)$. In figures, $T_s = 75 - (0.68 \times 0.29 \times 85)$, or 58.2. In the insulated house, on the other hand, with a wall U of 0.13, inside surface temperature is $75 - (0.68 \times 0.13 \times 85)$, or 75 minus 7.5, or 67.5; this is a comfortable surface temperature. Body radiation to a wall at this temperature is practically nil.

However, even in well-insulated houses, people will get chilled if they stand too close to a window for too long a time on a cold day, unless the window's cold is counteracted by a heating outlet immediately beneath it. This will be true, though to a lesser extent, even with storm windows affixed or double glazing installed.

SEASONAL HEATING COSTS

To estimate actual fuel requirements for a heating season, accurate estimates are needed of the average number of days per year during which the heating plant will be in use, and the extent to which it will be used each day. This information is not, of course, required for dimensioning the heating plant; for that purpose the

Summary of Heat Losses of Insulated Residence (Btuh)

Room or Space	Walls	Ceiling and Roof	Floor	Glass and Door	Infiltration	Totals
Bedroom A	2620	2770	—	1530	3080	10,000
Bedroom B	1720	1870	—	1530	2080	7,200
Bedroom C	1260	1470	—	1030	1580	5,340
Bedroom D	1300	1220	790	770	1350	5,430
Bathroom 1	330	610	—	540	670	2,150
Bathroom 2	870	280	250	340	430	2,170
Living Room	3630	—	—	1910	5730	11,270
Dining Room	1830	—	—	3300	3270	8,400
Kitchen	1430	—	—	1040	2440	4,910
Lavette	1520	—	—	1160	590	3,270
Entrance Hall	430	960	—	680	1700	3,770
Garage	−580[a]	−1040[b]	1180	4120	2120	5,800
Recreation	950	—	720	770	3080	5,520
Design Totals	17,310	8,140	2,940	18,720	28,120	75,230
Operating Totals[c]	17,310	8,140	2,940	18,720	14,060	61,170
Percentages[d]	28	13	5	31	23	100

[a] Wall heat loss of 1080 Btuh minus wall heat gains of 680,370 and 610 Btuh.
[b] Heat gains 790 and 250 Btuh.
[c] Based on 0.5 computed infiltration.
[d] Based on operating totals.

Table 3-34. (Reprinted with permission from the *1977 Fundamentals Volume, ASHRAE HANDBOOK & Product Directory*)

probable maximum heat loss at design temperature is all that is needed.

There are various methods of calculating fuel requirements and seasonal heat losses, but in residential work the traditional method has been, and still is to a considerable extent, the *degree-day* method. A degree-day is a unit of measure; one occurs for every degree that the average outside temperature is below the base of 65° F during each 24-hour period. This can be figured on an hourly basis, or by means of daily highs and lows. Suppose that the high temperature on a particular day is 52° F and the low is 22° F. The mean for that 24-hour period is, therefore, 37° F (52 + 22 ÷ 2 = 37). The mean is 28° F below the base of 65° F, and so 28 degree-days have piled up during that period. The reason 65° F is used as the average outdoor temperature above which no demands will be made on a house heating system is that the normal heat sources in the house—sunlight, artificial light, people, cooking, bathing, etc.—will keep the indoor temperature at 70° F or higher when it is 65° F outdoors. This is a pragmatic and not a theoretical figure and it has been established by many years of practical records kept by numerous organizations.

The total number of degree-days for a given locale can be obtained from local sources like the weather station, fuel suppliers, or building offices. They can be estimated from prepared degree-day maps, and figures may be obtained from the nearest National Weather Service office. Information for individual states is published by the U.S. Department of Commerce, and can be obtained from the National Climatic Center, Federal Building, Asheville, NC 28801. Or, the figures presented in Table 3-35 can be used directly for the cities listed or interpolated (with caution) for other areas in the general vicinity.

Seasonal heat loss equals the hourly heat loss (*HL*) in Btu's × 24 (hours in a day) × number of degree-days (*DD*), divided by the design temperature difference (Δ*T*) × the seasonal efficiency factor of the heating equipment (*Eff*). The latter factor, which generally varies from around 50 percent to 80 percent for fuel-fired equipment and is 100 percent for electric resistance heating equipment, can be obtained from the manufacturer of the specific product. This formula, which is similar to the one used in the NAHB *Insulation Manual*, is written:

$$S_{HL} = \frac{HL \times 24 \times DD}{\Delta T \times Eff}$$

Other slight variations on this formula are sometimes used, with the net result being approximately the same. Dividing the answer by the fuel heating value in Btu per unit (gallon, cubic foot, etc.) provides the seasonal fuel consumption.

This traditional method, though still in widespread use, does not give overly accurate results for a number of reasons: Many assumptions must be made; efficiencies of heating equipment can be highly variable; normal internal heat gains in modern houses have increased greatly over the years; residential insulation practices have greatly improved; the degree-day factor itself is a bit chancy; and so on. This means that there can easily be as much as a plus or minus variation of 20 percent from actual seasonal fuel usage, and the variation may be as high as 50 percent in the case of electric resistance heating. Such variations should be accepted as a possibility where this method is used.

The ASHRAE, in the *1976 Systems Volume, ASHRAE HANDBOOK & Product Directory*, recommends the use of the *modified degree-day procedure* for estimating residential heating energy consumption during this interim period while work proceeds to develop a simple but relatively accurate alternative method that one hopes will give better results. This procedure uses the formula:

$$E = \frac{H_L \times D \times 24}{\Delta t \times \epsilon \times V} (C_D)(C_F)$$

where

E = fuel or energy consumption for the estimate period

H_L = design heat loss, including infiltration, Btu per hour

D = number of 65 degree-days for the estimate period

Δt = design temperature difference, ° F

ϵ = rated full load efficiency, decimal

V = heating value of fuel, consistent with H_L and E

C_D = interim correction factor for heating effect vs degree-days

C_F = interim part-load correction factor for fueled systems only; equals 1.0 for electric resistance heating

The factor H_L is the maximum probable heat loss from the house under consideration. The rated efficiences of the heating equipment can be obtained from the manufacturer; they generally run about 50 to 80 percent. Values for C_D are listed in Table 3-36, and those for C_F are in Table 3-37. The heating value of fossil fuels varies somewhat; typical values are shown in Table 3-38, and specific values can be obtained from local fuel suppliers.

Assume that the insulated house in Syracuse, New York, used in the previous example, is heated with No. 2 fuel oil at 140,000 Btu per gallon. From Table 3-35, the number of degree-days for that area is 6756 for a full 365-day estimate period (shorter periods can also be determined from the Table). Assume further a

Average Monthly and Yearly Degree Days for Cities in the United States [a,b] (Base 65 F)

State	Station	Avg. Winter Temp[d]	July	Aug.	Sept.	Oct.	Nov.	Dec.	Jan.	Feb.	Mar.	Apr.	May	June	Yearly Total
Ala.	Birmingham .... A	54.2	0	0	6	93	363	555	592	462	363	108	9	0	2551
	Huntsville .... A	51.3	0	0	12	127	426	663	694	557	434	138	19	0	3070
	Mobile............................... A	59.9	0	0	0	22	213	357	415	300	211	42	0	0	1560
	Montgomery...................... A	55.4	0	0	0	68	330	527	543	417	316	90	0	0	2291
Alaska	Anchorage .... A	23.0	245	291	516	930	1284	1572	1631	1316	1293	879	592	315	10864
	Fairbanks .... A	6.7	171	332	642	1203	1833	2254	2359	1901	1739	1068	555	222	14279
	Juneau.............................. A	32.1	301	338	483	725	921	1135	1237	1070	1073	810	601	381	9075
	Nome .... A	13.1	481	496	693	1094	1455	1820	1879	1666	1770	1314	930	573	14171
Ariz.	Flagstaff .... A	35.6	46	68	201	558	867	1073	1169	991	911	651	437	180	7152
	Phoenix .... A	58.5	0	0	0	22	234	415	474	328	217	75	0	0	1765
	Tucson .... A	58.1	0	0	0	25	231	406	471	344	242	75	6	0	1800
	Winslow .... A	43.0	0	0	6	245	711	1008	1054	770	601	291	96	0	4782
	Yuma .... A	64.2	0	0	0	0	108	264	307	190	90	15	0	0	974
Ark.	Fort Smith .... A	50.3	0	0	12	127	450	704	781	596	456	144	22	0	3292
	Little Rock .... A	50.5	0	0	9	127	465	716	756	577	434	126	9	0	3219
	Texarkana......................... A	54.2	0	0	0	78	345	561	626	468	350	105	0	0	2533
Calif.	Bakersfield .... A	55.4	0	0	0	37	282	502	546	364	267	105	19	0	2122
	Bishop............................... A	46.0	0	0	48	260	576	797	874	680	555	306	143	36	4275
	Blue Canyon...................... A	42.2	28	37	108	347	594	781	896	795	806	597	412	195	5596
	Burbank .... A	58.6	0	0	6	43	177	301	366	277	239	138	81	18	1646
	Eureka C	49.9	270	257	258	329	414	499	546	470	505	438	372	285	4643
	Fresno............................... A	53.3	0	0	0	84	354	577	605	426	335	162	62	6	2611
	Long Beach .... A	57.8	0	0	9	47	171	316	397	311	264	171	93	24	1803
	Los Angeles .... A	57.4	28	28	42	78	180	291	372	302	288	219	158	81	2061
	Los Angeles C	60.3	0	0	6	31	132	229	310	230	202	123	68	18	1349
	Mt. Shasta C	41.2	25	34	123	406	696	902	983	784	738	525	347	159	5722
	Oakland .... A	53.5	53	50	45	127	309	481	527	400	353	255	180	90	2870
	Red Bluff .... A	53.8	0	0	0	53	318	555	605	428	341	168	47	0	2515
	Sacramento....................... A	53.9	0	0	0	56	321	546	583	414	332	178	72	0	2502
	Sacramento....................... C	54.4	0	0	0	62	312	533	561	392	310	173	76	0	2419
	Sandberg........................... C	46.8	0	0	30	202	480	691	778	661	620	426	264	57	4209
	San Diego.......................... A	59.5	9	0	21	43	135	236	298	235	214	135	90	42	1458
	San Francisco..................... A	53.4	81	78	60	143	306	462	508	395	363	279	214	126	3015
	San Francisco..................... C	55.1	192	174	102	118	231	388	443	336	319	279	239	180	3001
	Santa Maria .... A	54.3	99	93	96	146	270	391	459	370	363	282	233	165	2967
Colo.	Alamosa .... A	29.7	65	99	279	639	1065	1420	1476	1162	1020	696	440	168	8529
	Colorado Springs .... A	37.3	9	25	132	456	825	1032	1128	938	893	582	319	84	6423
	Denver .... A	37.6	6	9	117	428	819	1035	1132	938	887	558	288	66	6283
	Denver C	40.8	0	0	90	366	714	905	1004	851	800	492	254	48	5524
	Grand Junction .... A	39.3	0	0	30	313	786	1113	1209	907	729	387	146	21	5641
	Pueblo............................... A	40.4	0	0	54	326	750	986	1085	871	772	429	174	15	5462
Conn.	Bridgeport .... A	39.9	0	0	66	307	615	986	1079	966	853	510	208	27	5617
	Hartford .... A	37.3	0	12	117	394	714	1101	1190	1042	908	519	205	33	6235
	New Haven .... A	39.0	0	12	87	347	648	1011	1097	991	871	543	245	45	5897
Del.	Wilmington........................ A	42.5	0	0	51	270	588	927	980	874	735	387	112	6	4930
D.C.	Washington .... A	45.7	0	0	33	217	519	834	871	762	626	288	74	0	4224
Fla.	Apalachicola...................... C	61.2	0	0	0	16	153	319	347	260	180	33	0	0	1308
	Daytona Beach................... A	64.5	0	0	0	0	75	211	248	190	140	15	0	0	879
	Fort Myers .... A	68.6	0	0	0	0	24	109	146	101	62	0	0	0	442
	Jacksonville .... A	61.9	0	0	0	12	144	310	332	246	174	21	0	0	1239
	Key West .... A	73.1	0	0	0	0	0	28	40	31	9	0	0	0	108
	Lakeland........................... C	66.7	0	0	0	0	57	164	195	146	99	0	0	0	661
	Miami .... A	71.1	0	0	0	0	0	65	74	56	19	0	0	0	214

[a] Data for United States cities from a publication of the United States Weather Bureau, *Monthly Normals of Temperature, Precipitation and Heating Degree Days,* 1962, are for the period 1931 to 1960 inclusive. These data also include information from the 1963 revisions to this publication, where available.
[b] Data for airport stations, A, and city stations, C, are both given where available.
[d] For period October to April, inclusive.

Table 3-35. (Reprinted with permission from the *1976 Systems Volume, ASHRAE HANDBOOK & Product Directory)*

State	Station	Avg. Winter Temp[d]	July	Aug.	Sept.	Oct.	Nov.	Dec.	Jan.	Feb.	Mar.	Apr.	May	June	Yearly Total
Fla. (Cont'd)	Miami Beach C	72.5	0	0	0	0	0	40	56	36	9	0	0	0	141
	Orlando................... A	65.7	0	0	0	0	72	198	220	165	105	6	0	0	766
	Pensacola .... A	60.4	0	0	0	19	195	353	400	277	183	36	0	0	1463
	Tallahassee .... A	60.1	0	0	0	28	198	360	375	286	202	36	0	0	1485
	Tampa...................... A	66.4	0	0	0	0	60	171	202	148	102	0	0	0	683
	West Palm Beach.......... A	68.4	0	0	0	0	6	65	87	64	31	0	0	0	253
Ga.	Athens .... A	51.8	0	0	12	115	405	632	642	529	431	141	22	0	2929
	Atlanta .... A	51.7	0	0	18	124	417	648	636	518	428	147	25	0	2961
	Augusta .... A	54.5	0	0	0	78	333	552	549	445	350	90	0	0	2397
	Columbus................. A	54.8	0	0	0	87	333	543	552	434	338	96	0	0	2383
	Macon...................... A	56.2	0	0	0	71	297	502	505	403	295	63	0	0	2136
	Rome .... A	49.9	0	0	24	161	474	701	710	577	468	177	34	0	3326
	Savannah .... A	57.8	0	0	0	47	246	437	437	353	254	45	0	0	1819
	Thomasville C	60.0	0	0	0	25	198	366	394	305	208	33	0	0	1529
Hawaii	Lihue....................... A	72.7	0	0	0	0	0	0	0	0	0	0	0	0	0
	Honolulu.................. A	74.2	0	0	0	0	0	0	0	0	0	0	0	0	0
	Hilo........................ A	71.9	0	0	0	0	0	0	0	0	0	0	0	0	0
Idaho	Boise .... A	39.7	0	0	132	415	792	1017	1113	854	722	438	245	81	5809
	Lewiston .... A	41.0	0	0	123	403	756	933	1063	815	694	426	239	90	5542
	Pocatello .... A	34.8	0	0	172	493	900	1166	1324	1058	905	555	319	141	7033
Ill.	Cairo C	47.9	0	0	36	164	513	791	856	680	539	195	47	0	3821
	Chicago (O'Hare)........... A	35.8	0	12	117	381	807	1166	1265	1086	939	534	260	72	6639
	Chicago (Midway) .... A	37.5	0	0	81	326	753	1113	1209	1044	890	480	211	48	6155
	Chicago.................... C	38.9	0	0	66	279	705	1051	1150	1000	868	489	226	48	5882
	Moline .... A	36.4	0	9	99	335	774	1181	1314	1100	918	450	189	39	6408
	Peoria .... A	38.1	0	6	87	326	759	1113	1218	1025	849	426	183	33	6025
	Rockford................... A	34.8	6	9	114	400	837	1221	1333	1137	961	516	236	60	6830
	Springfield................ A	40.6	0	0	72	291	696	1023	1135	935	769	354	136	18	5429
Ind.	Evansville .... A	45.0	0	0	66	220	606	896	955	767	620	237	68	0	4435
	Fort Wayne .... A	37.3	0	9	105	378	783	1135	1178	1028	890	471	189	39	6205
	Indianapolis .... A	39.6	0	0	90	316	723	1051	1113	949	809	432	177	39	5699
	South Bend................ A	36.6	0	6	111	372	777	1125	1221	1070	933	525	239	60	6439
Iowa	Burlington .... A	37.6	0	0	93	322	768	1135	1259	1042	859	426	177	33	6114
	Des Moines .... A	35.5	0	6	96	363	828	1225	1370	1137	915	438	180	30	6588
	Dubuque .... A	32.7	12	31	156	450	906	1287	1420	1204	1026	546	260	78	7376
	Sioux City................. A	34.0	0	9	108	369	867	1240	1435	1198	989	483	214	39	6951
	Waterloo.................. A	32.6	12	19	138	428	909	1296	1460	1221	1023	531	229	54	7320
Kans.	Concordia .... A	40.4	0	0	57	276	705	1023	1163	935	781	372	149	18	5479
	Dodge City................ A	42.5	0	0	33	251	666	939	1051	840	719	354	124	9	4986
	Goodland .... A	37.8	0	6	81	381	810	1073	1166	955	884	507	236	42	6141
	Topeka .... A	41.7	0	0	57	270	672	980	1122	893	722	330	124	12	5182
	Wichita .... A	44.2	0	0	33	229	618	905	1023	804	645	270	87	6	4620
Ky.	Covington .... A	41.4	0	0	75	291	669	983	1035	893	756	390	149	24	5265
	Lexington .... A	43.8	0	0	54	239	609	902	946	818	685	325	105	0	4683
	Louisville .... A	44.0	0	0	54	248	609	890	930	818	682	315	105	9	4660
La.	Alexandria .... A	57.5	0	0	0	56	273	431	471	361	260	69	0	0	1921
	Baton Rouge .... A	59.8	0	0	0	31	216	369	409	294	208	33	0	0	1560
	Lake Charles .... A	60.5	0	0	0	19	210	341	381	274	195	39	0	0	1459
	New Orleans............... A	61.0	0	0	0	19	192	322	363	258	192	39	0	0	1385
	New Orleans............... C	61.8	0	0	0	12	165	291	344	241	177	24	0	0	1254
	Shreveport .... A	56.2	0	0	0	47	297	477	552	426	304	81	0	0	2184
Me.	Caribou.................... A	24.4	78	115	336	682	1044	1535	1690	1470	1308	858	468	183	9767
	Portland .... A	33.0	12	53	195	508	807	1215	1339	1182	1042	675	372	111	7511
Md.	Baltimore .... A	43.7	0	0	48	264	585	905	936	820	679	327	90	0	4654
	Baltimore C	46.2	0	0	27	189	486	806	859	762	629	288	65	0	4111
	Frederich .... A	42.0	0	0	66	307	624	955	995	876	741	384	127	12	5087
Mass.	Boston..................... A	40.0	0	9	60	316	603	983	1088	972	846	513	208	36	5634
	Nantucket .... A	40.2	12	22	93	332	573	896	992	941	896	621	384	129	5891
	Pittsfield .... A	32.6	25	59	219	524	831	1231	1339	1196	1063	660	326	105	7578
	Worcester .... A	34.7	6	34	147	450	774	1172	1271	1123	998	612	304	78	6969

Continued on next page

Table 3-35 continued

State	Station	Avg. Winter Temp^d	July	Aug.	Sept.	Oct.	Nov.	Dec.	Jan.	Feb.	Mar.	Apr.	May	June	Yearly Total
Mich.	Alpena .... A	29.7	68	105	273	580	912	1268	1404	1299	1218	777	446	156	8506
	Detroit (City) .... A	37.2	0	0	87	360	738	1088	1181	1058	936	522	220	42	6232
	Detroit (Wayne) .... A	37.1	0	0	96	353	738	1088	1194	1061	933	534	239	57	6293
	Detroit (Willow Run) .... A	37.2	0	0	90	357	750	1104	1190	1053	921	519	229	45	6258
	Escanaba........................ C	29.6	59	87	243	539	924	1293	1445	1296	1203	777	456	159	8481
	Flint .... A	33.1	16	40	159	465	843	1212	1330	1198	1066	639	319	90	7377
	Grand Rapids.................. A	34.9	9	28	135	434	804	1147	1259	1134	1011	579	279	75	6894
	Lansing.......................... A	34.8	6	22	138	431	813	1163	1262	1142	1011	579	273	69	6909
	Marquette....................... C	30.2	59	81	240	527	936	1268	1411	1268	1187	771	468	177	8393
	Muskegon....................... A	36.0	12	28	120	400	762	1088	1209	1100	995	594	310	78	6696
	Sault Ste. Marie .... A	27.7	96	105	279	580	951	1367	1525	1380	1277	810	477	201	9048
Minn.	Duluth .... A	23.4	71	109	330	632	1131	1581	1745	1518	1355	840	490	198	10000
	Minneapolis .... A	28.3	22	31	189	505	1014	1454	1631	1380	1166	621	288	81	8382
	Rochester .... A	28.8	25	34	186	474	1005	1438	1593	1366	1150	630	301	93	8295
Miss.	Jackson .... A	55.7	0	0	0	65	315	502	546	414	310	87	0	0	2239
	Meridian .... A	55.4	0	0	0	81	339	518	543	417	310	81	0	0	2289
	Vicksburg C	56.9	0	0	0	53	279	462	512	384	282	69	0	0	2041
Mo.	Columbia .... A	42.3	0	0	54	251	651	967	1076	874	716	324	121	12	5046
	Kansas City .... A	43.9	0	0	39	220	612	905	1032	818	682	294	109	0	4711
	St. Joseph .... A	40.3	0	6	60	285	708	1039	1172	949	769	348	133	15	5484
	St. Louis........................ A	43.1	0	0	60	251	627	936	1026	848	704	312	121	15	4900
	St. Louis........................ C	44.8	0	0	36	202	576	884	977	801	651	270	87	0	4484
	Springfield...................... A	44.5	0	0	45	223	600	877	973	781	660	291	105	6	4900
Mont.	Billings .... A	34.5	6	15	186	487	897	1135	1296	1100	970	570	285	102	7049
	Glasgow .... A	26.4	31	47	270	608	1104	1466	1711	1439	1187	648	335	150	8996
	Great Falls .... A	32.8	28	53	258	543	921	1169	1349	1154	1063	642	384	186	7750
	Havre .... A	28.1	28	53	306	595	1065	1367	1584	1364	1181	657	338	162	8700
	Havre C	29.8	19	37	252	539	1014	1321	1528	1305	1116	612	304	135	8182
	Helena............................ A	31.1	31	59	294	601	1002	1265	1438	1170	1042	651	381	195	8129
	Kalispell .... A	31.4	50	99	321	654	1020	1240	1401	1134	1029	639	397	207	8191
	Miles City .... A	31.2	6	6	174	502	972	1296	1504	1252	1057	579	276	99	7723
	Missoula .... A	31.5	34	74	303	651	1035	1287	1420	1120	970	621	391	219	8125
Neb.	Grand Island .... A	36.0	0	6	108	381	834	1172	1314	1089	908	462	211	45	6530
	Lincoln C	38.8	0	6	75	301	726	1066	1237	1016	834	402	171	30	5864
	Norfolk .... A	34.0	9	0	111	397	873	1234	1414	1179	983	498	233	48	6979
	North Platte.................... A	35.5	0	6	123	440	885	1166	1271	1039	930	519	248	57	6684
	Omaha .... A	35.6	0	12	105	357	828	1175	1355	1126	939	465	208	42	6612
	Scottsbluff...................... A	35.9	0	0	138	459	876	1128	1231	1008	921	552	285	75	6673
	Valentine........................ A	32.6	9	12	165	493	942	1237	1395	1176	1045	579	288	84	7425
Nev.	Elko .... A	34.0	9	34	225	561	924	1197	1314	1036	911	621	409	192	7433
	Ely .... A	33.1	28	43	234	592	939	1184	1308	1075	977	672	456	225	7733
	Las Vegas .... A	53.5	0	0	0	78	387	617	688	487	335	111	6	0	2709
	Reno .... A	39.3	43	87	204	490	801	1026	1073	823	729	510	357	189	6332
	Winnemucca.................... A	36.7	0	34	210	536	876	1091	1172	916	837	573	363	153	6761
N.H.	Concord .... A	33.0	6	50	177	505	822	1240	1358	1184	1032	636	298	75	7383
	Mt. Washington Obsv..............	15.2	493	536	720	1057	1341	1742	1820	1663	1652	1260	930	603	13817
N.J.	Atlantic City .... A	43.2	0	0	39	251	549	880	936	848	741	420	133	15	4812
	Newark .... A	42.8	0	0	30	248	573	921	983	876	729	381	118	0	4589
	Trenton........................... C	42.4	0	0	57	264	576	924	989	885	753	399	121	12	4980
N. M.	Albuquerque.................... A	45.0	0	0	12	229	642	868	930	703	595	288	81	0	4348
	Clayton .... A	42.0	0	6	66	310	699	899	986	812	747	429	183	21	5158
	Raton .... A	38.1	9	28	126	431	825	1048	1116	904	834	543	301	63	6228
	Roswell .... A	47.5	0	0	18	202	573	806	840	641	481	201	31	0	3793
	Silver City .... A	48.0	0	0	6	183	525	729	791	605	518	261	87	0	3705
N.Y.	Albany .... A	34.6	0	19	138	440	777	1194	1311	1156	992	564	239	45	6875
	Albany C	37.2	0	9	102	375	699	1104	1218	1072	908	498	186	30	6201
	Binghamton .... A	33.9	22	65	201	471	810	1184	1277	1154	1045	645	313	99	7286
	Binghamton C	36.6	0	28	141	406	732	1107	1190	1081	949	543	229	45	6451
	Buffalo .... A	34.5	19	37	141	440	777	1156	1256	1145	1039	645	329	78	7062
	New York (Cent. Park)........ C	42.8	0	0	30	233	540	902	986	885	760	408	118	9	4871
	New York (La Guardia) ...... A	43.1	0	0	27	223	528	887	973	879	750	414	124	6	4811

State	Station	Avg. Winter Temp[d]	July	Aug.	Sept.	Oct.	Nov.	Dec.	Jan.	Feb.	Mar.	Apr.	May	June	Yearly Total
	New York (Kennedy) .... A	41.4	0	0	36	248	564	933	1029	935	815	480	167	12	5219
	Rochester .... A	35.4	9	31	126	415	747	1125	1234	1123	1014	597	279	48	6748
	Schenectady C	35.4	0	22	123	422	756	1159	1283	1131	970	543	211	30	6650
	Syracuse .... A	35.2	6	28	132	415	744	1153	1271	1140	1004	570	248	45	6756
N. C.	Asheville...................... C	46.7	0	0	48	245	555	775	784	683	592	273	87	0	4042
	Cape Hatteras	53.3	0	0	0	78	273	521	580	518	440	177	25	0	2612
	Charlotte...................... A	50.4	0	0	6	124	438	691	691	582	481	156	22	0	3191
	Greensboro .... A	47.5	0	0	33	192	513	778	784	672	552	234	47	0	3805
	Raleigh .... A	49.4	0	0	21	164	450	716	725	616	487	180	34	0	3393
	Wilmington..................... A	54.6	0	0	0	74	291	521	546	462	357	96	0	0	2347
	Winston-Salem .... A	48.4	0	0	21	171	483	747	753	652	524	207	37	0	3595
N. D.	Bismarck....................... A	26.6	34	28	222	577	1083	1463	1708	1442	1203	645	329	117	8851
	Devils Lake C	22.4	40	53	273	642	1191	1634	1872	1579	1345	753	381	138	9901
	Fargo .... A	24.8	28	37	219	574	1107	1569	1789	1520	1262	690	332	99	9226
	Williston...................... A	25.2	31	43	261	601	1122	1513	1758	1473	1262	681	357	141	9243
Ohio	Akron-Canton .... A	38.1	0	9	96	381	726	1070	1138	1016	871	489	202	39	6037
	Cincinnati C	45.1	0	0	39	208	558	862	915	790	642	294	96	6	4410
	Cleveland .... A	37.2	9	25	105	384	738	1088	1159	1047	918	552	260	66	6351
	Columbus .... A	39.7	0	6	84	347	714	1039	1088	949	809	426	171	27	5660
	Columbus C	41.5	0	0	57	285	651	977	1032	902	760	396	136	15	5211
	Dayton .... A	39.8	0	6	78	310	696	1045	1097	955	809	429	167	30	5622
	Mansfield .... A	36.9	9	22	114	397	768	1110	1169	1042	924	543	245	60	6403
	Sandusky C	39.1	0	6	66	313	684	1032	1107	991	868	495	198	36	5796
	Toledo......................... A	36.4	0	16	117	406	792	1138	1200	1056	924	543	242	60	6494
	Youngstown .... A	36.8	6	19	120	412	771	1104	1169	1047	921	540	248	60	6417
Okla.	Oklahoma City.................. A	48.3	0	0	15	164	498	766	868	664	527	189	34	0	3725
	Tulsa.......................... A	47.7	0	0	18	158	522	787	893	683	539	213	47	0	3860
Ore.	Astoria .... A	45.6	146	130	210	375	561	679	753	622	636	480	363	231	5186
	Burns C	35.9	12	37	210	515	867	1113	1246	988	856	570	366	177	6957
	Eugene .... A	45.6	34	34	129	366	585	719	803	627	589	426	279	135	4726
	Meacham .... A•	34.2	84	124	288	580	918	1091	1209	1005	983	726	527	339	7874
	Medford .... A	43.2	0	0	78	372	678	871	918	697	642	432	242	78	5008
	Pendleton .... A	42.6	0	0	111	350	711	884	1017	773	617	396	205	63	5127
	Portland .... A	45.6	25	28	114	335	597	735	825	644	586	396	245	105	4635
	Portland C	47.4	12	16	75	267	534	679	769	594	536	351	198	78	4109
	Roseburg....................... A	46.3	22	16	105	329	567	713	766	608	570	405	267	123	4491
	Salem .... A	45.4	37	31	111	338	594	729	822	647	611	417	273	144	4754
Pa.	Allentown...................... A	38.9	0	0	90	353	693	1045	1116	1002	849	471	167	24	5810
	Erie .... A	36.8	0	25	102	391	714	1063	1169	1081	973	585	288	60	6451
	Harrisburg .... A	41.2	0	0	63	298	648	992	1045	907	766	396	124	12	5251
	Philadelphia .... A	41.8	0	0	60	297	620	965	1016	889	747	392	118	40	5144
	Philadelphia C	44.5	0	0	30	205	513	856	924	823	691	351	93	0	4486
	Pittsburgh .... A	38.4	0	9	105	375	726	1063	1119	1002	874	480	195	39	5987
	Pittsburgh C	42.2	0	0	60	291	615	930	983	885	763	390	124	12	5053
	Reading........................ C	42.4	0	0	54	257	597	939	1001	885	735	372	105	0	4945
	Scranton .... A	37.2	0	19	132	434	762	1104	1156	1028	893	498	195	33	6254
	Williamsport................... A	38.5	0	9	111	375	717	1073	1122	1002	856	468	177	24	5934
R. I.	Block Island .... A	40.1	0	16	78	307	594	902	1020	955	877	612	344	99	5804
	Providence .... A	38.8	0	16	96	372	660	1023	1110	988	868	534	236	51	5954
S. C.	Charleston .... A	56.4	0	0	0	59	282	471	487	389	291	54	0	0	2033
	Charleston C	57.9	0	0	0	34	210	425	443	367	273	42	0	0	1794
	Columbia .... A	54.0	0	0	0	84	345	577	570	470	357	81	0	0	2484
	Florence .... A	54.5	0	0	0	78	315	552	552	459	347	84	0	0	2387
	Greenville-Spartenburg .... A	51.6	0	0	6	121	399	651	660	546	446	132	19	0	2980
S. D.	Huron .... A	28.8	9	12	165	508	1014	1432	1628	1355	1125	600	288	87	8223
	Rapid City .... A	33.4	22	12	165	481	897	1172	1333	1145	1051	615	326	126	7345
	Sioux Falls .... A	30.6	19	25	168	462	972	1361	1544	1285	1082	573	270	78	7839
Tenn.	Bristol........................ A	46.2	0	0	51	236	573	828	828	700	598	261	68	0	4143
	Chattanooga .... A	50.3	0	0	18	143	468	698	722	577	453	150	25	0	3254
	Knoxville .... A	49.2	0	0	30	171	489	725	732	613	493	198	43	0	3494
	Memphis........................ A	50.5	0	0	18	130	447	698	729	585	456	147	22	0	3232

Continued on next page

Table 3-35 continued

State	Station	Avg. Winter Temp[d]	July	Aug.	Sept.	Oct.	Nov.	Dec.	Jan.	Feb.	Mar.	Apr.	May	June	Yearly Total
	Memphis C	51.6	0	0	12	102	396	648	710	568	434	129	16	0	3015
	Nashville .... A	48.9	0	0	30	158	495	732	778	644	512	189	40	0	3578
	Oak Ridge C	47.7	0	0	39	192	531	772	778	669	552	228	56	0	3817
Tex.	Abilene .... A	53.9	0	0	0	99	366	586	642	470	347	114	0	0	2624
	Amarillo .... A	47.0	0	0	18	205	570	797	877	664	546	252	56	0	3985
	Austin .... A	59.1	0	0	0	31	225	388	468	325	223	51	0	0	1711
	Brownsville .... A	67.7	0	0	0	0	66	149	205	106	74	0	0	0	600
	Corpus Christi .... A	64.6	0	0	0	0	120	220	291	174	109	0	0	0	914
	Dallas .... A	55.3	0	0	0	62	321	524	601	440	319	90	6	0	2363
	El Paso .... A	52.9	0	0	0	84	414	648	685	445	319	105	0	0	2700
	Fort Worth .... A	55.1	0	0	0	65	324	536	614	448	319	99	0	0	2405
	Galveston .... A	62.2	0	0	0	6	147	276	360	263	189	33	0	0	1274
	Galveston C	62.0	0	0	0	0	138	270	350	258	189	30	0	0	1235
	Houston .... A	61.0	0	0	0	6	183	307	384	288	192	36	0	0	1396
	Houston C	62.0	0	0	0	0	165	288	363	258	174	30	0	0	1278
	Laredo .... A	66.0	0	0	0	0	105	217	267	134	74	0	0	0	797
	Lubbock .... A	48.8	0	0	18	174	513	744	800	613	484	201	31	0	3578
	Midland .... A	53.8	0	0	0	87	381	592	651	468	322	90	0	0	2591
	Port Arthur .... A	60.5	0	0	0	22	207	329	384	274	192	39	0	0	1447
	San Angelo .... A	56.0	0	0	0	68	318	536	567	412	288	66	0	0	2255
	San Antonio .... A	60.1	0	0	0	31	204	363	428	286	195	39	0	0	1546
	Victoria .... A	62.7	0	0	0	6	150	270	344	230	152	21	0	0	1173
	Waco .... A	57.2	0	0	0	43	270	456	536	389	270	66	0	0	2030
	Wichita Falls .... A	53.0	0	0	0	99	381	632	698	518	378	120	6	0	2832
Utah	Milford .... A	36.5	0	0	99	443	867	1141	1252	988	822	519	279	87	6497
	Salt Lake City .... A	38.4	0	0	81	419	849	1082	1172	910	763	459	233	84	6052
	Wendover .... A	39.1	0	0	48	372	822	1091	1178	902	729	408	177	51	5778
Vt.	Burlington .... A	29.4	28	65	207	539	891	1349	1513	1333	1187	714	353	90	8269
Va.	Cape Henry C	50.0	0	0	0	112	360	645	694	633	536	246	53	0	3279
	Lynchburg .... A	46.0	0	0	51	223	540	822	849	731	605	267	78	0	4166
	Norfolk .... A	49.2	0	0	0	136	408	698	738	655	533	216	37	0	3421
	Richmond .... A	47.3	0	0	36	214	495	784	815	703	546	219	53	0	3865
	Roanoke .... A	46.1	0	0	51	229	549	825	834	722	614	261	65	0	4150
Wash.	Olympia .... A	44.2	68	71	198	422	636	753	834	675	645	450	307	177	5236
	Seattle-Tacoma .... A	44.2	56	62	162	391	633	750	828	678	657	474	295	159	5145
	Seattle C	46.9	50	47	129	329	543	657	738	599	577	396	242	117	4424
	Spokane .... A	36.5	9	25	168	493	879	1082	1231	980	834	531	288	135	6655
	Walla Walla C	43.8	0	0	87	310	681	843	986	745	589	342	177	45	4805
	Yakima .... A	39.1	0	12	144	450	828	1039	1163	868	713	435	220	69	5941
W. Va.	Charleston .... A	44.8	0	0	63	254	591	865	880	770	648	300	96	9	4476
	Elkins .... A	40.1	9	25	135	400	729	992	1008	896	791	444	198	48	5675
	Huntington .... A	45.0	0	0	63	257	585	856	880	764	636	294	99	12	4446
	Parkersburg C	43.5	0	0	60	264	606	905	942	826	691	339	115	6	4754
Wisc.	Green Bay .... A	30.3	28	50	174	484	924	1333	1494	1313	1141	654	335	99	8029
	La Crosse .... A	31.5	12	19	153	437	924	1339	1504	1277	1070	540	245	69	7589
	Madison .... A	30.9	25	40	174	474	930	1330	1473	1274	1113	618	310	102	7863
	Milwaukee .... A	32.6	43	47	174	471	876	1252	1376	1193	1054	642	372	135	7635
Wyo.	Casper .... A	33.4	6	16	192	524	942	1169	1290	1084	1020	657	381	129	7410
	Cheyenne .... A	34.2	28	37	219	543	909	1085	1212	1042	1026	702	428	150	7381
	Lander .... A	31.4	6	19	204	555	1020	1299	1417	1145	1017	654	381	153	7870
	Sheridan .... A	32.5	25	31	219	539	948	1200	1355	1154	1051	642	366	150	7680

heating equipment efficiency rating of 70 percent or 0.70. The operating heat loss from the house is 61,170 Btu/hr (Table 3-34). $H_L \times D \times 24$ equals $61,170 \times 6756 \times 24 = 9,918,348,480$. Then, $\Delta t \times \epsilon \times V$ equals $85 \times 0.70 \times 140,000 = 8,330,000$. Then 9,918,348,480 divided by 8,330,000 = 1190.68. Then C_D (from Table 3-36) multiplied by C_F (from Table 3-37) equals 0.64×1.56 (assumed) $= 0.9984$. This multiplied by 1190.68 equals 1188.77, or approximately 1189 gallons of No. 2 fuel oil required for the period. The total cost for fuel for the season is found by multiplying the price per gallon times the gallonage needed; at 95 cents per gallon, for example, the cost would be $1129.55. Other types of fuels can be calculated for in the same fashion, including electric resistance type equipment. For electric systems, the computations are often made directly in watts of electrical energy; to convert Btu/hr into watts, simply divide the number of Btu/hr by 3.413 (or, 1 Btu/hr = 0.293 w). This can then be converted to kwh by dividing watts by 1000 (1000 w = 1 kwh).

Similarly, *U*-factors can be expressed as *W*-factors, which denote heat flow in watts per square foot instead of Btu/hr. The conversion factor is $W = 0.293\ U$. Heat pumps, however, should be calculated by a rather complex procedure called the bin method, which we will not investigate here.

In cases where auxiliary equipment such as pumps or blowers are a part of the heating equipment in fuel-fired heating systems, the electrical energy required to operate the auxiliary equipment is properly considered a part of the total energy required for heating. This energy consumption is added to the fuel consumption for a grand total, and can be determined by the formula from the *1976 Systems Volume, ASHRAE HANDBOOK & Product Directory:*

$$E = (KW)\ (F)/S$$

where

E = energy required for auxiliaries, kilowatt hours

KW = connected load of fans or pumps

F = fuel estimate for annual heating season

S = size of heating unit in fuel units input

Heat Loss vs Degree-Days Interim Factor c_D

Outdoor Design Temp, F	−20	−10	0	+10	+20
Factor C_D	0.57	0.64	0.71	0.79	0.89

Table 3–36. (Reprinted with permission from the *1976 Systems Volume, ASHRAE HANDBOOK & Product Directory*)

Part-Load Correction Factor for Fuel-Fired Equipment[a]

Percent oversizing	0	20	40	60	80
Factor C_F	1.36	1.56	1.79	2.04	2.32

[a] Because equipment performance at extremely low loads is highly variable, it is strongly recommended that the values not be extrapolated.

Table 3–37. (Reprinted with permission from the *1976 Systems Volume, ASHRAE HANDBOOK & Product Directory*)

Energy Conservation Effects

The above calculations assume a steady indoor design temperature and ignore possible fuel/energy savings that might accrue from the use of various heat-conserving tactics, some of which have been mentioned earlier. And there are, of course, a great many possibilities along these lines, some effective and some a good deal less so. In this regard, comments made in chapter 43 of the *1976 Systems Volume, ASHRAE HANDBOOK & Product Directory* are worth quoting directly:

No simple, valid procedures have been developed for evaluating the effects of suggested residential energy conservation practices. Those suggestions that reduce heat loss per degree difference, such as storm windows or increased insulation, may be approximated using the modified degree-day procedure. Several studies indicate that reduction of thermostat set point may reduce fuel consumption by approximately 3% per degree. Reduced appliance and lighting usage will lower energy requirements but increase heating needs in winter. Evaluation of other suggestions is not yet on a base sufficiently valid to draw quantitative conclusions.

In other words, it is conservative practice to ignore those energy-saving practices that cannot be quantitatively entered into the calculations. This will give the overall estimate a certain amount of leeway, which it may well need if the house is damp the first year, or if a particular winter is unusually cold.

It should further be realized that this outline of estimating fuel/energy costs assumes ideal conditions. Actually there are several variables that may make these "book calculations" more or less erroneous. They range from differing heating plant efficiencies to different levels of relative humidity maintained in the house; from varying qualities of construction workmanship to wide variations in air infiltration because of opened doors and windows. Few of the components that are employed in the entire gamut of thermal efficiency and heat loss calculations are invariably steady-state. A scientifically accurate estimate would be possible only for a scientifically controlled building. No house is that.

Values of Various Fuels

Fuel	Unit	Btu
No. 2 oil	gal	140,000
Natural gas	cu ft	1,000
Propane gas	gal	91,500
Butane gas	gal	102,000
Coal, anthra.	ton	25.4 mil
Coal, bitum.	ton	26.2 mil
Lignite	ton	14.0 mil
Kerosene	gal	135,000
Electricity	Kwh	3,412
Wood	Cord	12–24 mil

Table 3–38.

Chapter 4

Principles of Moisture Control: Winter

In the science of chemistry, water is known as almost the most corrosive of all natural compounds. It will, sooner or later, decompose practically every terrestrial substance. Protective membranes, like polyethylene films or human skins, will stave off the deteriorating fury of water, but not indefinitely. Indeed, water is both essential to life, and, its eventual solvent.

The house has always offered relative dryness as well as an environment that can be artificially heated against the cold. Heat is not only the natural enemy of cold; in many of man's artificial surroundings it is also a formidable opponent of dampness, particularly in cold climates. In hot, moist regions, unfortunately, heat and water vapor are often additive, for the peculiar reason that the warmer the air is, the more moisture it can hold per cubic foot. Thus, the exquisitely miserable environments of hot-humid areas such as New Orleans—and, indeed, New York city or Chicago on a sweltering summer day.

However, in regions with cold winters, heat usually has the effect of decreasing humidity within an artificially warm space. Heated, humid spaces, such as in houses, lose moisture to the cold outer air because the *vapor pressure* indoors is higher than outdoors and this forces the vapor outwards.

VAPOR PRESSURE

Vapor moves from warm to cold areas because the greater quantity of moisture per cubic foot in the warm air compared with the outdoor cold air creates a vapor pressure differential that forces the moisture outward, regardless of the purely *thermal* barriers (i.e., building materials, including insulation) that compose the structural cross section. And as the invisible vapor moves outward, its temperature drops toward the low of the outdoor unheated space. During this reduction, the vapor will meet a crucial temperature at which it will condense into visible water droplets. This temperature, which is a highly irregular variable and which depends upon various internal and external conditions, is known as the *dewpoint;* this is the point at which the air containing the moisture becomes *saturated*. It cannot hold any more water in vapor form but changes it by condensation into a liquid.

A moment's thought will make it clear that many thermal insulations, which are constructed so that heat is impeded in its flow through them by millions of tiny air pockets, will—unless especially protected to prevent it—provide an efficient pathway for the outflow of vapor in cold weather. And as that vapor nears the outside of the structure, it will meet the dewpoint, condense into water, and saturate the material. If the outdoor cold is especially severe, the water will change into frost or ice.

But whichever it does, we know the result: extensive damage to walls, roofs, ceilings, paint films, and the like—*particularly* in tight and well-insulated houses that have no vapor barriers. In such structures, because the heat is impeded in its outward flow but the vapor is not, the drop in temperature to and below the dewpoint often occurs well within the building cross sections and even in the insulation. In loosely built, uninsulated houses, the dewpoint often is not reached by the water vapor until it is practically outside the building, particularly when most of the vapor escapes through cracks around windows and doors. But regardless of the specifics, condensation within the structure is intolerable.

It is true that almost everyone today knows that the problem of condensation exists. But it is also true, unfortunately, that in many instances they are not familiar with the best methods of preventing it. Some, furthermore, continue to follow obsolete practices in

4-1. The frosted window is single-glazed; the clear window is double-glazed. (Pittsburgh Plate Glass Co.)

order to save a few dollars, even though they are not afforded adequate protection. This combination of lack of knowledge and unwise economy results in an ever-mounting bill for remedial measures that adds unnecessarily to costs of maintenance.

Condensation control is just as important as control against heat loss, particularly in climates with outdoor design temperatures below 10° F (Figure 4-1).

WHAT IS A HEALTHFUL INTERIOR HUMIDITY?

The solution of the problem of condensation is not primarily one of reducing interior humidity. On the contrary, moderately high humidity indoors at all times is desirable during cold weather for human comfort—and, as medical evidence increasingly shows, for human health. A too-dry atmosphere can be very uncomfortable for most people, as those who have lived in steam-heated houses or apartments well know. (We must note, however, that there are some people who find fairly dry, even arid, atmospheric conditions both comfortable and beneficial.) Worse yet, such a condition can cause, or at least encourage, various types of respiratory ailments.

Indeed, there is substantial evidence that a definite relation exists between the dryness of air in artificially heated houses and the incidence of respiratory infections. Numerous tests and studies along these lines have been conducted. Some, for example, involved two identical buildings or rooms, with identical heating and ventilating systems, and subject to the same outdoor climate. The indoor temperature was kept constant, while the relative humidity in one space ranged from 20 to 40 percent, and in the other from 30 to 50 percent (the relative humidity was kept below 50 percent in all cases). The essential results of the tests were that the occurrences of upper respiratory infections were notably less for those people working or playing in the higher relative humidities than in the lower. The assumption was that the relative humidity was in large part responsible, though related factors such as change of dust level might also have played a part. But since humidity influences so many physiological functions of the respiratory tract, it seems logical that humidity is probably a significant factor in respiratory health.

The part that relative humidity plays in other diseases and illnesses is less certain and considerably less well known. There is little question that humidity can play a major role in viral and bacterial survival/infectivity, however. Studies of meningitis, poliomyelitis, cholera, and smallpox, for instance, indicate that humidity is an important factor. But the problem is that high humidities are favorable for cholera and poliomyelitis, while low humidity favors smallpox and meningitis. Thus, insofar as humidification of our homes is concerned, we are faced with a Catch-22 situation, where neither high nor low humidity can be specifically chosen as being the best course of action. In all probability, until or unless conclusive results from various experimentations and testing programs elicit specific and important guidelines for interior humidification, we shall proceed along our present course.

But while you cannot abolish respiratory infections, the most common of which is the cold, by maintaining a humidity of around 50 percent, statistically you should at least be able to decrease both their incidence and their severity. Furthermore, there are the known facts about the relationship between humidity and health for such hospital inmates as premature babies (very high humidity), post-operative patients (high), allergic people (moderately high and very clean, but upon occasions very low with little attention paid to air cleanliness in particular), and so on. That these special situations are not quite so special, that is, that they may also apply to us ordinary, cold-prone mortals, has been frequently pointed out by various luminaries in the medical profession. Comments have been made to the effect that low relative humidity may be in part responsible for respiratory diseases and perhaps for nervous disorders as well; that very low humidities are detrimental to the comfort of all subjects (an arguable point); and that there is a strong possibility that a relative humidity of as high as 70 percent in a house may be physiologically advantageous.

Very well. We must face the fact that artificial humidification of one sort or another is an excellent idea and probably is going to be used increasingly in houses as these facts become more widely known and become better verified. Why? Simply because many studies made over the years have shown that normal mean relative humidities in old houses are quite low when temperatures hover between the 0° F and 32° F mark, in the range of 10 percent to 30 percent. In more tightly built houses, the range of relative humidity is apt to be a bit higher, from around 30 percent to 40 percent (Figure 4-2). Of course, in many areas of the country the temperatures may hover around -20° F (or less) to 0° F for protracted periods of time, which is likely to depress relative humidities even further.

Thus, while it is true that tight modern construction tends to increase the mean relative humidity in houses, it still does not necessarily bring it up to the comfort level of 40 to 50 percent in cold climates. There are exceptions, of course, among those few houses that have recently been built to extremely tight tolerances, where the release of water vapor from assorted indoor activites and the installation of various types of heat-exchanging devices instead of direct outside ventilation does occasion relative humidity of fairly high levels. The first factor, the release of water vapor, has itself increased substantially over the years with the advent of various water-using appliances, our penchant for frequent bathing and showering, and like reasons. But in the main, humidification devices are obviously going to

be used more and more, to prevent the parching of the upper respiratory tract and also the drying-out and damaging of furniture and books. It is ironic that the most carefully controlled humidities (outside special areas in hospitals and manufacturing plants requiring unusually accurate humidity control) are maintained for valuable inanimate objects such as rare books and manuscripts. The range that keeps these commodities "healthy" is just about the same as that for man, i.e., 50 percent. To those who deprecate the need for higher average indoor humidities in cold weather for members of the human race, the idea seems to be that people are replaceable but rare books are not.

If there is any delusion left that humidity levels have little or no effect on human health, it is dispelled by the fact that steam-producing devices are almost invariably used to alleviate the discomforts (and often hazards to life) resulting from winter infections, whether it be croup or a mere stuffed nose or a sore throat. The house in which the sufferer is forced to stay is too dry, and the old-fashioned steam kettle or the modern electric humidifier or vaporizer adds vapor to the affected passages.

Many people, not understanding the benefits of high indoor humidity, have been working on the theory that the cure for condensation difficulties (paint failure, plaster failure, impaired effectiveness of insulation, and wood decay, to name a few) is to *reduce* the moisture-producing conditions that cause them. True, in the case of unvented household appliances, from the shower in the bathroom to the clothes dryer in the laundry, the concentration of vapor is too great and should be forced outdoors through special vents. Elsewhere, however, the only way to eliminate the danger of damage caused by healthful interior humidities is to design the structure so that vapor will not get into the parts of the house where it can cause trouble; in other words, through effective vapor barriers, double glazing to control window condensation, and carefully designed spot ventilation.

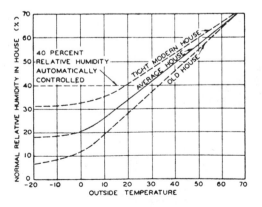

4-2. Relative humidity in dwellings. (Reprinted with permission from the *1977 Fundamentals Volume, ASHRAE HANDBOOK & Product Directory*)

How to Measure Relative Humidity and Other Properties of Air

It is often desirable to discover properties of air other than its regular temperature, the one that is read on a standard dry bulb thermometer. To make this possible, a psychrometric chart appears in Figure 4–5. Notes explaining the chart will make its use clear; all that needs further elucidation is the meaning of the term "psychrometer," and the use of the psychrometric—or hygrometric (the two are synonymous)—or *wet-bulb* thermometer.

A wet bulb thermometer is a special type in which the bulb is kept damp, either by means of a water reservoir and a cloth wick arrangement connecting the bulb to the reservoir (this is usually called a hygrometer—Figure 4-3), or else by a cloth kept damp by hand (a type called a sling psychrometer—Figure 4-4). If the air is fanned or blown over the first type, or if the second type is whirled around, a temperature will be registered that is affected by the actual amount of water vapor in the air. If *any two* properties of air are known, such as wet-bulb and dry-bulb temperatures, any other property of the air can be found on the psychrometric chart.

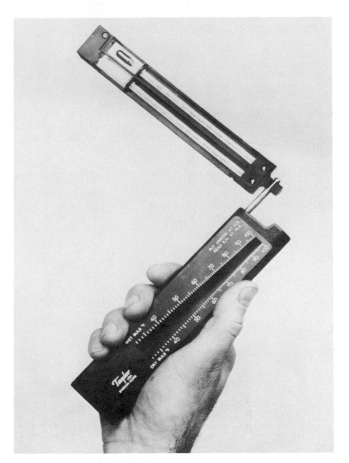

4–4. Sling psychrometer. (Courtesy, Taylor Instrument, Consumer Products Division, Sybron Corporation)

WHAT CONSTITUTES WINTER COMFORT?

In order to establish a standard of indoor temperature-humidity comfort, the ASHRAE has developed, through research running as far back as the early 1920's, a basic *comfort chart,* which is shown in Figure 4-6. The chart is applicable for all altitudes from sea level to about 7000 feet and for the most common special case for indoor thermal environments, where the mean radiant temperature is approximately equal to dry-bulb air temperature and the air velocity is less than 45 feet per minute.

Human comfort is, of course, at least partly a subjective matter: Not everybody is comfortable under identical conditions. The ASHRAE's experts have tested thousands of people over the years to determine optimum comfort levels at various indoor dry- and wet-bulb temperatures. The results, in percentages of people comfortable at various dry- and wet-bulb combinations, are shown in the comfort chart.

Effective Temperatures

The fine lines that rise vertically from the bottom of the chart (Figure 4-6) represent the dry-bulb temperature. The somewhat heavier straight lines that slant downward from left to right denote the wet-bulb

4–3. Relative humidity hygrometer. (Courtesy, Taylor Instrument, Consumer Products Division, Sybron Corporation)

EXPLANATION

If two properties of air are known, all properties may be found as follows:

DRY-BULB TEMPERATURE is read directly by following vertically down to the bottom scale.

WET-BULB TEMPERATURE (Fig. 1) is read directly at the intersection of the wet-bulb line with the 100 percent relative humidity line (saturation curve). The scale is marked along the 100 percent line.

RELATIVE HUMIDITY (Fig. 2) is read directly from the curved lines marked Relative Humidity. For a point between the lines, estimate by distance.

MOISTURE CONTENT, or Absolute Humidity (Fig. 3), is read directly from horizontal lines with scales to the right and left of the chart, and is the weight of water vapor contained in a quantity of air and water-vapor mixture which would weigh 1 lb if all water vapor were extracted.

DEW-POINT TEMPERATURE (Fig. 3) is read at the intersection of a horizontal line of given moisture content with the 100 percent relative humidity line.

TOTAL HEAT (Fig. 1) is read directly by following the wet-bulb line to the scale marked Total Heat. Total Heat refers to a quantity of air and water-vapor mixture which would weigh 1 lb if all water vapor were extracted, and includes the heat of the water vapor.

SPECIFIC VOLUME (Fig. 4) is read directly from the lines marked Cu ft per Lb of Dry Air. For points between lines, estimate by distance. Specific volume is the volume occupied by a quantity of air and water-vapor mixture which would weigh 1 lb if all water vapor were extracted.

VAPOR PRESSURE (Fig. 3) corresponding to a given moisture content is read directly from the left-hand scale marked Pressure of Water Vapor.

4-5. Psychrometric chart. (Reprinted with permission from ASHRAE)

ASHRAE PSYCHROMETRIC CHART NO. 1

NORMAL TEMPERATURE
BAROMETRIC PRESSURE 29.921 INCHES OF MERCURY
COPYRIGHT 1963
AMERICAN SOCIETY OF HEATING, REFRIGERATING AND AIR-CONDITIONING ENGINEERS, INC.

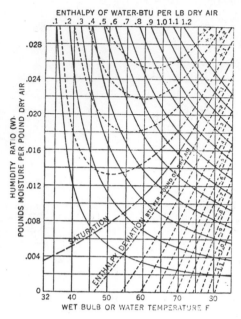

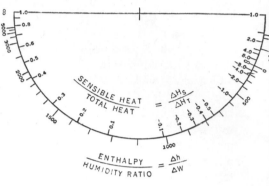

$$\frac{\text{SENSIBLE HEAT}}{\text{TOTAL HEAT}} = \frac{\Delta H_s}{\Delta H_T}$$

$$\frac{\text{ENTHALPY}}{\text{HUMIDITY RATIO}} = \frac{\Delta h}{\Delta W}$$

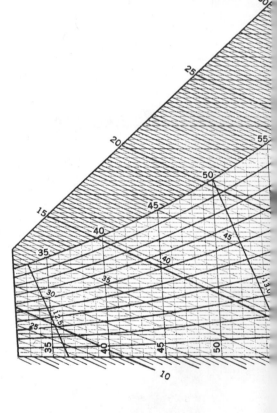

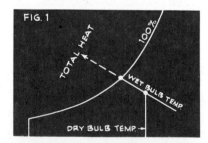

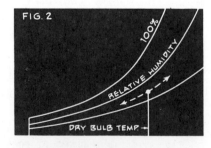

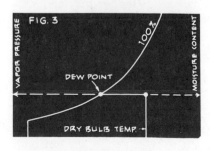

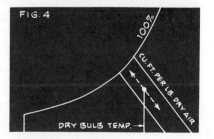

88

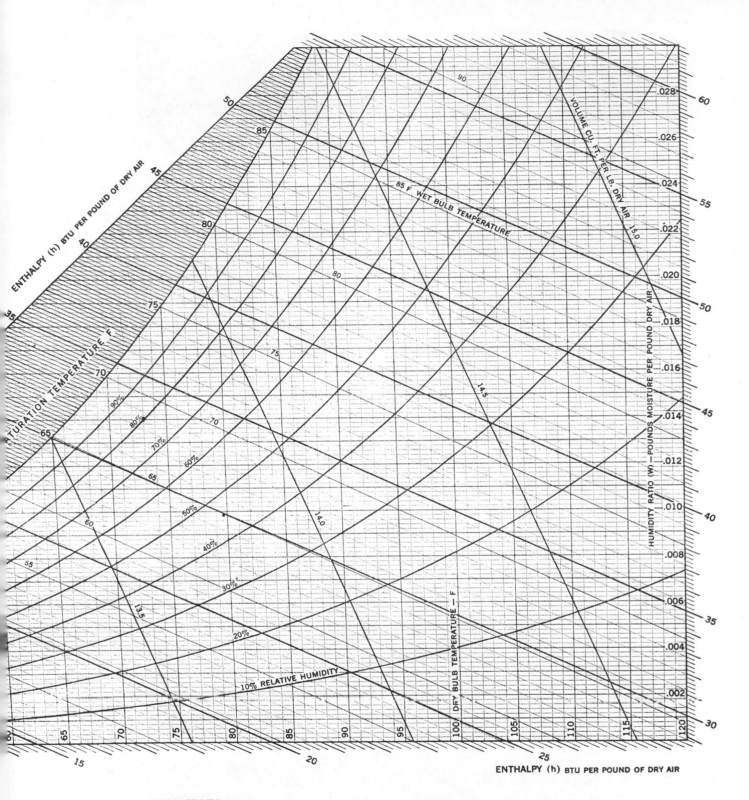

EXAMPLES

A. Air at 80 deg dry bulb and 65 deg wet bulb.

Relative Humidity............45 percent
Moisture Content............68.5 gr per lb
Dew Point...................56.8F
Total Heat (includes heat of
  1 lb of dry air and heat of
  68.5 grains of water vapor).. 30.0 Btu per lb
Specific Volume.............13.81 cu ft per lb
(Actual weight of 13.81 cu ft
= 1.0098 lb; 1 lb for the dry air
and 68.5 grains for the moisture
content, 7000 grains = 1 lb)
Vapor Pressure..............0.228 lb per sq. in.

B. Air at 75 deg wet bulb and 67 deg dew point.

Dry-bulb Temperature.........94.7F
Relative Humidity...........40.0 percent
Moisture Content............99.2 gr per lb
Total Heat..................38.5 Btu per lb
Specific Volume.............14.28 cu ft per lb
Vapor Pressure..............0.328 lb per sq in.

Continued on next page

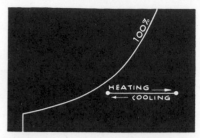

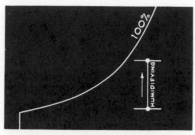

SENSIBLE HEATING AND COOLING of air are represented by a straight line between the dry-bulb temperature limits of the process, which is distinguished by a change in dry-bulb temperature and relative humidity, and by no change in vapor pressure.

HUMIDIFYING of air, with no temperature change, is represented by a straight line along the dry-bulb temperature line of the air between the moisture content limits of the process.

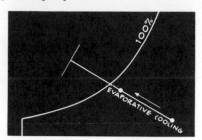

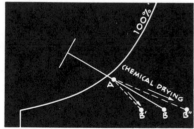

EVAPORATIVE COOLING of air, by bringing it in contact with water at a temperature equal to the wet-bulb temperature of the air, is represented by a straight line drawn along the wet-bulb temperature line of the air between the limits of the process. In this process the total heat of the air remains unchanged because the sensible heat extracted from the air is returned as latent heat.

COOLING AND DEHUMIDIFYING of air are represented by a straight line between the initial condition of the air and the point on the 100 percent line corresponding to the temperature of the cooling surface. This applies only when the surface temperature is below the initial dewpoint.

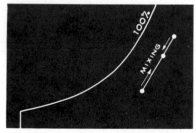

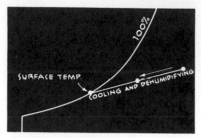

MIXING of air at one condition with air at some other condition is represented by a straight line drawn between the points representing the two air conditions. The condition of the resultant mixture will fall on this line at a point determined by the relative weights of air being mixed.

CHEMICAL DRYING of air is represented by a straight line along the wet-bulb temperature between the limits of the process (AB) only in case the drying is purely by adsorption and the drying agent does not retain much heat of vaporization. If much heat is retained, the process takes place on a line below the wet bulb (AB'). If the drying agent is soluble in water, the drying process is above (AB'') or below (AB') the wet bulb, depending on whether heat is liberated or absorbed when the agent is dissolved in water.

temperatures. The heavy solid lines that curve sharply upward from left to right are the relative humidity lines, and the heavy broken lines that slant downward represent the *effective temperatures* (ET*). The *1977 Fundamentals Volume, ASHRAE HANDBOOK & Product Directory* defines effective temperature as: "the dry-bulb temperature of a black enclosure at 50% relative humidity (sea level), in which a solid body or occupant would exchange the same heat by radiation, convection, and evaporation as in the existing non-uniform environment." Or, more understandably, "Effective Temperature . . . has been the best known and most widely used of all thermal indices. It combines the effect of dry-bulb, wet-bulb, and air movement to yield equal sensations of warmth or cold."

In the chart, for example, we find that a dry-bulb temperature of 70° F and a wet bulb of 60° F—which is about the same as 57 percent relative humidity—both cross at about the 72° F effective temperature line. But note that this line is completely outside the lined area that indicates the comfort zone that the ASHRAE's experiments have established and is set forth in the ASHRAE *Comfort Standard 55-74* (ASHRAE, New York, 1974).

But if we raise the dry-bulb temperature to about 75° F (lower the relative humidity from 57 percent to around 40 percent), the effective temperature is found to be between 76° F and 70° F, which is almost centered in the comfort zone.

The chart shows that almost all people will be comfortable with effective temperatures ranging from 73° F to 81° F. This means, approximately, from a dry-bulb temperature of 71° F and a wet-bulb of 65° F (relative humidity about 73 percent) up to a dry-bulb of 80° F and a wet-bulb under 55° F (relative humidity about 19 percent). The latter, of course, not only is drier than will be encountered in most modern houses; it also tends to be unhealthy, as we have pointed out.

4-6. (Reprinted with permission from the *1977 Fundamentals Volume, ASHRAE HANDBOOK & Product Directory*)

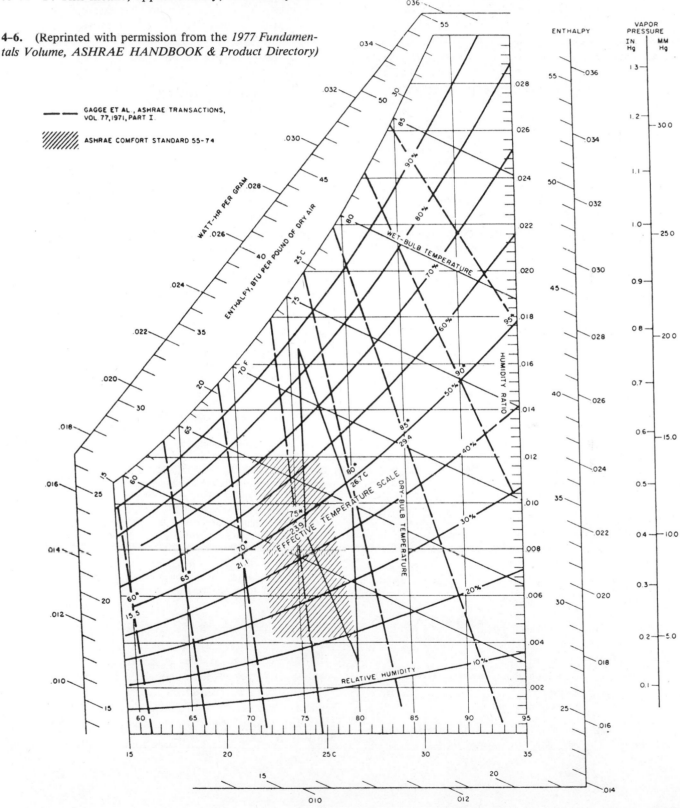

CAUSES OF MOISTURE DAMAGE

Condensation of warm, moist air is only one of four major sources of water-caused damage inside the house. It is the most prevalent, but the other three are not uncommon. One is too-damp basements, crawl spaces, or floor slabs. The second is snow backup or ice dams on the roofs of houses with no roof overhangs or with extremely shallow eaves. And the third results from wind-driven rain penetrating the walls of the house and saturating the sheathing.

The experience of the past few decades has shown that water damage resulting from condensation is most serious in Zone 1 of Figure 4-7 and not uncommon in Zone 2. It is relatively rare in Zone 3, but even there it occurs occasionally. For example, in the Tennessee Valley Authority region of Zone 3, condensation has been known to cause trouble in the TVA's small. tightly built plywood houses.

Moisture damage arising from damp undersides of houses and from wind-driven rain can, of course, occur in houses in any temperature zone. Indeed, sweaty slabs and dripping basement walls are phenomena of hot, humid summers rather than of cold winters, though moisture in crawl spaces can cause trouble the year round.

Protective measures against condensation and other forms of water damage in walls, roofs, and foundations of houses, should be provided in all three zones wherever the structural cross sections have overall U factors of 0.25 Btu or less. This is often the case even with poorly insulated houses. Note, however, that such protective measures are advisable under virtually any circumstances, if there is any possibility that condensation and other forms of water damage might occur.

Zones Include Areas with Design Temperatures about as follows: Zone I, −20 F and lower; Zone II, 0 F to −20 F; and Zone III above 0 F. Note that cross hatched areas are outside of Zones I and III.

4-7. (Reprinted with permission from the *1977 Fundamentals Volume, ASHRAE HANDBOOK & Product Directory*)

Furthermore, a problem that makes such protection equally important during hot weather has arisen along with the great increase in availability and popularity of mechanical cooling. This is the fact that vapor in the hot outdoor air penetrates an unprotected wall or ceiling and increases the mechanical load by adding to the latent heat within the building. Vapor barriers reduce or eliminate this latent heat gain, and they should be used in all climates with hot and humid weather. In hot-dry regions, they are not commonly necessary (but may be in winter).

It is always best to be on the safe side in this matter of moisture damage. Protect the house when it is built! Corrective measures "after the fact" are both expensive and inefficient. The cost of such protection for a new building is low, and the safety insurance value high.

Condensation Due to High Interior Humidity

Agriculture Information Bulletin No. 373, *Condensation Problems in Your House: Prevention and Solution,* published by the U.S. Department of Agriculture and available from the Forest Products Laboratory, nicely summarizes the basic reasons why indoor condensation is more of a problem today than it used to be years back:

Changes in design, materials and construction methods since the mid-thirties have resulted in houses that are easier to heat and more comfortable, but these changes have accentuated the potential for condensation problems. New types of weatherstripping, storm sash, and sheet material for sheathing in new houses provide tight air-resistant construction which restricts the escape of moisture generated in the house. Newer houses are also generally smaller and have lower ceilings resulting in less atmosphere to hold moisture.

Estimates have been made that a typical family of four converts 3 gallons of water into water vapor per day. Unless excess water vapor is properly removed in some way (ventilation usually) it will either increase the humidity or condense on cold surfaces such as window glass. More serious, however, it can move in or through the construction, often condensing within the wall, roof, or floor cavities. Heating systems equipped with winter air-conditioning systems also increase the humidity.

Most new houses have from 2 to 3-1/2 inches of insulation in the walls and 6 or more inches in the ceilings. Unfortunately, the more efficient the insulation is in retarding heat transfer, the colder the outer surfaces become and unless moisture is restricted from entering the wall or ceiling, the greater the potential for moisture condensation. Moisture migrates toward cold surfaces and will condense or form as frost or ice on these surfaces.

To this, one might add such factors as more extensive use of water and of appliances discharging water vapor than was formerly the case, and the forthcoming widespread use of heat-exchange systems instead of ventilation to the outdoors in order to conserve heat within the interior living spaces. Typical amounts of vapor produced by various causes in the home are shown in Table 4-1.

Moisture Production for Various Domestic Operations*

Operation	Pints of Moisture
Floor mopping	2.9 per 100 square feet
Tub bath	0.1
Shower	0.5
Dish washing	0.5—1.0
Clothes washing	3.0—5.0
Cooking	5.5 per day
House plants	1.5—2.5 per day
Humans	0.25 per hour

* Abstracted from several sources.

Table 4–1.

Condensation Due to Excessive Moisture Under The House

Because of the substantial cost of constructing full basements, it is common practice today to omit them entirely and either build upon a concrete slab or leave an enclosed crawl space below the building. If the crawl space is damp, or if there is excessive moisture beneath the slab, large quantities of water vapor may find their way into walls, attics, and living areas.

Much the same condition often occurs in houses with basements, when the basement walls and floors are not correctly waterproofed, and there is either standing water in the basement or at least a great excess of dampness in the air. It is also common in homes with part-basements, mainly in the unexcavated area. The problem is thus not limited to low-cost, basementless houses; it can arise in any home in which care has not been taken to assure dry conditions throughout the foundation area. For example, in many homes the part of the basement containing the furnace may be thoroughly dry while an adjoining section, used perhaps for laundry or for the storage of foods, may be damp enough to cause serious trouble. Excessive moisture behind walls or under floors of earth-sheltered houses, can, of course, be disastrous and is a critical design point of such structures.

Incorrectly designed and built slabs may also cause dangerous concentrations of moisture that can damage walls and ceilings and also make cemented wood floors buckle and rot. The addition of radiant heating lines or perimeter heating system ducts to a slab further complicates the problem.

Water Damage Due to Snow Backup

A common cause of paint and plaster failures and wood decay in areas of severe winter conditions is the backup of melting snow or ice at the roof eaves. This condition does not usually occur with houses that have moderately wide roof overhangs, though it can indeed happen. However, a house with little or no roof overhang may suffer severe damage to plaster, paint, and wallpaper inside the house as the backed-up snow or ice melts and the water seeps into the walls and ceilings.

Water Damage Due to Wind-Driven Rains

Failure of exterior paint or other finish, improper jointing, poor or failed caulk, and damage to the structure resulting from wind-driven rains is occasionally a problem. The condition is mentioned here because such damage is often erroneously attributed to vapor condensation resulting from inadequate protection of the building walls and roofs from indoor humidity, rather than to the real cause.

CONDENSATION CONTROL

No one device or material will guarantee foolproof condensation control, and no device or material for such a purpose will be of any use if it is incorrectly or carelessly applied. Vapor barriers, whether paint or membrane, will fail wherever there is incomplete coverage by the paint film or tears or gaps in the membrane. Means of ventilation will not work if they are too small, too tightly screened, or if they are so located that they can be clogged with leaves or snow.

Therefore, in the following discussion of materials, it must always be borne in mind that correct specification alone is only half the job. Proper supervision of application or installation is essential if future trouble is to be avoided.

Vapor Barriers

The question as to what constitutes an "adequate" vapor barrier is a complex one, and it would be profitless and tiresome to discuss it in detail here. On the other hand, a basic knowledge of this method of vapor control is important.

There has been in the past, and still is to some degree, a fair amount of confusion concerning vapor barrier standards and methods of testing, as well as in the accepted terminology. But from a practical point of view, experience plus an averaging out of innumerable materials tests have established certain materials in combination as sufficiently impermeable for use in house building. As to terminology, those terms that will be used here are the ones presently most commonly accepted in the building trades. The word *permeability* is a general term that means having a capability of being penetrable and especially in having pores or openings that permit liquids or gases to pass through. When that gas is water vapor, our only interest here, then the proper term is *water vapor permeability*. This phrase in turn is the equivalent of the word "permeance" (which has a different meaning in the field of magnetics). The unit of permeance is the *perm,* which is the equivalent of the passage of one grain of water vapor per hour per square foot per inch of mercury vapor pressure difference between the two surfaces of the material. Note that, for this term, the thickness of the material is indeterminate. But when water vapor permeability of *unit* thickness is being discussed, the unit of permeance is the *perm-inch.* Just as a material can admit the passage of water vapor, so can it resist that passage, and this resistance is in fact oftentimes of more interest than the conductance value. Resistance to vapor flow provided by a material is simply the reciprocal of the permeance, and the unit of resistance is designated as a *rep.* Defined, a rep is resistance to water vapor flow in inches of mercury vapor pressure difference per square foot per hour per grain.

The necessary vapor barrier resistance, or its maximum conductance, is not a fixed value and depends upon a number of factors. Much depends upon the specific construction of the building sections and the materials used therein, as well as upon the amount and type of insulation that is used. Whether or not the building is heated only, is heated and mechanically cooled, or is air conditioned the year round has a bearing, and so does the type of heat being used; heating by methods that do not require fuel combustion, such as electric heating or heat pumps, often means that there will be a greater amount of water vapor present than otherwise might be the case. The same is true of modern, extra-tight houses that are so well insulated and so completely enwrapped in a vapor barrier that virtually all of the moisture generated within the house remains therein, and condensation can become a problem unless additional ventilation and dehumidification takes place. Thus, in some cases it may be necessary to engineer vapor barriers to provide sufficient conductance to allow a certain amount of entrapped water vapor to escape, rather than using a high-rep value that turns the house into a terrarium.

So there is no approved standard for a good vapor barrier: This depends to a great extent upon circumstances and oftentimes the permeance of a barrier is best established upon the basis of various design factors. However, considerable experience in the northern parts of the United States has shown that, in houses of conventional frame construction that are sheathed with wood siding, a vapor barrier of 1 perm has been found to be satisfactory. (But as noted, there are occasions when 1 perm is insufficient.) The tentative present-day recommendation therefore, is that, in the words of the *1977 Fundamentals Volume, ASHRAE HANDBOOK & Product Directory,* " . . . the walls of every well-constructed modern dwelling include a vapor barrier when the construction includes any material that would be damaged by moisture or its freezing. This applies to all condensation zones in Figure [4–7] when the *U*-value for the wall is lower than 0.25 Btu/h Ft² (F), and in Zone I and II to walls of higher transmittance." There are numerous kinds of vapor barriers that can serve this purpose, and they can be classed in three categories: membrane, structural, and coating barriers. Table 4–2 shows the permeance and resistance values for a variety of materials, both good and bad for the purpose of vapor barriers; the discussion below deals only with low-permeance materials.

MEMBRANE VAPOR BARRIERS

The following sheet or membrane materials, alone or in combination, are acceptable as vapor barriers if they are warranted by a reputable manufacturer to have a permeance of less than 1 perm, and if there are no gaps, tears, or other vapor-admitting defects in them after installation.

Asphalt-saturated and coated vapor barrier or sheathing paper, 43 pounds per roll of 500 square feet. The perm rating for this material ranges from 0.2 to 0.3; differences are attributable to exact weight, manufacturer, and specific samples tested. None of these materials are absolutely uniform, so that there may also be some differences in permeance in different pieces from the same roll. Weights per 500 square feet of the material greater than 43 pounds will have a somewhat better resistance, while those of lighter weight will have lesser resistance to the passage of water vapor. Note that the uncoated asphalt-saturated sheathing paper at 22 pounds per 500 square feet does not perform well at all. Common dull-surface asphalt-saturated felts can be used and will perform marginally for a time, but lack durability and longevity. The 15-pound asphalt felt, weighing in at 70 pounds per 500 square feet, is rated with a perm of 1.0. But two layers of this material would doubtless result in a perm rating not of half, or 0.5, but probably somewhat less than that; it frequently occurs with vapor barrier materials that multiple layers increase the resistance of passage of water vapor more than would be expected. Ordinary tar felts, however, are wholly useless for the purpose.

Saturated and coated roll roofing, 326 pounds per 500 square feet. On average, their dry-cup permeance rates at 0.05, and thus they are excellent vapor barriers. However, their heavy weight and relatively high cost tend to limit their use to ground cover in crawl spaces or similar locations.

Reinforced and laminated kraft paper and asphalt, 34 pounds per 500 square feet. This material consists of a layer of asphalt between two sheets of paper, the whole reinforced with fibers. The paper listed is specified as a "30–120–30" paper (the first and last figures refer to the weights of the paper and the middle figure to the layer of asphalt, for a standard square footage per roll). This particular paper (others are available, with different ratings) has a perm rating 0.03, and makes a good vapor barrier.

Aluminum foil, either plain foil, foil-laminated-to-paper, or the inner sheet of multiple-layer reflective insulation. The foil should be of sufficient thickness so that microscopic holes do not permit vapor passage in excess of 1 perm. When a foil is 0.001 inch thick (1 mil), it is said to have a zero vapor transfer; however, a foil of this thickness is fairly expensive. The types usually found on the market are on the order of 0.00035 (.035 mil) inches thick, and these do often have microscopic holes in them. If intact, the perm rating is 0.05. If aluminum foil insulation is not being used, probably the best solution, if one wishes to specify foil as a vapor barrier, is to select one of the laminated products in which thin foils are asphalt-laminated to both sides of thin but strong paper. These products have permeance rates about as low as any other vapor barrier on the market (the type with aluminum foil on one side and weighing 43 pounds per 500 square feet has a perm rating of 0.002); they also have the added advantage, like all foil products, of providing a certain amount of reflective insulation performance when they are installed that there is an air space on one or both sides of the material.

Plastic films. These materials (Figure 4–8) are remarkably strong for their light weight, and in this respect are superior to aluminum foil, which tears easily. Membranes that are 0.002 inch thick (2 mil) have a good perm rating, but are so thin that they puncture or tear easily. Thicknesses of 0.004 (4 mil), however, are widely used as vapor barriers on walls and ceilings and have a perm rating of 0.08. The films may also be used as under-slab vapor barriers, since they are chemically inert as well as tough, and under almost all circumstances will remain effective for the life of the building. When used under slabs, it is advisable to lay

4-8. Polyethylene film vapor barrier. (Visking Corp.)

0.006 inch thick (6 mil) or heavier sheeting over a smooth sand base rather than coarse gravel, since this reduces the possibility of punctures by sharp stones. On the other hand, sand can lead to a wicking action of ground moisture if any appreciable quantities are present; gravel will not.

Vinyl and similar wall coverings, glossy-surfaced cloths, plasticized and foil-surfaced wall papers. These materials have widely variable vapor transmission rates, and many of them are well below the recommended 1 perm, depending upon type and manufacturer, but they are difficult to install so that they give adequate protection around doors and windows and at baseboards. They are, of course, particularly useful as vapor barriers in existing houses where moisture conditions have become troublesome. Where their use is contemplated for vapor barrier purposes, specific ratings should be obtained from the manufacturer.

Integral vapor barriers. Some vapor barriers of the membrane type are supplied as an integral part of a building material. Three examples of such combination vapor barriers are given below.

Vapor barrier sheets (nonreflective) on one side of blanket or bat insulation, with or without a suitable breather paper on the other side, are in common use. An asphalt-coated backing paper of this sort weighing 31 pounds per 500 square feet has a perm rating of 0.04, and others may be higher or lower, depending upon the specific paper and the manufacturer. Many such papers are well over the recommended 1 perm rating. Unfortunately, few manufacturers state the permeability rate of their papers, and it is therefore good practice to require a warranty—even safer—an actual test to prove the paper is a vapor barrier. The safest procedure of all is to disregard this vapor barrier and install another, separate barrier of polyethylene film over the insulation, for complete protection.

Aluminum foil on the back or face of gypsum wallboard or a similar product makes an excellent vapor barrier when correctly applied, and it also provides some insulating value if there is an air space behind the wallboard. Note, however, that foil backing is not recommended in air-conditioned buildings in the hot, humid climates of southern Atlantic and Gulf Coast areas; under such conditions the vapor barrier must often be placed on the exterior side of walls and ceilings, and the exact location should be determined by a qualified mechanical engineer. Depending upon the particular foil-covered product, other limitations may apply as well. For example, United States Gypsum places these restrictions on the use of their foil-backed gypsum wallboard products: not recommended for use where exposure to moisture is extreme and continuous; not to be used as a base for ceramic or other tile, vinyl-faced wallboard in double-layer assemblies, applied vinyl wall coverings, or any other highly water vapor resistant wall finishes; construction of partition and/or floor-ceiling assemblies must conform to designs as tested at certain fire testing facilities in order to attain fire-resistance ratings; and when the material is to be secured with an adhesive, only one that is specifically recommended for that purpose can be used. In addition, in order to prevent objectional sag in ceilings, U.S.G. specifies that the weight of overlaid unsupported insulation should not exceed: 1.3 pounds per square foot for 1/2-inch thick panels with frame spacing 24 inches on centers; 2.2 pounds per square foot for

1/2-inch thick panels with frame spacing 16 inches on centers and for 5/8-inch thick panels 24 inches on centers; 3/8-inch thick panels cannot be overlaid with unsupported insulation; the attic areas, if unheated, must be properly vented in all cases. There are also certain maximum spacings of frame members that must be followed in new, single-layer, wood-frame construction (Table 4–2A). Obviously, such limitations and restrictions will differ from product to product, but the important point to note is that all such building materials, especially if of a composite nature, must be correctly chosen for the job at hand, and then properly installed, if they are to be successful.

The effectiveness of thermal insulation with aluminum foil facing (Figure 4–10), like many others, is dependent upon correct installation. In cases where the maufacturer recommends that the insulation be dished between the studs or joists instead of being attached in overlapped fashion to the stud faces, the vapor barrier is imperfect because of gapping at the stapling flanges. Again, complete protection can only be afforded by adding a second, unbroken vapor barrier, such as polyethylene sheeting.

4–9. Installing U.S.G. foil-back gypsum panels. (Courtesy of U.S. Gypsum)

Maximum Spacing of Frame Members for Single-Layer, New, Wood-Frame Construction

thickness	location	application method(1)	max. frame spacing o.c.
3/8" (9.5 mm)	ceilings (2)	perpendicular(3)	16" (406 mm)
	sidewalls	parallel or perpendicular	16" (406 mm)
1/2" (12.7 mm)	ceilings	parallel (3)	16" (406 mm)
		perpendicular	24" (610 mm)(4)
	sidewalls	parallel or perpendicular	24" (610 mm)
5/8" (15.9 mm)	ceilings	parallel (3)	16" (406 mm)
		perpendicular	24" (610 mm)
	sidewalls	parallel or perpendicular	24" (610 mm)

(1) Long edge relative to framing. (2) Not recommended below unheated spaces. (3) Not recommended if water-based spray-texture finish is used. (4) Max. spacing 16" for water-based spray-texture finish application.

Table 4–2A. (Courtesy of U.S. Gypsum)

4–10. Foil-faced mineral wool insulation. (Duncan Photos)

STRUCTURAL VAPOR BARRIERS

Structural vapor barriers are comprised of various structural materials normally manufactured as rigid sheets or planks; they are relatively impervious to the transmission of water vapor because of their inherent composition and physical structure, and most can be sealed against water vapor passage at joints or edges. These materials obviously include such materials as sheet aluminum, copper, steel or other metals, fiberglass, acrylic or other plastic panels and the like, which in nearly all cases have an effective perm rate of zero. Ordinary 1/4-inch thick Exterior-type Douglas fir plywood has a perm rating of 0.7, largely because of its waterproof gluelines. Building sections sheathed with Exterior-type engineered grades of plywoods form a relatively effective vapor barrier in themselves, provided that the joints are properly sealed and especially if the panels are bonded to the framework with the proper type of adhesive. By comparison, the water vapor permeance of exterior Medium Density Overlay (MDO) plywood in a 3/8-inch thickness has a perm rating of 0.3, and exterior High Density Overlay (HDO) plywood in a 1/2-inch thickness has a perm rate of 0.1. These ratings are based on Douglas fir properties; the MDO overlay is on one side only, and the HDO overlay is on both sides of the panel.

Rigid thermal insulations. Though most thermal insulations are nonstructural and have no value as vapor barriers, there are a few rigid board forms that do have reasonable resistance to the passage of water vapor. For instance, expanded polyurethane board stock carries a perm-inch rating of 0.4 to 1.6, depending upon the specific material. Expanded polystyrene (extruded) has a perm-inch rating of 1.2. These materials, when used in sufficient thickness, and depending upon exactly how and where they are installed, can serve with reasonable effectiveness as vapor barriers. The latter is used as perimeter and masonry wall insulation (Figure 4–11). It is not a perfect vapor barrier, but it has been found that any condensation that takes place towards its cold side simply evaporates when the temperature rises, without damaging the material or the structure. As frame wall or roof deck insulation, it should always be accompanied by a vapor barrier placed on the side facing into the house. Alternatively, various kinds and thicknesses of rigid insulation are available with foil facing, which are listed as having an effective perm-inch rating of 0.0 For complete protection, all joints must be fully sealed.

COATING BARRIERS

There are several types of coating barriers in common use today. Some are of the semifluid mastic type, and others are of the hot melt type. The fully fluid paint type is usually referred to as a surface coating, although indeed the other two types are also. The basic composition of coating barriers may be polymeric, asphaltic, resinous or of some other material of similar qualities, and various pigments, solvents and vehicles may be included as necessary. Application of coating barriers may be made by trowel, roller, brush or spray, depending upon the type of surface and the type of coating.

Asphalt mastic is sometimes used as a vapor barrier on foundations, for instance, and is applied in thick layers by troweling the material onto the surface, where it adheres readily. This makes an extremely effective vapor barrier, when applied in sufficient thickness, but will degrade to some degree over a long period of time when in contact with ground moisture. In a 3/16-inch coating thickness, it has a perm rating of 0.0. Hot melt asphalt is also widely used as a damp-proofer for foundation walls, particularly on those made of concrete block. As a damp-proofer, it is relatively effective, but it should not be considered a waterproofer. Like the mastic, it will degrade over a period of time upon contact with moisture, and it also tends to become brittle and lacks the bridging capability to cover small cracks that might appear in the foundation. When applied at

4-11. Rigid plastic foam board insulation. (Courtesy, Georgia-Pacific Corporation)

the rate of 2 ounces per square foot, the perm rating is 0.5. However, if two applications are made, with complete and even coverage by spraying, the perm rating will drop below 0.1.

It has long been known that certain types and combinations of house paints are relatively impermeable. The usefulness of paints as the only vapor barrier in new construction is, of course, substantially reduced by the fact that (as in the case of wallpaper) it is well-nigh impossible to ensure a complete seal at windows, exterior doors, and baseboards. In existing houses, such materials are often the only economically feasible way of providing a moderately effective vapor barrier, but the greatest care must be taken to caulk all open cracks between the woodwork and the plaster or wallboard and to make certain that there is a solid and continuous paint film covering both surfaces and the joint between them.

Furthermore, ceilings as well as walls must be covered with the vapor resistant paints, not only under attics, but also between first and second floors. If this is neglected, vapor will migrate through the unprotected ceiling and out toward the cold walls along the joist spaces, causing spot condensation where the dewpoint is reached. The use of paints as a vapor barrier should be considered where no other method is practical or feasible, or simply as a bit of added protection when used in combination with a true vapor barrier. The following are types of paint applications that have tested well, both in the laboratory and in actual use.

For sealing plaster, plasterboard, or fiberboard, use a *pigmented* primer-sealer as a first coat, instead of glue

Permeance and Permeability of Materials to Water Vapor[a]

Material	Permeance (Perm)	Resistance[1] (Rep)	Permeability (Perm-in.)	Resistance/in.[1] (Rep/in.)
Materials used in construction				
Concrete (1:2:4 mix)			3.2	0.31
Brick masonry (4-in. thick)	0.8[f]	1.3		
Concrete block (8-in., cored, limestone aggregate)	2.4[f]	0.4		
Tile masonry, glazed (4-in. thick)	0.12[f]	8.3		
Asbestos cement board (0.2-in. thick)	0.54[d]	1.8		
Plaster on metal lath (0.75 in.)	15[f]	0.067		
Plaster on wood lath	11[e]	0.091		
Plaster on plain gypsum lath (with studs)	20[f]	0.050		
Gypsum wall board (0.375 in., plain)	50[f]	0.020		
Gypsum sheathing (0.5 in., asphalt impreg.)			20[d]	0.050
Structural insulating board (sheathing qual.)			20-50[f]	0.050-0.020
Structural insulating board (interior, uncoated. 0.5 in.)	50-90[f]	0.020-0.011		
Hardboard (0.125 in., standard)	11[f]	0.091		
Hardboard (0.125 in., tempered)	5[f]	0.2		
Built-up roofing (hot mopped)	0.0			
Wood, sugar pine			0.4-5.4[f,b]	2.5-0.19
Plywood (douglas fir, exterior glue, 0.25 in. thick)	0.7[f]	1.4		
Plywood (douglas fir, interior glue, 0.25 in. thick)	1.9[f]	0.53		
Acrylic, glass fiber reinforced sheet, 56 mil	0.12[d]	8.3		
Polyester, glass fiber reinforced sheet, 48 mil	0.05[d]	20		
Thermal insulations				
Air (still)			120[f]	0.0083
Cellular glass			0.0[d]	∝
Corkboard			2.1-2.6[d], 9.5[e]	0.48-0.38,0.11
Mineral wool (unprotected)			116[e]	0.0086
Expanded polyurethane (R-11 blown) board stock			0.4-1.6[d]	2.5-0.62
Expanded polystyrene—extruded			1.2[d]	0.83
Expanded polystyrene—bead			2.0-5.8[d]	0.50-0.17
Unicellular synthetic flexible rubber foam			0.02-0.15[d]	50-6.7
Plastic and metal foils and films[c]				
Aluminum foil (1 mil)	0.0[d]			
Aluminum foil (0.35 mil)	0.05[d]	20		
Polyethylene (2 mil)	0.16[d]	6.3		3100
Polyethylene (4 mil)	0.08[d]	12.5		3100
Polyethylene (6 mil)	0.06[d]	17		3100
Polyethylene (8 mil)	0.04[d]	25		3100
Polyethylene (10 mil)	0.03[d]	33		3100
Polyester (1 mil)	0.7[d]	1.4		
Cellulose acetate (125 mil)	0.4[d]	2.5		
Polyvinylchloride, unplasticized (2 mil)	0.68[d]	1.5		
Polyvinylchloride plasticized (4 mil)	0.8-1.4[d]	1.3-0.72		

Table 4-2. (Reprinted with permission from the *1977 Fundamentals Volume, ASHRAE HANDBOOK & Product Directory*)

Table 4-2 continued

Material	Permeance (Perm)	Resistance[i] (Rep)	Permeability (Perm-in.)	Resistance/in.[i] (Rep/in.)
Building paper, felts, roofing papers[g]				
Duplex sheet, asphalt laminated, aluminum foil one side (43)[h]	0.002	0.176	500	5.8
Saturated and coated roll roofing (326)[h]	0.05	0.24	20	4.2
Kraft paper and asphalt laminated, reinforced 30-120-30 (34)[h]	0.03	1.8	3.3	0.55
Blanket thermal insulation back up paper, asphalt coated (31)[h]	0.04	0.6-4.2	2.5	1.7-0.24
Asphalt-saturated and coated vapor barrier paper (43)[h]	0.2-0.3	0.6	5.0-3.3	1.7
Asphalt-saturated but not coated sheathing paper (22)[h]	3.3	20.2	0.3	0.05
15-lb asphalt felt (70)[h]	1.0	5.6	1.0	0.18
15-lb tar felt (70)[h]	4.0	18.2	0.25	0.055
Single-kraft, double (16)[h]	31	42	0.032	0.024
Liquid-applied coating materials				
Paint-2 coats				
Asphalt paint on plywood		0.4		2.5
Aluminum varnish on wood	0.3-0.5		3.3-2.0	
Enamels on smooth plaster		0.5-1.5		2.0-0.66
Primers and sealers on interior insulation board		0.9-2.1		1.1-0.48
Various primers plus 1 coat flat oil paint on plaster		1.6-3.0		0.63-0.33
Flat paint on interior insulation board		4		0.25
Water emulsion on interior insulation board		30-85		0.03-0.012
Paint-3 coats				
Exterior paint, white lead and oil on wood siding	0.3-1.0		3.3-1.0	
Exterior paint, white lead-zinc oxide and oil on wood	0.9		1.1	
Styrene-butadiene latex coating, 2 oz/sq ft	5.5		0.18	
Polyvinyl acetate latex coating, 4 oz/sq ft	5.5		0.18	
Chloro-sulfonated polyethylene mastic, 3.5 oz/sq ft	1.7		0.59	
7.0 oz/sq ft	0.06		16	
Asphalt cut-back mastic, 1/16 in., dry	0.14		7.2	
3/16 in., dry	0.0		—	
Hot melt asphalt, 2 oz/sq ft	0.5		2	
3.5 oz/sq ft	0.1		10	

[a] Table gives the water vapor transmission rates of some representative materials. The data are provided to permit comparisons of materials; but in the selection of vapor barrier materials, exact values for permeance or permeability should be obtained from the manufacturer of the materials under consideration or secured as a result of laboratory tests. A range of values shown in the table indicated variations among mean values for materials that are similar but of different density, orientation, lot or source. The values are intended for design guidance and should not be used as design or specification data. The compilation is from a number of sources; values from dry-cup and wet-cup methods were usually obtained from investigations using ASTM E96 and C355; values shown under *others* were obtained from investigations using such techniques as *two-temperature, special cell*, and *air-velocity*.

[b] Depending on construction and direction of vapor flow.
[c] Usually installed as vapor barriers, although sometimes used as exterior finish and elsewhere near cold side where special considerations are then required for warm side barrier effectiveness.
[d] Dry-cup method.
[e] Wet-cup method.
[f] Other than dry- or wet-cup method.
[g] Low permeance sheets used as vapor barriers. High permeance used elsewhere in construction.
[h] Basic weight in lb per 500 ft².
[i] Resistance and resistance/in. values have been calculated as the reciprocal of the permeance and permeability values, respectively.

size, shellac, or self-priming flats. In the case of wallboards, it is best to use a primer specifically formulated for that purpose. Glue size is useless as a vapor barrier and shellac is not much better. Aluminum paints are not advised as primers, both because their vapor resistance in one-coat applications is not particularly good and because some finish paints do not adhere well to them.

In general, oil-based paints make the best vapor barriers. Those formulations in which resins largely supplant oils are referred to as varnish-based paints, and those that have been modified without alkyd resins are referred to as oil-alkyds; both are classed as non-breathing paints. Rubber-based paints, which may be formulated with chlorinated natural rubber or styrene-butadiene resin, are also nonbreathing paints and can form a reasonably effective vapor barrier (compared to other paints). Latex paints, which are water-thinned and are made up of various resinous materials in numerous blends and modifications, are very poor indeed as vapor barriers. There are also sundry proprietary paint formulations that are designed specifically to be used as vapor barriers. If use of one of these formulations is contemplated, the purchaser would do well to obtain full particulars as to the worth of the material, preferably as determined by an independent testing laboratory, before purchasing.

If one specifies or applies a high-grade alkyd-resin primer-sealer that has been designed *as* primer-sealer, he will be practically certain of getting a prime coat that has just about as good vapor resistance as can be obtained in a paint. A few results of various paint applications are shown in Table 4-2.

For woodwork that is to be painted with a gloss or semigloss finish, specify an "enamel undercoat" as the sealer before the finish coats are applied.

For finish coats on plaster, plasterboard, and fiberboard any of the following types of paint can be used: standard flat paints, latex-rubber paints, alkyd-resin paints, in ascending order of vapor resistance; also, any other type of paint on which the architect can obtain, either from the manufacturer or the dealer, a positive assurance that its permeability to vapor is satisfactorily low. According to many tests, a one-coat application over a good primer-sealer will make nearly as satisfactory a vapor seal as a two-coat job if the paint is designed for one-coat use and if it is applied generously and is not spread out too thin. Several paint experts recommend using rollers instead of brushes for such applications, since the roller assures a thicker paint film.

Any reputable brand of gloss or semigloss paint provides good vapor barrier properties over a suitable enamel undercoat on woodwork.

Even when a high quality membrane vapor barrier is being used in new construction, it will do no harm at all to specify interior house paints with low permeability. The combination of membrane and paint vapor barriers may be a bit like the man who wears both a belt and suspenders—but the fact is that such a man never loses his pants!

On the other hand, a paint vapor barrier should never be used alone in new construction. Paint formulas are oftentimes changed, so that paint once showing good vapor resistance may decrease in value when the formula is changed. Furthermore, a membrane vapor barrier protects the structure somewhat during construction, something a coat of paint cannot do, since paint is not applied until a building is finished. .

There is another aspect to bear in mind when paint vapor barriers are applied over plaster: Paint should not be applied to newly plastered walls and ceilings while there is any great amount of moisture still present. Several months, at least, should pass to permit the plaster to dry out. Exactly the same situation obtains for interior masonry walls, whether they be above grade, below grade, part of a basement, or an earth-sheltered house. The reason is that vapor barrier paints make it difficult if not impossible for moisture to escape through the paint film; if there is a clear path, most of it may evaporate through the outer layers of the structure, but some will stay with the paint, causing blisters and other kinds of damage. If the outward path is blocked, paint damage will be severe.

Installation of Insulation and Vapor Barriers

The proper placement of these materials is shown in the following series of installation photographs and drawings. The importance of careful supervision of this work has been emphasized previously and is restated here: No matter how good an insulation or a vapor barrier, defective workmanship can drastically reduce their effectiveness. Here, perhaps more than anywhere else in the house, vigilance is essential for assuring good materials performance. The following series of illustrations points up some of the more important aspects of proper insulation installation (Figures 4–12 to 4–35).

4–12. Install nonreflective vapor barrier type with flanges lapping the face of the studs, joists, or rafters, making sure the vapor barrier side faces into the house. (Courtesy, Mineral Insulation Manufacturers Association, Inc.)

4–13. Install reflective vapor barrier type dished between the studs, joists, or rafters, making sure the breather side faces outward. *Always* dish in well up from the bottoms of the joist or rafter faces, so that the batt will not sag and close the air space between the foil and the ceiling. When placed too close to joist or rafter bottoms, the batt will soon droop and even touch the ceiling, thus eliminating the foil's insulating value. (Reflectal/Borg-Warner Corp.)

4–14. But *never* push batts in against roofing or flooring; this prevents ventilation behind the insulation. (Courtesy, Mineral Insulation Manufacturers Association, Inc.)

4-15. Make sure the stapler hits the flange squarely, otherwise the staple will not be driven flush. (Courtesy, Mineral Insulation Manufacturers Association, Inc.)

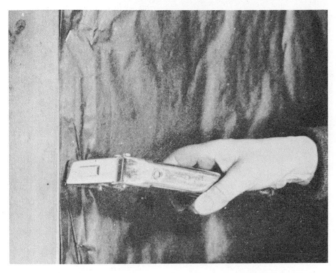

4-16. Use enough staples. . . (Courtesy, Mineral Insulation Manufacturers Association, Inc.)

4-17. (*Right*) To prevent gaps, i.e., no more than 6 inches apart. (Courtesy, Mineral Insulation Manufacturers Association, Inc.)

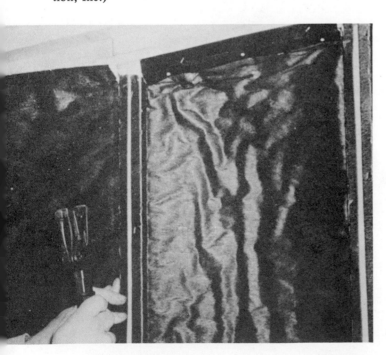

Comment #1. We have stated previously that a nonreflective vapor barrier that is integral with bat or blanket mineral wall insulation should be installed with the flanges lapping the faces of the studs, joists, or rafters. Sometimes, however, dishing of the insulation is recommended when wallboard is applied rather than a plaster finish. When insulation is dished, an added vapor barrier such as polyethylene film is necessary if the insulation itself is not very carefully fitted. In most climates, the usual recommendation is to add this extra vapor barrier anyway, even if the insulation *is* well fitted. The same is true, of course, where batt or blanket insulation covered with reflective foil is installed. In this case, the insulation must be dished in order to provide the 3/4-inch air space that affords the reflective barrier its effectiveness (with no air space, there is no reflectivity and the worth of the foil face is lost). An additional vapor barrier should be fitted to seal off the inevitable gaps that will occur along the stapling flange.

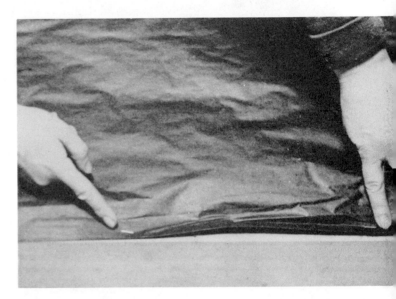

Comment #2. A special word of warning should be offered on the proper location of the vapor barrier. Occasionally the barrier is wrongly placed due to well-intentioned mistake. For example, in one instance the vapor barrier side of the insulation was marked "Install with this face to the warm side." It happened that it was a very hot day, and the inside of the house was considerably cooler than outdoors. The workmen not unnaturally were putting a vapor barrier face outwards, since it indubitably faced the "warmer" side that day! In view of the damage a vapor barrier on the wrong side of the insulation can do, it obviously is important to catch this sort of error while there still is time.

4-18. (*Left*) Staple to bottom sill and top plate or fire stop, as shown, allowing an extra length to ensure a tight vapor barrier fit at top and bottom. (Courtesy, Mineral Insulation Manufacturers Association, Inc.)

4–19. Stuff loose insulation in narrow spaces around windows and doors. . . (Courtesy, Mineral Insulation Manufacturers Association, Inc.)

4–20. Behind pipes. . . (Courtesy, Mineral Insulation Manufacturers Association, Inc.)

4–21. Ducts. . . (Courtesy, Mineral Insulation Manufacturers Association, Inc.)

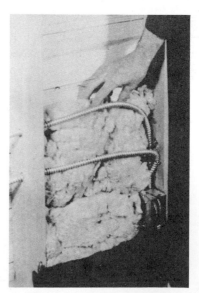

4–22. And electric cables, but leave a gap of at least 3 inches around and above flush-mount or recessed lighting fixtures . . . (Courtesy, Mineral Insulation Manufacturers Association, Inc.)

4-23. (*Left*) And fit vapor barrier snugly over pipes, ducts, around windows and doors, and over other narrow areas . . . (Wood Conversion Co.)

4-24. (*Left*) Around electric outlets. . . (Courtesy, Mineral Insulation Manufacturers Association, Inc.)

4-25. (*Right*) And heating ducts. (Baldwin-Hill Co.)

4-26. Make sure the vapor barrier completely seals the areas between parts of the structure. (*Progressive Architecture*)

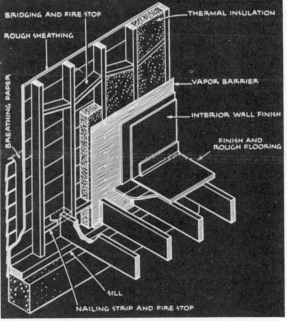

4-27. And at the floor joists, make sure the work is done *before* the subflooring is laid if balloon framing is used, or is tight to the sole plate in platform framing. (Courtesy, Mineral Insulation Manufacturers Association, Inc.)

4-28. Cut batts carefully to fit in odd angles. Note that this picture is wrong, since no flange has been left at the top to lap the end rafter. (Courtesy, Mineral Insulation Manufacturers Association, Inc.)

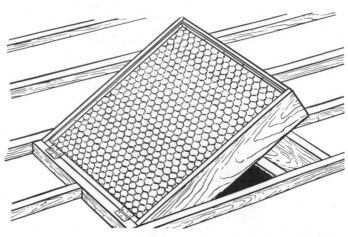

4-29. And do not forget to insulate the attic door or scuttle, including a good vapor barrier. (Celotex Corp.)

4-30. Wherever there are tears. . . (Courtesy, Mineral Insulation Manufacturers Association, Inc.)

4-31. Glue *and* staple patches over them. (Wood Conversion Co.)

4-32. When loose wool is being used in the attic floor, be sure a good vapor barrier is in place before the wool is poured and raked. . . (Courtesy, Mineral Insulation Manufacturers Association, Inc.)

4-33. And measure the depth to make sure there is enough material. (Courtesy, Mineral Insulation Manufacturers Association, Inc.)

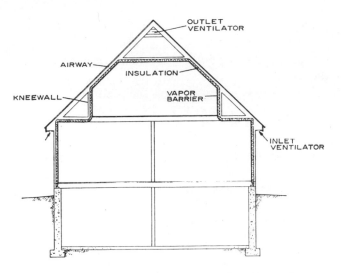

4-34. Never carry insulation to the roof peak; put it across collar beams.(USDA)

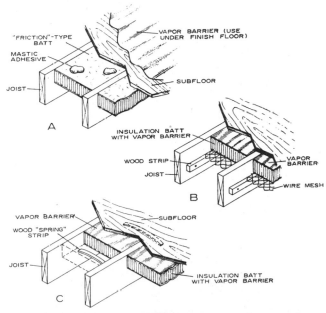

4-35. Installation of vapor barriers and insulation in floor (unheated crawl space): *A*, friction-type batts; *B*, wire mesh support; *C*, wood strip support. Note that an additional vapor barrier can be installed under the finish floor even if there already is one integral with the insulation.(USDA)

TIMING OF WORK

All special building trades that have to place pipes, ducts, and wires in the walls and ceilings *must finish the roughing-in before the insulation and the vapor barrier are applied.* A good insulation mechanic will always make sure that the materials surround or cover all pipes, ducts, and utility lines (given adequate supervision, of course). Plumbers or electricians—and even more commonly tinsmiths—never even think of replacing insulation or repairing cuts in the vapor barrier; it is not their job. Therefore, the work should be scheduled so that the insulation and vapor barrier, whether

separate or combined, are put in place *as late as possible* in the schedule. Not only will this avoid necessary damage by other trades, but it will minimize the danger of tears in the membrane resulting from materials handling or from carelessness on the part of people in the house. Ideally, the lath or wallboard should be placed immediately after the insulation and vapor barrier. In any event, before any of the insulation or vapor barrier is covered, it should be thoroughly inspected for damage, poor installation, or misplacement, and any necessary repairs or corrections should be made. Then that particular section should be immediately covered to prevent any further damage.

WEATHER AND VAPOR BARRIER INSTALLATION

There is another awkward headache in connection with these materials: This is the matter of season of building. There is always the danger that insulating materials and/or vapor barriers will become thoroughly soaked during stormy weather, absorb or retain excess moisture in buildings that are plastered during cold weather, or perhaps become frozen during cold weather. The structural materials may absorb great quantities of moisture—there may even be standing water—before the vapor barrier is installed; the moisture then becomes entrapped within the structure after the barrier is installed and paint is applied. Insulation, vapor barriers, or paint may be damaged, and the structure as well. Putting these and other similar possibilities together, we come up with an easy-to-say but virtually impossible-to-enforce rule: Build only during warm sunny weather!

There is, of course, no way to follow this rule in large subdivision and low-cost housing developments, and with today's high cost of labor and tight construction schedules it is extremely difficult under any circumstance. But in the individual home it can be managed to a reasonable degree by careful scheduling and by proper protection of the various sections and components of the partially-built house. Particularly in the regions of cold winters, this is a factor that definitely should be emphasized.

THE PROBLEM OF BUILT-UP ROOFS

The procedure of installing vapor barriers and insulation on built-up roofs with no hung ceiling below is even more important insofar as protection of the roof materials is concerned. It is common practice to rush through the roofing work as fast as possible, despite the fact that the specifications for such roofs almost invariably call for the requirement that the deck be dry before work begins. The urgency to complete closing-in of the structure results in ignoring this specification with great frequency and the result is trouble.

There is, however, a reasonable solution for this difficulty. Whenever it is important to get the roof deck covered-in as soon as possible, which is generally the case, the work can be done in two stages. First, the vapor barrier can be installed and protected in one operation; this can be rapidly accomplished. If the barrier has to be applied over a damp or wet roof deck, any blisters, bubbles, or other damage that result—they will show up over a short period of time—can then be repaired. Meanwhile, the barrier acts as a service roof until the deck, and the entire building, has been well dried by ventilation and sunshine, and work by other trades above the roof deck level can be completed. Later, at practically any convenient time, the roofer can then apply the insulation and roofing felts without being pressured by time or adverse weather conditions. There will be no further damage by other trades because their work is done, and, though the job has to be done in two steps rather than one, the fact that the roof will be fully serviceable and not require rework makes the process a cost-effective one.

In the case of smaller buildings such as moderate-priced houses, the two-step operation may not be feasible, particularly if the whole job is small enough to do in one day. In that case, the roofer should not come on the job until there has been a spell of good weather and the roof deck really is dry enough to install a vapor barrier, insulation, and roofing felts without the danger of water damage.

THE PROBLEM OF EXTERIOR FINISH

Most of the early evidences of condensation damage are seen in the exterior paint film. Certainly this is the source of most complaints. The result is that the paint industry is deeply interested in the whole condensation problem. Sometimes men in the industry tend to recommend practices that will protect the paint, regardless of what such practices will do to the wall or its inner surfaces.

Among the suggestions that have been made in the past by members of the industry (in addition to paint or membrane barriers) are backpriming of siding, development of more permeable outdoor paints, and wall ventilation. The first two are discussed below while the last is analyzed in a later section on ventilation in general.

Here are a few general ideas that may serve as guides in specifying exterior paints and their application. Some are positive recommendations; others are suggestions based on fairly limited testimony which, nevertheless, showed excellent results.

The first suggestion is that back-priming of siding is an unnecessary expense and a hazard to the wall cross section, since it essentially involves placing a vapor barrier on the wrong side of the wall. (This assumes that the paint being used is a nonbreathable type; if it were a breathable paint, then the whole operation would be pointless anyway.) It may help to keep condensed moisture out of the siding and thus reduce damage to the exterior paint, but the moisture it bars will obviously have to stay in the wall, where it can cause trouble. Edge-priming, on the other hand, is important and should always be done, particularly around dormer cheeks, windows, etc.

The next recommendation is that no prime coat containing zinc oxide or leaded-zinc oxide should be used. This will reduce the tendency of the paint to blister. The presence of zinc oxide in the paint also includes the presence of zinc soaps. Zinc soaps are soluble in water: When moisture comes through the wood from the inside, it attacks and dissolves the zinc soaps and the paint will lift. The primer should be a nonporous oil-base type specifically designed as an undercoat, and it must be relatively flexible and capable of absorbing swelling gases that develop on the wood surface. The primer should be applied in a thick coat, so that the wood grain is completely obscured; many painters habitually spread primer far too thinly.

A third suggestion is that the moisture vapor permeability of the outside wall paint should be higher than the inside wall paint. This would prevent entrapment of moisture within the wall section. A lesser amount of paint on the outside and more paint on the inside would accomplish this purpose. But, different paints have different permeability, and the rate of thickness to which inside and outside coat paintings are built up over the years would be most difficult, if not impossible, to control.

However, this leads to two separate ideas. First, exterior paints should be applied thinly. There are one-coat paints for outside application that result in a single, relatively thin paint layer. One possibility is applying two coats of a suitable paint on the sides of the house that "get a beating" from the sun, and a single coat elsewhere. Considering the frequency with which many houses are repainted, however, in many cases this would be an impractical suggestion.

The second idea is that paint with a higher inherent permeability might be used on the outside, provided this does not also involve poor wearing qualities. However, this also presents some problems. For protection of the wood surface, breathable paints *must* be applied over an impermeable primer, since they afford so little protection against moisture vapor penetration (a result of dew or rain) from the outside. Then too, repainting with a breathable paint over previous coats of nonbreathable paints would be pointless. And, there are so many other variables involved, such as the number of coatings, film thickness of each coating, type of pigment, type of vehicle, length of exposure period, weathering, absence of defects and voids in the paint film, and so on and on, that there seems to be no positive way to determine exactly what the permeability of a paint finish, either interior or exterior, might be at any given time. Note, too, that high-permeability paints also increase the likelihood of rusty nails and other metal parts. However, if all nails or staples are set and puttied (as they should be if they are ferrous) or else are made from nonrusting aluminum or stainless steel, and if all flashing is noncorrodable and tight, that problem will disappear.

Most masonry wall finishes do not present a serious problem in controlling wall condensation: Most masonry materials are more or less vapor permeable and the finishes commonly applied to them (except when oil paints are used over them—not an advisable procedure) are also permeable to vapor, though highly rain-resistant to water penetration. Condensation occurring in a masonry wall can cause damage; masonry materials are not subject to decay, but an accumulation of condensation within an improperly constructed masonry wall in cold climates could lead to freeze-up and cracking. However, instances have been known when wood furring strips and the insulation itself, as well as joists butted or countersunk into a masonry wall, have been damaged by such condensation. And, excess water vapor within a masonry wall will reduce its thermal insulating value. It will pay to make sure that the exterior finish of the masonry is properly vapor permeable to permit the escape of moisture from the wall during cold weather. This, of course, refers to above-ground masonry constructions; below-grade masonry is a different proposition.

Unpainted brick walls, either 8-inch solid or face brick with a 4-inch concrete masonry backup, are excellent for protection against water penetration and for vapor permeability, provided the brick, the mortar, and the workmanship are of top quality (see chapter 9).

WALL SHEATHING PAPER

Once in very common use, wall sheathing paper is seldom seen these days. This is because most walls are now sheathed with plywood, fiberboard sheathing, or rigid insulation, rendering an application of building paper unnecessary. But where the walls are sheathed using the old method of horizontal or diagonal boards, or behind a stucco or masonry veneer finish, sheathing paper should be used. The strips should be installed horizontally starting at the bottom of the wall, with each succeeding sheet overlapping by about 4 inches at the bottom. Strips of 8-inch or greater width can also be used around all window and door openings to help minimize air infiltration, regardless of what type of sheathing is applied. Sheathing paper must be breathable, water-resistant but not vapor-resistant Some authorities have asserted that these sheathing papers have a tendency to deteriorate by virtue of the very fact of their breathability; moisture can cause the paper to fail, with the result that the sheathing will become saturated with moisture, thus leading to decay of the wood and possible damage to the insulation and the interior finish of the wall. This, however, is a rather dubious assertion, and in fact many houses a century or more old that have been dismantled reveal the

sheathing paper to be in quite good condition, age notwithstanding, with no sign of decay in evidence. A number of different materials can be used for this purpose, including 15-pound asphalt felt, rosin, and similar papers. The sheathing paper should have a perm rating of 6.0 or more; nonbreathing materials of a lower perm rating are insufficiently permeable to the passage of water vapor, and they may actually constitute vapor barriers.

HOUSE ON A SLAB

In this type of construction, condensation damage can occur at any time of the year, particularly if the slab is insulated at the perimeter without an effective seal. To avoid various sorts of difficulties, ground moisture should not be permitted to enter the slab at any point.

Until recently, it has been standard practice to cover the smoothed gravel base for the slab with a heavy waterproof paper, such as 55-pound roll roofing. During recent years, the lightweight polyethylene membranes previously described have largely superceded roll roofing in this application, since the materials are lightweight, come in huge unbroken sheets, and are extraordinarily tough for their thinness (Figure 4–36). The membrane is easy to lay, has good puncture resistance (although considerable care must be taken during the installation and subsequent pouring operations), and is immune to attack by decay-producing fungi.

4-36. Polyethylene film vapor barrier (Visking Corp.)

The lighter asphalt felts that used to be employed for the purpose of vapor-proofing slabs are not serviceable over a period of time, since they tend to deteriorate once they are in contact with the ground. For instance, 15-pound asphalt-saturated felt will lose its effectiveness as a vapor barrier under a slab in a matter of about three years, possibly less.

Whenever a strip material is used, the strips should be lapped a minimum of 6 inches and each lap should be cemented with a hot or solvent-type cement. Any punctures caused during construction should be repaired with cemented patches. The strips should be turned up at the ends and along the sides where they butt on the foundation wall, so that they will extend to the top of the slab. The edge insulation should be placed *inside* this barrier, of course, as shown in Figure 4-37.

Concrete floor slabs that are built well above-grade present fewer problems with respect to ground moisture and condensation than do slabs that are built on-grade. Agriculture Handbook No. 73, *Wood-Frame House Construction* (Forest Products Laboratory, U.S. Department of Agriculture, slightly revised April 1975) recommends that the top of a concrete floor slab be no less than 8 inches above the ground. The perm rating of the vapor barrier should be less than 0.5, which can be achieved by using 55-pound roll roofing or heavy asphalt laminated duplex material, 6-mil or heavier polyethylene sheeting, three layers of heavy roofing felt mopped with hot asphalt, or heavy, asphalt-impregnated, vapor-resistant rigid sheet material with sealed joints. It might be added that where a building site has a high water table or is poorly drained, and especially when it is necessary to afford ample protection for a finish floor laid atop a concrete floor slab and made of wood or other material that can tolerate little moisture,

4-37. Styrofoam edge insulation. (The Dow Chemical Co.)

two or more layers of vapor barrier material known to have long life and a low perm rating can be installed.

It is also important that the base course, or cushion, be composed of compacted coarse gravel, and that it be placed sufficiently above grade and with the surrounding grades sloped away so that the slab area will be particularly well drained. Houses built on slabs whose gravel base is actually below grade can suffer extensive moisture damage; consequently great care should be taken to provide adequate drainage. Sometimes a layer of sand is added above the gravel. This will afford good protection against puncture for a sheet vapor barrier. On the other hand, in the event of a high water table the sand can also act as a wick, drawing ground moisture up into direct contact with the vapor barrier.

Perimeter insulation is a must in concrete slab construction. Heat loss takes place close to and along the perimeter edge, and proper insulation will cut that heat loss to practically nil. Special rigid insulation must be used and can be placed in either of two ways: the vertical type is placed against the inside of the foundation walls and extends 2 feet below floor level and at least 1 foot below outside grade level; or L-type, which is applied along the foundation wall and also laid on top of the slab vapor barrier and extending back at least 2 feet under the slab. The vertical type must be installed before backfilling and laying of the gravel cushion. The L-type is installed by preparing a recess in the gravel about 24 inches wide and laying the insulating board in it, butting against a vertical strip of the same material.

Insulation used for floor slabs must have high resistance to heat transmission, permanent durability when exposed to dampness and frost, and high resistance to crushing due to floor loads, weight of slab, or expansion forces. In addition, the material must be immune to fungus and insect attack, and should not absorb or retain moisture. Though a minimum thickness of 1 inch can be used, a 2-inch thickness is highly recommended for all installations. In the past, cellular-glass insulation board with an R factor of 1.8 to 2.2 per inch of thickness was widely used for this purpose. Another similar type was made of glass fibers with plastic binder; this material if exposed to constant groundwater must be coated with coal-tar pitch or asphalt. Both of these types, however, have been largely superceded by foamed plastic insulation board (usually molded or extruded polystyrene), typically available in thicknesses of 1/2, 1, 1 1/2, and 2 inches. R factors vary from 3.7 to over 5.0 for 1-inch thicknesses, depending upon the materials. Some care must be taken in selecting the specific type of board to use, since a few are low in crushing strength; crushing reduces thickness and also insulating qualities.

If heating pipes or ducts are to be laid under the slab, special types of protection must be used (Figure 4-38). These should follow the recommendations of the heating contractor or can be worked out on the basis of

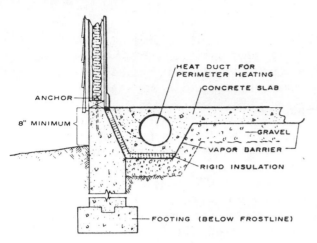

4-38. Perimeter heating ducts in a concrete slab must be insulated to reduce heat loss. (USDA)

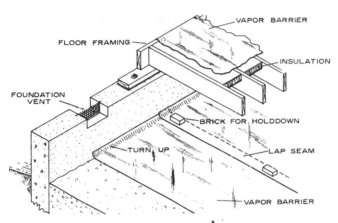

4-39. Installation of vapor barrier and insulation in heated crawl space. (USDA)

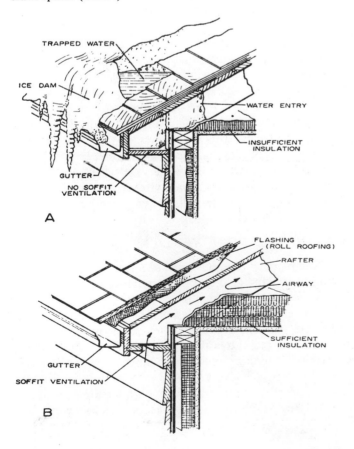

4-40. Ice dams: *A,* insufficient insulation and ventilation can cause ice dams and water damage; *B,* good ventilation, insulation, and roof flashing minimize problems. (USDA)

the principles given herewith. The main purpose of protection in this instance will be to prevent excessive heat loss, called *reverse* heat loss, into the ground. This heat loss is likely to amount to as much as 20 percent of total heat loss in many types of present-day houses, and it may exceed that figure if only 1-inch insulation is used at the slab perimeter.

HOUSES BUILT OVER CRAWL SPACES

Many small houses are being built partly or entirely over crawl spaces today; it is one practical way of reducing costs. Sometimes a part basement is included, the rest of the area under the house being unexcavated. Whether there is a part basement or no basement at all, it is of the greatest importance that protection from moisture rising from the ground into the floors and walls of the structure be provided when the house is built, for, if it is not, serious trouble will be inevitable.

All crawl spaces of whatever nature should be protected from moisture with a durable vapor barrier on the ground surface and with sufficient foundation wall ventilation to dispose of any vapor that may get through the vapor barrier or the walls. Vapor barriers suitable for use under slabs are also acceptable here. They should be well lapped but not necessarily cemented. Foundation wall vents are advisable even when ground cover is used, though they need not be as large as when the cover is omitted.

In cold climates, underfloor insulation together with a vapor barrier above it between the subfloor and the floor, as shown in Figure 4–39, should be used. Instead of a heavy asphalt paper vapor barrier to support the insulation, wire cloth may be used *provided* there is a good ground cover.

Exactly the same requirements for ground cover and ventilation should be observed in unexcavated areas of houses with part basements. The unexcavated part should be kept as dry as possible, particularly if the basement area is to be used for storage of perishable goods or is the site of a furnace or workshop. It is not good practice to have a continuous wall separating the basement from the crawl space. Either leave it open or, if there is a wall, build in plenty of vents so that air can circulate through the crawl space and keep it dry.

SNOW BACKUP AND ICE DAMS ON ROOFS

A reliable method of preventing water damage from these causes is to place a layer of heavy roll roofing (90-pound smooth mineral-surfaced works well) along the eaves and about 4 feet up the roof slope, or at least far enough to cover the sheathing well above the line where the wall below meets the roof (Figure 4–40). In addition, 1-inch spacer blocks or metal ties should be affixed every 16 inches behind the gutter to keep the gutter away from contact with the facia board. Sheet metal can be used instead of roll roofing provided it is rustproof.

Obviously, this type of precaution is used generally when overhangs are minimal and climatic conditions severe, though experience has shown that many ordinarily moderate climates may have bad winters at infrequent intervals, and that the problem may also occur on houses with eave overhangs of as much as 2 feet.

Roofing felts themselves are not suitable protection since they are not really waterproof and since they may deteriorate under adverse moisture conditions.

HEATING SYSTEMS AND CONDENSATION CONTROL

Mention has been made previously of certain types of forced warm air furnaces that are provided with humidifying equipment to add to winter comfort. If furnaces of this type are being installed there is one word of advice: *never* use the humidifier until the new house is thoroughly dried out—not until after two or three heating seasons at the least—and not after that unless the air in the house is uncomfortably dry. This is a particularly important point with regard to earth-sheltered houses constructed of poured concrete and largely covered by earth. Two or three years may pass before the excess moisture in the concrete, which can only enter into the living space of the house, is thoroughly dissipated. Meantime, it may actually be necessary to dehumidify in order to reduce undesirably high levels of moisture.

One thing that well-designed heating systems can do, particularly in modern houses with large glass areas, is reduce or eliminate the nuisance of window condensation during cold weather. This is achieved by using a perimeter outlet system, preferably continuous under the glass areas. Details of these perimeter systems are given in chapter 7. In severe climates, of course, the installation of double- or triple-glazed windows greatly aids in the elimination of the condition.

AIR-CONDITIONED HOUSES

For the most part no special problems other than those found in ordinary houses have yet been found to exist, from the condensation control point of view, with year-round air conditioning. Reverse condensation almost never occurs to a serious extent in summer since the interior temperatures are practically never kept so much lower than the outdoor temperatures that a dew-point could be reached by outside vapor penetrating inside the house.

Of course, in certain regions of the country where summer temperatures and humidities are very high, occasional reverse condensation might occur, though it is hard to imagine that it could do so frequently enough to cause any damage. In these regions, follow the recommendations of the air conditioning suppliers. If they suggest a vapor barrier on the outside (particularly if there is no winter problem), include one. Note too the discussion in this regard on pages 147 and 158.

Ventilation

There is literally no place in the United States where natural or forced ventilation of certain parts of the house is not of importance. In the warmer climates, room and attic ventilation is almost essential for hot-weather comfort; in regions where winters are cold, such ventilation is important not only for the summer comfort it gives but also for the reduction in vapor pressures inside the structure it creates in winter. In all climates, also, crawl space ventilation is important to keep moisture rising from the ground from entering the house and floors of the building.

It is largely ineffective, and therefore bad practice, to build so that the family will have to do its own ventilating for condensation control by opening and closing windows, doors, fireplace dampers, etc. They simply will not perform this function when it is most needed—when it is very cold outdoors. In any event, ventilation alone, when insulation is used, does not prevent condensation problems. Consequently, the house must be provided with good automatic, foolproof means of ventilating the roof or attic, the rooms, and the crawl spaces under the house.

There are few experts in the field who say that ventilation is all that is needed to eliminate the danger of moisture condensation damage and that no vapor barriers need be used. There are some who believe that, in certain houses and under particular conditions, complete vapor barriers are not necessary; this is especially true of ceiling barriers where the attic can be adequately ventilated in locales where winter design temperatures are higher than -20° F, or in homes where combustion air is not required (electrically heated homes, for instance). Actually, there is no single cure-all. Both vapor barrier and ventilating techniques are preferred in tight, relatively small, modern houses of today. In the case of the new, ultra-tight, highly energy-efficient homes now coming into vogue, special systems that make use of heat-exchangers while still allowing proper ventilation are now being developed.

ATTIC AND ROOF VENTILATION

The parts of the house most in need of ventilation in both warm and cold climates are the roof, and the attic area under it if that area is unheated. For many years, it has been customary to specify small gable or hip louvers or vents for the colder parts of the country, usually no more than the minimum size specified under various building code and other construction requirements.

Required vent sizes may differ from region to region, according to specific local codes, but the following constitute recommended good practices for lofts and attics. Below roofs that have a slope of 3 inches or less for every 12 inches of run, the total net area of free ventilation should be 1 square foot for every 300 square feet of ceiling area, with free circulation through all spaces. For a gable roof with a slope of over 3 inches in every foot of run, there should be 1 square foot for every 300 square feet of ceiling area, split between at least two louvers on opposite sides located near the ridge. For hip roofs, there should be 1 square foot for every 300 square feet of area, with 0.5 square foot distributed uniformly at the eaves and 0.5 square foot located at the ridge. This should be considered a minimum venting area; more can be provided if desired. The term "net free ventilating area" means a wide-open venting space—no screening or louvers. This, of course, is bad practice, since all vents must be screened, and many should be louvered as well. Thus, the actual size of the vent must be somewhat larger than the net free ventilating area itself would indicate. Commercially available vent units are designated in terms of net free area; simply use the correct listed sizes. For homemade vents covered with screening, sizes must be increased as shown in Table 4–3; various types of louvered vents are shown in Figure 4–41.

For all houses in which the attic insulation is placed between the rafters rather than between the floor joists, for all flat or shed roofs in which there are no attic spaces and no room for gabled louvers, and for many types of houses with irregularly shaped attics that gabled louvers cannot ventilate effectively, eave vents are a necessity. It is only in relatively recent years that provision for eave vents had to be made, since many older houses without attic insulation had open spaces under the roof overhang between the rafters. Various possibilities are shown in Figure 4–42. Eave vents consist of strips, perforations, or circular holes cut between each pair of rafters. Possible details for vents in the cornice of a flat roof and another detail for a hip roof are illustrated in Figures 4–43 and 4–44. In unfinished attics the eave vents may simply open into the attic space if there are adequate louvers, or, in hip roofs, good peak or hip vents.

Net Free Vent Area

Type Covering	Gross Opening
¼ " mesh	1 × net
¼ " mesh & louvers	2 × net
1/8" mesh	1.25 × net
1/8" mesh & louvers	2.25 × net
1/16" mesh	2 × net
1/16" mesh & louvers	3 × net

Table 4–3.

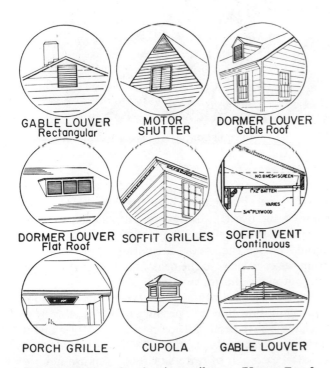

4–41. Types of roof and attic ventilators. (Hunter Fan & Ventilation Co.)

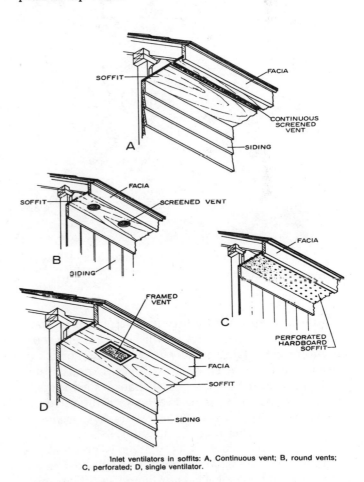

Inlet ventilators in soffits: A, Continuous vent; B, round vents; C, perforated; D, single ventilator.

4–42. Various inlet ventilators in soffits. (USDA)

111

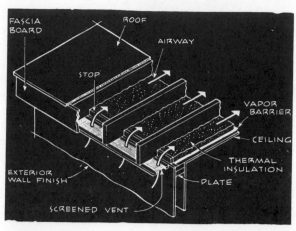

4–43. Cornice ventilation. (*Progressive Architecture*)

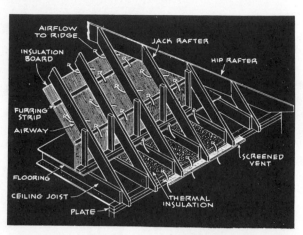

4–44. Hip roof ventilation. (*Progressive Architecture*)

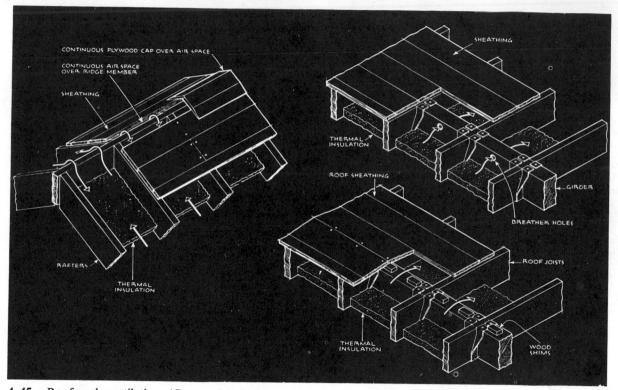

4–45. Roof peak ventilation. (*Progressive Architecture*) **4–46.** Flat roof ventilation. (*Progressive Architecture*)

However, special measures must be taken in many houses with finished attics in which there are no collar beams or gable louvers and where the insulation is carried between the rafters clear to the peak. Special provisions must also be made for all flat or shed roofs in which the insulation is packed between the rafters or across their bottoms and the rafters butt against a center girder rather than resting on it.

In the former case, peak venting is necessary. A method of providing air circulation in a peaked roof is illustrated in Figure 4–45. The topmost sheathing board is omitted and the roof cap is made sufficiently large (reinforced perhaps by a thin piece of plywood) so that

it will cover the space where the sheathing board is omitted and overlap the next board. At each end of the gable the space left by the omitted sheathing board should be screened. Air circulation is thus provided from the eave vents to the peak and then along the peak and out along the edges of the gable.

For flat or shed roofs of the type mentioned above, some provision that will permit air to pass through or over the center beam will be necessary. Holes about 2 inches in diameter bored near the top of the beam, one between each pair of rafters or roof joists, would probably be enough, as would 1-inch or 1 1/2-inch wood shims placed at regular intervals on top of the girder before the roof sheathing is put in place (Figure 4–46).

In many flat or shed roof contemporary houses, and in those with so-called vaulted or cathedral roofs, the ceiling joists or rafters are left exposed for visual effect, and the roof is built up directly on top. Here roof ventilation is impossible, unless a rigid type of finish roof covering is installed on furring strips, leaving a gap between the insulation decking and the finish roofing that is open from eave to peak; the peak can be covered with a special ventilating cap. Extra care must be taken to make sure that the vapor barrier is in perfect condition before the built-up roofing is finally finished.

Indoor ventilation at the ceiling line in houses of this type is almost essential. It can be obtained by using narrow, ceiling-level, awning-type windows, or small continuous louvers. In some pitched-roof designs, clerestory window arrangements, roof windows, and ventilating skylights are becoming increasingly popular. To ventilate the fixed-glass gable that is also becoming popular requires the same type of treatment: i.e., louvers at the top.

Even when sizable gable louvers are included in a roof, it may also be necessary to include eave vents as well. There have been many cases when houses have been located so that the prevailing winds did not blow against the gable louvers, and others where the houses were so close together that sufficient air motion was impossible. In such houses, even with brisk breezes very little air will pass through the louvered openings, and additional openings under the eaves must be installed to provide positive air movement. In many cases, the use of a venting system other than gable louvers might well be indicated. There are numerous different types of vents designed to be installed directly in the roof itself; some of them are "wind-powered" and provide a certain measure of forced draft. These units are generally located near the top of the roof, with provisions made for fresh air to enter through the eaves or along the lower portions of the roof.

It should, however, be borne in mind that too much ventilation can also cause problems. If there is not an adequate vapor barrier in the ceiling, the top of the insulation may be cooled to such an extent that vapor rising from the floor below will condense in the insulation; this is unlikely with a good vapor barrier. But cooling of the insulation also means that heat will travel upward at a faster rate, and thus heat loss will be increased. The *1977 Fundamentals Volume, ASHRAE HANDBOOK & Product Directory,* has noted that, "insulation requires added ventilation, which in turn necessitates adequate insulation." However, with the 6 to 12 inches or more of insulation being installed nowadays in new houses, normal or even over-adequate attic ventilation is unlikely to contribute much to excess heat loss, unless there is a veritable arctic gale swirling through the attic.

FORCED VENTILATION IN ATTICS

This is becoming increasingly common for summer comfort in all but the lowest-priced houses, and it is an excellent means of cutting down on, or escaping entirely, the high cost of mechanical cooling. Exhaust fans are located either in a gable or in a ceiling plenum. The gable type is suitable for houses with year-round air conditioning, but those in the ceiling are not. Further details on attic fans will be found in chapter 5.

These fans are not suitable for winter roof ventilation. They are too powerful and waste too much heat. Furthermore, in ceiling plenum installations the opening through which the air is pulled up by the fan from the rooms below in hot weather must be provided with a tight, insulated cover to prevent heat and vapor transfer during the winter. When an attic stairway or access scuttle is used for summer air circulation, the protection described earlier will be sufficient.

PERMEABLE ROOFING

There is one additional way of reducing condensation hazards in roofs, and that is through the use of relatively permeable roofing materials. The typical modern roof, with its heavy roofing felts and essentially impermeable asphalt shingles, built-up roofing, or fiberglass shingles, is a real vapor trap. However, if conditions warrant the use of a permeable material, one possible choice is either cedar shingles or cedar shakes. Cedar is an excellent roofing material, and may be obtained fully treated with a fire retardant. This by no means makes the shingles fireproof, but they are sufficiently fire-safe that they can be used in most locales. Local building codes, however, may militate against the use of cedar shingle roofing in any form.

WALL VENTILATING

All houses, except air-conditioned ones with fixed glazing, are provided with the most satisfactory means of winter ventilation known to man: windows. However, the point has already been made that these ideal ventilators will not be operated efficiently by the homeowner when the weather gets cold. Some other method of reducing interior humidities when they reach a point where they could damage the structure must be found. Theoretically, a good vapor barrier will handle the problem, but no barrier is perfect. Furthermore, too high a concentration of moisture inside the house can actually damage window frames as condensation on the window drips down, and it can cause mold and mildew in closets and elsewhere. The problem can be even worse in houses equipped with steel- or aluminum-framed windows, on which incredible quantities of condensation and frost can build up, only to melt away into the trimwork. In severe situations, mechanical dehumidification equipment must be installed to take care of the problems; ordinary ventilation simply will not do the job.

Of course, the major problem in most houses is keeping interior humidities up. Pans of water can be set out on radiators, humidifiers can be installed to work in warm air furnaces or in individual rooms, and, in extreme cases, kettles of water can be set to steaming on stoves, or hot showers turned on. Many of these methods, it must be noted, are hardly cost-effective.

This need for an increase in interior humidity has led to various expedients besides vapor barriers for reducing the vapor pressure on the walls of a dwelling. The most common of these are wall vents, either airing the outer side of the wall or actually venting the room directly to the outdoors, and automatic dehumidifying installations.

People in the paint industry, primarily concerned with the elimination of exterior paint failure, may recommend the use of some means of ventilating the siding or shingles so that the circulation of air will drive off the dangerous concentrations of moisture behind the material. Some types of siding with very narrow overlaps provide cracks between the strips that give a certain amount of air motion—but these types also permit wind-driven rain to damage the wall. When the siding has a wide overlap, small wedges have been known to be used to provide air circulation behind these siding strips. Finally, there are certain types of siding (wood, metal, or hardboard) that are made with shadow vents both for appearance and to provide ventilations; these may likewise permit the entry of wind-driven rains or fine snow.

The adequacy of these methods of venting the outer skin of the house is dubious. In a well-insulated house the dewpoint often will be *inside the sheathing* during cold weather; and while the exterior paint surface may be protected, the sheathing and the studs will not. Condensation may well damage them over a period of years. In moderate climates, air passages in walls can be employed to remove an unrestricted vapor supply, but these often are overly large and can be a source of considerable heat loss. Wall cavity ventilation can be effective in certain cases, if correctly designed and installed; but insufficient specific data exists by which informed judgments can be made on this.

VENTILATING THE INTERIOR

The only suitable method of reducing dangerous concentrations of humidity inside the house is interior ventilation, preferably by some automatic method. It can be shown that interior ventilation is actually much less wasteful of heat than one might imagine, *if the indoor relative humidity is kept at comfortably high levels.* Table 4–4 shows that for air entering a house at 32° F saturated, and leaving it 70° F and 30 percent relative humidity, 14,000 cubic feet are necessary to remove one pound of water, in the form of vapor, from the house.

This compares with only 4,070 cubic feet when the leaving air is 70° F and 45 percent relative humidity.

In other words, it costs *less* to ventilate a well-insulated and moisture-protected house than it does when the house is not protected at all. Real fuel savings also result when indoor humidities are high. This is a curious but pleasant fact of physics. A less pleasant fact is that ventilation is indeed responsible for some degree of heat loss, and in these days of high fuel costs and energy conservation, any heat loss that can be corrected by some cost-effective means must be considered. One method with considerable promise that doubtless will enjoy greatly increased use in the future is the installation of heat exchangers, which allow an input of fresh ventilating air with only a minimal loss of heat.

In any case, houses should be built so that their parts can withstand vapor pressures resulting from between 40 and 50 percent relative humidities. The trouble is, however, that in such houses, and especially in modern, ultra-tight houses, there is a marked tendency for humidity to rise *above* that level, until condensation occurs.

There are two simple methods, that do not call for operation by the occupants, of controlling excessive indoor humidities. One, which can be used only with warm air systems with automatic humidifiers, is to include a humidity controller, or humidistat. If the humidistat is set to turn the humidifier off when the humidity reaches 45 percent, condensation damage will be avoided. Such a device is shown in Figure 4–47. Another method is to connect a humidistat to automatic fans in the kitchen, bathroom, laundry room, and other places where excessive vapor is produced, so that when the "local" humidity reaches a danger point, the humidistat will start the exhaust fan, thus reducing vapor concentrations to a safe point.

The need for humidistats in a new house is hard to establish. Most people have no idea what humidity level they prefer, and even less of a notion what humidity levels their living habits may cause. Therefore, if a house is provided with built-in automatic fans where needed, it will always be possible to add humidistats later if the need arises.

Of course, if the family objects to these solutions because of fancied drafts and heat losses, or too high noise level from the fans, dehumidifiers with built-in humidistats can be used. This is an expensive alternative, and not one to resort to until the house has been lived in for a while and the structural parts have dried out, but it may be called for in exceptional instances. Likewise, in the case of a new super-energy-efficient house, plans may call for comparatively precise control of humidity, noise, drafts and heat losses through the use of specialized equipment, including heat exchangers, which certainly must be automatic and may well be computerized.

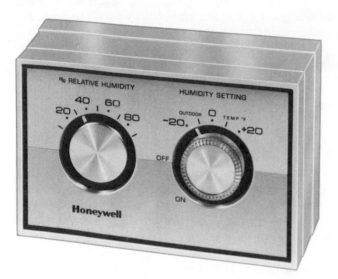

4-47. Humidistat, or electronic humidity controller. (Courtesy, Honeywell Inc.)

CRAWL SPACE WALL VENTILATION

The need for an impermeable vapor barrier ground cover in unheated crawl spaces has been emphasized; and the danger that crawl space vents may become clogged with leaves, snow, and tall grass only reinforces the importance of such a cover. As a matter of fact, it is not uncommon for vents to be closed by the occupants when the ventilation is needed most: in the winter. They do this to keep the floors warm, forgetting that this may saturate the joists and eventually rot them out.

Foundation vents should be placed as high in the wall as possible, so that air will pass directly over the bottoms of the joists, thus helping to keep them dry. At the same time, this location will help to prevent blockage. Properly, one vent should be located at each corner of the wall rather than toward the center as is frequently done. This will prevent the formation of damp pockets in the corner areas.

RELATION OF INDOOR RELATIVE HUMIDITY TO VENTILATION HEAT LOSS

	AIR IN	AIR OUT				
Temperature	32F	70F	70F	70F	70F	70F
Relative Humidity	Sat	24%	30%	45%	60%	Sat
Absolute Humidity (Lbs water/lb air)	0.00379	0.00380	0.00475	0.00712	0.00950	0.01582
Water Vapor Removed from House (Lbs water/lb air)		0.00001	0.00096	0.00333	0.00571	0.01203
Enthalpy (Btu/lb air)	11.758	20.986	22.026	24.636	27.516	34.090
Total Heat Removed from House (Btu/lb air)		9.228	10.268	12.878	15.758	22.332
Air Necessary to Remove 1 lb Water Vapor from House (Lbs air/lb water)		1,000,000	1,042	303	175	83
(Cu ft air/lb water)		13,450,000	14,000	4,070	2,350	1,020

If a house has a volume of 10,000 cubic feet and an infiltration rate of one air change per hour, which is considered typical, the water removal rate at 30 percent interior humidity is:

$$\frac{10,000}{14,000} = 0.714 \text{ lb per hr}$$

Then if the house is equipped with storm windows and vapor barriers and is otherwise arranged for a humidity of 45 percent, the ventilation rate necessary to remove the same amount of water in the form of vapor is:

$$4070 \times 0.714 = 2900 \text{ cu ft per hr}$$

The heat loss due to ventilation in the original case is approximately:

$$\frac{10,000}{13.5} \times (70F - 32F) \times 0.24 = 6750 \text{ Btu per hr}$$

The heat loss due to the same cause in the second case is:

$$\frac{2900}{13.5} \times (70F - 32F) \times 0.24 = 1960 \text{ Btu per hr}$$

The estimated saving is: $6750 - 1960 = 4790$ Btu per hr

If the total heat loss of the house is 50,000 Btu per hr for an outdoor temperature of 32F, the saving amounts to:

$$\frac{4790}{50000} = 9.6 \text{ percent of the total heat loss}$$

Table 4–4.

The vents need not be as large or as numerous when a durable ground cover is used, of course. The *1977 Fundmentals Volume, ASHRAE HANDBOOK & Product Directory* recommends that the total net free ventilating area of crawl space vents be calculated as follows:

$$a = (2L/100) + (A/300)$$

where

L = the perimeter of the crawl space, linear feet.
A = the area of the crawl space, square feet.
a = the total net area of all vents, square feet.

Because this amount of ventilation cools the first floor so much, insulation must be placed between the floor joists. However, if a good ground cover is installed, the net free venting area should be reduced to 10 percent of the amount calculated by the formula. The vents must be screened, of course, in order to keep out vermin and small animals; overall vent areas, as determined by the type of screening used, are shown in Table 4-3.

Of course, there is one way of eliminating the total problem of crawl space moisture at one stroke, and with it the need for wall vents. This is the use of the space as a plenum heating chamber. Information on this type of heat distribution will be found in chapter 7.

THE PROBLEM OF DOUBLE GLAZING

One minor annoyance that sometimes reaches the proportions of a problem is the condensation that occasionally shows up on the outer panes of double-glazed windows or storm windows. If storm windows are in question, there is a way of eliminating the condensation that is the essence of simplicity. If the outermost glass area is vented from the bottom, this alone will not successfully eliminate moisture from the window. But if a small vent hole about 1/4 inch in diameter is drilled at the top of the window, to allow circulation of air between the panes, condensation on the outer window will be completely eliminated and the likelihood of condensation on the inner window will not materially be increased. Naturally, such a trick cannot be worked with hermetically sealed insulating glass windows.

Figure 4-48 shows the surface temperatures on the warm side of various glass unit surfaces as well as the interior relative humidity at which condensation will appear on the glass. For instance, at 0° F, the temperature of the warm side of a single glazing 1/4-inch thick is 21° F and the indoor relative humidity at which condensation will occur is only 12 percent. With prefabricated double glazing, on the other hand, using 1/4-inch glass and a 1/2-inch air space, the inner surface temperature would be 47° F and the relative humidity condensation point 38 percent, satisfactorily within the comfort-and-health range of interior humidities.

These figures apply not only to hermetically sealed double glazing, but also to window-storm-window combinations, provided they are weatherstripped.

It should be borne in mind that if the window frames are of metal, the condensation point will be considerably lower around the window perimeter, due to the higher heat conductivity of the metal. Perimeter condensation may occur with such windows, even if they are double glazed.

Condensation Control in Old Houses

With the rapidly rising costs in heating fuels, along with higher standards for winter comfort that calls for warmer interior temperatures, higher humidities, and an absence of drafts, owners of old houses have in recent years been spending sizable sums of money to "winterize" their dwellings. This involves installing storm windows and doors, as well as weatherstrips; blowing insulation into the walls and finished attic floors, where membrane vapor barriers cannot be placed; using tight and relatively vapor-resistant exterior wall materials; and installing humidifying equipment to raise the interior humidity to what is considered a comfortable point. When all these things are done, or even only part of them, a moisture load that it cannot dispose of is put on the building and condensation damage results.

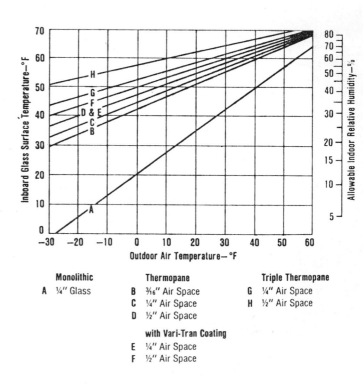

Monolithic	Thermopane	Triple Thermopane
A ¼″ Glass	B ³⁄₁₆″ Air Space	G ¼″ Air Space
	C ¼″ Air Space	H ½″ Air Space
	D ½″ Air Space	
	with Vari-Tran Coating	
	E ¼″ Air Space	
	F ½″ Air Space	

4-48. Inboard glass surface temperatures (no sun). (Courtesy, Libby-Owens-Ford Company)

The problem could, of course, be solved by educating the homeowner to open a window whenever condensation begins to appear on the glass, or to install powered fans at sources of greatest moisture production and turn them on when necessary. But few and far between are the homeowners who will, after spending all that money to achieve what they consider to be real winter comfort as well as low heating costs, open a window to let some of the valuable warm air escape. Actually, of course, little heat is lost if this is done right, as the example on page 115 shows.

The application of a suitable paint vapor barrier or wallpapers with high vapor resistance, as described earlier, may work. So may natural ventilation. And if conditions are not remedied by these methods, automatic dehumidifiers can be used. Ground moisture can be eliminated *if* the crawl space is deep enough for access; if not, the area may have to be excavated at considerable cost. Large foundation wall vents should also be built in. Floor temperatures can be kept comfortable if insulation can be placed between the floor joists—again, a costly job if the area is too shallow for easy access. But the work must be done when the situation is really severe; not to do it will mean the eventual rotting of joists and the collapse of the floor, together with damage to walls and roof resulting from moisture arising by stack action.

When snow backup damage occurs in an old house, the shingles will have to be taken up for several courses above the roof-wall line and replaced after the necessary waterproof layer has been put in. If the gutters are fastened directly to the fascia boards, they should be taken off and spacer blocks should be placed in between.

Chapter 5

Principles of Thermal Control: Summer

The human animal has a persistent habit of thinking traditionally. New ideas are harder to get used to, sometimes, than a new set of teeth or a new wife. The idea that summer comfort is almost as much of a problem in Montana or Illinois as it is in Texas or Florida can be a tough one to buy for many folks; almost all of the old building traditions of the northern states are firmly based on the concept that winter heating is the real problem to worry about. Summer comfort has, until comparatively recently, been almost entirely neglected.

Probably the easiest way to convince the unconvinced on the summer heat problem is to expose them to a few facts. These facts are shown in unarguable graphic form in Figure 5–1: the average amount of solar radiation in Btu that strikes one square foot of ground per day during the month of July throughout the United States. Note how the July isothermal lines connecting points of equal intensity tend to run more or less along

a north-south axis, as compared with the east-west axis of January pattern in Figure 5–2. Obviously, July is hot all over the United States!

That people have been doing something about the problem is made clear by a few statistics. In 1950, according to reliable estimates, central cooling units were built into about 3,500 new dwellings. By 1955, only five short years later, the number had increased to roughly 140,000. Since that time, the numbers have shot up amazingly, to the point where year-round heating and cooling is built into a large proportion of the one-family dwelling units that are constructed in this country. And, of course, one must also consider the tremendous number of cooling-equipment retrofits in existing houses, replacement of old heating systems with heating/cooling systems, the burgeoning use of small through-the-wall and portable or window air conditioners, and so on.

It is true that currently more and more people are at

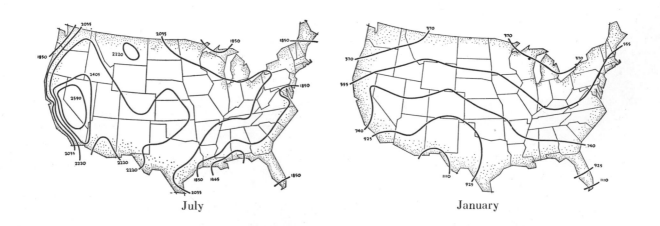

July   January

5–1 and 5–2. Average daily solar radiation received at the ground. (U.S. Weather Bureau)

least attempting to cut back on their use of mechanical cooling equipment, largely because of the increasingly high cost of operation but also in the interest of energy conservation. It is likewise true that many people who would, a few years ago, have automatically included central air conditioning systems in their new houses today are having some second thoughts, for much the same reasons. So even though summer cooling is obviously here to stay, and will continue to be installed in new houses all around the country, the portion of the new house market without mechanical cooling is and will also continue to be an important one. At least in parts of the northern tier of states, and in the high mountain country as well, it is possible with proper orientation, construction, and ventilation techniques to provide summer comfort *without* mechanical cooling for innumerable house locations and types.

Nevertheless, all houses should be built so that they will make economical cooling equipment installation and operation possible. This chapter will assume that every house should be designed for such economy, because this always means greater summer comfort whether the building is air-conditioned or not.

Heretofore, many people have hesitated to use these techniques unless summer cooling was actually a part of the picture, because this meant increased construction costs. We have, in other words, found ourselves in the peculiar position of underemphasizing the comfort aspects of a house unless several thousand dollars' worth of special equipment is to be put in to make that comfort mechanically possible. In that case, we say we must use every possible device to keep the cost down. We can afford to spend a few hundred dollars on structure, if it will cut cooling unit size, because by doing so we will save money. Ah, the $500 more for insulation, we might think, added to the original amount specified, along with a few minor structural modifications, will reduce the cost of the cooling equipment from $3000 to $2000 by cutting the required size of the unit, and that's a savings of $500 or so (or whatever). . . .

False economy. Think how much more could be saved, not only in operating costs and equipment costs but in energy as well, by not having any air conditioning at all—but only the materials and techniques that make mechanical cooling more economical! If a house can be made comfortable without air conditioning by effective use of known means of thermal control such as trees, cross ventilation, sun control devices, insulation, and so on, its occupants will be both happier and richer. And they can always install cooling later at no added structural expense, since the house is already an efficient heat barrier. If they want to sell, they can get more for it if it is ready for a cooling unit than if it requires alteration.

SUMMER COMFORT

Before we launch into an analysis of building for summer comfort and for cooling equipment economy, we should first establish what we mean by the phrase "summer comfort." It is not a fixed quantity; for not everyone is comfortable, say, at 90° F in the shade. People have differing internal thermostatic controls, many of them subjective. However, extensive experiments have, over the years, resulted in the establishment of maxima and minima of temperature and humidity within which most people will be comfortable. The comfort chart shown in chapter 4 (Figure 4–6) indicates the area within which indoor climates should be kept if the average person is to be at ease during hot weather; the comfort zone is the same as for cold weather.

In cases where the indoor thermal environment has a mean radiant temperature nearly equal to the dry-bulb air temperature, air velocity is less than 45 feet per minute, altitudes are less than 7000 feet, and the occupants of the thermal environment are lightly clothed and engaged in sedentary activity (light office work, for instance), the data shown on the chart are applicable. The shaded section represents the comfort zone recommended in the ASHRAE Comfort Standard 55-74. Most people will be comfortable in a range from an effective temperature of 72° F or a dry bulb of 71° F and a wet bulb of 65° F (relative humidity about 73 percent) up to an ET of 78° F, dry bulb of 80° F and a wet bulb of 56° F (relative humidity about 20 percent). Above and below these levels a majority of people become increasingly uncomfortable—either too chilly or too hot and damp. If we raise the dry bulb to 85° F and the relative humidity to 60 percent, a not uncommon summer situation, the ET is about 86° F, and very few people would be comfortable in that sweltering heat. But if the humidity is left at 60 percent and the dry bulb is dropped 10° to 75° F, the effective temperature becomes about 75° to 76° F, where almost everyone is comfortable.

The House for Summer Comfort

To keep indoor climates within this comfort zone under summer conditions, much can be done by varying the structure of the house. For example, it has long been known that the main sources of summer heat are roofs and windows. Unlike winter conditions, where low outdoor temperature is the major villain, the guiltiest party in increasing summer discomfort indoors is the sun itself, though high air temperatures and high humidity of course play an important part.

A useful and informative indication of the sources and relative amounts of heat entering a typical wood-frame house in the New York Metropolitan area during an average July day is presented in Figure 5–3. The

Olgyay brothers' study (Victor and Aladar Olgyay, et al., *Application of Climatic Data to House Design,* Housing and Home Finance Agency Study, 1954, reprinted in Olgyay and Olgyay, *Solar Control and Shading Devices,* Princeton University Press, 1957), from which this chart was taken, assumes average cloudiness and no window shading. Note that the radiation is both direct and diffuse; the direct radiation only enters through the windows when the sun is shining directly upon them, but diffuse radiation enters through all windows at all times during the daylight hours. Their findings suggest that diffuse radiation is a factor that should also be dealt with in an effort to decrease heat gain.

There are three *structural* techniques for controlling the entry of solar energy into a building: special roof treatments, shading, and heat-resisting materials. Orientation is of course also of great importance; it has been discussed in some detail in chapter 2, and in this chapter is reviewed under "Shade." Ventilation is primarily a matter of using powered fans in the attic, and consequently it is treated under "Roofs."

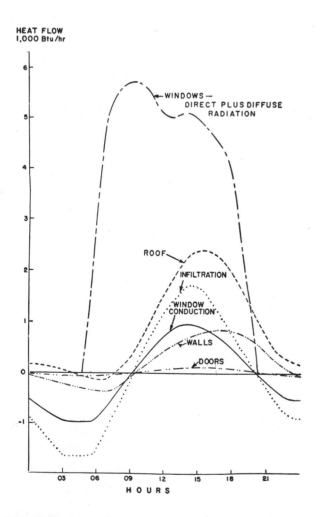

HEAT FLOW
1,000 Btu/hr

WINDOWS—
DIRECT PLUS DIFFUSE
RADIATION

ROOF
INFILTRATION
WINDOW
CONDUCTION
WALLS
DOORS

HOURS

5–3. Types and sources of heat entering a house during hot weather. (Olgyay and Olgyay, "Solar Control and Shading Devices," Princeton University Press, 1957)

ROOFS

The most important single element in the hot-weather heat load of a house is, of course, its roof. Readings in every part of the country show that uninsulated under-roof spaces can reach temperatures higher than 150° F when the outdoor temperature is only 90° F. Furthermore, this load is an invariable from the point of view of house location—unless the site has large trees that shade part or all of the roof during the summer weather. And, as will be seen, modern cooling load practices ignore this type of shade, since trees are impermanent and may be lost during a storm or from disease or old age.

It is true that a pitched roof has a variable heat load at various parts of the day. A western pitch will undergo heat penetration ranging from almost zero for some hours after sunrise to very high indeed during the afternoon. Similarly, a north pitch will at all times have a much smaller heat load than a south pitch. However, these variations in roof pitch are never taken into account in calculating cooling loads, and they are of minor importance in attic temperature control in a non-cooled house.

Roof Insulation

The best single way of achieving control of attic temperatures, summer as well as winter, is with roof insulation. For example, the ceiling-roof cross section described in Table 3-18 (chapter 3) has an overall U, or heat transmission coefficient, of 0.046 when constructed with 6 inches of R-19 blanket insulation, and only 0.159 with no insulation. This means that, in wintertime, the heat loss through an insulated 1,000-square foot roof, $U = 0.046$, would be only 46 Btu per hour per degree temperature difference. For the uninsulated roof, it would be 159 Btu.

The summer situation is equally dramatic but considerably more complicated. When calculating heat gain through a roof, it is essential to remember that the overall U-factor is not the only heat transfer mechanism that must be considered. In winter calculations, the effect of the sun's energy on the roof is always ignored for conventional heating systems, since heat losses must be figured for worst conditions: i.e., when there is no sun at all. But in the summer, the sun's energy becomes an addition to the thermal load.

Calculating the heat gain that occurs through roofs and walls, according to the *1977 Fundamentals Volume, ASHRAE HANDBOOK & Product Directory,* "involves the concept of sol-air temperature. *Sol-air temperature* is that temperature of the outdoor air which, in the absence of all radiation exchanges, would give the same rate of heat entry into the surface as would exist with the actual combination of incident solar radiation, radiant energy exchange with the sky and other outdoor surroundings, and convective heat exchange with the outdoor air."

Cooling Load Temperature Differences for Calculating Cooling Load from Flat Roofs

Roof No	Description of Construction	Weight lb/ft²	U-value Btu/(h·ft²·°F)	1	2	3	4	5	6	7	8	9	10	11	12	13	14	15	16	17	18	19	20	21	22	23	24	Hour of Maximum CLTD	Minimum CLTD	Maximum CLTD	Difference CLTD
															Without Suspended Ceiling																
1	Steel sheet with 1-in. (or 2-in.) insulation	7 (8)	0.213 (0.124)	1	−2	−3	−3	−5	−3	6	19	34	49	61	71	78	79	77	70	59	45	30	18	12	8	5	3	14	−5	79	84
2	1-in. wood with 1-in. insulation	8	0.170	6	3	0	−1	−3	−3	−2	4	14	27	39	52	62	70	74	74	70	62	51	38	28	20	14	9	16	−3	74	77
3	4-in. l.w. concrete	18	0.213	9	5	2	0	−2	−3	−3	1	9	20	32	44	55	64	70	73	71	66	57	45	34	25	18	13	16	−3	73	76
4	2-in. h.w. concrete with 1-in. (or 2-in.) insulation	29	0.206 (0.122)	12	8	5	3	0	−1	−1	3	11	20	30	41	51	59	65	66	66	62	54	45	36	29	22	17	16	−1	67	68
5	1-in. wood with 2-in. insulation	19	0.109	3	0	−3	−4	−5	−7	−6	−3	5	16	27	39	49	57	63	64	62	57	48	37	26	18	11	7	16	−7	64	71
6	6-in. l.w. concrete	24	0.158	22	17	13	9	6	3	1	1	3	7	15	23	33	43	51	58	62	64	62	57	50	42	35	28	18	1	54	63
7	2.5-in. wood with 1-insulation	13	0.130	29	24	20	16	13	10	7	6	6	9	13	20	27	34	42	48	53	55	56	54	49	44	39	34	19	6	56	50
8	8-in. l.w. concrete	31	0.126	35	30	26	22	18	14	11	9	7	7	9	13	19	25	33	39	46	50	53	54	53	49	45	40	20	7	54	47
9	4-in. h.w. concrete with 1-in. (or 2-in.) insulation	52 (52)	0.200 (0.120)	25	22	18	15	12	9	8	8	10	14	20	26	33	40	46	50	53	53	52	48	43	38	34	30	18	8	53	45
10	2.5-in. wood with 2-in. insulation	13	0.093	30	26	23	19	16	13	10	9	8	9	13	17	23	29	36	41	46	49	51	50	47	43	39	35	19	8	51	43
11	Roof terrace system	75	0.106	34	31	28	25	22	19	16	14	13	13	15	18	22	26	31	36	40	44	45	46	45	43	40	37	20	13	46	33
12	6-in. h.w. concrete with 1-in. (or 2-in.) insulation	75 (75)	0.192 (0.117)	31	28	25	22	20	17	15	14	14	16	18	22	26	31	36	40	43	45	45	44	42	40	37	34	19	14	45	31
13	4-in. wood with 1-in. (or 2-in) insulation	17 (18)	0.106 (0.078)	38	36	33	30	28	25	22	20	18	17	16	17	18	21	24	28	32	36	39	41	43	43	42	40	22	16	43	27
															With Suspended Ceiling																
1	Steel Sheet with 1-in. (or 2-in.) insulation	9 (10)	0.134 (0.092)	2	0	−2	−3	−4	−4	−1	9	23	37	50	62	71	77	78	74	67	56	42	28	18	12	8	5	15	−4	78	82
2	1-in. wood with 1-in. insulation	10	0.115	20	15	11	8	5	3	2	3	7	13	21	30	40	48	55	60	62	61	58	51	44	37	30	25	17	2	62	60
3	4-in. l.w. concrete	20	0.134	19	14	10	7	4	2	0	0	4	10	19	29	39	48	56	62	65	64	61	54	46	38	30	24	17	0	65	65
4	2-in. h.w. concrete with 1-in. insulation	30	0.131	28	25	23	20	17	15	13	13	14	16	20	25	30	35	39	43	46	47	46	44	41	38	35	32	18	13	47	34
5	1-in. wood with 2-in. insulation	10	0.083	25	20	16	13	10	7	5	5	7	12	18	25	33	41	48	53	57	57	56	52	46	40	34	29	18	5	57	52
6	6-in. l.w. concrete	26	0.109	32	28	23	19	16	13	10	8	7	8	11	16	22	29	36	42	48	52	54	54	51	47	42	37	20	7	54	47
7	2.5-in. wood with 1-in. insulation	15	0.096	34	31	29	26	23	21	18	16	15	15	16	18	21	25	30	34	38	41	43	44	44	42	40	37	21	14	46	29
8	8-in. l.w. concrete	33	0.093	39	36	33	29	26	23	20	18	15	14	14	15	17	20	25	29	34	38	42	45	46	45	44	42	21	14	46	32
9	4-in. h.w. concrete with 1-in. (or 2-in.) insulation	53 (54)	0.128 (0.090)	30	29	27	26	24	22	21	20	20	21	22	24	27	29	32	34	36	38	38	38	37	36	34	33	19	20	38	18
10	2.5-in. wood with 2-in. insulation	15	0.072	35	33	30	28	26	24	22	20	18	18	18	20	22	25	28	32	35	38	40	41	41	40	39	37	21	18	41	23
11	Roof terrace system	77	0.082	30	29	28	27	26	25	24	23	22	22	22	23	23	25	26	28	29	31	32	33	33	33	33	32	22	22	33	11
12	6-in. h.w. concrete with 1-in. (or 2-in.) insulation	77 (77)	0.125 (0.088)	29	28	27	26	25	24	23	22	21	21	22	23	25	26	28	30	32	33	34	34	34	33	32	31	20	21	34	13
13	4-in. wood with 1-in. (or 2-in.) insulation	19 (20)	0.082 (0.064)	35	34	33	32	31	29	27	26	24	23	22	21	22	22	24	25	27	30	32	34	35	36	37	36	23	21	37	16

1 Application: These values may be used for all normal air-conditioning estimates; usually without correction (except as noted below) in latitude 0° to 50° North or South when the load is calculated for the hottest weather.

2 Corrections: The values in the table were calculated for an inside temperature of 78 F and an outdoor maximum temperature of 95 F, with an outdoor daily range of 21 deg F. The table remains approximately correct for other outdoor maximums (93-102 F) and other outdoor daily ranges (16-34 deg F), provided the outdoor daily average temperature remains approximately 85 F, If the room air temperature is different from 78 F and/or the outdoor daily average temperature is different from 85 F, the following rules apply: (a) For room air temperature less than 78 F, add the difference between 78 F and room air temperature; if greater than 78 F, subtract the difference. (b) For outdoor daily average temperature less than 85 F, subtract the difference between 85 F and the daily average temperature; if greater than 85 F, add the difference.

3 Attics or other spaces between the roof and ceiling: If the ceiling is insulated and a fan is used for positive ventilation in the space between the ceiling and roof, the total temperature difference for calculating the room load may be decreased by 25%. If the attic space contains a return duct or other air plenum, care should be taken in determining the portion of the heat gain that reaches the ceiling.

4 Light Colors: Multiply the CLTD's in the table by 0.5. Credit should not be taken for light-colored roofs except where the permanence of light color is established by experience, as in rural areas or where there is little smoke.

5 For solar transmission in other months: The table values of temperature differences calculated for July 21 will be approximately correct for a roof in the following months:

North Latitude	
Latitude	Months
0°	All Months
10°	All Months
20°	All Months except Nov., Dec., Jan.
30°	Mar., Apr., May, June, July, Aug., Sept.
40°	April, May, June, July, Aug.
50°	May, June, July

South Latitude	
Latitude	Months
0°	All Months
10°	All Months
20°	All Months except May, June, July
30°	Sept., Oct., Nov., Dec., Jan., Feb., Mar.
40°	Oct., Nov., Dec., Jan., Feb.
50°	Nov., Dec., Jan.

Table 5-1. (Reprinted with permission from the *1977 Fundamentals Volume, ASHRAE HANDBOOK & Product Directory*)

Note that in determining *U*-values for roofs in summer conditions, downward heat flow figures must be substituted for the upward flow figures used for figuring winter conditions, since the heat flow is inward and not outward. This is exemplified in Table 3-20, chapter 3.

The Sol-Air Temperature

This is an hourly figure that varies with a number of climatic factors, listed by the HANDBOOK (and included in a rather complex formula) as follows:

The absorptance of the surface for solar radiation
The total solar radiation incident on the surface, in Btu per hour per square foot
The coefficient of heat transfer by long wave radiation and convection at the outer surface, in Btu per hour per square foot per degree Fahrenheit
The surface temperature in degrees Fahrenheit
The outdoor air temperature in degrees Fahrenheit
The hemispherical emittance of the surface
The difference between the long wave radiation incident on the surface from the sky and surroundings, and the radiation emitted by a blackbody at outdoor air temperature, Btu per hour per square foot

Once the sol-air temperature cycle has been determined and corrections made as necessary for specific conditions, further calculations can be made to determine particular cooling load temperature differences (CLTD) for different constructions. The CLTD can then be used to find the heat gain through a building section; correction factors are employed as necessary. The values shown in Table 5-1 are based on an indoor temperature of 78° F, an outdoor maximum of 95° F, and an outdoor mean of 85° F, with an outdoor range of 21° F and a solar radiation variation typical of 40° N latitude on July 21. Corrections can be made for other latitudes, months, sol-air temperature cycles, etc., as needed.

To calculate the total heat passing through a roof section per hour per square foot, multiply the overall *U* times the CLTD (corrected if necessary). To take an example, the first roof section listed has a *U* of 0.213 with 1 inch of insulation. For 10 A.M. solar time, multiply 0.213 times 49, for a result of 10.437 Btu, the heat flow per square foot into the building at that point. For 4 P.M. (1600 hours) multiply 0.213 by 70 CLTD, for 14.91 Btu heat flow per square foot. Thus, the heat gain for this construction in a 1000-square-foot roof would be 10,437 Btu at 10 A.M. and 14,910 Btu at 4 P.M.

With just 1 more inch of insulation added to this particular roof construction, the overall *U* becomes 0.124. Then the 10 A.M. heat gain is 0.124 × 49, or 6.076 Btu; and 4 P.M. gain is 0.124 × 70, or 8.68 Btu. Obviously, full insulation is a magnificent investment in summer comfort and low cooling load.

The foregoing information is actually oversimplified; making cooling load calculations on an hour-by-hour basis, especially for large and complex structures like office buildings, is an extremely complicated business that is loaded with variables. While such computations can indeed be used to determine residential cooling loads and the results can be very accurate, the process is an overkill. Because of the unique features that distinguish residences from other types of buildings, cooling load calculations for them are handled in a much more generalized, simplified fashion, sometimes called the 24-hour method. The comparison of total hourly heat gains above were given primarily to indicate the value of insulation during hot weather and not as a method of calculating heat gain.

Reflective Air Spaces

These increase the thermal efficiency in roofs even more than mass thermal insulation during hot weather, since heat flow down through such an air space is much less than when it is up. Table 3-3 of chapter 3 shows summer surface conductances and resistances, while Table 3-4 shows the thermal resistances of plane air spaces; note the substantial differences in values as the direction of heat flow changes. Table 3-20 graphically demonstrates the increase in total thermal resistance in a given pitched-roof construction when a reflective air space is included, and points out the differences between winter and summer conditions in the same circumstances. Interesting comparisons can also be noted between reflective and nonreflective surfaces in the effective heat resistance of ventilated attics, in Table 5-2. Used either alone or in conjunction with mass thermal insulation, the reflective type obviously is an efficient roof insulation for summer conditions.

5-4. Mass plus reflective insulation for maximum control of summer heat. (Dewey G. Mears)

Effective Resistance of Ventilated Attics (Summer Condition)

PART A. NONREFLECTIVE SURFACES

Ventilation Air Temp., F	Sol-Air[d] Temp., F	No Ventilation		Natural Ventilation		Power Ventilation[e]					
		Ventilation Rate, cfm/ft²									
		0		0.1[b]		0.5		1.0		1.5	
		1/U Ceiling Resistance, R[c]									
		10	20	10	20	10	20	10	20	10	20
80	120	1.9	1.9	2.8	3.4	6.3	9.3	9.6	16	11	20
	140	1.9	1.9	2.8	3.5	6.5	10	9.8	17	12	21
	160	1.9	1.9	2.8	3.6	6.7	11	10	18	13	22
90	120	1.9	1.9	2.5	2.8	4.6	6.7	6.1	10	6.9	13
	140	1.9	1.9	2.6	3.1	5.2	7.9	7.6	12	8.6	15
	160	1.9	1.9	2.7	3.4	5.8	9.0	8.5	14	10	17
100	120	1.9	1.9	2.2	2.3	3.3	4.4	4.0	6.0	4.1	6.9
	140	1.9	1.9	2.4	2.7	4.2	6.1	5.8	8.7	6.5	10
	160	1.9	1.9	2.6	3.2	5.0	7.6	7.2	11	8.3	13
PART B. REFLECTIVE SURFACES[f]											
80	120	6.5	6.5	8.1	8.8	13	17	17	25	19	30
	140	6.5	6.5	8.2	9.0	14	18	18	26	20	31
	160	6.5	6.5	8.3	9.2	15	18	19	27	21	32
90	120	6.5	6.5	7.5	8.0	10	13	12	17	13	19
	140	6.5	6.5	7.7	8.3	12	15	14	20	16	22
	160	6.5	6.5	7.9	8.6	13	16	16	22	18	25
100	120	6.5	6.5	7.0	7.4	8.0	10	8.5	12	8.8	12
	140	6.5	6.5	7.3	7.8	10	12	11	15	12	16
	160	6.5	6.5	7.6	8.2	11	14	13	18	15	20

Table 5–2. (Reprinted with permission from the *1977 Fundamentals Volume, ASHRAE HANDBOOK & Product Directory*)

Assume that in a roof with 6 inches of mass thermal insulation between the ceiling joists, a sheet of aluminum foil is stapled across the inside faces of the rafters, as in Figure 5-4. Now the overall U of the roof can be calculated with the inclusion of a reflective air space, and the roof itself becomes a part of the heat barrier. Without the reflective air space and surface resistances, however, the roof itself is in common practice ignored as a heat barrier.

Roof Ventilation

Cooling loads as calculated in the past have not been reduced in houses because of mechanical ventilation in the roof or attic, nor are they today. Conventional wisdom held that such ventilation, however, was nevertheless important for economic and efficient operation of a cooling system. Numerous recent tests have rather definitely disproved that notion. It is, of course, an essential for summer comfort in a nonair-conditioned house.

In air-conditioned houses, a powered exhaust fan set in a gable opening or elsewhere in the roof may sometimes be recommended. The idea is that this will help to forcibly eject excessive hot air from the attic, thereby lessening the load on the cooling equipment; the assumption is that the living space would be well sealed so that the fan could not draw air up from the conditioned space below. This forced ventilation was thought necessary because natural ventilation, even when a house is oriented so that the prevailing summer breezes can blow through the attic space, is rarely powerful enough to do the job.

It is true that the power fan will eject heat from the attic space, and it is likewise true that, at least in some instances, there can be a diminution of the cooling load and a consequent drop in energy demand and operating cost of the cooling equipment. This is doubtless not true in every case, but that it can occur is graphically shown in Figure 5-5. However, it is not true that the

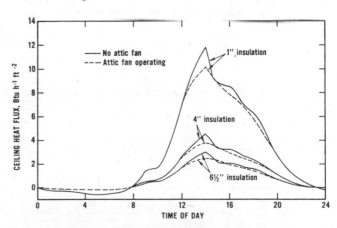

5-5. Ceiling heat gains for insulation thicknesses of 1, 4, and 6 1/2 inches. (National Bureau of Standards, *Summer Attic and Whole-House Ventilation*, 1979)

123

drop in heating load is sufficient to occasion a net saving in energy consumption, when the energy required to power the fan is also taken into account. The studies included in the National Bureau of Standards, *Summer Attic and Whole House Ventilation* (NBS Special Publication 548, U.S. Department of Commerce, 1979), as well as others, conclusively demonstrate that there is, in fact, either no appreciable benefit to be gained in the way of energy conservation, or a definite and sometimes substantial increase in total energy consumption, especially where the ceilings are well insulated. Typical test results, as compiled from test data, are shown in Table 5-3, for various insulation thicknesses, percentages of natural ventilation, and different outdoor wind speeds.

It is possible, though barely so, that the installation of ventilating devices that use no power, such as turbine vents or vent chimneys, can result in sufficient attic cooling to cause a slight drop in cooling load and a small net energy gain. It is also fairly obvious—and tests have supported the observation—that houses equipped with mechanical cooling equipment that also make use of whole-house ventilating fans whenever possible can be effectively cooled and at the same time enjoy a substantial net saving in energy consumption.

In non air-conditioned houses, attic ventilation takes on a much more important comfort function: It is essential to move as much of the air as possible up through the attic without creating unpleasant drafts. Here it is necessary to make some distinctions in terms. Today, the "attic fan" that used to be employed primarily to ventilate the attic, and sometimes the living spaces as well to a small degree, is considered only as a relatively low-volume (1000 to 1500 cubic feet per

Daily Reduction in Energy Required to Operate Air-Conditioning Equipment Due to Power Vent Fan Operation and Daily Energy Required to Operate Fan

Insulation thickness, in	0	1	4	6 1/2
Daily reduction in energy to operate AC unit, Btu	2093	2336	1289	1039
Daily energy consumption of power vent fan, Btu	8624	8624	8721	8818

Table 2a

Percentage of Natural Ventilation, Eq. (17)	100	75	50	25	0
Daily reduction in energy to operate AC unit, Btu	1289	2140	3219	4962	7066
Daily energy consumption of power vent fan, Btu	8721	8856	8982	9089	9138

Table 3a

Outdoor wind speed, mph	5	3.75	2.5	1.24	0
Daily reduction in energy to operate AC unit, Btu	1723	2486	4169	6962	11178
Daily energy consumption of power vent fan, Btu	8917	9014	9208	9596	9790

Table 5–3. (National Bureau of Standards, *Summer Attic and Whole-House Ventilation,* 1979)

minute) ventilating fan used solely to move hot air from the attic. As was just pointed out, this type of fan is useless, from a practical standpoint, in aiding the operation of mechanical cooling, some advertisements and popular opinions notwithstanding. Nor does it do much good, from the standpoint of cooling living spaces, when it operates in a sealed attic. The *whole-house* attic fan, on the other hand, is designed to draw cool air in from the outdoors through windows and doors in the living spaces, draw it up into the attic, and exhaust it to the outdoors again as heated air. It represents an efficient and effective cooling method that can be employed as the principal cooling means in the non air-conditioned house, or as auxiliary cooling in lieu of turning on the mechanical cooling in the houses so equipped.

The most efficient type of forced attic ventilation, or whole-house ventilation, is the plenum fan installation which draws air up through a ceiling grille (Figure 5-6). The fan should be set vertically, as shown, rather than horizontally, since in the latter position the installation is at its noisiest. The fan can be operated manually or by a timer set to turn the fan on at a predetermined time each evening and off again during the early morning hours. Automatic controls would doubtless prove more satisfactory for most home-owners, however: the fan turns on at a certain indoor temperature provided that the outdoor temperature is not higher than that, and it turns off again at a set indoor temperature.

Fan size, naturally, depends upon the volume of space to be ventilated, and the rate of air exchange desired. The former is determined by measuring the entire living space, or the space to be ventilated, and then computing the volume in cubic feet. For the rate of air change, experience has shown that fans should be of sufficient capacity to change the air in the rooms below once every one and a half minutes in most of the northern states. In all other parts of the country the fans should be powerful enough to change the air once every minute (Figure 5-7).

When a plenum installation is being planned, the ceiling grille should be located centrally, such as in a hall ceiling or at the head of a stairwell, so that it will pull air more or less equally from all of the rooms to be ventilated. The grille must be large enough, too, to satisfy the demands of the fan. Too small a grille will usually result in a high noise level, both from the rushing sound of the air and from the fluttering of the grille louvers. An alternative to the true plenum system is the currently popular method of mounting the fan face down in a frame cut into the attic floor. This is an acceptable (and less expensive) arrangement, provided that the fan is designed to operate in this manner. Here the entire attic in effect becomes the plenum, and the efficiency is about the same. In any case, *do not use cheap fans!* The small original saving will soon be dissipated in repair bills.

Fans set in pre-existing gable louvers or windows, or in wall or roof louvers cut especially to fit them, are also satisfactory for summer ventilation. They are less efficient than the plenum type, of course, since they must exhaust not only the downstairs air but also the air flowing through the attic from other louvers or windows.

Houses with flat or shed roofs, or with the vaulted or cathedral type—either with or without hung ceilings—are unsuitable for either plenum or gable-louver fan installations. They have no space for them. Usually the exhaust fan must be placed somewhere in a wall near the main living area so that sufficient air motion through the house is assured. An exhaust fan can be located in the outer wall of a recreation room, as shown in Figure 5-8, for instance. Naturally, the wall opening must be screened as well as louvered, and it should be set at least a foot (more if possible) above ground level in order to prevent muddy water or snow from getting in during storms.

5-6. Vertical plenum exhaust fan installation in an attic. (Ilg Electric Ventilating Co.)

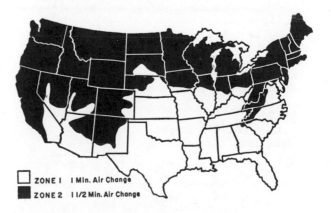

ZONE 1 1 Min. Air Change
ZONE 2 1 1/2 Min. Air Change

5-7. Ventilating air change requirements. (Hunter Fan & Ventilating Co.)

5-8. Exhaust fan installation in recreation room. (Hedrich-Blessing/Hunter Fan & Ventilating Co.)

Roof Color

Though many years ago residence roof coverings were almost uniformly dark in color, today light-colored roofing materials are both common and popular. One reason, of course, is that a wide range of roofing material colors has become readily available over the past several years, and oftentimes the lighter colors are preferred as a matter of taste. Another reason is that light colors reflect more solar energy than dark ones, as is shown in Table 5-4.

Standard calculations for overall cooling load in air-conditioned buildings take into account load reductions resulting from light-colored roofs. However, rather than going into the specific reflectance values of individual roofing materials, as has been done in Table 5-4, the differentiation is simply made between light

Solar Reflectivities of Roofs

Description	Reflectance value
Asphalt tab shingles, common lay	
Woodblend (GAF)	17%
Russet Blend (GAF)	9%
Autumn (Flintkote)	10%
Frosted Red (Flintkote)	20%
Canyon Red (Flintkote)	13%
Snow White (Flintkote)	24%
Dark Mahogany (GAF)	8%
Pastel Green (GAF)	16%
Earthtone Brown (GAF)	9%
Blizzard (Fire King)	34%
White (JM)	33%
Red (JM)	14%
Clover Green (Flintkote)	11%
Shake cedar wood shingles, new, unoiled	32%
Same but oiled	28%
Red clay mission tile	26%
Pea gravel covered	
Dark blend	12%
Medium blend	24%
Light blend	34%
White coated	65%
Crushed used brick, red, covered	34%
White marble chips covered	49%
Flexstone or mineral chip roof type, white	26%
Polyurethane foam, white coated	70%
Same with tan coating	41%
Silver, aluminum painted tar paper	51%
White coated, smooth, Kool Kote (Corbett Roofing Co./Tucson)	75%
Tarpaper, "weathered"	41%

Table 5-4. (National Bureau of Standards, *Summer Attic and Whole-House Ventilation,* 1979)

126

and dark surfaces. This situation obtains not only in the complex calculations made for large buildings, but in the simplified method used in making residential calculations as well.

The assumption is that whatever color roofing material is initially applied to a house, light or dark, will probably remain a constant for a sufficient length of time to be valid as a design criterion. Tests have shown that changing the color of a given house roof from dark to light does indeed result in a considerable reduction in summer roof heat gain. However, several points must be noted in this connection. First, there is no assurance that a light color will remain effective after a season or two, particularly in suburbs located near large cities, since air contaminants can easily reduce the reflectivity to only nominal values in short order. Second, even though a light-colored roof may remain clean, it still will not have much of a function on days of adverse weather conditions, as, for example, on hot but cloudy days when humidity as well as air temperature is high. Third, even though the reduction in roof heat gain is substantial, that reduction in most cases really has very little effect on summer total house heat gain; this is because the roof heat gain is generally rather small by comparison with the total.

Another point worth keeping in mind is that while a light-colored roof might, in some instances, be of some small help during the heat of the summer, for the remainder of the year the color serves no practical pur-pose. A light color does not diminish winter heat loss from within the house, nor does it cause any additional loss.

Therefore, in choosing between a light and a dark roof covering, the selection can well be made solely on esthetic grounds rather than practical ones since there is no compelling reason to choose on a basis of reflectivity. And in making cooling load calculations for a house with an existing light-colored roof, while one can indeed calculate on the basis of the light color, doing so on the basis of a dark color instead would result in a more conservative and perhaps more practical result.

Water Cooled Roofs

Large reductions in cooling load can be achieved through wetting or dampening roofs, with a reduction in heat gain of as much as 80 percent possible, depending upon the method used. Obviously, if a water-cooled roof can reduce the load on an air conditioner, it will also make the interior of a noncooled house a good deal more comfortable. Much, however, depends upon individual circumstances; one must remember that the roof heat gain represents only a small portion of the total heat gain of a house, especially where adequate thermal insulation is used.

Water-cooled roofs do add some maintenance problems to the homeowner's life, too. A roof pond (Figure 5-9) has to be drained periodically, and the roof must be cleaned of leaves, dirt, soot, and other debris. Fur-

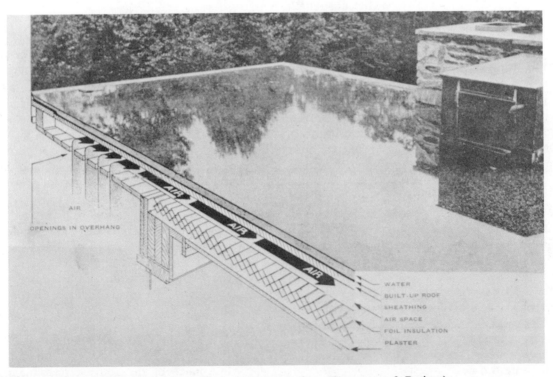

5-9. Method of open-pooled or ponded roof construction. (Pomerance & Breines)

thermore, it may become a breeding place for mosquitoes and other insects unless treated with inhibiting chemicals, which are both troublesome and costly to apply. If the ponding is done by means of large plastic bags, some of the open-pond problems disappear, but are replaced by others, such as the longevity of the bags themselves. As for roof sprays, which are more efficient than the 1-inch roof pond and are the only feasible water cooling method for pitched and shed roofs, the major problem is maintenance of the valves and pipes, which may become clogged or corroded from impurities in the water. The spray should be thermostatically operated, since otherwise it must be turned on and off by hand.

Of course, water-cooled roofs are feasible only in areas where there are no water shortages. Such areas are becoming increasingly hard to find in our overpopulated and overindustrialized urban and suburban centers; this is also the case in many rural and/or agricultural areas where domestic water uses are making strong inroads on the slender supplies from dug and drilled wells, and even upon creeks and rivers.

In addition to the two major types of water cooling systems, ponds and sprays, there is a third, which is basically a variant of the spray system. This is the trickle method, which is good only for shed or pitched roofs.

ROOF PONDS

In designing a flat-roof house for a pond, care must be taken to make sure that the structure will support the weight of the water. Most roofs have sufficient strength to carry the load of a 1-inch pond without reinforcement; but one of 6 inches will require larger ceiling joists and stronger wall framing. A cubic foot of water weighs a little over 62 pounds, so that a 6-inch pond on a 1000-square foot roof will weigh in the neighorhood of 31,250 pounds, or nearly 16 short tons—roughly 31 pounds per square foot. Though this great weight must be reckoned with, it does not create any drastic structural problems; by comparison, a poured concrete floor of the same thickness weighs approximately 70 pounds per square foot, a clay tile roof about 10 to 15 pounds per square foot, and a conventional asphalt shingle and wood sheathing roof about 10 pounds per square foot.

The waterproofness of a roof to be covered with water is also of obvious importance. Certainly no roof that has been exposed to the elements for a number of years can safely be used as a pond base unless it is carefully finished with a new layer of roofing paper and asphalt, or other similar waterproofing materials. The same situation prevails where the water will be contained in bags, because the possibility of container leakage is always present. A new roof, if well built, will of course be waterproof.

If an existing roof has a suitable coping, there is no reason why it cannot serve as a pond base, provided

that it has sufficient structural strength. However, if the coping must be added, the cost may make ponding uneconomical. A drain system will also be necessary—and costly if it has to be added. In the case of a new house, of course, both coping and drain must be included in the plans, and the roof design should be specifically oriented to ponding.

SPRINKLED ROOFS

The low cost of a sprinkler system, plus the fact that it is effective on pitched as well as flat roofs and requires no special copings, drains, or roof construction, makes it preferable for cooling residential roof surfaces. Since it relies on a high rate of evaporation, rather than on both evaporation and reflectivity as in the case of the pond, just enough water is needed to keep the surfaces slightly damp. Circumstances vary, but in many cases a gallon of water will keep 200 square feet of roof surface damp for a minute; at least some of the water can, in mechanically cooled houses, come from cooling equipment runoff.

Dust and soot will not affect the evaporation rate measurably, either; the cooling effect will be about as efficient in a location with a polluted atmosphere as in one where the air is clean.

Sprinkling systems can be controlled either by a thermostat that turns the water on and off as the surface temperature of the roof rises and falls, or by a clock that turns the water on and off morning and evening. The former is less wasteful of water, since the clock system will permit considerable runoff.

TRICKLE METHOD

The least expensive installation for water cooling pitched roofs is the trickle method. A perforated pipe or a sprinkler hose is placed along the ridge of the roof so that water will trickle down each face, just enough to keep the surfaces damp. The major difficulties with this system are that it often results in too much water on one end of the roof and not enough on the other; that it cannot effectively be controlled by a thermostat, since temperature changes will be unequal; and that, since efficient cooling demands dampness of the *complete* surface, some water will be wasted in runoff. Moreover, dirt on the roof, or irregularities in the surface, will cause the water to form rivulets, thus cooling only part of the surfaces. However, in rural and semirural areas where water supply is abundant and cheap, the atmosphere relatively clean, and low installation costs a decisive factor the trickle method of cooling may be useful.

SHADE FOR WALLS AND GLASS AREAS

While much of the above discussion on roofs has dealt implicitly with sun control, since the largest part of a roof's heat load in the summer is solar energy, the most important *specifically* radiant, or sun-control, problem is that which concerns glass areas and, to a lesser extent, walls and solid wood doors.

Control of hot-weather radiation entering windows exposed to the sun is one of the knottiest of all cooling problems. This is because of the highly complex nature of the sun's motion through the skies, which varies from day to day. Thus at noon on June 21 at a 40° north latitude, it is 71.5° above the south horizon; whereas at noon on December 21 it is only 24.5°. As Figure 5-10 shows, the sun will shine into a southward-oriented window almost from sunrise to sunset during the weeks around the winter solstice, but during the period around the summer solstice it will strike such a window only during the midday hours.

While this variation in angle makes calculations complicated, it also makes it possible to control the energy of the sun entering south windows effectively with overhangs or other sun control devices. You can keep solar radiation out almost all day long during hot weather and let it in during most of the day during cold weather, all with the same control devices.

It is important that the south-facing wall and its glass

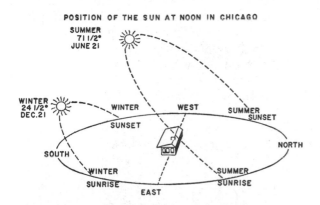

5-10. Sun angles at noon in Chicago. (Courtesy, Libby-Owens-Ford Company)

5-11. Exterior vertical sunshade. (Ben Schnall/FPG)

areas face as nearly as possible to the *true south*. In wintertime, a shift of a house of as much as 15° from true south will result in only minor losses of the total amount of solar heat that can be gained; but in summer a shift of only a few degrees from south to west can seriously diminish the value of an overhang during the hottest parts of the year. It is, of course, possible to rectify even a fairly large shift from true south by means of other control devices, such as the vertical sunshade shown in Figure 5-11. There are numerous highly effective possibilities; however, they are an added cost element.

Glass Houses

We have already discussed some of the problems of glass areas in chapter 3; but they have great merits, too, of course. The psychological benefits of glass walls bear remembering whenever an adjustment between living amenity and cooling load is being worked out. Large glass areas bring the outdoors in, open vistas and views to the otherwise boxed-in occupants of the building, engender a feeling of restfulness, and allow psychological relaxation. From an emotional and psychological point of view, windows are a necessary part of residences, though this has been found to be far less true of large public or commercial buildings. Surveys have shown that nearly all homeowners would very much like to have more and larger expanses of glass in their homes, rather than fewer and smaller.

With this in mind, serious objections can be raised to the current tendency in low- and medium-cost homes toward smaller glass areas, and particularly to proposed legislation in some areas of the country that would make relatively small glass areas mandatory in all new residential construction, in an effort to reduce energy consumption. The idea is that heating/cooling loads will be smaller and operating costs lower, with a concomitant saving in energy. And indeed, the idea most certainly will work. But if structural or other types of sun control devices are built into or around the house with care and judgement, the increases in energy consumption will be very small; in fact, they may be smaller than in many houses now being built with relatively small windows but with no effective sun control devices.

Problems of Sun Control

Whatever the size of windows in a house, sun control is not a matter susceptible to easy solution. This is made clear in the following summary of the problems of sun—and environment—control at glass openings: minimum of solar heat entering in summer; maximum of solar heat entering in winter; adjustment of solar heat entry to maximum efficiency of heating and cooling systems; control of condensation at windows in winter; minimum glare at all hours of the day; insect and dust control at openings; protection against rain, snow, and wind; provision of adequate ventilation in nonair-conditioned houses during hot weather; control of infiltration/exfiltration during cold weather and hot weather; minimum of heat loss during winter; control of cold-air convective currents during winter; arrangements for interior privacy when needed; maintenance costs balanced against original costs of sun control devices; and exterior appearance: the esthetic factor.

Every house presents a complex of many or all of these factors, and perhaps others as well, and no solution is automatic. It will take careful thought, particularly in view of the highly technical physics of solar radiation and optics of various glasses. The following summary of techniques for controlling solar heat makes it even more clear that a solution to the problem of sun control is not to be worked out in an afternoon.

Methods of Sun Control

There are five types of methods of sun control, primarily for windows but also for walls exposed to the sun:

Natural devices: building orientation, trees and shrubbery, shade of other buildings and projecting wings, topography—hills and valleys

Around windows, outside: balconies, arcades, canopies and overhangs, porches and verandahs, arbors, eggcrate overhangs, sungrids, solid horizontal and vertical fins, deep reveals, awnings of cloth, plastic or metal

Over windows, outside: shutters, fixed or movable louvers, fixed exterior venetian blinds, heat-absorbent and/or metallic-filmed storm windows or glass jalousies in addition to the regular window, venetian screening, paint or whitewash (used mainly in greenhouses and, rarely, in factories where glare has proved an annoying problem)

The window itself: Heat-absorbing and/or metallic-filmed glass, double glazing or triple glazing, with or without heat-absorbing and/or metallic-filmed glass, glass jalousies, glass block, frosted glasses, elimination or downsizing of windows

Over windows, inside: Single or double cloth roller shades, insulating roller shades, slatted bamboo shades, horizontal or vertical venetian blinds, draperies, glass curtains, venetian screens inside casement windows, insulating shutters or panels, thermal curtains, and similar devices

ORIENTATION

The sun itself must be faced and controlled from the very start of the design of a building, and this can best be done by beginning with intelligent orientation, together with logical placement of glass areas.

As stated above, major glass areas should whenever possible face true south. When they do, the sun can be controlled with great accuracy. When the orientation must be somewhat off south, the overhangs must be supplemented as necessary by vertical sun barriers such as tall plantings, or wood or masonry walls, or fences sufficiently close to the glass area to prevent entry of unwanted radiation (Figure 5-12).

A southern orientation does not, of course, require that all lots provide a good southern frontage. If it did, the whole subject would become absurd, since it is obviously impossible to subdivide land so that every lot would always have a good southern exposure facing the street. It is possible to maintain, with considerable effectiveness, a southern orientation for major glass areas in the living quarters (Figure 5-12), regardless of the direction the front of the lot faces. The layouts shown are, admittedly, optimistic in imagining that all lots will have southern frontages sufficiently wide to provide a nice, rambling elevation in that direction; but adjustments can be made, if necessary involving two-story design, to assure the best possible use of the south side.

With a true southern orientation, the east and west walls of the house (and their openings) will be exposed to the full power of the sun during early morning and late afternoon. To provide the needed shade, these elevations must also be shielded—but overhangs will not do all the job; other types of sun control are required.

The western elevation needs most shading, since at the time the sun strikes that side of the house the air temperature will already have been raised about as high as it will go. The added load of the sun's rays is still large, even though less than at noon, and the combina-

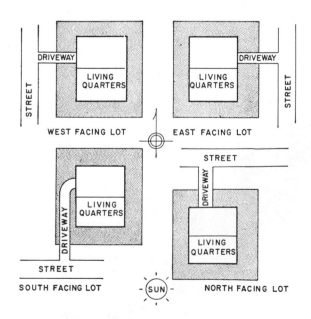

5-12. Method of achieving southward orientation regardless of location of street in relation to house. (Courtesy, Libby-Owens-Ford Company)

tion of sun and air heat can make the western wall a real heat trap.

To eliminate this problem, the narrowest elevations of the house should face east and west, provided that there are no other overriding environmental factors to be considered; and attached garages, carports, or workshops should be built on the western side, with a consequent omission of most if not all of the windows there. Of course, such structures can be placed on the eastern side too, if the western is not available for reasons of elevation, view, or existing landscaping.

SUN CONTROL DEVICES

Once a building is effectively located on its site, the problem then arises as to what device or combination of devices to control solar radiation should be used. The selection of methods will depend upon a wide variety of factors, of course; but as far as the relative merits of any particular device goes, it must be realized that none is perfect, technically speaking. All have their defects that must be compensated for.

One basic principle can, however, be applied to solar control in any part of the country: if a device is to control heat gain effectively, it must be located outside rather than inside the window. Monolithic (single-glazed) tinted float glass might be considered an exception to this; heavy-duty bronze-tint in a ½-inch thickness glass, for example, will transmit only about 24 percent of the total solar radiation reaching it. But

on the other hand, the glass is neither inside nor outside the window: It *is* the window. However, inside devices that are useful for eliminating glare have little effect on heat. Indeed, many of them have a tendency to store and reradiate any sun heat that comes through the window glass. Draperies, roller shades, blinds, shutters and like devices may or may not reduce heat, depending on the materials from which they are made; but this is done only by eliminating or at least drastically reducing light entering the room, thus defeating half the purpose of a well-windowed building.

Structural Sunshades

The use of structural sunshades or projections over or at the sides of windows and glass walls to serve as sun control devices first became popular in buildings erected in very warm climates, as in Brazil and Tel Aviv. Actually, of course, overhangs are no more and no less efficient in the north than they are in the south. They may consist of cantilevered overhangs or balconies, open eggcrate sun deflectors, deep reveals, and vertical or horizontal fins or visors that are either slatted or solid. The use of these devices presents a complex problem, the answer to which must be compounded out of economics, esthetics, and technology. Structural sun control devices add to the cost of a house, but they are attractive if well used.

Technically, of course, their value on south walls is very great—even though not perfect. No structural sun-

5-13. Projected second floor as sun control device, designed by Charles M. Goodman, Hollin Hills, Virginia. (Robert C. Lautman)

131

shade is ever 100 percent efficient, unless it is so wide that it becomes economically unfeasible and, from the point of view of livability, a darkness hazard whenever the sun is not shining. In particular, an overhang that is designed for minimum summer and maximum winter sunlight cannot, by itself, function perfectly for more than a very brief period, since it is designed in accordance with some optimum angle of solar radiation. When the solar angle is more horizontal than that, too much sun enters; when more vertical, the room may become gloomy. Even semiperfect operation can be expected for only three to four weeks a year, when the sun's relation to the overhang is at it most effective.

Nevertheless, south wall overhangs are essential for summer comfort and cooling economy. In single-story houses they may be made merely by extending the rafters as far out from the wall as desired. This is often accomplished by means of secondary members that are attached, frequently at an angle considerably different than the actual roof pitch, to the rafters themselves. Or else a horizontal solid or eggcrate canopy can be used; it permits good circulation around the openings while barring the sun. A first-floor setback, in combination with a roof overhang, is a good sun control device for a two-story house (Figure 5-13).

Permanent frames, over which a roll-up canvas can be spread during hot weather or leafy vines can be grown, are another excellent and human-scale device for sun control at the south elevation.

It should be emphasized that whenever a house is being designed for mechanical cooling, the structural overhang should extend the whole length of the south elevation and not just over the glass area. Heat penetrates a wall, though more slowly and to a lesser degree, just as surely as it does a piece of glass.

And one more point. Whenever clerestory windows are used, protect those glass and wall areas from solar radiation also. One individual built himself a modern house in the Southwest, and after occupying it for one season found he had to go to the considerable added expense of tacking overhangs above his clerestories; without them, the heat gain through the clerestory area was uncomfortably high.

Fixed or movable vertical louvers, either alone or in combination with horizontal elements, are used quite widely in the tropics, but largely in nonresidential buildings, since they interrupt, if they do not actually destroy, the view from the window. Such louvers sometimes are used in this country, too. But this particular type of sunshade is not particularly suited to residential applications, though they do work and can be installed if desired. They can even be automated to move their positions with relation to the sun's path, but this is a luxury that most homeowners would most probably be happy to forego.

Design of south-exposure structural overhangs is one of the toughest problems, especially for owner-designer-builders, in dealing with sun control on south exposures. The chief difficulty lies in selection of the optimum width of overhang to protect the area as much as possible from the summer sun, while at the same time permitting the winter sun to warm windows and walls—at least in latitudes north of 35°. Most of the methods used to calculate overhang widths are complex, making use of charts and tables and involve the calculation of individual angles for the particular latitude in which the house is being built and the shading-sunshine seasonal combination desired. But the following section, "Solar Window Overhang: Summer and Winter Effectiveness," by F. W. Hutchinson and M. O. Cotter, includes a series of simple tables which make it possible to select overhang widths without having to go through a series of time-consuming calculations.

It is true that these tables provide only *geometrical* relationships. They cannot reveal what is the *optimum* overhang for a given situation. A decision on the most suitable overhang is, indeed, one that will be controlled by various climatic and environmental conditions other than simple sun angle. For example, in high altitudes sun control is likely to be somewhat more urgent than in low altitudes, as it is in desert regions more than in humid ones, since the sun's energy is more direct and less diffused in high or dry atmospheres than in low and moist ones.

If more accurate determinations of solar angle than those provided in the next section are considered desirable, they can be obtained in any of several ways. One possibility is interpolation of the data contained in Tables 5-5 through 5-10. Sun path diagrams can be used in conjunction with shading masks and a shading mask protractor; this system allows the determination of vertical as well as horizontal shading patterns. The ASHRAE publishes tables of solar position and related angles for several north latitudes (*1977 Fundamentals Volume, ASHRAE HANDBOOK, & Product Directory,* Chapter 26), which can serve as a basis for both horizontal and vertical projections, and much more detailed tables of a similar nature can be found in the *Hydrographic Office Bulletin No. 214, Tables of Computed Altitude and Azimuth,* U.S. Government Printing Office. Or, one might use a sun angle calculating system or device, such as the Libbey-Owens-Ford Sun Angle Calculator (Figure 5-14). For example, if one wanted to determine the sun angle on a south wall at 9:00 A.M. on any given day, the Calculator would make it possible. The Hutchinson-Cotter tables are useful only for solar noon sun angles: Quite adequate for most residential applications, but perhaps insufficient if the glass areas are unusually large, and certainly so in large nonresidential "glass wall" buildings.

One word of warning: never forget that the following tables apply only to *true south.* For walls oriented— even slightly—away from true south (as little as 7°), special adjustments must be made, including vertical sunshades to keep the morning or afternoon sun out of the glass area during the hottest parts of the year. The tables have no application whatsoever to walls with an east or west orientation.

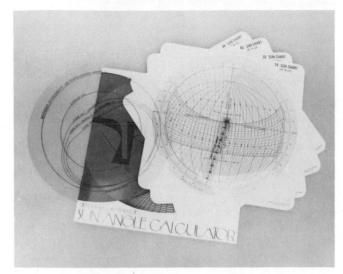

5-14. The Sun Angle Calculator. (Courtesy, Libby-Owens-Ford Company, Duncan Photos)

Solar Window Overhang: Summer and Winter Effectiveness

(The following material, written by F. W. Hutchinson and O. M. Cotter, has been slightly revised from the original that appeared in *Progressive Architecture,* June, 1955.)

The function of a solar window is to admit heat and light during the winter months, and to admit light but exclude heat during the summer months. This objective requires that the window be exposed to direct sunshine for a large fraction of the day during the winter, but shaded from direct sunshine for as large a fraction as possible of the summer day. Shading can, of course, be obtained through manual operation of blinds, draperies, louvers, adjustable drops, or various types of structural overhang; in many cases, however, such special devices are unnecessary due to the fortunate circumstance that solar mechanics assist the designer in providing automatic seasonal control of shading for south-wall windows.

In midwinter, the sun rises south of the east-west line and describes an arc which brings it to a maximum elevation (within the latitude range of the United States) of from 20° to approximately 40°, the value of the maximum varying with latitude. In midsummer the sun rises north of the east-west line and describes an arc which brings it to a maximum elevation (again for the range of latitude for the United States) of from, roughly, 65° to 85°. The ratio of maximum summer elevation to maximum winter elevation varies with latitude, but is of the order of 2 to 3. Hence, it is evident that by designing an overhang in conjunction with a south-wall solar window, it is possible to exclude the high midday summer sun while admitting the lower midday winter sun.

Control of shading during the morning and afternoon hours is less complete, but does retain a high degree of effectiveness due to the fact that from April 21 to August 21 the sunrise and sunset are north of the east-west line; hence, throughout this warm season, the sun does not irradiate a south window just as it crosses the horizon. In mid-June, for example, sunrise on the 40th parallel of latitude (corresponding roughly to the location of Denver, Columbus, and Philadelphia) is before 5 A.M., yet the sun does not shine on a south wall until after 8 A.M. and by that time it is already at an elevation of

nearly 40°; thus, in this case, the minimum elevation for midsummer is higher than the maximum for midwinter. This factor becomes of even greater significance when it is realized that (again at latitude 40°) throughout the greater part of May, June, and July, the minimum elevation at which irradiation of a south wall occurs is always greater than the elevation at solar noon throughout November, December, and January.

Basis of Overhang Design. The limiting cases of structural overhang obviously correspond to the extremes of excluding all summer sun or admitting all winter sun. Thus at latitude 40° the sun could be excluded from mid-April throughout mid-August, if a sufficient length of overhang were provided to shade the window when the solar latitude is 20°. If, however, complete irradiation is desired from mid-September through mid-March, the overhang would have to be short enough to admit sunlight for all elevations below 50°; obviously these two conditions are mutually incompatible. Thus some type of compromise is necessary if a fixed length of overhang is to be used. The basis for such a compromise is arbitrary and must, therefore, remain largely a matter of judgement and of esthetics.

In localities where the summers are particularly hot, greater amounts of overhang will often be used with resultant partial sacrifice of winter heating effect, whereas in localities characterized by cold winters and moderate summers, the overhang may be designed to provide a greater thermal gain in winter at the expense of some undesirable heat gain in summer . . . .

In establishing a basis for design of overhang, two relatively independent decisions must be made. The first is to select the solar elevation corresponding to which the entire window is to be irradiated, whereas the second is to select the elevation at which the window is to be entirely in the shade. A common selection for complete irradiation is the solar elevation, at the latitude of the particular installation, which occurs at solar noon on the shortest day of the year, December 21; on this basis the window would be partially shaded at noon on all other days of the year. A common alternative is to select the solar elevation at noon on the 21st of October or November. On either of these bases the window would be completely irradiated for all sunshine hours from October 21 through February 21, or from November 21 through January 21, but would be partially shaded the remainder of the year.

The decision with respect to complete shading may be based on the solar elevation at noon on the longest day of the year, June 21; in this event the entire window would be in the shade only (at solar noon) on this one day. If shading is based on the noon elevation for some later month, as the 21st of July or August, the window would then be completely shaded at noon from May 21 to July 21, or from April 21 to August 21. For times when the window is partially shaded, the fraction receiving direct sunshine will depend upon the full-radiation design condition as well as the full-shade condition, since for a fixed basis of full shading the height of the window will vary with the condition for complete irradiation.

Developed from the principles outlined above, [Table 5-5] gives the required geometrical relationship between length of overhang and base of the window for the more common summer-design criteria. Thus if full shading of a solar window is to be obtained at solar noon on June 21, for a structure located at latitude 30°, the value of b_8 is read from [Table 5-5] as 878. This number is equal to the required vertical distance from underside of overhang to bottom of window, the distance being expressed as a percentage of the overhang. Thus if the overhang for a particular window were 10 inches, the vertical distance would have to be 87.8 inches. Reversing the procedure, if the vertical distance is fixed as part of the architectural design, the required length of the overhang for June design can readily be calculated. Example: In a structure where the distance from floor to underside of overhang is 9 feet, the bottom of a solar window is to be arbitrarily located 1 foot above the floor. In this case the vertical distance from underside of overhang to bottom of window is 96 inches, so the required length of overhang will be 96/8.78 or slightly less than 11 inches.

[Table 5-6] is similar in form to [Table 5-5] but gives the vertical distance, c', expressed as a percentage of length of overhang, from underside of overhang to top of window for common winter-shading criteria. For example: In the previous example 11 inches of overhang were required for June shading of the window. If this same window were to be fully irradiated at solar noon on December 21, the window height would be determined as follows: From [Table 5-6] for December and for 30° latitude the distance c′ is read as 75; then, since overhang is already established as 11 inches, it follows that the vertical distance from underside of overhang to top of the window must be .75 × 11 or 8¼ inches; the required window height to meet the selected design conditions is therefore 96-8¼ or 87½ inches. (In practice a standard window height would be selected giving an approximation to the theoretical value.)

VALUES OF SHADING DISTANCE, B′, FOR SUMMER DESIGN (SOLAR NOON)

| | LATITUDE | | | |
	30°	35°	40°	45°
June 21	878	514	327	254
July 21	598	401	282	219
Aug. 21	317	236	192	156

Table 5-5.

VALUES OF SHADING DISTANCE, C′, FOR WINTER DESIGN (SOLAR NOON)

| | LATITUDE | | | |
	30°	35°	40°	45°
Oct. 21	115	97	81	67
Nov. 21	84	70	55	45
Dec. 21	75	60	47	40

Table 5-6.

The selection of the boundary shading values—as discussed above—is a very simple matter, since the actual elevation of the sun at solar noon is equal to its elevation measured in a vertical plane normal to a south-facing window. For any time of day other than solar noon, however, the effective solar altitude differs from the actual value and can be obtained only by trigonometric computation. Thus at solar noon on December 21, latitude 30°, the actual elevation is 37° and this is also equal to the effective elevation. At 9 A.M., 10 A.M., and 11 A.M. (correspondingly at 1 P.M., 2 P.M., and 3 P.M.) on this same day the actual solar altitudes are 21°, 29°, and 35°, respectively, whereas the corresponding effective solar altitudes are 28°, 33°, and 36°, respectively (refer to 3rd column of [Table 5-7]). Thus not only do the effective altitudes differ from the actual, but the variation increases nonlinearly as a function of the number of hours on either side of solar noon.

Insofar as the authors are aware, no published data exist on seasonal variation of effective solar altitude. [Note: There are, in somewhat different form. See for instance the ASHRAE tables of solar position referred to earlier.] Lacking such data it is a time-consuming task to calculate the effectiveness (whether with respect to partial shading or to partial irradiation) of a solar window. To correct this difficulty [Tables 5-7 through 5-10] have been prepared for latitudes 30°, 35°, 40° and 45° respectively. Each table provides hourly values, on the 21st day of each month, of the angle of incidence, i, of direct solar radiation on a south-facing window and of the effective solar altitude, H′, with respect to such a window.

To further reduce the effort needed in computing the instantaneous effectiveness of solar window overhang, the tables give values of three instantaneous constants, a, b, and c. By use of these constants, together with d from [Table 5-10B], the architect or engineer can immediately determine the fraction of a solar window that is "working" at any time during the winter months and the fraction that is directly irradiated (thus increasing cooling load) at any time during the summer months. Example: A south-facing solar window at 40° latitude is so designed that complete shading occurs at solar noon only on June 21 and complete irradiation at solar noon on December 21. At solar noon of any month other than December this window will be partially shaded; considering February, for example, the shading constant, c′, is read from the 10th column of [Table 5-9] (for 12 noon in either February or October) as 34. From [Table 5-10B] the value of d for June-December design conditions is read as 280. The shading conditions for this window at solar noon in either February or October is then:

$$\% \text{ Window shaded} = 100 \ (c/d)$$
$$= 100 \ (34/280)$$
$$= 12.2\%$$

If the seasonal effectiveness of this window as a source of winter heating is being investigated the shading factor would indicate that only 87.8 percent of the window area would be transferring direct solar radiation at solar noon in February. Conversely, if October cooling load were being checked the overhang would be only 12.2 percent effective in preventing the direct transmission and/or absorption of solar energy.

The irradiating percentage (87.8 percent) could also be obtained directly by noting from [Table 5-9] that the b value equals 246, hence:

$$\% \text{ Window irradiated} = 100 \ (b/d)$$
$$= 100 \ (246/280)$$
$$= 87.8\%$$

Referring to the fifth column of [Table 5-9], the b value at 9 A.M. in January or November is 287. Then:

$$\% \text{ Window irradiated} = 100 \ (b/d)$$
$$= 100 \ (287/280)$$
$$= 102.5\%$$

Since values in excess of 100 percent are obviously impossible, the above result must be interpreted as meaning that the shadow line is above the top of the window; hence an opaque wall depth of 2.5 percent of window height is subject to direct irradiation. Conversely from column 10 of [Table 5-9], the b value at 9 A.M. (or 3 P.M.) on May 21 or July 21 is 397. Then:

$$\% \text{ Window shaded} = 100 \ (c/d)$$
$$= 100 \ (397/280)$$
$$= 142\%$$

This result indicates that the shade line is below the bottom of the window; hence not merely is the window wholly protected from solar irradiation, but an opaque wall depth below the window (equal in distance to 42 percent of the window height) is likewise in shadow.

(This completes the paper by Messrs. Hutchinson and Cotter. A mathematical appendix has been omitted.)

Table 5–7.

Latitude: 30°, 21st day of the month

1	2	3	4	5	6	7	8	9	10
SOLAR TIME	ANGLE OF INCIDENCE i	EFFECTIVE SOLAR ALTITUDE H	a	b JUNE	JULY	AUG	c OCT	NOV	DEC
DECEMBER									
8 am, 4 pm	56°	19°	34	844	564	283	0	0	0
9 am, 3 pm	48	28	53	825	545	264	0	0	0
10 am, 2 pm	42	33	65	813	533	252	0	0	0
11 am, 1 pm	38	36	73	805	525	244	0	0	0
12 noon	37	37	75	803	523	242	0	0	0
JAN. OR NOV.									
8 am, 4 pm	58°	23°	42	836	556	275	0	0	0
9 am, 3 pm	51	33	65	813	533	252	0	0	0
10 am, 2 pm	45	37	74	804	524	243	0	0	0
11 am, 1 pm	41	39	82	796	516	235	0	0	7
12 noon	40	40	84	794	514	233	0	0	9
FEB. OR OCT.									
8 am, 4 pm	64°	36°	72	806	526	245	0	0	0
9 am, 3 pm	58	43	92	786	506	225	0	8	17
10 am, 2 pm	53	46	104	774	494	213	0	20	29
11 am, 1 pm	50	48	112	766	486	205	0	28	37
12 noon	49	49	115	763	483	202	0	31	40
MAR. OR SEPT.									
7 am, 5 pm	83°	56°	150	728	448	167	35	66	75
8 am, 4 pm	76	58	159	719	439	158	44	75	84
9 am, 3 pm	70	58	163	715	435	154	48	79	88
10 am, 2 pm	65	59	166	712	432	151	51	82	91
11 am, 1 pm	60	59	166	712	432	151	51	82	91
12 noon	60	59	166	712	432	151	51	82	91
APR. OR AUG.									
8 am, 4 pm	85°	81°	598	280	0	0	483	514	523
9 am, 3 pm	79	75	373	505	225	0	258	289	298
10 am, 2 pm	75	72	316	562	282	1	201	232	241
11 am, 1 pm	72	71	294	584	304	23	179	210	219
12 noon	71	71	290	588	308	27	175	206	215
MAY OR JULY									
8 am, 4 pm	—	—	—	—	—	—	—	—	—
9 am, 3 pm	70°	87°	2120	0	0	0	2005	2036	2045
10 am, 2 pm	84	83	801	77	0	0	686	717	726
11 am, 1 pm	81	81	602	276	0	0	487	518	527
12 noon	80	80	567	311	31	0	452	483	492
JUNE									
8 am, 4 pm	—	—	—	—	—	—	—	—	—
9 am, 3 pm	—	—	—	—	—	—	—	—	—
10 am, 2 pm	87°	86°	1610	0	0	0	1495	1526	1535
11 am, 1 pm	84	84	986	0	0	0	871	902	911
12 noon	84	84	951	0	0	0	836	867	876

Table 5–8.

LATITUDE: 35°, 21ST DAY OF THE MONTH

1	2	3	4	5	6	7	8	9	10
SOLAR TIME	ANGLE OF INCIDENCE	EFFECTIVE SOLAR ALTITUDE	a	b			c		
	i	H′		JUNE	JULY	AUG	OCT	NOV	DEC
DECEMBER									
8 am, 4 pm	55°	17°	30	484	371	206	0	0	0
9 am, 3 pm	46	23	42	472	359	194	0	0	0
10 am, 2 pm	38	27	52	462	349	184	0	0	0
11 am, 1 pm	33	30	58	456	343	178	0	0	0
12 noon	31	31	60	454	341	176	0	0	0
JAN. OR NOV.									
8 am, 4 pm	57°	19°	35	479	366	201	0	0	0
9 am, 3 pm	49	29	54	460	347	182	0	0	0
10 am, 2 pm	42	32	63	451	338	173	0	0	3
11 am, 1 pm	36	33	65	449	336	171	0	0	5
12 noon	35	35	70	444	331	166	0	0	10
FEB. OR OCT.									
8 am, 4 pm	63°	33°	65	449	336	171	0	0	5
9 am, 3 pm	57	40	84	430	317	152	0	14	24
10 am, 2 pm	50	42	91	423	310	145	0	21	31
11 am, 1 pm	45	43	93	421	308	143	0	23	33
12 noon	44	44	97	417	304	139	0	27	37
MAR. OR SEPT.									
7 am, 5 pm	82°	52°	129	385	272	107	32	59	69
8 am, 4 pm	74	53	134	380	267	102	37	64	75
9 am, 3 pm	66	54	135	379	266	101	38	65	75
10 am, 2 pm	61	54	135	379	266	101	38	65	75
11 am, 1 pm	56	54	136	378	265	100	39	66	76
12 noon	56	55	140	374	261	96	43	70	80
APR. OR AUG.									
8 am, 4 pm	83°	77°	432	82	0	0	335	362	372
9 am, 3 pm	77	71	292	222	109	0	195	222	232
10 am, 2 pm	72	69	260	254	141	0	163	190	200
11 am, 1 pm	67	66	227	287	174	9	130	157	167
12 noon	66	66	225	289	176	11	128	155	165
MAY OR JULY									
8 am, 4 pm	—	—	—	—	—	—	—	—	—
9 am, 3 pm	84°	82°	736	0	0	0	639	666	676
10 am, 2 pm	79	78	462	52	0	0	365	392	402
11 am, 1 pm	76	76	389	125	12	0	292	319	329
12 noon	75	75	373	141	28	0	276	303	313
JUNE									
8 am, 4 pm	—	—	—	—	—	—	—	—	—
9 am, 3 pm	87°	86°	1414	0	0	0	1317	1344	1354
10 am, 2 pm	82	81	650	0	0	0	553	580	590
11 am, 1 pm	79	79	520	0	0	0	423	450	460
12 noon	78	78	470	44	0	0	373	400	410

Table 5–9.

1 SOLAR TIME	2 ANGLE OF INCIDENCE i	3 EFFECTIVE SOLAR ALTITUDE H′	4 a	5 b JUNE	6 JULY	7 AUG	8 c OCT	9 NOV	10 DEC
DECEMBER									
8 am, 4 pm	55°	15°	27	300	255	165	0	0	0
9 am, 3 pm	44	19	34	293	248	158	0	0	0
10 am, 2 pm	35	23	42	285	240	150	0	0	0
11 am, 1 pm	28	25	46	281	236	146	0	0	0
12 noon	25	25	47	280	235	145	0	0	0
JAN. OR NOV.									
8 am, 4 pm	56°	16°	28	299	254	164	0	0	0
9 am, 3 pm	46	22	40	287	242	152	0	0	0
10 am, 2 pm	38	27	52	275	230	140	0	0	5
11 am, 1 pm	32	29	55	272	227	137	0	0	8
12 noon	29	29	55	272	227	137	0	0	8
FEB. OR OCT.									
8 am, 4 pm	63°	30°	57	270	225	135	0	2	10
9 am, 3 pm	53	34	68	259	214	124	0	13	21
10 am, 2 pm	46	37	76	251	206	116	0	21	29
11 am, 1 pm	41	38	79	248	203	113	0	24	32
12 noon	39	39	81	246	201	111	0	26	34
MAR. OR SEPT.									
7 am, 5 pm	82°	47°	107	220	175	85	26	52	60
8 am, 4 pm	72	48	110	217	172	82	29	55	63
9 am, 3 pm	63	48	111	216	171	81	30	56	64
10 am, 2 pm	57	49	115	212	167	77	34	60	68
11 am, 1 pm	51	50	118	209	164	74	37	63	71
12 noon	50	50	119	208	163	73	38	64	72
APR. OR AUG.									
8 am, 4 pm	80°	72°	302	25	0	0	221	247	255
9 am, 3 pm	74	67	232	95	50	0	151	177	155
10 am, 2 pm	67	64	201	126	81	0	120	146	154
11 am, 1 pm	63	62	189	138	93	3	108	134	142
12 noon	61	61	180	147	102	12	99	125	133
MAY OR JULY									
8 am, 4 pm	88°	86°	1340	0	0	0	1259	1285	1293
9 am, 3 pm	81	77	444	0	0	0	363	389	397
10 am, 2 pm	75	73	318	9	0	0	237	263	271
11 am, 1 pm	72	70	281	46	1	0	200	226	234
12 noon	70	70	275	52	7	0	194	220	228
JUNE									
8 am, 4 pm	—	—	—	—	—	—	—	—	—
9 am, 3 pm	84°	82°	686	0	0	0	605	631	639
10 am, 2 pm	78°	77	424	0	0	0	343	369	377
11 am, 1 pm	74	74	345	0	0	0	264	290	298
12 noon	74	73	334	0	0	0	253	279	287

Table 5–10A.

LATITUDE: 45°, 21ST DAY OF THE MONTH

1	2	3	4	5	6	7	8	9	10
SOLAR TIME	ANGLE OF INCIDENCE i	EFFECTIVE SOLAR ALTITUDE H'	a	b			c		
				JUNE	JULY	AUG	OCT	NOV	DEC
DECEMBER									
8 am, 4 pm	54°	5°	9	245	210	147	0	0	0
9 am, 3 pm	42	14	26	228	193	130	0	0	0
10 am, 2 pm	31	15	26	228	193	130	0	0	0
11 am, 1 pm	23	19	34	220	185	122	0	0	0
12 noon	22	22	40	214	179	116	0	0	0
JAN. OR NOV.									
8 am, 4 pm	55°	10°	17	237	202	139	0	0	0
9 am, 3 pm	45	18	32	222	187	124	0	0	0
10 am, 2 pm	34	19	35	219	184	121	0	0	0
11 am, 1 pm	27	23	42	212	177	114	0	0	2
12 noon	24	24	45	209	174	111	0	0	5
FEB. OR OCT.									
8 am, 4 pm	62°	25°	48	206	171	108	0	3	8
9 am, 3 pm	52	31	60	194	159	96	0	15	20
10 am, 2 pm	42	32	62	192	157	94	0	17	22
11 am, 1 pm	36	33	65	189	154	91	0	20	25
12 noon	34	34	67	187	152	89	0	22	27
MAR. OR SEPT.									
7 am, 5 pm	79°	41°	88	166	131	68	61	43	48
8 am, 4 pm	70	44	95	159	124	61	28	50	55
9 am, 3 pm	61	44	95	159	124	61	28	50	55
10 am, 2 pm	53	44	96	158	123	60	29	51	56
11 am, 1 pm	47	44	98	156	121	58	31	53	58
12 noon	45	45	100	154	119	56	33	55	60
APR. OR AUG.									
8 am, 4 pm	79°	69°	257	0	0	0	190	212	217
9 am, 3 pm	69	61	178	76	41	0	111	133	138
10 am, 2 pm	62	58	157	97	62	0	90	112	117
11 am, 1 pm	58	57	153	101	66	3	86	108	113
12 noon	56	56	148	106	71	8	81	103	108
MAY OR JULY									
8 am, 4 pm	85°	82°	670	0	0	0	603	625	630
9 am, 3 pm	77	72	306	0	0	0	239	261	266
10 am, 2 pm	71	68	249	5	0	0	182	204	209
11 am, 1 pm	66	62	188	66	31	0	121	143	148
12 noon	65	61	180	74	39	0	113	135	140
JUNE									
8 am, 4 pm	87°	85°	1120	0	0	0	1053	1075	1080
9 am, 3 pm	79	76	403	0	0	0	336	358	363
10 am, 2 pm	74	71	287	0	0	0	220	242	247
11 am, 1 pm	70	69	259	0	0	0	192	214	219
12 noon	69	69	255	0	0	0	188	210	215

Table 5–10B.

VALUES OF WINDOW HEIGHT, D, FOR SUMMER-WINTER OVERHANG DESIGNS

	LATITUDE			
	30	35	40	45
June–Oct	763	417	246	187
June–Nov	794	444	272	200
June–Dec	803	454	280	214
July–Oct	483	304	201	152
July–Nov	514	331	227	174
July–Dec	523	341	235	169
Aug–Oct	202	139	111	89
Aug–Nov	233	166	137	111
Aug–Dec	242	175	145	116

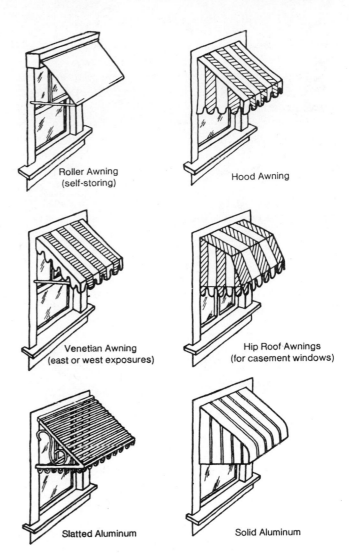

5-15. Types of awnings. (National Bureau of Standards, *Window Design Strategies to Conserve Energy*, 1977)

Nonstructural Sun Control Devices. Most structural overhangs can be effectively worked into the design of new buildings only; they often stick out like sore thumbs when added to old ones. All other methods of sun control discussed below, however, can be applied to old as well as new structures, and are especially useful when air conditioning is added to an existing house.

Awnings. One of the oldest sun control devices is the awning, which can be obtained in several different styles (Figure 5-15) and, of course, in a myriad of sizes and decorative effects.

The open-slat type provides effective control of the sun without seriously impairing the view or cutting down on natural ventilation. Metal or wood slatted

Heat Gain Through Single Glazed Windows with Awnings

Orientation of Window	Type of Awning	Heat Gain per 100 Sq Ft. Glass Surface, Btu/Day	Heat Excluded by the Awning	
			Btu/Day	Percent Reduction
South	No awning	62,200	0	0
	White canvas awning	22,500	39700	64
	Dark green canvas awning	27,700	34500	55
	Dark green plastic awning	35,600	26600	43
West	No awning	84,200	0	0
	White canvas awning	19,500	64700	77
	Dark green canvas awning	23,900	60300	72
	Dark green plastic awning	34,800	49400	59

Table 5-11. (National Bureau of Standards, *Window Design Strategies To Conserve Energy*, 1977)

139

awnings reflect the sun's heat *outside* the window from their upper surface more effectively than do canvas awnings, and they also reradiate heat getting through the slats; they thus keep much radiation out of the protected rooms.

Metal awnings are longer-lived than canvas, and they are less susceptible to weathering or damage. For the most part, they are fixed in place. Canvas awnings do deteriorate after a time and must be replaced, but they can also be removed for storing as desired. The roll-up awning is obviously more flexible than the metal type, in more ways than one, and some are self-storing.

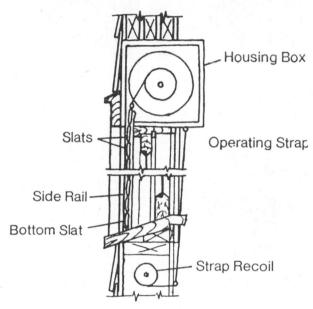

5–16. Installation of an external roll blind. (National Bureau of Standards, *Window Design Strategies To Conserve Energy,* 1977)

Typical *U*-Values of Roll Blinds in Combination with Various Types of Windows

Glass Type	Season	Glass Alone	Glass + 1/2 × 2" Roll Blind Slats	Glass + 1/8 × 1 3/8" Roll Blind Slats
Single	Winter	1.13	0.405	0.568
	Summer	1.06	0.395	0.550
Double (1/2" Air Space)	Winter	0.58	0.301	0.384
	Summer	0.56	0.297	0.376
Single + Storm Sash	Winter	0.56	0.297	0.376
	Summer	0.54	0.290	0.366

Table 5–12. (National Bureau of Standards, *Window Design Strategies To Conserve Energy,* 1977)

The extent to which awnings are effective in excluding heat from a house can be seen in Table 5-11, which establishes values for a design day representing August 1 at 40° latitude. South-exposure heat gain is totaled for 8 A.M. to 4 P.M., and west-exposure from noon to 5 P.M. The awnings are assumed to have a 70° drop, with a venting provision at the top; the foreground is dark. If the foreground were light, heat gain could be as much as double the values shown, due to heat reflection upward, beneath the awning.

Exterior Roll Blinds. Though exterior roll blinds have been used in Europe for a good many years, they have only recently been introduced in this country, notably on the NASA Technology Utilization House in Hampton, Virginia. Roll blinds are permanently fastened over the window (Figure 5-16). They consist of a series of wood, aluminum, or vinyl slats that run in vertical side tracks and store at the head of the window when not needed. Horizontal slots between the slats can be left open for good ventilation and the admittance of some light, or closed tightly to prevent the greatest amount of heat gain/loss. They can be adjusted to any level and disappear entirely from sight in the fully-opened position. Secondarily, they provide good protection for windows during stormy weather, and they also cause a considerable reduction in noise transmission from the outdoors.

Though roll blinds are relatively expensive and do require some maintenance, they also do a good job of solar heat management. Typical *U*-values for roll blinds in combination with various glazings are shown in Table 5-12.

Sun Screens. Sun screen or solar screen is a special type that consists of a series of tiny horizontal louvers, about 15 to 20 to the inch, held together with vertical wires. The louvers must be set at an optimum angle for efficient shading, while still allowing good visibility from within the building. The screening is coated with a heat-absorbing material to improve efficiency.

Though more costly than ordinary screening, solar screens, by killing two birds (insect *and* sun control) with one stone, often turn out to be a real economy.

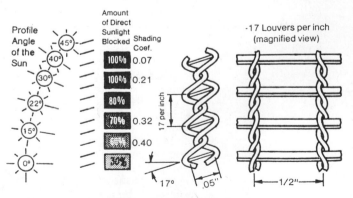

5–17. Sun penetration through a sun screen versus sun angle. (National Bureau of Standards, *Window Design Strategies To Conserve Energy,* 1977)

Figure 5-17 shows the geometry and the effectiveness of one particular brand of screen; others are comparable. The screens also serve to reduce glare, protect the glass, and provide daytime privacy, while at the same time allowing visibility as high as 86 percent.

Freestanding sun control devices. Overhangs are of little value on east and west walls, as we have previously pointed out, unless they are so wide that they constitute a barrier to adequate daylight. Freestanding elements, whether arbors, vertical lattices, high slatted fences, or hollow-masonry walls (with the decorative core patterns laid so that they serve as ventilating spaces) are required for sun control in these compass directions, as well as (though to a somewhat lesser degree) in southwest and southeast directions. If use of a garage as a sun barrier is not feasible, the freestanding element is a sound solution *unless* the best views are in the east or west direction. In that case a decision will have to be made whether to save the view and increase the cooling load and summer discomfort, or hinder the view and achieve sun control.

Trees. The really ideal freestanding sun control device is, of course, a deciduous tree. Not only is it effective and beautiful, but it is practically free. A tree needs no painting, washing, adjustment, seasonal removal or replacement, and only rarely any repair. It is ideal summer sun shade for houses—*while it lives.* As mentioned before, trees are not counted on as shading devices in cooling load calculations because of their perishability.

Sun control by the window itself. Exterior sun control devices can by a logical extension be made to include the actual glass used in the wall opening. Various kinds of glass and windows have been developed for the purpose. The simplest and oldest, as far as glass goes, is the frosted type that eliminates glare (and clear vision at the same time) but has little or no effect on the incoming heat. The more expensive glass block not only does away with glare, but it materially reduces the radiated heat of the sun, dissipating it in the dead air space inside the block. Glass block *U*-factors are given in Table 5-13; note that the larger the block, the better the performance.

However, none of these sight-barring glasses actually serves the major purpose of a wall opening: to permit vision out and light in while barring the violences of weather from the occupants of the room. Neither, of course, do the standard window glasses, double-strength, single-strength, or plate, which are transparent indeed, not only to visible radiation but also to heat.

Heat absorbing glass. One method of controlling the summer sun's heat without special devices is by the use of heat absorbing float glass. However, the cost of such glass is considerably higher than ordinary window glass.

Float glass, the successor to plate glass, is made in numerous thicknesses, including single-strength 3/32-inch and double-strength 1/8-inch. Even these thin layers of glass will block out some solar radiation, since their typical solar transmittance values are 86 and 84 percent, respectively; that is, 14 and 16 percent, respectively, of the solar irradiation striking the glass will be blocked out. As the thickness of the glass increases, its solar transmittance decreases. So, unfortunately, does the percentage of daylight that is admitted.

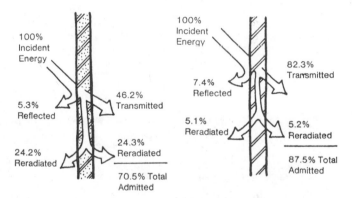

5-18. Solar energy transmission through heat-absorbing single glazing versus clear glass (summer). (National Bureau of Standards, *Window Design Strategies To Conserve Energy,* 1977)

Figure 5-18 shows a typical example of heat absorbing glass solar energy transmission as compared to standard glass. Note that in this case the glass is only moderately effective in the summer when installed in a regular single-pane thickness window frame—the reason being that while about 5 percent of the solar radiation is reflected and about 48 percent is absorbed, a good part of the absorbed heat is reradiated into the room. It should be noted, too, that these values are not absolute; they vary not only with the particular glass, but also with the sun angles.

A double-glazing arrangement, with the outer layer of heat absorbing glass and the inner of ordinary clear glass, will greatly improve the thermal efficiency of a given thickness of heat absorbing glass (Figure 5-19). Under normal circumstances, the chief disadvantage of such an arrangement, and for that matter of all heat absorbing glazing, is that it is just as effective in barring

U-Values for Glass Blocks*

Nominal Size	U-Value (single cavity)	U-Value (double cavity)
4 × 12 inch	0.60	0.52
6 inch sq.	0.60	—
8 inch sq.	0.56	0.48
12 inch sq.	0.52	0.44

* Note that the larger blocks provide better insulation.

Table 5-13. (National Bureau of Standards, *Window Design Strategies To Conserve Energy,* 1977)

solar radiation in the winter, when it is desirable in the rooms, as it is in the summer, when it is not. However, a special reversible double-glazed sash can be employed so that in winter the heat from the heat-absorbing glass can be discharged inside the room to serve a useful purpose instead of the outside, and wasted.

As can be seen in Table 5–14, the various sorts of tinted float glass are far more effective in controlling

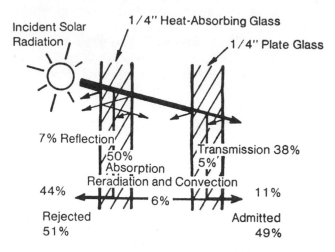

5–19. Solar energy transmission, heat absorbing insulating glass. (National Bureau of Standards, *Window Design Strategies To Conserve Energy,* 1977)

solar radiation than are the clear glasses, even in very heavy thicknesses. Glass that is coated with a metallic film is even more effective; not only is solar energy absorbed, but it is also reflected. Glare and penetration of ultraviolet rays are also reduced. This type of glass imparts a mirror-like appearance from the outside, but allows good visibility from the inside; it can be obtained in golds, greys, blues, bronzes, and silver.

The heat reduction that can be provided by glasses of this sort are substantial, but in residential applications they should not necessarily be employed as the sole protection against solar energy gain in the air-conditioned house. Overhangs and/or vertical sunshades should also be included. Indeed, in many instances a well-designed sun control device will reduce cooling load to a point where the heat resisting glass becomes an unnecessary added expense. A storm window or one of the prefabricated double- or triple-glazed windows will cut out a large portion of the convective heat, and the sun control overhang or freestanding wall or fence will handle the radiant heat.

Shutters. In the old days many houses had workable wooden shutters, many of them with movable slats, that could be adjusted to bar the hottest rays of the sun while still permitting air to enter. They were also useful in protection against rain and snow, and proved a nuisance to burglars, too, when bolted shut.

Typical Properties of Clear and Tinted Glass

FLOAT GLASS		THICKNESS in	THICKNESS mm	TRANSMITTANCE Average Daylight %	TRANSMITTANCE Total Solar %	REFLECTANCE Average Daylight %	RELATIVE HEAT GAIN Eng	RELATIVE HEAT GAIN Met	U VALUE SUMMER Eng	U VALUE SUMMER Met	U VALUE WINTER Eng	U VALUE WINTER Met	No Shade	Venetian Blinds Light	Venetian Blinds Med	Draperies Light	Draperies Med	Draperies Dark
CLEAR	SS	3/32	2.5	90	86		216	680			1.13		1.01			.56	.61	.70
	DS	1/8	3	90	84		212	668			1.13	6.4	.99		.64			
		5/32	4	89	82	8	210	662	1.03	5.8	1.12		.98	.55				
		3/16	5	89	80		206	649			1.12		.96			.55	.60	
		1/4	6	88	77		200	630			1.10	6.2	.93		63	.54	.59	.69
HEAVY DUTY CLEAR		5/16	8	87	74		196	618	1.03	5.8	1.09	6.2	.91	.55	.63	.53	.58	.68
		3/8	10	86	71	8	190	599	1.02		1.08	6.1	.88	.54	.62	.52	.56	.66
		1/2	12	84	65		182	574	1.01	5.7	1.06	6.0	.84		.61	.50	.54	.63
		5/8	15	82	60		172	542	1.01	5.7	1.04	5.9	.79	.54	.60	.49	.52	.60
		3/4	19	81	56	7	166	523	.99	5.6	1.02	5.8	.76	.53	.59	.47	.50	.58
		7/8	22	79	53		160	504	.98	5.6	1.00	5.7	.73		.58	.46	.49	.56
BLUE-GREEN		3/16	5	78	55	7	167	526	1.09	6.2	1.12	6.4	.76	.53	.59	.47	.50	.58
		1/4	6	74	48		155	489			1.10	6.2	.70		.57	.45	.47	.54
GREY		1/8	3	62	63	6	179	564	1.08	6.1	1.13	6.4	.82	.54	.60	.50	.53	.62
		3/16	5	51	53	5	165	520	1.09	6.2	1.12		.75	.53	.58	.47	.50	.57
		1/4	6	42	.44		149	470			1.10	6.2	.67	.51	.55	.44	.46	.52
HEAVY DUTY GREY		3/8	10	28	31	5	127	400	1.09	6.2	1.08	6.1	.56	.44	.46	.40	.42	.46
		1/2	12	19	22	4	113	356	1.08	6.1	1.06	6.0	.49	.39	.41	.35	.37	.39
BRONZE		1/8	3	68	65	6	183	577	1.08	6.1	1.13	6.4	.84	.54	.61	.50	.54	.63
		3/16	5	58	55		167	526	1.09	6.2	1.12		.76	.53	.59	.47	.50	.58
		1/4	6	50	46	5	153	482			1.10	6.2	.69	.52	.56	.45	.47	.53
HEAVY DUTY BRONZE		3/8	10	37	33	5	131	413	1.09	6.2	1.08	6.1	.58	.45	.48	.41	.43	.48
		1/2	12	28	24		117	369	1.08	6.1	1.06	6.0	.51	.41	.43	.37	.39	.41

Table 5–14. (Courtesy, Libby-Owens-Ford Company)

Today most of the shutters seen on "Cape Cods" and "Dutch Colonials" are fakes. The new house that has usable wood shutters is eccentric. This is unfortunate, because shutters, especially of the operable type, can indeed serve valuable energy conserving functions. At present the only shutters available are unfinished wood with fixed louvers, or prefinished aluminum with fixed slats. Though not as useful as those with adjustable slats or louvers, they are quite effective in barring the sun's rays. Four different types are shown in Figure 5-20.

Bahama Shutters

Sarasota Shutters

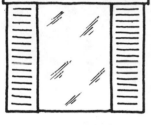
Rolling Shutters

Side-hinged Shutters

5-20. Types of shutters. (National Bureau of Standards, *Window Design Strategies To Conserve Energy,* 1977)

Double glazing. An effective method of sun control the year round in localities having both hot summers and cold winters is the double-glazed (or triple-glazed) window, which can be made even more efficient if the outer light is heat absorbing glass. However, exterior shading (whether trees, awnings, eggcrate overhang, or some other device) is also advisable to protect the interior from the hottest attacks of the sun. This is, of course, particularly true in mechanically cooled houses, where every Btu kept out of the structure is money saved. Actually, in such houses the use of special glazings, of whatever type, will be a matter of calculating whether it will save enough, when used in conjunction with good shading devices, to make its added cost justifiable.

Of course, the value of multiple glazing in reducing winter heat loss has already been described. Particularly in cold climates, such windows are, as we have seen, a real *winter* economy.

Inside Sun Control Devices. Methods of controlling solar radiation inside the room are well known and in wide use; they need not detain us long. They include roller shades, venetian blinds, and draperies; film

shades and insulating shutters are also possibilities. As noted previously, few of these techniques satisfactorily control solar heat inside the room—not, at least, without at the same time practically eliminating all sunlight.

One of the oldest methods of controlling glare and giving privacy, *roller shades* provide only a minimally effective method of solar heat control in a home, but do prove useful to a degree. As can be seen in Table 5-15, the opacity and the color of the shade has a great deal to do with performance; a reversible shade that is dark on one side and light on the other is the most functional, since it can be used to reflect the sun's energy in the summer and collect it in the winter. The result of one typical computation for roller shades is shown in Table 5-16; and it indicates that some savings can be gained from their installation. Making such determinations, however, is a complex business and must be carefully calculated for individual installations.

In many modern window-walled houses, wood- or plastic-strip roll shades are effectively used as interior glare-control and shading devices. Relatively durable and low-cost, strip shades also make an attractive

Typical Heat-Blocking Characteristics of Roll Shades

Characteristic	Transmitted	Reflected	Absorbed
Light-color, translucent	25%	60%	15%
White, opaque	0	80	20
Dark, opaque	0	12	88

Table 5-15. (National Bureau of Standards, *Window Design Strategies To Conserve Energy,* 1977)

Seasonal Energy Expenditure for a Window in New York City (Kbtu/Sq. Ft.) (− denotes energy input required from mechanical system)

Glazing	Shading	North		East		South	
		Wint.	Sumr.	Wint.	Sumr.	Wint.	Sumr.
Single	None	−84	−43	−38	−76	+29	−59
Single	roll						
	shade	−69	−15	−23	−26	+45	−20
	Savings	15	28	15	50	16	39
Storm/	None	−25	−37	+14	−65	+71	−51
double							
Storm/	roll						
double	shade	−19	−13	+21	−23	+81	−18
	Savings	6	24	7	42	10	33
Savings roll shade + double compared to no roll shade + single		65	30	17	53	52	41

Table 5-16. (National Bureau of Standards, *Window Design Strategies To Conserve Energy,* 1977)

decorating element. The same is true of freestanding *shoji* or similar screens. However, these devices do little to bar the sun's heat, and they are of limited value as radiation control devices.

Roll film shades, on the other hand, especially when sealed at bottom and sides, can afford substantial reductions in both heat loss and heat gain, as much as 60 percent in some cases.

Unlike other types of interior window coverings, *venetian blinds* have a high degree of adjustment flexibility, so that the amount of daylight entering a room can be controlled as well as can be the admittance of direct-beam sunlight. Standard metal or wood slat venetian blinds also have a reasonable degree of effectiveness against radiant heat gain, as can be seen in Table 5–17 where they are compared to roller shades in terms of their shading coefficient (SC).

Vertical venetian blinds, which are available in fabrics and plastics for various applications (Figure 5–21), provide a variable amount of protection against solar heat, depending upon exactly what material is used in them. The slats can be adjusted to regulate the entry of sunlight as it changes direction during the day.

For maximum prevention of the entry of solar radiation, light-colored and tight-fitting venetian blinds are most effective. Some types have a quite low shading coefficient, and they can reject as much as 75 percent of the solar radiation from the room. Nevertheless, their cost-effectiveness must be taken into consideration and compared with that of the excellent protection afforded by exterior devices.

Opaque *draperies* are useful mainly for decoration and, at night, for privacy. The nonopaque types do reduce solar radiation a little while admitting light, but their efficiency is low.

Summer heat gain can be reduced by the use of draperies. Their effectiveness depends primarily on the amount of solar energy absorbed by the material, the amount transmitted through it, and also, to some extent, its reflectivity. Double draperies will further improve thermal performance. However, in order to have a reasonable degree of effectiveness at all, the draperies should be enclosed at the top, sealed down both sides,

5–21. Vertical venetian drapery. (Courtesy, LouverDrape, Inc., Santa Monica, CA, Lee White Photography)

Shading Coefficients for Single Glass with Indoor Shading by Venetian Blinds or Roller Shades

	Nominal Thickness[a]	Solar Trans.[b]	Type of Shading				
			Venetian Blinds		Roller Shade		
					Opaque		Translucent
			Medium	Light	Dark	White	Light
Clear	3/32 to 1/4	0.87 to 0.80					
Clear	1/4 to 1/2	0.80 to 0.71					
Clear Pattern	1/8 to 1/2	0.87 to 0.79	0.64	0.55	0.59	0.25	0.39
Heat-Absorbing Pattern	1/8	—					
Tinted	3/16, 7/32	0.74, 0.71					
Heat-Absorbing[d]	3/16, 1/4	0.46					
Heat-Absorbing Pattern	3/16, 1/4	—	0.57	0.53	0.45	0.30	0.36
Tinted	1/8, 7/32	0.59, 0.45					
Heat-Absorbing or pattern	—	0.44 to 0.30	0.54	0.52	0.40	0.28	0.32
Heat-Absorbing[d]	3/8	0.34					
Heat-Absorbing or Pattern	—	0.29 to 0.15 0.24	0.42	0.40	0.36	0.28	0.31
Reflective Coated Glass							
S.C.[c] = 0.30			0.25	0.23			
0.40			0.33	0.29			
0.50			0.42	0.38			
0.60			0.50	0.44			

[a] Refer to manufacturer's literature for values.
[b] For vertical blinds with opaque white and beige louvers in the tightly closed position, SC is 0.25 and 0.29 when used with glass of 0.71 to 0.80 transmittance.
[c] SC for glass with no shading device.
[d] Refers to grey, bronze, and green tinted heat-absorbing glass.

Table 5–17. (Reprinted with permission from the *1977 Fundamentals Volume, ASHRAE HANDBOOK & Product Directory*)

Shading Coefficients for Single and Insulating Glass with Draperies

Glazing	Glass Trans.	Glass SC*	A	B	C	D	E	F	G	H	I	J
Single Glass												
1/4 in. Clear	0.80	0.95	0.80	0.75	0.70	0.65	0.60	0.55	0.50	0.45	0.40	0.35
1/2 in. Clear	0.71	0.88	0.74	0.70	0.66	0.61	0.56	0.52	0.48	0.43	0.39	0.35
1/4 in. Heat Abs.	0.46	0.67	0.57	0.54	0.52	0.49	0.46	0.44	0.41	0.38	0.36	0.33
1/2 in. Heat Abs.	0.24	0.50	0.43	0.42	0.40	0.39	0.38	0.36	0.34	0.33	0.32	0.30
Reflective Coated	—	0.60	0.57	0.54	0.51	0.49	0.46	0.43	0.41	0.38	0.36	0.33
(See Manufacturers' literature	—	0.50	0.46	0.44	0.42	0.41	0.39	0.38	0.36	0.34	0.33	0.31
for exact values)	—	0.40	0.36	0.35	0.34	0.33	0.32	0.30	0.29	0.28	0.27	0.26
	—	0.30	0.25	0.24	0.24	0.23	0.23	0.23	0.22	0.21	0.21	0.20
Insulating Glass (1/2 in. Air Space)												
Clear Out and Clear In	0.64	0.83	0.66	0.62	0.58	0.56	0.52	0.48	0.45	0.42	0.37	0.35
Heat Abs. Out and Clear In	0.37	0.56	0.49	0.47	0.45	0.43	0.41	0.39	0.37	0.35	0.33	0.32
Reflective Coated	—	0.40	0.38	0.37	0.37	0.36	0.34	0.32	0.31	0.29	0.28	0.28
(see Manufacturers' literature	—	0.30	0.29	0.28	0.27	0.27	0.26	0.26	0.25	0.25	0.24	0.24
for exact values)	—	0.20	0.19	0.19	0.18	0.18	0.17	0.17	0.16	0.16	0.15	0.15

*For glass alone, with no drapery.

**Shading Coefficient values for the SC lines for representative glazings. Substitute for SC index letters values on the line of the glazing selected.

SHADING COEFFICIENT INDEX LETTER

DRAPERIES ADD 100% FULLNESS
(Fabric width two times draped width)

Notes:
1. Shading Coefficients are for draped fabrics.
2. Other properties are for fabrics in flat orientation
3. Use Fabric Reflectance and Transmittance to obtain accurate Shading Coefficients.
4. Use Openness and Yarn Reflectance or Openness and Fabric Reflectance to obtain the Various Environmental Characteristics, or to obtain Approximate Shading Coefficients.

CLASSIFICATION OF FABRICS
I = Open Weave
II = Semi-open Weave
III = Closed Weave

D = Dark "Color"
M = Medium "Color"
L = Light "Color"

Table 5-18. (Reprinted with permission from the *1977 Fundamentals Volume, ASHRAE HANDBOOK & Product Directory*)

and sealed across the window sill or extend down to full contact with the floor. This is a situation that simply does not prevail with most draperies.

By and large, draperies that are thermally efficient are of more value in wintertime heat conservation than as a device for excluding summer heat. During hot daytime weather most people would prefer to have sunlight and a somewhat higher cooling load, and no matter how effective or efficient the draperies might be in reducing heat gain, their value when left open is zero. Table 5-18 shows various closed values.

THE WINDOWLESS BUILDING

Of the above solutions or devices, only one is absolutely perfect; that is the building without any windows at all. Perhaps the time will come when (as a result of factors very different from those an architect considers when designing a building) the windowless structure will be home for all of us—probably underground, at that. But until that time, buildings without windows are for most uses bad in every way. They tend to give their occupants a permanent feeling of claustrophobia. So says Mr. Conklin, and the comments are obviously based on experience as well as fact. He goes on:

A sizable proportion of this book was written in a one-room apartment on the basement level of an old New York brownstone. The two windows faced north, and directly on the street. It was necessary to keep the venetian blinds closed at all times to prevent passersby from peering in. The few months spent in this essentially windowless room gave an uncomfortable preview of what it would be like to live underground—including the constant hum of the air conditioner... It was a nerve-wracking experience. Men are not moles: they need the visual gymnastic of a view and the spiritual tonic of sunlight if they are to operate as civilized human beings.

The revision of this book, on the other hand, was done in a comfortable (albeit somewhat crowded) office located on the side of a ridge at the 7500-foot level in the Colorado Rockies. The large window and the sliding glass patio doors (double-glazed) face southeast, out over a long, pastoral valley 400 feet below with a mountain range as a backdrop. By leaving the drapes open, it was possible to watch the sun rise over the neighboring ridge, work in its warmth most of the morning, and watch the interplay of colors in the mountains as it sank during the afternoon. There was no noise save that of the leaves rustling in the breeze, and for the most part the passersby were Clark's nutcrackers, various hawks, and an occasional scrub jay. Men indeed are not moles; had the revision been done under the same circumstances as the original writing, the reviser would have been faced with a well-nigh intolerable situation. Mr. Conklin's conclusion must, for all practical purposes, be treated not as an opinion, but as a fact.

Reradiation From The Ground

Reradiation can be an important addition to the heat entering a house through its windows and, to a lesser degree, its walls. The total amount of diffuse radiation entering a building is shown in Figure 5-3, but the information is not broken down into its component parts of "sky-solar radiation" and "ground reradiation." No reliable table of measurements for ground reradiation is known to exist; in any event this is a highly variable condition. But Figure 5-22 indicates that, if ground conditions are adverse, it can be extremely high. The moral of this sketch is almost ridiculously obvious—and is ignored by hundreds of thousands of people!

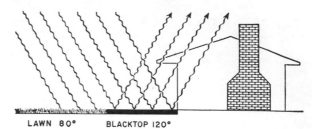

5-22. Effect of blacktop too near exposed wall of a house. (Building Research Advisory Board, "Weather and the Building Industry")

Locate paved or graveled driveways, terraces, and sidewalks a considerable distance from the south, east, and west walls of a house! And provide a moderately wide grassy area, flower bed, or bank of low shrubbery directly adjacent to these walls to serve as efficient absorbers of the solar radiation; or else make sure that the paved areas are completely protected from the sun's heat by trees, arbors, trellises, or other overhead sun control devices. (The shrubbery should be low, incidentally, so that in nonair-conditioned houses the plantings will not interfere with the passage of summer breezes through open windows.)

THERMAL INSULATION OF WALLS

As with roofs, walls should have a very low thermal conductivity for summer as well as winter conditions. The total heat gain through walls in hot weather can be determined in much the same way as that for roofs: by using sol-air temperatures and the proper tables for cooling load temperature differences. Without going into the complexities of this process (and there are many), it can be said that a south wall will have a much higher heat penetration than a north one, and a sunlit one more than a shaded one. Furthermore, wall color has a measureable effect, since a light wall color will reflect considerably more heat energy than will a dark one. This fact, however, is not taken into consideration in residential cooling calculations; wall colors are so unpredictable that the safest course is in assuming a dark color.

Unlike the summer situation in roofs, mass thermal insulation is just as effective in walls as reflective air spaces, summer as well as winter. Little will be gained by trying to squeeze a 1-inch foil-lined space into the stud area already occupied by 3 inches of mass insulation. It would be necessary to reduce the mass insulation to 2 inches to make sure the reflective space was wide enough; and the additional cost of installing two different materials is not warranted by any measurable difference in the overall *U* factors. Of course, other arrangements will work: a 2-inch insulation blanket with a reflective foil facing; a 3-inch insulation blanket with a reflective foil facing, *provided* that the insulation is dished in and the foil is kept at least 1 inch from the lath or wallboard; or a reflective foil-faced rigid material, provided that the inch air space is maintained. Multilayer all-aluminum foil insulation, dished between the studs, provides good insulation *and* vapor barrier the year round in some climates.

FLOORS

Except when a room is over an unconditioned space (garage) or open space (porch), it is common practice to assume that there is no heat gain from floors. Crawl spaces, cold basements, and slabs are considered to be at the same temperature as the cooling design temperature inside the house. They often are lower, but not enough to affect the cooling load measurably.

VAPOR BARRIERS

Air conditioning engineers state that an impermeable vapor barrier in all structural cross sections of a mechanically cooled house is as important in summer as it is in winter, at least in areas of the country with high outdoor humidity.

The summer problem is not, however, one of condensation. It is generally accepted, as pointed out previously, that summer condensation is an almost nonexistent phenomenon, and that, when it does occur in a few unusual cases, it is usually too transient to damage the structure. Some experts feel that a barrier in the *outer* layers of a structural cross section may be useful in such exceptionally humid regions as the Gulf area; but many others disagree, feeling that whatever condensation may occur will dry out again as nightfall comes and the temperature drops.

No, the vapor barrier is important during hot weather for an entirely different reason. The cooling load in any structure, houses included, is composed of two separate types of heat, sensible and latent, just as is the heating load in winter (chapter 4). But while the winter latent heat load requires vaporization of water, the summer load requires condensation of vapor for real comfort.

As pointed out previously, people can be quite comfortable in an air temperature of 90° F, provided the humidity is very low. On the other hand, air at no more than 75° F can be miserably uncomfortable if the humidity is up in the 70s or 80s. An air conditioning

unit, one might say, "feels" the same way; it has to work as hard if not harder to condense surplus vapor in the indoor air of a house into water as it does to add coolness to dry air. It is important, therefore, that indoor humidities be kept as low as possible during hot weather—a situation diametrically opposed to that existing in the winter season.

High indoor humidity in hot weather comes from cooking, washing, bathing; from people, animals, plants; and from high *outdoor* humidity. The temperature differential between the hot outdoors and the mechanically cooled indoors creates a vapor pressure in the walls which makes it possible for the outdoor vapor to penetrate into the house and add to the moisture load.

A good vapor barrier will keep almost all of the outdoor humidity outdoors. It will not only keep the cooling load down, but will also help eliminate the unpleasant problems of summer mildew, sticky salt, dank closets, and profusely sweating human beings—the inevitable results of high indoor humidities during hot weather.

No vapor barrier is needed in Arizona or elsewhere in the American desert or high altitude areas where humidities always remain low. But everywhere else where summer humidity is high they are essential parts of economical and comfortable "conditioned" living.

DAMP CELLARS AND CRAWL SPACES

Condensation, however, can—and always does in humid climates—occur in cellars and crawl spaces, where air temperatures are much nearer those of the ground (as low as 45° F) than of the outdoor air. Vapor barriers will help keep this moisture from coming up through the floor into the house, but they will not eliminate it from the cooler spaces themselves. In cellars, the vapor barriers should cover the bottoms of the floor joists, either in the form of a foil-backed lath or wallboard, or a separate membrane of high vapor resistance. In crawl spaces, the same treatment that is effective in cold weather is also good during hot: a heavy roll roofing, plastic film, or other relatively impermeable material laid over the ground and lapped 6 inches at the strip joints. However, a vapor barrier under the insulation across the bottom of the joists is also important, to keep airborne outdoor humidity entering the crawl space from condensing in the insulation.

Summer condensation in these beneath-the-house areas is not alleviated by ventilation. What happens, if the outdoor air is humid, is that ventilation merely adds moisture to the cool area, where it of course condenses. It is almost impossible to move enough of this outdoor air through these restricted spaces to drive the moisture out mechanically; the only cures are sealing the areas completely off from the outer atmosphere, heating the space until the moisture dries out, or using dehumidifying equipment. One would hardly recommend heating the spaces on hot days, so the only alternatives are hermetically sealing them, or using electronic or chemical dehumidification equipment. As long as the moisture in the basement or crawl space areas is kept out of the upper reaches of the house by vapor barriers, there is no reason to make any special efforts to dry it out—unless for some reason the occupants want it that way. °

CONTROL OF INDOOR HEAT SOURCES

Comfortable summer living and economical summer cooling can be considerably enhanced by the control of heat-producing sources inside a house, although much of this control will be a matter of occupant living habits rather than of design, construction, or equipment.

However, there are two indoor heat-producing conditions that can be controlled to some degree automatically. One we have already discussed in some detail in chapter 3: the built-in exhaust fans in kitchens, baths, laundries, and other moisture sources. During cold weather they reduce the danger of condensation; during hot, they not only drive out most of the unwanted heat, but also much of the vapor, thus cutting the latent heat load.

The other method of heat reduction indoors has to do with lighting devices. A fluorescent light, as everyone knows, is almost cold, by comparison with an incandescent bulb. It does produce some heat, but only a fraction of that cast off by the resistance-heated filament of a common light bulb, for about the same light intensity. A 100-watt incandescent bulb produces 341 Btu per hour, enough to destroy the value of a great deal of evening coolness. A fluorescent light of approximately the same brightness (32 watts) disperses only 109 Btu per hour into the room and is, therefore, a sizable comfort and economy improvement over the older form of illumination.

Obviously, the judicious use of modern fluorescent fixtures (as indirect lighting sources in the living areas as well as direct lights in baths, kitchens, workrooms, studies, and the like) will reduce the indoor evening heat load considerably. And now that these fixtures are made so that they produce their light nearly as instantaneously as incandescents, the old complaint about delayed activation and "flickering" is no longer valid. Nor is the complaint about the harsh, cold light; new fluorescent lamps are available in a variety of color-temperatures and tones, including matches to both daylight and incandescent light.

Though the equipment was at one time considerably more expensive than incandescent fixtures, that gap has now largely closed, and, in fact, in many instances the situation is reversed. Fluorescent bulbs are more expensive than the incandescent type, but far longer bulb life and much lower operating costs for the same level of il-

lumination pay worthwhile dividends over a period of time.

And, once again, the high cost of cooling makes a judicious use of fluorescent fixtures a sound investment. They will reduce cooling loads measurably, while their lower heat output in the winter will do little if anything to adversely affect overall heating costs.

MECHANICAL COOLING

As was mentioned earlier, the process of calculating cooling loads can be as complex and super-sophisticated as one cares to make it; computations for large buildings are best run on, and the results analyzed by, a computer. But this is unnecessary when dealing with residential cooling loads; a greatly simplified method can be employed that will give perfectly satisfactory results. The *1977 Fundamentals Volume, ASHRAE HANDBOOK & Product Directory* lists the reasons for this:

The unique features that distinguish residences from other types of buildings, with respect to cooling load calculation and equipment sizing, are:

1. Residences, unlike many other structures, are assumed to be occupied, and usually conditioned, for 24 hours a day, every day of the cooling season.

2. Residential cooling system loads are primarily imposed by heat flow through structural components and by air leakage or ventilation. Internal loads, particularly those imposed by occupants and lights, are small in comparison to those in commercial or industrial installations.

3. Most residences are cooled as a single zone, since there is no means to redistribute cooling unit capacity from one area to another as loads change from hour to hour.

4. Most residential systems employ units of relatively small capacity (from about 20,000 to 60,000 Btu/hr) which have no means for controlling capacity except by cycling the condensing unit. Since cooling load is largely affected by outside conditions, and few days each heating season are *design* days, a partial load situation exists during most of the season. An oversize unit with no capacity control is detrimental to good system performance under these circumstances.

5. Dehumidification is achieved only during periods of cooling unit operation, since there is only very limited use of reheat or bypass systems to directly control humidity under conditions of relatively light sensible load. Space condition control is usually restricted to use of room thermostats, essentially sensible heat-actuated devices.

6. Many residential systems are operated 24 hours a day, thus permitting full advantage to be taken of thermal *flywheel* effects of the structural members and furnishings within the structure. (This accentuates the partial load effects mentioned in item 4, above.)

Thus, though complex methods *can* be used for determining residential cooling loads, empirical data and various studies fully support the simplified procedures that will be discussed here.

Calculation of Cooling Load

The following outlines a method for calculating residential cooling loads that should be usable by practically anyone. It is applicable to almost every type and size of house, almost everywhere in the country.

Remember, however, that this information is applicable to *residential use only*. It will not be sufficient for large nonresidential buildings, particularly those with minimum roof insulation, oversize glass areas, and large and variable indoor heat gains. For such buildings, the more complicated but more accurate and comprehensive method outlined in the *1977 Fundamentals Volume, ASHRAE HANDBOOK & Product Directory,* Chapter 25, should be used.

There are several systems that can be used to calculate residential cooling load, all somewhat different in specific form, but all based upon the same premises and yielding approximately the same results. The ASHRAE Chapter mentioned above contains the basic information needed. The Hydronics Institute offers their Manual No. C-30, *Cooling Load Calculation Guide for Residences,* which includes tables, examples, and sample calculations. *Load Calculation for Residential Winter and Summer Air Conditioning,* Manual J, from the Air Conditioning Contractors of America, is quite similar but perhaps a bit more definitive. The *Insulation Manual* from the National Association of Home Builders Research Foundation likewise contains a comprehensive method, and those who are involved with all-electric homes might wish to consult the National Electrical Manufacturers Association's Standards Publication No. HE-1, *Manual for Electric Comfort Conditioning.* Though the following information largely derives from the ASHRAE HANDBOOK, any of the other manuals cited cover the necessary details equally well.

Before any calculations can be started, a certain amount of preliminary information must be gathered; there are also a few points with regard to mechanical cooling in general that must be noted.

The first step is to obtain accurate data and measurements of the structure. A full set of plans or blueprints of the house is needed; if these are not available, a series of scaled drawings of floor plans and elevations will serve. Window, door, and room dimensions should be listed and the exact positions of doors and windows noted. The construction details of the various building sections, including doors and windows, should be noted as well. Check the orientation of the structure, and list the directions in which each of the exterior walls face.

Other factors must be investigated as well. Determine what, if any, shading or solar control devices, such as draperies, roll shades, overhangs, and the like will be used to protect the window openings. If the devices are operable, determine how they will be used; i.e., if roll shades are installed, will they remain half open, fully open, or be closed during the heat of the day, as a general rule. If storm sash or triple glazing with removable outer panels is installed, determine whether or not the glass will remain in place during the entire cooling season. And finally, establish the number of oc-cupants of the house. This should include only those who are actually present on a regular basis; house guests are not normally included unless they are present more frequently than not, and entertainment of large groups is not usually included in the calculations, except in unusual circumstances.

In general cooling practice, concrete slab floors are not considered as having a heat gain, nor are wood floors over enclosed crawl spaces or basements, either ventilated or unventilated. As noted previously, any dampness or moisture conditions that exist, or might exist, in a crawl space should be corrected in order to avoid adverse effects upon the performance of the cooling equipment. Though bathrooms are included in the calculations, they are seldom actually cooled; instead, the bathroom cooling load is equally divided among the adjacent rooms. An exception to this might be a luxury-type bathroom of a size at least equal to a small bedroom, large enough that the room would not be adequately cooled by virtue of the door being open most of the time as is usually the case with a small bathroom.

Clothes dryers must always be provided with vents to the outdoors to minimize cooling loads when the units are in operation, and vent fans are recommended for bathrooms to remove moisture that accumulates during bathing. Vent fans should also be used in kitchens during periods of cooking of a nature that produces quantities of moisture and heat.

Certain unusual conditions may be present in a given house, and these too must be taken into consideration. For instance, a house may have an expandable attic, unfinished room or ell, or a basement that may at some time be converted into a family or recreation room. The cooling load should be included in the calculations, *provided that* the plans for expansion/finishing are reasonably definite and will expectably be carried out in the near future. If they are not, then the cooling equipment will be oversized for the actual cooling load, and performance will suffer.

Making The Calculations

Making the heating load calculations for a residence at first glance seems involved, but can be readily accomplished by following a series of simple steps. The use of a pocket (or other) calculator is recommended, since it makes the job so much easier.

Step one. Prepare a separate sheet of paper for each room of the house. Using measurements taken from the plans (or from the structure itself), determine the total area of all walls exposed to the outdoors. This includes door and window openings, as well as the back walls of any closets that might open into the room.

Step two. Determine the area of exterior doors, and enter the figure on the appropriate sheets. If the doors contain lights, treat the lights as windows and the remaining area as doors.

Step three. Similarly, determine the window areas, and enter them on the room sheets.

Step four. Total the window and door areas for each room, and subtract this from the gross wall area to arrive at the net wall area.

Step five. Find the total floor area that is exposed to any uncooled space, including closets.

Step six. Find the total ceiling area that is exposed to any uncooled space, including closets.

Step seven. Determine the total gross partition wall area that is exposed to any uncooled space (separating a garage from a kitchen, for instance).

Step eight. Set the room sheets aside for the moment, and determine the inside design temperature. The usual temperature is 75° F, and most cooling load tables and computations are based on this figure. Another temperature can be used, however, if desired, as will be explained a bit later. Note that the temperature chosen should be the same for every room of the house, and it should be the same for the entire cooling season.

Step nine. Determine the outside design temperature. This is done much in the same way as when calculating house heating load. Consult the summer conditions section of Table 3-7 (also review the material concerning the selection of a winter design temperature in that chapter) and choose an appropriate design temperature from Column 6. Since climatological characteristics change rapidly over short distances, local conditions should be considered and the chosen design temperature weighted appropriately

Step ten. Determine the design temperature difference by subtracting the inside design temperature from the outside design temperature. For example, if the chosen outside temperature and the inside temperature are 95° F and 75° F respectively, the design temperature difference is 20° F.

Step eleven. From Table 3-7, Column 7, determine the mean daily temperature range of your locale and, if necessary, temper the figure according to local climatological information. Then determine whether this outdoor temperature swing is in the low range (L—less than 15° F), the medium range (M—15° F to 25° F), or the high range (H—over 25° F).

Step twelve. Go back to the room sheets again, and determine (either from Tables or by calculation of the individual components) the *U*-value of each different building section, exclusive of glass areas. Where applicable, use summer conditions rather than winter ones. For instance, a frame exterior wall might have a *U* of 0.081, a partition wall 0.083, a pitched roof 0.141, and so on.

Step thirteen. For each room, determine the heat gain of the various building section areas, exclusive of glass, at the design temperature difference. This is done by consulting Table 5-19. To present an example, let us assume that you have chosen an outside design temperature of 95° F, and that the outdoor temperature swing for your locale is medium (M). The exterior wall

in Room A is of frame construction. Enter the Table at the left, and find the "Frame and veneer-on-frame" entry. Follow the line to the right, to the column headed "95," "M." The design equivalent temperature difference is listed as 23.6.

To complete the calculation for the wall section, multiply the wall *U* times the wall area times DETD. Assuming the wall to have an area of 1000 square feet and a *U* of 0.081, we have 1000 × 0.081 × 23.6, or 1911.6 Btu/hr for a total heat gain through that section.

Now suppose that the chosen outdoor design temperature is 93° F. The Table is set up in increments of 5, and the chosen temperature is not listed. In that case, the design equivalent temperature should be adjusted by 1° for each 1° difference from the tabulated values. Read the "95" column as 23.6 for a medium range, for instance, and subtract 2° from that figure, or 21.6. Or, choose the "90" column under "M" and add 3° for the same DETD.

Follow the same procedure to arrive at a total heat gain for all of the building sections in each room, then total all of the individual figures for each room. As noted previously, the total for the bathrooms should be split up and added equally to the immediately adjacent rooms.

Step fourteen. For each room, determine the heat gain through the windows. This is done by consulting Table 5-20. First locate the appropriate type of glazing, then the outside design temperature, the appropriate shading device, and finally the orientation of the window. For example, assume that the window is single-glazed, that the outside design temperature is 95° F, that the window is fitted with roller shades that normally will be half-drawn during the heat of the day, and that it faces southeast. The Table lists a value of 60 for this combination, which means that 60 Btu per hour is transmitted through the glass per square foot, on average.

To determine the heat gain for the window unit, multiply the area of the glass times the value listed. Most accurate results will be obtained if the calculations are carried out to at least two decimal places. (Example: Window area of 5.45 square feet times 60 equals 327 Btu/hr.)

Windows that are shaded from the outside by permanent devices such as overhangs are treated somewhat differently. If a window is always in the shade (facing onto a broad veranda, for instance), it is considered as a north-facing window for purposes of calculation, irrespective of the actual orientation. Windows that are capped by overhangs and face north, northeast, or northwest are treated without consideration for the overhang, which affords no shading in these orientations. However, windows that face in the other directions and lie beneath overhangs are partly sunlit and partly shaded, with the proportions variable during the course of each day.

Design Equivalent Temperature Differences

Design Temperature, °F	85		90			95			100		105	110
Daily Temperature Range[a]	L	M	L	M	H	L	M	H	M	H	H	H
WALLS AND DOORS												
1. Frame and veneer-on-frame	17.6	13.6	22.6	18.6	13.6	27.6	23.6	18.6	28.6	23.6	28.6	33.6
2. Masonry walls, 8-in. block or brick	10.3	6.3	15.3	11.3	6.3	20.3	16.3	11.3	21.3	16.3	21.3	26.3
3. Partitions, frame	9.0	5.0	14.0	10.0	5.0	19.0	15.0	10.0	20.0	15.0	20.0	25.0
masonry	2.5	0	7.5	3.5	0	12.5	8.5	3.5	13.5	8.5	13.5	18.5
4. Wood doors	17.6	13.6	22.6	18.6	13.6	27.6	23.6	18.6	28.6	23.6	28.6	33.6
CEILINGS AND ROOFS[b]												
1. Ceilings under naturally vented attic or vented flat roof—dark	38.0	34.0	43.0	39.0	34.0	48.0	44.0	39.0	49.0	44.0	49.0	54.0
—light	30.0	26.0	35.0	31.0	26.0	40.0	36.0	31.0	41.0	36.0	41.0	46.0
2. Built-up roof, no ceiling—dark	38.0	34.0	43.0	39.0	34.0	48.0	44.0	39.0	49.0	44.0	49.0	54.0
—light	30.0	26.0	35.0	31.0	26.0	40.0	36.0	31.0	41.0	36.0	41.0	46.0
3. Ceilings under unconditioned rooms	9.0	5.0	14.0	10.0	5.0	19.0	15.0	10.0	20.0	15.0	20.0	25.0
FLOORS												
1. Over unconditioned rooms	9.0	5.0	14.0	10.0	5.0	19.0	15.0	10.0	20.0	15.0	20.0	25.0
2. Over basement, enclosed crawl space or concrete slab on ground	0	0	0	0	0	0	0	0	0	0	0	0
3. Over open crawl space	9.0	5.0	14.0	10.0	5.0	19.0	15.0	10.0	20.0	15.0	20.0	25.0

[a]Daily Temperature Range
  L (Low) Calculation Value: 12 deg F. Applicable Range: Less than 15 deg F.
  M (Medium) Calculation Value: 20 deg F. Applicable Range: 15 to 25 deg F.
  H (High) Calculation Value: 30 deg F. Applicable Range: More than 25 deg F.

[b]Ceilings and Roofs: For roofs in shade, 18-hr average = 11 deg temperature differential. At 90 F design and medium daily range, equivalent temperature differential for light-colored roof equals 11 + (0.71)(39 − 11) = 31 deg F.

Table 5-19. (Reprinted with permission from the *1977 Fundamentals Volume, ASHRAE HANDBOOK & Product Directory*)

Design Transmitted and Absorbed Solar Energy and to Air-to-Air Temperature Difference, Btu/(h·ft²)

Outdoor Design Temp.	Regular Single Glass						Regular Double Glass						Heat Absorbing Double Glass					
	85	90	95	100	105	110	85	90	95	100	105	110	85	90	95	100	105	110
No Awnings or Inside Shading																		
North	23	27	31	35	38	44	19	21	24	26	28	30	12	14	17	19	21	23
NE and NW	56	60	64	68	71	77	46	48	51	53	55	57	27	29	32	34	36	38
East and West	81	85	89	93	96	102	68	70	73	75	77	79	42	44	47	49	51	53
SE and SW	70	74	78	82	85	91	59	61	64	66	68	70	35	37	40	42	44	46
South	40	44	48	52	55	61	33	35	38	40	42	44	19	21	24	26	28	30
Draperies or Venetian Blinds																		
North	15	19	23	27	30	36	12	14	17	19	21	23	9	11	14	16	18	20
NE and NW	32	36	40	44	47	53	27	29	32	34	36	38	20	22	25	27	29	31
East and West	48	52	56	60	63	69	42	44	47	49	51	53	30	32	35	37	39	41
SE and SW	40	44	48	52	55	61	35	37	40	42	44	46	24	26	29	31	33	35
South	23	27	31	35	38	44	20	22	25	27	29	31	15	17	20	22	24	26
Roller Shades Half-Drawn																		
North	18	22	26	30	33	39	15	17	20	22	24	26	10	12	15	17	19	21
NE and NW	40	44	48	52	55	61	38	40	43	45	47	49	24	26	29	31	33	35
East and West	61	65	69	73	76	82	54	56	59	61	63	65	35	37	40	42	44	46
SE and SW	52	56	60	64	67	73	46	48	51	53	55	57	30	32	35	37	39	41
South	29	33	37	41	44	50	27	29	32	34	36	38	18	20	23	25	27	29
Awnings																		
North	20	24	28	32	35	41	13	15	18	20	22	24	10	12	15	17	19	21
NE and NW	21	25	29	33	36	42	14	16	19	21	23	25	11	13	16	18	20	22
East and West	22	26	30	34	37	43	14	16	19	21	23	25*	12	14	17	19	21	23
SE and SW	21	25	29	33	36	42	14	16	19	21	23	25	11	13	16	18	20	22
South	21	24	28	32	35	41	13	15	18	20	22	24	11	13	16	18	20	22

Table 5-20. (Reprinted with permission from the *1977 Fundamentals Volume, ASHRAE HANDBOOK & Product Directory*)

First, determine where the shade line falls on the various walls of the house. Using Table 5-21, locate the shade line factor for your latitude and for each wall orientation. Multiply this factor times the width of the overhang. The result will be the distance from the bottom of the overhang to the line between sunlit and shaded wall. Compare this shade line with each individual window, and determine how much of the window is sunlit and how much shaded. If only a few inches at the top of a window are shaded, there is little point in taking any shading credit for it; simply treat it in the normal fashion, as explained above. However, if there is substantial shading, it should be included in the calculation.

Calculate the exact area of glass that is shaded, and subtract it from the total glass area to arrive at the sunlit area (or vice versa). Determine the heat gain of the sunlit area, using its true orientation, in Table 5-20. Determine the heat gain of the shaded portion by considering it as north facing, regardless of its true orientation, and by using an appropriate value from Table 5-20.

After finding the heat gain for each window, add the values to the total heat gain in each room.

Step fifteen. Calculate the cooling load attributable to infiltration and ventilation. Infiltration is assumed to be at a rate of approximately one-half air change per hour, a value that has been found to be satisfactory. Consult Table 5-22, and locate the appropriate outside design temperature and attendant infiltration factor.

Multiply this factor by the *gross* wall area (exposed) for each room. The result is the infiltration cooling load in Btu/hr; add this to the total cooling load for each room.

Ventilation is a highly variable factor from home to home. Only mechanical ventilating systems are considered; intermittently operated small exhaust fans are not. A separate assessment must be made in each individual case to determine the volume of air that is delivered by the ventilating equipment into the house, in cubic feet per minute (cfm), and the potential input of ventilating air into the structure every hour, on average. Much depends, of course, upon just how the equipment is operated. The appropriate factor in Table 5-22 can be used to determine the total sensible heat gain. This should be divided equally among all of the rooms in the house, and added to the total heat gain of each room.

Step sixteen. Determine the occupancy heat gain. Using your estimate of the number of occupants of the house, allow 225 Btu/hr of heat gain for each. In no case, however, should the total be less than 675 Btu/hr. The heat release of appliances should also be taken into consideration; a value of 1200 Btu/hr has been found to be satisfactory for residential cooling loads. This should be added to the kitchen total heat gain, while the occupant heat release should be divided equally among those rooms that are used as living areas as opposed to sleeping areas.

Step seventeen. Find the total sensible heat gain for each room by making a grand total of all of the values listed.

Step eighteen. Determine the latent heat gain for each room. Though this can be done separately, it is a rather difficult process and generally unnecessary. Experience shows that latent heat gain is approximately 20 to 30 percent of the calculated sensible heat gain in a residence. If the relative humidity is usually fairly high in your area, multiply the total sensible heat gain of each room by 0.30, and if quite low most of the time, use a multiplier of 0.20.

Step nineteen. Find the total cooling load for the house by adding all of the sensible and latent heat gain values of all the rooms.

Equipment Selection

To quote the *1977 Fundamentals Volume, ASHRAE HANDBOOK & Product Directory,* "Installed equipment capacity is based on three considerations: (1) calculated cooling load of the structure; (2) heat gain to the distribution system; and (3) the effects of inside temperature swing and outside design conditions. Equipment capacity multipliers, which relate outside design conditions to total equipment load (structure plus distribution system) and inside temperature swing, are given. . . for unitary equipment utilizing air-cooled, evaporatively cooled, or water-cooled condensing units.

Shade Line Factors

Direction	Latitude, Degrees						
Window Faces	25	30	35	40	45	50	55
E	0.8	0.8	0.8	0.8	0.8	0.8	0.8
SE	1.9	1.6	1.4	1.3	1.1	1.0	0.9
S	10.1	5.4	3.6	2.6	2.0	1.7	1.4
SW	1.9	1.6	1.4	1.3	1.1	1.0	0.9
W	0.8	0.8	0.8	0.8	0.8	0.8	0.8

• Note: Distance shadow line falls below the edge of the overhang equals shade line factor multiplied by width of overhang. Values are averages for 5 hr of greatest solar intensity on August 1.

Table 5-21. (Reprinted with permission from the *1977 Fundamentals Volume, ASHRAE HANDBOOK & Product Directory*)

Sensible Cooling Load Due to Infiltration and Ventilation

Design Temperature, F	85	90	95	100	105	110
Infiltration, Btuh/ft^2 of gross exposed wall area	0.7	1.1	1.5	1.9	2.2	2.6
Mechanical ventilation, Btuh/cfm	11.0	16.0	22.0	27.0	32.0	38.0

Table 5-22. (Reprinted with permission from the *1977 Fundamentals Volume, ASHRAE HANDBOOK & Product Directory*)

These values, when multiplied by the calculated equipment load, determine the equipment capacity requirement in terms of its standard rating."

These multipliers have been established for various kinds of equipment by organizations such as the Air Conditioning and Refrigeration Institute and can be obtained from the organizations, manufacturers of the equipment, dealers, and installers. They must be accurately used if the installation is to be a successful one, and the equipment must be sized quite closely to the total cooling load requirements for the structure, as comprised of the three principal considerations mentioned above.

Operating Costs For A Cooling System

Estimates of seasonal cooling load costs are, at best, only rough approximations. Some idea of costs for a given installation can be gotten with the aid of Table 5-23, which presents a list of average cooling requirements, in hours, for a few large cities. This information comes from a survey of electric utility companies, and it is based upon an inside design temperature of 75° F. As a general rule, residential cooling hours are toward the lower end of each range.

To calculate cooling costs with the aid of this Table, proceed as follows:

Find the total hourly power requirements of the cooling equipment. These figures must be obtained for the specific cooling system being used; averages are not reliable enough.

Multiply the hourly power requirement times the number of hours the cooling equipment will be operating, from Table 5-23. If necessary or desirable, modify the hourly figures for local conditions.

Multiply this kwh figure by the applicable power rate; note that it is important to use the correct rate step of the utility residential rate structure to get a reasonably accurate estimate. Note too that this will be the rate for power consumption that would be *in addition* to the amount of power used for other purposes in the home, which may vary from perhaps 200 to 500 or more kwh depending upon the type and usage of electrical appliances.

If the unit is water cooled, the total amount of water actually consumed should be multiplied by the applicable water rate and added to the power cost. If a gas-fired unit is used, the operating costs would be calculated similarly; the electric power to operate the fan(s) must of course be included along with the gas for the unit.

In areas where cooling equipment is in common use, the best way to determine the approximate operating costs of a particular proposed cooling system is to consult with the power company that serves the area. Most companies have accumulated data over the past few years from actual meter readings, and they are able to develop specific estimates on this basis. These estimates are far more likely to have a reasonable degree of accuracy than those obtained by any other method.

Estimated Equivalent Rated Full-Load Hours of Operation for Properly Sized Equipment During Normal Cooling Season

City	Hours	City	Hours
Albuquerque, NM	800–2200	Indianapolis, IN	600–1600
Atlantic City, NJ	500–800	Little Rock, AR	1400–2400
Birmingham, AL	1200–2200	Minneapolis, MN	400–800
Boston, MA	400–1200	New Orleans, LA	1400–2800
Burlington, VT	200–600	New York, NY	500–1000
Charlotte, NC	700–1100	Newark, NJ	400–900
Chicago, IL	500–1000	Oklahoma City, OK	1100–2000
Cleveland, OH	400–800	Pittsburgh, PA	900–1200
Cincinnati, OH	1000–1500	Rapid City, SD	800–1000
Columbia, SC	1200–1400	St. Joseph, MO	1000–1600
Corpus Christi, TX	2000–2500	St. Petersburg, FL	1500–2700
Dallas, TX	1200–1600	San Diego, CA	800–1700
Denver, CO	400–800	Savannah, GA	1200–1400
Des Moines, IA	600–1000	Seattle, WA	400–1200
Detroit, MI	700–1000	Syracuse, NY	200–1000
Duluth, MN	300–500	Trenton, NJ	800–1000
El Paso, TX	1000–1400	Tulsa, OK	1500–2200
Honolulu, HI	1500–3500	Washington, DC	700–1200

Table 5-23. (Reprinted with permission from the *1976 Systems Volume, ASHRAE HANDBOOK & Product Directory*)

Chapter 6

Special Problems of Hot Climates

While the bulk of the United States is primarily concerned with staying comfortably warm during the winter season, the fact is that perhaps a third or more of the citizenry is much more concerned with the problem of maintaining bearable comfort levels during hot weather. And this number is increasing annually as people remove from the northern climes in an effort to escape high heating costs and the rigors of a harsh, cold climate by moving to the Sun Belt states.

It is a common misconception of many inhabitants of the 40th Parallel Zones—in this country, at least—that peoples living in warmer climates are adjusted to the higher temperature and do not need special devices to keep them comfortable. Unless the siesta can be called a "special device" (it is not; it is a way of living, of making mid-day heat bearable), it simply is not true that residents of the tropical and subtropical zones can adapt themselves comfortably to that much heat.

As many automobile and truck drivers, especially those who pull camping trailers or haul heavy loads, are well aware (often to their sorrow), vehicles oftentimes have a great deal of difficulty in getting rid of the heat that they generate during operation, and they are prone to abrupt overheating and consequent mechanical breakdown, always accompanied by inconvenience and often by damage as well. Much the same is true of the human body, which produces heat in proportion to activity and method of operation. The difference is that while the permissible rise in temperature in a vehicle can run to 50° F, or more, that of the human body is more on the order of 2° F to 3° F, and that rise is governed by intricate and involuntary heat-regulating devices of great sensitivity. And as with a vehicle, damage ranging from mild to irreparable (death) can be the consequence of overheating. A good many studies, as well as simple statistics, have shown that the death rate even in northern cities like Chicago and New York increases markedly during the hot summers and especially during heat waves; the very young and the very old are most affected by high temperatures. The interminable, record-breaking heat that blanketed a large portion of the country during the summer of 1980 resulted in well over 1,000 deaths that were attributable to heat or heat-related causes.

There is no pretense of offering in this chapter a complete manual on the subject of hot climates. That would be a book by itself; and, indeed, some excellent ones are available. Studies continue in this field, especially in the tropical areas of the world, and new data are constantly being added to our fund of information. What *is* offered is a brief guide to the general principles of keeping as comfortable as possible in hot climates, as learned over the centuries by tropical people and modified in recent decades by modern technology.

Unless a great deal of care in the design and construction of houses is taken to provide positive defenses against the heat, man in hot climates can be more uncomfortable indoors than out. Too often, as was emphasized in the introduction to chapter 2, houses designed originally for the rigors of a New England winter are built in the middle of a Texas plain, and indoor comfort is either achieved by inordinately expensive mechanical cooling, or is to all intents and purposes abandoned as a concept (particularly in low-cost houses), as electric fans are set to do the impossible task of cooling the air. All a fan does is move air, not cool it. And air motion alone, though slightly palliative in that it encourages evaporation of perspiration, is no cure-all for the discomforts of a really hot thermal environment.

What is needed, of course, is a house designed specifically for hot climates. People have lived in such regions since prehistory and have developed relatively comfortable houses for them. Yet one of the stumbling blocks in the way of rational hot climate design is that there are no standards that can be established for all such regions. Climatic conditions vary enormously from area to area, even though they may lie in very nearly the same latitude. A house for comfortable living in hot, dry El Paso, with less than 9 inches of rain per year, should be quite differently designed than one in hot, wet Houston, with over 47 annual inches of rain. The two cities lie only 2 degrees of latitude apart, and both have average July temperatures of around 82°F.

What Are Hot Climates?   These two cities cited above present the basic climatic differences in the torrid zones: the hot-dry and the hot-humid. And these differences are of great importance in building design. The hot-dry climate is characterized by exceedingly hot days and relatively cool nights, as the sun's heat is quickly reradiated to the clear, "transparent" night sky, a phenomenon known as radiational cooling. The hot-humid climate is characterized by slightly lower daytime and considerably higher nighttime temperatures, since high humidity prevents full insolation during the day and limits reradiation of daytime heat out to the sky at night. Mixtures of the two are found in some areas: hot-dry regions, for instance, with definite rainy seasons, as in Lake County, California, where average monthly precipitation varies from as low as 0.1 inches in July to as high as 20.5 inches in January.

One of the common characteristics of hot climates in the southern United States, unlike the true tropics, is a short winter season during which some artificial heat is needed. The cold is rarely severe but is enough to be uncomfortable without heating. In many of these regions, homes are designed for hot-climate comfort rather than cold, and the necessary warmth is provided by inexpensive space heaters of one sort or another. Central heating in such climates is generally an economic waste.

These are the most important variations in hot-climate conditions, and they are wide. Obviously, the problems of designing and building for hot-climate comfort are many and diverse, and among the more important is the determination of the actual nature of the climates in a particular location.

ESSENTIAL CLIMATIC FACTS

If houses are to be designed and built intelligently for hot-climate comfort, even more detailed information is needed about certain aspects of the local weather than with the average temperate climate situation. The basic types of weather data have been described in chapter 2. Some are reviewed here with special emphasis on the data for hot climates.

Outdoor dry-bulb temperature averages and extremes. This is essential, basic data, particularly on a 12-month basis.

Wet-bulb temperatures. These temperatures are especially important in hot-humid climates. Wet-bulb readings at maximum dry bulb will give a very real measure of the extent of the comfort problem in such climates.

Day and night temperatures. The temperature ranges between hot days and cool nights are important, and they should be obtained at least for a week or so during the hottest part of the year. When there is wide variation, the assumption is that the climate is of the hot-dry type; when it is small, that the climate is hot-humid.

Wind velocities and direction. Wherever there is a good prevailing breeze, particularly in hot-humid climates, buildings should be oriented, and building openings placed, so as to take every possible advantage of it. In hot-dry regions it is often more important to deflect both direct and diffuse solar radiation from the inside of the building; but in hot-humid areas, where still air is more of a punishment than scorching sunlight, natural ventilation can be invaluable. This is particularly true of the nonair-conditioned house, of course; it must be meticulously designed to take advantage of any breeze, if it is to be at all livable.

On the other hand, the possibility of catastrophic winds during certain seasons of the year must be ascertained, especially in hurricane regions, and suitable solid closures for the wall openings must be provided. Data on wind velocities and directions are not always easily available on a microclimatic basis; information from local sources, particularly in rural areas, must be relied on.

(Hurricane-resistant construction is too large and specialized a subject for presentation in this chapter. People in areas subject to hurricanes can use local building regulations as minimal guides. New designs and constructions presently coming into use, such as total truss-framing, afford greater protection against hurricanes than in the past, and the latest details should be investigated. *See also* page 17.)

Angles of solar incidence the year round. A general fault of many modern houses in hot climates is that protection against the sun is inadequate on exposed sides. When the major climatic problem is heat, shielding from the sun's radiation at *all* times of the day and *all* seasons of the year is a basic factor in comfort and also, of course, in the economical operation of cooling equipment. Tables and charts of solar positions and of clear-day insolation can be of some help in this respect, but these must be adjusted to reflect microclimatic variables, clearness of the air, ground reflection and similar factors.

The average number of cloudy and rainy days a year. This information can help identify climates in which the hot-humid problems of mildew, materials deterioration, and insect infestation will be especially serious. Insects are a hazard in any hot climate, but particularly so when there is a great deal of dampness. In addition, this data, plotted against average temperatures and humidity data, can often help in arriving at pragmatically sound decisions on types and sizes of sun-control devices and on other factors that depend on solar heat and glare.

Local data about the site. Information that will affect the microclimate of the dwelling itself includes: natural shade; site contours and their relation to prevailing winds; nearness of streams or lakes; position relative to nearby hills or valleys; type of soil, to judge its suitability for shade and windbreak plantings; and so on.

DESIGN FOR HOT CLIMATES

At present it is no more possible to offer absolute standards for the design of buildings in hot-dry or hot-humid climates than it is in temperate climates. There are fairly wide differences of opinion among people who are experienced in building in hot climates about what types of materials, equipment, and building techniques are best. And, of course, research and experimentation is a constant process, resulting in continual development of new techniques, procedures and materials, as well as new applications of old information. Some feel, with good reasons, that the wisest practice is to follow the local traditions for hot-climate building, an especially valuable course in under-developed regions where native materials and methods often make possible quite comfortable homes. Others believe that while some of the old methods remain viable, others are obsolete and should be superceded by more modern technology and designs. One must realize, too, that just as with houses in the temperate zones, there is an incredible number of variables that must be taken into consideration from area to area; these concern not only the problems of correct construction of dwellings for localized conditions, but also the socio-economic ramifications that may be involved in any particular locale.

Actually, the only safe thing is to present a consensus, covering as much as possible the areas of agreement. The whole problem is too new, in terms of modern research, for much positive or scientifically certain data to be obtainable on many of the most debatable points, and the following paragraphs are more a compilation of some of the available experience in these areas than an exact statement of ascertained facts.

Hot-Dry Climates

Here traditional or native buildings are usually built with extremely thick masonry, stone, or earth walls and roofs (Figure 6–1). Small openings with deep reveals are characteristic of such houses. In addition, many houses have sheltered areas outside the structure, such as patios, courtyards, or areas enclosed by fence or arbor where, open to the sky, the family can sleep.

This living pattern is quite logical, for the walls and the roof are thick enough to prevent the sun's energy from warming the interior of the building during the day. Some heat may penetrate, but it will be dissipated overnight through reradiation to the night sky and

6–1. Taos Pueblo, New Mexico. (Arthur Rothstein/Library of Congress)

through natural ventilation. Meanwhile the family is sleeping comfortably in the open patio. Indeed, the idea of sleeping outdoors with the body directly exposed to the night air (except for insect screening) is particularly sound in hot-dry climates, since one can become cooler faster in such regions by permitting body heat to radiate to the clear night sky than by many other ways more common in the North.

Today, thick-walled construction is usually too expensive to be practical and is no longer commonly used in this country. There is, however, a resurgence of interest in heavy-walled structures in both hot and cool climates, and such constructions can be made to suit various climatic parameters with logs, stone, conventional framing in a shell design, heavy masonry, double-wall, and other methods. And yes, even adobe is enjoying something of a comeback in the United States, and is particularly suited to, and surprisingly common in, the areas shown in Figure 6–2. Complete details of adobe construction can be found in Leaflet No. 535, *Building with Adobe and Stabilized-Earth Blocks,* put out by the U. S. Department of Agriculture (slightly revised 1972, available from the USDA, Washington, D. C. 20250).

6–2. Areas of the United States in which adobe construction is practiced. (USDA)

If it is to be effective, thick-walled construction, especially adobe, must be correctly done. Architects from the Southwest like to tell of the northern builder who observed the comfortable temperatures maintained in the adobe structures of the desert Native Americans, and who set about manufacturing standard 8-inch blocks out of adobe. Of course, he was miserably disappointed when his homes became unbearably hot toward the end of the day! He had ascribed to the material a quality that was entirely dependent on thickness. Concrete or stone, or adobe, has about as high a heat

transmission coefficient as any nonmetallic substance—as high as 16 Btu per inch as compared with 0.27 Btu for mineral wool—but heat will take so long to penetrate a very thick layer (12 to 18 inches or more) that it will flow back out during the cool nights and will be diminished by night ventilation. With only 8 inches of thickness the time lag, or thermal lag, is insufficient to keep the heat out. At the opposite extreme, it seems quite reasonable that a deep-set earth-sheltered house, with a carefully designed ventilating system, by its very nature would serve nicely under hot conditions. However, there are yet so few constructions of this nature that no significant body of practical or experiential data has been developed.

Adobe and other materials of a similar nature have been largely replaced by modern insulating materials and construction techniques that permit only a small portion of the heat to enter the wall or roof exposed to the sun or the hot air. Similarly, since sleeping in the open is rarely feasible in most urban and suburban areas, either air conditioning or artificial ventilation with attic or bedroom exhaust fans, or both, takes over the task of keeping the rooms and their occupants cool at night. It has been proposed that sections of the roof over bedrooms in modern houses built in hot-dry climates be made retractable so that they could be pulled back at night, thus exposing the occupants to the cool night sky. This might well be useful, but its practicality and its cost-effectiveness probably are somewhat less than optimum.

With the thin walls and shallow windows of most modern houses in hot-dry climates must go special devices for providing shade, or else an intelligent use of existing natural shade, since thick walls are not present to keep out the solar energy by means of deep reveals and thermal lag.

EVAPORATIVE COOLING

Comfort coolness in hot-dry climates can of course be achieved by regular air conditioning. Indeed, refrigeration cooling is commonplace in such regions. But there is a less costly (and less efficient) alternative to this type of cooling in truly arid hot climates, and that is the technique known as "evaporative" or "adiabatic" cooling. Such systems can be either mechanized or natural, and though they see little use in this country, nonetheless they can be effective. Evaporation of water indoors increases relative humidity and decreases the dry-bulb temperature of the air. The evaporative process requires heat energy; sensible heat flows from the air to the water, thus lowering the dry-bulb temperature and providing the latent heat of evaporation, thus increasing the humidity.

The result is increased comfort resulting from a lower indoor temperature and somewhat higher humidity. If the system is well designed, that humidity should stay around 50 percent.

The usefulness of evaporative cooling is quite limited

157

in this country. Only desert areas and certain regions high in the western mountains where the air is dry, hot, and clear are suitable for it. For this reason no extensive analysis of the design and installation of the systems are offered here.

Hot-Humid Climates

Here the most common characteristic of nonair-conditioned houses is their openness. They are designed to catch every vagrant breeze that passes; for comfort in humid climates is most satisfactorily achieved by ventilation.

The well-balconied, high-ceilinged, large-windowed Louisiana mansion (Figure 6–3); the loosely-woven structures of the natives in the wet tropics; the deep-veranda, post-and-lintel, fabric-walled homes of the Equatorial African planters; and the paper-thin walls of the dwellings in southern Japan: all are designed to admit breezes. The houses are so placed that whatever air there is in motion passes through the living quarters. Outdoor sleeping is rare and is not missed since night sky radiation is a small factor in humid climates. One sleeps on screened porches or verandas instead.

Artificial ventilation, whether by native boys waving punkahs or by electric fans, is one of the few sure ways of obtaining a bit of comfort in a hot-humid climate. The slow-moving, large, ceiling-hung electric fan is the only kind for this climate.

Actually, of course, for genuinely comfortable living in hot-humid climates, air conditioning is a basic essential, not only because it reduces temperatures to bearable levels, but also, and perhaps even more importantly, because it cuts indoor humidity below the point

6–3. St. Emma, Assumption Parish, Louisiana. (Frances Benjamin Johnson/Library of Congress)

where it can damage both living and nonliving matter. Strange things can happen to inanimate objects in hot-humid climates, as anyone who has served military time in the Pacific or folks who live along the seacoasts or in other particularly humid regions can well attest. Furniture becomes rickety as the glue in the joints softens, wood floors swell and warp, wood in the mechanisms of pianos swells up so that the keys will not work, and musical instruments containing wood can be virtually destroyed. Doors stick in their jambs, drawers cannot be opened if they are closed, or cannot be closed if they are open. Paint may become discolored because of mildew or mold growths, or may peel off because of moisture absorbed by the wood underneath. Wallpaper can droop and come loose from the plaster, or break out in a rash of mildew spots. Plaster ceilings can commence to sag, and rugs or mats can collect enough moisture to be ruined. Mold will grow on practically anything, a person feels sweaty and sticky ten minutes after a shower, and one's clothes never do feel dry and crisp. In many cases, dessicants, mildew-proofing sprays and powders, low-wattage electric heaters, and portable dehumidifiers must be employed for protection.

Extremes of moisture, therefore, are more than just an annoyance; they become a serious problem—not only to things, but to people. Any coastal resident from Blaine, Washington, clear around to Eastport, Maine, and a lot of inlanders as well, are only too well aware that on a humid ("muggy") day, one's skin stays sticky and moist even when the temperatures are only at the 60° F mark or less, and one can feel quite uncomfortable, the more so if relatively active. Evaporative cooling from the skin surface cannot take place because of the high moisture content of the air—it has little or no "drying power."

All these problems can be brought under complete control by a well-designed air-conditioner. But air conditioning in humid climates can exacerbate one problem that is of lesser import up North: and that is pipe or duct condensation. This results when air-conditioning ducts or cold-water pipes pass through nonair-conditioned air, as in attics and walls. In the humid South, even more than in the North, such ducts must be protected with vapor barriers outside the insulation. Vapor barriers might also be needed in floors and ceilings under some conditions in hot-humid climates; in unusual circumstances hot weather condensation can occur within building sections, particularly in masonry or brick-veneered structures fitted with a good vapor barrier. Studies are currently being conducted in this area; in the meantime, in lieu of more definitive data, follow local air conditioning practices as to vapor barrier protection, as well as recommendations by consulting or manufacturers' engineers for houses that are to be mechanically cooled.

In situations where cost or other factors preclude the installation of air-conditioning systems, various combinations of dehumidification, building sections that are thermally efficient, and both natural and mechanical ventilation can often be employed with good results. Natural ventilation, as has been stated, is of great importance, and air flow design can be critical. In order to achieve reasonable bodily comfort, the velocity of the air flow is of greater importance than its volume, and in hot-humid conditions that velocity should approach 400 feet per minute, whether natural or mechanically induced.

BUILDING METHODS FOR HOT CLIMATES

Some of the more important structural techniques and materials used for heat control in hot climates are outlined below. These suggestions, though brief, should serve as general guides to good practice in such regions and, it is hoped, will make unlikely the repetition of such egregious errors as the unshaded Cape Cod Colonial in the grip of a blazing desert sun.

Roofs

The problem of keeping sun and air heat out of attics or roofs differs somewhat from that in northern climates, where the roof is designed primarily to keep heat in during the winter. For one thing, the problem is more difficult and calls for sterner measures to reduce the amount of heat entering through the roof. One needs more insulation, not less, to improve comfort under a hot sun. It must be said, however, that the new practice of employing extremely heavy or high-R-value insulations in roof constructions is indeed as effective in blocking out the sun's heat as it is in retaining internally generated heat; primarily it is the older and the less energy-efficient houses that fall short in this respect.

No single insulating material and no one construction technique should be considered as wholly adequate in reducing downflow of heat to a bearable proportion in hot-climate regions. Rather, the most cost-effective, readily available, and best-constructed, under the given conditions, combinations of materials and techniques should be employed. For example, irrespective of whatever other methods are used, normal reflectors of solar radiation, such as light-colored roof surfacing materials and as much natural shade as the environment affords, should always be utilized. In addition, a combination of devices and materials should be used in the roof and ceiling, so designed that they will keep a large part of both the radiant and the conducted heat from passing down into the rooms below. Straight reflective insulation is considerably more efficient in hot climates, dollar for dollar, than the mass type.

Natural ventilation alone, though valuable, is not of course adequate as a method of drawing heat out of the top of the structure. All methods of eliminating heat that do not require excessive operating and maintenance costs should be used to keep the roof as cool as possible. Particularly in hot-humid climates, care must be taken to use inorganic insulating materials, such as reflective foil, which are impervious to attack by the biological enemies of the house.

In hot climates attic ventilation should be powered. Electric bills for exhaust fans are not excessive and the original investment for the fan is likely to prove a sound one, provided it is installed in accordance with the principles of air flow. In areas where daytime breezes are relatively constant, the wind-powered "turbine" type of exhaust ventilators can often be used to good effect, with no operating cost.

Water-cooled roofs, either spray or pool type, are often used in hot climates to reduce the amount of heat entering the building. Evaporative cooling from a water spray is very effective in excluding solar radiation and so is ponding, provided that the water on the roof is deep enough (at least 1 inch). Though situations will vary, a depth of 6 inches or more of water in a roof pond is approximately the equivalent, in solar radiation exclusion, of a roof spray system. Another possibility now being experimented with consists of large plastic bags filled with water and laid out across a flat rooftop. This system is being utilized for solar heating in winter (in relatively mild climates), as well as for summer cooling. Though somewhat complex and unorthodox, the idea does work.

Water-cooling of roofs, however, is not always possible or desirable in hot climates. In hot-dry regions, there is likely to be a shortage of water that will make the technique uneconomical; in hot-humid areas, it may prove of only minor value since it adds to the natural humidity of the atmosphere. There is also the possibility of vegetable and fungus growths, as well as insect breeding, particularly in the hot-humid regions. And, roofs designed for ponding must be extremely stout and well-constructed in order to bear the substantial weight of the water and also to minimize the potential danger of leakage.

A not uncommon type of construction in hot climates outside the United States is the double roof. One example of this construction is the house that Admiral William F. Halsey occupied in the Solomon Islands during World War II (Figure 6–4). This type of native building is particularly useful in those parts of the world where there are moderately strong winds, but rarely gales, to provide natural cooling between the layers.

The double roof is an ancient concept; it has been employed, and still is today, by the Arabs in their tents, which are actually made up of an inner and an outer tent with a space between the layers through which air can circulate and heat can be carried away. This same principle is used in some of the present-day tents used in this country by backpackers and mountain climbers, and the form of the so-called "double walled" and flyed designs (in a tent, often as not the walls are actually the roof). The principle is that of a heat shield.

The outer layer absorbs a quantity of the solar radiation, which then reradiates downward from the bottomside of the shield; ideally, the shield should be highly reflective, in which case a good portion of the energy will be reflected back into space. The lower layer of the roof must lie at least an inch below the upper one, and it must be arranged so that there is continuous free air movement between the two layers. This serves to carry away the superheated air between the panels, and thus the lower one absorbs only a small fraction of the total amount of heat energy received.

Various methods and materials can be used for this purpose. For instance, a built-up pitched roof might consist of a plywood decking atop the rafters, upon which is laid a 3-inch to 4-inch layer of polyisocyanurate rigid insulation. As a final layer, one might place ribbed, natural-finish aluminum roofing panels upon supporting stringers, with an inch or so of clearance between the panels and the insulation. The air space should be open at the eaves, so that fresh, relatively cool air can circulate upward through the spaces to the ridge, where the heated air can disperse into the atmosphere through a ventilating ridge cap (Figure 6–5).

6–4. Munda, New Georgia. Upper roof is made of ivory leaves. (U.S. Army)

If there are to be clerestories in flat or shed roofs to permit light to enter the central area of the structure, adequate overhangs to keep the sun from the windows should of course be provided and the roof of the clerestory should be as carefully insulated as the rest of the building.

Two further points must be mentioned. First, note that a pitched roof has a greater area than a flat roof on the same size of structure and that it can permit considerably more heat gain than a flat roof will in identical conditions. The degree of pitch, of course, will influence the amount of heat gain per square foot of roof area. Second, the orientation of the roof with respect to the sun's angle can also make a substantial difference in the amount of heat gain through the roof sections. By way of illustration, in a house with a pitched roof oriented with the ridgeline in an east-west direction, the south-facing roof will be exposed to considerably more insolation than the north-facing surface. It goes without saying, of course, that the surface of the finished roof covering should be white or very light-colored in order to effect long-wave radiation back to the sky (a highly reflective surface is even better).

Walls

Very few houses built back in the 1950s in the hot-climate regions of the United States had insulation of any type in their walls, and, until very recent years, that situation did not markedly improve. Though the benefits of insulation are now becoming better-known to the public in general, it still is largely associated with heating problems rather than with cooling. Is the fact that so few houses in our hot-climate regions have insulated walls an indication that (at least in the nonair-conditioned house) wall insulation is of relatively small value?

As we know, quite the opposite is true. Any wall construction that will keep a sizeable amount of heat out of the structure is worthwhile in hot climates, and insulating materials do just that. Just as interior surface temperatures of walls must be kept close to the ambient air temperature in winter heating conditions to achieve bodily comfort, so must they also be kept well below

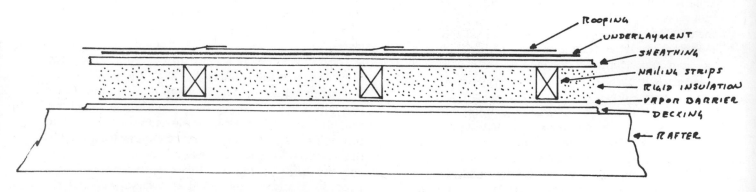

6–5. Typical built-up insulated roof construction.

the normal temperature of the human skin during the cooling season. If the wall surfaces approach the average skin surface temperature of the occupants—83°F—people in the room suffer because their bodies cannot lose heat by radiation to the walls. Even if the air is kept moderately cool by ventilation, the hot walls will make the room's occupants very uncomfortable; in hot climates the interior wall temperatures, especially if the wall is a typical thin frame construction or even brick veneer, can easily rise into the discomfort zone.

There is a technique common with older houses in the Caribbean that involves the first floor of the house being built of thick masonry and the second floor of much lighter frame construction. Thus, during the day the first floor will remain relatively cool, and at night the lightly built second floor will be cool. This is a design that might possibly be used, at least in more expensive houses, in this country.

However, since massive masonry walls are not economically feasible in most parts of the country (and for most would-be homeowners), insulation must provide the barrier to heat in such houses, just as in roofs. It is a sound investment in comfort wherever climates are hot, and a genuine long-term economy for air conditioning.

One simple method of building walls of great thermal efficiency is to erect stud walls of conventional design around the perimeter of the house. Then erect another, identical stud wall, set back from the first by a matter of 1 to 4 inches (Figure 6–6). Both stud walls can be filled with batt or blanket insulation in the usual fashion and the air space between may be left open, filled with additional mineral wool, or sheets of rigid foam insulation can be installed. Using this general technique in one combination or another can lead to R-values reaching into the 40s and 50s, with commensurately low U-values for the wall sections when the other various wall elements such as doors and windows are taken into account. A variation on this theme, well-proven in practice (though primarily intended for cold climates) is shown in Figure 6–7. Because of the considerably greater thermal lag inherent in solid-wood construction of this sort, interior temperatures can be maintained at relatively even levels, whether heating or cooling is involved.

A rather novel way of increasing the hot-climate effectiveness of wall insulation was developed for certain factories built in the South during World War II; this method (Figure 6–8) could also be applied to residential design. This is the provision of vertical ventilation between the outer layer of wall material and the insulation. The general construction principles are not unlike that of the built-up roof discussed earlier, and the principle again is that of a heat shield. Since hot air rises, a considerable amount of air motion will occur if one merely leaves continuous openings at the bottom and top of the wall; cooler air will enter the wall cavities at the bottom and the heated air will exhaust at the top. But this method is *not recommended* where winters are severe!

Unfortunately, no reliable test data on the value of this sort of wall ventilation for houses is available. However, the technique should be usable in hot-climate houses, provided care is taken to prevent the entry of insects and small animals into the space by screening the vents top and bottom.

6–7. Solid wood double-wall construction for highest thermal efficiency. (Courtesy, Pan Adobe Cedar Homes)

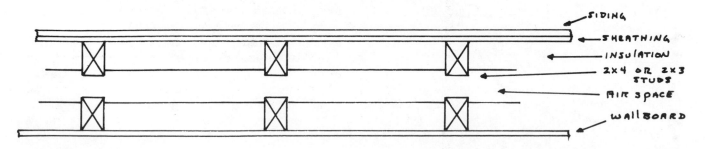

6–6. Double stud wall construction.

SIDING
SHEATHING
INSULATION
2X4 OR 2X3 STUDS
AIR SPACE
WALLBOARD

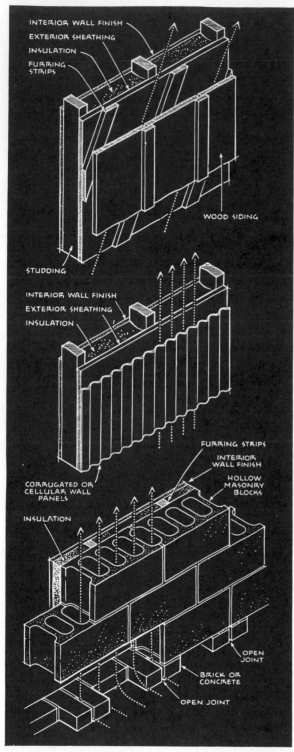

6–8. Methods of ventilating walls in hot climates.
(*Progressive Architecture*)

Openings

With the exception of the more primitive dwellings, no common type of home is completely windowless. There are nearly always wall openings to admit light and (in hot climates) air currents and to permit the evacuation of stale air and unpleasant odors inside the structure.

However, in nonair-conditioned houses particularly, too many openings and poor opening designs and placement can have very harmful effects upon hot-climate comfort; in air-cooled buildings these defects can add appreciably to the cost of operating the cooling equipment. The number of window placement factors that can be mishandled by those unfamiliar with hot-climate design is surprisingly large. Windows and fixed-glass areas can be too openly exposed to the sun's heat, incorrectly shaded, wrongly placed in the building, ineffectively glazed, and too big, to name just a few problems. It is true that special sun-control devices of a wide variety are available, but in many instances they are costly. Good building design often could reduce the expense of these items. Considerable research has been initiated in the past few years by the U. S. Department of Energy, the National Bureau of Standards, and various other agencies and organizations, in the area of energy-effective windows. This work continues apace and will do so in future years; data is just now becoming available concerning effective window design and construction with respect to energy conservation, acoustic properties, air infiltration, and ventilation. Numerous important contributions will soon be forthcoming in this field, ones that are likely to affect fenestration in new houses to a considerable degree.

The more important factors to be considered in planning openings of houses in hot climates are as follows:

Orientation is basic. Whenever possible, the wall with the largest openings, usually the living room with its view windows, should be oriented (in the northern hemisphere) more or less to the north, a situation opposite to that in the temperate zone with cold winters, where solar-house design calls for southern or southwestern exposures. If factors such as view and prevailing winds are also favorable, a north orientation can be extremely effective in increasing comfort in the most-occupied and largest-windowed rooms of the house.

All openings exposed to the sun should be shaded. If natural shade cannot be provided, whether trees, tall shrubbery, or vines growing over arbors near enough to the windows to keep out most of the sun's heat, artificial shade must be built in. Particularly in hot-dry climates where solar glare as well as solar heat are often a serious problem, shade is important on all sides of the house. Verandas and wide balconies furnish shading for windows and at the same time make possible outdoor living, particularly if adequately screened. Wood, concrete, or metal overhangs can be made a part of the structure, as can pivoted vertical louvers that can be turned or automatically operated to bar the sun's rays as their direction changes position throughout the day. Wood, metal, or glass exterior hoods or venetian blinds, or wood or glass jalousies are also effective. When properly oriented and positioned, attractive screen walls of decoratively patterned concrete block can serve the purposes of providing shading for large glass areas, of privacy, and of wind protection as well.

Window types are often important. The double-hung window is never as satisfactory in hot climates as casement, hopper, and awning types (if correctly oriented), or the sliding window that disappears entirely into the wall. In many regions, a single outswinging side-hinged window, correctly oriented in terms of prevailing winds, can act as an efficient wind scoop to bring the breezes into the structure. However, single and double casements should be avoided in areas where high winds and hurricanes are known to occur. Here glass jalousies are of particular value.

Glazing to be selected is not difficult to determine, since the decision will be largely an economic one. If windows are shaded adequately, heat-absorbing glass is not worthwhile, since the only heat that such glass bars more efficiently than any other kind of glass is radiant heat. The so-called solar-control, nonglare, or other tinted glazing may be of value, depending upon the circumstances.

As for double glazing, whether of the integral type or composed of inner window and outer storm window, there is conflicting evidence of its value as a heat gain reducer. The same pros and cons that were described in chapter 5 apply here as well. Under very hot conditions and for an air-cooled house, double glazing, with one pane heat-absorbing, might pay for itself, particularly if the openings are to be very large. In naturally cooled houses, the less glass the better. Indeed, in really subtropical spots, as in the Caribbean, it is common for openings not to be glazed at all. They are screened, usually, but experience has shown that glass serves no purpose in those regions of permanent summers. Very wide balconies keep out the sun and rain, and heavy wood or metal shutters protect against hurricanes.

Windows versus artificial light and high wattage versus low wattage should be considered. One frequently finds in hot climates that picture windows are sometimes installed where they serve as solar heat traps (this is a potential problem with passive solar heating designs in cooler climes, too); large areas of natural window lighting are used in spots where artificial lighting sources would serve better insofar as summer comfort is concerned; and high-wattage incandescent lamps are frequently installed where low-wattage and much cooler-running fluorescent fixtures could readily provide more light with far less power consumption. Similar errors, of course, are just as often made in the temperate zones, but their effects, at least as far as summer comfort is concerned, are likely to be more substantial in the hot climates.

Glass-fronted solar heat traps are to be avoided, and fluorescent lighting fixtures are much to be preferred over incandescent types. Substituting low-wattage fluorescent lights in nonair-conditioned houses for large window areas, however, must be done with very careful judgement. In hot-humid climates especially, the maximum intake and movement of air is desirable. Unless relatively costly artificial ventilation is brought in to replace normal air movement, the large operable window in hot-humid climates should not be abandoned. Of course, it should be shaded completely.

Cellars and Crawl Spaces

The problem of condensation in cellars and crawl spaces is aggravated in hot climates with high outdoor humidity. In addition to the techniques of controlling this trouble outlined in chapter 4, it is quite proper in climates with no winter cold problems to install insulation and a vapor barrier with the barrier facing *outward*. Double-glazed cellar windows might also be economically feasible, especially if the basement area is to be used extensively for living purposes.

In hot-humid climates, the best—and often the only—solution to the sweaty cellar or crawl space is the house on stilts. This not only keeps the underside of the house dry, but it also adds considerably to the comfort of the occupants. For one thing, it adds coolness by permitting the full force of whatever breezes there are to move under the house, thus reducing any effect from heat and moisture stored there. And for another, it considerably reduces the hazard of animal infestations, from snakes to land crabs, from ants to centipedes. Some sort of poison must be applied to the stilts so that the insects and other hot climate pests will not crawl up them. The space beneath the house can be used for storage or for shady seating during the hottest part of the day (in which case it should usually be screened). And of course it makes a wonderful carport, at no extra cost. Two types of stilt houses, one primitive and the other modern, are shown in Figures 6–9 and 6–10.

Latent Heat

Since an increase in humidity in hot climate houses always increases the discomfort, even though the temperature may not rise at all, specific methods of reducing humidity at points of its origin are always helpful additions to comfort in such regions. Individual exhaust fans in kitchens, bathrooms, laundry and other dampness-producing areas are essential in the tropical and semitropical regions if natural ventilation is inadequate to dispose of the surplus humidity.

THE PROBLEM IN TEMPERATE CLIMATES

That the problem is not entirely one of the true tropics may not have been emphasized in this chapter, but it is perfectly true that "40th parallel thinking" has resulted in bad errors in hot-weather design as far north as the Mason-Dixon line. One has only to look around in the Washington, D.C., area to note hundreds of houses whose thermal characteristics and designs are totally unfitted for the area, where the summer climate approaches the semitropical.

But one thing does remain as a common bond between cold-climate and hot-climate design for thermal efficiency and that is the use of thermal insulating materials and methods. These are important not only in air-conditioned houses in the South, where they have a large economical function, but also in nonair-cooled dwellings, where their comfort-producing values make them decidedly worth the relatively small extra expenditure (in comparison to the total cost of the structure) that their use involves.

For the old truism still holds: it is easier to keep warm in cold climates than it is to get cool in hot climates. And anything that will help to increase the net comfort of man in an overheated environment is a positive contribution to the health and happiness of a large part of the world—even if its values cannot at first be counted in immediate dollars and cents.

6-9. Native stilt houses near Port Moresby, New Guinea. (U.S. Army)

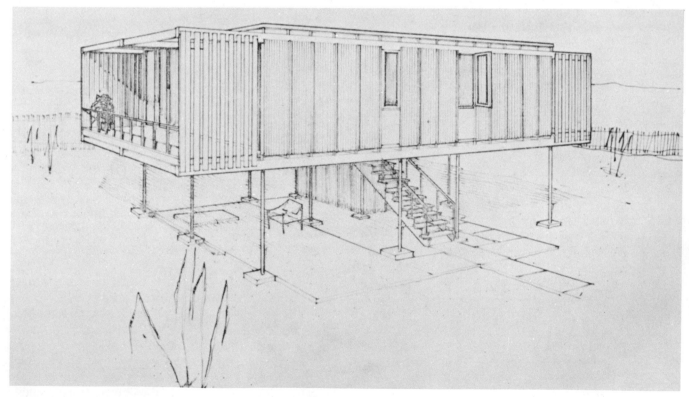

6-10. Modern stilt house design. ("Fabricating Houses from Component Parts," N. Cherner, Reinhold Publ. Corp.)

Chapter 7

Heating and Cooling Systems

No one who is not professionally schooled as a mechanical engineer should be expected to be able to lay out the details of thermal control systems. On the other hand, many inveterate home-builders and do-it-yourselfers do exactly that, and successfully, by dint of considerable research and study. For others, who may only have a passing interest in the field, it is not only easily possible but also desirable to know something of the principles of heat and cold generation and distribution, and of the types of available equipment. This is important not only from the point of view of costs, but also because it affects the design of the structure, its insulation, its protection against moisture, its fire safety and its durability.

There are two basic ways of analyzing thermal control systems for houses: technical efficiency and occupant satisfaction. Both must be carefully studied if the resultant installation is to deliver trouble-free and complaint-free performance.

Technical Aspects. A good heating and cooling system requires study of: unit selection, to deliver the necessary heating and cooling effectively, using the most reliable and inexpensive available fuels; unit location, for the best possible thermal distribution, operating silence, safety, and accessibility for maintenance and repairs; layout of distribution systems, to carry the thermal loads efficiently to outlets located correctly in accordance with external climatic conditions; relation of units and distribution system selection and locations to local building regulations, fire laws and insurance requirements; and specification of structural details and materials to assure the most effective performance of the system and the safety and the durability of the building.

Comfort Aspects. Occupant satisfaction with heating and cooling systems depends on ten factors. An acceptable heating and cooling system should: maintain uniform comfort air temperatures; be draft-free; maintain indoor relative humidity within reasonable limits; neither circulate nor introduce impurities into the air, either at the unit or through pipes or ducts; be quiet; be economical to operate and maintain; be automatic; provide heating and cooling sources adjacent to window areas and other walls; lend itself to zoning so temperatures can be varied in different parts of the house; and be unobtrusive and pleasing in appearance.

It should be noted that not all of these aspects are always incontrovertible. For instance, in many new heating installations nowadays there is a move away from automation and toward simpler, manually operated heating equipment and associated devices. A wood/coal stove, which has become a common choice as a back-up source of heat for some solar-heated houses, is certainly not automatic in operation; fuel must be fed by hand and, in most cases, temperature regulation, such as it is, is also manual. When considering the design and specifications, and the equipment selection, of any given heating/cooling system installation, all of the aspects just mentioned, both technical and comfort, must be tempered to meet the demands of the situation.

In our review of this subject we will first discuss fuels and energy sources; next, heating systems and distribution methods; and last, cooling systems.

FUELS AND ENERGY SOURCES

Little more than a century ago the world knew only one method of keeping warm: by burning wood or coal in stoves or fireplaces in each important room of a house. Those rooms that were not important from the daytime living aspect, such as bedrooms, usually just got cold, and beds were warmed by putting heated stones or crocks of hot water between the sheets.

But the industrial revolution and, later, the evolution in power technology changed all of that. First came coal-fired central heating systems; then petroleum; later, gas; followed by low-cost electricity. Now comes the advent of practical solar energy and, tomorrow, widespread solar energy as well as alternative sources—geothermal, wind, biomass fuels and the like.

Since coal was the fuel for the first central heating systems, we shall examine it first.

Coal

One of the most plentiful resources of naturally stored energy, coal, is, of course, found in two major forms: anthracite (or hard) and bituminous (or soft). There are also two types of lesser importance found in this country: sub-bituminous and lignite. Soft coal is available in varying degrees in almost all parts of the country, whereas hard coal is commercially mined mostly in eastern Pennsylvania (there are small amounts in a few other states as well). All told, coal is presently being mined in twenty-seven of the fifty states, and there are recoverable reserves in at least thirty-five states (Figure 7–1).

Coal was widely used as a fuel in residences before World War I but began to languish somewhat afterward because of the discovery and development of enormous petroleum reserves. But a number of automatic or semiautomatic coal-stoking and ash-removal systems for domestic use were developed, and coal transportation and home delivery systems, storage yards, and all the ancillary aspects of a huge and steady business grew up around coal-fired home heating

U.S. Coal Data

Recoverable resources	1429 billion short tons
Demonstrated reserve base	434 billion short tons
Low sulfur resource base	100 billion short tons
Coal productions–1974	0.596 billion short tons
Annual increase in domestic production 1960–74	2.3%
U.S. coal consumption–1974	0.014 Q (10^{18} Btu)
Total U.S. energy consumption–1974	0.072 Q (10^{18} Btu)
Heat content of coal resources	
total resources	36.5 Q (10^{18} Btu)
demonstrated resource base	11.5 Q (10^{18} Btu)
low sulfur resource base	2.7 Q (10^{18} Btu)

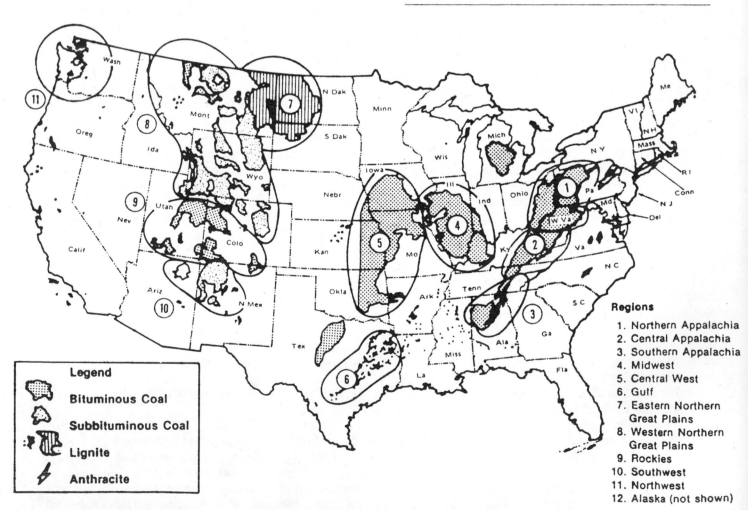

Legend

Bituminous Coal

Subbituminous Coal

Lignite

Anthracite

Regions

1. Northern Appalachia
2. Central Appalachia
3. Southern Appalachia
4. Midwest
5. Central West
6. Gulf
7. Eastern Northern Great Plains
8. Western Northern Great Plains
9. Rockies
10. Southwest
11. Northwest
12. Alaska (not shown)

7–1. United States coal supply regions. (*Energy Handbook,* Van Nostrand Reinhold, 1978)

166

systems. Nonetheless, coal eventually became unfashionable because of its dustiness, equipment maintenance problems, the labor required to stoke a boiler or a furnace and remove the ashes, and similar problems. Using fuel oil was cheaper and easier, all in all, and then came natural gas systems that provided another excellent fuel source, followed by clean, flameless electric heating systems; the competition was simply too much, and the public quickly turned away from coal as a home-heating fuel.

Today, the far-flung retail coal distribution system that used to serve countless thousands of homes throughout huge sections of the country has almost entirely disappeared. The likelihood that it will ever again be established is very remote; there are comparatively few homes today that are heated with coal, and their numbers are unlikely to increase sufficiently to justify such a program. In addition, there are numerous problems of a practical, economical, and environmental nature involved in burning coal as a primary house-heating fuel, problems that, most likely, are insurmountable. Consider, for instance, the horrendous difficulties that would be encountered today in disposing of the resulting ashes generated by all of the dwelling units in the city of New York.

Though coal will, doubtless, never become a primary house-heating fuel again, nonetheless it is still being used. Kitchen ranges that burn either wood or coal are becoming increasingly popular, as are prefabricated fireplaces and wood-coal stoves of various types. A good many thousands of Americans are turning to these heating devices as supplementary units, or as back-up units, that will give them ready heat when needed, as well as a flexible choice as to the type of fuel that they can use. The same principle has been extended recently to central heating systems, in the form of multifuel boilers.

Yet, coal may once again enter our lives as a home-heating fuel in relatively widespread use, but in one or another of several disguises. Instead of being directly burned to produce heat in the individual home, it will be changed to a synthetic fuel (commonly called synfuel at central locations) and transported through a distribution network that already exists. A process called gasification produces a synthetic gas that can be used as a direct replacement for our shrinking supplies of natural gas. By another process called liquification, coal can be converted to diesel fuel, gasoline, and also heating fuel, among other products. And, of course, coal is widely used today in the generation of electricity, which in turn can be utilized as energy to operate residential electric comfort heating systems. In effect, then, coal is virtually as important as a fuel today, though largely in an indirect manner, as it was decades ago. And from that standpoint, coal probably will remain of great importance for some time to come.

Oil

Oil remains a widely used domestic fuel in some areas of the country, particularly the New England states. Its use, however, is now declining for reasons of high price, problems of availability, and declining supplies; plus the disadvantages that fuel oil has always had, such as odor, relatively noisy operation of burners, relatively expensive maintenance of equipment, storage problems, fire hazard, and the like. Fuel oil can be burned equally well in central heating plants or in various types of unit heaters and is a familiar and still relatively cost-effective fuel, depending upon geographic locale. Consumption for home-heating purposes, however, seems to have peaked about 1972 and has declined steadily since then. All indicators point to the fact that, while fuel oil will continue to be used for residential heating purposes, the number of new installations of this type of equipment will probably continue to decline. Its use will eventually become severely limited from a practical standpoint because of high cost and low (or lack of) availability, and, probably, the appearance of synthetic fuel oils will do little to change this.

Gas

Gas has enjoyed great popularity as a heating fuel for some years now. Natural gas has understandable appeal: no storage problems, great cleanliness, less expensive burners, silent operation. Cost at one time was also a compelling factor, since home heating could be done quite inexpensively with natural gas. This fuel is still relatively cost-effective today, and natural gas service is available throughout much of the country in urban, suburban, and even some exurban areas. However, like oil, peak consumption seems to have been reached in 1972 and has dropped since that time. And like oil, supplies are becoming a bit unpredictable, costs are rising rapidly, and, in the future, general availability may be curtailed from lack of supplies. However, there is the possibility that it will be replaced to some extent by synthetic gas.

The so-called "bottled gas," or liquified petroleum gas (LPG), has also enjoyed a certain amount of popularity as a domestic fuel, even for heating purposes. In many semirural and rural areas of the country, virtually the only choices of fuel for automatic home-heating systems are bottled gas (which actually is stored in large outside tanks for heating purposes) and electricity. And in many areas, bottled gas is less expensive and nearly as convenient as electric energy for heating.

Gas burners can be used with all types of furnaces and boilers, as well as with freestanding unit or space heaters. Bottled and natural gas are not interchangeable as fuels in the same burner, however, since a different size of orifice must be used for each type of gas.

Electricity

Electricity is not, by strict definition, a fuel; it is direct energy. Nevertheless, two decades or so ago, electricity enjoyed considerable popularity as a source of energy for home comfort heating and, at one time or another and in various parts of the country, competed directly with the more conventional solid, liquid, and gaseous fuels. All considered, it was (and in a few places still is) cost-effective in light of the advantages offered: flameless, even heat, great flexibility of zoning and control, low initial installation cost, low maintenance, and so on. Today, those same advantages remain worthy of serious consideration, but electric power costs have risen in many areas of the country to such an extent that electric comfort heating is very expensive. In spite of that, this source of energy will become even more important to domestic heating. With new techniques and materials for thermal control of houses, electric heating systems can be made a more viable choice than they are, on average, today. The gap in the cost of heating by electricity and by heating with fossil fuels, on a heat unit basis, will narrow somewhat, perhaps considerably, and the availability of electric power may well be less problematical in the future than will that of fossil fuels. Domestic use of the latter will doubtlessly continue to dwindle, while consumption of electric power in the residential/commercial sector, as well as overall electric power generation, is expected to rise; some of that electrical energy, a larger proportion than is used today, will be consumed for residential comfort heating and cooling.

Predictions vary considerably, but it seems reasonable to expect that electric power consumption by the residential/commercial sector will be approximately four times greater in the year 2000 than it was in 1980. This is due not only to population increase, but also to an increasing dependency on electric power to serve our various needs in lieu of other, more traditional energy sources that are in increasingly short supply. High costs or no, electrical energy generated in one fashion or another (there are a good many possibilities) will be a mainstay for domestic heating and cooling purposes in years to come.

Solar Energy

The term "solar energy," as we use it today, generally is taken to mean either direct heat from the sun, as when it shines in through windows, or indirect heat from the sun gathered by means of solar collectors and transferred/stored within the building for comfort heating purposes. Actually, the term is a misnomer, since solar energy is represented by fossil fuels, wind power, geothermal power, and so forth. However, since the first meaning of the term seems to be firmly stuck in the public mind, this is the one that we will use.

Solar energy, so inexhaustible (Figure 7-2) and so wasted, has only recently become a viable and worthwhile method of heating houses, and it shows all signs of becoming equally useful for cooling purposes in the not too distant future. Indeed, solar cooling is being accomplished right now with considerable success in a good many houses, but this is not yet a nationwide accomplishment. Solar heating, on the other hand, has become a most successful method in virtually every part of the country, and techniques are now being used that will provide anywhere from just a few percent of the total heating needs to as much as 100 percent, though in most cases the practical maximum is about 75 to 80 percent. The collection and storage of solar energy continues to involve relatively expensive and, in many cases, rather overly high-technology equipment. Earlier solar houses (and many present-day designs as well) were obviously just that: ungainly and peculiar-looking for the most part, with a huge collecting area where the sun's heat is stored or turned into power often the most prominent and dazzling part of the structure (Figure 7-3). This is no longer necessarily the case. Some new solar houses are still obviously solar-heat oriented, but many more contemporary designs of both active and passive solar modes of heating appear in a wide variety of designs and styles that look only a bit different from their conventional counterparts.

There is nothing new about the use of solar energy, of course. According to legend, Archimedes successfully set fire to an attacking Roman fleet back in 212 B.C. by concentrating the sun's rays on a solar reflector made of polished brass discs and by aiming it at the sails of their ships. That the sun was used to light temple fires during that same time period is a fact. Various other solar-powered devices appeared over the centuries, including solar concentrators used to drive pumps and distill water, various kinds of solar engines, solar cookers and water-pumping systems, solar stills, and the like. In France, one Abel Pifre assembled a collection of equipment that consisted of a steam engine fired by a 100-square-foot parabolic solar collector, which in turn operated a printing press, which in turn was used to publish *Le Journal Soliel* ("The Sunshine Journal") (Figure 7-4).

The most common commercial use of solar energy in this country has been in solar water heaters. Though they have been in the news a good deal recently, there is nothing new about them, either. By 1900, southern California was rife with solar water heaters, and practically one out of every three houses had one. Models large enough (and designed) for heating swimming pools were even available. But apparently the American penchant for eschewing simple, low-technology, solutions to various problems in favor of high-technology, sophisticated, and complex gadgetry, as well as very inexpensive alternative fuels of ready availability, slowed the development of solar energy to a standstill. Except, of course, that a few thousand solar water heaters have continually and quietly gone about their business of providing their owners with ample and, oftentimes, free hot water for the past several decades.

The solar industry of late has redeveloped and is starting to show signs of life, but is unfortunately fraught with poorly designed systems, materials of dubious quality, manufacturers of questionable integrity, design and installation mistakes and cost-cutting, and the inevitable big-business competition in terms of high-technology controls, "black boxes," sophisticated plumbing, and such, instead of reliance upon and refinement of well-known, low-cost, reliable designs.

Solar comfort heating for houses is now a reality and solar cooling almost so. There is no question whatsoever that it can do an efficient and effective job in heating houses, including existing ones. Until the present, its use has not been practical, especially from a broad-scale standpoint, for two major reasons. First, in the past, several heating fuels were cheap and easily available, and burning cheap fuel at a profligate rate was a lot easier than going to the expense and bother of fitting a solar energy arrangement. The second reason is that for many years the building industry, which like all others tends to be highly resistant to change in any appreciable degree anyway, has been largely geared, as it

7-2. Distribution of solar energy over the United States, in Btu per square foot per average day. (*Energy Handbook,* Van Nostrand Reinhold, 1978)

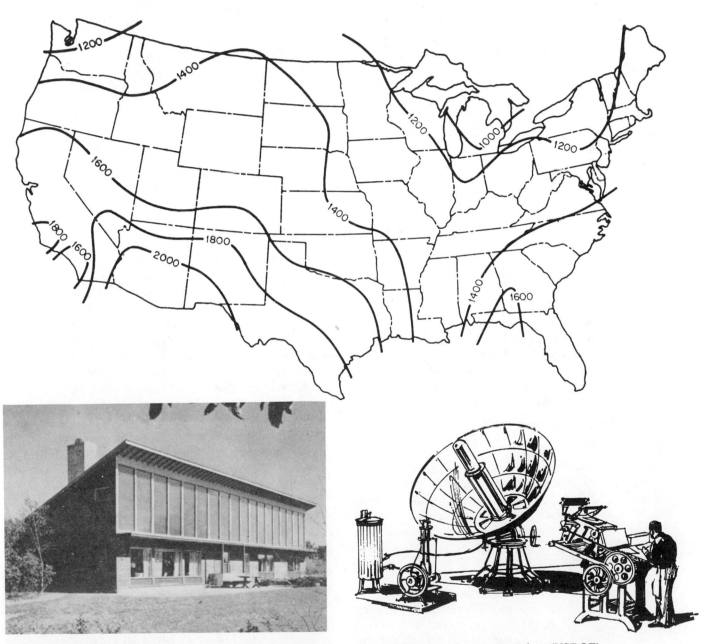

7-3. Solar-heated house at Dover, Massachusetts, designed by Maria Telkes. (Maria Telkes)

7-4. The Pifre solar steam engine. (USDOE)

is today, to producing houses with the lowest possible initial cost. The primary attention has been focused upon making a home inexpensive to purchase. How much the cost of operating it might be for the subsequent owners over the next twenty or forty or one hundred years has been no concern whatsoever of the building contractors.

The fact is that today a house powered fully, or nearly so, by solar energy for heating and cooling is substantially more expensive than a conventionally equipped house. Thus, the initial price may be $10,000 to $15,000 higher for an architect-designed, contractor-built solar house. But, it is equally true that a solar heated house, despite its higher initial cost, is more cost-effective in most instances over a long period of time than is a conventional house. This is true *today* and, as the years go by, will become a more and more important factor as the availability of other fuels and energy sources continues to dwindle and their cost continues to escalate.

For these and a number of other reasons, solar energy will undoubtedly become tremendously important to us all, in various ways. It has been calculated that enough solar energy reaches the surface of the earth every fifteen minutes to supply the current energy requirements for a full year for the entire world. Unfortunately, most of this energy cannot be effectively harnessed. The mean insolation in any one locale varies greatly from day to day, from month to month, from season to season. Latitude, weather patterns, and length of day all have their effect in determining the possible amount of sunshine that falls upon a given point, and, of that amount, only a small part can be used due to the inefficiency of our present-day solar equipment. But use it we must, and over the next few decades we will see amazing developments in home heating and cooling through passive, active, and hybrid solar modes, residential "power plants" that will generate electricity from solar-powered photovoltaic cells, and widespread commercial and industrial use of solar energy, including the generation of electricity for general consumption.

Atomic Energy

It was once thought that atomic energy might be the answer as a source of domestic heating and cooling. Obviously, there is little chance that this will ever come about, insofar as individual domestic systems are concerned, not only because of the tremendous costs involved, but also because of the general unreliability of atomic technology at present and the incredible dangers that are involved therein. Atomic energy is, of course, being used to generate substantial quantities of electricity; this energy can be used for home consumption in heating, cooling, and everyday purposes. Whether or not atomic power generation will continue to grow in this country is an open question; certainly the industry at this point is at a practical standstill. The

rest of the world continues to develop their atomic generating capabilities, but in any event the supplies of the necessary raw materials for production of atomic energy are in somewhat limited supply and certainly finite. Without substantial new breakthroughs in atomic technology, this is not a source of power upon which we should place any great amount of dependence.

Air and Water

In the heat pump, air and water are sometimes used as heat and cold sources. Though this interesting device has been around for many years, it is only since about 1947 that it has become practical enough to be put into regular and relatively widespread use. The heat pump is still more a theoretical than a practical device for very cold climates, but much progress is being made in perfecting the units, and the time is not far off when they will be competitive with other heating systems, even in severe climates. In the southern states, where winter heating loads are small and cooling is the major objective, heat pumps are fairly popular, particularly where electric rates are relatively low.

In this country, the great proportion of heat pump installations make use of air as a primary energy source, though some are designed to operate with water as a source, and they can also be solar-assisted. There are other possibilities as well, as can be seen in Table 7-1. In the heating mode, the heat pump extracts heat energy from an outside source and pumps it into the house, while in the cooling mode it extracts heat from the house itself and exhausts it outdoors. However, the ability of a heat pump to produce heat diminishes as the temperature of the heat source lowers. This means that, in most installations, an additional source of energy for comfort heating—usually electricity—must be included in the equipment in order to provide sufficient overall heating capacity when outside temperatures are particularly low. Thus, as with many solar heating installations, the primary heating system cannot always be depended upon to fulfill total heating requirements, and a backup system must be included. Oftentimes, the backup system is of nearly the same capacity as the primary system, and it is always integral with the unit.

The heat pump can be an economical device in any area where heating requirements are relatively low. Units using air as the heat source are less efficient and use more electricity than those using water, as is also true of mechanical cooling units. However, they undoubtedly will be improved with further research—and air is inexhaustible, which water is not.

The advantage of using an electric-powered heat pump for heating over straight electric resistance heating lies in the fact that the ratio of power used to heat obtained, given as unity with resistance heating, can be as high as 3 or even 4 with a heat pump if the air or water temperatures are moderately high.

Heat Pump, Heat Sources and Sinks

Heat Source	Air	City Water	Well Water	Surface Water	Waste Water	Earth	Solar
Source classification	Primary	Primary or auxiliary	Primary	Primary	Primary or auxiliary	Primary or auxiliary	Auxiliary
Suitability as heat sink	Good	Good	Good	Good	Variable with source	Usually poor	May be used to dissipate heat to air
Availability (location)	Universal	Cities	Uncertain	Rare	Limited	Extensive	Universal
Availability (time)	Continuous	Continuous—except local shortages	Continuous—check water table	Continuous	Variable	Continuous, temperature drops as heat is removed, slowly rises when pump stops	Intermittent, unpredictable, except over extended time
Expense (original)	Low, less than earth and water sources except city	Usually lowest	Variable, depending on cost of drilling well	Low	Variable	High	High
Expense (operating)	Relatively low	High, usually prohibitive	Low to moderate	Relatively low	Low	Relatively moderate	Unexplored. Promising as auxiliary for reducing operating cost
Temperature (level)	Favorable 75–95% of time in most of United States	Usually satisfactory	Satisfactory	Satisfactory	Usually good	Initially good—drops with time and rate of heat withdrawal	Excellent
Temperature (variation)	Extreme	Variable with location (10 to 25 F deg)	Small	Moderate	Usually moderate	Large—less than for air, however	Extreme
Design information	Usually adequate	Usually adequate	Usually adequate	Usually adequate	Adequate if source is constant in supply and temperature	Inadequate	Practically available
Size of equipment	Moderate	Small	Small (except for well)	Small	Variable (usually moderate)	Small (except ground coils)	Available in some areas
Adaptability to standard product	Excellent, can be factory assembled and tested	Excellent	Excellent (except for well)	Excellent	Poor	Poor	Poor
Sources it may augment		Air, earth					
Special problems	Least heat available when demand greatest. Coil frosting requires extra capacity, alternate source, or standby heat. May require ductwork.	Scale on coils. Local use restrictions during shortages. Disposal. Water temperature may become too low to permit further heat removal.	Corrosion, scale may form on heat transfer surface. Disposal may require second well. Water location, temperature, composition usually unknown until well drilled. Well may run dry.	Water may cause scale, corrosion, and algae fouling.	Usually scale forming or corrosive. Often insufficient supply. Very limited application, hence required individual design. Freeze-up hazards.	Limited by local geology and climate. Installation costs difficult to estimate. Requires considerable ground area, may damage lawns, gardens. Leaks difficult to repair.	Probably will require heat storage equipment at either evaporator or condenser side.

Table 7–1. (Reprinted with permission from the *1976 Systems Volume, ASHRAE HANDBOOK & Product Directory*)

Alternative Sources

There are a number of alternative sources of fuel or energy for comfort heating and cooling. None of them will ever be universally used in this country for one reason or another, but all of them are important from several standpoints. First, some of them are of particular interest to many homeowners, especially to those who have adopted one or the other of the so-called "alternative life-styles," because the source oftentimes can be controlled independently on a one-to-one basis, with no dependence upon commercial interests for supply. Individual self-sufficiency is quite possible, a thought that appeals to many. Second, some of the sources are infinitely renewable or constantly available, unlike the more conventional fuels such as oil and gas. Third, energy obtained from these sources and put to use wherever possible release just that much more energy of more conventional kinds for use where, at least for the present, only conventional fuels are practical. This, in effect, stretches and also makes more useful our dwindling reserves of conventional fuels. Fourth, several alternative sources can readily be used to provide auxiliary heat when used in conjunction with more conventional heating systems; can be used to provide a safeguard in the event of disruption of fuel supplies for conventional systems; and can be arranged to offer secondary sources that can be quickly turned to whenever they are more cost-effective than conventional fuels. And last, some of the sources are capable of being exploited by commercial interests, so that the energy derived from them can be made available on a relatively wide-scale basis to a network of consumers, thus easing the strain somewhat on conventional fuels in short supply. For these and several other lesser reasons, alternative fuel and energy sources have attracted a considerable amount of interest, both from individuals and from government, and are worthy of investigation.

WOOD

Wood, which is actually a form of solar energy, was widely used as a home-heating fuel many years ago throughout extensive portions of the country and has always been relied upon to a certain degree. And, of course, it has long been popular as a fireplace fuel, largely for ambiance rather than for heat. But over the past few years there has been an explosion of interest in wood as a backup heat source and often as a primary source when used in airtight stoves. Fuel wood is not universally available, of course, but where it is, wood is one of the few fuels that can be gathered and used on an individual basis, often at no cash cost, and in many areas it can be purchased at a price low enough to make it competitive with, or cheaper than, other types of fuel. It is not, however, a fuel that can be burned "automatically" and requires a considerable amount of

effort and attention on the part of the user.

As with other fuels, wood has its advantages and disadvantages, but under the proper circumstances does deliver good heat. Different species of wood have slightly different burning qualities and characteristics, but any kind of wood, including those of no commercial value, can be burned as fuel. Regardless of species, wood will provide just under 8,000 Btu per ovendry pound—this is the so-called "low heat value" that discounts the latent heat in the wood—when burned properly in an airtight stove. This figure, which is based upon an assumed moisture content of approximately 20 percent for normal air-cured firewood, decreases as the moisture content rises. A pound of red maple and a pound of eastern white pine will produce approximately the same amount of heat when burned, assuming that their moisture content is the same. But the heat yield is a function of wood density, and since the maple is much denser than the pine, a cord of maple will produce considerably more Btu's than will a cord of pine. This total is in turn variable, since, while a cord of wood theoretically contains 128 cubic feet, in actual practice the amount can range anywhere from 60 to 90 or so cubic feet, depending upon how the wood is stacked and the volume of the air voids between the logs. Thus, the best way to purchase wood for fuel is by the ton, or, if the price per cord between two species of wood is the same, choose the species of higher density for a greater yield in Btu's. As with other heating fuels and systems, the net amount of usable heat that is delivered into the living area depends upon the design and efficiency of the heating equipment; it is always considerably less than unity. Whether the wood is a hardwood or a softwood makes no difference.

An excellent discussion of wood as a fuel and the various ramifications of using it as such can be found in Shelton and Shapiro's *The Woodburner's Encyclopedia* (Vermont Crossroads Press, 1977).

HYDROPOWER

Flowing water has long been utilized as a source of power throughout the world. From the very beginnings of this country, water power has been an important source of energy. Early on, water was widely used as a source of mechanical energy to power mill wheels and the like, and later as the prime mover for all kinds of industrial machinery. With the advent of effective electrical generating systems that could be powered by water, the use of other hydropower applications dwindled rapidly, and in its stead there appeared a substantial network of hydroelectric generating stations of considerable capacity. The use of hydropower by individuals or small groups largely disappeared.

Today, however, there is a resurgence of interest in hydropower, both to generate electricity and, in some instances, to provide mechanical power. Large, hydroelectric power plants remain an extremely important part of our overall national electric generating system. But in addition, many of the small hydroelectric plants or hydropower sites that have long been abandoned are now being rebuilt in order to provide power in small communities or for certain commercial applications. For individual purposes, hydropower is now of limited practicality and available to only a very few rural residents. But, in some cases, hydropower can serve a definite purpose as an alternative energy source, either mechanical or electrical. For some individuals who choose to lead an alternative life-style and where conditions are right, this is a source well worth investigating.

Though small hydropower operations can provide only a tiny fraction of our total national energy needs, nonetheless they may well have increasing importance in the future; whatever additional power is produced by individuals or small groups simply means that that much less must be produced by or obtained from other sources. From the standpoint of the individual, it is possible, for instance, to generate sufficient hydroelectric power from a small powerhouse to serve the needs, though perhaps somewhat minimally, of a farm or a rural dwelling. There are problems involved, of course. There must be sufficient year-round water flow, the generating capability must be both reliable and cost-effective, and the equipment is neither easy to buy nor to assemble. In many cases, the undertaking will not be worthwhile, but, where it is, the developer of the power plant will enjoy a measure of energy independence that few of us will ever realize.

On a much larger scale, the many, large, utility-owned hydroelectric generating plants scattered throughout the country provide others of us with large amounts of electrical energy that is developed through intensive use of a renewable energy resource—falling water—and is not dependent upon dwindling supplies of fossil fuels for its production. This important point has not, of course, gone unnoticed by those who are engaged in the struggle to meet our ever-increasing national energy demands and consumption. As the chart in Table 7-2 shows, although the United States has developed a larger percentage of its available hydroelectric power potential than most of the rest of the world, there still remain substantial undeveloped reserves. New hydroelectric generating capacity is being developed continuously in an effort to tap some of this energy, and doubtlessly this process will go on for many years to come. Thus, while few individuals can directly take advantage of hydropower, a great many of us will indefinitely continue to be served by hydropower in the form of the electrical energy that reaches us through the transmission lines for our various domestic purposes. To this one might add the potential energy that may some day be developed by harnessing the kinetic energy of tidal currents. The technology for tidal power plants is available today—such plants have been used intermittently in various parts of the world, including the United States, for some three centuries—but the idea has gained little acceptance because of the practical problems and the economics involved. However, the day may well come when a certain small proportion of our electrical generating capacity derives from this source.

United States Hydroelectric Power by Region, 1973

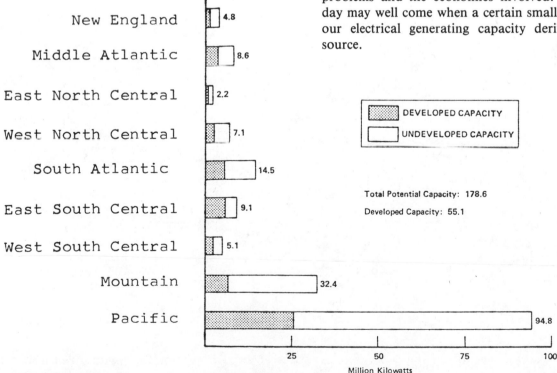

Total Potential Capacity: 178.6

Developed Capacity: 55.1

Table 7-2. (*Energy Handbook,* Van Nostrand Reinhold, 1978)   Source: Federal Power Commission, 1974.

WIND POWER

As with water, man has long used the kinetic energy available in the wind as a source of power for a variety of purposes. Early on, of course, these purposes were largely mechanical, such as grinding grain or pumping water from the ground. As our ability to manufacture equipment for the generation of electricity grew, wind generators or wind-driven power plants became quite popular. In fact, during the 1930s and 1940s, there were many thousands of individual, small-capacity, wind-electric systems in use all over the United States on homesteads, farms, and ranches where electricity was otherwise unavailable. These systems performed well, and many of them are still in operation, though the rural electrification program in large measure superceded them. But the present high cost of electrical energy, as well as the various energy crises of the past few years, has sparked renewed interest in the possibilities of wind-electric systems of all kinds, and has spurred a surprising amount of research and development work in the field. And certainly, as Figure 7–5 shows, there is a substantial amount of electrical power that can be derived from the wind, a constantly renewable resource of solar origin. In fact, it has been determined by the NSF/NASA Solar Energy Panel that

by the year 2000, if the proper program were instituted with available technology, wind power plants could generate 1.536×10^{12} kilowatt hours of electrical energy annually, or approximately 19 percent of our total projected electrical energy requirement for that year.

Obtaining usable electrical energy from wind power is a perfectly feasible method that has been well tested and well proven; good technology is now available, as is the necessary equipment, and further development continues apace. However, wind-power energy production is not achieved without some difficulties. First, of course, one must be in a location where there is suitable wind velocity that can be relied upon over long periods of time. There is the problem of efficiency; in theory, only 59.3 percent of the wind energy passing through the area swept by a rotor can be extracted, and, in practice, an excellent rotor can manage to capture only about 70 percent of that amount. Thus, one can expect to capture only about 40 to 45 percent of the available wind energy, given the current state of technology. Proper siting can be difficult, and, as yet, the storage of electricity, to compensate for times when the wind is down and generation is not taking place, is also problematical. The cost-effectiveness of electrical generation by wind power is quite variable and, oftentimes, not

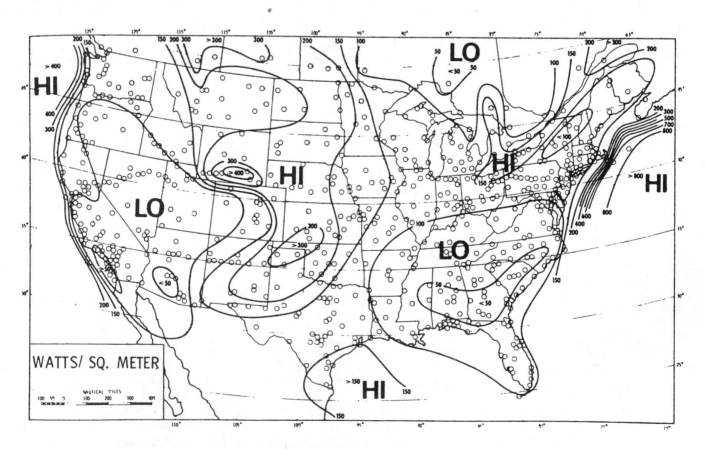

7–5. Available wind power in the United States, annual average. (*Energy Handbook,* Van Nostrand Reinhold, 1978)

favorable; however, there is every likelihood that this situation will change for the better.

Electrical generation by wind power can be accomplished on either an individual or a public-utility basis. Perhaps the most famous of the large wind generators in this country was the system installed at Grandpa's Knob in Vermont. This huge rotor, fitted with two 8-ton blades and 175 feet in diameter, was designed to produce 1250 kilowatts of electricity. The unit was tested back in 1941, and the test pointed out the commercial potential of wind power. More recently, NASA has built a wind-generating system called Mod-Zero, a 100-kilowatt, 125-foot system near Sandusky, Ohio; other systems, with capacities of several million watts, are being studied. Thus, it is entirely possible that large electric utilities may be able to add to their generating capacity through the use of on-line wind-power systems. At present, however, small wind generators are more practical for individual homeowners, most especially those in rural areas.

Small systems are commercially available, either complete or as assorted component parts, for home installation. Though similar to the systems used several decades ago, they are much improved and quite capable of providing several kilowatts of power to individual households. They can be coupled with electrical energy storage systems, and may also be installed in such a manner that electrical power is supplied by the utility company when needed, while the wind generator provides energy the rest of the time. During periods of excess generation, unused power can actually be fed back to the utility company for use elsewhere. In years to come, it is quite likely that individual wind generators will provide a fair amount of energy to many homeowners around the country.

GEOTHERMAL POWER

The possibilities of harnessing geothermal power for various applications, not only commercial electrical generation but also direct heating of both commercial buildings and residences, has lately created some excitement. In a few isolated areas of the country, geothermal power has been used successfully for various purposes for a good many years. It is apparent that this resource can be developed to a certain extent, though geothermal power will never represent a very substantial portion of our total consumption. As can be seen in Figure 7–6, its potential is almost entirely restricted to the western part of the United States. In present use, power is derived from both steam and, for the greater

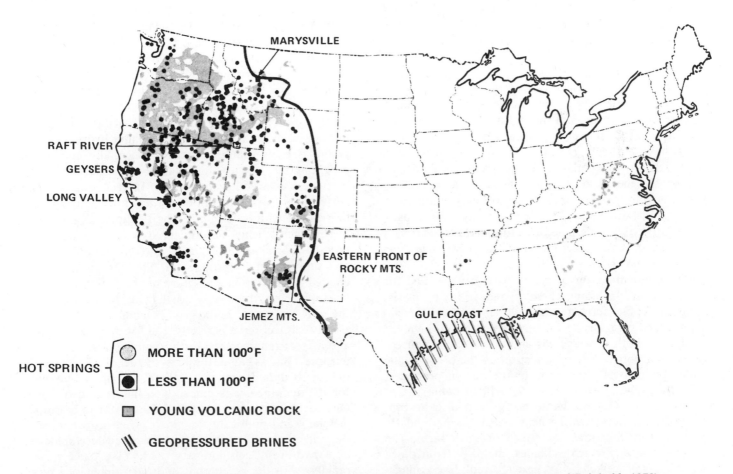

7–6. United States geothermal resources, areas of promise. (*Energy Handbook,* Van Nostrand Reinhold, 1978)

part, hot water. Another potential source is the heat entrapped in dry, hot rock below the earth's surface, but as yet no way has been found to tap it.

Geothermal energy has been and will continue to be developed and produced by commercial operations, including electrical generation; there is little possibility here for individual uses. However, in a certain few areas the value of geothermal energy may become of considerable importance to a few thousands of individual homeowners. For example, a huge hot spring is located in the city of Glenwood Springs, Colorado, and it has been determined that the source has more than enough capability to provide every dwelling and commercial building within the city limits with hot-water heat for an indefinite time. The project is basically feasible, and it is quite possible that it will also become cost-effective in due course.

FUTURE POSSIBILITIES

The various fuels and energy sources that have just been discussed are either quite conventional or at least relatively well known. For numerous reasons, however, we cannot place our hopes upon any one of them, or even combinations thereof, to serve our future needs exclusively. We must look ahead, and continually investigate other possibilities that will help in meeting our rapidly increasing demand for energy. There are several such possibilities, all of which exhibit potentials ranging from excellent to more or less reasonable. Some, in fact, are in the experimental stages of evaluation and production at the present.

Organic waste is a resource that is now being recognized in this country as a potential source for energy. Organic wastes such as paper, wood, animal dung, food residues, and the like are utilized to a considerable extent in many other parts of the world, since they have a heating value. In this country waste materials, until recently, have received little attention as a potential energy source. Now, however, a good many waste-energy recovery projects are being undertaken throughout the nation. Though, for the most part, these projects are designed to utilize solid wastes *as* a fuel, in some cases other fuels are being processed *from* the waste material.

There are numerous processes that can be used for this purpose, including chemical reduction, pyrolysis, and anaerobic fermentation. When recovery is accomplished on a large scale and by somewhat involved processes, both methane gas and oil can be produced. There is a potential for production on the order of 200 million barrels of oil per year by the various processes, and a production of close to 1.5 trillion cubic feet of methane gas. Organic waste energy can also be captured by the individual homeowner and is particularly adaptable to the rural homestead or small farm. The organic waste, which includes manure from farm animals, is processed by a digester, a tank-like arrange-

ment with associated equipment that breaks the material down. As the biomass material is "digested," bio-gas, a mixture of about two parts methane gas to one part carbon dioxide by volume, is produced. This gas can be used to run natural-gas appliances, including stoves, refrigerators, water heaters, and space heaters, and can also be used to operate internal combustion engines. Thus, for the individual interested in energy independence or self-sufficiency, biomass conversion represents another arrow in his quiver.

Methane gas, just mentioned as one of the principal products of organic waste recovery system projects, is somewhat similar to natural gas and is one of the commoner volatile gases in nature. Generally it is a product of decomposition of organic matter, hence the popular name, "swamp gas." But a theory has recently been propounded that methane may be found in much greater volume than heretofore suspected, and that tremendous reserves of the gas may lie entrapped deep within the bowels of the earth. Whether or not this is true remains to be seen, of course, but there is sufficient evidence to support this belief and investigation will be undertaken over the next few years in an attempt to arrive at the truth of the matter. If the theory is proven and the proper technology can be developed, methane gas may one day become an important fuel.

Hydrogen is another gas that is very common, relatively easy to manufacture, and makes an excellent fuel. The technology for producing hydrogen gas has existed for many years, and the gas has been used to some small extent as a fuel. But because of the scarcity and high price of other fuels, additional research is now going on that may well result in the use of hydrogen fuels as an everyday matter. For instance, experiments are now under way in the use of hydrogen to fuel commercial airliners. In California, a liquid hydride compound is being manufactured commercially, and test programs are being undertaken to determine its usefulness as an automotive fuel. In fact, it seems to perform very well and will power any internal combustion engine with only minor modifications.

This fuel is being manufactured at considerably less cost than gasoline, for instance, and requires only water and sunlight for its production. There is no pollution created during the manufacture of the fuel nor during its combustion, there is no waste from the process, and the only byproduct is oxygen. In addition, hydrogen-based fuels can serve perfectly well for heating, drying, and a great range of residential/commercial/industrial purposes, just as can natural gas or fuel oil. The potential supply of hydrogen is unlimited, and the technology for its manufacture is currently being upgraded. The only deterrents to its widespread use appear to be commercially and politically oriented; given proper incentive and a favorable economic climate, the development of a hydrogen fuels industry could take place quite rapidly, with the result that hydrogen might one day become an ordinary, commonplace, and very important fuel for the average citizen.

Synfuels is the term given to synthetic fuels developed by any one of a number of sophisticated manufacturing processes. These processes involve the conversion of coal by means of carbonization, gasification, and liquifaction. The first process is used primarily to develop coke, coal tar, light oils, and coal gas, which in turn are used in the production of plastics, motor fuels, explosives, drugs and dyes, and a great many other products. Gasification produces a synthetic gas that can be in turn used for producing other synthetic materials or for replacing our dwindling supplies of natural gas. Liquifaction produces synthetic liquid fuels such as gasoline, diesel fuel, and heating fuel.

These processes are by no means new, and the technology for them is well known. However, insofar as liquifaction and gasification in particular are concerned, there is much research and development activity, both in the laboratories and in the field, aimed at improving yields of synthetic fuels and in turn decreasing our dependence upon natural gas and oil. But, in view of the fact that the derivation of these synthetic fuels is from a fossil fuel—coal—and even though that fuel is in reasonably good supply, nonetheless it is a finite supply and we would do well to place only modest dependence upon it. Synfuels will, however, continue to be an important source of energy in the near future.

Shale oil is a term that has been much on the minds of many people, particularly those who live in the shale regions of Colorado, for the past several years. Shale oil is properly a synfuel. The shale in which it is found is a sedimentary rock that contains an insoluble, organic material called kerogen. When the shale is heated, the kerogen transforms and yields a refinable crude oil that can be utilized in much the same way as natural crudes. Experimentation in the production of shale oil has been going on now for many years, with various processes being developed and refined in an attempt to establish a workable, cost-effective process.

This goal has been nearly reached, aided in part by the sudden rise in the price of natural crudes, and development proceeds apace. The industry is presently centered largely on the Western Slope of the Colorado Rockies, where present plans by one major concern alone call for the production of two million barrels of synthetic crude oil per day by the year 2000. There are, however, a good many economic, political, and environmental roadblocks standing in the way of such production, and, in all likelihood, development of this resource will continue to be somewhat slow, as it has been in the past. It may be, however, an important adjunct to our other energy resources.

Photovoltaic cells—or solar cells, if you prefer—were developed by the Bell Telephone Laboratories in 1954, and until recent years, not much further refinement took place, nor were photovoltaic cells much used. One reason for that, of course, is that until just lately an array large enough to light up a single 100-watt light bulb carried a price tag of approximately $50,000. But that situation is about to change, and dramatically. The U. S. Department of Energy, largely through the Solar Energy Research Institute, has embarked on a program to reduce the cost and increase the effectiveness of photovoltaic arrays to the point where they will be affordable for residential (as well as for commercial and industrial) power applications.

Photovoltaic cells generate electricity when sunlight strikes them. They can be mounted in any appropriate position—a rooftop, for instance, just as is a solar heat collector—and can be used to provide the electrical power needs of a household. There are still many barriers to be broken down, many hurdles to be leaped, but there is a strong possibility that affordable photovoltaic cells will make the modern, ultra-energy-efficient house of the 1990s not only self-sufficient as regards electrical generation for in-house purposes, but even producers of electrical energy being fed back into a power grid system.

The reader will note that none of these fuels or energy sources, conventional or unconventional, are a panacea. No single one of them will serve all of our needs or fulfill every purpose, even when considered on a residential basis alone. All of them have advantages, all of them have drawbacks. Solar heating is simply not workable in some places; oil is very expensive and sometimes in short supply; gas reserves are running low; photovoltaics are out of the question presently; wind power is adaptable only on a limited individual basis and has not yet been developed on a commercial basis; and so on and on.

In the past, a homeowner could install an oil-fired hot-water heating system in his home, or a gas-fired warm-air system, or whatever else he chose, and that would be the end of it—one house, one heating system. This circumstance has changed. Today the homeowner cannot, and should not, depend upon one fuel or energy source, or one heating system, to supply his comfort heating needs (the same holds true, of course, for comfort cooling). Many homeowners, although a very small minority, have already reached that conclusion and have increased their heating flexibility by installing backup and/or multiple-fuel systems, in both new and existing houses.

The houses of the future—and that includes the immediate future—will be so constructed as to require the most reasonable minimum of energy to heat and/or cool; they will be equipped with heating/cooling systems that have built-in flexibility and precise control mechanisms and that are not dependent upon any one fuel or energy source. In most houses, there probably will be no such thing as a "main" fuel or system.

Rather, there will be combinations of equipment that can be operated in two or more modes, or under differing control systems. Thus, a house might be fitted with a passive solar system backed up by radiant glass panels and a wood stove; or with a central heat-pump air-conditioning system with solar assist and backed up by a central wood/coal furnace; or with a combination electric/gas/coal central furnace combined with passive solar comfort heating, natural and mechanical cooling, and active solar water heating; or with any one of numerous other possibilities.

Bear in mind, as we discuss heating and cooling systems in the following pages, that while many of the systems, or the different kinds of equipment, can stand alone as complete heating or cooling installations, they can also be used in combination with one another to provide the flexibility and variety of options that will be necessary through the coming years for comfortable, cost-effective home heating/cooling.

HEATING SYSTEMS

Residential heating systems can be broken down into two distinct types. One is the central heating system, whereby the heat is produced in a central location within the building by a single heat-generating means, and the heat is then transferred via an exchange medium running through a system of ducts or pipes to all other areas of the house. The other kind of system is the decentralized or area scheme, whereby several heat-producing units are placed at appropriate points throughout the house, with each unit heating only its particular area. Of the two systems, central heating has long been favored by residents in this country, and we probably use it to a greater extent than any other country. In most other parts of the world, area heating is the rule rather than the exception. However, many homeowners in this country are coming to the realization that decentralized heating is an effective and versatile method that has a great many advantages, particularly given today's high fuel costs and occasional tenuousness of supply.

Heating systems can further be classified in two major categories: wet and dry. Wet or hydronic heat makes use of a liquid as a medium of heat exchange from the heat-producing unit to the area being heated. Dry-heating systems, on the other hand, use no liquids; in the case of warm-air heating systems, convective air currents are relied upon as the medium of heat exchange, while with radiant heating, the radiating heat energy strikes and warms the surfaces in the heated area, which in turn heat the air itself. In fact, convection and radiation frequently work in concert in a dry-heating system, and conduction is also responsible for some degree of heat transfer. Note that both wet and dry heating systems may be either centralized or decentralized.

Central Heating

Central heating systems depend upon a single piece of heat-generating equipment to produce sufficient Btu's of heat to replenish the entire heat loss of the house. The heat is ducted or piped to individual rooms, where it is dispersed into the area via air outlets, radiant panels, radiators, or similar devices. Several different kinds of arrangements can be used for this purpose.

FORCED HOT WATER

One of the most popular systems for centralized residential heating for the past several decades has been the forced hot water arrangement. The heart of this system is a boiler that raises water temperatures to at least 170° F. Any fuel can be used in a boiler—even electricity in regions of very low power rates.

Boilers are of two major types: cast iron and steel. Probably the best way to select a boiler is on a price basis, giving due consideration to the guarantees or warranties provided by the manufacturer. *Conversion* boilers are often selected if it is felt that a change of fuel may become necessary during the boiler's life. However, a much more satisfactory solution, in the light of high fuel costs and possible supply interruptions, is to install a special multifuel boiler of the sort shown in Figure 7-7. Such a boiler includes a combustion chamber for either oil or gas, electric heating elements if desired, and a large firebox for wood. The boiler can be operated with whichever fuel is most cost-effective or available. There are also, of course, boilers especially designed for oil (Figure 7-8) and for gas (Figure 7-9). If the fuel source is dependable, it is generally best to select a boiler specifically designed for a given fuel. However, given present-day circumstances and the fact that multifuel boilers are entirely depend-

7-7. Multifuel boiler burns oil or gas in the left-hand chamber, coal or wood in the right-hand firebox, or utilizes electric elements in the center. (Courtesy, Tekton Corporation)

7-8. Typical oil-fired boiler. (*Home Heating,* Farmers' Bulletin No. 2235, USDA)

7-9. Typical gas-fired boiler. (*Home Heating,* Farmers' Bulletin No. 2235, USDA)

able as well as being versatile, one can conceive of many situations where installation of a multifuel boiler would be advisable.

All boilers carry a rating. Years ago, cast iron coal- or oil-fired boilers were rated by the Institute of Boiler and Radiator Manufacturers—the so-called IBR rating. Steel boilers, on the other hand, were rated by the Steel Boiler Institute, Inc.—the SBI rating. Then, in the years just prior to 1980, boiler ratings were published by The Hydronics Institute, in a publication called *The Testing and Rating Standard for Cast Iron and Steel Heating Boilers.* Under this arrangement, the Institute tested all oil boiler series, while the American Gas Association (AGA) Laboratories tested the gas-fired boiler series. Now, however, all residential boilers are being tested by the individual manufacturers according to test procedures established by the U.S. Department of Energy (DOE). The Institute and AGA Laboratories continue to make verification tests for confirmation.

The new testing procedures are better than the old; the Btu input and the steady-state efficiency are measured, and then the input is multiplied by the percentage of efficiency to arrive at an official gross rating category called "Heating Capacity." Heat that passes through the boiler jacket is not counted as a loss because it is of value within the house. Each boiler model is also tested to determine its approximate annual fuel utilization efficiency. This results in a specific rating, so that the consumer can compare two or more units to determine which has the better efficiency for a given size and presumably choose the one that in theory will have the lowest fuel consumption and the highest energy conservation. The purchaser of a boiler should be guided by the "Net Rating," and match that rating to the total heat losses of the house. Boilers that meet DOE requirements and pass the required tests will be given a seal and rating by the Hydronics Institute: SBI for steel boilers and IBR for cast iron boilers. All gas-fired units will carry the AGA seal.

Distribution. Once the water in the boiler has been heated, it has to be distributed. And here the ingenuity of the heating engineers has produced a proliferation of types of piping and outlets that is often bewildering. The major ones are discussed below. Many of the special variations available are ignored in this simplified presentation, not because they are not of value, but because they are beyond the scope of this book.

A forced hot water system requires a good pump, which uses power and may require periodic maintenance. If a pump fails, particularly when the family is out, the whole system could freeze up during their absence. For this reason, many forced hot water systems are not, in fact, filled with water, but with an antifreeze solution. However, modern pumping equipment is quite reliable. The system also requires an expansion tank to permit the volume of fluid, as it heats, to expand into something. This tank can be placed nearly anywhere in the system, but usually is located near the boiler. The expansion tank remains about half-filled with fluid and half with air, which compresses when the heated water expands. This permits the use of a sealed system, which in turn allows higher pressure and a higher boiling point of the liquid. Thus, higher temperatures can be maintained without the problem of steam in the radiation outlets, and those outlets can consequently be physically smaller.

Piping layouts for forced hot water systems include the series-loop baseboard system, the one-pipe system, the two-pipe reverse return system, the two-pipe direct return system, and various kinds of panel systems. The two-pipe direct return system is not recommended for residential heating. The two-pipe reverse return system, once in common use, no longer offers sufficient advantages in most residential applications to be useful, but is still sometimes installed; such an installation is shown in Figure 7–10.

The series-loop baseboard system uses a single pipe that enters directly into a baseboard radiation unit and continues from the opposite end of the unit into the next one, and so on, until all of the radiation units are connected in a loop (Figure 7–11). This system has the advantage of reducing materials and labor to a minimum. The potential disadvantage is that each succeeding radiation unit receives water that is a bit cooler than the last, and by the time the heated water has reached the final radiation unit on the line, the heating

capabilities of that unit are reduced. On the other hand, the first one in the line may radiate too much heat. However, in a small, properly balanced system, this often is not a serious drawback.

The one-pipe system (Figure 7–12) is commonly used in house installations; it has a single pipe that makes the circuit from boiler outlet to boiler return. Each radiation unit is connected to the main pipe by a pair of smaller branch pipes. One of the branches is connected to the main pipe with an ordinary tee, but the other is connected by means of a special tee called a one-pipe fitting. These fittings are so designed as to cause only a part of the water circulated through the main to go through the radiation units and back into the main again. This successfully minimizes the problem of ever-diminishing temperatures in successive radiation units, a difficulty formerly associated with such systems.

A simple panel system is diagrammed in Figure 7–13. Such systems can be installed in ceilings or floors. Balancing valves and vents must be placed in an accessible position at the head of the return main so that the panels can be properly balanced.

Piping layouts can be split into two or more circuits; Figure 7–14 shows a typical multiple-circuit arrangement for a one-pipe system. Note that the circulating pump is not shown here. With one pump in the supply pipe, both circuits can be operated as one heating zone. However, with some piping modification and the introduction of a second circulating pump, the system

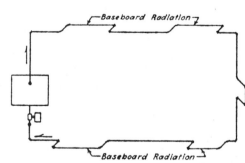

7–11. Series loop piping system. (The Hydronics Institute)

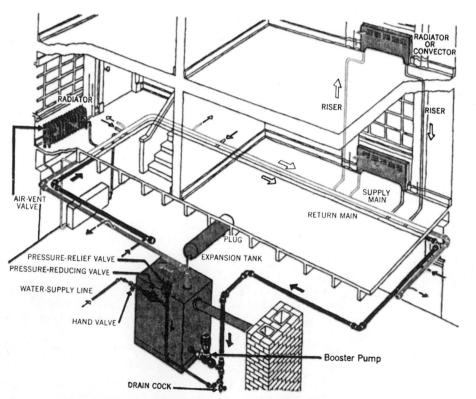

7–10. Typical two-pipe forced hot water system. (*Home Heating,* Farmers' Bulletin No. 2235, USDA)

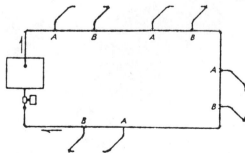

7–12. One-pipe system. (The Hydronics Institute)

180

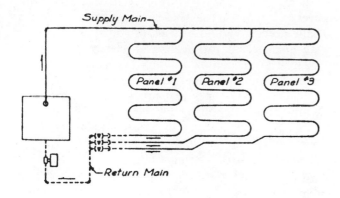

7-13. Simple panel piping system. (The Hydronics Institute)

could be set up in two zones. All piping layouts can be broken into two or more zones, a particularly useful arrangement in large or rambling houses. The number of zones in a forced hot water heating system is rarely more than three, but in actuality any number can be used.

The preferred piping material in American houses is copper. Though it is fairly expensive, it suffers little if any corrosion, is more pliable and easy to install than steel, and is smaller in diameter than ferrous pipe. However, steel and wrought iron are also used, particularly in floor radiant-heating layouts, snow-melting systems, and other outdoor ground-heating applications.

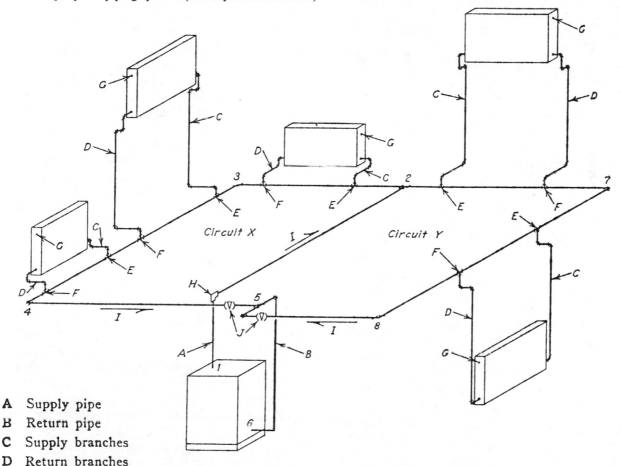

A   Supply pipe
B   Return pipe
C   Supply branches
D   Return branches
E   If one pipe fitting is designed for *supply* connection to heat distributing units, install here
F   If one pipe fitting is designed for *return* connection from heat distributing units, install here
G   Air vent on each unit
H   Flow control valve required if an indirect water heater is used and optional if an indirect water heater is not used
I   Direction of flow of water
J   Balancing cocks

Trunk: 1-2 and 5-6
Circuit **X**: 1-2-3-4-5-6
Circuit **Y**: 1-2-7-8-5-6
Circuit **Main (X)**: 2-3-4-5
Circuit **Main (Y)**: 2-7-8-5

2   Trunk split into two circuits
5   Circuits connected into return trunk

7-14.   One-pipe forced hot water heating system, multiple circuit. (The Hydronics Institute)

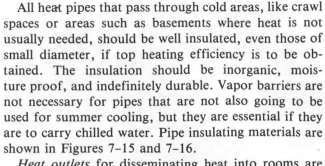

7-15. Wrap-type pipe insulation. (Duncan Photos)

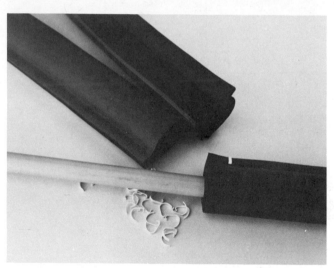

7-16. Preformed molded foam jacket type of pipe insulation. (Duncan Photos)

7-17. Typical hot-water convector unit. (*Home Heating,* Farmers' Bulletin No. 2235, USDA)

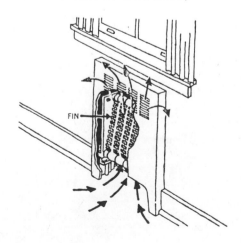

FIN

All heat pipes that pass through cold areas, like crawl spaces or areas such as basements where heat is not usually needed, should be well insulated, even those of small diameter, if top heating efficiency is to be obtained. The insulation should be inorganic, moisture proof, and indefinitely durable. Vapor barriers are not necessary for pipes that are not also going to be used for summer cooling, but they are essential if they are to carry chilled water. Pipe insulating materials are shown in Figures 7-15 and 7-16.

Heat outlets for disseminating heat into rooms are of four distinct varieties: radiators; convectors or radiator-convectors; baseboard radiant or radiant-convector strips; and floor, ceiling, or wall panels.

In the old days, radiators were the only method of distributing steam or hot water heat. In 1940, of all wet heat installations in houses, 70 percent used straight radiators; by 1950, the number had dropped to 8 percent. Convectors of various sorts largely replaced radiators, and now baseboard heating has largely replaced them both. Floor and ceiling panels are difficult and expensive to install and they have largely taken a back seat.

Convectors (Figure 7-17) are typically made up of a metal cabinet, with an opening at the bottom and louvered openings near the top, enclosing a series of finned tubes. As the hot water circulates through the tubes, air comes in through the bottom of the cabinet, passes over the tubes and fins, and transfers the heat into the room. Some types of convectors have low-volume circulating fans built into them, particularly useful for summer cooling when a chiller is added to the system. Convector units may be installed against an outside wall or recessed into the wall.

Baseboard units are shown in Figure 7-18. The unit on the left is a radiant strip, while the other two are radiant-convector strips. The advantages of these inconspicuous heat-distributing elements are obvious. They are almost invisible and can be painted to match any decorative scheme. They are designed to spread an even layer of heat across the lower part of the room, especially at the outer wall where it usually is coldest, and they will heat a well-insulated room uniformly, with little temperature difference between floor and ceiling. They also free wall or window space heretofore devoted to radiators or convectors for other uses.

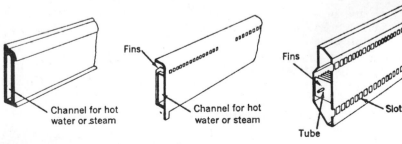

Fins

Fins

Channel for hot water or steam

Channel for hot water or steam

Slots

Tube

7-18. Typical baseboard radiation units. (*Home Heating,* Farmers' Bulletin No. 2235, USDA)

There are a couple of points to bring out concerning radiation versus convection. One is: Some air movement is desirable in any room. In older, all-radiator-heated houses, this movement is provided by wasteful infiltration through loose windows and doors. And indeed, this infiltration is by no means confined to old houses; unfortunately, many newer ones are afflicted with the same problem. However, in most modern, tightly built houses infiltration is reduced. Radiant heat in such a room can make it stifling if there is not enough air motion, and this is possibly one of the reasons for the popularity of convectors. Furthermore, since well-designed convectors beneath windows direct part of their flow of air across the glass area, the largest volume of cold entering the room, i.e., through the glass, is warmed before it has a chance to chill the occupants. Radiators do not perform the same task as well, since radiation is not directed, but takes place equally in all directions unless a special arrangement of fans is used—in which case the radiator is modified into a sort of *ad hoc* convector. There is, of course, some convection with a plain radiator, as the currents of hot air rise, but this is not enough air motion.

It must be noted that few conventional convectors have fans. The convection is natural in these outlets, not forced. It is often, therefore, only mildly effective as a means of distributing warmed air, when compared with forced warm air systems. Only special individual room units like the year-round hot-water heating/cooling convectors referred to above, have fans or blowers as an integral part of their construction. It should also be noted that in some instances (where houses equipped with radiation units or radiant/natural-convection units have been thoroughly weather-conditioned by the installation of insulation of vapor barriers, caulking, and weatherstripping) small low-volume fans have had to be introduced in order to provide enough air movement within the heated area to make the heat units effective and to help distribute the heat more or less uniformly. The loss of that infiltration that formerly caused air movement has resulted in some peculiar heating difficulties!

Radiant panel hot water heat, which is suitable for new construction only, has a number of advantages: there are no exposed radiation elements; the water in pipes is kept at relatively low temperatures (80° to 85° F in the floor, 105° to 110° F in the ceiling, and 110° to 115° F for the not-often-used wall panels). If walls are thoroughly insulated, room air temperatures need be no higher than 68° F, rather than around 74° F, since panel radiation delivers even heat from a large square-foot area throughout the room rather than, as with other types of radiant heat emitters, producing it in concentrated or narrow-strip flows. A 68° air temperature, plus radiant heat from a large area directly to the occupant, plus a relative humidity of 40 to 50 percent, will deliver what is probably the highest degree of human comfort possible under winter conditions.

But panel radiation also has its defects: It is the slowest of all systems to heat a room, since before the panels will radiate into the room they must heat up the material in which they are embedded (particularly true in floor panels embedded in concrete slabs); it is the slowest of all to cool for the same reason: the panel encasement will continue to radiate heat long after the need for it has ceased; ceiling radiation sometimes dries out and crumbles the plaster in which the pipes are embedded, and to avoid this the plaster over ceiling radiant panels should be formulated in accordance with Standard Specification ASA A42-1, available from either the American Standards Association or the American Society for Testing Materials; rugs, draperies, and furnishings sometimes upset the balance of floor panel systems; the need for air motion in rooms that are intensively used, such as kitchens, may not be satisfied by a panel system, and a convective unit, a fan, or a window opened a bit may be needed; and the high initial cost of installation must be considered. (However, in consideration of the comfort value gained in such an installation, in many cases the advantages outweigh the disadvantages.)

The best radiant panel systems are designed so that the water enters the panel at the outer perimeter of the wall (Figure 7-19) where it is coldest. Independent circuits for each major room, and sometimes more than one for a really large room, will keep cold zones from occurring toward the end of overlong circuits.

The decision on where to locate panel radiation should be based on several criteria. The first is heating efficiency; and here the ceiling panel seems to have the edge (Figure 7-20). In houses over heated basements, where cold floors are no problem, ceiling radiation would obviously be better. It is less expensive to install ceiling panels in such a house than to put them in floors, since floor pipes should be buried in concrete, and a concrete first floor is unnecessary over a basement. In a ceiling application, plaster is troweled on over the pipes in exactly the same way (except for the special formulation) as it is in conventional work.

If the house is to be built on a slab, the cost of floor radiation may be lower than it would be in the ceiling, since the concrete embedment for the pipes is part of the slab.

Copper tubing, or wrought iron or black steel pipes, can be used for any wet radiant heating system. Wrought iron and steel goes in floors, and copper tubes in ceilings, more often than not, but this is more a matter of convention than necessity. Copper tubing, being lighter, does put less of a load on the ceiling construction; it is also an easier material to work with and contains no leak-prone threaded connections, which is probably why it is used there more often than other materials.

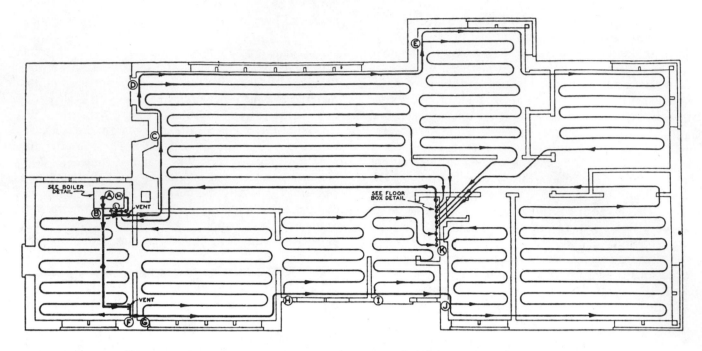

7-19. Typical piping plan for a floor panel heating system. (The Hydronics Institute)

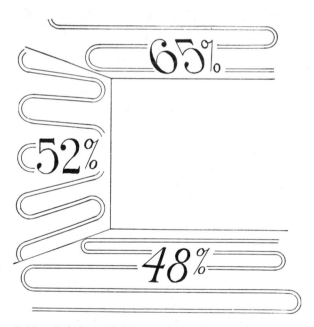

7-20. Relative efficiencies of panel heating systems. (Chase Brass & Copper)

7-21. Wrought iron piping for snow melting. (A. M. Byers Co.)

In general, wall radiation is suitable only for bathrooms and other areas where the ceiling or floor area alone is not large enough to deliver enough heat. It is not a good idea to use it in other rooms. Though there are some advantages to radiant wall panels, they are outweighed by disadvantages. For one thing, when people get too close to them they become overly conscious of heat only on one side of their bodies, which causes uncomfortable sensations. In addition, there is always the possibility that a wall pipe can be punctured much more easily by an errant picture-hanging nail, or some such, than would be the case with either floor or ceiling installations.

This does not, of course, apply to sidewall radiation in a bathroom for supplementary heat. The room is usually small, and the temperature differentials across it will not be large.

Copper tubing or steel or wrought iron pipe can also be used for snow-melting under driveways, front and side walks, and terraces, as in Figure 7-21. This pleasant addition to a house heating plant requires special valves, connections, and controls, and should be laid in strict compliance with the pipe manufacturer's instructions and under the direction of a heating engineer. The cost of such an installation is relatively high, as are the operating expenses, but on the other hand the level of convenience is high as well. Nor is the installation an energy-conservative one. However, neither of these considerations are likely to be factors with anyone who wants and can easily afford a snow-melting installation. The heating medium in the pipes or tubes, incidentally, must be separate from that in the house system, because it is necessary to include a proper amount of a permanent antifreeze in the liquid. Of course, if the house system is also filled with a similar solution, separation is not necessary. The antifreeze used in the systems must be of a proper, approved type; additives like kerosene or alcohol should never be introduced into the system.

HYDRONIC BASEBOARD SYSTEM

The electrically heated hydronic baseboard system is an effective and efficient means of heating a house. This arrangement consists of a series of fluid-filled baseboard radiation units which may be connected together to form a single-loop installation. Water is circulated through the entire system by a circulating pump, which, along with a compact set of controls, heat exchanger, expansion tank, and accessory items, may be wall-mounted at any convenient location (Figure 7-22). The individual baseboard units of a typical system, shown in Figure 7-23, contain separate heating elements, so that the circulating water will be maintained at a uniform temperature throughout the system. Though this is a central heating system in that many of the component parts of the system are centrally located, and single-point control is used for the entire system, it differs in that the heat source is not centrally located. This kind of arrangement has the advantage of being quite easily expanded if necessary.

GRAVITY WARM AIR SYSTEM

Everybody knows that warm air rises, and this principle can easily be put to work in a central gravity-type warm air heating system. In grandfather's day such installations were very common and were of the wood- or coal-fired variety (Figure 7-24). The furnace was located in the basement; and often as not the bonnet was positioned directly under a register and the warm air simply drifted upward into the living room space above. Two-story houses were fitted with floor registers cut through the first-floor ceilings, so that warm air would also be carried into the upper story. Meanwhile, the cold air would fall, by gravity, back to the lower regions of the house to be reheated.

The gravity furnace is still an efficient means of heating a small, well-insulated, compact home with a basement. Unlike forced warm air systems, the warm air outlets are installed on the inside walls of the house, with the return air inlets installed on outside walls. The direct register system is seldom used, and instead a rudimentary ducting system is installed (Figure 7-25).

7-23. Electrically heated hydronic baseboard system. (*Home Heating,* Farmers' Bulletin No. 2235, USDA)

7-22. Heat exchanger, expansion tank, and controls for an electrically heated hydronic system are especially compact. (*Home Heating,* Farmers' Bulletin No. 2235, USDA)

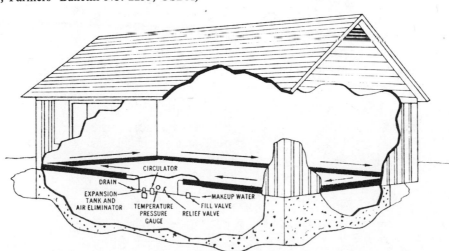

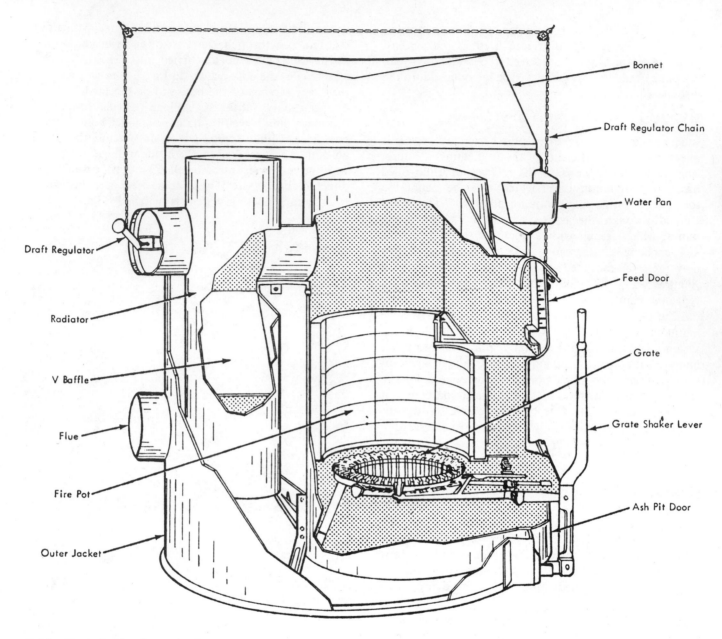

Bonnet

Draft Regulator Chain

Water Pan

Draft Regulator

Feed Door

Radiator

V Baffle

Grate

Flue

Grate Shaker Lever

Fire Pot

Outer Jacket

Ash Pit Door

7-24. Typical old-style gravity furnace. (Air Conditioning Contractors of America)

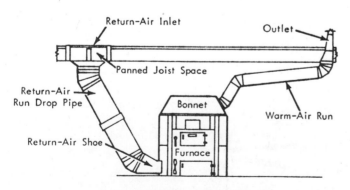

Return-Air Inlet

Outlet

Panned Joist Space

Return-Air
Run Drop Pipe

Bonnet

Warm-Air Run

Return-Air Shoe

Furnace

7-25. Basic elements of a gravity warm air heating system. (Air Conditioning Contractors of America)

The light warm air rises to the outlets, displacing the heavier, colder air which flows down through the return-air drop pipe and back into the furnace. Air circulation is continuous as long as there is a fire in the furnace.

Gravity furnaces can be fired by coal, gas, oil, or wood. Various elementary automatic controls can be added, but there is no blower. There are a good many drawbacks to this kind of system, of course, including the fact that cooling cannot be added. But there are occasions when a gravity system will serve rather well.

FORCED WARM AIR SYSTEM

Because of their many advantages over the gravity warm air system, forced warm air systems are almost universally used in preference to them in modern houses.

Furnaces for warm air heating are generally made of steel, with enameled steel cabinets. They are in one piece, at least in the domestic sizes, and in a variety of shapes and designs suitable for all types of fuels, air flow, and location. Figure 7–26 shows a "highboy" upflow unit for location in utility rooms. A typical gas-fired basement unit is shown on Figure 7–27, and a horizontal gas-fired unit for installation in attics or crawl spaces is shown in Figure 7–28. A downflow, or counterflow unit, in which the warm air is forced downward to supply airflow for duct systems, is shown in Figure 7–29. Though the system is generally used only in areas of low electric power costs, the electric upflow furnace (Figure 7–30) makes an excellent central heating plant. This unit makes a clean, neat, and unobtrusive installation, as can be seen in Figure 7–31. A similar arrangement can be achieved by installing special electric heaters (Figure 7–32) directly in the ductwork; this can be done to increase flexibility of the heating energy source utilized, or for supplementary heat capacity in a heat pump installation in extremely cold climates.

7–26. Typical upflow furnace. (Courtesy, Carrier Air Conditioning, a subsidiary of United Technologies Corporation)

7–27. Gas-fired basement furnace. (Courtesy, the Johnson Corporation, Division of Magic Chef, Inc.)

7–29. Oil-fired counterflow unit forces warm air downward into under-floor ductwork. (Courtesy, the Johnson Corporation, Division of Magic Chef, Inc.)

7–28. Gas-fired horizontal furnace for installation in attic or crawl space. (Courtesy, the Johnson Corporation, Division of Magic Chef, Inc.)

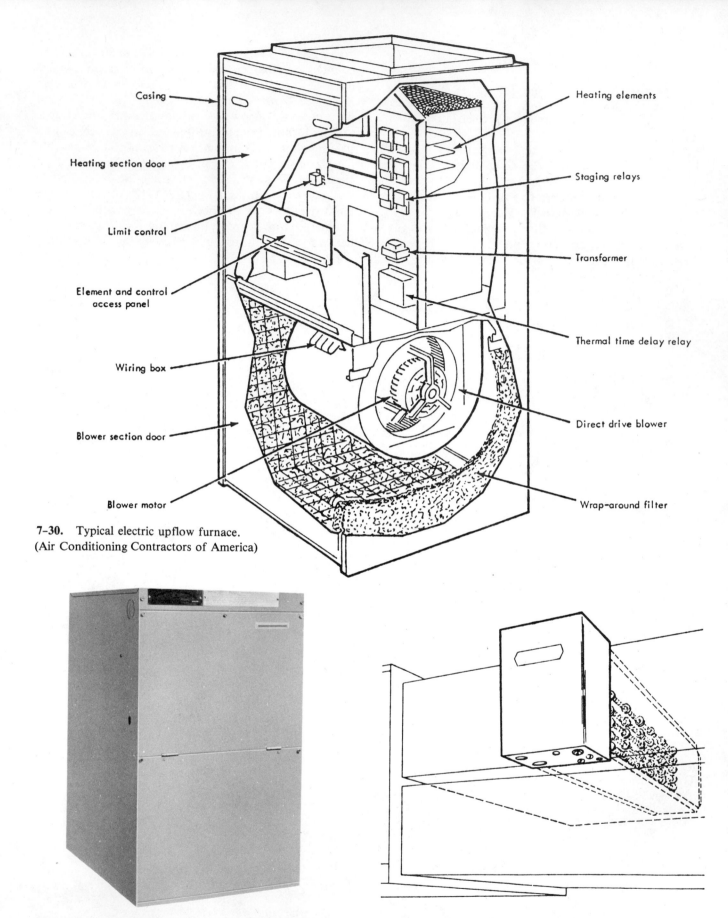

Casing

Heating section door

Limit control

Element and control access panel

Wiring box

Blower section door

Blower motor

Heating elements

Staging relays

Transformer

Thermal time delay relay

Direct drive blower

Wrap-around filter

7-30. Typical electric upflow furnace. (Air Conditioning Contractors of America)

7-31. Encased electric furnace for residential application. (Courtesy, the Johnson Corporation, Division of Magic Chef, Inc.)

7-32. Electric duct heater installed in duct. (Air Conditioning Contractors of America)

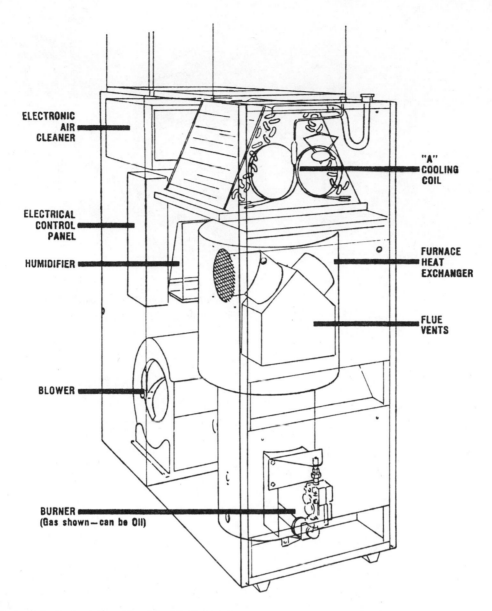

ELECTRONIC AIR CLEANER

ELECTRICAL CONTROL PANEL

HUMIDIFIER

BLOWER

BURNER
(Gas shown—can be Oil)

"A" COOLING COIL

FURNACE HEAT EXCHANGER

FLUE VENTS

7-33. Forced warm air furnace is equipped with electronic air cleaner and summer cooling coils. (*Home Heating,* Farmers' Bulletin No. 2235, USDA)

The prospective furnace purchaser should be aware that, from time to time, a great many cheap warm air furnaces are offered on this highly competitive market. It goes without saying that the small savings for one of these competitive units is soon wiped out in expensive repairs, heating inefficiency, and higher fuel costs. Furthermore, the cheaper units are noisy and sometimes dirty, and their controls may be so insensitive that wide variations in indoor temperature may occur, with resultant cold drafts and much human discomfort. In buying a warm air furnace, the best grade is a good investment at relatively small additional cost.

A point previously made in chapter 4 should be restated here; it has to do with built-in humidifying systems in residential warm air furnaces. These automatic humidifiers should never be operated during the first year or so of completion of the house, particularly if the house's walls are plaster. It will take at least that long for the structure to dry out, and adding humidity *before* this has happened can only increase the possibility of deterioration of the house.

Combined furnaces and summer cooling units in one package are readily available today, and for houses planned for year-round air conditioning such unitary designs have much merit. They have been carefully engineered for maximum operating efficiency and are almost wholly automatic (Figure 7-33). Details on the summer cooling side of these units are given later in this chapter.

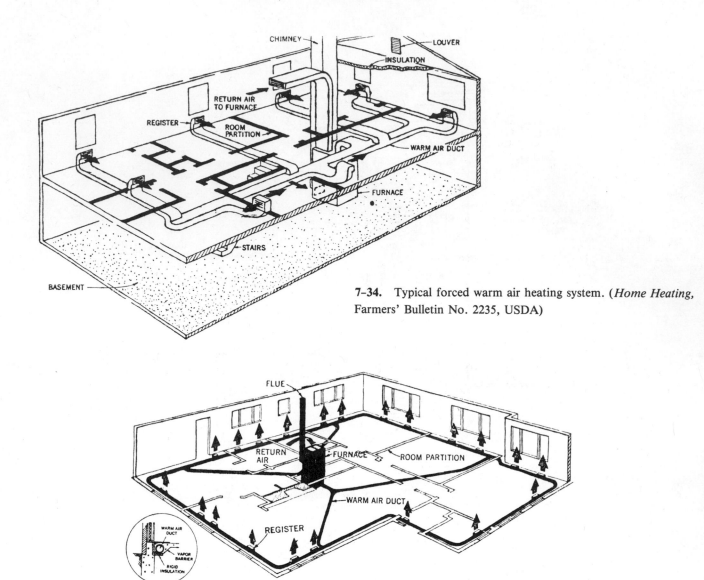

7-34. Typical forced warm air heating system. (*Home Heating,* Farmers' Bulletin No. 2235, USDA)

7-35. Perimeter loop heating system in a house built on a slab. (*Home Heating,* Farmers' Bulletin No. 2235, USDA)

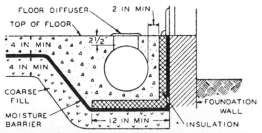

The minimum thickness of concrete over the loop duct should be 2.5 in., and continuous mesh reinforcing not less than 6×6—10 gage and 18 in. wide should be placed in the concrete and centered over the duct.

7-36. Cross section of perimeter heating system duct installed in concrete slab. (Reprinted with permission from the *1976 Systems Volume, ASHRAE HANDBOOK & Product Directory)*

Duct Systems. Duct systems for forced warm air circulation are of many varieties. The most efficient warm air distribution systems bring the air across the underside of the house to the outer walls, at the floor level. A number of designs for these perimeter installations have been developed over the years, and for cold-winter heating all are preferable to the overhead systems, where the supply registers are mounted high on the inside walls. If the furnace is in a basement, the standard upflow type is proper. But if the ductwork is in a floor slab or a crawl space, a downflow furnace like that in Figure 7–29 must usually be used. A typical residential ducting system is shown in Figure 7–34. For a house on a slab, the loop perimeter system (Figure 7–35) is both efficient and effective, if properly installed. Round ductwork is used in these systems, and Figure 7–36 shows a detail of how the ducts should be placed.

Filters. All warm air systems without exception use filters to remove dirt and impurities from the air before it enters the furnace to be heated. The standard filter supplied with most such systems is a disposable glass fiber unit (Figure 7-37) which should be replaced once or twice a year, or more often in polluted atmospheres. Also available are relatively low-cost washable filter units of various types. The impingement filter, for instance, is commonly made of woven aluminum mesh. Although this type of filter costs anywhere from twice to five times as much as the disposable variety, it will last almost indefinitely. The filtering element is held in a rigid metal frame and is coated before use with a sprayed-on dust-attracting filter coater, to which the dust particles in the air adhere, made especially for the purpose. For effective filtering, the unit should be washed periodically with soap and water, dried thoroughly, and then resprayed with filter coater in accordance with the manufacturer's instructions.

Electronic air cleaners, operating on the ionizing principle, provide far and away the highest efficiency in air cleaning, but at relatively high cost. They must be used where very pure air is essential from a medical point of view, as when there are sufferers from asthma or other bronchial allergies, and are advisable in any circumstances where the electronic cleaner's far greater efficiency makes the investment worthwhile. They are rated up to 90 percent efficient in the removal of pollen, tiny particles, and dust, whereas the standard disposable air filters are rated at 15 percent efficency in removing dust particles only. Obviously such a filter reduces housekeeping chores, lengthens the life of fabrics and furnishings, and greatly increases comfort and health, particularly in regions with polluted atmospheres.

The proper name of this air cleaning process is "electrostatic precipitation." As air passes through the ductwork in the heating/cooling system, it moves into the air cleaner and passes through an electrical field that is established between a series of electrodes and ionizing wires. The particulates in the airstream pick up a strong positive electrical charge. As the air moves into the collecting section of the cleaner, it enters another electrical field established between a series of metal plates that carry alternate negative and positive charges. The particulates, with their positive charges, are attracted to the negative-charged plates and stick fast (Figure 7-38).

Electronic air cleaners are automatic in operation but must be periodically cleaned. This is easily accomplished with the manual-wash electronic air cleaner of the type shown in Figure 7-39. All that is required is to periodically open the door of the unit, slide the electronic cell from the frame in the ductwork, soak the cell in detergent, rinse, and replace. Drying is not necessary, since the cleaner will go through a drying cycle automatically when it is returned to its position. Various kinds of automatic systems are also available,

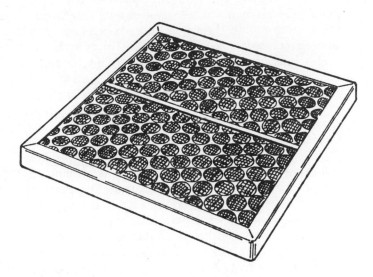

7-37. Disposable type of furnace filter. (Air Conditioning Contractors of America)

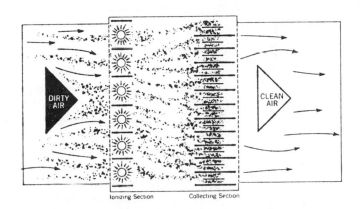

7-38. Electrostatic precipitation. (Air Conditioning Contractors of America)

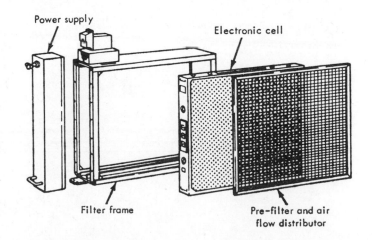

7-39. Manual-wash electronic air cleaner. (Air Conditioning Contractors of America)

wherein the electronic cell is periodically cleaned with a built-in hot water spray at periodic intervals. These may be semi-automatic and operated by a push button, or completely automatic and controlled by a time clock.

It is also possible, through the use of air system filtration, to combat a common problem in most households—that of odor. Odors from cooking, cleaning, smoking, pets, and a hundred other sources are present to one degree or another in nearly all houses; this is especially true in today's tight, practically infiltration-proof homes, where stale and odoriferous air may have a tendency to stay about for an annoyingly long period of time. This problem can be combated by the installation of a special type of ductwork filter containing activated charcoal as a filtering medium. The charcoal will absorb the unwanted odors, leaving the air clean and fresh-smelling. Charcoal filters must be used in conjunction with another filter that will remove particulates from the airstream; ordinary mesh-type dust filters are marginally effective, but it is strongly recommended that an electronic precipitator be used in order to keep the charcoal filter as clean as possible. In all cases, the charcoal filter must be installed a short distance downstream from the air cleaner, so that it receives only cleaned air.

Duct Materials for warm air systems are of many types. The most common still is galvanized steel, perhaps because of the price factor. However, sheet metal ducts are not always quiet, unless they are exceptionally well installed and, if necessary, fitted with acoustical insulation. But many other materials may be used in constructing ductwork.

Duct materials are classified by types, of which there are five. Ducts made of Type I materials will float when concrete is being poured, are subject to corrosion by concrete, and are noncombustible; an example is the galvanized sheet metal just mentioned. Ducts made of Type II material will also float when concrete is being poured, are *not* subject to corrosion by concrete, and are noncombustible; an example is stainless steel ductwork. Ducts made of Type III material will float when concrete is being poured, are subject to moisture transmission, and are combustible; examples of this type are laminated paper or organic fiber ducts, which must satisfy certain criteria having to do with crushing strength, deterioration, etc. Ducts constructed of Type IV material are subject to moisture transmission, are not subject to corrosion by concrete, will not float when concrete is being poured, and are noncombustible; examples of this type are ceramic and concrete pipe. Ducts made of Type V material are not subject to moisture transmission, are not subject to corrosion by concrete, will not float when concrete is being poured, and are noncombustible; an example is asbestos-cement pipe or ceramic pipe.

All of these various types and materials must conform to certain minimum criteria, and the ductwork manufactured from them must also fulfill certain requirements and meet certain standards, depending upon the specific application. Installation procedures also vary and are dependent upon particular job specifications.

Warm air radiant systems for floors of houses on concrete slabs are sometimes used, and prove very effective when properly constructed. The crawl space plenum system, which uses the entire crawl space as an integral supply or return chamber for heated air, gained some popularity in years past, but has since been discredited for several reasons and now is unacceptable heating practice. However, it is possible to use an extended plenum system whereby a warm air supply is fed into a properly prepared crawl space to warm that area and consequently the floor above as well, while an extended plenum type of trunk feeds additional warm air into the living quarters in the usual fashion. This gives a comfortably warm floor, making possible lower room

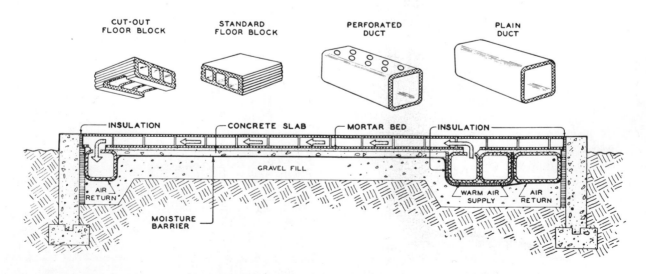

7-40. Schematic of a radiant warm air tile floor. (Natco)

air temperatures, just as with wet-heat radiant floors. Another radiant system consists of a floor made out of special structural clay tiles with a vitreous, exposable upper surface (Figure 7–40). In these floors the air temperature should be quite low, since the warm air is only half an inch or so under one's feet and is quickly conducted to the top surface of the tiles. Various other systems have also been devised for under-floor heating, particularly with respect to solar-heating installations.

Duct insulation is necessary whenever ducts pass through unheated spaces (attics and crawl spaces) without other thermal insulating protection. When ducts are run through dropped ceilings *under* a thick layer of attic insulation, no duct insulation is needed, of course. All insulation for ducts should be at least 1 inch thick. And when ducts are to be used for cool air in summer air conditioning systems, the insulation must be protected with a good vapor barrier on the outside.

Some ducts are self-insulating, and need no added material (except, in some instances, an outside vapor barrier—if it is not an integral part of the duct). There are several ducts of this type.

Warm air outlets, called grilles, registers, or diffusers, are available in a wide range of types and styles. Certain kinds of outlets are likewise used as inlets for cold air return ducts. They are available for installation in floors, walls, and ceilings. Many warm air outlets contain adjustable dampers with which the amount of air entering can be varied, its direction changed, and the whole house system balanced. An even better method of system balancing involves dampers in the ducts themselves. Of particular note is the type of return grill that includes an electronic air cleaner (Figure 7–41).

The correct application, engineering, and design of these various warm air distribution systems is extremely important if the system is to be effective and efficient. It should be emphasized that this book makes no attempt to present technical information on the layout of warm air systems—or of any heating or cooling systems at all, for that matter. That is beyond its scope. Such layouts present many highly technical and often obscure problems even to heating engineers, who spend a good share of their time solving various complex problems and answering numerous difficult questions concerning the engineering and design data of heating systems. Do not rely on the data in this chapter to provide answers to such questions!

HEAT PUMP SYSTEMS

The heat pump is a unique mechanism that is reversible to provide either heating or cooling. It operates along the lines of a mechanical refrigerating system when used for air cooling in the summer, and it is in this mode (Figure 7–42) that the system is most effective and efficient. However, when the effects of the evaporator and condenser are reversed, the heat pump absorbs heat from an outside source and raises it to a higher potential, to be employed for indoor winter heating (Figure 7–43). As previously noted, the efficiency of a heat pump in the heating mode diminishes as the temperature lowers, so in many installations an auxiliary heat source must be used in combination with it.

7–41. Air return grille incorporating electronic air cleaner. (Courtesy, Carrier Air Conditioning, subsidiary of United Technologies Corporation)

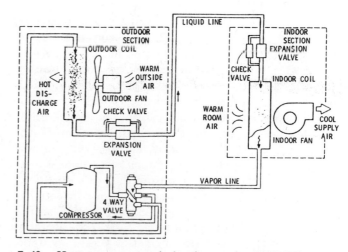

7–42. Heat pump system in heating mode. (USDOE)

193

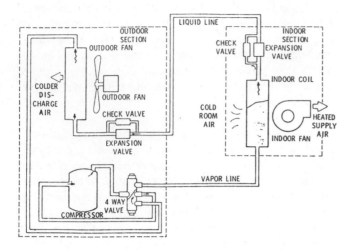

7-43. Heat pump system in cooling mode. (USDOE)

The most commonly used type of heat pump in this country is the *air-to-air* system, wherein heat is absorbed from outside air, upgraded, and then distributed indoors with air as a medium. However, other systems are also possible, and are in use; the most common of them are shown in Table 7-3.

The heart of a heat pump is a specially built compressor, which may be of the centrifugal, reciprocating, or rotary variety. In addition, there must be various heat exchange components, which are similar to heat exchangers used in present air conditioning practice. The refrigeration components, which include piping, receiving, expansion devices, and various accessories are also largely the same as those used in other types of air-conditioning and refrigeration systems. An air-source heat pump must also have a defrosting control system to rid the outdoor coil of accumulations of frost that periodically build up and reduce air flow. Supplementary electric resistant heaters may also be incorporated in the unit or placed in the ductwork. The heat distribution system within the house is constructed much along the lines of those previously discussed for hydronic and warm air heating systems, i.e., ductwork or piping; installation details vary considerably, of course, depending upon the specific job requirements.

As was pointed out earlier in the book, heating systems that are fueled by fossil fuels generally have a relatively low order of efficiency, which may vary anywhere from 40 to 80 percent or so. Electric resistance heating, on the other hand, has an efficiency of unity; all of the electrical energy going into a resistance heating unit comes out as heat—none is lost. For every watt of power consumed, 3.413 Btu/hr of heat is produced: no more, no less. Of the conventional heating systems, then, electric resistance heating has the best efficiency. But the heat pump can do considerably better than that. Its efficiency varies depending upon operating conditions, type of machine, and numerous other factors, but the system can indeed have an effi-

ciency of as much as 300 to 400 percent. This is often expressed as the Coefficient of Performance (COP), which is the ratio of useful heat output of the heat pump to the energy input to the pump, expressed in the same units. Thus, a heat pump can actually produce more heat than the energy required to power the unit represents. This is possible because the additional amount of heat is "free" and is extracted from the heat sink (earth, air, water, solar). To quote *Heat Pump Equipment Selection & Application,* Manual H (Air Conditioning Contractors of America, 1977): "The principal advantage of a properly sized and installed heat pump system is that it has lower energy use characteristics than any other conventional heating system. Another advantage is that it will have a lower cost of operation as compared to an electric resistance heating system (either baseboard, duct heater, or electric furnace). Depending on fuel prices, the heat pump may show an operating cost advantage over heating systems fueled solely with fossil fuels." The COP of a heat pump is not a constant, but rather it rises and falls throughout the heating season with the variations in temperatures. For this reason, a heat pump system must be evaluated in terms of the Seasonal Performance Factor (SPF). This is the ratio of the total system output of useful heat to the total energy input, for an entire heating season. The SPF is always lower than the best COP for a given heat pump installation, and yearly operating cost estimations must be based on the SPF.

The primary function of a heat pump actually is in cooling, and in order that proper temperature and humidity control can be achieved during the cooling season, a heat pump must be chosen on the basis of its cooling capacity. This nearly always means that the heat pump has insufficient capacity to properly meet the heating requirements of a house. This is the lesser of two evils; overcapacity in cooling means numerous difficulties, while undercapacity in heating can readily be made up with supplementary heat sources.

By graphing the effective heat loss of a house, the indoor design temperature, the design heat loss, and the outdoor design temperature it is possible to arrive at what is called the first thermal balance point. It is at this point on the graph where the heating capacity of the heat pump will be reached. The difference between this point and the total design heat loss must be made up from another source (Figure 7-44). This situation is particularly problematical in areas of severe winter conditions, and it has, in the past, rendered the heat pump essentially ineffective in those areas—other systems have been more frequently installed. However, the difficulty has been substantially overcome by new developments in the field—specifically a 2-stage or dual-compressor heat pump unit that extends the limit of operation to a considerably higher thermal balance point, and in many cases will be either totally or nearly sufficient to take care of the entire heating load of a

Common Heat Pump Types

HEAT SOURCE AND SINK	DISTR FLUID	THERMAL CYCLE	DIAGRAM
AIR	AIR	REFRIGERANT * CHANGEOVER	
AIR	AIR	AIR CHANGEOVER *	
WATER AIR	AIR WATER	REFRIGERANT * CHANGEOVER	
EARTH	AIR	REFRIGERANT * CHANGEOVER	
WATER	WATER	WATER CHANGEOVER *	

* ALL SINGLE STAGE COMPRESSION

Table 7-3.   (Reprinted with permission from the *1976 Systems Volume, ASHRAE HANDBOOK & Product Directory*)

house (Figure 7–45). Such a unit is pictured in Figure 7–46; the grilled cylindrical unit is the outdoor section of the pump, while the remaining two cabinets are installed within the house.

Developmental work on heat pump systems is proceeding rapidly, and the changes are that in the near future such systems will come into widespread use all over the country. Evidence of this continued development can be seen in the solar-assisted heat pump system diagramed in Figure 7–47. Here, the sun's heat is collected and carried to the water storage tank, and is then transferred as needed to the coil. When the water temperature is sufficiently high, a fan transfers the air into the house by means of a ductwork system. If the water temperature is insufficient, the heat pump automatically takes over, extracting heat from the outdoor air, compressing it and elevating its temperature in the indoor compressor section, and then transferring it

to the coil for distribution into the house. In the event that neither the heat pump nor the solar collector can provide sufficient heat to meet the heating requirements of the house, a standby electric heater takes over and provides supplemental heat. Note that water is also taken from the water storage tank and transferred to a heat exchanger to preheat the domestic hot water

7-46. Two-stage heat pump system has increased effectiveness in cold-weather heating. (Courtesy, Carrier Air Conditioning, subsidiary of United Technologies Corporation)

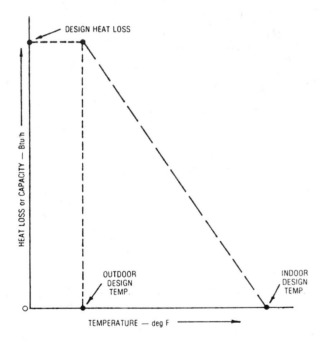

7-44. Heat pump heating system first balance point. (Air Conditioning Contractors of America)

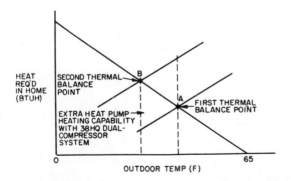

7-45. Heat pump system second balance point for a two-stage unit. (Courtesy, Carrier Air Conditioning, subsidiary of United Technologies Corporation)

SOLAR-ASSISTED HEAT PUMP

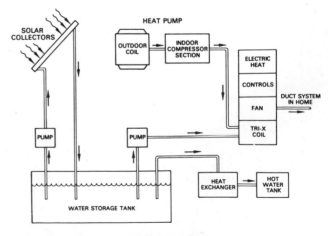

7-47. Schematic of solar heat pump system. (Courtesy, Carrier Air Conditioning, subsidiary of United Technologies Corporation)

supply, thus reducing the cost of domestic water heating. Such symbiotic relationships of various heating methods, devices, and sources will become more and more commonplace in the future years.

SOLAR HEATING SYSTEMS

The principle of solar heating is disarmingly simple: Just gather up all that lovely free heat from the sun, bring it indoors, and spread it around. But the mechanics of solar heating can be extremely complex, the array of equipment and accessories produced for the purpose is seemingly endless, and at present the state of the art is in somewhat of a turmoil. Even a sketchy investigation of the field would be well beyond the scope of this book. In any case, there is currently a plethora of information available on the subject, covering it in every possible (and doubtless some impossible) detail. Any library or bookstore, however small, can surely produce at least two or three volumes for the interested reader to peruse. But in order to round out our picture of heating systems, it is necessary for us to look briefly at some solar basics.

The basis of a solar heating system is not merely collection of solar heat for immediate warmth, but also proper distribution of that heat for effective, comfortable, whole-house heating, as well as storage of the collected heat for use when the sun is not shining. Solar heating methods can be broken down into three basic categories.

The first is the *direct solar* method, which turns the house into a sort of greenhouse. The house itself is used as a solar collector by allowing sunshine in through extensive glass areas. The house then becomes a heat storehouse. Heavy insulation prevents the escape of undue amounts of heat, and heavy, massive building materials store the heat within the house envelope for reradiation into the living space after the sunlight disappears and cooling begins.

The second method is most commonly called *passive solar,* or integrated solar, and a good many ingenious systems have been developed along these lines. The method makes use of natural thermal properties of materials of all kinds, both building materials and otherwise. In this situation, sunshine is admitted into the living area through windows, but also heat is directly absorbed by drums of water, huge water bags located on the rooftop, massive concrete walls or floors, or what have you. The solar components actually are built into, and frequently are indistinguishable from, the house itself. Simplicity of system is a watchword with this method, and though house designs are likely to be somewhat different, even radical, nonetheless they are extremely efficient from a thermal standpoint when properly constructed. In addition, they use few if any mechanical devices, electrical or other power, or automatic controls to collect, store, and distribute heat.

The third variety is commonly called *active solar,* or sometimes indirect. This system is far more complex than the other two types, since it relies largely upon high-technology equipment and controls for collection, storage, and distribution of the heat. Such systems are also far more expensive and much more prone to failure of one sort or another. The system operates by first collecting solar heat in special collectors, whence it is moved via piping or ductwork by pumps or fans into a heavily-insulated storage container such as a tank of water or a vault of rock. More piping or ductwork and more fans or pumps, as well as temperature sensing controls, are required to distribute the heat from storage to the living area as needed.

In most instances, an auxiliary heating system or a supplementary heat source must be included to meet the overall heating needs of the solar house. Such systems may be complete heating systems of a conventional kind, or area unit heaters of more or less conventional design, or perhaps just a wood stove. Auxiliary heating means used with active solar heating systems are quite often integrated into the solar system by means of yet more controls, piping, and ductwork.

A great many existing houses can take some advantage of solar heat by making a few minor structural changes and by the addition of certain kinds of solar equipment. For the most part, though, for maximum utilization of solar energy the house must be specifically designed and constructed with that particular fact in mind. While most conventional mechanical heating systems are simply add-ons, any one of which can be installed in one fashion or another in virtually any house, the same simply is not true of solar heating systems. To be fully effective, the heating system and the house must be totally integrated. The heating system is the house, and the house is the heating system.

As can be seen from Figure 7–48 the direct gain system is by far the simplest. Sunlight comes in through the glass, turns directly into heat, and some of that heat is stored in the concrete (or other) mass. To increase thermal efficiency, the glass should be covered with an insulating material at night.

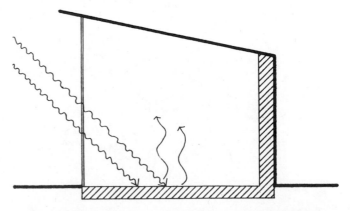

7-48. Simple direct gain solar heating system. (USDOE)

A passive-system thermal storage wall is shown in Figure 7-49; the wall is made of concrete about a foot thick, and it is painted a dark color. As the sun passes through the glass and strikes it, the wall heats up; heat is radiated directly into the living space, and an air flow can be arranged by constructing ports at the top and bottom of the wall. Dampers can be installed to prevent a nighttime reverse air flow that would cool the space. Insulating shutters are used to cover the glass at night to reduce heat loss. Two somewhat similar arrangements can be made by building a water drum thermal storage wall (Figure 7-50), usually referred to simply as a drum wall, or by installing a thermal curtain and water tube storage system, as shown in Figure 7-51.

Active solar heating systems are of a much higher level of complexity and technology. The initial cost of such a system, however, may or may not be more than that of an integrated or passive system when the whole-house costs are taken into consideration. Operating costs, of course, are indeed higher. Perhaps the most important, and often the most obvious, part of an active solar system is the collector. An exploded cross section of a typical collector is shown in Figure 7-52. In the interest of efficiency, as well as for varying applications, there are a good many different collector designs, and a multitude of minor variations in construction and materials used (Figure 7-53). Some of them use air as a

collecting medium, while others use liquid. A typical complete single-family residential heating system is shown in simplified schematic form in Figure 7-54.

Such systems have now been developed to a relatively high degree and are coming into widespread use throughout the country. In due course, they will doubtless play a prominent part, in any number of

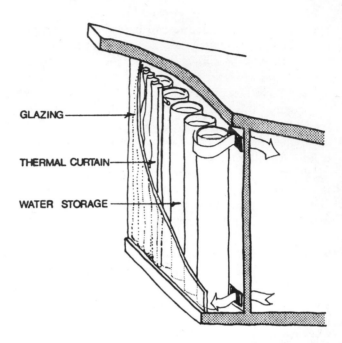

7-51. Solar heating system using water tube heat storage. (USDOE)

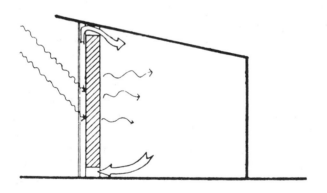

7-49. Solar heating system employing thermal storage wall. (USDOE)

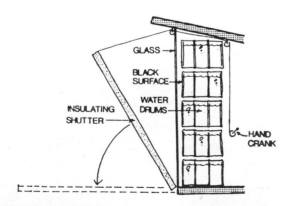

7-50. Solar heating system employing drum wall for heat storage. (USDOE)

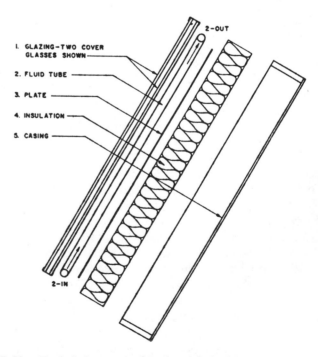

7-52. Exploded cross section through double-glazed solar collector. (Reprinted with permission from the *1978 Applications Volume, ASHRAE HANDBOOK & Product Directory*)

198

specific variations, in our residential heating applications. In fact, more advanced, integrated systems such as the one installed in the NASA Tech House (a contemporary experimental residence constructed at the Langley Research Center in Hampton, Virginia, a few years ago by the National Aeronautics and Space Administration) will probably be more the rule than the exception (Figure 7-55).

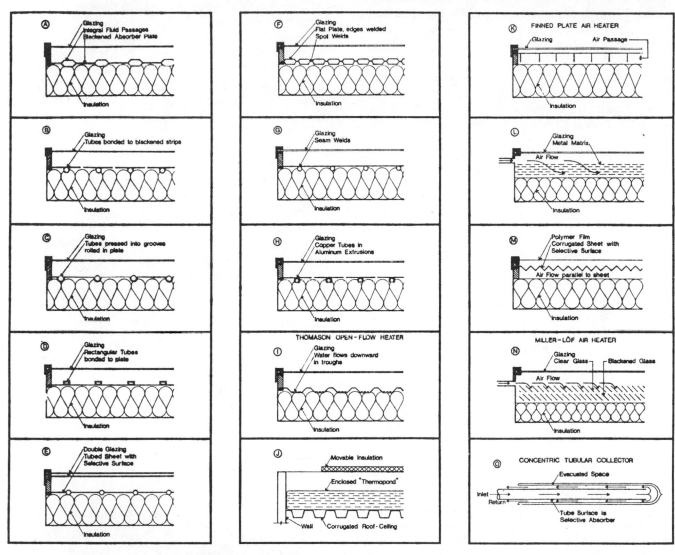

7-53. Variations of solar collectors employing both water and air as collecting media. (Reprinted with permission from the *1978 Applications Volume, ASHRAE HANDBOOK & Product Directory*)

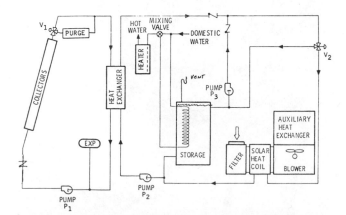

7-54. One of many variations of a typical solar heating system. (USDOE)

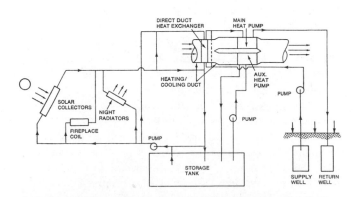

7-55. Simplified diagram of solar heating and cooling system as installed in the NASA Tech House. (NASA)

Area Heating Systems

Area heating systems are oftentimes less systems than they are collections of comfort space heating units, sometimes rather diverse, that can be used singly or in concert to achieve whatever degree of house heating is needed at any given moment. Unlike central heating systems, there is no single source of heat, no centralized mechanical equipment, and no distribution system *per se*. This type of heating has a number of advantages. The initial cost is generally fairly low, installation is simple enough and also usually inexpensive, and, for the most part, maintenance of the equipment is also minimal. There is a great deal of flexibility in area heating systems: heat output can be regulated or controlled from area to area as required; the units themselves can be entirely different from one another as regards size, type, fuel and so on; units can be completely shut down when not needed; and units can be added in whatever manner is most convenient if the living quarters are expanded. Space heating units can also be tailored to exactly fulfill whatever needs are paramount at the moment. There are drawbacks, too, of course, and chief among them is the fact that, except in one instance (the unit heat pump), mechanical cooling must be accomplished by other means, since it cannot be made integral with the area heating system. However, many homeowners find that the advantages of this type of heating far outweigh the disadvantages.

FIREPLACES

With the advent of central heating and cheap fuels, these old, traditional means of heating a house became largely ornamental rather than functional and were seldom used for anything other than spasmodic enjoyment. In recent years, however, many people have turned to using their fireplaces in an attempt to augment their conventional heating systems and to reduce the cost of heating system operation. For the most part, that effort is a futile one.

Virtually all existing open masonry fireplaces must be classed as among the biggest heat wasters in the house. If the fireplace has a large, open flue with no damper, vast quantities of heat that is produced by the conventional heating system simply sails right up the flue and is exhausted to the outdoors, increasing rather than decreasing heating costs. Fireplaces that have dampers are better, but are still heat wasters. Because of their construction, most of the heat generated when the fireplace is operating goes up the chimney rather than into the room. Average operating efficiency when a fireplace is used only occasionally is estimated to be just about 0 percent, and in many cases, because the damper must be left open for a period of time after the fire has died down and no longer produces much heat, there may well be a net loss of heat. If the fireplace is used on a more or less continuous basis, efficiency may run from approximately 15 percent to 35 to 40 percent; part of this is due to the fact that the masonry mass of the chimney will eventually warm up and radiate into the living space some of the heat that would otherwise be lost up the chimney. But in all cases, fireplaces will burn anywhere from five to ten times as much wood to produce the same amount of useful heat as an efficient wood-burning stove.

However, recent developments in the field have made it possible for the owners of existing fireplaces to upgrade the installation by the addition of various kinds of equipment that allow a considerably greater useful heat production and the consumption of less fuel. For instance, tube grates or similar accessories can be installed directly in the fireplace opening (Figure 7–56) with no effort whatsoever. As the fire burns, cold air is pulled in through the bottoms of the tubes, passes through the heated tubes, and is expelled into the room as hot air from the orifices at the top. For a small additional amount of work and expense, such accessories can be equipped with small blowers, so that the air is forcibly sucked through the tubes and exhausted into the living space as hot air in much greater volume.

One can also add heat-proof glass doors in a tight-fitting decorative frame that mounts across the face of the fireplace opening. A drawback to glass doors is that they must frequently be cleaned, but they do apparently improve the net efficiencies of most fireplaces, particularly by preventing the escape of warm interior air up the flue when the fire is very low or out. And, of course, they provide a fine safety factor that is well worth considering. Such a unit equipped with a blower and/or tube grate (Figure 7–57) will do much to improve the efficiency of a fireplace.

A different situation obtains in cases where the intent is to construct a new fireplace. There are masonry

7-56. Tubular grate assembly for installation in an existing fireplace opening. (Courtesy, Envirostyle Direct)

fireplace designs that are very efficient and that can provide the decorative features of a fireplace as well as a reasonable amount of supplementary heat. The Count Rumford fireplace is one example, and the massive Russian type, which has a particularly high efficiency (comparatively speaking), is actually capable of heating a sizable volume of living space, and can be used for cooking and baking as well, is another example. Much work has also been done with unconventional massive masonry designs of fireplaces that outwardly appear to be rather conventional.

7-57. Tubular grate, blower, and glass door installation for existing fireplace. (Courtesy, Envirostyle Direct)

For those who wish to build an ordinary-looking fireplace installation, the prefabricated circulating fireplace shell makes an excellent starting point. These steel units are designed to be emplaced on a masonry base, following which the masonry is built up around them. They can be obtained with numerous different accessories; they are frequently equipped with blowers, cold air inlets, tight-fitting glass doors, various damper and control arrangements; and they often use outside air for combustion. Even accessory water heaters are available. These installations are potentially as efficient and effective as freestanding wood/coal stoves when properly installed and operated.

The freestanding metal fireplace has become relatively popular over the past few years, and it has the advantage of simplicity of installation: Since it needs only a proper hearth and backboard and a metal chimney package, the installation can be made by the homeowner himself. The efficiency of such fireplaces is rather low, but by and large is considered to be better than that of conventional open masonry fireplaces.

They do consume substantial quantities of wood, but they also radiate substantial quantities of heat from their metal bodies. These units are available in a great many decorator styles and in several sizes.

For those who wish to retrofit an existing conventional fireplace to achieve far greater efficiency and heat production than is possible with even tube grates and similar fireplace accessories, the answer is a fireplace insert unit. This consists of what is actually a closed wood stove that is set within the masonry fireplace opening or on the hearth and connected to the fireplace flue, with a faceplate surround installed to close off the gap between the unit and the fireplate walls. These units are available in many sizes and styles, and they can be fitted to virtually any conventional fireplace. They have a sufficient degree of efficiency and heat-producing capability to make an excellent auxiliary heat source.

WOOD/COAL STOVES

These were of equal importance to fireplaces as sources of comfort heating in early-day homes, and largely succeeded them as designs and availability improved during the 1800s. However, like fireplaces, both heating and cooking stoves were largely dispensed with as new and inexpensive fuels and central heating systems came into being. But suddenly, wood/coal stoves have created a great stir throughout the country as an inexpensive and effective (and also nostalgic) means of providing auxiliary or supplementary heat. Indeed, the demand for these units has become so great that an entire new industry in stoves and stove-related products has grown up practically overnight, and the consumer can today choose from dozens of different brands that encompass a tremendous variety of stove types and designs (Figure 7-58).

Wood/coal stove technology, designs, efficiencies, combustion methods, operating characteristics, flue designs, and a host of other details are lengthy and complex, not to mention somewhat confusing, and are well outside the scope of this book; the reader should refer to volumes specifically devoted to this subject for comprehensive information. However, there are a few basic points that should be brought forth here.

Perhaps the most important one is that the person who is contemplating the purchase and installation of a wood/coal stove should thoroughly investigate the field before proceeding. A successful, efficient, and worthwhile installation depends upon a great many different factors, and knowledge of the subject is the best defense against possible disappointment. Much also depends upon the way in which stoves are operated, insofar as heat production, efficiency, and safety are concerned, and the prospective stove owner would do well to learn as much as possible about these details. None of these units are automatic, and they must be operated manually.

7-58. One of many typical wood stoves currently available. (Courtesy, Envirostyle Direct)

Expectable efficiencies of wood/coal stoves run anywhere from about 40 percent to as high as 80 percent under optimum conditions; the average is probably somewhere around the 50 percent mark, though there is no way to make a definite ascertainment. The efficiency, and the production of useful heat, is dependent to some degree upon the type of stove, which can be roughly broken down into three categories. Generally speaking, the nonairtight or "open" stove, sometimes called the "Franklin" type, will have the lowest efficiency range, largely due to air leakage into the stove through the unsealed joints. Airtight stoves (which are not *fully* air tight) have considerably greater efficiencies, and they are currently the most popular. Circulating stoves, the third category, also have a relatively high degree of efficiency. The reader must realize, however, that efficiency and heat production of stoves are dependent upon a great many additional factors.

There are two further points of note. The first is that, in choosing a stove for a particular application, the buyer should have some realistic idea of how much heat output he wants and how much area, or volume, must be heated, and to what degree. There is a definite tendency to buy a stove that is actually oversized by a substantial amount, which invariably leads to excessive heat production, or inefficient, low-grade burns, the use of more fuel than is necessary, and various other problems that ultimately lead to dissatisfaction with the unit.

The second point is that wood stoves are often erroneously considered by their owners to be wood/coal stoves. This is seldom the case, and burning coal in most wood stoves is a potentially dangerous practice that can lead to all manner of difficulty. If a stove is designated as a wood stove and contains a wood-burning grate (or no grate at all), it should be used only for burning wood. If the stove is designated as wood/coal, it probably will be fitted with a coal-type grate, which is of considerably smaller mesh than a wood grate, and the manufacturer's literature will doubtless spell out the fact that the stove can indeed be used with coal. If the unit is designated as a coal stove, of course coal can be fired in it with no compunctions, and wood can be used as well.

A final word of caution—in fact, a warning. The installation of wood/coal stoves, and their attendant metal appliance chimneys, is a relatively simple job. It is a job that has been enthusiastically undertaken by home mechanics and do-it-yourselfers all over the country. But that simplicity has been misleading for many people, because the sad fact is that probably half, and maybe more, of the wood/coal stove installations in this country are thoroughly unsafe and are nothing less than house fires waiting for a good opportunity to start. An improperly installed stove installation can be extremely dangerous, and the job must be done just right to avoid future problems. Any person desiring to make his own stove installation should thoroughly check all of the details, particularly with regard to fire safety, and know exactly what he is about before he begins (see also chapter 9).

SPACE HEATERS

These are familiar to practically everyone, and not much needs to be said about them. They are available in an incredible profusion of styles, sizes, and heat output ratings, and they are available in department and hardware stores everywhere. Perhaps the most popular are the small portable electric heaters, some of which are purely radiant and others of which include a small, low-volume fan to convey heat away from the unit. However, other styles and fuels are available as well: the electrically operated quartz heaters, kerosene heaters, catalytic units, propane-fueled units, and so on.

The chief use of space heaters is for short-term auxiliary or supplementary heat in specific and usually small areas, and they are particularly helpful on those few extra-cold days of the year when the total heat load of the house exceeds the capacity of the main heating system.

ELECTRIC AREA HEAT

This is undoubtedly the most popular kind of area heating, perhaps because of its great flexibility and the wide variety of devices that can be used to provide the heat. Electric resistance heating is a special variation of dry heat that uses centrally generated power rather than a primary fuel. In certain parts of the country where the average rate per kilowatt hour of electricity energy is relatively low, it can compete fairly well with most fuels. This is especially true when savings in construction resulting from the use of electric heating units are taken into account. These days there are few regions with relatively low electric rates. However, some people want electric heat even though operating costs may be higher than for the more conventional fuels. The reasons are easy to state.

With a *fully* insulated house, plus double- or triple-glazed and weatherstripped windows and doors, the operating cost of electric heat is bearable enough even though it may still be higher than for other energy sources; on the other hand, in some areas it may be comparable or even a bit less.

Electric heating systems are generally cheaper to install than conventional heat. There are no furnaces or boilers, no ducts or pipes, no chimneys, no complicated pumps, fans, and other controls, except thermostats. Maintenance costs are almost nil. There is nothing to get out of order except the thermostats, though very occasionally a heating element may go bad.

Electric heat units are very unobtrusive, for the most part, and take up little space. In addition, they can generally be positioned so that they do not interfere with furnishings.

Electric heat is quiet, fire-safe if correctly designed, as clean as an electric light bulb, and very rapid in its response to heating demand.

Against electric area heating is the fact that air cleaning and circulation as well as humidity control are not parts of electric resistance heating systems. Independent forms of cleaning and ventilation will be required, and dry winter air may call for separate humidifying devices. Furthermore, a separate summer cooling system is necessary. Electric heating systems are listed in Table 7-4. The more common ones are described below.

Wires or cables in the ceiling (Figure 7-59) provide an invisible and safe heating system. Floor cables are almost as easy to put in, except that they must go under the floor, embedded in a layer of concrete. This makes them suitable only for new construction and mainly for new houses on slabs. Embedded resistance heating cables are also suitable for snow melting installations (Figure 7-60), although the cost of operation is something to be reckoned with; and cables of a slightly

Principal Types of Electric Space Heating Systems

Decentralized Systems

A. Natural Convection Units
  1. Floor drop-in heaters
  2. Wall insert and surface mounted heaters
  3. Baseboard convectors
  4. Hydronic baseboard convectors with immersion elements

B. Forced Air Units
  1. Unit ventilators
  2. Unit heaters
  3. Wall insert heaters
  4. Baseboard heaters
  5. Floor drop-in heaters

C. Radiant Units (high intensity)
  1. Radiant wall, insert or surface mounted; open ribbon or wire element
  2. Metal-sheathed element with focusing reflector
  3. Quartz tube element with focusing reflector
  4. Quartz lamp with focusing reflector
  5. Heat lamps
  6. Valance heaters

D. Radiant Panel-Type Systems (low intensity)
  1. Radiant ceiling with embedded conductors
  2. Pre-fabricated panels
  3. Radiant floor with embedded conductors
  4. Radiant-convector panel heaters

Centralized Systems

A. Heated Water Systems
  1. Electric boiler
  2. Electric boiler, with hydronic off-peak storage
  3. Heat pumps
  4. Integrated heat recovery systems

B. Steam Systems
  1. Electric boiler, immersion element or electrode type

C. Heated Air Systems
  1. Duct heaters
  2. Electric furnaces
  3. Heat pumps
  4. Integrated heat recovery systems
  5. Unit ventilators
  6. Self-contained heating and cooling units

Table 7-4. (Reprinted with permission from the *1976 Systems Volume, ASHRAE HANDBOOK & Product Directory*)

7-59. Plastering over electric radiant ceiling wires. (General Electric Co.)

7-60. Electric resistance wiring for snow melting. (Edwin L. Wiegand Co.)

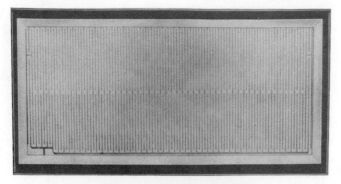

7-61. Glass radiant electric heating panel. (Courtesy, Continental Radiant Glass Heating Corporation)

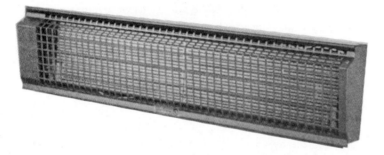

7-62. Glass radiant electric baseboard panel. (Courtesy, Continental Radiant Glass Heating Corporation)

7-63. Convective electric heating panel. (Westinghouse Electric Co.)

different type can be installed to keep roof eaves and guttering free from ice during the winter.

Radiant glass panels provide economical electric radiant heat and are particularly appropriate as backup units in solar heat installation. Glass panels are available for installation on baseboards, walls, or ceilings, and they come in numerous sizes, styles, shapes, and wattages. Some contain integral thermostat units, while others are designed to be attached to separate wall thermostats. Typical units are shown in Figures 7-61 and 7-62. Because they are surface-mounted, full insulation thickness can be maintained in the walls behind them.

Electric wall heaters of the convection type are also available. These units, which include a fan along with the resistance coils (both protected from prying hands by a metal grill (Figure 7-63) have a very large output—4,000 watts (13,660 Btu/hr) from a 15 by 22 inch wall area is typical. Of course, the blast of hot air may be uncomfortable unless the grill has fins that direct the hot air upwards or that are adjustable.

Electric baseboards are available in a convective style as well as in radiant glass. The appearance is that of any convective metal baseboard; though this type of unit delivers more heat, length for length, than glass radiant baseboard panels, the larger convective currents can cause dust streaks.

Calculating electric heat loads involves converting kwhr rating into Btu/hr figures, since most electric heat equipment is sold on a wattage basis. A kilowatt contains 3,413 Btu. For a house with a calculated heat loss of 45,000 Btu/hr, the heat loss in kwhr would be 45,000 divided by 3,413, or about 13.2 kwhr.

To estimate annual electric heating costs, proceed as outlined in chapter 3, except that a constant must be figured into the final calculations. The ASHRAE recommends that until a better method for calculating seasonal heat losses for electrically heated houses is developed, the formula taken from the NEMA *Manual for Electric Comfort Conditioning* be used. This formula is stated:

$$kwh = \frac{(HL) \times (DD) \times C}{(TD)}$$

where

kwh = annual kilowatt-hour consumption.
C = constant.
HL = heat loss of residence in kilowatts (Btu/hr divided by 3415).
DD = annual degree days.
TD = difference between indoor and outdoor design temperature, ° F.

The constant, C, is called an experience factor and it is dependent upon several variables: the type of equipment chosen, how frequently outside doors are open, orientation and design of the house, and so on. Further information can be obtained from the NEMA *Manual* cited above. Experience has shown that a figure of 17 is not atypical, and in that case, the calculation for the house mentioned previously would be as follows:

$$\frac{13.2 \; (kw \; \text{heat loss}) \times 4,626 \; (\text{deg days}) \times 17 \; (C)}{70° \; F \; (\text{temp diff})}$$

or 14,830 annual kwhr. The degree-day number, 4,626, was chosen by the simple expedient of locating our example house in the city of Washington, D.C.

The constants used in this and similar formulas depend primarily upon the different types of electric heating equipment, but also on less ponderable variables: differences in climates, location and design of house, and living habits of the occupants, among others. There obviously is some inaccuracy in estimating annual electric heating costs; but then this is also true with calculations for more usual forms of heat.

HEAT PUMP AREA UNITS

These are comparatively new on the area or space heating scene. As can be seen in Figure 7-64, the unit looks much like an ordinary window-mounted air conditioner. It is, however, a complete, through-the-wall heat pump installation that, unlike other area units, can be used for both heating and cooling. This sort of heat pump system is ideal for use as a backup to another type of heating system; for primary heating and cooling in a relatively small area; for primary cooling and auxiliary heat for an area supplied with another type of heat but no cooling; or as heating and cooling in an addition to a house where an extension of the existing conventional heating system is impractical or impossible.

7-64. Through-the-wall heat pump unit. (Courtesy, Carrier Air Conditioning, subsidiary of United Technologies Corporation)

COOLING SYSTEMS

As with most other products in the building trades area these days, there is a proliferation of cooling units and distribution systems that makes the task of selection a confusing one; and price competition, as usual, engenders a good many inadequately engineered and poorly built units in the marketplace.

If there is one major rule to follow in buying residential cooling systems, it is this: use only equipment from a well-known, responsible manufacturer; insist on a performance guarantee or warranty against defects; and make sure installation instructions are meticulously followed. Installation should either be done by the supplier or, at least, be approved in writing by him.

Cooling System Principles

These are basically the same, whatever the type. With the exception of the extremely rare layout that uses naturally cold water from the ground or from municipal supplies, all systems include a refrigeration cycle that reduces air temperatures and humidities either directly, as with "dry" air conditioners, or indirectly, by chilling water and then circulating it to individual room convectors.

There are five basic methods of cooling air or water: compression, which is used in nearly all house cooling systems; absorption, with gas or oil as the energy producer, which is used to only a limited degree in houses; ice, in which air is actually blown over a mass of ice to cool it and, except in an extremely rare instance, is of no value for residential cooling; and the heat pump, basically the same as a compression system. The last, evaporative coolers, are usable only in those regions of the country where the climate is extremely dry during the hot season; these units reduce indoor temperatures by evaporating moisture by means of a fan blowing air through a water spray or drip, thus raising indoor humidity, which in turn reduces air temperatures.

Rating of Air Conditioners

Until 1956, air-conditioning units were generally rated in terms of tons of cooling they provided. A ton of refrigeration theoretically equals 12,000 Btu, which is the amount of heat needed to melt a ton of ice. In addition, some manufacturers also publicized their units in terms of compression motor horsepower. Not infrequently the two were equated, even though there was known to be a considerable differential in efficiency between types of compressor motors and designs.

In 1956, twenty-one of the largest manufacturers of room coolers agreed to re-rate their units in terms of actual Btu of heat removed per hour from the conditioned space. The ratings were based on a standard method of testing, which was developed by the Air Conditioning and Refrigeration Institute (A.R.I.) and carried out by an independent testing laboratory.

Today, cooling units are rated on the Btu basis, and in accordance with A.R.I. Standard 210, and approved models are also Underwriters Laboratories listed. Where applicable, they are also tested by the American Gas Association (AGA), and their seal of approval will be found on gas-fired equipment. The performance specifications of modern cooling units are completely spelled out; these include the A.R.I. Cooling Capacity in Btu/hr, the air-handling capacity in cubic feet per minute, and various other technical and mechanical data. The machines also carry two performance ratings. One is called the energy efficiency ratio, or EER, and the other is the seasonal energy efficiency ratio, or SEER. By comparing these figures, it is possible for the consumer to determine which of two or more cooling unit models has the better overall performance characteristics, other specifications being equal.

Cooling Methods

COMPRESSION SYSTEM

The elements of a standard compression type of air conditioning system (Figure 7–65) are as follows. Warm, damp, indoor air is blown over the cooling coils (Figure 7–66) by a fan and out into the conditioned space cooled and dry. The refrigerant, heated by the warm room air, leaves the coils and flows to the compressor (Figure 7–67) where it becomes a high-pressure superheated gas, and from there to the condenser where the heat is "squeezed out" by the condensing medium. The gas then becomes a liquid and moves on to the cooling coils again through an expansion valve that returns it to a low-pressure state, ready to absorb more heat from the room air as it "boils" back into gaseous form. By reducing the refrigerant liquid to normal

7–65. Schematic diagram of refrigeration cycle, compression system. (Air Conditioning Contractors of America)

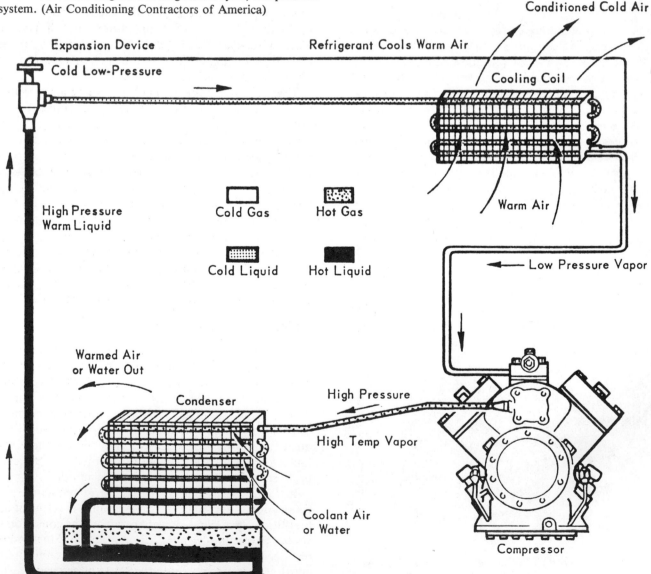

pressure, the expansion valve also reduces the temperature of the liquid to its normal (or atmospheric-pressure) boiling point, making it very "heat-hungry" indeed.

Power requirements for compression systems vary with unit size. Small window units usually require 220-volt 3-wire service; but this should cause no difficulties in new houses, since such wiring is standard in any residence with the usual power consumption for large appliances (stoves, heaters, washers, power tools, and the like). In residences designed for energy self-sufficiency, where one of the objects is the consumption of as little electrical energy as possible, conditioning equipment of this sort generally cannot be included in the house equipment package.

Central compression air conditioners work better with three-phase current rather than the usual single-phase that is standard in most parts of the country.

7-66. Cooling coil. (Courtesy, the Johnson Corporation, Division of Magic Chef, Inc.)

7-67. Typical compressor/condenser unit. (Courtesy, the Johnson Corporation, Division of Magic Chef, Inc.)

Motors running on three-phase current are simpler, less expensive, longer-lasting, and often less costly to maintain. Three-phase current is not readily available in residential areas, however, and the local power company should be queried on the matter before a central cooling unit is specified. The lack of three-phase current will not interfere with one's choice of central compression units, however, since more equipment is offered in a single-phase mode than in a three-phase one.

ABSORPTION SYSTEM

In the process of refrigeration using a gas or oil flame, the heat from the gas flame is used as the energy source to circulate the refrigerant rather than a mechanical compressor. There are four major components in an absorption system: generator, absorber, chiller, and condenser (Figure 7-68). Other lesser components are required (such as the analyser, rectifier, and heat exchanger) to improve the operating efficiency of the system. In a typical system, a solution of liquid and refrigerant is first heated in the generator by a gas or oil flame. The gas that is dissolved in the fluid boils off and passes into a condenser, which may be either air or water cooled. The gas gives up its heat in the condenser and becomes a liquid; it then passes through the chiller, where it absorbs heat from the air or water being cooled, and changes back to a gas. The gas then travels to the absorber, where it goes back into solution and moves on to the generator, to repeat the cycle.

The advantages of the absorption system are: the same fuel is used year-round and if the fuel is relatively inexpensive, operating costs will be less than for electric-powered coolers; the system is entirely silent except for the air-circulating fans since there is no compressor pump; there are no moving parts except fans to get out of order so the unit has a long life. The disadvantages include: need for a flue connection and fuel and water piping; the unit is obtainable only with both heating and cooling cycles.

COMBINATION SYSTEMS

These are oftentimes employed where a structure is to be equipped for both heating and cooling. In this case, the cooling unit is generally incorporated either wholly or partly into the heating equipment, and the cooling air is circulated through the same ductwork system. Various arrangements are possible, such as a split system, two separate or compatible units, or a year-round unit that is manufactured especially to serve both heating and cooling purposes (Figure 7-69). Note that absorption cooling systems can be used in combination with warm air furnaces to provide both heating and cooling. In many instances, the heat pump can prove satisfactory for this purpose, provided that electricity as a heating energy source is practical.

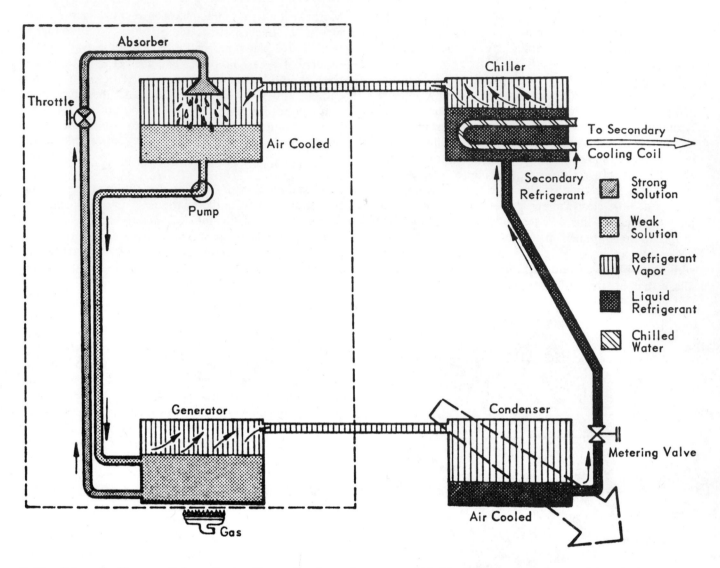

7–68. Schematic diagram of absorption cooling cycle, absorption system. (Air Conditioning Contractors of America)

REFRIGERANT COOLING

This takes place in the condenser and is done in one of two ways: by air or by water. Water-cooled condensers were at one time the most common in-house units, since water is more efficient than air as a heat remover. But water for high-side cooling must be cheap, plentiful, cold, and expendable, or else it must either be recirculated through a cooling tower, which is expensive and bulky, or it must be used as a spray in what is known as an "evaporative condenser." Both cooling towers and evaporative condensers save from 90 to 95 percent of the cooling water otherwise wasted and are thus economical in operation.

However, in addition to cost, size, the attendant unattractiveness and difficulty of installation, and the necessity for a good, constant source of cold water, they have another defect. Unless the water is chemically pure, it may deposit salts and various encrustations on the surfaces of the units, leading to costly maintenance,

repairs, and replacements. Furthermore, even though these units reduce water costs greatly, there still is an annual expenditure for water that, in some areas, may be a sizable addition to the overall operating expense. And, of course, in some areas, water is becoming a more and more precious commodity.

Air-cooled condensers are the units of choice in residential cooling work today, not only because of the various installation, maintenance, and cost problems involved with the water-cooled condensers, but also because of the increasingly widespread national shortage of water. Condensers that are cooled by air work well, though they are not as efficient as the water-cooled types, pratically at the hottest time of the year when the cooling load is heaviest. Since the air used as the cooling medium is the regular air of the hot outdoors, it obviously must be handled in large volumes and at relatively high speeds if it is to draw enough heat out of the refrigerant to do much good. The specifica-

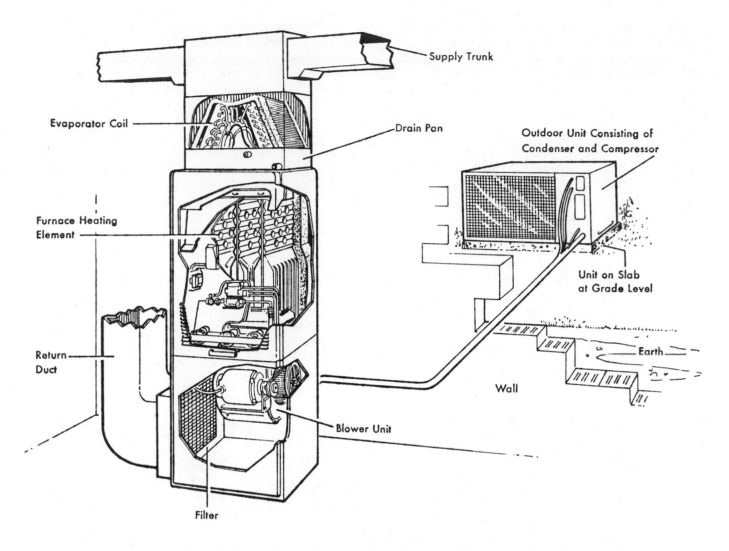

Evaporator Coil

Furnace Heating Element

Return Duct

Filter

Supply Trunk

Drain Pan

Outdoor Unit Consisting of Condenser and Compressor

Unit on Slab at Grade Level

Earth

Wall

Blower Unit

7–69. Combination unit for year-round air conditioning. (Air Conditioning Contractors of America)

tions of cooling units, however, are based upon standard rating conditions of 90° F outside dry-bulb, 80° F inside dry-bulb and 67° F inside wet-bulb temperatures. Thus, a unit with a 35,000 Btu/hr capacity can handle a cooling load up to those rated conditions. If the exceptable load for a particular cooling application will be in excess of the rating condition, higher cooling capacity will be needed.

For most efficient operation of an air-cooled condenser, the refrigerating part—compressor and condenser—is best located out-of-doors, so that it can make use of free air volumes. Units installed in attics, as has been done upon occasion in the past, are not as effective as they would be outdoors, since attics can become so unbearably hot, nor are they as convenient for service work. Outdoor refrigerating units, seperate from the cooling coils, are available in compact and attractive weatherproof cabinets that can be successfully concealed in a breezeway, courtyead, surrounded by

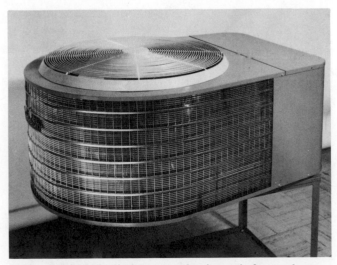

7–70. Vertical air discharge condensing unit for outdoor installation. (Courtesy, the Johnson Corporation, Division of Magic Chef, Inc.)

shrubbery in the yard, or even mounted upon a flat roof (Figure 7–70). As shady location as possible is helpful in the operation of the unit, but shrubbery should not be so close to the equipment as to restrict air flow. Units with vertical discharge of air are frequently chosen for this purpose, since they are quieter and the hot air is kept away from grass and plants.

UNIT COOLERS

These are air cooled and are usually bought to cool one room in an existing house; however, it is entirely feasible to use two or three or more of these self-contained units either installed in window openings, or, preferably, built into the other walls at convenient locations, for partly or completely air conditioning a house (Figure 7–71). There are, natually, advantages and disadvantages in this system. There is no ductwork, nor is a remote compressor system needed. It is easy to cool only one room at a time, as needed. But this is also true with a well-designed central system that is carefully zoned, and the latter also has the merit that one can concentrate all of the cooling output in the living room, say, when a large party is being given, letting the other rooms temporarily get hot. This cannot be done with the individual room units. One the other hand, this consideration may not be of concern.

With automatic thermostats, the units will go on and off in accordance with the load. When the sun is beating into one room, the unit will stay on, cooling only that room until the temperature drops. The others will stay off as long as the room temperature is at or below the thermostat setting. However, much the same thing can be done with a well-zoned central system in which multiple thermostats control ducting dampers.

Installation charges are small, since no special piping, drains, or ducts are needed. The extra carpentry work around the wall built-ins is only a small-cost item, and electrical connections are not generally exorbitant.

Maintenance is easy, since the units are at all times available for inspection and repair, which is not always the case when the central unit is located in a shallow crawl space, attic, or tight closet. However, an individual-unit system requires multiple filter replacement or cleaning, and it requires maintenance of several motors, pumps, and fans rather than just one. Furthermore, there may be somewhat higher power costs, since more electricity is needed to run several fractional-horsepower motors than to run one 3- or 4-horsepower

7–71. Room-type air conditioning unit. (Courtesy, Carrier Air Conditioning, subsidiary of United Technologies Corporation)

motor. Equipment costs *may* be higher, too, though the savings on ductwork and piping may be large enough to account for the difference.

Economical spot cooling is obviously possible with this system; but really good balance throughout the house will be difficult to obtain automatically. Achieving even moderately level house-wide cooling may require frequent manual adjustment of thermostats.

Heat pump through-the-wall units. These are available for those who wish to use one unit for both room cooling and light-load room heating, as for example on cool mornings and evenings during spring and fall seasons when it would be wasteful to turn on the central heating equipment.

Through-the-Wall Cooling Units with Resistance Heating Coils. These units are completely self-contained and present an unobtrusive appearance both inside and outside, while offering individually controlled, completely automatic electric heating and electric air conditioning for relatively small areas, either single rooms or apartments. Cooling capacities of nearly 30,000 Btu/hr are available in conjunction with heating capacities of approximately double that amount.

Evaporative Coolers. These are available in numerous styles for window-mounting, as well as in fully portable units.

Distribution Systems

The systems for summer cooling are designed in accordance with essentially the same basic principles as those for winter heating. However, it should be noted that just because a ductwork installation will work well for winter heating does not necessarily mean that it will work well for summer cooling also. One must consider, for instance, that warm air rises while cool air falls; this and numerous other conflicting details must be considered when a heating/cooling ductwork system is designed. Regardless of how good a commercial heating/cooling unit may be, if it is connected to a badly designed ductwork system, the results will be both unsatisfactory and expensive. The ductwork should be designed and installed either in accordance with the information set forth by the manufacturer of the heating/cooling equipment, or in accordance with the instructions offered in Manual K, *Equipment Selection and System Design Procedure,* put out by the Air Conditioning Contractors of America, and available from them.

Filters for summer cooling systems are identical with those used with warm air systems; either disposable fiber, impingement, or electronic.

DUCT MATERIALS

These are the same as those used for warm air. The traditional types for years have been galvanized iron or aluminum sheet; other materials may also be used, pro-

vided that they are acceptable and conform to the requirements of the National Fire Protection Association.

DUCT INSULATION

This is even more important for heating/cooling or cooling-only systems than it is for heating systems. Ducts must be insulated against heat gain in the summer wherever they pass through unconditioned spaces in attics, crawl spaces, warm rooms, etc. The ductwork should be insulated with at least 2 inches of blanket-type duct insulation, or covered with rigid sheet insulation at least 1-inch thick. When the latter type is used in attics or other areas where the surrounding ambient temperature is likely to be quite high, as in an attic, be sure to select an insulation type that is satisfactory for such usage and will not degrade under the high temperatures. Commercially available insulating ducts can also be used. The insulation must be covered with an effective vapor barrier and all of the joints in the material must be properly sealed to prevent moisture migration. If this is not done, dampness in the insulation can reduce its effectiveness.

OUTLETS

For central cool air, outlets are in every respect identical with those used for warm air heat. They include registers with either fixed or adjustable louvers, diffusers, and grills. Selection of these devices and their locations is particularly important in achieving good distribution of both warmed and cooled air. Inside-wall systems frequently use registers that discharge air in a horizontal direction from either low sidewall outlets or high sidewall outlets; the latter are suitable for both heating and cooling, but the former are recommended only for heating. Baseboard or floor diffusers that discharge air vertically are the preferred type for perimeter heating/cooling systems, and the units must be sized to handle cooling-air velocities. Ceiling diffusers may be used (located near the centers of rooms or near outside walls) in climates where winter conditions are relatively mild. They are not recommended for winter air conditioning in severe climates unless additional means for providing warm floors are included in the system.

Cooling System Problems

CONDENSATION

Condensation is one of the continuing problems in all summer air conditioning with the exception of window units. Most of these latter have "slinger rings" on the fan that cool the condenser. These rings collect the water as it condenses and sling it back over the coils, cooling them somewhat and thus cutting electric current requirement to a small degree at the same time that they evaporate most if not all of the water. Only in regions of unusually high humidity, combined with high temperatures, will water from the window units be produced in such quantities that it cannot be entirely evaporated on the hot coils. In these exceptional cases, it may be advisable to provide a drip block at the ground level to carry the water away from the foundation and keep it from penetrating the cellar or crawl space, or from causing a permanently muddy spot on the ground surface.

All central cooling units, on the other hand—even those located remote from the house—should be provided with drain lines, *not* drain pans that have to be emptied. On a humid day a central conditioner may remove as much as 100 quarts of water from the indoor air, and this water must be safely disposed of. Units located in attics, closets, and utility rooms can be drained to the regular plumbing drain line; those in basements usually have a line leading the condensate down a cellar drain or into the main house drain. When a central conditioner is located in a crawl space without a drain to the sewer line or other safe disposal place, it is necessary to specify a cooling unit that includes a small pump for moving the condensate upwards to flow into a surface drain inside or outside the house.

NOISE

This is often an annoying problem with summer air cooling units, especially those using adapted warm air ducts. The faster-moving air cannot help but make a noise, and that noise is magnified if the air moves through poorly designed, loosely built, and inadequately insulated ducts. To be effective acoustically, the insulation should line the inside of the ducts, rather than the outside. However, it is rare in houses that the noise problem is acute enough to call for duct linings of this sort; the insulation on the outside does reduce noise somewhat, and—if the ducts are well put together—this probably will be enough. For methods of attenuating sound in ducts, see chapter 8.

The pumps that compress the refrigerant may also be noisy; and their noise and vibration can "build" additional noise into the building. All floor-mounted units should use properly designed sound and vibration deadeners, and similar protection should be provided for noise units in attics and suspended in crawl spaces, as described in chapter 8. Remote condensers probably need no such protection if they are far enough from the house.

Chapter 8

Principles of Sound Control

Comfortable living is not only a matter of privacy and of protection against the thermal environment. It is also affected by noise—increasingly so in recent years, with the enormous growth and the number, variety, and loudness of modern noise-producing devices. From the rattle of a loose fan belt in the home air conditioning unit to the hollow shriek of a jet plane ripping jagged holes in the atmosphere (and our peace of mind), we are ever more menacingly confronted with noise as a factor that we either have to get used to or to control. The purpose of this chapter is to outline the methods of controlling noise hazards from outside the house as well as from inside.

In discussions of residential acoustics, the tendency too often is to think only in terms of sounds originating in an enclosed space and their control within that space by sound *absorption*, and to underemphasize the importance of sound transmission through walls, roofs, and floors and its control by sound *isolation*. Both are important, of course. A low noise level within rooms is essential for peace of mind, whether in a 10- by 12-foot kitchen, or a 100- by 150-foot theater. The science of acoustical design and the development of efficient sound-absorbing materials are both in an advanced state, and it is not difficult to achieve good noise control *within* rooms today.

But a house almost never needs protection against unpleasant noises within the room of origin as much as it needs reduction of the passage of noise from outdoors to indoors, or from noisy rooms to quiet rooms. Therefore, while not ignoring sound absorption, we will place special emphasis on planning methods, types of construction, and varieties of materials that can reduce sound transmission annoyances to a minimum.

Why Noise Control Is Important

It has only been during the last two decades or so that much attention has been paid to the problems of noise in and around the house. In the past, people have simply borne with the noises their neighbors or the general environment produced, or else they have moved away. But with the advent of smaller and more lightly constructed houses, and with the great increase in noise in the newer, more closely built-up communities, psychologists and physiologists have had occasion to examine the hazards to emotional and physical health caused by excessive noise in and around the dwelling.

In most cases, random sounds commonly encountered in residential areas do not cause serious or permanent physiological disabilities, except occasionally with persons who are already ill. However, there is a very real possibility of hearing damage and partial hearing loss, either temporary or permanent, for persons engaged in various activities in and around the home. Such difficulties are generally suffered at the hands of the operators of the noise-producing equipment themselves, though they can extend as well to others in the immediate vicinity. If the human ear is exposed to noise levels of greater than 85 dBA over extended periods of time, damage can result. This can easily happen in residential and recreational pursuits when people use home workshop power tools, ride motorcycles and snowmobiles, shoot rifles, or listen endlessly to highly amplified music. Unfortunately, the effects of excessive noise are cumulative, so that the impact of noise exposure in one's occupation must be added to that experienced at home and during recreational pursuits; thus, many more people are risking permanent hearing damage than they perhaps realize.

In addition, temporary psychological and physiological disturbances do occur when one hears an unusually loud or sudden noise and, if such noises are common in the environment, decreased levels of health may possibly result. Fatigue is very difficult to quantify, qualify, and measure; however, excessive loud noise, or spasmodic, sudden noises, are annoying, and annoyance leads to fatigues of various kinds. There is general agreement that this exacts a heavy toll in frayed nerves and physical exhaustion. Researchers have long since proven that sleep, and, more particularly, what we term "a good night's sleep," is essential to both emotional and physical health. Numerous studies have shown that noise at various levels has varying impact on sleepers, disturbing their sleep and causing a shift in sleep level to the point of awakening. When sleep is thus disturbed by sound, the results are detrimental.

There is another aspect of the noise problem, and that is the fact that most of us are used to a continual background of noise. We find a complete absence of noise unnatural and, quite possibly, bothersome until we become accustomed to the situation. Furthermore, the level of background noise that we will tolerate varies with different circumstances and in different areas of the house. The sound of a popcorn popper might be exasperating when we are absorbed in classical music, but would never be noticed in the hubbub of a televised football game. The whine of a vacuum cleaner seems perfectly normal during the daytime hours, but very unwelcome during the evening when we are trying to relax. High sound levels are perfectly acceptable in kitchens and workshops, but seldom are in bedrooms or nurseries. And, depending upon the state of our physical and/or emotional health at any given moment, most of the time we never notice the refrigerator turning on and off, or the wall clock ticking, but at other times such sounds are intrusive and irritating. Furthermore, we often prefer to have a certain amount of background noise that will effectively mask intruding noises that we do not want to hear. Thus, a radio playing comforting music covers the shrill noises of children playing in the yard.

In general, however, too little noise is rarely a problem in modern houses, although complaints have been registered by occupants of tightly sealed air-conditioned houses that, when the unit turns itself off, "the silence becomes oppressive." How common a problem this is we have no way of knowing. Too much noise, on the other hand, particularly of a discontinous, sudden, or shrill type, is an increasingly common complaint. Noise of this sort means sleeplessness, irritability, nervousness, and lowered personal effectiveness. Furthermore, noises that are almost automatically accepted in an office or a factory, whether they are loud conversations, operation of office equipment, running of various types of machinery, intruding sounds of street traffic, or combinations of all of these, are ruinous in the much quieter atmosphere of a house.

Noise Standards

The admittedly complex subject of noise control in the house is made still more difficult by the fact that one person's annoying noise may be another person's quiet. One may be almost unaware of the fact that noises can be bothersome, while another may demand a standard of silence approximating that of the famous French author, Marcel Proust, to whom the sound of a fly buzzing in his study was sheer torture.

This means that the problems of acoustical control are such that one is almost forced to analyze what the individual reactions of members of the family are to various types of noise. For example, a nervous person who wakes up at the slightest noise should have a bedroom that is protected against every sort of sound annoyance, while someone who is not bothered by average noises would not need this sort of protection.

It is thus literally impossible to establish criteria for noise control for the "average" family. However, it is possible—and almost essential—to establish the basic criteria for a quiet environment, both outdoor and indoor, since many of these desiderata can be obtained at almost no cost by careful advance planning. Environmental sound control means careful selection of community, site, and the house location, and equally careful planning of the house for segregation of noise-producing areas from quiet ones. Sound control by means of structural techniques and materials selection will cost money; planning is less expensive.

ENVIRONMENTAL SOUND CONTROL

Even if the site is already selected, it still makes good sense to draw up a list of the most important causes of noise affecting it for guidance in laying out sound control procedures. Such a list should consist of pertinent elements for Table 8-1. If the site is still to be selected, this table will be a good sound-control guide.

One of the most objectionable noise problems in our modern air-age society arises from airfields and regular air lanes. Low-flying planes on regular routes, planes roaring up from a nearby field, and sonic booms are about the most inescapable and nerve-racking noise producers of our time. This is likely to be especially true in the newer suburbs, since airfields, like such suburbs, tend more and more to be located in outlying areas away from urban centers and from the older, inner belts of suburban development—usually too built up to provide the room needed for an airfield. A great deal of future discomfort can be avoided if some attention is paid to the problem of airplane noise, although it is true that it is not always possible to be sure that at some future time an intrusive jetport may not be located in the area. Community protests will be the only means of preventing such future noise hazards. It should be noted that regulatory efforts by various agencies are increasing yearly in order to abate objectionable noises from airports and air traffic, and that public anger concerning such noise has grown to such an extent that there is a very real possibility that future growth of the industry may well be hindered.

HOUSE PLANNING

The principles of segregation of function in the modern house are well understood and are listed in Table 8–2. One of the more common problems in this connection is the location of children's bedrooms. Parents sometimes want these rooms near the living quarters so that if, during the evening, the youngsters awake and start crying they can be heard. The fact that most children can sleep through an amount of racket that would keep the average adult sitting on the edge of the bed is sometimes used by thoughtless parents as a further reason for this unsound locations of bedrooms: "The children don't mind the noise." But physicians generally agree that children need quiet when they sleep, just as much as adults do. Too much noise can make a child irritable and unhappy after he wakes, even though he may seem to be sleeping soundly through it. The best program for planning a modern house is to isolate all bedrooms from noise-producing areas, wherever possible.

But even in ideal circumstances, it is not usually possible to eliminate all noise hazards by site selection or by house planning. There still will be areas—and times—where and when noise must be produced on a high enough level to be noticeable, and often annoying: home workshop, frequent parties, noisy street, playground, airport, neighbors, etc. Its control is the function of special materials and construction techniques.

ENVIRONMENTAL SOUND CONTROL FACTORS

COMMUNITY

1. Restrictive zoning regulations, rigidly enforced, against noise-producing, nonresidential uses such as through truck traffic, commercial and industrial establishments, public institutions of various types, etc.

2. Adequate distance from shopping centers, railroads, truck routes and toll highways, etc.—"adequate" in the sense that the noise produced by these elements will be almost indistinguishable from the background noise level of the community.

3. Avoidance of airports and regular air lanes.

SITE

1. Location on a street with a minimum of through traffic, a cul-de-sac being preferable.

2. Reasonable distance from noise-producing community buildings such as schools, hospitals, fire houses, churches with bells or carillons, etc.

3. Restrictions in the zoning ordinance or deed of sale making it impossible for future homes to be built so close to existing houses that noises from neighbors' activities could be annoying.

LOCATION

1. Suitable distance from street to reduce possibility of street noises becoming bothersome.

2. Orientation, when possible, so that existing contours and existing or future plantings will serve as acoustical barriers.

3. Safe distance from possible noises at rear of lot, in particular to protect against children's play yards and adults' workshops near existing or future homes.

4. When necessary, planning for outdoor acoustical barriers between the house and noise sources. Brick or stone walls, solid-wood fences, earth embankments, thick plantings of nondeciduous, densely foliaged shrubs or trees, or combinations of these, are suitable for the purpose.

Table 8–1.

Sound Control Factors in House Planning

---

1. Windowless wall and/or garage located as sound barrier against the greatest source of noise (street, neighbors, shopping center, etc.).

2. Segregation of quiet rooms from noise-producing rooms by distance: bedrooms away from living, food preparation, and utility areas; studies isolated from play areas, hobby rooms, party rooms, workshops, etc.; places for quiet conversation protected from general living area or from music room by separation or by placing in an alcove off the main living room, etc.

3. Placement of bathrooms, hallways, utility rooms, and other usually quiet areas so that they serve as sound barriers between various quiet rooms and the noise-producing areas; location of fireplace and any other interior masonry walls to serve the same purpose.

4. Insulation against sound transmission between bedrooms by closets.

5. In plans and specifications for noise-producing rooms, provision for adequate sound absorbing treatment, whether by design of furnishings or specification of acoustical materials, or both; provision for adequate sound isolation from surrounding quiet rooms by design and construction, including special sound-isolation procedures and materials if and as necessary. This is particularly important in moderate-sized homes with open kitchens, combined living-dining room areas, general "family rooms," children's playrooms, and adult workshops or hobby rooms.

6. Provide for adequate control of impact noises in first-floor construction over occupied basements, and in second-floor construction over living spaces.

7. Elimination, by design and construction, of all potential sound paths and noise leaks in the entire structure.

Table 8–2.

SOUND CONTROL TERMINOLOGY

Before we can even begin to discuss the relative merits of different materials and structural systems from the point of view of sound absorption and insulation, it is essential to have some understanding of acoustic terminology and of the various types of sound measurements used in the acoustical profession. Sound is an astonishingly complex physical phenomenon; beside it heat (and cold) and light, and their measurement and control, are relatively simple. For instance, sound can be measured for its magnitude of intensity (or power, or pressure) in decibels; for its loudness in phons; for its frequencies in cycles per second; and for its "annoyance level," for which, up to the present, there is no reliable measure except the subjective reactions of each individual. Definitions of these and other associated terms used in measuring the sound-control properties of materials and structures are given in Table 8-3. The booklet, *About Sound*, published by the Office of Noise Abatement and Control of the U.S. Environmental Protection Agency (Washington, DC 20460) is recommended for further technical definitions and a bibliography of books on noise, vibration, and sound control.

Glossary of Major Acoustic Terms

Decibel: Equivalent to the smallest change in sound intensity that can be detected by the human ear. . . cannot be measured directly and has no fixed absolute value (Olin, Schmidt & Lewis). The unit used to express sound pressure level and sound power level (AACA). A measure, on a logarithmic scale, of the magnitude of a particular quantity (such as sound pressure, sound power, intensity) with respect to a standard reference value (0.0002 microbars for sound pressure and 10^{-12} watt for sound power (EPA).

Sound Level: Also noise level—the weighted sound pressure level obtained by use of a sound level meter having a standard frequency-filter for attenuating part of the sound spectrum (EPA).

Loudness: The judgement of intensity of a sound by a human being, depending primarily upon the sound pressure of the stimulus (EPA).

Loudness Level: The loudness level of a sound, in phons, is numerically equal to the median sound pressure level, in decibels, relative to 0.0002 microbar, of a free progressive wave of frequency 1000 Hz presented to listeners facing the source, which in a number of trials is judged by the listeners to be equally loud (EPA).

Sound Pressure: At a given distance from a source, the force of moving air molecules spread over a spherical area, generally expressed in dynes, which are units of force, per square centimeter (Olin, Schmidt & Lewis). The minute fluctuatio s in atmospheric pressure that accompany the passage of a sound wave. For a steady sound, the value of the sound pressure averaged over a period of time (EPA).

Sound Pressure Level: The ratio on a logarithmic scale of the measured sound pressure to a reference pressure of 0.0002 microbars, expressed in decibels.

Sound Absorption: The reduction of sound levels within an enclosed space by the use of surface materials with high sound absorbing qualities.

Noise Reduction: The numerical difference in decibels of the average sound pressure levels in two areas or rooms, combining the effect of the transmission loss performance of structures separating the two areas or rooms, plus the effect of acoustic absorption present in the receiving room (EPA).

Sound Insulation: The reduction of sound levels in spaces adjacent to those in which the sounds originate by the use of materials and structural cross sections with low sound transmission characteristics.

Sound Absorption Coefficient: The fraction of incident sound energy at specific frequencies that is absorbed by a surface; the remaining fraction is reflected. Used to specify sound absorbing materials and surfaces.

Impact Insulation Class: A single-figure rating that is intended to permit the comparison of the impact sound insulating merits of floor-ceiling assemblies in terms of a reference contour (EPA).

Sound Transmission Class: The preferred single-figure rating system designed to give an estimate of the sound insulation properties of a partition (EPA).

Sound Transmission Loss: A measure of sound insulation provided by a structural configuration (EPA).

Frequency: The number of pulsations per second produced by a sound source (AACA). Expressed in cycles per second (cps) or in Hertz (Hz).

Reverberation: The persistence of sound in an enclosed space, as a result of multiple reflections, after the sound source has stopped (EPA).

Table 8–3.

SOUND ABSORPTION

Acoustical tiles and plasters, heavy draperies and thick carpets, and even many types of furnishings can be used with great effectiveness to control reverberation in noise-producing areas such as halls, stairways, kitchens, living/dining areas, music rooms, workshops, recreation rooms, and children's playrooms. Indeed, the necessity for special sound absorbing treatments of surfaces in the typical house is questionable, with the possible exception of the kitchen, the workshop, and the children's playroom. The reason for this is simple.

Annoyance from discordant noises within a room arises from the high reflectivity of the room surfaces, which may cause the sound to shuttle back and forth, reverberating, echoing, clattering. In bare rooms, this annoyance is common enough, as it also is in poorly designed public rooms, such as restaurants, that have a high noise level and inadequate absorbing surfaces.

But the fortunate fact about most rooms in houses is that the very things that make them livable from the point of view of comfort and attractiveness also help to keep reverberation and clatter under control. Carpets and rugs, draperies, books, upholstered furniture, even, though to a lesser extent, tables and non-upholstered chairs, and finally the people themselves who are in the room, all absorb sound and almost always reduce reverberation to unnoticeable levels.

It is true that in the living rooms and dining rooms of modern houses with the large glass areas and the nonabsorptive furniture surfaces, as well as the broad, flat expanses of walls, floors and ceilings, that are typical of much contemporary design, reverberation and too-sharp sound may be noticeable. And if much entertaining is contemplated in such rooms, it may be advisable to use some sort of acoustical treatment, probably on the ceiling, as recommended below. However, this will be the exception and not the rule.

Similarly, special acoustical treatments for music rooms are only infrequently necessary. For one thing, hearing acuity in such rooms is considerably more important than a low reverberation time, and absorptive materials will tend to deaden the music and also to change the quality of the musical sound. The higher pitches, in which various combinations give the distinctive character or timbre of various instruments and vocal sounds, are more readily absorbed both by the furnishings and the synthetic acoustical materials. Furthermore, the room's furnishings and its occupants will adequately keep reverberation well under control. (For music room or listening area shape, see below.)

Indeed, the only rooms in which special sound absorptive treatments will, infrequently, be needed are those mentioned above (kitchens, workshops, playrooms), hallways and stairwells, and, occasionally, large dining rooms. In these rooms, which usually have highly "reflective" surfaces, acoustical materials may profitably be used.

Sound is a form of energy, and when it strikes the surface of a material part of that energy is reflected back toward the sound source, while the remainder penetrates the material itself, glances about in tiny fissures and air spaces, and eventually is dissipated as heat; in effect, it is trapped, or absorbed. All materials, regardless of their makeup, reflect a certain portion of the sound energy that hits them and absorb a certain portion. The ratio of the amount of absorbed energy to the amount of reflected energy is known as the *sound absorption coefficient*. Materials that have a sound absorption coefficient of approximately 0.20 or greater are generally called sound *absorbers*, while those with smaller coefficients are known as sound *reflectors*. Different materials, however, will absorb or reflect sound energy to a greater or lesser degree depending upon the particular frequency of the sound waves. Thus, in determining an overall capability for any particular material, it is necessary to test the material at a number of different frequencies to arrive at an average value; conversely, sound-absorbing materials can be chosen on the basis of absorption performance at whatever certain sound frequencies it is desirable to damp.

For convenience in assessing many of the more common building and decorative materials, a value called the *noise reduction coefficient* (NRC) is used (Table 8–4). This value is the average of the absorption coefficients noted at 250, 500, 1000, and 2000 Hz, the middle range of the six frequencies at which materials are generally tested for their absorption coefficients (the remaining two are 125 and 4000 Hz) and is expressed to the nearest multiple of 0.05. While the NRC is valuable for average and noncritical design purposes, introduction of coefficients resulting from tests at other frequencies (either higher or lower) may result in an entirely different NRC. Sound-absorptive materials are oftentimes introduced into a design or interior decor specifically for acoustic damping, and they are widely referred to as acoustic materials. Note, however, that because these materials will absorb sound is no indication that they will also insulate against sound; and generally they should not be used for that purpose. In fact, good acoustic materials for the most part have quite poor sound-insulating properties.

Sound-absorbing materials are quite valuable in reducing room noise produced by highly reflective surfaces. Such noise is a combination of direct noise from the source and reflected noise from the surfaces, which can actually build up and exceed the noise level of the source. And since the source is in the room, ergo, no amount of sound-absorbing material can reduce the noise level in the room to a point below that of the source. In fact, the noise-reduction capabilities of sound absorbing materials are actually quite limited,

Sound Absorption Coefficients for Common Materials

No.	Material	125	250	Frequency (Hz) 500	1K	2K	4K	NCR rating
	Walls							
1	Brick	0.03	0.03	0.03	0.04	0.05	0.07	0.05
2	Concrete painted	0.10	0.05	0.06	0.07	0.09	0.08	0.05
3	Window glass	0.35	0.25	0.18	0.12	0.07	0.04	0.15
4	Marble	0.01	0.01	0.01	0.01	0.02	0.02	0.00
5	Plaster on concrete	0.12	0.09	0.07	0.05	0.05	0.04	0.05
6	Plywood	0.28	0.22	0.17	0.09	0.10	0.11	0.15
7	Concrete block, coarse	0.36	0.44	0.31	0.29	0.39	0.25	0.35
8	Heavyweight drapery	0.14	0.35	0.55	0.72	0.70	0.65	0.60
9	Fiberglass wall treatment, 1 in (2.5 cm)	0.08	0.32	0.99	0.76	0.34	0.12	0.60
10	Fiberglass wall treatment, 7 in (17.8 cm)	0.86	0.99	0.99	0.99	0.99	0.99	0.95
11	Wood paneling on glass fiber blanket	0.40	0.90	0.80	0.50	0.40	0.30	0.65
	Floors							
1	Wood parquet on concrete	0.04	0.04	0.07	0.06	0.06	0.07	0.05
2	Linoleum	0.02	0.03	0.03	0.03	0.03	0.02	0.05
3	Carpet on concrete	0.02	0.06	0.14	0.37	0.60	0.65	0.30
4	Carpet on foam rubber padding	0.08	0.24	0.57	0.69	0.71	0.73	0.55
	Ceilings							
1	Plaster, gypsum, or lime on lath	0.14	0.10	0.06	0.05	0.04	0.03	0.05
2	Acoustic tiles 0.625 in (1.6 cm), suspended 16 in (40.6 cm) from ceiling	0.25	0.28	0.46	0.71	0.86	0.93	0.60
3	Acoustic tiles 0.5 in (1.2 cm), suspended 16 in (40.6 cm) from ceiling	0.52	0.37	0.50	0.69	0.79	0.78	0.60
4	The same as (3), but cemented directly to ceiling	0.10	0.22	0.61	0.66	0.74	0.72	0.55
5	Highly absorptive panels, 1 in (2.5 cm), suspended 16 in (40.6 cm)	0.58	0.88	0.75	0.99	1.00	0.96	0.90
	Others							
1	Upholstered seats	0.19	0.37	0.56	0.67	0.61	0.59	0.55
2	Audience in upholstered seats	0.39	0.57	0.80	0.94	0.92	0.87	0.80
3	Grass	0.11	0.26	0.60	0.69	0.92	0.99	0.61
4	Soil	0.15	0.25	0.40	0.55	0.60	0.60	0.45
5	Water surface	0.01	0.01	0.01	0.02	0.02	0.03	0.00

Table 8–4. (*Noise Control Handbook of Principles and Practices,* Van Nostrand Reinhold, 1978)

and reductions of 10 dB are very nearly the maximum, though in some instances the reduction may go as high as 12 to 13 dB. While this is not a great deal, the importance of the installation of such materials is not to be underestimated. In the first place, a reduction of only 5 to 8 dB will doubtless be quite noticeable (and quite comforting) to the occupants of the room. The pleasurability of previously more difficult conversation, or concentration, will be markedly enhanced. And second, even a small reduction of this sort can change the ambience of a room or area from annoying and irritating, perhaps even hazardous, to acceptable or better. And, the improvement can be brought about in either new construction or existing houses without benefit of intricate and extensive design details or major renovation.

Typically, sound-absorbing materials are best placed on ceilings in houses, largely because ceiling acoustic materials are readily available and the ceiling presents a large, open expanse of surface area that can be easily covered without interfering with decor, furnishings, and normal living patterns. Acoustic materials for walls are considerably less practical. Generally speaking, the installation of acoustic tile or similar material is not a particularly difficult or expensive chore, though upon occasion changes must be made to ceiling lighting systems and/or ventilating systems. However, the walls of long, narrow, and high-ceilinged rooms, such as hallways or entryways open to the second floor, might well be covered, at least on their upper portions, with sound-absorbing materials. In this instance, the relatively small ceiling area as compared with the wall area, especially where the walls are parallel, will not admit the installation of sufficient acoustic material to be effective. Or, of course, if additional absorptive capacity is needed in a room that has already had the ceiling covered, the upper portions of the walls, or even the entire walls, can also be covered. Carpeting, especially of the wall-to-wall variety, makes an excellent adjunct to acoustic materials in a room. Though the carpeting itself does not have particularly good absorptive characteristics, it does much to soften footsteps or any other surface-generated noises that might occur on a hardwood or masonry floor. Because such noises are effectively diminished to a substantial degree, there is considerably less sound energy ricochetting around the room for the acoustic materials to handle, and this automatically lessens the noise level.

Oftentimes people unfamiliar with the properties and characteristics of sound-absorptive materials will attempt to use ordinary mineral wool or fiberglass batt or blanket thermal insulation, which does have sound-absorptive qualities, for both sound insulation and thermal insulation. Unless properly done, which it seldom is, this trick does not work. If the thermal insulation is fitted with a foil or kraft paper vapor barrier, or if another barrier such as polyethylene film is installed (and in most cases there must be a vapor barrier of some sort on exterior walls), the sound-absorbing qualities of the insulation are completely negated. And, of course, if the insulation has no vapor barrier, then the thermal effectiveness of the insulation is likely to be at least diminished. Such installations have been made with perforated wall-covering like tile or hardboard to cover the insulation; however, if the insulation lies directly against the inside surface of the perforated material, even though there is no vapor barrier to interfere, there still will be no effective reduction of noise level. There must be a substantial air space between the thermal insulation and the perforated material, so that sound waves can enter through the perforations and move into, and around and about within, the air space and the thermal insulation.

One might, however, achieve reasonable results, say in a ceiling, by first installing 6 inches or more of fiberglass thermal insulation between the rafters with the vapor barrier facing downward, into the room.

Below this, a layer of unfaced fiberglass insulation about 2 inches in thickness could be friction-fitted between the joists. Then, an air space should be left at the bottom of the joist bays. The ceiling could be covered with perforated acoustic tile. The fact is, though, that approximately the same results can be achieved by installing the proper type of suspended acoustic ceiling, with a good deal less fuss and bother. Various types of acoustical tiles are shown in Figures 8-1 to 8-4. Figure 8-5 suggests the value of carpeting as a good acoustical material.

8-2. Perforated acoustical ceiling tile. (Courtesy, Armstrong World Industries)

8-1. Acoustical ceiling tile. (Courtesy, Armstrong World Industries)

8-3. Residential acoustical tile ceiling installation. (Courtesy, Armstrong World Industries)

219

8-4. Plank-type acoustical tile ceiling. (Courtesy, Armstrong World Industries)

8-5. Carpeting for sound control. (Carpet Institute, Inc.)

ROOM SHAPE

With one exception, the *shape* of rooms as a method of controlling noise in rooms is to all intents and purposes never considered in house design and building. It is important in the planning of auditoriums, music halls, theaters, and the like, but not in houses—except for a room specifically designed for music reproduction. Here the problem is not sound reduction or absorption, but clarity, plus reverberation or echo management.

There are two or three basic principles to be observed in designing a music room for a house. The major objective is to achieve as high a degree of sound fidelity with as low an amount of distortion due to room shape and surfaces as possible. The first and perhaps the most important of these principles is that walls and, if possible, floor and ceiling, should not be parallel or unbroken. A modern house with a shed-type roof and exposed-beam ceiling automatically makes for good music reproduction as far as the "top and bottom" of the room goes. As for walls, nonparallelism need not be achieved by the expensive and sometimes unesthetic method of setting the walls at odd angles, as is often done in auditoriums. Any room with an ell, such as a living room with a dining alcove off it, provides adequate discontinuity of surfaces to break up echos and reverberation. A living room with an angled fireplace in one corner will also provide sufficient irregularity in wall surfaces to assure the best possible music reception. In fact, if the builder gets his walls a bit out of alignment, the floor just a little off-level, and the ceiling slightly askew (and this happens more often than not, even in top-grade, careful construction), no more need be done. Those fractions of inches of nonparallism are sufficient.

For the most part, however, even most audiophiles do not pay a great deal of attention to the specific design of a music listening room or area when a new house is being built; usually other considerations are overriding. Virtually all "normal" living rooms, dens, and such that have irregular wall surfaces due to bookcases or shelves, furnishings and other paraphenalia, the standard carpeting and drapes, and the usual upholstered furniture and other appurtenances are perfectly adequate for music listening. In fact, today's stereophonic and quadraphonic sound reproduction systems are so versatile, can be regulated and adjusted to such a great degree, and are of such excellence (assuming top-quality equipment is purchased) that they can be made to sound superb in practically any residence room of practically any size and characteristics.

There are three important factors involved: the system components (amplifier, preamplifier, tuner, receiver, turntable, tape deck) must be of high quality; the loudspeaker system must be properly engineered, matched to the equipment, and placed to the greatest advantage in the room; and the signal sources (radio stations, records, tapes) must be as high-grade as possible. The speaker system is particularly important and should be fitted with the correct crossover systems and housed in proper enclosures; acoustic suspension (sealed) systems are best for small rooms or areas, while vented systems tend to perform better in large spaces.

Very little in the way of specific standards can be suggested for the treatment of room surfaces. Since every person's requirements will differ, much of the room treatment should be left until the music unit has been played enough so that the occupant can decide what is needed in the way of sound-deadening material. If the system is a sophisticated one that includes audio equalization and audio processing controls, there is an excellent possibility that no sound-absorptive materials will have to be introduced. Be aware, too, that it is possible (though unlikely) for a room to become so full of acoustic materials, thick carpeting, overstuffed furniture, heavy drapes, and similar accoutrements, that the music may sound as though it emanates from the bottom of a rain barrel and reaches your ears through a heavy fog. Top-quality reproduced sound will indeed lose its presence, brilliance, and sparkle if it is damped too much.

SOUND ISOLATION

In almost every type of dwelling unit, single-family as well as two-family and multiple-dwelling, the major noise control problem is not absorption. It is isolation. Sound isolation involves the use of structural and design procedures that will effectively reduce noise transmission in a building. This transmission of sound is separated into two categories: *airborne* noise, where the medium that spreads the noise begins with air, and *structure-borne* noise, which arises through direct mechanical contact with structural parts of the building by the sound source, such as footsteps. In residential (and other) construction, special attention is paid to a type of structure-borne noise called *impact noise,* which occurs when something strikes a partition wall, floor, or other part of a building and generates a sharp, annoying, intrusive noise that can be particularly upsetting to the building occupants, largely because of its abrupt and discontinuous characteristics.

Sound isolation is achieved through the use of building materials, most of which are perfectly ordinary, in certain combinations and designs that will prevent or reduce noise transmission through materials. Acoustic materials—sound absorbers—are of little or no value for this purpose, since, as previously noted, for the most part these materials do not insulate against sound effectively and will not isolate noise transmission. Sound isolating materials and structures are integral parts of the house and must usually be included when it is first built. The reduction of sound transmission through building sections after the structure is finished always involves extensive and costly alterations.

Sound Isolation Requirements

In this chapter, we are concerned entirely with freestanding suburban or rural residences, and not with urban rowhouses or apartments. The problems of isolation from sounds occurring outdoors in urban areas are greatly complicated by the higher levels of outdoor noise in cities, the very wide variations in the pitch of such noise, code requirements that often make adequate sound isolation very costly, unusual requirements for party walls, etc. For effective sound isolation in suburban and country locations, the problem is considerably simpler, since for outer walls the only important element is the background noise level of the community.

Different constructions of building sections have varying ability to transmit or resist the passage of sound waves. Obviously, the sound intensity on the source side of the building section will be greater than that on the opposite side; there will be some loss in intensity as the sound waves pass through the building section. This loss is called *transmission loss* (TL) and is the ratio of airborne sound intensity on the source side of an infinitely large wall to the sound intensity on the opposite side. This difference in sound pressure levels is expressed in decibels. If there is a 40 dB noise level on the source side of a wall, and none of that sound can be distinguished on the inside (0 dB), that particular wall section has a TL of 40 dB. If the sound pressure intensity is raised to 60 dB on the source side of the wall, a sound level of 20 dB will be distinguishable on the inside. However, if a background noise level of 20 dB is introduced on the inside of the wall, it will completely mask the outside sound and render it unobjectionable. On the other hand, if the intent were to maintain a 0 dB level on the inside against a 60 dB outside source of sound, then it would be necessary to improve the TL of the section to at least 60 dB.

The TL ratings of various building constructions is obtained by testing the section at certain particular sound frequencies, varying from six to nine in number. The TL can be employed for a specific frequency or averaged for the various frequencies tested. A TL of 35 to 40 dB may be adequate for outer walls of peripheral suburban, exurban, and rural residences. A TL of 40 to 45 dB, however, might be only barely adequate in urban and suburban areas and could go as high as 55 dB or more in some locales. In extreme circumstances either of exterior noise or of sensitivity on the part of the occupants, these figures must be adjusted upward. Indoor walls and floors, when they must serve a sound-isolation function greater than normal, should have a TL of at least 40 dB. In unusual circumstances, the loss should be as much as 45 to 50 dB. This does not include impact sounds, which are covered later.

The TL is not a sufficiently definitive rating for many purposes, for a variety of reasons, and so have been largely superceded by a rating called the *sound transmission class* (STC). The figures are arrived at by a rather complex testing and graphing procedure, and the result is a single number that represents the transmission loss performance of a building section such as a floor, ceiling, or wall at all of the test frequencies, appropriately weighted to reflect certain other factors. The STC is a more reliable indicator than the TL, and STC values are assigned to the various kinds of typical and common building constructions for ready

higher the STC number, the more effec-
ction is as a sound barrier (Table 8–5).
f structures and materials will provide
ound insulation? There are several, and
t be combined with proper planning, as
construction, for good results. The

planning should include control of the potential noise at its source, if possible, as well as maximum separation between the potential source and the listener, and the inclusion of sound-reducing construction as barriers wherever and whenever the two first factors cannot be satisfactorily controlled to produce the desired low levels of sound transmission. Table 8–6 lists transmission loss values in decibels for numerous common building constructions.

One source of information for details on exactly how this can be done is L. O. Anderson's *Wood-Frame House Construction* (Agriculture Handbook, No. 73, slightly revised April 1975), available from the Forest Products Laboratory. A major source of information, which goes into considerable detail of a very practical nature with respect to design, planning and construction in residences and light commercial structures is the "106 Sound Control" section of *Construction Principles, Materials & Methods* (by Harold B. Olin, A.I.A., John L. Schmidt, A.I.A., and Walter H. Lewis, A.I.A., 4th Edition, published 1980 jointly by the Institute of Financial Education and the Interstate Printers and Publishers, Inc.; available from the Institute, 111 East Wacker Drive, Chicago, IL 60601).

Comparative Effectiveness of STC Numbers

STC Number	Effectiveness
25	Normal speech easily understood
35	Loud speech audible
45	Loud speech just barely audible
48	Loud speech almost entirely inaudible
50	Loud speech cannot be heard

Table 8–5. (Abstracted from *Wood-Frame House Construction,* Agriculture Handbook No. 73, USDA)

Transmission Loss in Decibels for Common Building Constructions

No. Material	Total Thickness (inch)	(cm)	125	250	500	1K	2K	4K	STC Rating	IIC Rating
Walls[a,b]										
1. Solid concrete	3	8	35	40	44	52	59	64	47	–[c]
2. Concrete (6, 15), layers of plaster	7	18	39	42	50	58	64	66	53	–
3. Concrete wall (6, 15), wood-wool + plaster on furring	10	25	31	40	52	58	60	60	52	–
4. Solid concrete blocks, layers of plaster	16	41	50	54	59	65	71	68	63	–
5. Brick (4.5, 11), layers of plaster	5.5	14	34	34	41	50	56	58	42	–
6. Brick (9, 23), layers of plaster	10	25	41	43	49	55	57	59	52	–
7. Brick (12, 30) without plaster	12	31	45	44	52	58	60	61	56	–
8. Stone (24, 61), layers of plaster	25	64	50	53	52	58	61	68	56	–
9. Hollow concrete block wall	12	34	47	43	45	52	54	56	48	–
10. Hollow concrete block	6	15	32	33	40	48	51	48	43	–
11. Cinder block (4, 10), layer of plaster	5.25	13	36	37	44	51	55	62	46	–
12. Cement block painted at both sides	3.75	10	40	40	40	48	55	56	44	–
13. Hollow gypsum block (3, 8), layers of plaster	4	10	39	34	38	43	48	46	40	–
14. Hollow gypsum block (3, 8), resilient one side, plaster	5	13	38	37	44	51	56	59	46	–
15. Hollow gypsum block (4, 10), gypsum lath + resilient clips	6	15	25	37	46	53	56	63	47	–
16. Hollow concrete (9.25, 23), layers of fiberboard	10.25	27	41	42	47	51	52	39	43	–
17. Double brick (4.5, 11) wall, cavity (2, 5), layer of plaster	12	31	37	41	48	60	60	61	49	–
18. Double brick (4.5, 11) wall, cavity (6, 15), layer of plaster	18	46	48	54	58	64	69	75	62	–
19. Wooden studs (4, 10), gypsum wallboards	5	13	22	30	35	40	41	40	39	–

Table 8–6. (*Noise Control Handbook of Principles and Practices,* Van Nostrand Reinhold, 1978)

Table 8-6 continued

No. Material	Total Thickness (inch)	(cm)	Frequency (Hz) 125	250	500	1K	2K	4K	STC Rating	IIC Rating
20. Wooden studs (4, 10), gypsum laths + plaster layers	5.75	15	32	36	42	48	48	62	46	–
21. Steel truss studs (3.75, 8), metal lath, plaster	5.25	13	30	28	35	40	43	53	39	–
22. Steel truss studs (3.75, 8), double layers gypsum boards	4.75	12	35	38	44	50	50	51	48	–
23. Metal channel studs (1.625, 4), gypsum wallboards	2.625	7	20	30	38	47	48	45	39	–
24. Solid sanded gypsum plaster	2	5	36	28	35	39	48	52	36	–
25. Solid sanded gypsum plaster with metal channels	2	5	35	25	32	38	47	54	36	–
26. Solid gypsum core movable partition	2.25	6	34	34	37	38	39	45	36	–
Floors-ceilings										
1. Reinforced concrete slab	4	10	48	42	45	55	57	66	44	25
2. Reinforced concrete as above + carpeting and pad	4.5	11	48	42	45	55	57	66	44	80
3. Reinforced concrete slab (6, 15), layer of plaster	7.5	19	42	39	44	49	54	60	47	31
4. Concrete (4.5, 11), wood flooring, layer of plaster	7	18	35	37	42	49	58	62	46	47
5. Concrete (4.375, 11), screed, suspended plaster ceiling	10	25	38	41	45	52	57	59	48	47
6. Concrete (6, 15), wood, battens floating on glass wool, layer of plaster	9.5	24	38	44	52	55	60	65	55	57
7. Concrete (6, 15) with hollow blocks, wood on screed, plaster	8.165	21	40	42	46	52	58	60	50	48
8. Concrete (5.5, 14), floating floor, suspended ceiling	15.25	38	40	46	54	59	62	68	55	53
9. Hollow tile beam (5, 13), screed + linoleum, plaster	6.75	17	36	40	43	49	55	60	47	40
10. Hollow concrete slab (6, 15), cement mortar + cement finish, plaster	7.5	19	39	38	43	49	54	57	46	30
11. Concrete channel slab, sand cement finish	6.25	16	34	34	38	46	55	61	42	32
12. Ribbed concrete (7.25, 18) screed, wooden lath + plaster	9.50	24	33	37	42	52	58	62	46	42
13. Hollow concrete beam (6, 15), screed + floor, plaster	7.50	19	32	41	43	44	54	64	45	31
14. Wooden joists (8, 20), floor, gypsum wallboard	9.50	24	19	24	31	35	45	42	34	32
15. Wooden joists (7, 18), wood + linoleum, reeds + plaster	9.50	24	24	27	35	44	52	58	39	40
16. Wooden joists (10, 25), paperboard + pad + carpet, wallboard	12.5	32	27	32	38	44	49	60	38	57
Windows										
1. Sliding, aluminum frame	0.09375[d]	0.2	10	14	17	18	18	20	–	–
2. Projected (awning), aluminum frame, exceptionally good weather strip	0.09375[d]	0.2	16	22	25	28	32	28	–	–
3. Double window 0.09375[d], 0.2), air-space (0.1875, 0.5)	0.375	1.0	18	21	19	24	27	18	–	–
4. A's (3) with a storm window, air-space (2, 5)	2.375	6.0	16	24	27	33	37	29	–	–
Doors										
1. Hollow-core flush, 30 lb (6.7 kg)	1.75	4	11	16	16	16	21	23	–	–
2. Solid-core flush, 95 lb (21.1 kg)	1.75	4	20	25	23	25	25	28	–	–

[a] Numbers in parentheses indicate thickness of layer, in inches and centimeters, respectively.
[b] Data for walls and floors-ceilings from Berendt et al., 1967. Data for windows and doors from Bishop and Hirtle, 1968.
[c] Not applicable.
[d] Conventionally described as $^3/_{32}$ inch.

This publication is quite complete and contains sufficient information on acoustics (as well as practically everything else) for virtually all residential construction purposes. The data included on sound performance for wall and floor/ceiling systems are based primarily upon results obtained by various nationally recognized acoustical laboratories, including the National Bureau of Standards, in accordance with test procedures established by the American Society for Testing and Materials (ASTM E90) and the International Organization for Standardization (ISO Recommendation R-140). Much information is also included in the *Noise Control Handbook of Principles and Practices,* edited by Lipscomb and Taylor (Van Nostrand Reinhold Company, 1978). The data in Table 8–6 on transmission losses in decibels for numerous common building constructions are taken from that work.

One general warning must be offered: It is important that sound-insulating walls and floors be of the best possible workmanship and of top-grade materials. All cracks and sound paths should be eliminated by tight construction and, if necessary, by special sound-deadening strips or pads. Sounds can travel through cracks to a degree that can reduce the insulating value of the structure almost to uselessness. Special attention should be given to the elimination of sound—path cracks around baseboards, electrical outlets, plumbing pipes, ducts, doors and windows, and other discontinuous elements in the structure. This is because of a phenomenon known as *flanking transmission,* whereby airborne noise can follow certain flanking noise paths that often are not particularly obvious. Such paths include open areas over walls and across vaulted ceilings, outdoors from window to window, along a hall and through openings under doors, through ductwork, through built-in cabinets, and so on. Noise leaks also allow the transmission of airborne noise through poor masonry mortar joints, porous masonry blocks, back-to-back cabinets, poor seals at floor edges, back-to-back electrical outlets, gaps at wall joints, and the like. All flanking noise paths and noise leaks must be eliminated, or the beneficial effects of constructions designed for high STC's will be at least in part nullified and the introduction of acoustic material will do little good.

EXTERIOR WALLS

The selection of exterior wall construction with adequate soundproof qualities is not a difficult chore. This is done by subtracting the level of the background noise on the "hearing" side of the section from the sound level that strikes, or may strike, the other side of the section. The difference represents the minimum required STC. Incidentally, the same can be done in terms of the TL of various constructions. Thus, it can be seen from Table 8–7 that if a wall construction has a STC of 40 to 50 and there is no background noise whatsoever, normal speech can be easily understood from one side of the wall to the other; obviously this construction would be entirely unsatisfactory wall construction under absolutely quiet circumstances. However, such circumstances seldom obtain; consider, for instance, that the rustle of leaves in a gentle breeze represents a sound level of 10 decibels, and an average whisper at a distance of 4 feet is about 20 decibels. Even a slight interior noise level of 20 decibels or so would do much to mask intrusive sounds. On the other hand, a wall section of STC of 60 to 70 obviously would be far quieter.

If the TL of a wall construction is 30 decibels or less, then normal speech can be understood easily through the wall; this is much the equivalent of an STC of 40 to 50. An ordinary stud wall frame covered on only one side with wood drop siding is in this category. The common exterior-wall residential construction of a two-by-four stud framing, covered on the outside with plywood or some similar siding and on the inside with gypsum wallboard, has an STC, as tested, of 32 to 36; and sometimes a bit higher, depending upon the specific tests. Another common construction, similar but with the exterior both sheathed and covered with siding and the interior covered with a double layer of gypsum board, has an STC of 38 to 41. If insulation is added to either of these constructions, there is an expectable increase of only 2 to 4 decibels in performance, and the thickness or density of the insulation makes little difference. Thus, two of the most common exterior wall constructions used today are relatively ineffective as sound barriers, though the latter arrangement is more satisfactory. The combination of a wood-frame wall

Hearing Conditions in the Listening Side of Walls with Varying STC

Speech	Background Noise		
	0 dB	20 dB	30 dB
Normal—easily understood	40–50	25–35	15–25
Loud—easily understood	50–60	35–45	25–35
Loud—half understood	60–70	45–55	35–45
Loud—faintly heard	70–80	55–65	45–55
Loud—inaudible		65–75	55–65

Table 8–7. (Abstracted from *Construction Principles, Materials & Methods,* the Institute of Financial Education, 1980)

covered with exterior siding on one side and gypsum lath plus layers of plaster on the inside is even better, with an STC of 46. Other constructions of even greater effectiveness can be adopted where necessary. Attention is directed to the data on masonry partitions in Table 8-6, since these have good sound-insulating qualities and can be readily constructed as exterior-residential walls (they are not, of course, normally used as interior partitions).

As a general rule, the denser a material and the heavier a building cross section, the better its sound insulating properties. There are important exceptions to this generality, however. A heavy building material which nevertheless is porous, such as a cinder block, has little sound-insulating value unless the wall in which it is used is plastered or stuccoed. Then the weight of the block plus the density of the plaster gives the wall quite good sound insulating values, and these can be improved slightly with the addition of thermal insulation. On the other hand, a lightweight wood frame wall in which some of the elements are discontinuous may have good sound-insulating value. For example, a regular stud wall on which plaster lath is attached with resilient clips can be a good sound barrier, and so can one in which the studs are staggered, half of them touching one inner wall surface and the other half the other surface.

For airborne sound transmission, the weight-density rule usually holds. Of course, any window or door will, when open, almost totally destroy a wall's sound insulating value. Even when closed they cut it considerably, though not enough to negate the value of a well-designed and well-built sound insulating wall. Windows and doors, of course, have their own sound transmission loss characteristics. Wherever minimum sound transmission is essential, those with the best properties should be chosen. In addition, edges and frames should be sealed, and caulking and insulation placed around the frames. Soft weatherstripping is an excellent choice for doors, along with an automatic threshold closure at the bottom.

Rooms that require particular quiet either should have shallow windows high in the walls or, if ventilation can be achieved by other methods, no openable window at all; and the permanently closed windows should be weatherstripped, tightly caulked around the frames, and double- or triple-glazed and provided with tight-fitting storm sash. Doors should be solid and heavy and they should be insulated with vinyl or felt strips to keep noise from entering through cracks between the door and its frame.

The problem of outdoor noise entering through open windows and doors is almost eliminated in the house with year-round air conditioning, particularly if the windows are double glazed—as they should be for economical air conditioning. The windows will be generally kept closed and outdoor noises will be prac-tically unnoticeable against the quiet background murmur of the air-conditioning unit.

SOUND INSULATION INSIDE THE HOUSE

A complicating factor in the control of sound transmission through walls and floors inside the house is the fact that there are two distinctly different types of sound to be considered, and that the effective control of one often does nothing to alleviate the other. Transmission of airborne sound from one room to another can be controlled by one sort of structural method; transmission of impact sounds resulting from the striking of hard objects (from heels to children's toys against a surface) or from vibration of machinery and equipment fastened to a surface requires quite different methods of construction and types of materials for adequate sound deadening.

CONTROL OF IMPACT NOISES

Constructions that must effectively reduce impact-sound transmission (floor-ceiling sections in particular) are rated by a different system than those that must contend only with airborne noise, since they must be evaluated in terms of reduction of both airborne noise and structure-borne impact vibrations. The performance of such sections is rated by its *impact insulation class* (IIC), which is arrived at by measuring the sound pressure level at sixteen particular test frequencies, followed by some fairly complex comparisons with a special reference contour—the procedure is a bit similar to that used for determining STC's. Constructions may also be rated in terms of *impact noise rating* (INR), which is somewhat comparable to the TL, but is used specifically for impact sound transmission. Of the two, the IIC is preferable and has become a standard. The larger the IIC rating, the more effective the construction is in resisting the transmission of impact sound. Sections that are INR-rated can be converted to an approximate IIC rating by adding 51.

In all houses, but particularly in two-story structures, the control of impact noise transmission to other rooms is a matter of considerable importance. Various types of floor constructions and finishes have been tested for their impact noise reducing qualities, and some of the more important results are listed in Table 8-6, together with the values for reduction of airborne noise. Figure 8-7 shows cross sections of some typical floor/ceiling constructions. Note that the installation of carpeting and padding, which serves to cushion impact on floors, is a very effective means of reducing impact sound transmission, since the carpeting serves to greatly diminish the amount of impact energy transmitted to the structural system of the building.

There is an important point to make on the *lateral transmission* of sound along floors from one room to another on the same level. Oftentimes the joint between walls and floors can provide natural paths for both airborne and structure-borne sound, both of which can travel along or through poorly made or designed jointures. Even if construction is correct, flanking paths may still exist. Where sound isolation is specifically part of a design, both the floor/ceiling and the wall systems should have comparable and compatible sound isolating capabilities. If they do not, the weaker or less effective of the two systems will diminish the effectiveness of the stronger. Spaces between floor joists must be blocked where the walls and floors join, and joints at both top and bottom of the partition where it meets the floor and the ceiling must be sealed with a resilient, nonhardening caulk or sealer. There should also be a break in the subflooring directly beneath the partitions in order to break the transmission of structure-borne impact noise from room to room. Other special precautions must be taken with floated floor constructions.

DETAIL	DESCRIPTION	ESTIMATED VALUES	
		STC RATING	APPROX. INR
A	FLOOR ⅞" T. & G. FLOORING CEILING ⅜" GYPSUM BOARD	30	-18
B	FLOOR ¾" SUBFLOOR ¾" FINISH FLOOR CEILING ¾" FIBERBOARD	42	-12
C	FLOOR ¾" SUBFLOOR ¾" FINISH FLOOR CEILING ½" FIBERBOARD LATH ½" GYPSUM PLASTER ¾" FIBERBOARD	45	-4

8–6. Cross sections of floor-ceiling constructions for sound control. (*Wood-Frame House Construction,* Agriculture Handbook No. 73, USDA)

DETAIL	DESCRIPTION	ESTIMATED VALUES	
		STC RATING	APPROX. INR

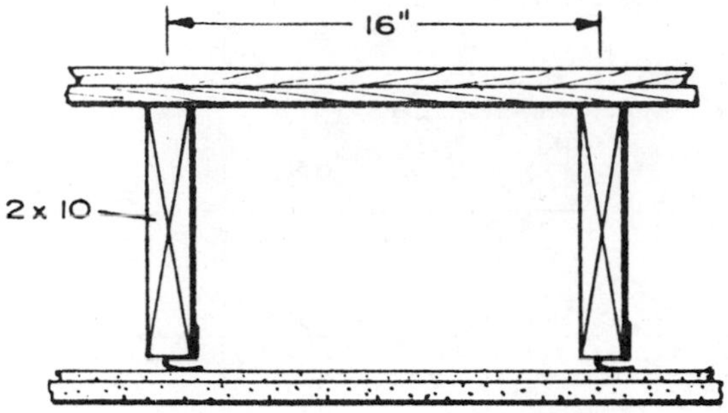 A	FLOOR
	  ¾" SUBFLOOR
	  (BUILDING PAPER)
	  ¾" FINISH FLOOR
	CEILING
	  GYPSUM LATH AND
	  SPRING CLIPS
	  ½" GYPSUM PLASTER
		52	-2

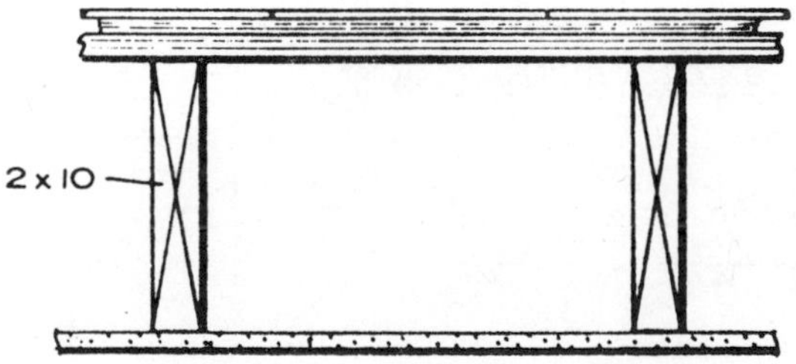 B	FLOOR
	  ⅝" PLYWOOD SUBFLOOR
	  ½" PLYWOOD
	  UNDERLAYMENT
	  ⅛" VINYL-ASBESTOS
	  TILE
	CEILING
	  ½" GYPSUM WALLBOARD
		31	-17

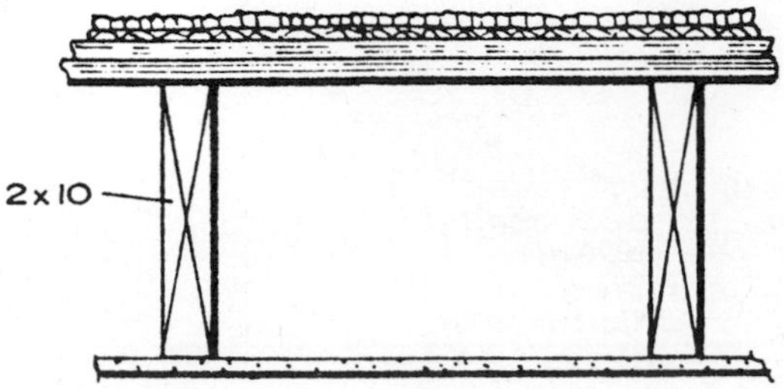 C	FLOOR
	  ⅝" PLYWOOD SUBFLOOR
	  ½" PLYWOOD
	  UNDERLAYMENT
	  FOAM RUBBER PAD
	  ⅜" NYLON CARPET
	CEILING
	  ½" GYPSUM WALLBOARD
		45	+5

227

CONTROL OF AIRBORNE NOISES

The passage of airborne noises through interior walls or floors, when not reduced by distance, can be controlled by construction with an STC of at least 40 and (around bathrooms, utility rooms, and particularly noisy playrooms or workshops) occasionally 52 or more (Table 8-8). The wall separating an active workshop from a bedroom, for instance, might well be on the order of 60 or higher. In practice, special sound-insulating construction is rarely used in private homes, except around such rooms. For suitable wall cross sections, see Figure 8-7. Because the constructions are more costly than standard wall designs, adequate insulation from noise should be achieved whenever possible by area segregation.

Noise-producing rooms should be provided with relatively soundproof doors, as well as efficient sound-insulating walls and floors. In these rooms, of course, windows to the outdoors are either nonexistent (as in

WALL DETAIL	DESCRIPTION	STC RATING
A 16" 2 x 4	½" GYPSUM WALLBOARD	32
	⅝" GYPSUM WALLBOARD	37
B 16" 2 x 4	⅜" GYPSUM LATH (NAILED) PLUS ½" GYPSUM PLASTER WITH WHITECOAT FINISH (EACH SIDE)	39
C	8" CONCRETE BLOCK	45
D 16" 2 x 4	½" SOUND DEADENING BOARD (NAILED) ½" GYPSUM WALLBOARD (LAMINATED) (EACH SIDE)	46
E 16" 2 x 4	RESILIENT CLIPS TO ⅜" GYPSUM BACKER BOARD ½" FIBERBOARD (LAMINATED) (EACH SIDE)	52

most utility rooms) or unimportant, since the noise level in such rooms when in use is likely to be higher than the background noise level outside.

The lateral movement of sound includes both airborne and structure-borne sound, and can take place through rigid wood floors as well as through concrete slabs. It is not likely to be a serious problem in houses, unless a workshop, hobby room, or playroom adjoins a "quite" room. Should this be made necessary by special requirements of the plan, it would be advisable to break the continuity of the floor by some means, but this involves special design and construction problems that are outside the scope of this chapter.

Transmission Loss Standards for Houses

Separating Section	Min STC	Opt STC
Living room/bedroom	50	57
Bedroom/bedroom	48	55
Kitchen/bedroom	52	58
Dining room/bedroom	52	58
Bathroom/bedroom	52	59
Family room/bedroom	52	58
Living room/bathroom	52	57
All floor/ceiling	48	60

Table 8–8.

8–7. Cross sections of wall constructions for sound control. (*Wood-Frame House Construction,* Agriculture Handbook No. 73)

WALL DETAIL	DESCRIPTION	STC RATING
A	½" GYPSUM WALLBOARD	45
B	⅝" GYPSUM WALLBOARD (DOUBLE LAYER EACH SIDE)	45
C	½" GYPSUM WALLBOARD 1½" FIBROUS INSULATION	49
D	½" SOUND DEADENING BOARD (NAILED) ½" GYPSUM WALLBOARD (LAMINATED)	50

VIBRATION NOISE TRANSMISSION

The transmission of this type of noise through and along floors, and through walls, is often a problem in small houses with warm-air furnaces, year-round air conditioners, various types of kitchen and laundry appliances, etc., that are rigidly fastened to the floors or walls. Special felt, cork, or rubber mounts (Figure 8–8) are available; these can greatly reduce this type of impact noise transmission if it is thought necessary. Often the problem can be avoided by selecting equipment that is known to be quiet in operation.

For the reduction of vibration and air-motion noise through pipe and duct systems, various methods of sound attenuation can be used (Figure 8–9). However, best practice is to avoid the need for such treatments by

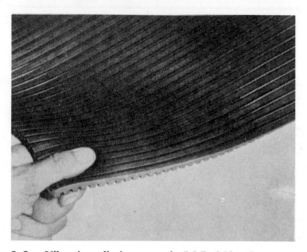

8–8. Vibration eliminator pad. (M.B. Mfg. Co.)

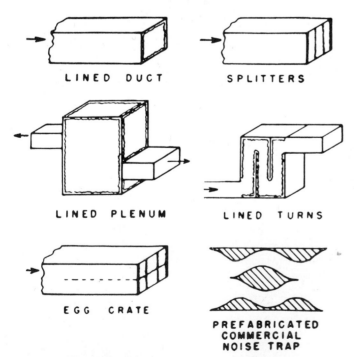

LINED DUCT   SPLITTERS

LINED PLENUM   LINED TURNS

EGG CRATE   PREFABRICATED
                    COMMERCIAL
                    NOISE TRAP

8–9. Acoustical baffles for duct lines in order of effectiveness. (R. D. Lemmerman, Koppers Co., Inc.)

making sure that the ductwork is tight and rattle-proof, that fans and blowers in the air conditioning units are very quiet, and that there is at least one right-angle turn in each duct line. These turns of themselves attentuate the noise quite satisfactorily—*provided* the ductwork is tight and does not itself add to the noise level.

Plumbing noises can be annoying, and precautions should be taken to minimize these sounds as much as possible. The worst noise usually comes from toilets, and for quiet the "hushed-flush" type of equipment should be used. It costs only a few dollars more, and it can eliminate a lot of embarassment. Drain lines should be isolated from the structure—that is, they should be freestanding and not in direct contact with the walls or floors. If this is not possible, they should be insulated with felt or some form of asphalt damping compound. A complete plumbing layout for a residence is a complex system, and the design, materials, and installation must be carefully considered and accomplished if acoustically satisfactory results are to be obtained. The design of a truly quiet system calls for consultation with an expert on the subject. Along these lines, it sould be noted that the new varieties of plastic pipe and fittings, which are now coming into widespread use for both drain-waste-vent systems as well as cold and domestic hot water supply and distribution systems, are considerably quieter than their metal counterparts if properly installed.

A point that is often ignored is that the rooms in which telephones are located should be free of excessive reverberation, so that conversation can be conducted without difficulty. It is also important that the phone not be located so that its bell or the user's conversation will annoy others, and also so that the user of the telephone can enjoy a reasonable degree of privacy and not be bothered by the conversation of others or from extraneous noises occurring in the vicinity. Best practice is to provide a special nook or recess, acoustically treated, for the phone, if necessary, so that sounds will not reverberate excessively or pass through the walls of the recess into adjacent rooms.

Summary

The techniques for sound insulation described in this chapter are somewhat condensed and simplified—the field has broadened considerably over the past few years, and new information and data is being developed and put into practice continuously. However, in most cases the information given should be adequate to solve all but the most recalcitrant conditions. If such conditions are unavoidable, further research in the latest findings in the residential acoustic field may well prove of value. If not, the recourse is to call in an acoustic engineer with special experience in sound-isolation work. The subject, particularly when it concerns stubborn problems, is forbiddingly complex, and the expert, in unusual situations, will prove an economy in the long run.

Chapter 9

Principles of Deterioration Control

Webster defines deterioration as "the growing worse in quality or state"—of anything from a piece of wood to a man's character. That is a safely broad definition for this chapter, wherein we propose to discuss not only gradual deterioration brought about by moisture and by insect and animal invasion, but also the much swifter "deterioration" caused by lightning and by fire. Our assumption will be that the deterioration of materials and of structure can be *positively* controlled. A really well-built house *can* be made to endure indefinitely, in livable and easy-to-operate condition, and with very low maintenance cost.

DETERIORATION DUE TO MOISTURE

Of the enemies of the house, the most pervasive and persistent is water. We have already examined several aspects of moisture control (in chapter 4, on condensation) and, when necessary, the pertinent sections of that chapter will be referred to in the following pages.

But water attacks houses in many other ways besides indoor condensation. In its various forms of rain, snow, exterior humidity, groundwater, and surface runoff, it is a difficult-to-control element; and only too often, in modern houses the techniques for managing it are scanted because they are time- and labor-consuming, finicky, and often expensive.

Indeed, there is no easy solution to the problem of preserving a house from deterioration due to moisture. This calls for constant vigilance during the design, specification, and construction periods, and, even under the best of conditions, for a certain amount of maintenance in the years that follow. But the fact is that extra care in the selection and use of materials and in the supervision of building techniques, preceded by careful design, can very sizably reduce maintenance costs and materials damaged later on.

Fortunately, proper control of water damage potentialities also constitutes good control of attack by the organic enemies of the house. In only a few cases, such as termite control in heavily infested areas, are special control techniques required in addition to those needed for keeping the house and its component parts dry.

The discussion of moisture deterioration control will follow this pattern: concrete and masonry; wood, both structural and finish; and metals, including structural members, pipes, sheet metal, electrical components, etc.

CONCRETE AND MASONRY

We study these materials first, because they comprise the part of the house most commonly subject to damage by water: the foundation. Though this would be difficult to prove statistically, many people doubtless would agree that more annoyance and discomfort, more actual property damage, and more maintenance expense are involved in the repair of poorly designed and built foundations than of any other part of the house. This is because the structure is buried largely if not entirely in the earth, and it is very expensive indeed to get at it from the outside. Interior waterproofing of cellars and basements to stop existing leaks is often just as expensive. At best, this is a palliative, and at worst, impossible. There is no substitute for proper construction at the outset.

Foundations

Long before modern technology ever attacked the problem, journeyman builders knew that foundation walls should go down at least to the deepest line of frost penetration and preferably somewhat below. Whether the house is built on a concrete slab, over a shallow crawl space, or on top of a full basement, its "roots" should lie in permanently unfrozen ground. In any structure whose foundations are above the frost line, the movement of the earth expanding and contracting as it freezes and thaws can literally throw the building off its base, if the condition is serious enough.

There are exceptions, of course, to this approved procedure of carrying foundation walls downward to the frost line. In parts of Alaska, for instance, the presence of permafrost (ground that is permanently frozen to great depths and which thaws only to shallow surface levels for a short period each year) require special and quite involved construction practices. Even within the continental United States there are many mountain areas with high water tables that result in frost depths of 9 or 10 feet or more during the long and severe winters experienced there. Different procedures are used here, too, frequently involving no more than a "floating foundation" comprised of only two or three courses of unmortared concrete blocks set in a shallow trench with no footing. And, of course, there are some warm areas of the country where there *is* no frost line; in these areas, foundations generally are sunk to whatever depth is desirable, with the usual minimum being 12 to 18 inches.

But when footings are below the frost line, or are sunk to any considerable depth in warm-weather areas, they inevitably are subject to the possibility of penetration of subsurface water. And with earth-sheltered houses, this possibility is of major concern in both design and construction, especially for those houses that are almost entirely covered by earth and are set to substantial depths.

Construction to prevent cellar leaks has been developed pragmatically over the years; today it is possible to build *any* foundation so that it will be water resistant. Experimentation and study continues today in the matter of achieving fully *waterproof* foundations that will remain so indefinitely—with reasonably encouraging successes reported so far. However, achieving such waterproofness takes considerable advance knowledge of the soil conditions at the site, not to mention careful planning and foundation design, some rather esoteric building materials, much attention to detail, and skilled, top-grade workmanship. Innumerable houses have been built on inadequately studied ground, and the result has been wet basements. The only cure for this problem often has been an automatically operating sump pump, with constant expense for power and for maintenance, the always possible damage from water if the pump breaks down, and a permanently damp cellar.

The major causes of wet foundations can be summarized as follows: poorly drained sites, either too low and level, or sloping in toward the cellar on one or more sides; inadequate or nonexistent gutters and downspouts; leaky plumbing, indoors and out, including outdoor sillcocks; moisture trapped behind dense shrubbery and vines too close to the foundation wall; condensation on cold surfaces, especially during hot weather; groundwater, both from surface drainage and from a too-high water table (When the water table is just below the bottom of the foundation floor, the area becomes damp through capillarity; i.e., moisture rising through the ground in the form of vapor. When it is above the floor level, as may happen during the early spring, when the frost is melting, the area under the house can become flooded, as the water literally forces its way through the floor and the lower part of the foundation wall); and poor design, which sooner or later can lead to foundation settling and cracking, allowing moisture penetration.

In addition, of course, faulty construction techniques and inadequate or incorrectly-mixed materials may also lead to wet basements. Poor workmanship is one of the more common causes of such trouble; this applies especially to sloppy or substandard damp-proofing or waterproofing of the outer wall of the foundation itself. And, poor planning and/or cost-cutting often means no thought at all is given to even minimal damp-proofing or foundation drains.

SITE SELECTION

The best way to insure a dry foundation is to locate the house on a moderately elevated site, with good natural drainage on all sides (Figure 9–1). Hillside locations, though desirable, can cause trouble because the high head of groundwater on the upslope side of the foundation builds up a hydrostatic pressure that can easily penetrate the structure.

In addition, the soil should be moderately porous. A clayey soil requires more drastic moisture control than one that is sandy, gravelly, or loamy. Such soils provide natural drainage within themselves, since water moves freely through them and is not stored as it is in a more impervious clay.

9–1. Farmstead at Marcellus, N.Y. (USDA)

Of course, these principles are only too often counsels of perfection. Particularly with the increasing scarcity and high cost of desirable building sites, people are being forced to buy lots that are far from adequate from a drainage point of view. A survey of the potentialities for damage from water in any site should be made before the foundation is specified and the requisite protective devices against surface and groundwater should be built into the specifications and the structure.

GUTTERS AND DOWNSPOUTS

It should be unnecessary, at this late date in the history of modern building technology, to have to urge the importance of these proven water protection devices. However, a glance at many mass-produced subdivisions will show how frequently they are omitted.

There is no substitute for a gutter-downspout system. Admittedly, these systems can be a bit troublesome; they require a certain amount of maintenance (though the latest vinyl systems with polypropylene screening actually need very little), and they can be problematical in areas of severe winter weather because of freezeup and ice accumulation. However, such maintenance as is needed is relatively easy and inexpensive, and both gutters and downspouts can be kept open by fitting them with low-density ice-melting heat tapes that will keep them clear at quite low cost. Both of these mild disadvantages are far preferable to leaky basement walls and possible foundation damage from roof runoff.

9-2. Downspout installation: *A,* downspout with splash block; *B,* drain to storm sewer. (USDA)

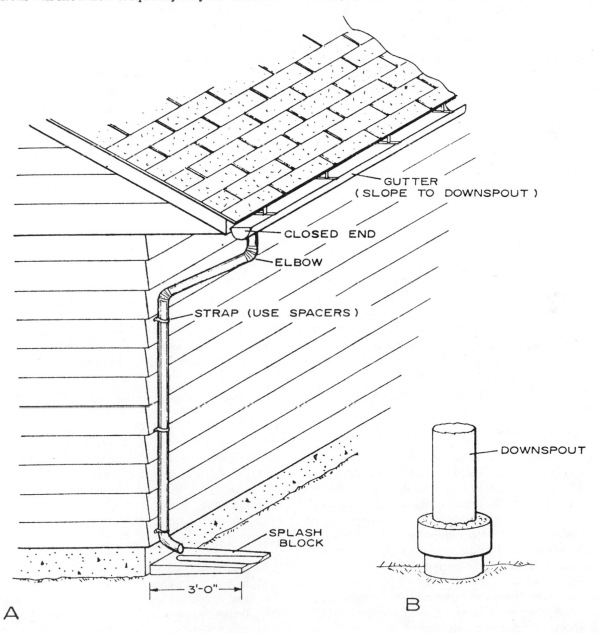

GUTTER
(SLOPE TO DOWNSPOUT)

CLOSED END

ELBOW

STRAP (USE SPACERS)

DOWNSPOUT

SPLASH BLOCK

3'-0"

A

B

Two alternatives to gutter-downspout systems are sometimes used: rainways, and gravel "drip strips." Neither is a good solution to the problem. Rainways, which are slightly off-pitched concrete or asphalt paths or walks around the perimeter of the house beneath the roof edges, are expensive, unattractive, also require maintenance, do not remove excessive runoff far enough away from the foundation, splatter great quantities of moisture onto the exterior siding, and also reflect heat into the house during hot weather. Gravel paths are even less effective, since they build in an extra head of water directly at the foundation wall; this may cause serious leakage and consequent damage to the masonry and to the wooden parts of the structure. In cold climates, the seriousness of the situation is compounded because of the possibility of freezing; the freeze-thaw cycle coupled with the enormous pressure imposed by the freezing soil can do great damage.

Guttering is readily available, and it usually comes in 4-inch to 5-inch size and in 10-foot sections for both gutters and downspouts. The guttering should be installed along the entire length of the roof eave edge, and should be fitted with end caps for a closed system. One downspout should be installed at any convenient point for every 700 square feet of roof area being drained into the gutters. Commercially available systems are made of either aluminum, galvanized steel, or vinyl plastic. They can also be custom-made of copper, or homemade of wood that is asphalt-coated on the inside faces (the wood should preferably be cedar, cypress, or redwood for longevity). Of them all, the vinyl plastic guttering is best, with aluminum and copper standing second. Galvanized steel rusts sooner or later unless painted on a regular schedule, and unprotected wood (except for the species mentioned) rots. A proper shielded gutter and downspout with a splash block is shown in Figure 9–2. Splash blocks should be long enough and so located as to carry the runoff well away from the foundation. Better yet, the downspout should be joined to an underground drainaway pipe that extends a considerable distance from the foundation before changing from solid to perforated leaching pipe, or emptying into a dry well or drainage ditch.

LEAKS IN PLUMBING

If there is a leak in a cellar pipe or fixture, it will sooner or later be spotted and repairs made. But concealed pipes in crawl spaces may leak undiscovered for years, eventually causing decay in the wood joists and flooring; and in slabs a leak's first manifestation may be actual wet spots on the concrete floor of the house. In both of these cases the damage caused by the time of discovery may already be extensive. It is obviously of special importance to make sure that all plumbing and wet-heating connections and pipes that are concealed in slabs or crawl spaces be installed with such care that nothing short of an earthquake could cause them to leak. The leaky outdoor sillcock can also go undetected for a long time, particularly if the house is not inspected periodically by the homeowner.

While the proper design and construction of *septic tanks* is not a part of the general subject covered by this book, mention should be made of the problem because of the costly and unpleasant maintenance and repair troubles that are incurred by poorly functioning installations. Everyone concerned with the design and building of new houses in rural areas without central sewage systems should be familiar with all of the pertinent design, construction, and installation data, as well as with the rules and regulations currently in effect, that govern installation in their specific areas. Many changes are now being made in residential sewage disposal systems, so the current, up-to-date information is the only data that should be relied upon; this can be obtained from local building department offices, and local or state health department authorities. To ensure proper operation and avoid leakage and other difficulties, residential sewage disposal systems must be built *exactly right*.

Dense shrubbery and vines too close to the house have already been warned against, in chapter 1. They should be placed far enough from the foundation wall to permit drainage and also to let the sun's rays in to dry out the area after a rain.

Condensation inside foundation areas was discussed in chapter 4. Some of the remedial measures will be mentioned in the following section since they can be useful against condensation as well as groundwater.

Groundwater, and surface water that becomes groundwater by seepage, constitute the major causes of damp or flooded basements. The best precaution is, as stated above, judicious site selection. But inasmuch as almost no site in the north temperate zone is always truly dry, it will be advisable to protect most foundations, at least to a minimal degree, from such water penetration. For sites with moderate water conditions, construction rating as water-resistant or damp-proof can be used; but for wet sites, particularly those located in clayey soils, construction rating as waterproof should be specified. It would, of course, be a waste of good money to include waterproofing protection if every indication of experience and testing for the given area points against it. On the other hand, the cost of a waterproof foundation represents only a small fraction of the total cost of a new residence, and if there is any indication that moisture might at some time become even a minor problem, the money will be well spent.

Waterproof and Water-Resistant Basements

In general, a poured concrete basement wall provides a more water-resistant construction than a masonry unit wall (other things, such as quality of workmanship, being equal). It is harder to waterproof masonry joints than it is to prevent leaks through monolithic concrete. However, it *is* possible to achieve a high degree of waterproofness with either type of wall if special materials and techniques are used.

The Portland Cement Association's *Concrete Masonry Handbook* states, "the elements of watertight concrete masonry walls. . . include sound masonry units, proper mortar, and a high standard of construction." They go on to say, "ASTM and CSA specifications for concrete brick and block do not specify water permeability, but they do note that protective coating may be required to prevent water penetration." And further, "Leaky walls are not confined to any one type of masonry construction. Leaks can occur in walls built of the best materials. The percentage of those that leak is small, but receives a disproportionate amount of attention." Quite so; and with good reason, as far as the affected homeowners are concerned. As to poured concrete foundations, the Portland Cement Association states flatly in a recent bulletin, *Concrete Facts About Basements,* "Dryness is the result of the drainage system—a gravel base or draintile—not the foundation material. Properly constructed concrete basements do not leak." The *Concrete Manual* (Bureau of Reclamation, U.S. Department of the Interior, 1975) tells us, "Hardened concrete might be completely watertight if it were composed entirely of solid matter." But, the *Manual* goes on the say that water used in mixing creates voids and also the cement shrinks as it dries. Thus, ". . . it is evident that hardened concrete is inherently somewhat pervious to water which may enter through capillary pores or be forced in by pressure. Nevertheless, permeability may be so controlled that construction of durable watertight structures is not a serious problem." Unless, of course, *your* basement has leaky walls.

Two points are obvious. First, properly constructed masonry foundations have a high degree of water resistance when constructed and installed to the highest standards, always assuming that no mechanical damage occurs. And second, for various reasons that include a lack of good quality control in the field, a masonry basement *may* leak, and the *possibility* of water leakage is ever-present and worth considering. Water leakage in a nicely finished basement that is used for living quarters, or in an earth-sheltered house, is not only dismaying, but also can be a disaster that is best insured against.

The first step, then, is to construct the foundations with the best of materials and workmanship. In the case of concrete blocks, this involves using quality Grade N blocks conforming to ASTM C90, Standard Specification For Hollow Load-Bearing Concrete Masonry Units, and ASTM C145, Standard Specification For Solid Load-Bearing Concrete Masonry Units. The mortar used to bond the units should be either Type M or S, under ASTM C270, mixed on the job with just enough water to produce a workable consistency during con-

struction. The water used for mixing must be clean and of a quality fit to drink; however, no appreciable amount of alkalies, sugars, or sulfates should be present. Joints must be properly tooled. And, of course, the design of the foundation itself must be proper and include a substantial footing amply sized to prevent settling or shifting and subsequent cracking of the mortar joints; reinforcing must be included if and as necessary. Joints should be properly cured before further construction continues.

Poured concrete foundations must likewise be made of the best materials and completed with the best techniques and workmanship. A great deal depends upon the specific mix of concrete used; i.e., the exact proportions of cement, aggregates, water, and admixtures. The use of generalities here can be misleading, and the specifics should be detailed for each individual job for best results. According to the Portland Cement Association's publication, *Admixtures for Concrete,* "The water tightness of concrete depends primarily on the amount of cement and mixing water used and the length of the moist-curing period. Concrete made with a water-cement ratio of less than 0.49 by weight will be watertight if it has low slump and is properly placed and cured." The slump (which is a test used as a measure of the consistency of concrete) in this case may run from a minimum of 1 inch to a maximum of 3 inches. Proper curing of the emplaced concrete is extremely important and, unfortunately, is a factor often disregarded. Concrete forms should be left in place for at least three to seven days, and the exposed tops of concrete walls or footings must be kept continuously damp, or even wet, by covering them with burlap sacking that is kept soaked or by running a length of soaker-type hose along the top and letting the water run continuously. Concrete slabs may be ponded, or covered with a layer of water; covered with soaked burlap and kept wet; sprayed on a continuous basis with a mist from a hose; or completely covered with a layer of polyethylene film that will seal moisture in (Figure 9-3).

9-3. Curing concrete by covering with polyethylene sheeting. (Courtesy, Portland Cement Association)

In all cases, curing should continue for three days minimum (seven is much better), and no part of the concrete should be permitted to become dry. A bit of sprinkling from time to time will not effect a proper cure, and the concrete will inevitably be of inferior quality. If it is possible to extend the curing period, so much the better; compressive strength will be greatly increased.

The second step is to reduce or eliminate the possibility of water contacting the masonry surfaces at all, a chore more easily talked of than accomplished. Moisture can enter a basement in two ways: as a result of temporary water pressure on the walls or floor, and by a process known as capillary draw. (A third mechanism, vapor transmission, is sometimes mistakenly thought to account for dampness in a basement, but in fact does not.) Temporary water pressures on the outside of foundation walls can occur whenever there is any appreciable amount of groundwater in the area. The cause may be a rise in water table, heavy rainfalls, lack of a proper guttering system, spring thaw of frozen ground, natural surface runoff courses or basins too close to the house, or other factors. Even a lawn sprinkler running for too long can cause slight hydrostatic pressures against a foundation wall. Such pressures are frequently unpredictable. They may result in direct leaks into the basement, or at times they may not. They can occur at virtually any time of year and for varying reasons. Sometimes they can happen suddenly, where no problems have apparently existed previously. For this reason, following the old adage that an ounce of prevention is worth a pound of cure, adequate damp-proofing of foundation walls is usually a good idea.

Capillary draw generally results in dampness problems rather than out-and-out (or "in-and-in") leakage, though water accumulations can also occur. Capillary draw through a foundation wall works in exactly the same manner as kerosene being drawn up a wick in an oil lamp or as ink being soaked up by a blotter. Moisture in the ground is drawn through the masonry wall, resulting at least in a substantial increase in the humidity within the basement and, at worst, in obvious dampness on the walls, perhaps even to the extent of some beading and puddling.

Where there is no likelihood of temporary hydrostatic pressures on the foundation walls, moisture can be blocked from entering by employing any of several methods of *damp-proofing*. If the presence of hydrostatic pressure is a possibility, *waterproofing* methods should be used. The latter, of course, will serve to prevent capillary draw as well. Damp-proofing is considerably less effective than waterproofing, and, though it will stop moisture penetration, it will not deter water penetration. The longevity of the materials tends to be less than those for waterproofing, and there is no real guarantee that, once installed, a damp-

proofing system will remain effective. On the other hand, damp-proofing is less expensive than full waterproofing, and it is less problematical to apply or install. Waterproofing methods are more complex and more expensive, but also can be long-lived and generally effective. A number of methods are well recognized, but it should be noted that experimentation in these and other methods as well are proceeding continuously, particularly with respect to earth-sheltered houses. There is a considerable degree of variability in the effectiveness of waterproofings; the quality of materials and workmanship, the design conditions, and the design of the waterproofing system are definite factors in effectiveness. The nature of the hydrostatic pressures also has a bearing; while many waterproofings are capable of withstanding low hydrostatic pressures on a periodic, temporary basis, few, if any, can withstand constant, high hydrostatic pressures with any great success.

DAMP-PROOFING CONCRETE

In cases where little or no ground moisture is present and there is no reason to suspect that even capillary draw will occur, or will present any problems if it does so occasionally and in mild form (or where moisture on the inside of the foundation walls is irrelevant), the usual procedure is as follows: simply pour a concrete footing and then pour a plain concrete foundation wall atop the footing, or build up a unit masonry wall. Other than using good workmanship and good materials, no specific precaution against moisture is taken.

However, if capillary draw might be expected to introduce unwanted moisture, there are several damp-proofing methods that can be employed. One possibility is to mix the concrete with an admixture intended to increase watertightness. There are two types: those that reduce permeability and those that reduce capillary flow. However, according to the Portland Cement Association, permeability-reducing agents sometimes act to increase rather than decrease permeability, and many of the admixtures used to reduce capillary flow, often called damp-proofers, are ineffective, especially against water under pressure.

Pargeting, or parging, is a well-known damp-proofing technique that consists of applying a coating of dense cement plaster to the exterior of the foundation wall. The technique is used mostly on concrete masonry walls, but may be applied to poured concrete as well (Figure 9-4). The National Concrete Masonry Association suggests applying the parging in two 1/4-inch coats. The first coat is troweled directly onto the concrete block, using a portland cement plaster. After the first coat has partly hardened, its surface is roughened with a scratcher to provide good purchase for the second coat, and then it is moist-cured for at least twenty-four hours. Prior to application of the second coat, the surface is lightly dampened with a water spray, then the second coat is plastered on and packed to a firm density by steel-troweling. This coating should also be damp-cured to ensure proper strength and water-resistance. Other thicknesses and coating methods are also used, such as three-coat on metal lath, single direct application, and so on.

9–4. Parging to damp-proof a masonry wall. (Courtesy, Portland Cement Association)

Parging can be used alone, but is frequently coated with another waterproofing material after the plaster cures. There are two in common use, and they are widely used on either concrete masonry or poured concrete foundation walls with or without parging. A bituminous or asphalt coating can be applied either hot or cold and can be sprayed or brushed on. Hot spraying has better penetration and covering capabilities, but the coatings are rather thin and hot asphalt tends to become brittle when cold. At least two coatings should be applied. Cold brushed asphalt coatings are thicker, but have neither the bridging nor the penetration qualities of hot asphalt. In either case, asphalt emulsions will slowly dissolve when in contact with water over a period of years. A general-purpose asphalt pitch is more stable than asphalt emulsions, but it remains brittle and will not reseal itself after cracking. A substitute material that works reasonably well is a heavy, dense coat of cold, fiber-reinforced asphaltic mastic applied in a thick layer with a trowel.

One material that is very inexpensive, easy to use, and effective is polyethylene sheet. This material must be carefully applied so as to avoid punctures and tears, but, if correctly placed so that its integrity is complete, 6-mil black polyethylene should last indefinitely when below-grade; it does degrade when exposed to sunlight.

Polyethylene sheet also has the capability of easily bridging cracks and defects in the foundation walls, and is an adequate and commonly-used damp-proofing protection when laid beneath a concrete floor; in the latter case, however, puncturing is always a possibility and the installation must be made with care.

From time to time various kinds of liquid seals have been offered up as exterior foundation wall damp-proofers, with claims ranging from merely remarkable to absolutely fantastic in the way of protection. However, such seals are in fact generally quite a bit less than adequate, and all of them, like most damp-proofers, lose their sealing capabilities when cracks in the concrete appear.

WATERPROOFING CONCRETE

When there is some hydrostatic pressure in the ground, even if only on a short-term and periodic basis, all concrete masonry foundation walls and even poured concrete walls must be built to the most exacting specifications, and they require waterproofing treatments of the exterior surfaces as well. The same is true of the underside of a concrete floor (Figure 9–5).

Considerable information on the business of waterproofing foundation walls, as well as damp-proofing them, can be found in The Underground Space Center's *Earth-Sheltered Housing Design* (Van Nostrand Reinhold Company, 1979). Since old data is constantly being reevaluated and new information is coming along continuously, anyone faced with the problem of fully waterproofing foundation walls should obtain up-to-the-minute details from this and/or other sources before establishing final design and construction specifications. At present, there are several methods of waterproofing, all with various capabilities, advantages, and disadvantages. The basics of some of those methods follow.

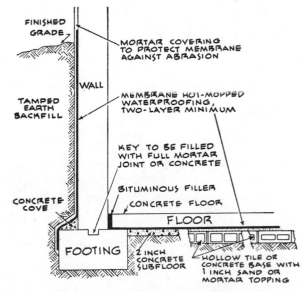

9–5. One method of waterproof foundation construction. (HHFA)

The *built-up membrane* is one method that has been in use for a number of years and has proven to be successful on many occasions. In fact, this is the first choice of some specialists in the field. The process consists of building up layers of asphalt or pitch alternated with a reinforcing membrane such as fabric or roofing felt. Fiberglass cloth or matt has been a recent choice, because this material is impervious to rot, fungus, and similar problems. However, proper adhesion of the materials to one another and to the foundation wall surface can be a problem, and so can the lack of elasticity and resealing or self-healing capabilities. Membranes are also susceptible to damage during the construction process. But, if carefully designed and engineered and correctly installed, they constitute a workable solution.

The same *polyethylene sheeting* mentioned earlier—a 6-mil or heavier black sheeting is frequently used—can be sealed to the foundation walls with a thick, heavy mastic. The overlaps between sheets must be substantial and also fully sealed with mastic. This combination, if properly installed, will provide adequate protection against periodic high ground water pressures. In fact, the same system, with the sheeting sealed down with any one of several specific adhesives, has been used successfully for a number of years in the All Weather Wood Foundation (AWWF) system. In combination with the treated wood members and sheathing and the particular construction techniques of the system, AWWF foundation walls are virtually watertight bulkheads (Figure 9–6).

9–6. Typical all weather wood foundation.

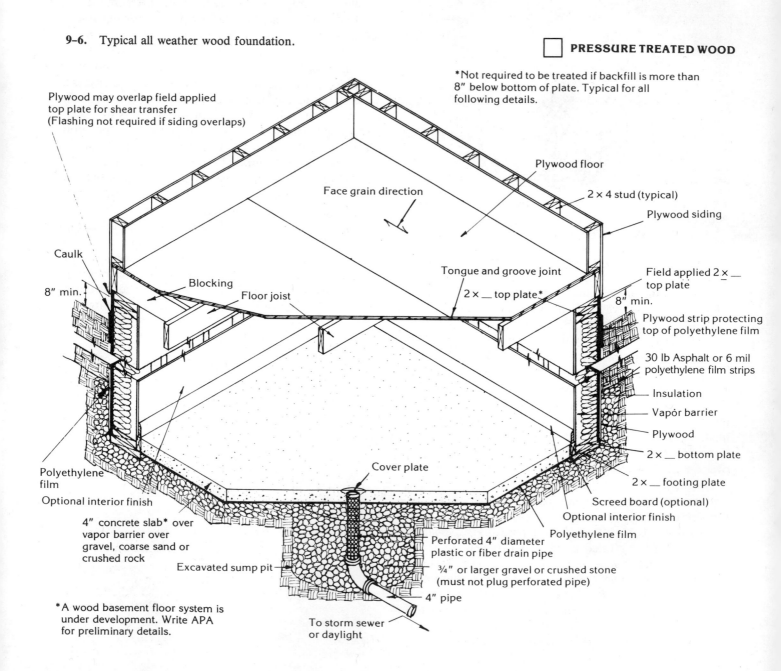

☐ **PRESSURE TREATED WOOD**

*Not required to be treated if backfill is more than 8" below bottom of plate. Typical for all following details.

Plywood may overlap field applied top plate for shear transfer (Flashing not required if siding overlaps)

Plywood floor

Face grain direction

2 × 4 stud (typical)

Plywood siding

Caulk

Tongue and groove joint

Blocking

Floor joist

8" min.

2 × __ top plate*

Field applied 2 × __ top plate

8" min.

Plywood strip protecting top of polyethylene film

30 lb Asphalt or 6 mil polyethylene film strips

Insulation

Vapor barrier

Plywood

2 × __ bottom plate

2 × __ footing plate

Polyethylene film

Cover plate

Optional interior finish

Screed board (optional)

Optional interior finish

Polyethylene film

4" concrete slab* over vapor barrier over gravel, coarse sand or crushed rock

Perforated 4" diameter plastic or fiber drain pipe

¾" or larger gravel or crushed stone (must not plug perforated pipe)

Excavated sump pit

4" pipe

*A wood basement floor system is under development. Write APA for preliminary details.

To storm sewer or daylight

238

Bentonite panels consist of cardboard covers that are filled with a particular clay soil called bentonite, much like a sheet of wallboard. Bentonite has the peculiar quality of greatly expanding upon contact with water, to the point where it seals out further moisture penetration. In many applications, this system constitutes one of the best waterproofing techniques now in use. It has the advantage of being easily installed (the sheets are merely nailed in position), the cost is not excessive, the material has some degree of bridging and self-healing capabilities, and it does not deteriorate with time. A somewhat similar method is sometimes used wherein bentonite clay is mixed with a mastic binder and sprayed directly onto the surfaces to be waterproofed. The layer can be 3/8-inch to 1/2-inch thick, and it has self-healing and bridging capabilities. To be effective, a proper mix and correct application procedures must be followed, and coverage and sealing must be complete. However, the system appears to have many advantages, few disadvantages, and is in general an effective method.

Flexible membranes are now being used with some success, though experimentation continues, especially in the matter of application techniques. These membranes may be of butyl rubber, neoprene or some similar material that has the advantages of good bridging characteristics and a certain amount of flexibility and elasticity. Making the proper seams can be a problem and requires great care; accidental damage can also destroy the membrane integrity. The membrane must be fully bedded and sealed to the foundation wall in order to be effective.

FOUNDATION DRAINS

Regardless of whether a wall is built with no moistureproofing considerations, with damp-proofing materials, or with full waterproofing, a complete footing drainage system (Figure 9–7), and sometimes an under-floor drainage system as well, should be a part of the foundation design. Typically, a modern footing drainage system consists of lengths of perforated plastic drainpipe or slotted plastic drain tubing, 4 to 6 inches in diameter, laid in a gravel bed alongside the footing around the entire perimeter of the foundation. The gravel bedding should continue for a considerable distance above the pipeline (minimum 2 inches above the footing top) to act as a filter that will prevent silt and sediment from settling down into the drainage area and clogging it. In severe cases, the pipeline should be wrapped with special filter fabrics. The pipelines must be graded slightly in order to effect adequate drainage flow, and the system must be connected at one or more points to a solid drainpipe line that leads to daylight on a sloping site, to a drainaway channel, to a storm sewer, or to a properly sized dry well (but *never* to a septic tank). Such a drainage system will allow drawdown of the water table, minimizing and often eliminating

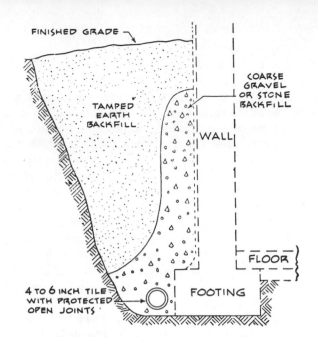

9–7. Foundation drain tile at footings. (HHFA)

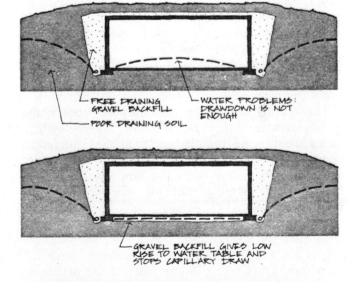

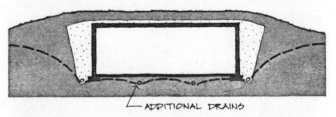

9–8. Drainage techniques showing moisture drawdown curbs. (*Earth Sheltered Housing Design*, Van Nostrand Reinhold, 1979)

239

hydrostatic pressures against the foundation walls themselves (Figure 9-8). This eases the load on the damp-proofing or waterproofing of the foundation walls, rendering them more effective and less prone to deterioration or other fault. In some cases, the presence of a complete drainage system may also mean that the foundation walls can be constructed and waterproofed to a somewhat lower level of potential performance because of the lowered possibility of substantial positive groundwater pressures; this in turn reduces costs and construction problems. Numerous methods for constructing under-floor drainage systems are used, among them: a layer of coarse gravel 4 to 6 inches thick; 4-inch clay tile or concrete block laid flat in a network or grid; or runs of perforated plastic drainpipe or slotted drain tubing.

A final point: A damp-proofing course 6 to 18 inches above the finished outside grade line will prevent moisture from rising into the wall by capillary action. This might consist of parging, an applied membrane, a layer of slate or similar material, tin or copper, or some other impervious and noncorrodable material. Some may also serve as a termite shield.

There is, of course, more to the design and construction of dry foundations than this. For example, if a house is to be built over a crawl space in wet ground, the technique of laying strips of roll roofing or polyethylene sheeting on the ground to keep out water *vapor* will not be adequate. A concrete lining, together with some form of membrane waterproofing, should be placed over the whole ground surface, and drain lines should also be put in around the footings. Similar tiles or drainpipes will also be needed in damp ground where houses are built on slabs, and the slab itself should be underlaid with a strong, durable waterproof and vapor-proof sheet material, as was described in chapter 4.

This chapter includes no data on waterproofing the *inside* surfaces of foundation walls. There are three damp-proofing mixtures that can be applied with fair to good success: portland cement and sand brush coating; portland cement, iron dust, and sand coating applied by troweling; parging coats of mortar or cement plaster.

Various proprietary materials are marketed at any given time for this purpose, but in most instances the results are not particularly good and many have not been thoroughly tested in any case. If use of one of these products is contemplated, a thorough investigation of its worth and effectiveness is suggested.

Exposed Masonry

From the point of view of protecting masonry from the elements and of keeping moisture from leaking through it into the inner layers, the type of wall cross section is of lesser importance than the actual surface itself. Note, however, that of the five common standard masonry wall constructions (solid masonry, hollow masonry, composite, cavity, and veneered), cavity walls offer the advantage of prohibiting passage of water or moisture completely through the wall assembly, and so is a good choice in areas of severe weather conditions. The major problems encountered with masonry houses include the following: leaks through masonry joints because of improper design or specifications, poor workmanship, poorly-formulated or imcompatible mortars, or shrinkage of mortar, brick, or block over a period of time; cracking because of improper design and/or specifications, aging, shifting ground, mechanical damage, and the like; and disfigurement and eventual deterioration of the masonry because of efflorescence, resulting in blisters, bulges, and spalling. This latter problem is actually much more likely to be detrimental to appearance than to structural integrity, especially if it is cleaned away promptly.

Efflorescence is, according to the Portland Cement Association (see Bibliography), "a crystalline deposit, usually white, that may develop on the surfaces of masonry or concrete construcion." This deposit often appears soon after construction of the masonry, and, while unattractive, it is usually harmless. But circumstances can occur where the surface of the masonry is disrupted. "A combination of circumstances causes efflorescence. First, there must be soluble salts in the material. Second, there must be moisture to pick up the soluble salts and carry them to the surface. Third, evaporation or hydrostatic pressure must cause the solution to move. If any one of these conditions are eliminated, effloresence will not occur." Further information on the causes of and the cures for efflorescence, as well as procedures designed to minimize or eliminate the possibility of efflorescence, can be obtained from the Portland Cement Association.

BRICK WALL CONSTRUCTION

The average exposed brick wall receives no special waterproofing treatment. To put it plainly, a well-built one does not need such treatment, except under extraordinary conditions. Water, in the form of rain, snow, or excessively high outdoor humidity will not penetrate so deeply that it will damage the inner layers of the structure *if*—and this is a big "if"—the materials and workmanship are of the highest quality. High-quality brick construction means, in summary form:

Bricks especially designed for use as exterior wall facing. The brick must be of high strength and density; texture selection is important, and, where weathering conditions are bad, deeply textured bricks should not be used. For double assurance, choose bricks that have been made in accordance with the pertinent specifications of the American Society for Testing Materials (ASTM Specification C62 for building brick; ASTM Specification C216 for facing brick).

Masonry mortars designed as such. Some of the worst troubles from moisture in brick walls arise from using cement mortars that are improperly formulated or mixed or that may be incompatible with the materials from which the bricks are made. Either use one of the proprietary brick cement mortars on the market; or formulate your own in accordance with the proper specifications, such as ASTM's Mortar for Unit Masonry, C270 (for plain masonry) or C476 (for reinforced masonry), and Aggregate for Masonry Mortar, C144.

Top-grade workmanship. It is appalling how many brick walls, even those using the best materials, perform poorly because of bad workmanship. Good workmanship means plenty of mortar between each brick (*no voids at all*) horizontally and vertically.

9-9. Top-grade brick workmanship. (Portland Cement Association)

Although top-grade workmanship (Figure 9-9) may cost somewhat more, the results in permanent wall durability and dryness will "write off" the extra expense in a short while. In this connection, note should be made of the fact that, as stated in the *Concrete Masonry Handbook* (Randall and Panarese, Portland Cement Association, 1976), "While workmanship is the most important element, it isn't fair to always hold the mason responsible for leaks due to poor workmanship. The owner, architect, and builder share the responsibility because they govern the type of workmanship desired."

Good flashing around all openings and at joints between dissimilar materials. One of the common causes of brick streaking and eventual deterioration is water dripping from badly designed window sills and caps, stone courses, fascia boards, exposed metal components, and the like. A noncorrodable, durable flashing, protruding outward and downward about an inch to form a drip edge, will keep most the water away from the wall surface.

Concave mortar joints. Unless the esthetic effect of a struck (or flush) joint is desired, all mortar joints should be pointed with a special tool, as in Examples 1 and 2 of Figure 9-10, so that the mortar is pushed tight against the bricks on both sides. Struck (No. 5 in Figure 9-10) and raked (No. 6) joints are quite unsuitable; and flush (No. 4) and weathered (No. 3) are not as good as Nos. 1 and 2, since the mortar is not pushed firmly into the joints.

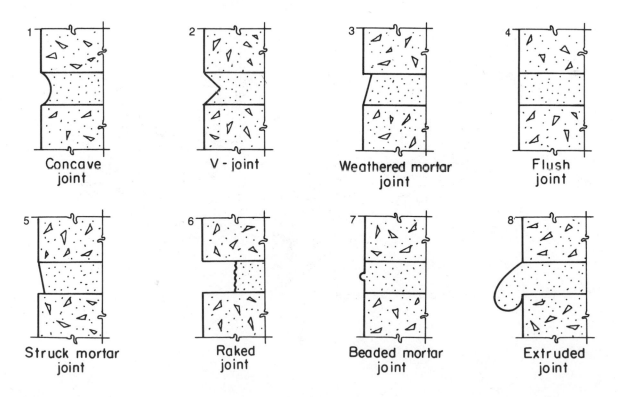

9-10. Types of brick of block mortar joints. (Portland Cement Association)

Vapor-permeable waterproof coatings for brick walls are rarely necessary when the wall is of top-grade quality in materials and workmanship, unless exterior conditions are unusually harsh, as may happen with exposed walls on the north side in winter. And, of course, exterior brick facings are sometimes painted for the decorative effect; in fact, this is by far the most prevalent reason, usually in conjunction with providing a fresh appearance and perhaps also a change in color and/or texture of the surface. But whatever the specific reasons, when waterproof coatings are used, they *should be vapor-permeable*. There are several different kinds of applied finishes that can be used with good success, and they will be briefly reviewed later in this chapter.

BRICK VENEER CONSTRUCTION

Proper construction of brick veneer over a wood frame is shown in Figure 9–11; stone is handled in the same way. L. O. Anderson, in his *Wood Frame House Construction* (USDA Agricultural Handbook No. 73,

available from the Forest Products Laboratories), from which this figure was taken, writes:

> If masonry veneer is used . . . the foundation must include a supporting ledge or offset about 5 inches wide. . . . This results in a space of about 1 inch between the masonry and the sheathing for ease in laying the brick. A base flashing is used at the brick course below the bottom of the sheathing and framing, and should be lapped with sheathing paper. Weep holes, to provide drainage, are also located at this course and are formed by eliminating the mortar in a vertical joint. Corrosion-resistant metal ties—spaced about 32 inches apart horizontally and 16 inches vertically—should be used to bond the brick veneer to the framework. Where other than wood sheathing is used, secure the ties to the studs.
>
> Brick and stone should be laid in a full bed of mortar; avoid dropping mortar into the space between the veneer and sheathing. Outside joints should be tooled to a smooth finish to get the maximum resistance to water penetration.
>
> Masonry laid during the cold weather should be protected from freezing until after the mortar has set.

And, of course, materials and workmanship for masonry veneer should be just as high quality as for an all-masonry wall.

9–11. Wood-frame construction with masonry veneer. Note 1/2-inch space between brick and sheathing. (USDA)

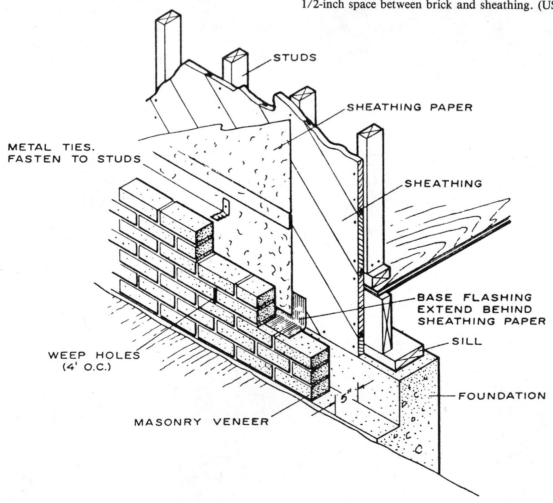

STUDS

SHEATHING PAPER

SHEATHING

METAL TIES. FASTEN TO STUDS

BASE FLASHING EXTEND BEHIND SHEATHING PAPER

SILL

WEEP HOLES (4' O.C.)

5"

FOUNDATION

MASONRY VENEER

CHIMNEY CONSTRUCTION

It hardly need be pointed out that masonry chimneys should be built with the same care as any other masonry, and in fact must comply with a number of rigid specifications and regulations. In addition, good noncorroding flashing and conterflashing must be used. Chimney leaks not only damage the masonry, but also the house itself. For details on chimney construction for fire safety, see pages 258-263.

CONCRETE BLOCK CONSTRUCTION

Exactly the same high standards of materials and workmanship should be used for exterior walls of masonry blocks made of concrete as for brick (Figures 9–12 and 9–13). But the much greater porosity of these materials makes exterior surface treatment essential, while in the case of concrete or brick they are optional. The somewhat lower cost of this type of construction, compared to brick or poured concrete, plus the variety of facing designs possible, make them a good substitute for clay brick walls. And, the two materials are often

9-12. Top-grade concrete block construction. (Portland Cement Association)

9-13. Tooling joints in concrete block construction. (Portland Cement Association)

used in concert. Of course, surface coatings must be renewed at periodic intervals, just like paint on wood: an element of maintenance not usually necessary with brick. However, a really good cement paint has great longevity and only needs washing occasionally to renew its cleanliness.

The pertinent concrete block specifications issued by the ASTM are: Concrete Masonry Units, Hollow, Load Bearing C90; Concrete Masonry Units, Hollow, Nonload Bearing C129; and Concrete Masonry Units, Solid, Load Bearing, C145. For concrete building brick, the specification number is C55.

Stucco over concrete masonry or over concrete provides a high-grade water-resistant surface if the stucco is correctly formulated and applied. However, a good stucco job is not inexpensive when added to the original cost of the masonry wall. It does make a weatherproof and moderately durable surface coating over metal lath on a wood-frame wall if well applied, and here the costs are usually comparable with brick veneer. Stucco can crack as the frame shrinks, but the inclusion of properly designed and placed control joints will usually minimize or eliminate this problem. A full discussion of stucco, which is simply a portland cement plaster, can be found in the Portland Cement Association's *Plasterer's Manual.*

MASONRY COATINGS

Numerous kinds of applied coatings can be used on concrete and masonry, both inside and out. Our chief concern here is with exterior finishes, which must be "breathable" and should be reasonably durable and weather-resistant as well.

Portland cement base paints have been used for many years and have a good record. Those made under Federal Specification TT-P-21 should be used. This specification provides for two types of paint: Type I, which is a general-purpose paint that contains a minimum of 65 percent portland cement by weight; and Type II, which has maximum durability and must contain at least 80 percent portland cement by weight. Each Type is further divided into two classes: Class A, which is general-purpose and contains no aggregate filler; and Class B, which is intended for use on open-textured surfaces and may contain anywhere from 20 to 40 percent of siliceous sand filler. These paints are also sometimes modified with latex. The surface created by a portland cement is tough and vapor-permeable, and the presence of alkalies in the concrete or concrete masonry will not affect them. These paints are sometimes job-mixed, but better results can be obtained by using a proprietary prepared paint made to the aforementioned Federal Specification.

Latex paints can also be used on exterior masonry surfaces and have the advantages of being easy to apply, odorless, and relatively inexpensive. Under normal circumstances they are quite durable and relatively colorfast. Those that are formulated with acrylics appear to give the best performance.

Various kinds, formulations, and brands of urethanes, epoxies, and polyesters have been (and are being) successfully used, but in varying degrees, upon exterior masonry surfaces. Likewise, rubber-based paints, which may be made with styrene-butadiene resin or chlorinated natural rubber, are also used on both interior and exterior masonry surfaces. These paints, however, while having much greater resistance to the entrance of moisture than do the latex paints, form skin that is so water-resistant as to be virtually impermeable. Thus, the possible consequences of using an applied finish that will not breathe must be carefully assessed before proceeding.

Oil-based, varnished-based, and oil-alkyd paints are susceptible to damage from alkalies, are not particularly durable under many circumstances, and are non-breathing to various degrees. Their use on concrete masonry surfaces cannot be recommended.

Clear coatings are sometimes specified to improve water resistance, to make cleaning easier, and to help to protect the surface from dirt and grime. In sum, of these coatings, some are reasonably effective, while others are not. Those that are based on a methyl methacrylate form of acrylic resin appear to be the most effective.

Concrete and concrete masonry walls can also be stained, though this does little to improve water-resistance and is not nearly as durable as coloring the concrete during mixing. Either organic dye stains, oil stains, or metallic salt stains can be employed, and the results can be good from a decorative standpoint.

Proprietary applied-finish products come and go, and some are good while others are less so. If the use of any such product is contemplated, a thorough investigation of the properties and characteristics of the particular product is suggested. A few of these products have been tested, and results may be obtainable from various agencies such as the National Bureau of Standards. Application of a finish that does not perform as advertised or specified can do more harm than good, and is both discouraging and expensive.

The fact should be recognized, too, that proper preparation for and application of a finish has as much or more to do with the ultimate effectiveness of that finish than does the material itself. All applied finishes must be used under the right conditions and in the proper circumstance, and upon surfaces that are correctly prepared to receive the finish. These details vary tremendously with the type of finish being applied and also with the specific product. If every aspect of the application is not attended with great care, the final results will surely be less than satisfactory.

Finally, note that no coating will permanently render a concrete or concrete masonry wall entirely waterproof or completely weatherproof. Some coatings intended for the purpose do not work at all, while others can be expected to serve only moderately well, from a long-term standpoint. This is especially true as moisture or weather conditions become more severe. The only *really* satisfactory way to make a water-resistant and weather-resistant brick or concrete masonry wall is to construct it with top-grade workmanship and materials and to keep the masonry joints repointed with a high grade of mortar as the years go by.

WOOD

Over the years, a body of information on wood and wood preservation has been collected which is almost embarrassing in its richness. The Forest Products Laboratory's *Wood Handbook* (revised 1974, available from the Laboratory) is a compendium of over 500 pages of compact, tested, and reliable data on this most common of all building materials. In addition, there are numerous government and private publications in the field, some of which will be quoted from in the following pages, that supplement the *Handbook* data.

We do not intend this section to compete with these publications. Rather, the purpose is to present some of the most important generally accepted data on wood preservation in simplified form. Fuller details can be obtained from the source publications. The major aspects of the problem fall into two categories: prevention of dampness, with its attendant evils of mildew, molds and stains, surface deterioration, and structural weakening; and elimination of attacks by insects and animals, from termites to rats.

Many types of wood treatment are useful in the control of both these hazards; but some are important only for one, and are required only when that hazard alone is present.

Prevention Of Decay

There are three ways of reducing or eliminating decay dangers: dryness, surface protective coatings (such as paint), and wood preservative treatments. All of these may be necessary under severe conditions, but usually only the first two are called for.

DRYNESS

This is of basic importance in all structural and finishing wood. Since wood is an organic material, it is a highly desirable food to a host of microscopic decay organisms, most of which find it inedible when it is relatively dry. Therefore, wood should have a moisture content, when used in house construction, that is below a maximum above which its enemies find it appetizing, and above a minimum that might cause shrinkage, warping, honeycombing, and loosening of knots. When knots become loose, they usually fall out, weakening the wood and opening it to leakage.

The *Wood Handbook* states: "Ideally, house framing lumber should be seasoned to the moisture content it will reach in use, thus minimizing future dimensional changes due to frame shrinkage. . . . If, at the time the wall and ceiling finish is applied, the moisture content of the framing lumber is not more than about 5 percent above that which it will reach in service [Table 9-1], there will be little or no evidence of defects caused by shrinkage of the frame. In heated houses in cold climates, joists over heated basements, studs, and ceiling joists may reach a moisture content as low as 6 to 7 percent. In mild climates the minimum moisture content will be higher." *The Handbook* also says: "The moisture content requirements are more exacting for finish lumber and wood products used inside heated and air-conditioned buildings than those in lumber used outdoors or in unheated buildings." Figure 9-14 indicates recommended moisture content averages for interior use of wood products, and recommended moisture content values for various wood items are listed in Table 9-1. *The Handbook* continues: "General commercial practice is to kiln-dry wood for some prod-

ucts, such as flooring and furniture, to a slightly lower moisture content than service conditions demand, anticipating a moderate increase in moisture content during processing and construction. . . . Common grades of softwood lumber and softwood dimension are not normally seasoned to the moisture content values indicated in [Table 9-1]. When they are not, shrinkage effects should be considered in the structural design and construction methods."

Wood dried to the recommended moisture contents will, under usual climatic conditions and with good construction practices, be relatively safe from decay. Of course, any exposed wood, such as siding, shingles, facias, window and door frames and window sashes, exposed porch floors and posts, and so on must usually be protected from water by preservative, paint or stain, although a few species carry their own waterproofness with them. These include cypress, redwood, and several types of cedar; and these woods are also, and probably for the same reason, most easily painted and most durable when painted.

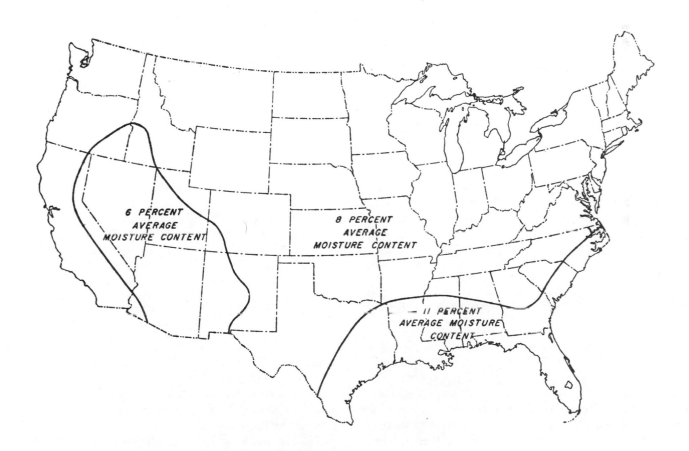

9-14. Recommended average moisture content for interior use of wood products in various areas of the United States. (Forest Products Laboratory)

Use of wood	Moisture content for—					
	Most areas of United States		Dry southwestern area		Damp, warm coastal areas	
	Average [2]	Individual pieces	Average [2]	Individual pieces	Average [2]	Individual pieces
	Pct.	Pct.	Pct.	Pct.	Pct.	Pct.
Interior: Woodwork, flooring, furniture, wood trim, laminated timbers, cold-press plywood	8	6–10	6	4–9	11	8–13
Exterior: Siding, wood trim, framing, sheathing, laminated timbers	12	9–14	9	7–12	12	9–14

[2] To obtain a realistic average, test at least 10 pct. of each item. If the amount of a given item is small, several tests should be made. For example, in an ordinary dwelling having about 60 floor joists, at least 10 tests should be made on joists selected at random.

Table 9–1. (Forest Products Laboratory)

Dry storage. It is not enough, of course, that wood should be of acceptable dryness when delivered to a building site. If it is incorrectly stored, it will swiftly absorb all of—and sometimes more than—the moisture that had previously been removed. All lumber should be carefully stored in stacks, preferably bundled and wrapped, and preferably in closed sheds. Lumber stored out-of-doors should be in roofed racks, or it should be in piles and covered at the top. In all cases, the piles or stacks should be arranged so that air can circulate between each layer. Theoretically, only as much lumber should be delivered to a job site as is needed on a given day, but this is very difficult to achieve in practice, given the conditions under which most houses are built. And, one must also take into consideration that storage conditions at a local yard frequently are little different than those at the site and may indeed be somewhat worse.

Dry construction. It is, of course, a counsel of perfection to recommend building only during dry weather. The job must go forward even when it means part or all of the wood may get wet. What *is* possible is to permit enough time to pass after putting the wood into a building for it to dry out before it is finally concealed from the dehydrating effects of sunlight and air by other parts of the structure or by protective paint coatings. Over-damp wood has been the cause of innumerable original-coat paint failures, not to mention various other difficulties; permitting sufficient drying time is good insurance against such problems.

In the house itself, conditions for wood are most severe when the timbers or finishing boards are very near to, or in actual contact with, the ground. A general rule that should always be followed is that no wood should be less than 8 inches above the grade level, unless it is thoroughly protected by a high-quality wood preservative. The exceptions, which have been noted before, are redwood, cedar, and cypress, which can withstand ground contact for a good many years. Below the bottom part of the wood structure, masonry foundation walls should be sealed off from the wood by a 4- to 6-inch impervious poured concrete cap or a solid brick or block masonry top layer.

SURFACE PROTECTIVE COATINGS

Paints will make almost all woods (even those most durably selfprotected as noted above) last longer and, to many people's tastes, look better. Table 9–2 indicates how the most commonly used building woods rate as to paintability, classes them as to weathering capabilities, and notes the appearance of the wood. This makes a good guide to the best kinds of wood to use wherever wood is exposed, both outdoors and indoors as well, and also to the qualities of the finishes.

Note must be made, however, of the fact that exterior wood surfaces need not *necessarily* be coated with an applied finish. Indeed, the so-called "natural" exterior sidings and trimwork, particularly redwood and cedar planking and also plywoods made of those materials, have gained a substantial amount of popularity in recent years. With top-quality construction, as well as proper application and fastening with only stainless steel or aluminum nails or other types of noncorrodable fasteners, unprotected exterior wood surfaces will change somewhat in color and texture over a period of anywhere from a few months to a few years;

Characteristics of Woods for Painting and Finishing

Wood	Ease of keeping well painted; I—easiest, V—most exacting [1]	Weathering		Appearance	
		Resistance to cupping; 1—best, 4—worst	Conspicuousness of checking; 1—least, 2—most	Color of heartwood (sapwood is always light)	Degree of figure on flat-grained surface
SOFTWOODS					
Cedar:					
Alaska-	I	1	1	Yellow	Faint
California incense-	I	--	--	Brown	Do.
Port-Orford-	I	--	1	Cream	Do.
Western redcedar	I	1	1	Brown	Distinct
White-	I	1	--	Light brown	Do.
Cypress	I	1	1	_____ do _____	Strong
Redwood	I	1	1	Dark brown	Distinct
Products [2] overlaid with resin-treated paper	I	--	1	--	--
Pine:					
Eastern white	II	2	2	Cream	Faint
Sugar	II	2	2	_____ do _____	Do.
Western white	II	2	2	_____ do _____	Do.
Ponderosa	III	2	2	_____ do _____	Distinct
Fir, commercial white	III	2	2	White	Faint
Hemlock	III	2	2	Pale brown	Do.
Spruce	III	2	2	White	Do.
Douglas-fir (lumber and plywood)	IV	2	2	Pale red	Strong
Larch	IV	2	2	Brown	Do.
Lauan (plywood)	IV	2	2	_____ do _____	Faint
Pine:					
Norway	IV	2	2	Light brown	Distinct
Southern (lumber and plywood)	IV	2	2	_____ do _____	Strong
Tamarack	IV	2	2	Brown	Do.
HARDWOODS					
Alder	III	--	--	Pale brown	Faint
Aspen	III	2	1	_____ do _____	Do.
Basswood	III	2	2	Cream	Do.
Cottonwood	III	4	2	White	Do.
Magnolia	III	2	--	Pale brown	Do.
Yellow-poplar	III	2	1	_____ do _____	Do.
Beech	IV	4	2	_____ do _____	Do.
Birch	IV	4	2	Light brown	Do.
Gum	IV	4	2	Brown	Do.
Maple	IV	4	2	Light brown	Do.
Sycamore	IV	--	--	Pale brown	Do.
Ash	V or III	4	2	Light brown	Distinct
Butternut	V or III	--	--	_____ do _____	Faint
Cherry	V or III	--	--	Brown	Do.
Chestnut	V or III	3	2	Light brown	Distinct
Walnut	V or III	3	2	Dark brown	Do.
Elm	V or IV	4	2	Brown	Do.
Hickory	V or IV	4	2	Light brown	Do.
Oak, white	V or IV	4	2	Brown	Do.
Oak, red	V or IV	4	2	_____ do _____	Do.

[1] Woods ranked in group V for _ease of keeping well painted_ are hardwoods with large pores that need filling with wood filler for durable painting. When so filled before painting, the second classification recorded in the table applies.

[2] Plywood, lumber, and fiberboard with overlay or low-density surface.

Table 9–2. (Forest Products Laboratory)

they will then remain attractive for many, many years. Rot, decay, and fungus attack must, of course, be avoided; but, in many areas of the country, this poses few problems of any consequence, again assuming that application and installation are correct. Natural weathering itself does not harm the structural integrity of the wood, at least from a practical standpoint, since the erosion and gradual wearing away of the surface takes place at a rate of only about 1/4 inch per century. Naturally-weathered wood is considered most attractive by many people, and it certainly has the advantages of lower initial cost, no maintenance cost, and virtually no upkeep.

Years back, the fact was generally accepted that penetrating stains, plain varnishes, and other clear finishes that would enhance the natural grain and texture of exterior wood were of a luxury type, usually needing renewal yearly or, at the most, every other year, both for appearance's sake and for protection of the wood. However, relatively recent improvements and innovations in applied finishes have changed this fact to some degree and will continue to do so in future years. Some transparent coatings, especially those left by conventional spar or marine varnishes, quickly become brittle with exposure to weather and will crack and peel in a very short period of time; their use is to be avoided as exterior house finishes. The same is true of numerous other proprietary types of clear finishes. However, research in polymers proceeds apace, and new clear finishes that do not absorb ultraviolet light, with consequent degradation, can be expected to have excellent longevity. Specific data on such coatings should be obtained, if possible, before using them, preferably from an independent testing laboratory.

Pigmented penetrating stains for exterior use, commonly called semitransparent stains, have proven their worth. These stains are particularly suitable for heavily textured, rough-surfaced, and the so-called resawn woods, and they also give excellent results when applied to naturally weathered woods. The Forest Products Laboratory (*Wood Handbook*) has determined that "a finish life of close to ten years can be achieved initially on rough surfaces by applying two coats of stain." They further state that in a two-coat finish, the second coat must be applied within about thirty to sixty minutes of first-coat application, allowing both coats to penetrate thoroughly into the wood. Similar exterior stains of a heavier nature that actually form a film on a wood surface are likewise very effective. These stains are variously known as opaque, heavy-bodied, or solid-bodied stains; again, best results are obtained on rough wood surfaces, though they can be applied to smooth surfaces as well.

The Forest Products Laboratory has itself developed, over a long period of time, a natural finish of low hiding power, simple formulation, and excellent durability and appearance. The FPL Natural Finish, as it is known, is currently (1980) being manufactured and retailed in ready-to-use form by several manufacturers, and the product meets Federal Specification TT-S-708a, "Stain, Oil; Semi-Transparent, Wood Exterior." With the proper precautionary measures, FPL Finish also can be easily "cooked up" at home by following the recipe for any of the three different finish colors in Table 9–3. Preparation should be done outdoors or in an open garage—use a hotplate—and is done as follows. Pour the paint thinner into a 5-gallon pail or open can; melt the paraffin in a double boiler or in a

FPL Natural Finish Formulas

Ingredients for slightly less than 5 gallons of finish	Quantity of ingredient for—		
	Cedar color	Light redwood color	Dark redwood color
Boiled linseed oil.....gal.	3.0	3.0	3.0
Mineral spirits or paint thinner...........gal.	1.0	1.0	1.125
Penta concentrate, 10:1 ....gal.	.5	.5	.5
Paraffin wax.........lb.	1.0	1.0	1.0
Zinc stearate.........lb.	.125	.125	.125
Burnt sienna tinting colors............pint	1.0	2.0	.333
Raw umber tinting colors.......:....pint	1.0	None	.333
Indian red iron oxide colors......pint	None	None	.667

Table 9–3. (Research note: FPL–046, Forest Products Laboratory)

can placed in a pan of water. Slowly pour the completely melted paraffin into the paint thinner, stirring vigorously meanwhile. Allow this solution to cool to about 70° F, and add the pentachlorophenol concentrate, the zinc stearate (if used), and then add the linseed oil, stirring meanwhile. (*Do not* inhale the zinc stearate powder.) And last, stir in the pigment, a little bit at a time. Application can be made by any method, and a single coat at the rate of 400 to 500 square feet per gallon is recommended for smooth-planed wood surfaces. This first coat may last only two or three years, but a subsequent recoat should last eight to ten years. Two coats can be applied, no more than four hours apart, on weathered or rough-sawn wood surfaces at the rate of 1 gallon to 200 to 250 square feet. Excess stain should be wiped off within an hour after application, or glossy spots will result. Modifications to this formula, color variations, and a good deal of further information can be obtained from the USDA Forest Service Research Note FPL-046, in its latest revision, available from the Forest Products Laboratory.

Paint is perhaps the most popular exterior finish for residences, and it definitely provides the maximum of protection against weathering. And, of course, the wide range of colors available affords the greatest flexibility of decorative emphasis. Paint should not be considered as a preservative, since it will not prevent decay or fungus attack in and of itself. And though paint is often applied in an attempt to prevent penetration of moisture into the wood, this at best is only partly effective and at worst is of no consequence whatsoever. This is true of all types of applied finishes, as is shown in Table 9–4 which lists some of the typical values of the moisture-excluding effectiveness of various finishes.

However, paints do give excellent service and will afford good protection against erosion of the wood, as well as some protection against moisture absorption in some cases. The keys to a long-lasting, effective, and attractive painted exterior surface lie in selection of a top-quality paint product, proper preparation of the surface to be painted, and correct application techniques. This is true of repainting as well as of applying an initial finish. In simplified form, the following three-step procedure is recommended by L. O. Anderson in *Wood-Frame House Construction* (slightly revised April 1975, available from the Forest Products Laboratory). The first step for new wood is a complete treatment with water-repellent preservatives; pretreated wood materials may be used during construction, or a preservative can be applied by brush or spray after construction. The second step is a heavy coat of nonporous oil-base primer, applied as soon as the water-repellent preservative is thoroughly dry. The third step consists of two coats of top-quality alkyd, oil-base, or latex exterior house paint; the first topcoat should be applied within two weeks of the primer application, and the second topcoat within two weeks after the first. The finish painting, especially with dark colors, should always be done on a cool surface that will remain cool and not be struck by hot sunlight shortly after painting. Temperatures should always be above 40° F for oil-base paints and above 50° F for latex paints. Painting should not be carried on during cool evenings when dews are expectable. More detailed information on the entire subject of painting and finishing is contained in *Wood-Frame House Construction*.

Some Typical Values of Moisture-Excluding Effectiveness of Finishes

Coatings	Effectiveness
INTERIOR FINISHES	*Pct.*
Uncoated wood	0
3 coats of phenolic varnish	73
2 coats of phenolic varnish	49
1 coat of phenolic varnish (sealer)	5
3 coats of shellac	87
3 coats of cellulose lacquer	73
3 coats of lacquer enamel	76
3 coats of furniture wax	8
3 coats of linseed oil	21
2 coats of linseed oil	5
1 coat of linseed oil (sealer)	1
2 coats of latex paint	0
2 coats of semigloss enamel	52
2 coats of floor seal	0
2 coats of floor seal plus wax	10
EXTERIOR FINISHES	
1 coat water-repellent preservative [1]	0
1 coat of FPL natural finish (penetrating stain)	0
1 coat house paint primer	20
1 coat of house primer plus 2 coats of latex paint	22
1 coat of house primer plus 1 coat of TZ [2] linseed oil paint, 30 percent PVC [3]	60
1 coat of house primer plus 1 coat of TL [2] linseed oil paint, 30 percent PVC	65
1 coat of T-alkyd-oil, 30 percent PVC	45
1 coat of T-alkyd-oil, 40 percent PVC	3
1 coat of T-alkyd-oil, 50 percent PVC	0
2 coats of exterior latex paint	3
1 coat aluminum powder in long oil phenolic varnish	39
2 coats aluminum powder in long oil phenolic varnish	88
3 coats aluminum powder in long oil phenolic varnish	95

[1] The same product measured by immersing in water for 30 min. would have a water-repellency effectiveness of over 60 pct.

[2] The letters *T*, *L*, and *Z* denote paint's pigment with titanium dioxide, basic carbonated white lead, and zinc oxide, respectively.

[3] PVC denotes pigment volume concentration which is the volume percent of pigment in the nonvolatile portion of the paint.

Wood was initially conditioned to 80° F and 65 percent relative humidity and then exposed for 2 weeks to 80° F and 97 percent humidity.

Table 9–4. (Forest Products Laboratory)

CHEMICAL WOOD PRESERVATIVES

In regions with much groundwater, high humidity, inadequate insolation, and, especially, with moderate to heavy termite infestation, preserving wood from deterioration becomes more difficult. Particularly when separation of the wood from the ground plus the usual paint coatings are known from regional experience to be insufficient protection, special chemical wood preservatives must be used. There are many proprietary preservative chemicals on the market, and there are several methods of applying them to wood. Application may be made on the job site, but treatment is usually (and most effectively) done by special plants designed for such operations.

For effective decay prevention and termite control, preservative materials and methods should be in accordance with pertinent Federal Specifications and the standards of the American Wood Preservers Association (AWPA); there are numerous such standards for various types of preservatives and their applications. Information and recommendations are also available from the Forest Products Laboratory.

Approved methods of application that are in current use include: pressure treatment, both full-cell and empty-cell processes, used primarily for all wood in contact with or buried in the ground; diffusion and double-diffusion processes, reasonably effective and sometimes used for poles and posts; vacuum, cold-soaking, and steeping processes, for wood in less exposed locations; superficial applications (brushing, spraying, dipping), which provide very limited protection to wood used in contact with the ground, and used where a water-repellent preservative is more important than actual avoidance of decay hazards.

Brush or spray treatments, according to the *Wood Handbook* (Forest Products Laboratory, revised 1974), "should be used only when more effective treatments cannot be employed. The additional life obtained by such treatments over that of untreated woods will be affected greatly by the conditions of service; for wood in contact with the ground, it may be from one to five years."

Pressure treatment is the most effective and most costly. Vacuum or soak treatments have good resistance to decay, with the specifics depending upon the particular treatment. Pine posts may be cold-soaked in No. 2 fuel oil containing 5 percent pentachlorophenol, for instance, to extend their effective life to as much as sixteen to twenty years; the vacuum process is sometimes used to treat millwork with water-repellent preservatives to aid in excluding moisture and dimensionally stabilizing the component parts.

There are two major types of preservative materials, as follows: preservative oils (coal-tar and other creosotes, coal-tars and water-gas-tars, creosote solutions, pentachlorophenal solutions, and water-repellent preservatives); water-borne preservatives (acid copper chromate, ammoniacal copper arsenite, chromated copper arsenate Types I, II, and III, chromated zinc chloride, and fluor chrome arsenate phenol, all of which are mixed in water solution). All of these various types of preservatives are employed in different ways for different purposes, ranging from protection of wood in contact with the ground at all times, immersed or submerged wood, marine work, and similar severely hostile-environment conditions, to light water-repellency treatments for interior millwork.

Treating structural members. The wood components of a house that are concealed from view are the ones most likely to suffer damage from decay, since they cannot dry out thoroughly once they have become damp. Particularly in regions where ground conditions are such that moisture may penetrate regardless of other design or structural techniques, wood pressure-treated with an approved preservative should be used. The parts needing treatment include wood girders, joists, sills, sole plates, headers, and (in severe conditions and with houses built over crawl spaces) sub-flooring and outer wall studs.

Treating exposed wood. While paints protect the *outer surface* of siding, shingles, fascia boards, and other wood members open to the weather, they are often ineffective in preventing wind-driven rain from getting inside of the material, either through the paint itself or through cracks between the wood pieces. Either of two treatments can be used to minimize this problem: a water repellent (WR) or a water-repellent preservative (WRP). For best results, all of the wood applied to the exterior of a house, including trimwork and window and door frames, should be treated with a WR or WRP before installation; all cut ends or edges should then be treated on the job with an identical or similar solution by brushing or, preferably, by dipping. At the very least, all of the exterior surfaces of untreated lumber and millwork should be brushed or sprayed with a WR or a WRP before installation. Note that none of these preservatives should *ever* be used indoors unless the particular product is both *approved and tested* as being suitable for that purpose. When properly applied, a WR or WRP will reduce water damage to the wood, prevent fungus attack, prevent excessive water penetration (and so minimize cracking, peeling and blistering of paint), and resist decay. Their effectiveness is excellent and will extend the life of exterior woodwork by a considerable margin, as well as minimizing maintenance problems.

Painting treated wood. Not all preservatives can be successfully painted over; creosote is one notable example. Though most water-repellent preservatives, and most water repellents, are paintable after drying, some are not. In most cases, if a WR or WRP has been applied with a brush, only two days of warm weather favorable to drying are required before painting can begin. If a dip treatment was used for 10 seconds or more, a full week of good drying weather is necessary.

In many instances involving preservatives that cannot be painted over immediately or even within a short time after their initial application, if the surface is left to weather for about a year, then paint *can* be successfully applied. Even certain creosotes can be painted after a year or so of weathering, with aluminum paint being used as a primer coat.

If the intention is to paint over the preservative, whatever its specific type, the particulars in that regard should always be obtained from the manufacturer, together with any details that might help to make the paint application fully successful. Additional information on wood finishing with water repellents and water repellent preservatives can be found in Research Note FPL-0124 (revised 1978), available from the Forest Products Laboratory

PREVENTION OF DETERIORATION DUE TO INSECTS

Wood in buildings is the edible goal of termites and a few other insects; but masonry, though inedible, often serves as a route by which these insects reach the wood, even when it is well out of reach of the ground. Termites are the only major insect enemies of wood that is used in houses, although in some areas carpenter ants, powder-post beetles (or "old house borers," usually troublesome only in the seasoned pine of older houses), and, near water, marine borers have also been destructive. In general, methods of preventing termite attack are effective against the other insects and, therefore, the following discussion will deal with termites alone—particularly since they are far and away the largest insect hazard in houses.

Termite Distribution

Of the two most common varieties of termites, subterranean (Figure 9–15) and nonsubterranean, those that live in the ground are by far the most common. They infest at least 75 percent of the United States to a greater or lesser degree. The distribution of these devouring insects is shown in Figure 9–16, which also delineates the very narrow areas in which non-subterranean termites are a problem.

There are several species of nonsubterranean termites, and damage from them is principally confined to a small part of southern California, parts of southern Florida, and Hawaii. The total amount of destruction caused is much less than that of the subterranean termites, but because dry-wood termites can live in dry wood without any contact with the ground or outside moisture, they present a definite hazard. They do not work rapidly and so can be readily controlled through regular inspection; if an infestation goes unnoticed, however, they can make short work of even heavy timbers.

Most termite damage in this country is done by subterranean termites. These insects colonize in the ground and must have a constant source of moisture. They build tunnels through the earth and over or around any obstructions to get at the wood they must have for food. Since most of their activity is so well hidden, strong measures of prevention, as well as regular inspection, must be undertaken to avoid damage, especially in areas where the general infestation level is high.

Termite control—and that of other insects as well—is achieved through the practice of three basic principles: isolation, starvation, and eradication. Isolate the structural wood they want to eat, starve them by making wood inedible and by removing all cellulose from the ground where they live, and poison the surrounding soil to make it uninhabitable for them.

Preventive measures against *subterranean termites* can be summarizd as follows:

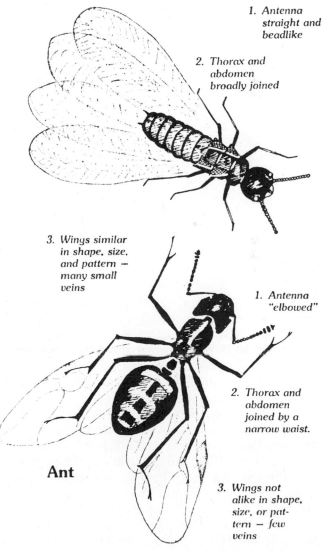

Termite

1. Antenna straight and beadlike
2. Thorax and abdomen broadly joined
3. Wings similar in shape, size, and pattern — many small veins

Ant

1. Antenna "elbowed"
2. Thorax and abdomen joined by a narrow waist.
3. Wings not alike in shape, size, or pattern — few veins

9–15. Distinguishing differences between flying termites and flying ants. (USDA)

251

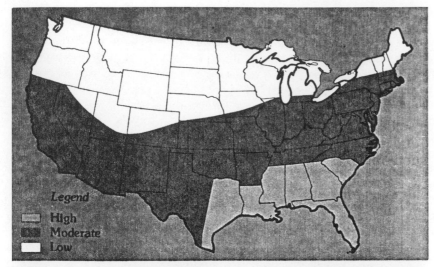

Incidence of subterranean termite damage in the United States.

Legend
High
Moderate
Low

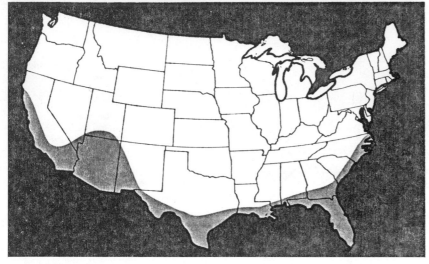

Incidence of drywood termite damage in the United States.

9–16. Incidence of termite damage in the United States. Above, subterranean; below, drywood.

Make a careful survey of the building site, to discover whether termites are already present. Remove all organic materials (stumps, roots, wood debris, form boards, grade stakes, building litter, and any other dead cellulose materials) from the building site and from the soil removed for the foundation before it is backfilled. Use a foundation that termites cannot penetrate. Void-free poured concrete is best, but other types can be made almost as good. Allow plenty of ventilation under the house. When it is built over a crawl space, make the space deep enough to permit periodic inspection of the area. Provide adequate drainage under the house and through the foundation so no water will accumulate. Isolate all wood from the ground. Porch posts and wooden stairways must be placed in concrete piers or foundations, and wood shingles or siding must be at least 8 inches above the top of the *final* grade. The old method of installing non-corrodable metal termite shields is still sometimes used,

especially when isolating a wood structure from a concrete porch slab (Figure 9–17), but termite shields of this sort also create their own set of problems. In many cases they have been found to be relatively ineffective, meanwhile giving the building occupants an entirely false sense of security. The builder should be guided by local practices and techniques. If necessary, specify and use wood pressure-treated with decay- and termite-resisting chemicals, especially in damp regions and areas known to be heavily infested with termites. Soil poisoning should be resorted to in areas with dense infestations, but with care and caution.

For *nonsubterranean termites,* which attack wood directly by flying to it through the air, the best preventive measures are:

Inspect all lumber before use to make sure that it is not already infested with the insects. If construction takes place during the swarming season, keep careful watch that the insects do not infest the construction materials as the job proceeds. Screen all openings in the house, including foundation and attic vents. Remove all wood debris, old stumps, posts, and the like from the premises. Coat all exposed wood surfaces (unless preservative-treated) with primer and paint, taking care to putty all cracks and joints first; in addition, in regions of heavy infestation, use lumber that has been commercially treated with chemicals that resist decay and termites.

There are very few indigenous woods that are proof to even a small degree against termite attack of either subterranean or nonsubterranean types. From a practical standpoint, as far as house construction is concerned, no woods should be considered as having any resistance against them. Where protection against ter-

mites is of prime importance, unless cost forbids, use concrete, stone, or brick for building rather than wood.

Most of these methods of termite control are undoubtedly familiar. The trouble is that too many people have tended in the past to avoid the problem by assuming that "their" houses will be lucky and escape attack. That does not work. Subterranean termite infestations are growing, not diminishing. The insects are spreading into areas heretofore immune, and no one can operate on the hope that chance will protect a structure from termite trouble.

Most of the techniques of termite control listed above are self-explanatory. Three of them, however, deserve further explanation.

Foundations should be laid resistant to termites as

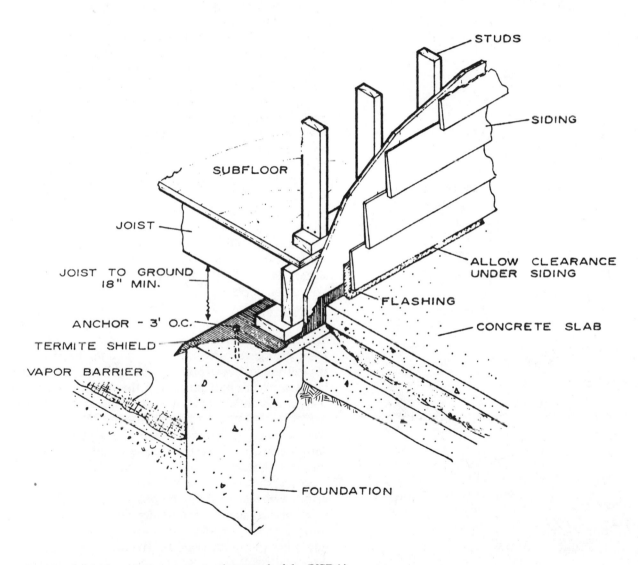

9-17. Metal shield used to protect wood at porch slab. (USDA)

follows: poured concrete, with expansion joints filled with coal tar pitch, elastomeric sealing compound, etc. (Figure 9–18); masonry walls capped with at least 4 inches of reinforced poured concrete reinforced with two No. 3 bars with the top at least 8 inches above finished grade (solid masonry units are unacceptable as a substitute), with masonry units joined only with cement mortar; first-floor girder support posts of concrete, if they bear directly upon the ground; basement floor covered with 4 inches of poured concrete, with all joints sealed with coal tar pitch, elastomeric sealing compound, etc.; first-floor girder support posts of untreated wood in a basement must rest upon short, poured concrete piers (Figure 9–19) that extend a few inches above the concrete floor (pressure-treated posts can rest upon the floor); wood floor joists in a crawl space foundation must be kept at least 18 inches above grade level, and girders must be 12 inches above grade, with good ventilation provided.

Termite shields have in most cases proved unsatisfactory. Unless installed exactly right, they do not do the job and may indeed lead to other difficulties. At the same time, they can give the homeowner the impression that he is safe from termites, when in fact they may already be marching through the timbers in quick-time. Some of the common faults with termite shields include: loose joints between sections of metal; improperly cut and soldered angles; strip shields on top of rather than embedded in the foundation walls; anchor bolt holes through shield not sealed properly; not enough clearance between shield and woodwork or pipes; shields too close to grade lines (or buried by grading operations); edges of shields damaged during construction; shields of corrodable or easily-torn materials.

And, of course, even the best of termite shield installations will in due course suffer from aging, mechanical damage, and similar problems; and there is always the possibility that the termites will get around them anyway. For this reason, other control measures are less problematical and more effective, and termite shields are falling into disfavor except for a few specialized applications.

Soil poisoning of the ground around and under a house is the principal method of protecting buildings, especially in high termite hazard areas. This is not a permanent preventive, since the poisons leach out of the soil and lose their potency after a time. However, an initial application of poisons in the soil near the foundation, and under the entire slab if and as necessary, is sufficient at the outset of construction. This should be followed by regular applications on a periodic basis, with full inspection of the premises made at somewhat greater frequency.

Several different poisons have been found to be very effective against termites; among them are water emulsions of heptachlor, chlordane, dieldrin, and aldrin. Many of the poisons that once were widely used for this and other purposes, such as DDT, are now restricted. No specific recommendations for soil poisoning will be given here, for two major reasons. The first is that pesticides undergo continuous review by the U.S. Department of Agriculture, specific varieties come and go from time to time, and the regulations that apply to their use change frequently. Only pesticides that bear

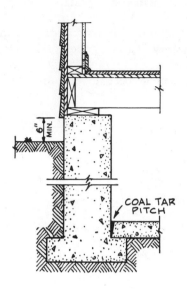

9–18. Poured concrete foundation walls protect against termites. (USDA)

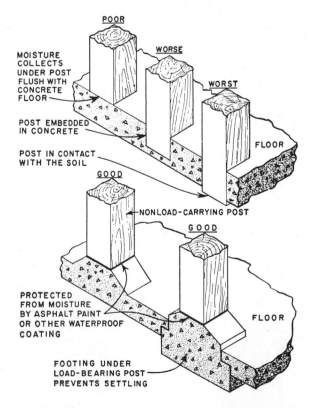

9–19. Termite-proof construction for wood posts. (USDA)

the USDA registration number and carry complete instructions should be used. The second reason is that pesticides, all of them, are highly dangerous, not only to humans but also to plants and animals. They must be stored, handled, and applied exactly right, and even then they can be extremely hazardous. We cannot, in good conscience, recommend that the homeowner undertake to establish and carry out his own soil poisoning program; rather, the job should be done by qualified professionals who are fully equipped and trained to do the job safely and correctly with the latest approved pesticides and techniques.

The problem of termite prevention can best be summarized in the following sentence from the USDA Farmers' Bulletin 1911 (unfortunately no longer available), which was printed in boldface in that publication: "If no wood is left in or on the soil, the danger of a large population of termites developing in the soil and later attempting to infest the building is practically eliminated." The trouble is, human frailty is such that cellulose-free earth around a house is an extreme rarity. It is not only, or always, those that are doing the building who are at fault; for the homeowner is even more careless in this respect than they are. For this reason, it is probably unwise to rely on clean earth alone as a termite preventive.

PREVENTION OF DETERIORATION DUE TO OTHER ANIMALS

Prevention of damage to houses by larger animals such as rats, mice, squirrels, and even certain types of birds can be described very briefly. The hazards of this type of animal infestation are in direct proportion to the quality of building construction. Fortunately, a house that is well designed and built for prevention of decay and termite attack is also basically proof against damage of these larger forms of animal life.

Mention of rodent control immediately brings to mind that perennial dreaded enemy of man, the rat. But, in this context, the rats that are unfortunately still common in many urban areas, particularly slums, are of little concern insofar as the necessity for taking special rat-proofing measures is concerned. There are two reasons for this. First, any modern house that is well-constructed according to present-day building practices, and especially if tightly built according to the standards suggested by this book, will be proof against rats as it is. And second, the likelihood of a new house being built in a rat-infested area, or in a natural rat habitat, is remote; should a new house perchance come under siege by rats, the sight and sounds of attempted entrance should provide ample warning to allow timely and direct protective and preventive measures to be taken.

Of much greater practical concern is the friendly neighborhood fieldmouse and his many cousins of several species. No building site is without them, or the potential for them, and they have the ability to find their way through the tiniest imaginable crannies and cracks into the living quarters of the house. But again, if the house is well and properly constructed, it will also be mouse-proof. This should be taken into consideration during construction because, while mice are unlikely to cause personal injury as rats can, they can nonetheless be disease carriers, are frequently destructive, are almost always disconcerting, and are never to be tolerated.

Many of the western mountain areas are inhabited by a creature called the bushy-tailed woodrat (often known as the packrat). These handsome and playful rodents, about the size of a squirrel, can raise absolute havoc with the insides of a house, since they can gnaw through anything (including full-sized logs), can squeak through tiny openings, and have a penchant for sampling everything that looks as though it might be edible, including electrical wiring. They are a particular problem for camps and vacation homes that are left unattended for long periods of time. Chipmunks and squirrels can also cause considerable amounts of damage, especially if they cannot find their way out again, panic, and go into a destructive frenzy. Even birds from time to time can find their way into houses, usually down unscreened flues or through unscreened louvers or vents.

Good construction to prevent animal ingress includes not only the normal high-quality building materials and practices, but also requires careful screening of all windows, vents, and doors; providing coarse wire-mesh barriers within or across the tops of chimney flues or proper caps on appliance chimneys, particularly those connected to open fireplaces; using floor drains in cellars and basements that are an absolute barrier to animals; and sealing of all holes in masonry or wood structures where pipes and wires enter.

Probably the only other useful generalization about animal-proofing houses has to do with the spaces between inner and outer layers of walls and between ceilings and second floors or attics; whether or not these spaces are filled with thermal insulation (except for rigid or foamed types) is immaterial. Such areas should include firestopping and must be completely and permanently sealed off with impervious materials against the entry of any form of wildlife—not only decay fungi and termites, but also the larger wild enemies of the house. Of particular importance in this connection is an absolutely tight foundation, with screened ventilating areas, especially in a house built over a crawl space or unfinished basement. Houses built on piers should have the first-floor joists firestopped, and the entire floor frame should be tightly covered with a suitable sheathing. If mice and other assorted small critters cannot get in through such areas, obviously they can do no damage. Care and common sense during construction will make their entry impossible.

METALS

The control of deterioration of metals used in house construction calls for the use of materials and methods that will prevent condensation, which, when excessive, causes corrosion.

Corrosion is the enemy of all ferrous metals, and its prevention is almost ridiculously simple: do not use ferrous metals in locations exposed to moisture. Copper or aluminum of the proper alloys, asbestos-cement, or plastic—PVC (polyvinyl chloride), CPVC (chlorinated polyvinyl chloride), PE (polyethylene), PB (polybutylene), ABS (acrylonitrile butadiene styrene), and the like—should be used instead of even the best galvanized iron or steel pipes if good performance and durability, with no maintenance costs for painting or for patching leaks, is desired.

It is true that the best grades of galvanized iron or steel have a relatively long life in exposed spots, compared to these metals ungalvanized; but they are not impervious. The zinc coating will wear through eventually, unless it is continuously protected by paint on invisible surfaces, or by asphalt, tar, or red lead on surfaces not exposed to the public view but still subject to the deteriorating effects of the weather. Therefore, for best results all metals used on the exterior of a house (including not only flashing and gutters and downspouts, but also, in certain circumstances, nails) should be of noncorrodable metals. Where applicable, plastics can be an excellent choice. Though the original cost may be higher when such materials are installed (often it is not), maintenance will be almost nil and the danger of leaks and holes caused by rust will be eliminated.

The problem of what nails to use to fasten shingles or siding to the outside of a house depends upon the type of exposure. Most shingles on roofs and walls are fastened so that the nails are concealed by the next course above; in such a location, rust-resisting galvanized nails are usually satisfactory. But when bevel siding or any other type of material with very shallow overlap (or none at all) is used, the nails must be exposed to the weather. Galvanized nails will eventually rust and leave stains (Figure 9–20), and they are unsightly in a natural finish; they may rust through even a well-painted surface in due course. The alternative, where nails will be exposed to weather, is to use either aluminum or stainless steel nails.

Galvanized steel is widely used for warm and cold air ducts, and, since the ducts are not exposed to the weather, they will last indefinitely if water *in any form* is kept from the metal. Cold-air ducts, therefore, must be protected from condensation by proper vapor barriers (see chapter 7). When ducts are inside the cool area, as in hung ceilings below insulated attics, the temperature differentials almost never will be great enough to cause surface condensation. But when they pass through attics above the insulation, through crawl spaces or through other uncooled areas, they should be insulated and provided with a vapor barrier.

Ducts used only to carry warm air need no protection other than that which automatically accompanies good building practices: isolation from moisture-producing areas, and proper insulation and vapor barriers in crawl spaces, slabs or unheated attics, as outlined previously.

Galvanized iron or steel ventilating louvers for attics, and cast iron ventilators in foundation walls both require paint and a certain amount of maintenance. However, prefabricated aluminum vents and louvers are available for virtually any purpose, and some plastic sorts are available as well; both need no painting, of course.

Another minor point: screening for roof and foundation louvers, as well as for windows and doors, should be corrosion-proof and, therefore, be made of copper, aluminum, glass fiber, or plastic. Particularly in foundations, corrodable galvanized screening may rust through in a year or so, if the exposure is intense.

Corrodable pipes are a major cause of failure in plumbing systems (Figure 9–21). No modern house that is designed and built in accordance with good practice uses ferrous metal waterlines today, not only because of their limited life, but also because rust on the inside of pipes can, after a few years, pollute the water. Ferrous metal wastelines—if they are of the best quality—are acceptable and sometimes required by building codes, in even the most expensive homes. They will rust somewhat, of course, but the rust will usually not interfere with the system's operation—not, at least, for decades—because their walls are so thick. Nonetheless,

9–20. Corrodable nails will eventually leave rust streaks on exterior siding. (Duncan Photos)

there is a marked swing toward the use of plastic piping of various sorts, not only for drain-waste-vent systems, but also for hot and cold water supply systems in residences; this is because corrosion, electrolysis, and numerous other problems that afflict metallic piping systems do not exist with these materials. When these advantages are considered in combination with the many other positive qualities and properties of plastic plumbing systems, one must conclude that eventually almost all new homes will be plumbed either partly or entirely with plastic.

9-21. Pipe corrosion. (USDA)

Condensation on cold water pipes is a common phenomenon and is usually ignored in most buildings. It will not damage the pipe, and the dripping condensate usually evaporates quickly. Pipe condensation can be troublesome, however, when the pipes pass through organic materials, or when they deposit their condensate within building cavities that have little or no ventilation. A considerable amount of hidden damage in the way of fungus attack, rot, and the like can be caused after a period of time. Insulation and protection of metallic pipelines prone to "sweating" is recommended as a precautionary measure; several types of pipe insulations are made for this purpose. This is a useful refinement that can further minimize the possibilities of unnecessary water vapor and potential structural damage, and it also adds to the house's overall quality.

PREVENTION OF "DETERIORATION" BY FIRE

An incombustible house made of metal and masonry throughout would be prohibitively expensive (though experimental houses of this sort have been constructed) and is actually no guarantee against fire. The furnishings can burn. On the other hand, good construction can reduce the danger of fire and, just as important, slow down its spread after it has started. The checklist that follows indicates the standard methods of achieving fire-resistant house construction and also various fire protection techniques. Every construction item on the list should be a part of any well-designed house. In many communities some or all of the items are required by building codes, but a code should not necessarily be followed as an ultimate in fire safety, particularly since so many codes are obsolete in terms of modern building practices. Some of the fire protection techniques suggested will be needed only in rural and semirural areas with poor public fire-fighting facilities. But most of them should be included as a matter of course in all houses, wherever they are located.

Fire Protective Checklist

The best fire protection is prevention. However, it is only good practice to provide warning and quenching systems in addition to nonflammable design and construction. All three methods of prevention are outlined in the following checklist.

PREVENTION

The site. Make sure that there is adequate community fire protection; this should include fire hydrants, good equipment, professional firemen, and a well-maintained street fire alarm system. Select sites that, while well landscaped with trees and shrubbery, are not too closely surrounded by unkempt meadows and (particularly in semiarid regions) flammable woods or brush. Lay out the site so that there is a belt of open lawn around the house. Particularly in rural and semirural regions, where the house may have several outbuildings, orient the house so that a line connecting it and the outbuildings is more or less at right angles to the prevailing winds; this will help to keep fire from spreading from one building to another.

Cellars and crawl spaces. Allow enough headroom to permit safe installation and inspection of heating units. Provide noncombustible materials at least on the area over the heating unit, and preferably over the whole underside of the house. Plaster on metal lath, or gypsum board with a fireproof cover on the exposed side, can be used in basements. In crawl spaces, it is necessary to use corrosion-resistant metal or an asbestos-cement material over the bottom of the joists, since plasters and plasterboards deteriorate in these

257

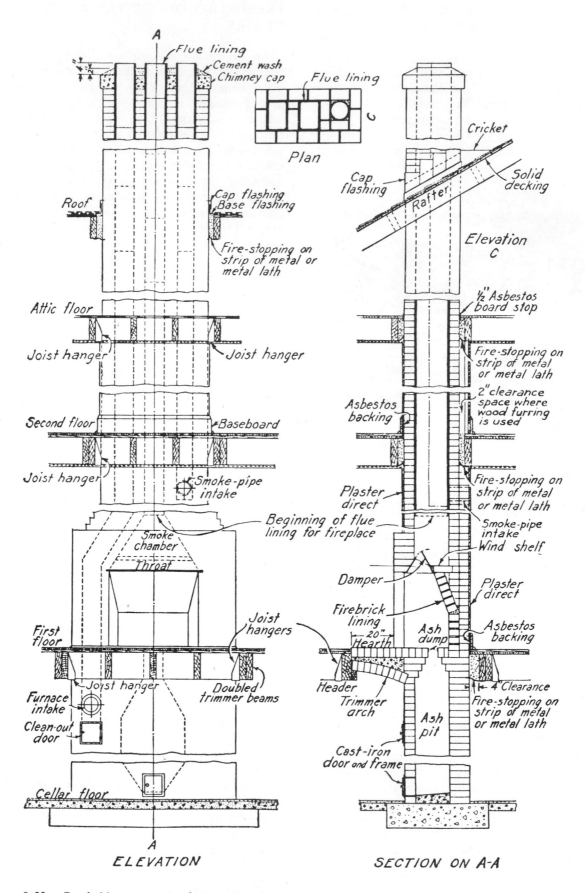

ELEVATION

- Flue lining
- Cement wash
- Chimney cap
- Flue lining
- Roof
- Cap flashing
- Base flashing
- Fire-stopping on strip of metal or metal lath
- Attic floor
- Joist hanger
- Joist hanger
- Second floor
- Baseboard
- Joist hanger
- Smoke-pipe intake
- Smoke chamber
- Throat
- Beginning of flue lining for fireplace
- First floor
- Joist hangers
- Joist hanger
- Doubled trimmer beams
- Furnace intake
- Clean-out door
- Cellar floor

Plan

SECTION ON A-A

- Cricket
- Cap flashing
- Rafter
- Solid decking
- *Elevation C*
- ½" Asbestos board stop
- Fire-stopping on strip of metal or metal lath
- 2" clearance space where wood furring is used
- Asbestos backing
- Fire-stopping on strip of metal or metal lath
- Plaster direct
- Smoke-pipe intake
- Wind shelf
- Damper
- Plaster direct
- Firebrick lining
- Asbestos backing
- 20"
- Hearth
- Ash dump
- Header
- Trimmer arch
- 4" Clearance
- Fire-stopping on strip of metal or metal lath
- Ash pit
- Cast-iron door and frame

9–22. Good chimney and fireplace construction. (USDA)

damp locations. Use masonry, reinforced concrete, or steel posts and piers, rather than wood. For highest grade of protection, metal columns and girders should be covered with concrete to keep them from buckling during a fire. Wood joists framed into masonry walls should be cut diagonally at the ends and tied with metal wall anchors. Joists so framed will not pull down the walls above should the joists collapse during a fire.

Chimneys and fireplaces. Chimneys (Figure 9–22) should always rest on foundations carried below the frost line, and not on wall brackets. No joists, studs, furring, or other combustible materials should be within 2 inches of the chimney. Joists should be framed away from the masonry with headers protected by incombustible material, such as loose mineral wool insulation between them and the chimney (Figure 9–23).

All masonry chimneys must be constructed of solid masonry units or reinforced portland or refractory cement concrete. The walls must be no less than 4 inches thick for those materials, or not less than 12 inches thick for rubble stone masonry. All joints must be completely filled with mortar. Figure 9–24 shows typical solid-unit masonry chimney layout patterns. All masonry chimneys must be lined with fire-clay flue lining (these should be no less than 5/8 inches thick) made to ASTM C315 specifications or with some other liner of similar approved material. The liner must be carefully bedded as installed, with tight joints that are smooth on the inside surface. If prefabricated chimneys (Figure 9–25) are specified, they must be of an approved type for residential installation, *applicable to the type of fuel being used*.

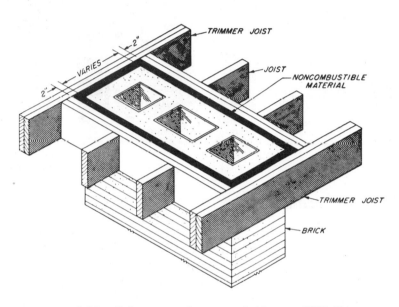

9–23. Safe construction around chimney. (USDA)

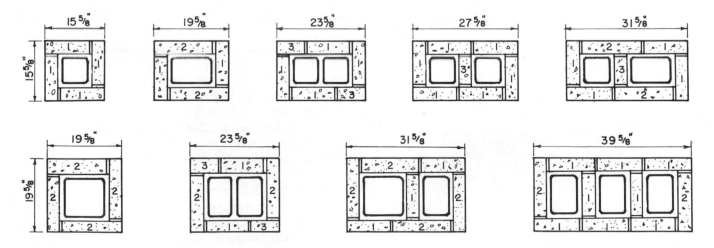

9–24. Typical concrete masonry chimney sections. (Portland Cement Association)

Through a High Pitch or Chalet Ceiling

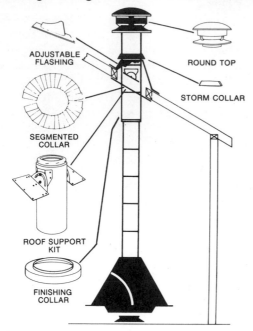

Through an Exterior Wall

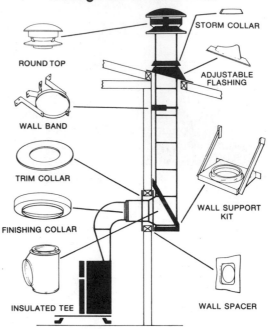

Through a Ceiling & Normal Pitch Roof

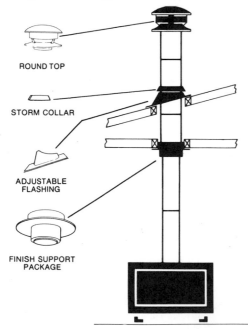

9-25. Typical metal appliance chimney.
(Courtesy, Metalbestos)

Chimney connectors (smoke pipes) must be of a suitable size, metal thickness and type, and be kept as short and straight as possible, and must be well supported. All connectors entering a chimney should be flush with the inner lining and not project into the flue, and they must be firmly cemented in place. The joints should be absolutely airtight (see information that follows on smoke test). Chimney connectors should never slope downward toward the chimney. Chimney connector clearances are variable, depending upon the specific circumstances. The minimum clearance from combustible wall surfaces, which in this context include lath-and-plaster or gypsum wallboard, is 18 inches. With certain types of protection, however, this clearance can be reduced substantially (Table 9-5).

The chimney termination must stand at least 3 feet above the roof and at least 2 feet above any portion of any building within 10 feet (Figure 9-26). Flashing around the joints between the chimney and the roof should be in accordance with the standards shown in Figure 9-27. Chimneys should be equipped with a standard screen/spark arrestor, which not only reduces the hazard of flying sparks, but also keeps out wildlife in the summer. The screening, and the chimney, should be cleaned at least once a year.

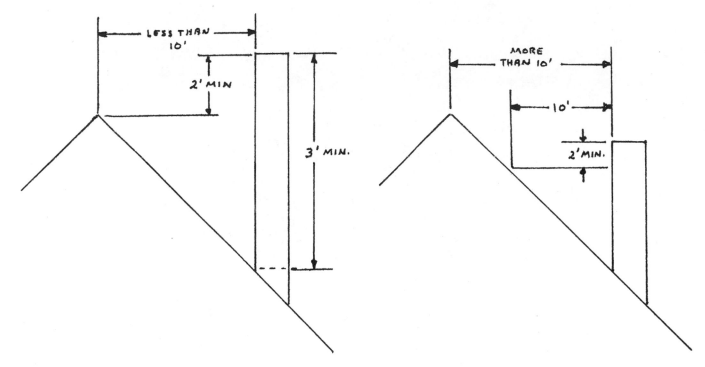

9-26. Chimney termination clearances.

Chimney Connector Clearance (in Inches) With Specified Forms of Protection

Type of Protection	Where the required clearance with no protection is:			
Applied to the combustible material and covering all surfaces within the distance specified as the required clearance with no protection. Thicknesses are minimum.	36 inches (914 mm) (in./mm)	18 inches (457 mm) (in./mm)	9 inches (229 mm) (in./mm)	6 inches (152 mm) (in./mm)
(a) ¼ in. asbestos millboard spaced out 1 in.	30/762	12/305	6/152	3/ 76
(b) 0.013″/0.330 mm (28 gage) sheet metal on ¼ in. asbestos millboard	24/610	12/305	4/102	2/51
(c) 0.013″/0.330 mm (28 gage) sheet metal spaced out 1 in. .	18/457	9/229	4/102	2/51
(d) 0.013″/0.330 mm (28 gage) sheet metal on ⅛ in. asbestos millboard spaced out 1 in. . .	18/457	9/229	4/102	2/51
(e) ¼ in. asbestos millboard on 1 in. mineral wool bats reinforced with wire mesh or equivalent .	18/457	6/152	4/102	2/51
(f) 0.027″/0.686 mm (22 gage) sheet metal on 1 in. mineral wool bats reinforced with wire or equivalent	12/305	3/76	2/51	2/51

Notes to Table

1. Spacers shall be of noncombustible material.

2. Methods (a), (c) and (d) require ventilation between sheet material and protected combustible material. If ventilation may be impaired use method (b), (e) or (f).

3. Mineral wool bats (blanket or board) shall have a minimum density of 8 lb per ft³ (0.128 g/cc) and a minimum melting point of 1500°F (816°C).

Table 9-5. (Reproduced by permission from NFPA 211, Standard for Chimneys, Fireplaces, and Vents, Copyright © 1977, National Fire Protection Association, Boston, MA)

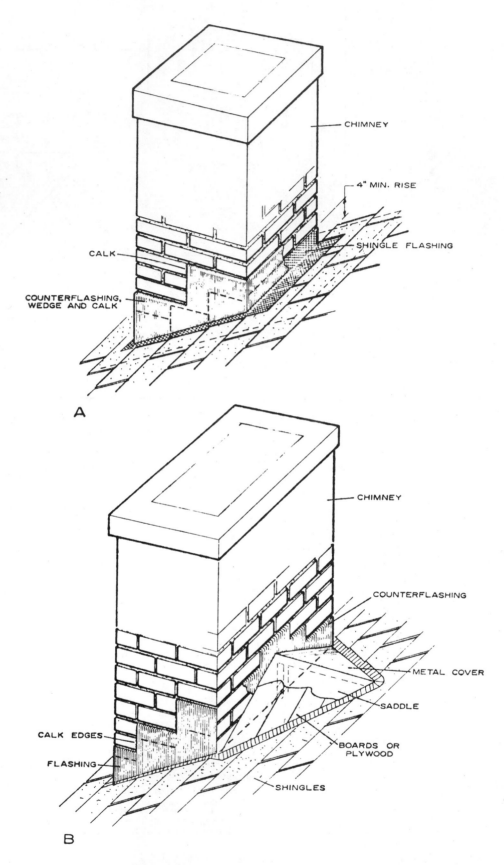

9–27. Chimney flashing: (*A*) flashing without saddle; (*B*) chimney saddle. (USDA)

There are a good many details, recommendations, and regulations that pertain to the construction of a masonry fireplace and/or chimney, as well as to the installation of furnaces, heaters, stoves, and prefabricated fireplaces. Masonry construction must be undertaken with the best of workmanship and materials, following approved and proven designs, procedures, and techniques and in full compliance with all building and fire code regulations. Installation of furnaces, heaters, wood/coal stoves, prefabricated fireplaces, and metal appliance chimneys must be made in strict accordance with building codes and the manufacturers' instructions, and it should be done with great care and top-grade workmanship. Current general standards can be found in the National Fire Protection Association's *Standard For Chimneys, Fireplaces, and Vents,* NFPA 211. Construction and installation details for this equipment can be found in such references as Randall and Panarese's *Concrete Masonry Handbook* (Portland Cement Association, 1976), Shalton and Shapiro's *The Wood Burners Encyclopedia* (Vermont Crossroads Press, 1977), and Zack Gould's *The Owner-Built Fireplace* (Van Nostrand Reinhold Company, 1978).

The smoke test mentioned above must be run on every new masonry chimney, and could well be run on new metal appliance chimney installations as well. In fact, the test can be repeated periodically through the years to make sure that the flue remains tight. Proceed as follows: Build a small paper and wood chip fire at the base of the flue. When a substantial column of smoke begins to come out of the chimney, block the outlet at the top by laying a board or a wet sack over it. If there are any leaks in the masonry, smoke will appear at those points. If leakage is found, the defect must be remedied before the chimney is used. Since this method is usually a difficult chore, paying close and careful attention to the construction of the chimney is a wise idea.

Walls and ceilings. All frame walls, whether of balloon, platform, or post-and-beam construction, and all furring spaces behind masonry walls should be fire-stopped at or between each floor and at the attic level, using wood blocks or (preferably) tightly fitted masonry, gypsum board, or other approved noncombustible materials. If wood blocks are used, they must be of nominal 2-inch thickness, or two thicknesses of 1-inch nominal material with staggered joints; two thicknesses of 3/4-inch plywood with staggered joints may also be used. Use incombustible insulations if possible.

Other things being equal, gypsum wallboard, or gypsum or metal lath and plaster are better fire retardants than the vegetable fiberboards. Masonry exterior walls are obviously better fire protection than those made of wood. Fire-retardant-treated wood or softwood plywood can also provide good fire resistance, but may be problematical due to eventual loss of effectiveness due to ageing of the chemicals.

The fire resistance of many of the new interior paints, wall coverings, and similar materials is not adequately known. At any given time, some of these new products, and indeed some of the old as well, may not be fire-resistant. Investigate to make sure, insofar as is possible, that interior treatments are not fire-hazardous.

Stairways. All stairways, including those from basement to first floor, should have enclosed and plastered or otherwise fireproofed soffits. Heavy wood headers at top and bottom and a firestop at midpoint of the stair run are also good practice. In addition, the stair from the basement to the first floor should be entirely enclosed so that it will be protected to some degree if a fire breaks out in the furnace room or elsewhere in the area. Basement and cellar stairs should have a tight-fitting door, preferably of metal or other fireproof construction at the top.

Roofs. Joints between roof and chimney and between rafters and tops of walls should be built in accordance with good fire-resistant design. The top plate should *completely* seal off the hollow space between inner and outer wall surfaces, and a fire-resistant vapor barrier or some other incombustible material should be placed across the area of connection between wall and roof.

Roofing should preferably be of incombustible material such as tile, slate, rustproof metal, etc. Isolated houses should use these roofing materials, which conform to Underwriters' Laboratories Class A rating; those in suburbs and smaller towns, where fire-fighting establishments are relatively nearby, can use Class B roofing assemblies, which are also considered fire-retardant under the Uniform Building Code. Wood shakes or shingles, a very popular roofing material, are normally quite combustible, but in some cases may have a Class B rating. Despite the fact that they can be made fire-retardant with proper treatment, in some areas they are not allowable roofing under local building codes.

Heating and Cooking Equipment. All furnaces, boilers, space heaters, stoves, and so on should be placed on an incombustible foundation, preferably concrete. Use of sheet metal, insulated or uninsulated, on a wood floor is not adequate protection. Wood/coal stoves and ranges must be placed on a proper stove board or hearth, and the hearth arrangement for fireplaces and stoves must extend for a substantial distance in front of and to the sides of the unit. Proper clearances between heat-producing equipment and surrounding combustible surfaces must be maintained, and heat shields installed as necessary. Warm air ducts should be so arranged that the heated air must travel at least 6 feet from the furnace and make a sharp bend before entering walls or floors.

Electric wiring, etc. All electric wiring should conform to the requirements of the National Electrical

Code (sponsored by the National Fire Protection Association under the auspices of The American National Standards Institute, and available from the Association at 470 Atlantic Avenue, Boston, MA 02210).

In many areas, all electrical work must be done by, or under the supervision of, a licensed electrician. In areas where local codes do not require this, the work should still be done by a qualified electrician. The only exceptions to this should be homeowners who have been trained in electrical work (or happen to be electricians themselves), or do-it-yourself homeowners who are *competent* and *knowledgeable* in the field; even in this instance, the homeowner is well advised to have his work thoroughly checked by a qualified, practicing electrician. All wiring should be inspected by an authorized inspector before it is closed in.

Enough current-carrying capacity (ampacity) in the service drop or lateral and in the main entrance panel and a large enough number of circuits should be provided to handle any possible future expansion *as well as* immediate needs. Adding circuits to an existing house, or changing the main entrance panel to a larger one, is a costly undertaking.

Floor or wall outlets should be provided so that at no place in a room need there be extension, appliance, or fixture cords longer than 6 feet. The National Electrical Code establishes, in Section 210-25, required receptacle placement for all parts of the living quarters of the house, to this effect.

Circuit breakers are safer than fuses; where plug fuses are used, noninterchangeable Type S fuses should be installed (these are now required in new equipment). In addition, ground-fault circuit protection, by means of ground-fault current interrupters, must be provided for all receptacles installed in bathrooms and garages and in all outdoor receptacles as well. Since they afford such excellent protection, they should likewise be installed in kitchens, workshops, and any other areas of the house where shock hazard is a potential.

Radio and television aerials should be mounted on sturdy masts or towers, strong enough to withstand any expected wind or ice loads—particularly if they are near any powerlines. They should be protected from lightning (see below), and their lead-in conductors should be at least 6 feet from any part of a lightning rod system. They should be well grounded, never attached to chimneys, and installed in strict accordance with the National Electrical Code (Article 810—Radio and Television Equipment).

Storage of flammables. Fuel oil tanks should be outdoors and preferably underground. Bottled gas installations, and aboveground gas and oil tanks, should be strongly fenced off so that children and animals cannot get to them. Paints, flammable cleaning fluids, gasoline, kerosene, oily rags, machine oils and greases, and the like should be stored in a building separate from the house, such as in a workshop or garage. They should never be kept in cellars, utility rooms, attached garages, or similar areas.

Attached garages. Walls and ceilings of garages adjoining a part of the house should always be of fireproof construction. Masonry or poured concrete should be used for all walls, and a heavy ceiling with a thick layer of gypsum or metal lath and plaster should be specified when there are occupied areas above the garage. Metal fire doors or their equivalent, fitted with self-closers, should be installed in passageways. These and other fire-retardant or fireproof construction techniques are required in many areas under local building codes or national standards such as the Uniform Fire Code.

Lightning protection. Lightning rod systems should be installed on isolated houses in all parts of the country where thunderstorms are frequent. They are advisable in *all* parts of the country if the house is so far from the fire department that the building could burn down before help arrives. Studies conducted in various parts of the country over a period of many years have shown that rural fires caused by lightning occur much more frequently in unprotected houses than in those fitted with lightning rods. Lightning rod systems should be installed by trained specialists and should follow the National Fire Protection Association's NFPA No. 78, *Lightning Protection Code* (approved by The American National Standards Institute and designated ANSI C5.1). Installation of a lightning rod system should be made with top-grade workmanship and with the latest approved materials and techniques in effect at the time. Get competitive bids on installation and deal only with well-established, reputable firms; this field has been plagued from time to time with shoddy practices, scams, and cons that can easily lead to disastrous results, not to mention an expensive but worthless installation. A poor lightning rod installation can be just as dangerous as none at all, and in some instances more so. A proper job is shown in Figure 9–28.

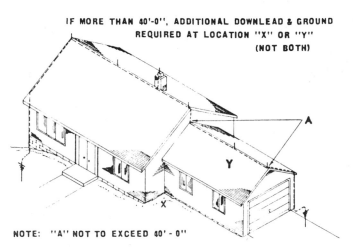

IF MORE THAN 40'-0", ADDITIONAL DOWNLEAD & GROUND REQUIRED AT LOCATION "X" OR "Y" (NOT BOTH)

NOTE: "A" NOT TO EXCEED 40'-0"

9–28. Proper lightning rod installation. (Courtesy, Thompson Lightning Protection, Inc.)

FIRE WARNING

The importance of including fire warning systems in houses is underlined by the shocking and virtually unknown fact that fire is the third-ranking cause of accidental death in this country, that most of the deaths occur in residential occupancies, and that nearly all of those occur when the occupants are trapped while sleeping. In many cases the fire does not do much damage; the deaths are caused by smoke inhalation. This problem is such a serious one that, in most areas today, local building codes require that smoke detectors powered from the building wiring must be installed in new houses and dwelling units. Alarms and alarm systems for houses should meet the standard of the National Fire Protection Association's NFPA No. 74, *Household Fire Warning Equipment*. All equipment should bear the Underwriters' Laboratories label, or equivalent, and be installed with top-grade workmanship and in accordance with the latest recommended practices.

Household fire warning systems must be capable of sounding the alarm under two completely different sets of fire conditions: one is a slow, smoldering fire, and the other is a high-heat, fast-spreading fire. Either one can produce highly dangerous smoke and toxic gases. House fires are particularly dangerous at night, when the sleeping occupants can so easily be overcome, and also when dense smoke reduces visibility to zero. Most house fire casualties are victims of these conditions rather than of burns. To provide effective warning, at least one smoke detector should be located between the sleeping occupants and the rest of the house, and heat or smoke detectors should be installed in all other major areas of the house as well.

In a residence, fire warning equipment can be installed on several different levels of protection, depending upon the locations and number of heat and smoke detectors used. These may consist of simple, self-contained units, or sophisticated, zoned networks in whole-house coverage. Either type should be tested at least every three or four months, oftener if desired. Those that are battery-operated or contain stand-by battery packs should be checked frequently to ensure that power will be available when needed. And, of course, a complete family escape plan that is based upon several contingencies, has several variables, and is well practiced is an essential adjunct to a fire warning system.

FIRE QUENCHING

Automatic sprinkling systems are economically out of the question for all but the most lavish of houses. For them, such a system would be a good investment, particularly if they are isolated. They would cut insurance rates considerably and prevent total loss in case a fire started.

Strategically located fire extinguishers, on the other hand, should be part of the equipment of every house,

no matter what its size or cost. Good ones are not cheap, but cheap ones are worse than useless, since they give a false sense of security. There are several different types and sizes of fire extinguishers (Figure 9–29) that might be placed at strategic locations in the house. Your local fire department, whether professional or volunteer, will be happy to recommend which types and sizes might best fit specific purposes, and further information can also be obtained from the National Fire Protection Association.

Good extinguisher locations include: near the heating plant (if oil-fired, add a couple of pails of sand to absorb oil leaks *before* a fire starts; outside the entrance to the heating-plant room, so it can be reached before approaching a fire inside; in the kitchen, either at the stove or near the entrance to the room; near the fireplace or wood/coal stove; at or near the front and back doors; near the television and/or stereo sets; in the master bedroom, ready at hand should a fire start at night; in the garage and in outbuildings wherever flammable materials are stored, preferably near or outside the entrance door; and in the workshop.

It is important that extinguishers be installed before the house is occupied. Most homeowners tend to let the purchase of extinguishers go by the board. They do not want to think about fire or to spend the money, so they ignore the problem. Furthermore, all the members of the household should be shown how the extinguishers

9–29. Fire extinguishers of the type that can be used in the home. (Duncan Photos)

265

work, and the units must be checked periodically and maintained in proper working order.

If country houses are located near ponds (Figure 9-30), running streams, or dug wells, it is excellent practice to include in the equipment that goes with the house a sturdy pump and sufficient lengths of durable hose, together with ladders tall enough to reach the roof. Most fires starting outdoors cannot be fought with extinguishers, particularly those on roofs, and the pond, pump, hose and ladders are the only recourse the occupants of isolated houses have if they are to put such fires out, or keep them under control until the fire equipment arrives.

Much progress has been made in the past few years in the areas of fire prevention and fire extinguishing. Homeowners are well advised to investigate thoroughly all of the procedures and techniques involved that may be of service to them, and to make every possible effort to minimize fire hazard (and to be well prepared, both physically and mentally, in case the circumstance does arise) in their home, be that house, mobile home, apartment, or condominium.

9-30. Fire control pond on farm in New Hampshire. (USDA) (Reprinted with permission from the *1977 Fundamentals Volume, ASHRAE HANDBOOK & Product Directory*)

Metric Conversions

The units of measurements used in this text conform to present practice for building technology in this country; that is, the customary and familiar U.S., English, and occasionally centimeter-gram-second (cgs) units. There is, however, a slow movement toward the use of metric units in this country. In particular, the SI (*Systéme International d'Unités* or International System of Units) metric system is now recognized as the international measurements language in building (and other) technology.

Educators in this country with considerable experience and expertise in the teaching of measurement systems have found that people who have been fully inculcated in one system, and who think and express themselves in terms of that system, encounter considerable difficulty in using a second system via the conversion method. Thought and expression take place through the accustomed system, then the conversion follows as a mechanical matter that often creates more problems and frustrations than it solves. The only effective course for most people seems to be to thoroughly learn the second system to the extent that thinking and expression takes place with the same facility as in the first, and the two systems can be used separately or interchangeably without conscious thought.

We suggest that those who customarily have worked with the U.S. system continue to do so and attempt conversions to the SI system only if necessary. For those necessary conversions, and for those who are familiar with the SI system and would prefer to use it, a conversion table of the basic units for transposition from one system to another is presented below. Additional conversion factors for the lesser used and more obscure units can be found in the *ASHRAE HANDBOOK & Product Directory,* in any of various standard engineering handbooks, or in manuals compiled for the purpose, such as William D. Johnstone's *For Good Measure* (New York: Holt, Rinehart and Winston, 1975).

Conversion Factors to SI Metric Units

Physical Quantity	Symbol	To Convert from	To	Multiply by
Length	x	in.	m	2.540 000* E-02
		ft	m	3.048 000* E-01
Area		$in.^2$	m^2	6.451 600* E-04
		ft^2	m^2	9.290 304* E-02
Volume		$in.^3$	m^3	1.638 706 E-05
		ft^3	m^3	2.831 685 E-02
Temperature		F	°C	$t_C = (t_F - 32)/1.8$
		F	K	$t_K = (t_F + 459.67)/1.8$
Pressure		in. Hg (60 F)	Pa	3.376 85 E + 03
Mass		lb	kg	4.535 924 E- 01
Mass/unit area	M	lb/ft^2	kg/m^2	4.882 428 E + 00
Moisture content rate		$lb/(ft^2)(week)$	$kg/(m^2 \cdot s)$	8.072 793 E - 06
Density	P	lb/ft^3	kg/m^3	1.601 846 E + 01
Thermal conductivity	k	$(Btu \cdot in.)/(hr \cdot ft^2 \cdot F)$	$W/(m \cdot K)$	1.442 279 E - 01
Thermal conductance	C	$Btu/(hr \cdot ft^2 \cdot F)$	$W/(m^2 \cdot K)$	5.678 263 E + 00
U-value	U	$Btu/(hr \cdot ft^2 \cdot F)$	$W/(m^2 \cdot K)$	5.678 263 E + 00
Thermal resistance	R	$(hr \cdot ft^2 \cdot F)/Btu$	$(m^2 \cdot K)/W$	1.761 102 E - 01
Thermal resistivity	r/in.	$(hr \cdot ft^2 \cdot F)/(Btu \cdot in.)$	$(m \cdot K)/W$	6.933 471 E + 00
Heat flow	q	$Btu/(hr \cdot ft^2)$	W/m^2	3.154 591 E + 00
Water vapor: permeability (23°C)	μ	$\dfrac{grain}{(hr)(ft^2)(in. Hg/in.)}$	$kg/(Pa \cdot s \cdot m)$	1.459 29 E - 12
permeance (23°C)	p,P	$\dfrac{grain}{(hr)(ft^2)(in. Hg)}$	$kg/(Pa \cdot s \cdot m^2)$	5.745 25 E - 11

*Exact factor.

Glossary

Absorption: a process whereby a material extracts one or more substances present in an atmosphere and takes it in to become a part of the material; physical and/or chemical change in the material is part of the process (swelling from absorption of water, for instance).

Acoustics: the science of sound, including its production, transmission, and effects. An acoustical material is defined as one that absorbs sound, or baffles or attenuates it; sound insulating materials have no special name. All terms dealing with sound, sound insulation, and sound absorption will be found in Table 8-3.

Adiabatic: as used in this book, a synonym for *evaporative*. Its general meaning is: descriptive of a process such that no heat is added to, or taken from, a substance or system undergoing the process.

Adsorption: the action, associated with the surface adherence, of a material in extracting one or more substances present in an atmosphere. Unlike the process of absorption, this one is not accompanied by physical or chemical change. Silica gel is one example of an adsorbant material that will take up great quantities of moisture.

Air, Ambient: generally, the air surrounding an object.

Air Change: introducing new, cleansed, or recirculated air to conditioned living space, measured by the number of complete changes per unit time, usually an hour or a fraction thereof, and expressed as ACH (air changes per hour).

Air Cleaner: a device, such as an electrostatic precipitator, used to remove airborne impurities.

Air Conditioning: correctly, the term should refer to the simultaneous and continuous control of all the following factors in an atmosphere: temperature, humidity, air motion, air distribution, air pressure, dust, bacteria, odors, toxic gases, and ionization. It is widely, but incorrectly, used to refer to summer cooling systems and techniques. In usual correct terms, an air-conditioning system includes a prime source of refrigeration for cooling and dehumidification and a means for circulating and cleaning air; it also contains means for ventilating and heating.

Air Cooler: a factory-encased assembly of elements whereby the temperature of air passing through the device is reduced.

Air, Saturated: moist air in which the partial pressure of water vapor equals the vapor pressure of water at the existing temperature. This occurs when dry air and saturated water vapor coexist at the same dry-bulb temperature.

Air Washer: a washer spray system or device for cleaning, humidifying, or dehumidifying the air.

Ambient Temperature: *see* Temperature, Ambient.

Area, Free: the total minimum opening area in an air inlet or outlet through which air can pass.

Atmospheric Pressure: the pressure due to the weight of the atmosphere as indicated by a barometer. *Standard atmospheric pressure* is equivalent to 29.921 inches of mercury at 32° F.

Barometer: instrument for measuring atmospheric pressure.

Biomass: the amount of living matter in a unit area of volume; usually taken as plant material, crop residues, animal manures, etc.

Biomass Fuels: the production of synthetic fuels, such as methane hydrogen, from terrestrial and sea plants and from animal wastes.

Boiler: a closed vessel in which a liquid is heated or vaporized; in this book, taken to mean a packaged boiler that is equipped and shipped complete with fuel burning equipment, mechanical draft equipment, and automatic controls and accessories, and is used for the purpose of residential comfort heating with a hydronic system.

British Thermal Unit: the quantity of heat required to raise 1 pound of water 1° Fahrenheit. Abbreviated as Btu.

Calorie: the quantity of heat needed to raise the temperature of 1 gram of water 1° Centigrade.

C Factor: *see* Conductance, Thermal.

Chimney Effect: the tendency of air or gas in a duct or other vertical passage to rise when heated; in buildings, the tendency toward displacement (caused by temperature differential) of internal heated air by unheated outside air because of the difference in density of outside and inside air. Also called *stack effect*.

Clo: a unit measuring the insulating effect of clothing on a human subject.

Coefficient of Expansion: *see* Expansion, Coefficient Of.

Coefficient Of Performance: *see* Performance, Coefficient Of.

Coefficient of Thermal Transmission: *see* Thermal Transmittance.

Comfort Cooling: refrigeration for comfort as opposed to refrigeration for storage or manufacture.

Comfort Zone—average: the range of effective temperatures over which the majority (50 percent or more) of adults feels comfortable; *extreme*: the range of effective temperatures over which one or more adults feel comfortable.

Condensation: the change in state from water vapor to liquid or to ice. More generally it refers to a similar change of state of any vapor.

Conductance, Surface: the amount of heat transferred from a unit area of a surface to the air, given in Btu/hr/sq ft/° diff. Also called *film conductance.*

Conductance, Thermal: the time rate of heat flow through a unit area of a substance of given thickness, symbolized as *C*. It is given as Btu/hr/sq ft/° diff/unit thickness.

Conduction, Thermal: heat tranferred through a substance in such a way that there is no gross displacement of the particles of the substance, as through the metal structure of a radiator.

Conductivity, Thermal: the time rate of heat flow through a unit area of a homogeneous substance, symbolized as *k*. It is given as Btu/hr/sq ft/° diff/in thickness.

Convection: the motion resulting in a fluid from density differences and the action of gravity. In this book, it is limited to *thermal convection,* the transfer of heat by the motion of air molecules: the faster the motion, the greater the heat.

Cooling Load: *see* Load, Cooling.

Degree Day: for any one day when the mean temperature is less than 65° F, there are as many degree days as there are degrees difference between the mean temperature for the day and 65° F. The degree-day unit is used in estimating fuel consumption and specifying nominal heating load of a building in winter. A *summer* degree-day unit is sometimes used in the same manner with respect to comfort cooling, and it can be based on the number of degrees between the mean temperature of the day and 75° or 80° F, but thus far the usage is not general.

Dehumidification: the condensation of water vapor from air cooling below the dew point; or, removal of water vapor from air by chemicals or by physical methods. The latter process is performed by a mechanical dehumidifier.

Density: ratio of the mass of a specimen of a substance to the volume of the specimen; the mass of a unit volume of a substance.

Design Cooling Load: *see* Load, Design Cooling.

Design Heating Load: *see* Load, Design Heating.

Design Temperature: *see* Temperature, Design.

Dew Point: *see* Temperature, Dew Point.

Diffusivity, Thermal: equals the *k* divided by the density of a material times the specific heat. It is given as Btu/sq ft/hr. A building having walls and roof of low diffusivity will be cooler in the daytime than one with high diffusivity, other things being equal.

Dry-bulb Temperature: *see* Temperature, Dry-Bulb.

Effective Temperature: *see* Temperature, Effective.

Emissivity: the capacity of a material to emit radiant energy; the ratio of the total radiant flux emitted by a body to that emitted by an ideal black body at the same temperature.

Emittance: the ratio of the radiant energy (heat) emitted from a surface to that emitted by an ideal black body at the same temperature.

Enthalpy: a thermal dynamic property of a substance defined as the sum of its internal energy plus the quantity Pv/J *(where P* = pressure of the substance, *v* = its volume, and *J* = the mechanical equivalent of heat); formally called *total heat* and *heat content;* expressed in Btu per pound.

Evaporation: the changing of a liquid to a vapor, during which process heat is used. An evaporative cooler and an evaporative condenser both decrease the dry-bulb temperature by increasing the relative humidity.

Exfiltration: air flow outward through a wall, leak membrane, etc.

Expansion, Coefficient Of: the change in length per unit length or the change in volume per unit volume, per degree change in temperature.

Film Conductance: *see* Conductance, Surface.

Furnace: an enclosed structure in which heat is produced; in this book, taken to mean such a unit equipped and shipped complete with fuel burning equipment, mechanical draft equipment, and automatic controls and accessories needed to provide residential warm air comfort heating.

Geothermal: relating to the heat of the earth's interior; geothermal power is produced by hot water or steam drawn from deep within the earth where it is stored from volcanic activity.

Gravity, Specific: density compared to density of standard material; it usually refers to water or to air.

Heat: form of energy that is transferred by virtue of a temperature difference.

Heat Capacity: the quantity of heat required to raise the temperature of a unit quantity of a substance 1° F. Used to determine the amount of heat per unit volume that various building materials are able to store, and usually expressed in Btu per cubic foot per degree Fahrenheit.

Heat Exchanger: a device specifically designed to transfer heat between two physically separated fluids.

Heat Gain: increase in the amount of heat in an enclosed space due to radiation, convection, conduction, and infiltration from a warmer space outside it, to latent heat from outside and inside of it, and to sensible heat created within it.

Heat, Humid: the ratio of increase of enthalpy per pound of dry air, with its associated moisture, to the rise of temperature under conditions of constant pressure and specific humidity.

Heating Load: *see* Load, Heating.

Heat, Latent: change of enthalpy during a change of state, usually expressed in Btu per pound; the heat added to the atmosphere when water is turned into vapor. It is usually given as 1060 Btu per pound of water when the water is at 212° F.

Heat Load: *see* Load, Heating.

Heat Loss: decrease in the amount of heat in an enclosed space due to radiation, convection, and conduction to a colder space outside of it.

Heat, Sensible: heat that is associated with a change in temperature; specific heat exchange of temperature; in contrast to a heat interchange in which a change of state (latent heat) occurs. This is heat added to the atmosphere by a heating source, natural (the sun, fire, etc.) or artificial (burning of fuels or conversion of electric energy to heat).

Heat, Specific: the number of Btu required to raise 1 pound of a given material 1° F. Water has a specific heat of 1.0, therefore 1 Btu is required to raise the temperature of 1 pound of water by 1° F.

Heat Transmission: any time rate of heat flow; usually refers to conduction, convection, and radiation combined.

Heat Transmission Coefficient: any one of a number of coefficients used in calculating heat transmission by conduction, convection, and radiation through various materials and structures. *See* also Transmittance, Thermal.

Horsepower: unit of power in the foot-pound-second system; work done at the rate of 745.7 W (550 ft lb per sec); equal to 42.40 Btu/min.

Humidify: to add water vapor to the atmosphere; the process is accomplished mechanically by a humidifier.

Humidistat: a regulatory device, activated by changes in humidity, used for automatic control of relative humidity.

Humidity: the amount of water vapor within a given space.

Humidity, Absolute: the weight of water vapor per unit volume in lb/cu ft.

Humidity Ratio: in a mixture of water vapor and air, the weight of water vapor per pound of dry air.

Humidity, Relative: the ratio of the actual partial pressure of the water vapor in a space to the saturation pressure of pure water at the same temperature.

Hydronic: a system of heating or cooling that involves transfer of heat by a circulating fluid in a closed system of pipes.

Hydropower: power produced by moving water.

Hydrostatic Pressure: *see* Pressure, Hydrostatic.

Hygrometer: an instrument for measuring relative humidity.

Hygroscopic: absorptive of moisture; readily absorbs and retains moisture.

Infiltration: passage of air into a building through window and door frames, through interstices in the structure, through fireplace chimneys, etc.

Insolation: solar radiation that has been received; the rate of delivery of all direct solar energy per unit of horizontal surface.

Insulation, Sound: acoustical treatment of fan housing, supply ducts, space supply enclosures, and other parts of a system and equipment to isolate vibration or reduce noise transmission.

Insulation, Thermal: a material having a relatively high resistance to heat flow and used principally to retard heat flow.

k Factor: *see* Conductivity, Thermal

Kilowatt: a unit of electric energy equal to 1,000 watts. It is equal to 56.88 Btu/min, and is abbreviated kw.

Kilowatt Hour: equals 60 x 56.88, or 3,413 Btu/hr.

Langley: a measure of solar radiation, equal to 1 calorie per square centimeter.

Latent Heat: *see* Heat, Latent.

Load, Cooling: the various factors that combine to total the amount of heat that a cooling unit must remove from a space to keep it at a desired temperature; it is equal to the heat gain.

Load, Design Cooling: the maximum probable space cooling needs of a building.

Load, Design Heating: the maximum probable space heating needs of a building.

Load, Heat: *see* Load, Heating.

Load, Heating: the factors that combine to total the amount of heat that an energy source must supply to a space to keep it at a desired temperature. It is equal to the heat loss.

Load, Refrigeration: the amount of heat per unit time imposed on a refrigerating system, or the required rate of heat removal.

Mass: a fundamental property of matter, which, for practical purposes, can often be equated with weight; more exactly, the quantity of matter in a body as measured by the ratio of the force required to produce a unit acceleration to the acceleration.

Mass Insulation: *see* Insulation, Thermal.

Megawatt: a unit of power equal to 1000 kilowatts, or 1 million watts.

Performance, Coefficient Of: the ratio of effect produced to the energy supplied, expressed in the same thermal units.

Performance Factor: the ratio of the useful output capacity of a system to the input required to obtain it. Units of capacity and input need not be consistent.

Perm: the unit of permeance; given as 1 grain per square foot per hour per inch of mercury.

Permeability, Water Vapor: the property of a substance that permits passage of water vapor and equals the permeance of a 1-inch thickness of the substance. Permeability is measured in perm-inches.

Permeance, Water-Vapor: the ratio of the water-vapor transmission of a material to the vapor-pressure difference between the two surfaces.

Perm-inch: a unit of permeability; the rate at which water vapor will flow through a material with a thickness of 1 inch.

Power: the rate of performing work; common units are watt, horsepower, and Btu.

Power Consumption: the power used, multiplied by time, measured in watts, horsepower, etc.

Pressure, Hydrostatic: the normal force per unit area that would be exerted by a moving fluid on an infinitesimally small body immersed in it if the body were to be carried along with the fluid.

Pressure, Saturation: the saturation pressure for a pure substance for any given temperature is that pressure at which vapor and liquid, or vapor and solid, can coexist in stable equilibrium.

Pressure, Vapor: the pressure exerted by the molecules of a given vapor.

Psychrometer: instrument for measuring relative humidities by means of wet- and dry-bulb temperatures.

Psychrometry: the branch of physics relating to the measurement or determination of atmospheric conditions, particularly regarding the moisture mixed with the air.

Radiation, Thermal: transmission of heat through space by wave motion; passage of heat from one object to another without warming the space between. Radiated heat is that portion of the total amount of heat that passes directly from source to heated surface, and does not include conducted or convected heat.

R Factor: *see* Resistance, Thermal

R-Value: an additive and comparative value assigned to thermal insulating materials, whereby one material can be compared to another with ease. R-values are established by means of laboratory tests to determine resistance to temperature changes or heat flow through them. The higher the R-value, the greater the thermal efficiency. R-value, however, does not indicate the rate of heat transfer, nor the quantity of heat transfer.

Reflectivity: the extent to which a body reflects heat striking it.

Refrigeration Load: *see* Load, Refrigeration.

Refrigerant: the fluid used for heat transfer in a

refrigerating system: the system absorbs heat at a low temperature and a low pressure of the fluid and rejects heat at a higher temperature and a higher pressure of the fluid; usually involves changes of state of the fluid.

Relative Humidity: *see* Humidity, Relative.

Resistance, Thermal: the reciprocal of thermal conductance; its symbol is *R*.

Resistivity, Thermal: the reciprocal of thermal conductivity.

Saturation, Degree Of: the ratio of the specific humidity of humid air to that of saturated air at the same temperature and pressure, usually expressed as a percentage; also called *Saturation Ratio*.

Saturation Pressure: *see* Pressure, Saturation.

Sensible Heat: *see* Heat, Sensible.

Sling Psychrometer: *see* Psychrometer.

Solar Absorptance: the ratio of the amount of solar radiation absorbed by a surface to the amount of radiation incident on it.

Solar Collector: a device used to gather and accumulate the sun's energy or solar radiation.

Solar Heating/Cooling, Active: the development, design, construction, and operation of systems that utilize and/or store the radiant energy of sunlight to provide comfort control and heated water for household and other uses with the aid of mechanical equipment and automatic controls.

Solar Heating/Cooling, Passive: same function as the active system, but without the use of mechanical equipment and automatic controls.

Solar Irradiation: the amount of radiation, both direct and diffuse, that can be received at any given location.

Solar Power: useful power derived from solar energy.

Solar Radiation: the total electromagnetic radiation emitted by the sun.

Solar Radiation Intensity: the amount of free energy outside the earth's atmosphere, averaging 442 Btu per square foot-hour.

Sound Insulation: *see* Insulation, Sound.

Specific Gravity: *see* Gravity, Specific

Specific Heat: *see* Heat, Specific.

Surface Conductance: *see* Conductance, Surface.

Synfuels: fuels produced by artificial means from other materials, such as synthetic natural gas through coal-gasification, synthetic crude oil produced by the hydrogenation of coal, etc; used for heating and other purposes.

Temperature: the thermal state of matter with reference to its tendency to communicate heat to matter in contact with it. In this book, temperature is always referred to in degrees Fahrenheit, with the freezing point of water at 32° and the boiling point at 212°

Temperature, Ambient: temperature of the atmosphere surrounding a particular location.

Temperature, Design: the temperatures used in calculating heating and cooling loads. Outside design temperatures are the lowest *average* temperatures in various parts of the country (or the highest, when calculating cooling loads). Indoor design temperatures in residential work are usually established at 70° F in the winter (though this temperature is becoming less universal as a guide than it used to be) and either 80° or 75° F in the summer.

Temperature, Dew Point: the temperature at which vapor begins to condense. It is equal to 100 percent relative humidity and is a variable depending on the state of the dry-bulb and wet-bulb temperatures at a given time.

Temperature, Dry-Bulb: the temperature of a gas or a mixture of gases indicated by an accurate thermometer after correction for radiation.

Temperature, Effective: an index combining the effects of temperature, humidity, and air motion on the sensations of warmth or cold felt by people. The numerical value is that of the temperature of still, saturated air that would induce the same sensation. By strict definition, it is the dry-bulb temperature of a black enclosure at 50 percent relative humidity (sea level) in which a solid body or occupant would exchange the same heat by radiation, convection, and evaporation as in the existing nonuniform environment.

Temperature, Room: the air temperature of any room, but the term is used colloquially to mean the ordinary temperature one is accustomed to find in dwellings.

Temperature, Wet-Bulb: a measure of the amount of humidity in the air. It is obtained by keeping a thermometer bulb moist and then passing air rapidly across it. Technically, it is the temperature at which water, by evaporating into the air, can bring the air to saturation adiabatically at the same temperature.

Therm: a unit of heating value equivalent to 100,000 Btu; one therm equals 100 cubic feet of natural gas.

Thermal Inertia: the tendency of a large mass of material to remain at the same temperature and to fluctuate comparatively slowly when influenced by higher or surrounding temperatures; also called *thermal flywheel effect*. See also Thermal Lag.

Thermal Insulation: *see* Insulation, Thermal.

Thermal Lag: the time that it takes for the inside air temperature of a space to heat up or cool to that of the surrounding outside temperature.

Thermal Mass: the total heat storage capacity of a given mass of materials, such as the building sections of a house.

Thermal Radiation: *see* Radiation, Thermal.

Thermal Resistance: *see* Resistance, Thermal.

Thermal Resistivity: *see* Resistivity, Thermal.

Thermostat: a device for controlling temperature by automatically turning on and off a heating or cooling source as the dry-bulb temperature changes.

Ton of Refrigeration: a refrigerating effect equal to 3516 watts (12,000 Btu/hr); seldom-used term today.

Transmission: in thermodynamics, a general term for heat travel; properly, heat transferred per unit of time.

Transmittance, Thermal: the transfer of heat by radiation, convection, and conduction through a material or combination of materials and air spaces. The rate of transmittance is abbreviated as *U*, and for individual materials or for combinations of materials the *U* is called the *coefficient of thermal transmission* or the *heat transmission coefficient*.

U Factor: *see* Transmittance, Thermal.

Vapor Barrier: a moisture-impervious layer applied to the surfaces enclosing a humid space to prevent moisture travel to a point where it may condense due to lower temperature.

Vapor Pressure: *see* Pressure, Vapor.

Ventilation: the process of supplying or removing air by natural or mechanical means to or from any space. Such air may or may not have been conditioned.

Wet-Bulb Temperature: *see* Temperature, Wet-Bulb.

Bibliography

Practical manuals and design guides that are frequently revised do not bear the year of publication in this Bibliography, but only the source. Readers requesting copies of these titles will always receive the latest versions if the requests are made directly to the originating agencies. Few, if any, of the titles are free, and the prices change from time to time; write to the agencies involved and ask for the current postpaid prices of the titles you are interested in, or request a current publications list and order blank.

Obtaining government publications can sometimes be confusing because there are several approaches, and because many titles come and go and prices change. One approach is to contact the department or bureau involved and request a current list of publications available, or the current status of those particular titles that you might want. A few titles are best obtained in this way, such as those listed for the Forest Products Laboratory. However, most titles are available through the United States Government Printing Office (USGPO), regardless of the originating agency. Address a request directly to the U.S. Goverment Printing Office, Superintendent of Documents, Washington, DC 20402, for the current status and price of specific titles; identify them by name and stock number or catalog number. If you do not have this information, or wish to see what else is available (there are over 24,000 titles with a turnover rate of 3,000 titles a year), request #SB-999 *Subject Bibliography Index,* which is free. From this list you can choose the subject bibliographies of interest, which in turn list all of the available titles for each subject; ordering is done directly from these lists.

If you do not wish to purchase the government titles, or want to research some that are no longer available, you can find them at any of the Regional Depository Libraries; each state has several such libraries, and you can obtain specific information at any public or institution library.

AIR CONDITIONING CONTRACTORS OF AMERICA (ACCA). *Heat Pump Equipment Selection & Application,* Manual H. (1228 17th Street, N.W., Washington, DC 20036)
> *Installation Techniques for Perimeter Heating & Cooling,* Manual 4.
> *Introduction to the Installation of Residential Ducted Heating and Air Conditioning Systems.*
> *Load Calculation for Residential Winter and Summer Air Conditioning,* Manual J.
> *Noise in the Neighborhood.*
> *Principles of Air Conditioning,* Manual B.
> *What Makes A Good Air Conditioning System,* Manual C.

AMERICAN PLYWOOD ASSOCIATION. *All Weather Wood Foundation System* (P.O. Box 11700, Tacoma, WA 98411)
> *Plywood Construction for Fire Protection.*
> *Plywood Construction for Noise Control.*

AMERICAN SOCIETY OF HEATING, REFRIGERATING AND AIR-CONDITIONING ENGINEERS, INC. *ASHRAE HANDBOOK & Product Directory* (1791 Tullie Circle N.E., Atlanta, GA 30329)

AMERICAN SOCIETY FOR TESTING MATERIALS (ASTM). *Index to Standards* (1916 Race Street, Philadelphia, PA 19103)

ANDERSON, BRUCE. *The Solar Home Book.* Andover, MA: Brick House Publishing Co., Inc., 1976

BELL, E. R., SEIDL, M. G., and KRUEGER, N. T. "Water-Vapor Permeability of Building Papers and Other Sheet Materials." *Heating, Piping and Air Conditioning Magazine,* December 1950. (Available from Forest Products Laboratory, P.O. Box 5130, Madison, WI 53705).

BURBANK, NELSON L., and PFISTER, HERBERT R. *House Construction Details.* New York: Simmons-Boardman, 1968

BUREAU OF RECLAMATION, U.S. DEPARTMENT OF THE INTERIOR. *Concrete Manual.* U.S. Government Printing Office, #024-003-00092-2
> *Paint Manual.* U.S. Government Printing Office, #024-003-00104-0.

DAVIS, ALBERT J., and SCHUBERT, ROBERT T. *Alternative Natural Energy Sources in Building Design.* New York: Van Nostrand Reinhold Company, 1977

DEPARTMENTS OF THE AIR FORCE, THE ARMY, AND THE NAVY. *Engineering Weather Data.* U.S. Government Printing Office, AFM88.29, TM5•785, NAVFAC P.89

FOREST PRODUCTS LABORATORY, U.S. DEPARTMENT OF AGRICULTURE, FOREST SERVICE. *Forest Products Laboratory Natural Finish,* USDA Forest Service Research Note FPL-046, 1979. (P.O. Box 5130, Madison, WI 53705)

> *List of Publications.* (P.O. Box 1530, Madison, WI 53705).
>
> *Wood Handbook.* U.S. Government Printing Office, #001-000-03200-3.

HAND, A. J. *Home Energy How-To.* New York: Popular Science/Harper and Row, 1977

HOUSE BEAUTIFUL. *Regional Climate Analyses and Design Data.* (717 Fifth Avenue, New York, NY 10022)

HUNT, V. DANIEL. *Energy Dictionary.* New York: Van Nostrand Reinhold Company, 1979

INTERNATIONAL CONFERENCE OF BUILDING OFFICIALS. *Uniform Building Code.* (5360 South Workman Mill Road, Whittier, CA 90601)

JOINT ECONOMY COMMITTEE, CONGRESS OF THE UNITED STATES. *The Economics of Solar Home Heating.* U.S. Government Printing Office, 1977

KERN, KEN. *The Owner Built Home.* New York: Charles Scribner's Sons, 1975

LECKIE, JIM; MASTERS, GIL; WHITEHOUSE, HARRY; and YOUNG, LILY. *Other Homes and Garbage.* San Francisco: Sierra Club Books, 1975

LIBBEY-OWENS-FORD COMPANY. *Glass For Construction.* (811 Madison Avenue, Toledo, OH 43695)

> *Sun Angle Calculator.*

LIPSCOMB, DAVID M., and TAYLOR, ARTHUR C., JR. *Noise Control Handbook of Principles and Practices.* New York: Van Nostrand Reinhold Company, 1978

LOFTNESS, ROBERT L. *Energy Handbook.* New York: Van Nostrand Reinhold Company, 1978

LOUVERDRAPE, INC. *A Study of the Performance of Interior Shading Devices in Reducing Energy Consumption and Air-Conditioning Equipment Costs.* (1100 Colorado Avenue, Santa Monica, CA 90401)

LUCAS, TED. *How to Use Solar Energy in Your Home and Business.* Pasadena, CA: Ward Ritchie Press, 1977

MINERAL INSULATION MANUFACTURERS ASSOCIATION. *A Close, Careful, Official Scrutiny of Cellulose Insulation,* Insulation Facts #2. (382 Springfield Avenue, Summitt, NJ 07901)

> *Home Insulation Checklist,* Insulation Facts #1.
> *How To Save Money By Insulating Your Home.*
> *Insulation and Fire Safety,* Insulation Facts #5.
> *Mineral Wool "Blowing Wool."*
> *Three Reports Analyze UF Foam, Set Rules For Its Acceptance,* Insulation Facts #3.

NATIONAL AERONAUTICS AND SPACE ADMINISTRATION. *An Inexpensive Economical Solar Heating System for Homes,* NASA Technical Memorandum TM X-3294. U.S. Government Printing Office, 1976, F-033-000-00632-2

NASA Tech House. U.S. Goverment Printing Office, 1977, #033-000-00704-3.

NATIONAL ASSOCIATION OF HOME BUILDERS RESEARCH FOUNDATION, INC. *Insulation Manual.* (627 Southlawn Lane, P.O. Box 1627, Rockville, MD 20850)

NATIONAL BUREAU OF STANDARDS, U.S. DEPARTMENT OF COMMERCE. *Acoustical and Thermal Performance of Exterior Residential Walls, Doors and Windows,* NBS Building Science Series No. 77. U.S. Government Printing Office, 1975, Cat.#C13.29/2:M

> *Building Research Translation, "Ventilation Air Inlets for Dwellings,"* NBS Technical Note No. 710-6. U.S. Government Printing Office, 1973, Cat. #C13.46: 710-6.
>
> *Energy-Effective Windows,* NBS Special Publication No. 512. #003-003-01929-1. U.S. Government Printing Office, 1978.
>
> *Geographical Variation in the Heating and Cooling Requirements of a Typical Single-Family House, and Correlation of These Requirements to Degree Days,* NBS Building Science Series No. 116. U.S. Government Printing Office, 1978, #003-003-01992-5.
>
> *Standards on Noise Measurements, Rating Schemes, and Definitions: A Compilation,* NBS Special Publication No. 386. U.S. Government Printing Office, 1976, #003-003-01593-8.
>
> *Summer Attic and Full-House Ventilation,* NBS Special Publication No. 548. U.S. Government Printing Office, 1979, #003-003-02089-3.
>
> *Thermal Analysis—Human Comfort—Indoor Environments,* NBS Special Publication No. 491. U.S. Government Printing Office, 1977, 003-003-01849-0.
>
> *Ura-Formaldehyde Based Foam Insulations: An Assessment of Their Properties and Performance,* NBS Technical Note No. 946. U.S. Government Printing Office, 1977, #003-003-01801-5.
>
> *Window Design Strategies to Conserve Energy,* NBS Building Science Series No. 104. U.S. Government Printing Office, 1977, #003-003-01794-9.

NATIONAL ELECTRICAL MANUFACTURERS ASSOCIATION. *Manual for Electric Comfort Conditioning,* NEMA Pub. No. HE 1. (2101 L Street, N.W., Washington, DC 20037)

NATIONAL FIRE PROTECTION ASSOCIATION. *Chimneys, Fireplaces, and Vents,* NFPA No. 211. (Batterymarch Park; Quincy, MA 02269)

> *Household Fire Warning Equipment,* NFPA No. 74.
> *Lightning Protection Code,* NFPA No. 78.
> *National Electrical Code,* NFPA No. 70.

NATIONAL OCEANIC AND ATMOSPHERIC ADMINISTRATION, U.S. DEPARTMENT OF COMMERCE. *Climates of the United States.* U.S. Government Printing Office, 1974, #003-017-00211-0

NATIONAL SOLAR HEATING AND COOLING INFORMATION CENTER, U.S. DEPARTMENT OF HOUSING AND URBAN DEVELOPMENT. *Solar Bibliography.* (P.O. Box 1607, Rockville, MD 20850)

OLGYAY, ALADAR, and OLGYAY, VICTOR. *Solar Control and Shading Devices.* Princeton: Princeton University Press, 1957

OLIN, HAROLD B.; SCHMIDT, JOHN L.; and LEWIS,

WALTER H. *Construction Principles, Materials and Methods*. Chicago: The Institute of Financial Education and Interstate Printers and Publishers, Inc. 1980

PORTLAND CEMENT ASSOCIATION. *Admixtures For Concrete*. (5420 Old Orchard Road, Skokie, IL 60076)
    Curing of Concrete.
    Efflorescence.
    Painting Concrete.
    Recommended Practices for Laying Concrete Block.
    The Concrete Approach to Energy Conservation.

RANDALL, FRANK A., Jr., and PANARESE, WILLIAM C. *Concrete Masonry Handbook*. Skokie IL: Portland Cement Association, 1976

RUFFNER, JAMES A., and BAIR, FRANK E. *The Weather Almanac*. New York: Avon Books, 1977

SHELTON, JAY, and SHAPIRO, ANDREW. *The Woodburners Encyclopedia*. Waitsfield, VT: Vermont Crossroads Press, 1976

SUMNER, JOHN A. *Domestic Heat Pumps*. Dorset, England: Prism Press, Dorchester, 1976

THE HYDRONICS INSTITUTE. *Cooling Load Calculation Guide for Residences,* Manual C-30. (35 Russo Place, Burkeley Heights, NJ 07922)
    Heat Loss Calculation Guide, Manual H-21.
    Installation Guide for Residential Hydronic Systems (Hot Water and Steam), Manual 200.

THE UNDERGROUND SPACE CENTER, UNIVERSITY OF MINNESOTA. *Earth Sheltered Housing Design*. New York: Van Nostrand Reinhold Company, 1979

U.S. DEPARTMENT OF AGRICULTURE, FOREST SERVICE. *Condensation Problems in Your House: Prevention and Solution,* Agriculture Information Bulletin No. 373, U.S. Government Printing Office, 1974, #001-000-03318-2

U.S. DEPARTMENT OF AGRICULTURE. *Fireplaces and Chimneys,* Farmers' Bulletin No. 1889. U.S. Government Printing Office, 1977

U.S. DEPARTMENT OF AGRICULTURE. *Home Heating: Systems, Fuels, Controls,* Farmers' Bulletin No. 2235. U.S. Government Printing Office, 1977

U.S. DEPARTMENT OF AGRICULTURE, FOREST SERVICE. *Wood-Frame House Construction,* Agriculture Handbook No. 73. U.S. Government Printing Office

U.S. DEPARTMENT OF AGRICULTURE, FOREST SERVICE. *You Can Protect Your Home from Termites.* U.S. Government Printing Office, #001-001-00420-1

U.S. DEPARTMENT OF ENERGY. *An Assessment of Thermal Insulation Materials and Systems for Building Applications.* U.S. Government Printing Office, 1978, #061-000-00094-1

U.S. DEPARTMENT OF ENERGY. *Introduction to Solar Heating and Cooling Design and Sizing.* U.S. Government Printing Office, 1978, #061-000-00152-2

U.S. DEPARTMENT OF THE INTERIOR, MINING ENFORCEMENT AND SAFETY ADMINISTRATION. *Safety Manual No. 1, Coal Mining.* U.S. Government Printing Office, 1975, #024-019-00011-0

U.S. ENVIRONMENTAL PROTECTION AGENCY, OFFICE OF NOISE ABATEMENT AND CONTROL. *About Sound.* (Washington, DC 20460, 1976)

Index

ABOUT THE AUTHOR

The late **Groff Conklin** was a free-lance writer and editor who specialized in the fields of architecture, construction, medicine, and science fiction. He was the author of several books and a contributor to more than twenty magazines, including *Science Illustrated* and *Better Homes and Gardens*. At the time of his death he was the science editor for *American Heritage Dictionary.*

S. Blackwell Duncan, who revised and updated this book, is an active writer with a life-long interest as well as personal experience in various aspects of home-building. He is an inveterate do-it-yourselfer and has built, rebuilt, and remodeled houses. The house in Snowmass, Colorado, where he and his wife now reside, was designed and built by them.